Glencoe Medical Assisting Review

Passing the CMA and RMA Exams

Jahangir Moini, M.D., M.P.H.
Medical Department Chairman
Florida Metropolitan University, Melbourne, Florida

Glencoe McGraw-Hill

New York, New York   Columbus, Ohio   Woodland Hills, California   Peoria, Illinois

This book is fondly dedicated to:

The living memory of my father.

My loving and caring family:
Mother, wife and daughters

My colleagues, staff, and past and present students at
Florida Metropolitan University

Library of Congress Cataloging-in-Publication Data

Moini, Jahangir
    Glencoe medical assisting review / Jahangir Moini.
        p. cm.
    Includes index.
    ISBN 0-07-821288-X
    1. Medical assistants--Examinations, questions, etc. 2. Physicians'
assistants--Examinations, questions, etc. I. Title: Medical assisting review. II.
Glencoe/McGraw-Hill. III. Title.

R728.8 .M65 2001
610.73'7'076--dc21

00-067216

Glencoe/McGraw-Hill

A Division of The McGraw·Hill Companies

Glencoe Medical Assisting Review: Passing the CMA and RMA Exams

Send all inquiries to:
Glencoe/McGraw-Hill
8787 Orion Place
Columbus, OH 43240-4027

 2 3 4 5 6 7 8 9 10   066   07 06 05 04 03 02 01

Preface

Glencoe Medical Assisting Review: Passing the CMA and RMA Exams is a comprehensive approach to reviewing the key competencies of a medical assisting program for the student preparing to take the CMA or RMA Medical Assistant certification exams. The book is divided into three parts: *Theory Review, Self-Evaluation,* and *Answers and Rationales.*

Theory Review

The first part, *Theory Review*, provides easy-to-read essential material summaries, which highlight key areas of a Medical Assistant's program. The chapters are organized into three sections that cover general, administrative, and clinical medical assisting knowledge. Chapters 1 through 7 cover General Medical Assisting, Chapters 8 through 10 cover Administrative Medical Assisting, and Chapters 11 through 18 cover Clinical Medical Assisting.

COMPETENCY CORRELATIONS

Each chapter correlates to the AAMA Role Delineation Competencies and RMA (AMT) Certification Exam Topics.

AT A GLANCE Tables

At a Glance tables throughout the chapters summarize key information for quick review.

STRATEGIES TO SUCCESS

We have collected a number of tips that will help students study for and pass the certification exams. We

call these tips *Strategies to Success*. There are two *Strategies to Success* features placed in every chapter, one at the beginning and one at the end of the chapter. In each chapter, the first tip will provide material to help improve a student's study skills and the second tip will enhance a student's test-taking skills. These skills are as essential as the material covered in this book.

CHAPTER REVIEW

At the end of each chapter, there are 20 to 40 multiple choice review questions that correlate with actual CMA and RMA-style questions. Each chapter review is followed by an answer key, so the book can be easily used for self-study.

Self-Evaluations with Answers and Rationales

This book contains three self-evaluations—General, Administrative, and Clinical—which correspond not only to the chapter divisions but also to the actual parts of the certification exams. The test for general medical assisting knowledge contains 250 questions, and it covers material contained in the first seven chapters of the book, as well as some communication and professionalism content covered in Chapter 8. The test for administrative medical assisting knowledge contains 225 questions, and it covers material reviewed in Chapters 8, 9, and 10. The last test covers the clinical medical assisting part of the book in 250 questions. Similar to the quizzes at the end of each chapter, these questions also follow both the CMA and RMA style. We recommend students answer as many of the questions as possible to familiarize themselves with the content covered on the exams. Practicing answering exam-style questions will increase the student's understanding of the material and raise confidence and test-taking abilities.

After students have taken a self-evaluation exam, they can find the correct answer and rationale for each question in the last section of the book. These rationales are not intended to be a complete review of the material; however, they can be used to refresh a student's memory about a specific topic and help focus on areas that need improvement through further study and review.

HOW TO USE THIS BOOK

This book is intended for use in a Medical Assistant review course or for self-study before taking either the CMA or RMA exam. There are a number of ways to use this book.

In a classroom, it might be best to teach the *Theory Review* chapter by chapter, and, at the end of the course, allow students to take the exams contained in the *Self-Evaluation* section to assess their knowledge. Instructors can tear out the perforated sheets and give students timed exams in the classroom or ask students to answer questions at home and check their own answers. Students can then come back to class with questions, and the class can review the material together.

A student using this book for self-study might find it more useful to begin with the *Self-Evaluations*, which can pinpoint strengths and weaknesses. If the answers and rationales are not sufficient in answering the student's questions, the student can consult the *Theory Review* section to refresh his or her memory about a specific topic.

STUDENT TUTORIAL AND TEST PREP CD-ROM SYSTEM REQUIREMENTS

To get the optimal results with the CD, your computer should have:

- Pentium processor or equivalent
- Windows 95 or higher
- 16 MB of RAM, 32 MB or higher recommended
- 8.5 MB hard drive storage
- 600 x 800 color monitor

- CD-ROM drive, 16x or higher recommended
- Mouse

INSTALLATION

Insert the CD-ROM into your CD-ROM drive. All installation and start-up operations are automatic. Once the software is installed, simply open the CD-ROM drive and close it again to start the application or double-click on your CD-ROM icon.

If your installation doesn't start automatically, go to the Start menu, choose Run, and type in D:\setup.exe, where D stands for your CD-ROM drive.

ABOUT THE CD-ROM

The software contains 1200 questions, which are a combination of questions taken from the text and new questions. Students will be able to take multiple chapter quizzes as well as comprehensive RMA- or CMA-style practice exams. The comprehensive practice exams are randomly generated from a database of questions so students can take as many practice tests as they want. Students can even choose the exact number of questions they want to answer. If they have only a short amount of time, they can take a quick 25-question exam. If they want to simulate a complete certification exam they can take a 300-question exam or, for a full night of practicing, they can go through the entire database of 1200 questions. We recommend that after reading each chapter, the student take at least one quiz for the chapter. After completing all the chapters in the *Theory Review* section, the student can start taking practice exams. If the student's scores are below 60% on these practice exams, the student should return to the appropriate chapters in the book to review the material. Please consult the help files on the CD-ROM for more information.

THE CMA AND RMA EXAMS

The Certified Medical Assistant (CMA) and Registered Medical Assistant (RMA) are voluntary, national credentials for a medical assisting professional. The CMA is awarded by the Certifying Board of the American Association of Medical Assistants (AAMA), and the RMA is given by the American Medical Technologists (AMT).

THE CMA EXAM

The CMA exam is offered biannually, in January and June. Graduating students and graduates of medical assisting programs accredited by the Commission on Accreditation of Allied Health Education Programs (CAAHEP) are eligible to take the CMA examination. Students thinking about taking the exam should go to the AAMA's web page at http://www.aama-natl.org or they can call the AAMA Certification Department at (312) 424-3100 to find out about locations, registration deadlines, and exact dates for the exam. There will be a fee for the exam, as well as a nonrefundable administration fee for registering. As of writing this book, it is cheaper to take the exam within 12 months of graduation from a CAAHEP-accredited institution. Please note that CMAs are required to recertify their credential every five years, by either continuing education or examination.

The exam content is based on the occupational analysis known as the AAMA Role Delineation Study, which covers general, administrative, and clinical aspects of a medical assistant's job. Each section of the exam consists of 100 questions, and the examinee has no more than four hours to answer every question. There are no penalties for guessing, and each question is assigned equal weight in the final scoring. It is important to remember that the candidate has to get a minimum number of questions correct in each section in order to be certified. If the student fails even one section, he or she will not get the CMA credentials. As with a lot of standardized tests, the scores for the CMA exam are calculated on a curve comparing every candidate's score with scores in the past and those of current test-takers.

THE RMA EXAM

Similar to the CMA exam, the RMA exam certifies medical assisting professionals. In order to be eligible to take the exam, the applicant should have graduated from a medical assistant program or institution accredited by a Regional Accrediting Commission or by a national accrediting organization approved by the United States Department of Education or from a formal medical services training program of the United States Armed Forces. The applicant should also have been employed in the profession of Medical Assisting for a minimum of five years, no more than two years of which may have been as an instructor in a postsecondary medical assistant program.

AMT certification examinations consist of 200 to 210 multiple-choice items with four answer choices. Examinees need to select the single best answer from among the four alternatives. Test items may require examinees to recall facts, interpret graphic illustrations, interpret information presented in case studies, analyze situations, or solve problems. While the CMA questions are weighted equally, RMA questions are weighted according to their difficulty when scoring the exam and, as on all standardized tests, the examinee's scaled score, not raw score, is what determines passing.

Unlike the CMA exam, which is offered only twice a year, the RMA exam is administered throughout the year at Cogent testing center locations. Although most centers offer tests every week of the year, several locations administer tests only on specific days of the year. A complete and up-to-date list of Cogent sites will be forwarded when the candidate's application is approved. Most examinations may be scheduled within three days of application completion. To find out more about the RMA exam, visit the AMT web page at http://www.amt1.com or call the AMT's Registrar's Office at (847) 823-5169.

AMT Certification examinations are intended to evaluate the competence of entry-level practitioners. The tests address content areas defined and validated by subject-matter experts, educators, and individuals working in their respective fields. As the tests provide only one source of information regarding examinee competence, they are used in conjunction with other indicators of training and experience in the granting of certification. The approximate percentages of questions according to content areas on the RMA certification exam are represented below:

I. General Medical Assisting Knowledge – 42.5 %
    A. Anatomy and physiology
    B. Medical terminology
    C. Medical law
    D. Medical ethics
    E. Human relations
    F. Patient Education

II. Administrative Medical Assisting Knowledge – 22.5%
    A. Insurance
    B. Financial bookkeeping
    C. Medical secretarial-receptionist

III. Clinical Medical Assisting – 35.0%
    A. Asepsis
    B. Sterilization
    C. Instruments
    D. Vital signs
    E. Physical Examinations
    F. Clinical pharmacology
    G. Minor surgery
    H. Therapeutic modalities
    I. Laboratory procedures
    J. Electrocardiography
    K. First aid

Acknowledgements

Special thanks go to the following Glencoe staff for their considerable efforts, invaluable advice, and vital guidance during the development of this book: Emese Gaal, Susan Cole, Linda Jefferson, Lowell Hoover, and Denise Phillips. The author would also like to thank the contributions of Sybil Sosin, whose input and insights made this text a more valuable tool in exam preparation.

Additionally, we would like to express our appreciation to WCB/McGraw-Hill for the artwork that helped illustrate this book.

REVIEWERS

The author gratefully acknowledges the following advisors and reviewers, whose comments and suggestions helped shape the manuscript into a comprehensive and useful review book.

Janet Roberts-Andersen, BS, MS, MT
Director of the Medical Assistant Program
Hamilton College
Urbandale, Iowa

Susan Boulden, BSN, RN, CMA
Medical Assisting Program Director/Instructor
Mt. Hood Community College
Gresham, Oregon

Michael L. Decker, BS, MA
Instructor
Omaha College of Health Careers
Omaha, Nebraska

Deborah E. Holmes, RN, CMA, MLT
Medical Assistant Program Coordinator
Nebraska Methodist College
Omaha, Nebraska

Charlotte A. Jensen, BS, MPS/HAS, CMA
Director of the Medical Assistant Department
Cabrillo College
Aptos, California

Barbara Lato, BSN, CMA
Program Director of the Medical Assistant
    Program
Mid-State Technical College
Marshfield, Wisconsin

Pat Gallagher Moeck, BA, MBA, CMA
Director of the Medical Assisting Program
El Centro College/ Mountain View College
Dallas, Texas

Susan Perreira, BS, CMA, RMA
Assistant Professor
Capital Community College
Hartford, Connecticut

Teri A. Provenzano, CMA
VP, Owner, and Program Coordinator of the
    Medical Assistant Program
Medical Careers Training Center
Somerville, New Jersey

Dyiane Saban, CMA
Medical Program Director
Bryman College
Gardena, California

Susan Schilling, BS, AA, CMA
Dean of Instruction
Bryant & Stratton
Syracuse, New York

Janet Sesser, BS, CMA, RMA
Corporate Director of Education, Allied Health
    Programs
Hightech Institute
Phoenix, Arizona

Lynn G. Slack, CMA
Director, Medical Programs
ICM School of Business and Medical Careers
Pittsburgh, Pennsylvania

Dana Stidham, BS, MS, TC
Medical Assisting Program Chair
Ivy Tech State College
Columbus, Indiana

Sylvia Taylor, AS, BS
Assistant Professor/MOA Director
Cleveland State Community College
Cleveland, Tennessee

Barbara Ulto
Branford Hall Career Institute
Branford, Connecticut

Bennita W. Vaughans, BA, MS
Medical Assisting Technology Program Director
H. Councill Trenholm State Technical College
Montgomery, Alabama

Brenda Vetere, BS, MT
Externship Coordinator/Adjunct Faculty
Capital Community College
Hartford, Connecticut

The author also appreciates the generosity and hard work put forth by the following contributors:

Domenick DiGregorio, AAS, BS, ARRT
Administrative Director of Diagnostic Imaging
Sebastian River Medical Center
Sebastian, Florida

Adjunct Professor
Florida Metropolitan University
Melbourne, Florida

Denise L. Barnes, AA/AS, BS, MBA, RMA
Adjunct Professor
Florida Metropolitan University
Melbourne, Florida

Richard L. Allard, BSEE, MSSM
Adjunct Professor
Florida Metropolitan University
Melbourne, Florida

Hengameh Moini, BS, MS, Office Manager
Neurological Medical Practice
Melbourne, Florida

George R. Jackow, Sr., BA, MA
Environmental Health Consultant/EPI
Brevard County Health Department

JoAnn Holzlohner, Administrative Assistant
Brevard County Health Department

Greg Vadimsky, Medical Student, FMU (Typist)

Alicia Demyan, CMA (Typist)

Stacy Meyers, Medical Student, FMU (Typist)

AAMA Role Delineation Study Areas of Competence (1997) Correlation Chart

Areas of Competence	Chapters
I. CLINICAL	
A. Administrative Procedures	
1. Perform basic clerical functions.	8
2. Schedule, coordinate, and monitor appointments.	8
3. Schedule inpatient/outpatient admissions and procedures.	8
4. Understand and apply third-party guidelines.	10
5. Obtain reimbursement through accurate claims submissions.	10
6. Monitor third-party reimbursement.	10
7. Perform medical transcription.	8
8. Understand and adhere to managed care policies and procedures.	10
B. Practice Finances	
1. Perform procedural and diagnostic coding.	10
2. Apply bookkeeping principles.	9
3. Document and maintain accounting and banking records.	9
4. Manage accounts receivable.	9
5. Manage accounts payable.	9
6. Process payroll.	9
II. CLINICAL	
A. Fundamental Principles	
1. Apply principles of aseptic technique and infection control.	4, 11, 12, 17, 18
2. Comply with quality assurance practices.	11, 12, 18
3. Screen and follow up patient test results.	8, 18
B. Diagnostic Orders	
1. Collect and process specimens.	12, 18
2. Perform diagnostic tests.	12, 14, 15, 18
C. Patient Care	
1. Adhere to established triage procedures.	8, 17
2. Obtain patient history and vital signs.	12
3. Prepare and maintain examination and treatment areas.	12, 14
4. Prepare patient for examinations, procedures, and treatments.	12, 14, 15, 16
5. Assist with examinations, procedures, and treatments.	12, 15, 16
6. Prepare and administer medications and immunizations.	13
7. Maintain medication and immunization records.	5, 13
8. Recognize and respond to emergencies.	8, 17
9. Coordinate patient care information with other health care providers.	8

Areas of Competence	Chapters
III. GENERAL (TRANSDISCIPLINARY)	
A. Professionalism	
1. Project a professional manner and image.	7, 8
2. Adhere to ethical principles.	7, 8, 9
3. Demonstrate initiative and responsibility.	7, 8, 9, 10, 12, 13, 17
4. Work as a team member.	7, 8, 9, 10, 12, 13
5. Manage time effectively.	8, 9, 10
6. Prioritize and perform multiple tasks.	8, 9, 10
7. Adapt to change.	8, 9, 10
8. Promote the CMA credential.	7, 8, 9, 10
9. Enhance skills through continuing education.	7, 8, 14, 15
B. Communication Skills	
1. Treat all patients with compassion and empathy.	6, 7, 8, 9, 12, 16
2. Recognize and respect cultural diversity.	6, 7, 8
3. Adapt communications to individual's ability to understand.	6, 8, 12
4. Use professional telephone technique.	7, 8
5. Use effective and correct verbal and written communications.	8
6. Recognize and respond to verbal and nonverbal communications.	7, 8, 12
7. Use medical terminology appropriately.	1, 2, 3, 4, 5, 6
8. Receive, organize, prioritize, and transmit information.	8
9. Serve as a liaison.	8, 9, 10
10. Promote the practice through positive public relations.	7, 8, 9, 10
C. Legal Concepts	
1. Maintain confidentiality.	7, 8, 9, 12
2. Practice within the scope of education, training, and personal capabilities.	7, 12, 13, 14, 15, 16, 17
3. Prepare and maintain medical records.	7, 8, 12, 13
4. Document accurately.	7, 8, 10, 12
5. Use appropriate guidelines when releasing information.	7, 8
6. Follow employer's established policies dealing with the health care contract.	7, 10
7. Follow federal, state, and local legal guidelines.	5, 7, 11
8. Maintain awareness of federal and state health care legislation and regulations.	5, 7, 11
9. Maintain and dispose of regulated substances in compliance with government guidelines.	5, 11, 13, 18

AAMA Role Delineation Study Areas of Competence (1997) Correlation Chart, continued

Areas of Competence	Chapters
10. Comply with established risk management and safety procedures.	11
11. Recognize professional credentialing criteria.	7, 8
12. Participate in the development and maintenance of personnel, policy, and procedure manuals.	8
D. Instruction	
1. Instruct individuals according to their needs.	6, 8, 12, 15, 16
2. Explain office policies and procedures.	8, 12
3. Teach methods of health promotion and disease prevention.	6, 8
4. Locate community resources and disseminate information.	6, 8, 12
E. Operational Functions	
1. Maintain supply inventory.	9, 17
2. Evaluate and recommend equipment and supplies.	9, 17
3. Apply computer techniques to support office operations.	8, 9

AMT Registered Medical Assistant (RMA) Certification Exam Topics Correlation Chart

Areas of Competence	Chapters
I. General Medical Assisting Knowledge	
A. Anatomy & Physiology	
1. Body systems—Know the structure and function of the: Skeletal system Muscular system Endocrine system Urinary system Reproductive system Gastrointestinal system Nervous system Respiratory system Cardiovascular system Integumentary system Special senses system	2
2. Disorders of the body—Identify various diseases, conditions, and syndromes.	3, 6, 17
B. Medical Terminology	
1. Word parts–Identify word parts—root, prefixes, and suffixes.	1
2. Definitions—Define medical terms.	1, 2, 3, 4, 5, 6
3. Common abbreviations and symbols—Know medical abbreviations and symbols.	1
4. Spelling—Spell medical terms correctly.	1, 2, 3, 4, 5, 6
C. Medical Law	
1. Medical law—Identify the various types of consent, and how and when to obtain each; know disclosure laws (i.e., what information must be reported to the proper agency); what constitutes confidential information; what information may be disclosed under certain circumstances; recognize legal responsibilities of the medical assistant; know the various medically related laws (i.e., Good Samaritan, Anatomical Gift Act, drug storage and maintenance, Drug Enforcement Agency Regulations).	5, 7, 8, 17
2. Licensure, certification, and registration—Know credentialing requirements of medical professionals.	7
D. Medical Ethics	
1. Principles of medical ethics—Know the principles of medical ethics established by the American Medical Association; define terminology associated with medical ethics.	7
2. Ethical conduct—Identify the ethical response for the various situations in a medical facility; recognize unethical practices.	7
E. Human Relations	
1. Patient relations—Identify emotional reactions of various age groups; respond appropriately to emotional needs of patients.	6, 7, 8
2. Other interpersonal relations—Employ appropriate interpersonal skills in the workplace.	7, 8

Exam Topics	Chapters
F. Patient Education	
1. Patient instruction—Employ various methods to instruct patients (i.e., echo method, verbal, and written instructions); instruct patients, as directed, in areas of nutrition, diet, medications, body mechanics, and treatment procedures; document patient instruction properly.	6, 8, 12, 15
2. Patient resource materials—Maintain patient resource materials.	6, 8, 12
II. Administrative Medical Assisting	
A. Insurance	
1. Terminology—Assist patients with insurance inquiries; know terminology associated with health and accident insurance in the medical office.	10
2. Plans—Know the major types of medical insurance programs encountered in the medical office, including government-sponsored, group, individual, and workers' compensation programs.	10
3. Claim forms—Complete and file forms for insurance claims; evaluate claims rejection; complete "first" reports.	10
4. Coding—Know coding systems used in insurance processing; code diagnoses and procedures.	10
5. Financial aspects of medical insurance—Know billing requirements for insurance programs; process insurance payments; track unpaid claims.	10
B. Financial Bookkeeping	
1. Terminology—Know terminology associated with financial bookkeeping in the medical office.	9
2. Patient billing—Maintain and explain physician's fee schedules; collect and post payments; manage patient ledgers; make financial arrangements with patients; prepare and mail itemized statements; know methods of billing; cycle billing procedures.	9, 10
3. Collections—Identify delinquent accounts; take appropriate steps for collection; perform skip tracing; perform telephone collection procedures; know collection as related to bankruptcy and small claims cases.	9
4. Fundamental medical office accounting procedures—Employ appropriate accounting procedures (i.e., pegboard); employ daily balancing procedures; prepare monthly trial balance; know accounts payable/receivable.	9

Exam Topics	Chapters
5. Banking—Manage petty cash; prepare and make bank deposits; reconcile bank statements; use and process checks appropriately (including NSF and endorsement requirements); maintain checking account; process payables (office bills).	9
6. Employee payroll—Prepare employee payroll; maintain payroll tax deduction records; prepare employee tax forms; prepare payroll tax deduction reports; know terminology pertaining to payroll and taxes.	9
7. Financial mathematics—Perform calculations related to patient and practice accounts.	9
C. *Medical Secretarial-Receptionist*	
1. Terminology—Know terminology associated with medical secretarial and receptionist duties.	8
2. Reception—Receive and greet patients and visitors under nonemergency conditions; screen visitors and sales persons requesting to see physician; obtain patient information; call/assist patients into examination room.	8
3. Scheduling—Employ appointment scheduling system (maintain appointment book, type daily schedule, review schedule with physician); prepare information for referrals; arrange hospital admissions and surgery; schedule patients for outpatient diagnostic tests; manage recall system and file; employ procedures for handling cancellations and missed appointments.	8
4. Oral and written communications—Answer and place telephone calls employing proper etiquette; manage telephone calls requiring special attentions (including lab and x-ray reports, angry callers, and personal calls); instruct patients by telephone regarding emergency treatment and medications; inform patients of laboratory results; employ effective intra-office communication skills (including employee supervision and patient handling); compose correspondence according to acceptable business format; type bills, statements, medical records, and other written materials, and proofread written material; manage mail; employ effective written communication skills.	7, 8, 12
5. Records management—Manage complete patient medical records system; file records according to appropriate system (master calendars, tickler files, correspondence, financial records, physician's records, non-patient files); transfer files; protect, store, and retain medical records according to appropriate conventions.	7, 8

Exam Topics	Chapters
6. Charts—Arrange contents of patient charts in appropriate order and perform audits for accuracy; record laboratory results and patient communication in charts; maintain confidentiality of medical records and test results (e.g., HIV, pregnancy tests); observe special regulations regarding the confidentiality of HIV results.	7, 8, 12, 18
7. Transcription and dictation—Transcribe notes from Dictaphone or tape recorder; transcribe notes from direct dictation.	8
8. Supplies and equipment management—Maintain inventory of medical and office supplies and equipment (reordering, order new supplies); arrange for equipment maintenance and repair, and maintain warranty/services files.	9, 12
9. Computers for medical office applications—Use computer for data entry and retrieval; use computer for word processing; use computer for billing and financial transactions; employ procedures for ensuring the integrity and confidentiality of computer-stored information.	8
10. Office safety—Maintain office cleanliness and comfort; maintain office safety (maintain office safety manual and post-emergency instructions); maintain records of biohazardous waste and hazardous chemicals; know and comply with Occupational Safety and Health Act (OSHA) guidelines and regulations.	11, 12
III. Clinical Medical Assisting	
A. Asepsis	
1. Terminology—Know terminology associated with asepsis.	4, 11
2. Universal blood and fluid precautions—Know transmission and prevention of transmission of microorganisms, know and follow OSHA guidelines for blood-borne pathogens.	4, 11, 17
3. Medical asepsis—Know and follow aseptic procedures when working; employ hand washing and gloving procedures.	4, 11, 12, 17
4. Surgical asepsis—Know and perform surgical aseptic techniques; employ surgical hand washing and gloving procedures.	4, 11, 12, 17
B. Sterilization	
1. Terminology—Know terminology associated with sterilization procedures.	4, 11
2. Sanitization—Know the procedures for sanitization of various equipment found in the medical office; know the various chemicals used for sanitization.	11, 12

Exam Topics	Chapters
3. Disinfection—Know procedures for disinfection of various disinfection chemicals; know the names of, and uses for, various disinfection chemicals.	11, 12
4. Sterilization—Employ procedures for sterilizing items (gloves, instruments, tubing, jars, solutions, and drapes); know proper sterilization methods for items (e.g., autoclave, chemical sterilization); know the procedures for wrapping items; know the various types of wrapping materials; describe the various types of indicators.	11, 12
C. Instruments	
1. Identification—Know various instrument parts (i.e., handles, locks, teeth, and serrations); know instrument classifications; name commonly used instruments; name specialty instruments.	12
2. Usage—Know the use of each of the commonly used instruments (i.e., forceps, hemostats, scissors); know the instruments used for various types of examinations (i.e., gynecological, pediatric, neurological, and physical examinations).	12
3. Care and handling—Know the procedure for care of nondisposable instruments; know the procedure for discarding disposable instruments.	11
D. Vital Signs	
1. Blood pressure—Obtain blood pressure (select proper cuff size, employ appropriate and accurate procedure); record measurement; recognize normal and abnormal blood pressure readings.	12
2. Pulse—Obtain a pulse, know various locations that can be used; record pulse; recognize normal and abnormal pulse.	12
3. Respiration—Obtain a respiratory rate; record respirations; recognize normal and abnormal respiration rate.	12
4. Height and weight—Obtain height and weight; record height and weight; know terminology associated with abnormal measurements; obtain and record pediatric height and weight.	12
5. Temperature—Know the types, care, and handling of thermometers; obtain temperatures via oral, rectal, and axillary methods; know normal temperature ranges for each method; record temperature; know fever classifications.	12
E. Physical Examinations	
1. Problem oriented records—Obtain medical history; employ appropriate terminology and abbreviations; differentiate between subjective and objective information (describe what constitutes each); understand SOAP procedure for recording information.	12

Exam Topics	Chapters
2. Positions—Know positions used for examinations; know when to utilize each; drape patient for each examination.	12, 15
3. Methods of examination—Know methods used for physical examinations; know when to employ each method.	12
4. Specialty examinations—Know procedures for pediatric examination, including Apgar scoring, head circumference measurements, and growth charts; know procedures for gynecological and obstetric examinations, including Pap smears, breast examinations, and routine obstetric examinations; know procedures for proctological examinations, including rectal, proctoscopy, and sigmoidoscopy; know procedures for genitourinary tract examinations.	12, 15
5. Visual acuity—Know procedures for obtaining near and far visual acuity (employ adult and pediatric charts); know procedures for obtaining color vision acuity; know normal and abnormal measurements.	12
6. Allergy testing—Know procedure for performing scratch test; know procedure for performing intradermal skin test; know terminology associated with allergy specialty.	12
F. Clinical Pharmacology	
1. Terminology—Know terminology associated with pharmacology; know commonly used abbreviations.	5, 13
2. Injections—Know procedures for performing intramuscular, subcutaneous, intradermal, and z-track injections; know sites and amounts used for each type; know procedure for obtaining a drug from a vial or ampule; know needle sizes and syringe types necessary for each injection type; perform calculations required for dosages, including conversion factors; prepare documentation.	13
3. Prescriptions—Know drug schedules and legal procedure for each; know procedures for completing prescriptions, refills, and patient documentation.	5, 13
4. Drugs—Know regulation of medications, including proper record maintenance and Drug Enforcement Agency regulations; know categories, forms, and uses of drugs; know commonly used drugs; know methods of administration other than injections: rectal, topical, vaginal, sublingual, oral, and inhalation; know procedure for ear instillation, eye drops, and ointments; know drug storage requirements (i.e., narcotics, locked cabinets, refrigeration, etc.); know procedure for using *Physician's Desk Reference*.	5, 13

Exam Topics	Chapters
G. Minor Surgery	
1. Surgical supplies—Know supplies used in minor surgery, including drapes, dressings, bandages, sutures, anesthetics, and antiseptics; identify by name, and use, instruments common to office surgery.	12
2. Surgical procedures—Know procedure for surgical tray preparation, including the use of sterile packs, transfer forceps, and sterile containers; know procedure for patient preoperative and postoperative skin care; handle sterile equipment using aseptic technique; identify potential contamination through personnel, moisture, and equipment handling; employ aseptic technique for hand washing and gloving; know procedures for removing all types of sutures; know dressing and bandaging procedures; know other surgical procedures; know care of equipment, skin preparation, and patient care for electrosurgery; know precautions, preparation, and patient care for laser surgery; dispose of contaminated disposable instruments.	12
H. Therapeutic Modalities	
1. Modalities—Know procedures for performing heat treatments, including hot pack, moist compress, hot water bottle, heat lamp, paraffin bath, and whirlpool bath; know procedures for applying ice pack and cold compress; know procedures for performing ultrasound treatments; know range-of-motion joint exercises.	16
2. Patient instruction—Instruct patients in the use of crutches, canes, wheelchairs, etc.; instruct patient regarding therapeutic treatments at home, as directed by physician.	16
I. Laboratory Procedures	
1. Safety—Employ universal blood and body fluid precautions and OSHA guidelines.	11, 18
2. Quality control—Establish and perform quality control procedures.	18
3. Laboratory equipment—Employ proper care and use of laboratory equipment, including microscopes, centrifuges, refractometer, and glassware.	18
4. Urinalysis—Know procedures for obtaining sterile, clean catch, timed, and drug screening specimens; know procedures for performing urinalysis, including physical characteristics, chemical (dipstick), and microscope preparation.	18

Exam Topics	Chapters
5. Blood—Obtain a blood specimen by venipuncture and fingerstick (including selection of proper specimen container); perform microhematocrit, hemoglobin, blood glucose (by reagent strips or Accu-Check™), sedimentation rate; know procedures for proper disposal of blood products.	18
6. Other specimens—Obtain a swab throat culture; obtain a stool specimen for occult blood and parasite determination; assist in obtaining cerebral spinal fluid; know procedure for obtaining sputum specimen.	18
7. Specimen handling—Label and handle reference laboratory specimens; complete request forms.	18
8. Records—Know appropriate record and documentation procedures.	7, 18
9. Microbiology—Identify microorganism categories; know names and growth patterns of pathogenic organisms; know procedures for obtaining laboratory specimens; know procedures for preparing slides for physician microscopic examination (i.e., wet mount).	4
J. Electrocardiography	
1. Standard, 12-lead ECG—Know procedures for patient preparation, lead placement, and obtaining a 12-lead ECG; identify and eliminate artifacts; know ECG lead marking codes.	14
2. Mounting techniques—Know procedures for mounting an ECG; identify abnormal readings for mounting.	14
3. Other ECG procedures—Know procedures for obtaining a rhythm strip; identify special ECG procedures (i.e., Holter monitor, treadmill examinations, etc.)	14
K. First Aid	
1. First aid procedures—Perform CPR and Heimlich maneuver; maintain a crash tray; identify first aid emergencies and associated procedures (i.e., strokes, heart attacks, fractures, animal bites, shock, asthma, poisoning, seizures, sprains, strains, burns, head injuries, lacerations, epistaxis, hemorrhages, injuries, and foreign bodies); know terminology and abbreviations associated with first aid.	17
2. Legal responsibilities—Know legal responsibilities as they apply to the medical assistant (i.e., reporting, action to be taken); report emergencies as required by law.	17

Brief Table of Contents

Expanded Table of Contents

Theory Review

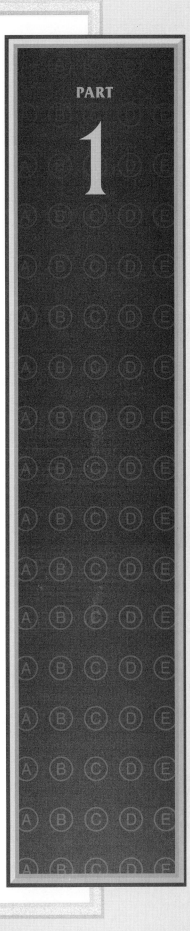

PART

1

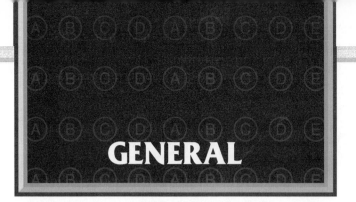

GENERAL

MEDICAL ASSISTING KNOWLEDGE

Theory Review

SECTION OUTLINE

Chapter 1 – Medical Terminology

Chapter 2 – Anatomy and Physiology

Chapter 3 – Pathophysiology

Chapter 4 – Microbiology

Chapter 5 – Pharmacology

Chapter 6 – Nutrition

Chapter 7 – Law and Ethics

CHAPTER 1

Medical Terminology

CHAPTER OUTLINE

Word Building

Spelling

Common Medical Abbreviations

Pharmaceutical Abbreviations

Medical Terminology in Practice

Common Terms Related to Disease
Integumentary System
Musculoskeletal System
Nervous System
Sensory System
Endocrine System
Cardiovascular System
Respiratory System
Digestive System
Urinary System
Reproductive System

AREAS OF COMPETENCE

AAMA—ROLE DELINEATION STUDY AREAS OF COMPETENCE

General (Transdisciplinary)

Communication Skills

• Use medical terminology appropriately

AMT—RMA CERTIFICATION EXAM TOPICS

Medical Terminology

- Word parts
- Definitions
- Common abbreviations and symbols
- Spelling

STRATEGIES TO SUCCESS

▶ *Study Skills*

Organize and manage!
  Organize your notes after class. Doing so will not only help you review material but also make it easier to understand your notes when you go back to them to study for an exam. Organizing your notes right away will also give you plenty of time to ask your instructor to clarify something you didn't understand.

Word Building

Root: The main part of a word that gives the word its central meaning. The root is the basic foundation of a word that can be made more complex through the addition of other word parts.

Prefix: A structure at the beginning of a word that modifies the meaning of the root. Not all medical words have a prefix. An example of a prefix can be found in the word *hypolipemia*. *Hypo-* is the prefix, *lip* is the root, and *-emia* is the suffix. For a list of common prefixes, see Table 1-1.

Suffix: A word ending that modifies the meaning of the root. Not all words have a suffix. An example of a suffix can be found in the word *ganglionectomy*. *Ganglion* is the root and *-ectomy* is the suffix. For a list of common suffixes, see Table 1-2.

Combining vowels: When a medical term is formed from many different word parts, these parts are often joined by a vowel. This vowel is usually an *o* and occasionally an *i*. For example, *o* serves as a combining vowel in the word *hyperlipoproteinemia* (*hyper* / *lip* / *o* / *protein* / *emia*). The vowel *o* is the most common combining vowel. The combining vowel is used to ease pronunciation; therefore only medical terms that need them have combining vowels.

Guidelines for using combining vowels:

- When a root and a suffix beginning with a vowel are connected, a combining vowel is usually not used.
- Connecting a word root and a suffix that starts with a consonant usually requires a connecting vowel.
- When two roots are connected, a combining vowel is usually used even if vowels are present at the junction.
- Most common prefixes can be connected to other word parts without a combining vowel.

Combining form: A root coupled with a combining vowel, which may be separated in writing by a vertical slash: *arthr* / *o*, *oste* / *o*, *ven* / *o*. Most medical terms contain at least one root or combining form and a suffix.

Prefix	Meaning	Example	Definition
a-	Without	Aphonia	Inability to produce sound
ab-	From, away from	Abduct	To move away from the midline of the body
ad-, ac-, af-, ag-, al-, an-, ap-, ar-, as-, at-	Toward, increasing	Adduct	To move toward the midline of the body
alb-	White	Albinism	Whiteness of skin, hair, and eyes caused by the absence of pigment
ambi-	Both	Ambidextrous	Able to use both hands effectively
ana-	Up, upward, toward	Anaphylactic	Characterized by an exaggerated reaction to an antigen or toxin
ante-	Before	Antepartum	Before childbirth
anti-	Against	Antibiotic	Acting against microorganisms
auto-	Self	Autodermic	Of the patient's own skin (said of skin grafts)
bi-	Two, both	Bilateral	Pertaining to both sides
bio-	Life	Biology	Study of life
circum-	Around	Circumcision	Removal of the skin around the tip of the penis
con-, col-, com-, cor-	Together, with	Congenital	Accompanying birth, present at birth
contra-	Against	Contraceptive	Preventing conception
de-	From, down, not	Decalcify	To decrease or remove calcium
dia-	Through	Diagnosis	Knowledge through testing
dis-	Apart, separate	Dislocation	Removal of any part of the body from its normal position
dys-	Bad, difficult, painful	Dysuria	Painful urination
ec-	Out, away	Ectopic	Pertaining to something outside its normal location
ecto-	Outside	Ectoplasm	Outermost layer of cell protoplasm

Table 1-1

Prefix	Meaning	Example	Definition
en-, em-	In	Endemic	Occurring continuously in a population
		Empyema	Pus in a body cavity
endo-	Within	Endoscope	Instrument to examine something from within
epi-	Upon, over	Epidermal	Upon the skin
eu-	Good	Eupnea	Normal, good breathing
ex-, e-	Out, away	Exhale	To breathe out
		Emanation	Something given off
hemi-	Half	Hemicardia	Half of the heart
hyper-	Excessive, beyond	Hyperlipemia	Condition of excessive fat in the blood
hypo-	Below, under	Hypoglycemia	Low blood sugar
in-, il-, im-, ir-	Not	Impotence	Inability to achieve erection
infra-	Below, under, beneath	Inframammary	Below the breast
inter-	Between	Intercellular	Between cells
intra-	Within	Intravenous	Within a vein
iso-	Equal	Isometric	Of equal dimension
juxta-	Near, beside	Juxtaarticular	Near a joint
mal-	Bad	Malaise	Discomfort
mega-, megal- / o	Large	Megacephaly	Abnormal enlargement of the head
mes- / o	Middle	Mesoderm	Middle layer of the skin
meta-	Beyond, after	Metastasis	Spread of disease from one part of the body to another
micro-	Small	Microscope	Instrument used to view small organisms
milli-	One-thousandth	Milliliter	One-thousandth of a liter
mono-	One, single	Mononuclear	Having only one nucleus
multi-	Many	Multidisciplinary	Pertaining to many areas of study

Table 1-1, continued

Prefix	Meaning	Example	Definition
neo-	New, recent	Neonatal	Pertaining to the period after birth
non-	Not	Noninvasive	Not invading the body through any organ, cavity, or skin (said of a diagnostic or therapeutic technique)
para-	Near, beside, beyond, opposite, abnormal	Paramedic	Person who provides emergency medical care (alongside other medical personnel)
per-	Through	Percutaneous	Through the skin
peri-	Around	Perianal	Around the anus
poly-	Many	Polyarthritis	Inflammation of many joints
post-	After	Postmortem	After death
pre-	Before	Premature	Before maturation
primi-	First	Primiparous	Having given birth for the first time
re-	Again, back	Reactivate	To make active again
retro-	Back, backward, behind	Retrograde	Going backward
rube-	Red	Rubella	Viral disease characterized by red rashes, among other things
semi-	Half	Semiconscious	Half conscious
sub-	Under, below	Sublingual	Under the tongue
super-	Above, excessive	Superficial	Near or above the surface
supra-	Above, over	Suprapubic	Above the pubic area
syn-, sym-	Together	Symbiosis	Mutual interdependence
tri-	Three	Triceps	Muscle with three heads
uni-	One	Unicellular	One-celled
ultra-	Beyond, excessive	Ultrasound	Sound with a very high frequency, used to obtain medical images

Table 1-1, continued

Suffix	Meaning	Example	Definition
-ac	Pertaining to	Cardiac	Pertaining to the heart
-ad	Toward	Cephalad	Toward the head
-al	Pertaining to	Thermal	Pertaining to the production of heat
-ar	Pertaining to	Articular	Pertaining to a joint
-desis	Binding	Arthrodesis	Surgical binding or fusing of a joint
-e	Noun marker	Dermatome	Instrument used to cut the skin
-ectomy	Excision, removal	Hysterectomy	Removal of the entire uterus
-emesis	Vomit	Hyperemesis	Excessive vomiting
-form	Resembling, like	Vermiform	Shaped like a worm
-genic	Beginning, originating, producing	Toxigenic	Producing toxins
-genetic	Beginning, originating, producing	Virogenetic	Caused by a virus, having a viral origin
-gram	Record	Electrocardiogram	Record of the variations in electrical potential caused by the heart muscle
-graph	Instrument for recording	Electrocardiograph	Instrument for making electrocardiograms
-graphy	Process of recording	Electrocystography	Process of recording the changes of electric potential in the urinary bladder
-iasis	Condition, formation of	Lithiasis	Formation or presence of stones
-iatric	Pertaining to medical treatment	Pediatric	Pertaining to the treatment of children
-iatry	Study or field of medicine	Psychiatry	Study of the human psyche
-ic	Pertaining to	Thoracic	Pertaining to the thorax
-ical	Pertaining to	Neurological	Pertaining to nerves
-ism	Condition	Cryptorchidism	Condition of undescended testes

Table 1-2

Prefix	Meaning	Example	Definition
-ist	Specialist	Gynecologist	Physician who specializes in the female reproductive system
-itis	Inflammation	Appendicitis	Inflammation of the appendix
-logist	Specialist in the study of	Microbiologist	Biologist who specializes in the study of microorganisms
-logy	Study of	Microbiology	Study of microorganisms
-lysis	Destruction, breaking down	Hemolysis	Breaking down of blood
-megaly	Enlargement	Cardiomegaly	Enlargement of the heart
-meter	Instrument used to measure	Scoliosometer	Instrument for measuring the curves of the spine
-oma	Tumor	Carcinoma	Cancerous, malignant tumor
-ory	Pertaining to	Auditory	Pertaining to hearing
-osis	Condition, disease	Leukocytosis	Condition of increased leukocytes in the blood
-pathy	Disease	Hemopathy	Disease of the blood
-penia	Abnormal reduction	Leukocytopenia	Decrease in the number of white blood cells
-philia	Attraction	Necrophilia	Attraction to dead bodies
-phobia	Abnormal fear	Photophobia	Fear of light
-plasia	Molding, formation	Dysplasia	Faulty formation
-plasty	Molding, surgical repair	Rhinoplasty	Surgical repair of the nose
-ptosis	Drooping, prolapse, falling	Mastoptosis	Drooping of the breast
-rrhage	Excessive flow, discharge	Hemorrhage	Bursting forth of blood
-rrhea	Discharge, flow	Amenorrhea	Absence of menstrual flow
-rrhexis	Rupture	Cardiorrhexis	Rupture of the heart

Table 1-2, continued

Prefix	Meaning	Example	Definition
-scope	Instrument used to view	Oscilloscope	Instrument that displays visual representation of electrical variations
-scopy	Process of viewing with a scope	Opthalmoscopy	Process of examining the interior of the eye using an opthalmoscope
-stasis	A standing still, control, stoppage	Hemostasis	A stopping of the flow of blood
-stomy	Surgical creation of a new opening	Colostomy	Creation of an opening between the colon and the surface of the body
-tomy	Incision, cutting	Phlebotomy	Incision into a vein

Table 1-2, continued

Spelling

Spelling: Medical terminology is important because it enables you not only to better communicate with your colleagues but also to write professional letters in which you use and spell medical terminology correctly. Throughout the chapters, pay attention to the way specialized medical terms are spelled and be prepared to answer spelling-related questions on the exam. Some commonly misspelled words:

- Abscess
- Aerobic
- Aneurysm
- Asepsis
- Asthma
- Benign
- Capillary
- Chancre
- Clavicle
- Defibrillator
- Desiccation
- Dissect
- Epididymis
- Fissure
- Glaucoma
- Hemorrhoid
- Homeostasis
- Humerus
- Ischium
- Occlusion
- Osseus
- Parenteral
- Parietal
- Perineum
- Specimen
- Surgeon
- Vaccine

Plural forms: Here are some general rules. Remember, there are almost always exceptions.

- Add an *s* or *es* to most singular nouns to make them plural.

- When a medical term in the singular form ends in *is*, drop the *is* and add *es* to make it plural (metastasis/metastases).
- When the term ends in *um* or *on*, drop the *um* or *on* and add *a* (atrium/atria, ganglion/ganglia).
- When the term ends in *us*, drop the *us* and add *i* (bronchus/bronchi). Exceptions to this rule involve mainly certain words of Latin origin (corpus/corpora, genus/genera, sinus/sinuses, virus/viruses)
- When the term ends in *ma*, add *ta* (stoma/stomata).
- When the term otherwise ends in *a*, drop the *a* and add *ae* (vertebra/vertebrae).

Possessive forms: For singular nouns and plural nouns that do not end in *s*, add an apostrophe and an *s*. For plural nouns that end in *s*, just add an apostrophe but no additional *s*.

Common Medical Abbreviations

Abbreviations: As a medical professional, you will be required to know a lot of abbreviations. The most common abbreviations used in association with medical care facilities are presented in Table 1-3. The most common medical record abbreviations are listed in Table 1-4, abbreviations associated with the metric system are listed in Table 1-5 on p. 11, and common prescription abbreviations are listed in Table 1-6 on p.11. Tables of relevant abbreviations are also included for each body system.

AT A GLANCE — Medical Care Facility Abbreviations

Abbreviation	Meaning
CCU	Coronary care unit
ECU	Emergency care unit
ER	Emergency room
ICU	Intensive care unit
IP	Inpatient
OP	Outpatient
OR	Operating room
PAR	Postanesthetic recovery
postop	Postoperative
preop	Preoperative
RTC	Return to clinic
RTO	Return to office

Table 1-3

AT A GLANCE — Medical Record Abbreviations

Abbreviation	Meaning
BP	Blood pressure
C	Celsius, centigrade
c/o	Complains of
CP	Chest pain
Dx	Diagnosis
F	Fahrenheit
H&P	History and physical
Ht	Height
Hx	History
L	Left

Table 1-4

Abbreviation	Meaning
L&W	Living and well
P	Pulse
PE	Physical examination
pH	Hydrogen concentration (acidity/alkalinity)
PI	Present illness
PMH	Past medical history
pt	Patient
Px	Physical examination
R	Right
R/O	Rule out
T	Temperature
Tx, Tr	Treatment
VS	Vital signs
Wt	Weight
WDWN	Well-developed and well-nourished
y.o.	Year old

Table 1-4, continued

Pharmaceutical Abbreviations

Metric system: A system of measurement based on the decimal system. Its units include the meter, gram, and liter. It is the most commonly used system of measurement in health care. For a list of common abbreviations used in the metric system, see Table 1-5. **Conversion factors for the metric system:** The meter (m), used for length, equals approximately 39.37 inches; the liter (L or l), for volume, equals approximately 1.056 U.S. quarts; and the gram (g or gm), for weight, equals approximately 0.035 ounce.

Apothecaries' system: An old system of measurement in which the weight measure is based on one grain of wheat and the liquid measure is based on one drop of water. The apothecaries' system measures weight by grains (gr), scruples (scr), drams (dr), ounces (oz), and pounds (lb). It uses minims (min), fluidrams (fl dr), fluidounces (fl oz), pints (pt), quarts (qt), and gallons (gal) to measure volume. In the apothecary system, dosage quantities are written in lowercase Roman numerals (i = 1, ii = 2, iv = 4, v = 5, vi = 6, ix = 9, x = 10, xi = 11, xx = 20, xl = 40, l = 50, lx = 60, xc = 90, c = 100, cx = 110, cc = 200, d = 500, m = 1000, mm = 2000, etc.). A bar written above a numeral multiplies its value by 1000 ($\bar{v}$ = 5000, $\bar{c}$ = 100,000, $\overline{m}$ = 1,000,000, etc.).

Conversion factors for the apothecaries' system: There are approximately 15 grains to a gram.

grains $\times$ 60 = milligrams

grains $\div$ 15 = grams

AT A GLANCE	Common Abbreviations Used in the Metric System
Abbreviation	**Meaning**
cc	Cubic centimeter (1 cc = 1 mL)
cm	Centimeter (2.5 cm = 1 inch)
km	Kilometer
mm	Millimeter
g, gm	Gram
kg	Kilogram (1 kg = 1000 gm = 2.2 pounds)
L or l	Liter = 1000 ml (1 gallon = 4 quarts = 8 pints = 3.785 L; 1 pint = 473.16 ml)
deca-	× 10
hect- / o	× 100
kilo-	× 1000
deci-	÷ 10
centi	÷ 100
milli-	÷ 1000
micro-	÷ 1,000,000

Table 1-5

AT A GLANCE	Common Abbreviations Used in Prescriptions
Abbreviation	**Meaning**
a	Before
a.c.	Before meals
ad lib.	As desired
AM, a.m.	Morning
amt	Amount
aq	Water
b.i.d., BID	Twice a day
buc	Buccal

Table 1-6

Common Abbreviations Used in Prescriptions

Abbreviation	Meaning
c̄	With
cap	Capsule
d	Day
Fl.	Fluid
h, hr	Hour
h.s.	At bedtime, at the hour of sleep
ID	Intradermal
IM	Intramuscular
IV	Intravenous
noc., n.	Night
NPO	Nothing by mouth
oint., ung.	Ointment
p̄	After
p.c.	After meals
per	By, through
PM, p.m.	After noon
p.o., PO	By mouth
PR	Through the rectum
p.r.n., PRN	As needed
PV, vag.	Through the vagina
q)	Every
q.d., QD	Every day
qh	Every hour
q2h	Every two hours
q.i.d., QID (*q* for *quarter,* "four times")	Four times a day
q.o.d.	Every other day

Table 1-6, continued

Abbreviation	Meaning
q2h	Every two hours
®	Right; registered trademark
Rx	Prescription, take
s̄, s	Without
SC, sub-Q, SQ, subcu	Subcutaneous
Sig:	Instruction to patient
soln.	Solution
sp.	Spirits
ss	One half
stat	Immediately
supp., suppos	Suppository
syr.	Syrup
T	Topical
tab	Tablet
t.i.d., TID	Three times a day
x	Times, for

Table 1-6, continued

Medical Terminology in Practice

Common Terms Related to Disease

AT A GLANCE	Common Terms Related to Disease
Term	**Meaning**
Benign	Noncancerous
Degeneration	Change of tissue to a less functionally active form
Etiology	Cause of a disease
Malaise	Not feeling well (the first indication of illness)
Malignant	Cancerous
Prognosis	Prediction about the outcome of a disease
Prophylaxis	Protection against disease
Remission	Cessation of signs and symptoms

Table 1-7

Integumentary System

AT A GLANCE	Integumentary System—Common Combining Forms		
Combining Form	**Meaning**	**Example**	**Definition**
adip / o	Fat	Adipose tissue	Layer of fat beneath the skin
albin / o	White	Albinism	Condition caused by the lack of melanin pigment in the skin, hair, and eyes
cry / o	Cold	Cyrosurgery	Surgery that uses liquid nitrogen to freeze tissue
cutane / o	Skin	Subcutaneous	Beneath the skin
derm / o	Skin	Dermatitis	Inflammation of the skin
erythr / o	Red	Erythrodermatitis	Inflammation of the skin marked by redness and scaling
hidr / o	Sweat	Hidradenitis	Inflammation of a sweat gland
hist / o	Tissue	Histology	Study of tissues

Table 1-8

Integumentary System—Common Combining Forms

Combining Form	Meaning	Example	Definition
kerat / o	Hard skin, horny tissue, keratin	Keratosis	Lesion formed from an overgrowth of the horny layer of skin
leuk / o	White	Leukoplakia	Raised, white patches on the mouth or vulva
lip / o	Fat	Lipoma	Common benign tumor of the fatty tissue
onych / o	Nail	Onycholysis	Separation of the nail from its bed
seb / o	Sebum (oil)	Seborrhea	Excessive secretion of sebum
squam / o	Scale	Squamous	Scale-like
trich / o	Hair	Trichopathy	Any disease of the hair
xanth / o	Yellow	Xanthoma	Yellow deposit of fatty material in the skin
xer / o	Dry	Xerosis	Abnormal dryness of the eye, skin, and mouth

Table 1-8, continued

Integumentary System—Suffixes

Suffix	Meaning	Example	Definition
-malacia	Softening	Onychomalacia	Softening of the nails
-phagia	Eating, swallowing	Onychophagia	Nail-biting

Table 1-9

Integumentary System—Abbreviations

Abbreviation	Meaning
Bx	Biopsy
Derm	Dermatology
SC, sub-Q, SQ, subcu, subq	Subcutaneous

Table 1-10

Musculoskeletal System

Musculoskeletal System—Common Combining Forms

Combining Form	Meaning	Example	Definition
ankyl / o	Stiff	Ankylosis	Complete loss of movement in a joint
arthr / o	Joint	Arthralgia	Pain in the joint
bucc / o	Cheek	Buccinator	Cheek muscle
burs / o	Bursa	Bursolith	Stone in a bursa
calc / o	Calcium	Hypercalcemia	Excessive amount of calcium in the blood
carp / o	Wrist	Carpal	Pertaining to the wrist
cervic / o	Neck	Cervical	Pertaining to the neck
chondr / o	Cartilage	Osteachondroma	Benign bone tumor
cost / o	Rib	Intercostal	Between the ribs
crani / o	Cranium (skull)	Cranial	Pertaining to the skull
dors / o	Back	Dorsal	Pertaining to the back
fasci / o	Band of fibrous tissue	Fasciotomy	Operation to relieve pressure on the muscles by making an incision into the fascia
fibr / o	Fiber	Fibroma	Benign tumor of the connective tissues
kyph / o	Hump	Kyphosis	Excessive curvature of the spine, "humpback"
lamin / o	Lamina	Laminectomy	Surgical removal of the lamina
lei / o / my / o	Smooth muscle	Leiomyoma	Benign tumor of smooth muscle
lord / o	Curve	Lordosis	Inward curvature of the spine
my / o, myos / o	Muscle	Myalgia	Muscle pain
myos / o	Muscle	Myositis	Inflammation of muscle tissue
my / o / cardi / o	Heart muscle	Myocardial	Pertaining to the heart muscle
oste / o	Bone	Osteoporosis	Condition in which bones become porous and fragile
pector / o	Chest	Pectoral	Pertaining to the chest

Table 1-11

Musculoskeletal System—Common Combining Forms

Combining Form	Meaning	Example	Definition
rhabd / o / my / o	Striated, skeletal muscle	Rhabdomyolysis	Destruction of muscle tissue accompanied by the release of myoglobin
spondyl / o	Vertebra	Spondylitis	Inflammation of the joints between the vertebrae in the spine
synov / i	Synovia	Synovial membrane	Membrane lining the capsule of a joint
ten / o, tend / o, tendin / o	Tendon	Tendinitis	Inflammation of the tendons

Table 1-11, continued

Musculoskeletal System—Suffixes

Suffix	Meaning	Example	Definition
-asthenia	Lack of strength	Myasthenia gravis	Disorder of neuromuscular transmission marked by weakness
-clasia	Breaking	Arthroclasia	Artificial breaking of adhesions of an ankylosed joint
-desis	Binding	Arthrodesis	Surgical binding or fusing of a joint
-physis	Growth	Metaphysis	The growing portion of a long bone
-schisis	Splitting	Rachischisis	Failure of vertebral arches and neutral tube to fuse
-trophy	Development	Hypertrophy	Excessive development

Table 1-12

Musculoskeletal System—Abbreviations

Abbreviation	Meaning
C1, C2, . . . C7	Individual cervical vertebrae (first through seventh)
Ca	Calcium
CTS	Carpal tunnel syndrome
EMG	Electromyography
fx	Fracture

Table 1-13

AT A GLANCE **Musculoskeletal System—Abbreviations**

Abbreviation	Meaning
ortho	Orthopedics
ROM	Range of motion
SLE	Systemic lupus erythematosus

Table 1-13, continued

AT A GLANCE **Actions of Muscles**

Motion	Meaning
Abduction	Movement away from the midline
Adduction	Movement toward the midline
Extension	Increase in the angle of a joint
Flexion	Decrease in the angle of a joint
Pronation	Act of turning downward or inward
Rotation	Act or process of turning on an axis
Supination	Act of turning upward or outward

Table 1-14

Nervous System

AT A GLANCE **Nervous System—Common Combining Forms**

Combining Form	Meaning	Example	Definition
cerebell / o	Cerebellum	Cerebellar	Pertaining to the cerebellum
cerebr / o	Cerebrum	Cerebral cortex	Outer layer of the cerebrum
dur / o	Dura mater	Subdural hematoma	Bleeding between the dural and arachnoidal membranes
encephal / o	Brain	Encephalitis	Inflammation of the brain
mening / o	Membrane	Meningomyelocele	Protrusion of the spinal cord through a defect in the vertebral column
myel / o	Spinal cord	Myelogram	Radiographic study of the spinal subarachnoid space

Table 1-15

Nervous System—Common Combining Forms

Combining Form	Meaning	Example	Definition
neur / o	Nerve	Neuralgia	Pain in a nerve
poli / o	Gray matter	Poliodystrophy	Wasting of gray matter
psych / o	Mind	Psychosomatic	Pertaining to the influence of the mind on the body

Table 1-15, continued

Nervous System—Prefixes

Prefix	Meaning	Example	Definition
hemi-	Half	Hemihypesthesia	Diminished sensation in one side of the body
tetra-	Four	Tetraparesis	Weakness of all four extremities

Table 1-16

Nervous System—Suffixes

Suffix	Meaning	Example	Definition
-algesia	Excessive sensitivity to pain	Analgesia	State in which painful stimuli are no longer as painful
-algia	Pain	Neuralgia	Nerve pain
-esthesia	Feeling neural sensation	Anesthesia	Loss of sensation
-kinesia	Movement	Bradykinesia	Decrease in spontaneity and movement
-kinesis	Movement	Hyperkinesis	Excessive muscular activity
-lepsy	Seizure	Epilepsy	Chronic brain disorder, often characterized by seizures
-paresis	Slight paralysis	Hemiparesis	Weakness on one side of the body
-phasia	Speech	Aphasia	Impairment of language ability
-plegia	Paralysis	Hemiplegia	Paralysis of one side of the body
-praxia	Action	Apraxia	Impairment of purposeful movement

Table 1-17

Abbreviation	Meaning
AD	Alzheimer's disease
ALS	Amyotrophic lateral sclerosis
CAT	Computed axial tomography
CNS	Central nervous system
CP	Cerebral palsy
CSF	Cerebrospinal fluid
CT	Computed tomography
CVA	Cerebrovascular accident
EEG	Electroencephalogram
LP	Lumbar puncture
MRI	Magnetic resonance imaging
MS	Multiple sclerosis
TIA	Transient ischemic attack

Table 1-18

Sensory System

The Eye

AT A GLANCE   The Eye—Common Combining Forms

Combining Form	Meaning	Example	Definition
aque / o	Water	Aqueous	Containing, or like water
blephar / o	Eyelid	Blepharitis	Inflammation of the eyelids
conjunctiv / o	Conjunctiva	Conjunctivitis	Inflammation of the conjunctiva, pinkeye
cor / o, core / o	Pupil	Corepraxy	Procedure to widen a small pupil
dacry / o	Tear, tear duct	Dacryoadenitis	Inflammation of the lacrimal gland
ir / o	Iris	Iritis	Inflammation of the iris

Table 1-19

Combining Form	Meaning	Example	Definition
dipl / o	Double	Diplopia	Condition in which one object is perceived as two objects
glauc / o	Gray	Glaucoma	Eye disease that may result in blindness
lacrim / o	Tear	Lacrimal	Pertaining to tears
mi / o	Smaller, less	Miosis	Contraction of the pupil
nyct / o	Night	Nyctalopia	Poor night vision
ocul / o	Eye	Intraocular	Inside the eye
opt / o	Vision	Optometer	Instrument for determining refraction of the eye
ophthalm / o	Eye	Ophthalmologist	Physician who specializes in treating eyes
palpebr / o	Eyelid	Palpebral	Pertaining to the eyelid
phot / o	Light	Photophobia	Fear and avoidance of light
presby / o	Old age	Presbyopia	Loss of accommodation in the eye resulting from aging
pupill / o	Pupil	Pupillary	Pertaining to the pupil
retin / o	Retina	Retinitis	Inflammation of the retina
scot / o	Darkness	Scotoma	Blind spot in which vision is absent or depressed
uve / o	Vascular layer of the eye	Uveitis	Inflammation of the uveal tract
vitre / o	Glassy	Vitreous humor	Fluid component of the transparent vitreous body

Table 1-19, continued

Suffix	Meaning	Example	Definition
-opia	Vision	Hyperopia	Farsightedness
-tropia	A turning	Esotropia	Inward turning of the eye, toward the nose

Table 1-20

The Eye—Abbreviations

Abbreviation	Meaning
ast	Astigmatism
IOP	Intraocular pressure
OD	Right eye
OS	Left eye
OU	Each eye
PERRLA	Pupils equal, round, reactive to light and accommodation
REM	Rapid eye movement
VA	Visual acuity
VF	Visual field

Table 1-21

The Ear

The Ear—Common Combining Forms

Combining Form	Meaning	Example	Definition
acou, acous / o	Hearing	Acoustic	Pertaining to hearing
audi / o	Hearing	Audiometer	Instrument for measuring hearing
audit / o	Hearing	Auditory	Pertaining to the sense or organs of hearing
aur / i	Ear	Aural	Pertaining to the ear
cochle / o	Cochlea	Cochlear	Pertaining to the cochlea
mastoid / o	Mastoid process	Mastoiditis	Inflammation of the mastoid process
ot / o	Ear	Otic	Pertaining to the ear
tympan / o	Eardrum	Tympanoplasty	Operation on a damaged middle ear

Table 1-22

The Ear—Suffixes

Suffix	Meaning	Example	Definition
-cusis, -acousia	Hearing	Presbycusis, presbyacousia	Nerve deafness due to aging
-otia	Ear condition	Macrotia	Enlarged ears

Table 1-23

The Ear—Abbreviations

Abbreviation	Meaning
AD	Right ear
AS	Left ear
AU	Each ear
EENT	Eyes, ears, nose, and throat
oto	Otology

Table 1-24

Endocrine System

Endocrine System—Common Combining Forms

Combining Form	Meaning	Example	Definition
aden / o	Gland	Adenectomy	Excision of a gland
andr / o	Male	Androgen	Hormone produced by the testes in males and by the adrenal cortex in males and females
adrenal / o	Adrenal gland	Adrenalectomy	Removal of one or both adrenal glands
calc / o	Calcium	Hypercalcemia	Elevated concentration of calcium in the blood
cortic/ o	Cortex, outer region	Corticosteroid	Steroid produced by the adrenal cortex
crin / o	Secretion	Endocrinologist	Physician who specializes in endocrinology
dips / o	Thirst	Polydipsia	Prolonged excessive thirst

Table 1-25

Endocrine System—Common Combining Forms

Combining Form	Meaning	Example	Definition
epinephr / o	Adrenal gland	Epinephritis	Inflammation of an adrenal gland
glyc/ o	Sugar	Hyperglycemia	High blood sugar
gonad / o	Sex gland	Gonadotropin	Hormone that promotes gonadal growth
home / o	Like, similar	Homeostasis	State of bodily equilibrium
hormon / o	Hormone	Hormonal	Pertaining to hormones
kal / i	Potassium	Hypokalemia	Lack of potassium in the blood as a result of dehydration, excessive vomiting, and diarrhea
lact / o	Milk	Prolactin	Hormone that stimulates milk production during pregnancy
natr / o	Sodium	Hyponatremia	Low concentration of sodium in the blood
parathyroid / o	Parathyroid gland	Parathyroidectomy	Excision of the parathyroid gland
somat / o	Body	Somatotropic	Having a stimulating effect on body growth
ster / o	Solid structure	Steroid	Pertaining to the steroids, some of which increase muscle mass
thyr / o	Thyroid gland	Thyrotropin hormone	Hormone that stimulates growth of the thyroid gland
thyroid / o	Thyroid gland	Thyroiditis	Inflammation of the thyroid gland

Table 1-25, continued

Endocrine System—Prefixes

Prefix	Meaning	Example	Definition
oxy-	Rapid, sharp	Oxytocin	Hormone that influences contractions of the uterus
pan-, pant- / o	All	Panhypopituitarism	State of inadequate or absent secretion of pituitary hormones
		Pantophobia	Fear of everything
tri-	Three	Triiodothyronine	Hormone secreted by the thyroid gland that regulates metabolism

Table 1-26

Endocrine System—Suffixes

Suffix	Meaning	Example	Definition
-agon	Assemblage, a gathering together	Glucagon	Hormone produced by the pancreas that causes an increase in blood sugar
-in, -ine	A substance	Epinephrine	Stress hormone secreted by the adrenal gland
-uria	Urine condition	Glycosuria	Urinary excretion of sugar

Table 1-27

Endocrine System—Abbreviations

Abbreviation	Meaning
ACTH	Adrenocorticotropic hormone
BMR	Basal metabolic rate
Ca	Calcium
DI	Diabetes insipidus
DM	Diabetes mellitus
FBS	Fasting blood sugar
FSH	Follicle-stimulating hormone
GH	Growth hormone
GTT	Glucose tolerance test
IDDM	Insulin-dependent diabetes mellitus
K	Potassium
Na	Sodium
PRL	Prolactin
TFT	Thyroid function test

Table 1-28

Cardiovascular System

Cardiovascular System—Common Combining Forms

Combining Form	Meaning	Example	Definition
angi / o	Vessel	Angiogram	X-ray image of a blood vessel
aort / o	Aorta	Aortic stenosis	Narrowing of the aorta
arter / o, arteri / o	Artery	Arteriosclerosis	Thickening of arterial walls
atri / o	Atrium	Atrial	Pertaining to an atrium
bas / o	Base	Basophil	Cell with granules that stain specifically with basic (alkaline) dyes
cardi / o	Heart	Cardiomegaly	Enlargement of the heart
coagul / o	Clotting	Anticoagulant	Drug that prevents clotting of the blood
coron / o	Crown, circle	Coronary arteries	Blood vessels encircling the heart
cyto / o	Cell	Cytology	Study of cells
hem / o, hema, hemat / o,	Blood	Hemorrhage	Abnormal discharge of blood
		Hematology	Study of blood
is / o	Same, equal	Anisocytosis	Abnormality of red blood cells that are of unequal size
kary / o	Nucleus	Eukaryote	Cell that contains membrane-bound nucleus with chromosomes
lymph / o	Lymph	Lymphadenitis	Inflammation of the lymph nodes
phleb / o	Vein	Phlebotomy	Incision in vein to draw blood
plasm / o	Plasma	Plasmapheresis	Removal of plasma from the body, separation and extraction of specific elements, and reinfusion
thromb / o	Clot	Thrombolysis	Dissolving of a clot
valv / o, valvul / o	Valve	Valvoplasty	Surgical reconstruction of a cardiac valve
vas / o	Vessel	Vasoconstriction	Narrowing of the blood vessels
ven / o	Vein	Venous	Pertaining to a vein

Table 1-29

Cardiovascular System—Suffixes

Suffix	Meaning	Example	Definition
-apharesis	Removal	Plasmapheresis	Removal of plasma from the blood using a centrifuge
-blast	Immature stage, germ, bud	Monoblast	Certain type of immature cell
-crit	Separation	Hematocrit	Percentage of volume of a blood sample that is composed of cells
-cytosis	Abnormal condition of cells	Poikilocytosis	Presence of large, irregularly shaped blood cells
-globin	Protein	Hemoglobin	Protein of red blood cells

Table 1-30

Cardiovascular System—Abbreviations

Abbreviation	Meaning
AF	Atrial fibrillation
AS	Aortic stenosis
ASD	Atrial septal defect
BP	Blood pressure
CAD	Coronary artery disease
CHD	Coronary heart disease
CHF	Congestive heart failure
ECG, EKG	Electrocardiogram
ECHO	Echocardiography
MI	Myocardial infarction
MVP	Mitral valve prolapse
PDA	Patent ductus arteriosus
PVC	Premature ventricular contraction
VT	Ventricular tachycardia

Table 1-31

Respiratory System

Respiratory System—Common Combining Forms

Combining Form	Meaning	Example	Definition
adenoid / o	Adenoid	Adenoidectomy	Operation to remove adenoid growths
alveol / o	Air sac	Alveolar	Pertaining to a small cell or cavity
bronch / i, bronch / o	Bronchus	Bronchitis	Inflammation of the mucous membrane of the bronchial tubes
capn / o	Carbon dioxide	Hypercapnia	Excessive carbon dioxide in the blood
coni / o	Dust	Pneumoconiosis	Pulmonary disease caused by prolonged inhalation of fine dust
cyan / o	Blue	Cyanosis	Bluish discoloration of the skin caused by a deficiency of oxygen in the blood
laryng / o	Larynx	Laryngitis	Inflammation of the mucous membrane in the larynx
lob / o	Lobe of the lung	Lobectomy	Excision of a lobe
nas / o	Nose	Paranasal sinuses	Accessory sinuses in the bones of the face that open into the nasal cavities
ox / o	Oxygen	Hypoxia	Deficiency of oxygen in tissue cells
phon / o	Voice	Dysphonia	Hoarseness
phren / o	Diaphragm	Phrenohepatic	Pertaining to the diaphragm and liver
pneum / o, pneuma, pneumat / o	Breath	Pneumatosis	Abnormal presence of air or other gas
pneum / o, pneumon / o	Lung	Pneumonia	Inflammation of the lung parenchyma
pulmon / o	Lung	Pulmonary	Pertaining to the lungs
rhin / o	Nose	Rhinorrhea	A watery discharge from the nose
spir / o	Breathing	Spirometer	Gasometer used to measure respiration
tonsill / o	Tonsil	Tonsillectomy	Removal of the tonsil

Table 1-32

Respiratory System—Suffixes

Suffix	Meaning	Example	Definition
-ema	Condition	Empyema	Condition of having pus in a body cavity as a result of a lung infection
-oxia	Oxygen	Anoxia	Absence of oxygen from blood or tissues
-pnea	Breathing	Apnea	Inability to breathe
-ptysis	Spitting	Hemoptysis	Coughing up and spitting out blood
-sphyxia	Pulse	Asphyxia	Impairment of oxygen intake
-thorax	Chest	Hemothorax	Blood in the pleural cavity

Table 1-33

Respiratory System—Abbreviations

Abbreviation	Meaning
ARDS	Acute respiratory distress syndrome
CPR	Cardiopulmonary resuscitation
CXR	Chest X-ray
PFT	Pulmonary function test
TB	Tuberculosis
URI	Upper respiratory infection

Table 1-34

Digestive System

Digestive System—Common Combining Forms

Combining Form	Meaning	Example	Definition
an / o	Anus	Perianal	Located around the anus
append / o	Appendix	Appendectomy	Surgical removal of the appendix
bucc / o	Cheek	Buccalabial	Pertaining to the cheek and lip
cec / o	Cecum	Cecal	Pertaining to the cecum
cheil / o	Lip	Cheilosis	Dry scaling and fissuring of lips

Table 1-35

Combining Form	Meaning	Example	Definition
chol / o, chole	Bile	Choledochus	Bile duct
cholecyst / o	Gallbladder	Cholecystectomy	Surgical removal of the gallbladder
col / o	Colon	Colostomy	Creation of an artificial opening into the colon
colon / o	Colon	Colonic	Pertaining to the colon
enter / o	Intestine	Enteropathy	Intestinal disease
gastr / o	Stomach	Gastritis	Inflammation of the stomach
gingiv / o	Gum	Gingivitis	Inflammation of the gums
gloss / o	Tongue	Hypoglossal	Below the tongue
hepat / o	Liver	Hepatitis	Inflammation of the liver
lapar / o	Abdomen	Laparoscopy	Examination and often surgery of the abdominal cavity with a laparoscope
or / o	Mouth	Oral	Pertaining to the mouth
peritone / o	Peritoneum	Peritonitis	Inflammation of the peritoneum
rect / o	Rectum	Rectocele	Prolapse of the rectum
sphing-, sphinc-	Binding, constricting	Sphincter	Circular muscle constricting an orifice

Table 1-35, continued

Suffix	Meaning	Example	Definition
-ase	Enzyme	Amylase	Class of digestive enzymes that act on starch
-chezia	Defecation	Hematochezia	Passage of bloody stools
-iasis	Abnormal condition	Choledocholithiasis	Stones in the common bile duct
-pepsia	Digestion	Dyspepsia	Upset stomach
-prandial	Meal	Postprandial	Following a meal

Table 1-36

Digestive System—Abbreviations

Abbreviation	Meaning
BE	Barium enema
EUS	Endoscopic ultrasound
GERD	Gastroesophageal reflux disease
GI	Gastrointestinal
IBS	Irritable bowel syndrome

Table 1-37

Urinary System

AT A GLANCE **Urinary System—Common Combining Forms**

Combining Form	Meaning	Example	Definition
albumin / o	Protein	Albuminuria	Protein in the urine
bacteri / o	Bacterium, bacteria	Bacteriuria	Bacteria in the urine
cali / o	Calix (calyx)	Caliectasis	Dilation of the calices
cyst / o	Urinary bladder	Cystitis	Inflammation of the urinary bladder
ket / o	Ketone bodies	Ketosis	Enhanced production of ketone bodies
lith / o	Stone	Nephrolithiasis	Presence of a renal stone or stones
meat / o	Opening, passageway	Meatoscope	Speculum for examining the urinary meatus
nephr / o	Kidney	Nephropathy	Disease of the kidney
olig / o	Scanty, few	Oliguria	Scanty urine production
pyel / o	Renal pelvis	Pyelolithotomy	Operation to remove a stone from the kidney
ren / i, ren / o	Kidney	Renography	Radiography of the kidney
ur / o, urin / o	Urine, urinary tract	Urodynia	Pain on urination
vesic / o	Urinary bladder	Perivesical	Surrounding the urinary bladder

Table 1-38

Urinary System—Suffixes

Suffix	Meaning	Example	Definition
-tripsy	Crushing	Lithotripsy	Crushing of a stone in the renal pelvis, ureter, or bladder
-uria	Urination	Dysuria	Difficulty or pain in urinating

Table 1-39

Urinary System—Abbreviations

Abbreviation	Meaning
ADH	Antidiuretic hormone; vasopressin
ARF	Acute renal failure
BUN	Blood urea nitrogen
Cath	Catheter
CFR	Chronic renal failure
HD	Hemodialysis
IVP	Intravenous pyelogram
KUB	Kidney, ureter, and bladder
PKU	Phenylketonuria
UA	Urinalysis
UTI	Urinary tract infection

Table 1-40

Reproductive System

Reproductive System—Common Combining Forms

Combining Form	Meaning	Example	Definition
amni / o	Amnion	Amniocentesis	Aspiration of amniotic fluid for diagnosis
balan / o	Glans penis	Balanitis	Inflammation of the glans penis
cervic / o	Cervix, neck	Endocervicitis	Inflammation of the mucous membrane of the cervix

Table 1-41

Combining Form	Meaning	Example	Definition
colp / o	Vagina	Colporrhaphy	Repair of a rupture in the vagina
culd / o	Cul-de-sac	Culdocentesis	Aspiration of fluid from the cul-de-sac
crypt / o	Hidden	Cryptorchism	Failure of one or both testes to descend
epididym / o	Epididymis	Epididymitis	Inflammation of the epididymis
galact / o	Milk	Galactorrhea	Abnormal, persistent discharge of milk
gon / o	Generation, genitals	Gonorrhea	Contagious inflammation of the genital mucous membrane
gynec / o	Female	Gynecomastia	Excessive development of the mammary glands in a male
hyster / o	Uterus	Hysterectomy	Removal of the uterus
lact / i, lact / o	Milk	Lactation	Production of milk
mammo / o	Breast	Mammogram	Breast X-ray
mast / o	Breast	Mastectomy	Excision of the breast
men / o	Menses	Amenorrhea	Absence or abnormal cessation of menses
metr / o	Uterus	Metrorrhagia	Irregular bleeding from the uterus between periods
nat / i	Birth	Neonatal	Pertaining to the first month of life
orchi / o, orchid / o	Testis, testicle	Orchiectomy	Removal or one or both testes
ov / o	Egg	Ovum	Female sex cell, or egg
prostat / o	Prostate gland	Prostatitis	Inflammation of the prostate
terat / o	Monster	Teratoma	Neoplasm composed of tissues not normally found in the organ
test / o	Testis, testicle	Testicular	Pertaining to the testes
vagin / o	Vagina	Vaginitis	Inflammation of the vagina
vas / o	Vessel, duct	Vasectomy	Removal of a section of the vas deferens
vert / i, vers / i	A turning	Cephalic version	Turning of the fetus so that the head is correctly positioned for delivery

Table 1-41, continued

Reproductive System—Suffixes

Suffix	Meaning	Example	Definition
-arche	Beginning	Menarche	Time of the first menstrual period
-gravida	Pregnant	Primigravida	Woman in her first pregnancy
-one	Hormone	Testosterone	Hormone related to masculinization and reproduction
-pexy	Fixation, fastening	Orchiopexy	Surgical treatment of an undescended testicle
-stomy	(New) opening	Vasostomy	Surgical procedure of making a new opening into the vas deferens
-tocia	Labor, birth	Dystocia	Difficult childbirth

Table 1-42

Reproductive System—Abbreviations

Abbreviation	Meaning
AB	Abortion
AIDS	Acquired immunodeficiency syndrome
BPH	Benign prostatic hyperplasia
CS, C-section	Cesarean section
CX	Cervix
D&C	Dilation and curettage
ECC	Endocervical curettage
EMB	Endometrial biopsy
FHT	Fetal heart tones
FSH	Follicle-stimulating hormone
GYN	Gynecology
HCG	Human chorionic gonadotropin
HIV	Human immunodeficiency virus
HSV	Herpes simplex virus
LH	Luteinizing hormone

Table 1-43

Abbreviation	Meaning
Multip	Multipara
Pap smear	Papanicolaou smear (test for cervical or vaginal cancer)
PMS	Premenstrual syndrome
PSA	Prostate-specific antigen
STD	Sexually transmitted disease

Table 1-43, continued

STRATEGIES TO SUCCESS

▶ *Test-Taking Skills*

Think success!
Approach the exam with confidence. It's unlikely that you will get all the questions right. Don't panic or become stressed when you can't answer a question. Relax, and imagine yourself doing wonderfully. A positive attitude will help you stay in control and allow you to focus on all the questions that you do know.

CHAPTER 1 REVIEW

Instructions:

Answer the following questions. Check your answers in the *Answer Key* that follows this section.

1. A prefix is
    A. The first part of a word
    B. A word structure at the end of a term that modifies the root
    C. A word structure at the beginning of a term that modifies the root
    D. Found on all medical terms
    E. The last part of a word that gives the word its root meaning

2. Which of the following suffixes means "inflammation"?
    A. -iasis
    B. -trophy
    C. -itis
    D. -osis
    E. -desis

3. The abbreviation for the word *diagnosis* is
    A. Diag
    B. DG
    C. dgs
    D. D
    E. Dx

4. The most common combining vowel is
    A. i
    B. u
    C. a
    D. e
    E. o

5. The prefix *ab-* means
    A. Without
    B. Toward
    C. Against
    D. Away from
    E. Previous or before

6. The combining form is the
    A. Word root
    B. Word root with the combining vowel attached (written with a separating vertical slash)
    C. Word root with the prefix and suffix attached (written with a separating vertical slash)
    D. Word root with the prefix and suffix attached (written without a slash)
    E. Combining vowel

7. Which of the following suffixes means "lack of strength"?
    A. -algia
    B. -tomy
    C. -asthenia
    D. –trophy
    E. -phasia

8. Which of the following words is misspelled?
    A. Abscess
    B. Homostasis
    C. Venous
    D. Prostate
    E. Integumentary

9. When the combining form *cyan / o* is used, it means that
    A. The skin is involved
    B. The object is blue
    C. The object is oily
    D. The muscles are involved
    E. Something is poisonous

10. The combining form *oste / o* means
    A. Tendon
    B. Vertebra
    C. Muscle
    D. Calcium
    E. Bone

11. Which of the following abbreviations means "every day"?

    A. b.i.d.
    B. q.e.d.
    C. t.i.d.
    D. q.i.d.
    E. q.d.

12. The prefix *intra-* means

    A. Between
    B. Below
    C. Within
    D. Beside
    E. Above

13. The abbreviation *stat* means

    A. Immediately
    B. Do not change
    C. Stay on alert
    D. Daily
    E. Statistics

14. The suffix *–stasis* means

    A. Condition
    B. Control
    C. Destruction
    D. Discharge
    E. Unchanged

15. The suffix *-pathy* means

    A. Disease
    B. Spasm
    C. Treatment
    D. Tumor
    E. Excision

16. Which of the following combining forms refers to the brain?

    A. myel / o
    B. encephal / o
    C. cortic / o
    D. alveol / o
    E. psych / o

17. The combining form *audi / o* means

    A. Speaking
    B. Hearing
    C. Seeing
    D. Learning through personal experience
    E. Learning from reported experience, or "book-learning"

18. The prefix *epi-* means

    A. Good
    B. Out
    C. Off
    D. Within
    E. Upon

19. *Nephr / o* and *ren / o* both refer to which of the following?

    A. The lungs
    B. The heart
    C. The bladder
    D. The kidney
    E. The rectum

20. The suffix *-gravida* refers to

    A. A pregnancy
    B. The condition of aging
    C. A serious condition
    D. A stomach ache
    E. A malignancy

21. The prefix *peri-* means

    A. Behind
    B. Underneath
    C. Inside
    D. Half
    E. Surrounding

22. The underlined portion of the words *pneumo-coniosis* and *pneumonoconiosis* represents which of the following word parts?

    A. Prefix
    B. Root
    C. Suffix
    D. Combining form
    E. None of the above

23. Which of the following contains the central meaning of a word?

    A. Prefix
    B. Suffix
    C. Root
    D. Combining form
    E. Both A and B

24. The abbreviation *q.o.d.*, as used in prescriptions, means

    A. Every hour
    B. Every two hours
    C. Twice a day
    D. Four times a day
    E. Every other day

25. The prefix *retro-* means

    A. Behind
    B. Around
    C. Below
    D. Before
    E. Above

26. The underlined portion of the word *hypolipemia* represents which of the following word parts?

    A. Prefix
    B. Root
    C. Suffix
    D. Combining form
    E. None of the above

27. Which of the following words is misspelled?

    A. Peritoneum
    B. Dissect
    C. Homerous
    D. Metastasis
    E. None of the above

28. Which of the following words is misspelled?

    A. Vacsine
    B. Sphincter
    C. Parietal
    D. Osseous
    E. Asthma

29. Which of the following prefixes means "bad, difficult, painful"?

    A. ex-
    B. dis-
    C. dys-
    D. dia-
    E. meta-

30. The suffix *–kinesia* means

    A. Mind
    B. Muscle
    C. Pain
    D. Touch
    E. Movement

31. The combining form *cheil / o* means

    A. Cheek
    B. Lip
    C. Gum
    D. Tongue
    E. Mouth

32. The prefix *rube-* means

    A. Rotation
    B. Small
    C. Spots
    D. Abnormal
    E. Red

33. Which of the following words is misspelled?

    A. Neruon
    B. Malaise
    C. Humerus
    D. Desiccation
    E. Glaucoma

34. The prefix *milli-* means

    A. One-thousandth
    B. Many
    C. One
    D. One-hundredth
    E. One-tenth

35. Which of the following suffixes means "beginning, origin, production"?

    A. -iasis
    B. -genic
    C. -genetic
    D. Both B and C
    E. Both A and B

36. The suffix –scope means an instrument for

    A. Measuring
    B. Viewing
    C. Creating a new opening
    D. Recording
    E. Illuminating

37. The combining form xer / o refers to something

    A. Dry
    B. Yellow
    C. Multiple
    D. Pertaining to hair
    E. Pertaining to X-rays

38. The combining form ot / o means

    A. Hearing
    B. Seeing
    C. Light
    D. Eye
    E. Ear

39. The plural of diverticulum is

    A. Diverticulums
    B. Diverticuli
    C. Diverticulae
    D. Diverticulumes
    E. Diverticula

40. The plural of calculus is

    A. Calculus'
    B. Calcula
    C. Calculi
    D. Calculuses
    E. Calculus

ANSWER KEY

1.	C		21.	E
2.	C		22.	D
3.	E		23.	C
4.	E		24.	E
5.	D		25.	A
6.	B		26.	A
7.	C		27.	C
8.	B		28.	A
9.	B		29.	C
10.	E		30.	E
11.	E		31.	B
12.	C		32.	E
13.	A		33.	A
14.	B		34.	A
15.	A		35.	D
16.	B		36.	B
17.	B		37.	A
18.	E		38.	E
19.	D		39.	E
20.	A		40.	C

Anatomy and Physiology

CHAPTER OUTLINE

Cell Structure

Organelles
Cell Division
Movement of Substances Across the Cell Membrane

Chemistry

Tissues of the Body

Body Membranes

Division Planes and Body Cavities

Division Planes
Body Cavities

Integumentary System

Musculosketal System

Skeletal System
Muscular System

Nervous System

Nerve Cells and Neurotransmitters
Central Nervous System
Peripheral Nervous System

Sensory System

Smell
Taste
Sight
Hearing
Endocrine System

Cardiovascular System

The Blood
Blood Cell Types

The Heart and Blood Vessels
Lymphatic System

Respiratory System

Digestive System

Additional Organs and Processes Involved With Digestion

Urinary System

Body Fluids
Organs and Function of the Urinary System

Reproductive System

Male Reproductive System
Female Reproductive System

AREAS OF COMPETENCE

AAMA—ROLE DELINEATION STUDY AREAS OF COMPETENCE

General (Transdisciplinary)

Communication Skills

- Use medical terminology appropriately

AMT—RMA CERTIFICATION EXAM TOPICS

Anatomy and Physiology

- Body systems

Medical Terminology

- Definitions
- Spelling

STRATEGIES TO SUCCESS

▶ *Study Skills*

Find a good place to study!
Think about what atmosphere you study best in. Are you distracted by the slightest noise? Do you like a certain level of noise to keep you going and focused? Do you like studying alone or in groups? Also consider how comfortable you want to be. Do you find yourself drifting off when you study on your bed or in a comfortable chair? Is studying at a desk too uncomfortable? There's no right place or way to study. Some people pace the halls, while others find a secluded place in their house where their family and friends can't bother them. We do suggest that you find a place that is well lighted. Unnecessary eye strain could cause you to become tired too soon. Whatever place you pick, make sure it's right for you and make it a habit to study there regularly.

Cell Structure

Cell: The basic structural unit of all organisms. Cells have three main parts: the cell membrane, the cytoplasm, and the nucleus. See Figure 2-1.

Cell membrane: A bilayer of phospholipid and protein molecules that controls the passage of materials in and out of the cell.

Cytoplasm: The medium for chemical reactions in the cell. It contains water, dissolved ions, nutrients, and different organelles. The cytoplasm surrounds the nucleus and is encircled by the cell membrane.

Nucleus: The largest and innermost organelle in the cell. It is a roughly spherical body near the center of the cell, and it contains DNA, which regulates the cell's activities.

DNA: Deoxyribonucleic acid. DNA consists of long chains of chemical bases along a sugar-phosphate backbone; the chains are joined in pairs by bonds between complementary bases and twist around each other in a double helix. This pattern of bases carries genetic information that directs all cell activities.

Chromatin: The genetic material contained in the nucleus of a nondividing cell. It consists primarily of chromosomes, made of DNA bound in clumps to proteins.

Nucleolus: A dense body within the nucleus, also known as the little nucleus, composed of DNA, RNA,

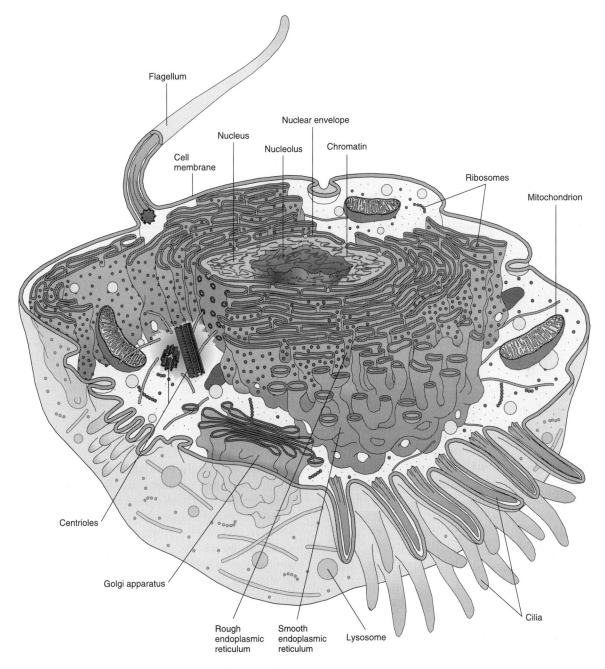

Figure 2-1. *A composite cell. Organelles are not drawn to scale.*

and protein molecules. It is the site for synthesis of ribosomal RNA (rRNA).

RNA: Ribonucleic acid. RNA consists of long, single chains of chemical bases along a sugar-phosphate backbone. RNA molecules are transported from the nucleus into the cytoplasm, where they direct the formation of proteins.

Organelle: A specialized part of a cell that performs a particular function.

Organelles

Ribosome: A granular cytoplasmic organelle composed of RNA. Ribosomes provide enzymes that link amino acids for protein synthesis.

Mitochondrion: A small, rod-shaped organelle that serves as the power plant of the cell because it provides energy.

Lysosomes: Cytoplasmic particles that digest material that comes into the cell. They are often referred to as the garbage disposals of the cells because they break down nutrient molecules and foreign particles.

Endoplasmic reticulum: A network of tubules that transports material through the cytoplasm and aids in the synthesis of proteins and lipids.

Golgi apparatus: A small membranous structure found in most cells that forms the carbohydrate side chains of glycoproteins. The Golgi apparatus consists of a stave of about six, flattened membranous sacs that refine and alter glycoproteins. It is also called the Golgi body or Golgi complex.

Cytoskeleton: The cytoplasmic elements that coordinate the movement of organelles.

Centriole: An intracellular, rod-shaped body involved with cell division and organizing mitotic spindles.

Cilium: One of numerous small, hairlike extensions that move substances across the surface of a cell.

Flagellum: A long, whiplike extension from a cell that aids in movement.

Cell Division

Mitosis: The division of a somatic cell to form two new cells, each identical to the parent cell.

Meiosis: A type of nuclear division in which the number of chromosomes is reduced to one-half the number found in a normal body cell. It results in the formation of an egg or sperm.

Cytokinesis: Division of the cytoplasm, exclusive of the nuclear division. Cytokinesis describes the total of all the changes that occur in the cytoplasm during mitosis, meiosis, and fertilization.

Movement of Substances Across the Cell Membrane

Diffusion: The movement of molecules from a region of higher concentration to a region of lower concentration.

Osmosis: The diffusion of water through a selectively permeable membrane in response to the concentration gradient.

Facilitated diffusion: Diffusion through a membrane by means of proteins acting as carrier molecules.

Filtration: The movement of fluid through a membrane in response to hydrostatic pressure.

Active transport: The movement of substances against a concentration gradient, from a region of lower concentration to a region of higher concentration. It requires a carrier molecule and uses energy.

Endocytosis: The formation of vesicles in the cell membrane to transfer particles and droplets from the outside into the cell. Phagocytosis (ingestion of solids) and pinocytosis (ingestion of liquids) are two such processes.

Exocytosis: The discharge from a cell of particles too large to pass through the cell membrane by diffusion.

Isotonic solution: A solution that has the same concentration (osmotic pressure) as the fluids within a cell.

Hypertonic solution: A solution that has a higher concentration (osmotic pressure) than the fluids within a cell.

Hypotonic solution: A solution that has a lower concentration (osmotic pressure) than the fluids within a cell.

Chemistry

Element: The simplest form of matter with unique chemical properties. Oxygen, iron, gold, and other elements cannot be broken down into different substances by ordinary chemical means. All matter, living and nonliving, is composed of elements.

Atom: The smallest particle of an element, consisting of electrons surrounding a nucleus composed of protons, neutrons, and other entities.

Atomic number: The number of protons in the nucleus of the atom. The hydrogen atom, for example, has one proton and its atomic number is 1. Carbon has six protons and its atomic number is 6.

Atomic weight: The relative weight of an atom, determined by the number of protons and neutrons together and compared to the standard carbon atom (which has a mass of 12 and an atomic weight of 12).

Ionic bond: A relatively weak attraction formed when one or more electrons are transferred from one atom to another. It is easily disrupted in water.

Covalent bond: The chemical bond formed when two atoms share a pair of electrons. It is the strongest type of chemical bond.

Ion: An atom that has acquired a charge through the gain or loss of one or more electrons.

Anion: A negatively charged ion.

Cation: A positively charged ion.

Ionization: The separation of a compound into its constituent ions.

Molecule: Two or more atoms chemically bonded together, such as the common form of oxygen (O_2).

Compound: A molecule composed of two or more different elements, such as carbon dioxide (CO_2).

Chemical reaction: The process by which atoms or molecules interact to form new chemical combinations.

Mixture: A combination of substances that are not chemically combined and can be separated by physical means.

Solution: A liquid mixture in which the components are evenly distributed and cannot be distinguished.

Solute: A substance that dissolves in a solution.

Solvent: A liquid in which a substance dissolves.

Suspension: A mixture in which a solid is distributed but not dissolved. It will separate unless it is shaken.

Electrolyte: A substance that permits the transfer of electrons in solution. Common electrolytes include acids, bases, and salts.

pH: The number used to indicate the exact strength of an acid or base.

pH scale: A scale, ranging from 0 to 14, that measures the hydrogen ion concentration of a solution.

Acid: A substance with a pH less than 7.0 that ionizes in water to release hydrogen ions. Because a hydrogen ion consists of a proton, an acid is referred to as a hydrogen ion donor or a proton donor.

Base: A substance with a pH greater than 7.0. It is referred to as a hydrogen ion acceptor or a proton acceptor. Bases contain higher concentrations of hydroxyl ions (OH^-), whereas acids contain higher concentrations of hydrogen ions (H^+).

Buffer: A substance that prevents or reduces changes in pH and counterbalances the addition of an acid or base.

Buffer system: A system that uses chemical reactions occurring in body fluids to maintain a particular pH.

The acid-base balance is regulated by two buffer systems in the body: the lungs and the kidneys.

ATP: The abbreviation for adenosine triphosphate. ATP is the primary provider of energy for a cell.

Tissues of the Body

Histology: The microscopic study of tissues.

Tissue: A collection of similar cells acting together to perform a particular function. Types include epithelial (see Table 2-1), connective, muscular, and nervous.

Gland: An organ that contains special cells that secrete substances. Some glands lubricate; others produce hormones (see Table 2-2 on p. 46).

Unicellular glands: Consist of only one cell.

Multicellular glands: May be classified on the basis of structure (simple or compound), type of secretion (mucous, serous, or mixed), presence or absence of ducts (exocrine or endocrine), characteristics of secreting units (alveolar or acinar), and manner of secretion (merocrine, apocrine, or holocrine).

Goblet cell: The only unicellular exocrine gland. Goblet cells produce mucus in digestive, respiratory, urinary, and reproductive tracts.

Connective tissue: Tissue that connects, protects, supports, and forms a framework for all body structures. Connective tissue includes loose fibrous tissue, adipose tissue, dense fibrous tissue, cartilage, bone, and blood.

Loose fibrous tissue: Fills spaces in the body and binds structures together.

Adipose tissue: A specialized form of loose fibrous tissue that provides insulation; it is commonly called fat.

Dense fibrous tissue: Connective tissue that forms tendons and ligaments.

Cartilage: A hard, dense connective tissue consisting of cells embedded in a matrix that can withstand consid-

AT A GLANCE	Types of Epithelial Tissue	
Type	**Description**	**Location**
Simple squamous	Single layer of thin, flat cells	Alveoli of lungs, capillary walls
Simple cuboidal	Single layer of cube-shaped cells	Ovary, thyroid gland
Simple columnar	Single layer of tall cells	Intestines, stomach
Stratified squamous	Several layers with flat cells at the free surface	Skin, vagina, anus
Transitional	Specialized to change in response to increased tension; cells become thinner when distended	Urinary bladder

Table 2-1

AT A GLANCE	Summary of Glandular Modes of Secretion	
Secretion Mode	**Meaning**	**Examples**
Merocrine	Pertaining to a secretory cell that remains intact during secretion	Salivary glands, certain sweat glands, pancreatic glands
Apocrine	Pertaining to a secretory cell that contributes part of its protoplasm to the secretion	Mammary glands and certain sweat glands
Holocrine	Pertaining to a secretory cell that produces secretions consisting of altered cells of the same gland	Sebaceous glands

Table 2-2

erable pressure and tension. It provides support, a framework, and attachment; protects underlying tissues; and forms structural models for many developing bones. It's bluish-white or gray and semi-opaque. Cartilage does not contain any nerves or blood supply. There are three types of cartilage: hyaline, fibrous, and elastic.

Bone: A hard, connective tissue consisting of specialized cells embedded in a matrix of hardened mineral salts. It is the most rigid connective tissue.

Blood: The only type of connective tissue that is liquid, composed of cells suspended in a fluid matrix called plasma.

Nervous tissue: Found in the brain, spinal cord, and nerves.

Muscle tissue: Provides movement, maintains posture, and produces heat. Muscle tissue is composed of elongated muscle fibers that can contract and thereby move body parts. There are three types of muscle tissue: skeletal, smooth, and cardiac. Skeletal muscles attach to bones and are controlled voluntarily. Smooth muscles, which lack the striations of skeletal muscles, line the walls of hollow internal organs. Cardiac muscles, which are striated, are found only in the heart. Both smooth and cardiac muscles are controlled involuntarily.

Sarcoma: A malignant tumor that forms in connective tissue.

Body Membranes

Membrane: A layer of tissue that lines body cavities, covers organs, or separates structures.

Cutaneous membrane: The membrane that covers the body. It is also known as the skin.

Epithelial membranes: Mucous and serous membranes.

Serous membranes: The pleura, pericardium, and peritoneum.

Connective tissue membranes: Synovial membranes and the meninges.

Meninx: One of three connective tissue coverings, or meninges, around the brain and spinal cord. The three layers, from the outermost to the innermost, are the dura mater, arachnoid, and pia mater.

Adenoma: A benign tumor of glandular epithelial cells.

Adenocarcinoma: Malignant tumor originating in glandular epithelium.

Division Planes and Body Cavities

Division Planes

Division plane: One of three imaginary planes (frontal, sagittal, and transverse) used as references in describing positions of the body or of parts of the body. See Figure 2-2.

Frontal plane: A plane that divides the body into front and back halves. This plane is also referred to as coronal or lateral.

Sagittal plane: A plane that divides the body into left and right halves. This plane is also referred to as median.

Transverse plane: A plane that divides the body into upper and lower halves. This plane is also referred to as horizontal.

Body Cavities

Body cavity: Either of two main cavities in the body, the dorsal and the ventral. See Figure 2-3.

Dorsal cavity: The main body cavity consisting of the cranial cavity, which contains the brain, and the spinal cavity, which contains the spinal cord.

Ventral cavity: The main body cavity consisting of the thoracic, the abdominal, and the pelvic cavities. It is much larger than the dorsal cavity.

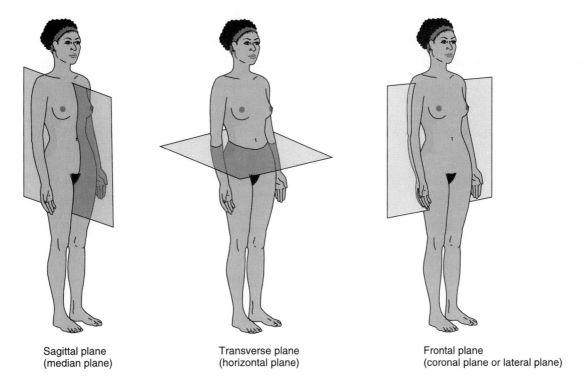

| Sagittal plane (median plane) | Transverse plane (horizontal plane) | Frontal plane (coronal plane or lateral plane) |

Figure 2-2. *Sectioning the body along various planes.*

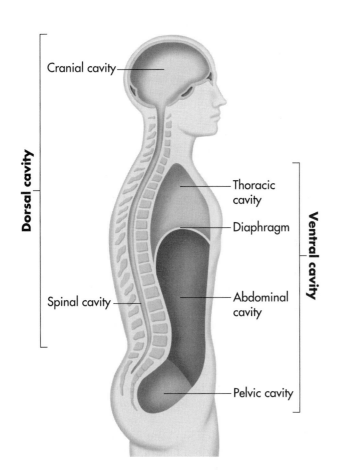

Figure 2-3. *The two main body cavities are dorsal and ventral.*

Integumentary System

Integumentary system: The skin and its derivatives. Functions of the skin include protection, regulation of body temperature, sensory reception, and the synthesis of vitamin D.

Cutaneous membrane: The medical term for skin. It consists of three layers: the epidermis, the dermis, and subcutaneous tissue. See Figure 2-4 on p. 48.

Epidermis: The outermost layer of the skin. It contains no blood vessels, but it does contain melanin, which gives skin its characteristic color, and keratin, which is a waterproof barrier against pathogens and chemicals. The more melanin in skin, the darker its color. The epidermis consists of five layers, or strata. They are, from outermost to innermost, the stratum corneum, the stratum lucidum, the stratum granulosum, the stratum spinosum, and the stratum germinativum.

Dermis: The layer of skin containing hair follicles, nails, glands (that secrete oil or sebum), fibers, sense receptors, and blood vessels. It is also called true skin.

Subcutaneous tissue: The bottom layer of the cutaneous membrane, beneath the true skin.

Stratum lucidum: A translucent band that is seen best in thick, glabrous skin.

Stratum corneum: Dead, keratinized cells located on the outer surface of the epidermis.

Keratinization: A process by which epithelial cells lose their moisture, which is replaced by keratin (protein).

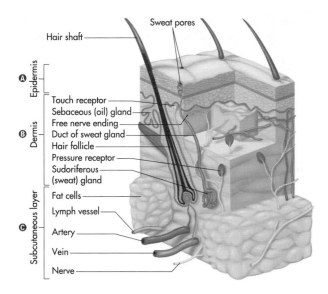

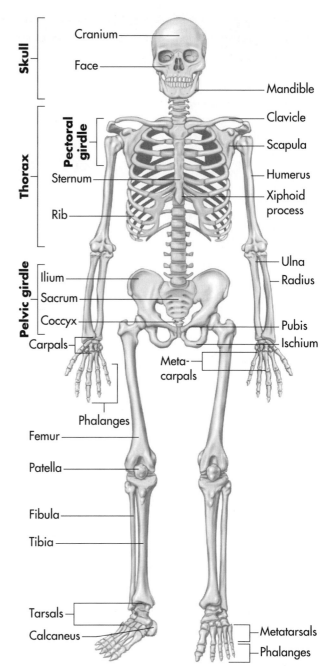

Figure 2-4. *The skin consists of three layers. A. The epidermis (outer layer) is made entirely of epithelial cells. B. The dermis (middle layer) contains connective tissue, nerve endings, hair follicles, and the sweat and oil glands. C. The subcutaneous (innermost) layer contains fat cells, loose connective tissue, and blood and lymph vessels.*

Sebaceous gland: An oil gland, associated with hair follicles. Sebaceous glands secrete sebum and are abundant in the scalp, external ear, face, nose, mouth, and anus.

Sweat gland: A gland that secretes sweat, either directly to the skin's surface (eccrine type) or indirectly through hair follicles (apocrine type). Also called sudoriferous glands, sweat glands are widely distributed over the body, except for the lips, nipples, and parts of the external genitalia.

Musculoskeletal System

Skeletal System

Bone: An individual unit of osseous tissue, part of the body's supporting framework. Although they appear hard and lifeless because of the calcium contained in them, bones are living tissue. Bones also produce blood cells, act as a storage area for calcium, and protect delicate organs of the body.

Types: There are two types of bone tissue: compact and sponge. The three types of cells in bone are osteoblasts, osteoclasts, and osteocytes.

Classification: Bones are classified into four types according to their shape: long, short, flat, and irregular. The femur, radius, and humerus are long bones. The carpals and tarsals are short bones. The ribs, scapula, skull, and sternum are flat bones. The vertebrae, sacrum, and mandible are irregular bones. The adult human skeleton is made up of 206 named bones. See Figure 2-5 and Table 2-3.

Figure 2-5. *The skeletal system is composed of bones, joints, and related connective tissue.*

Diaphysis: The shaft of a long bone, located between the epiphyses.

Epiphysis: Spongy bone tissue, located at the ends of a long bone.

Articulation, or **joint:** A place of junction between two or more bones of the skeleton. There are three types of articulation: immovable (synarthrosis), slightly movable (amphiarthrosis), and freely movable (diarthrosis).

Hyoid bone: A U-shaped bone in the neck that supports the tongue. This bone does not articulate directly with any other bone.

The Distribution of Bones in the Body

Axial skeleton	80 bones
Skull, consisting of: a. Cranial bones b. Facial bones c. Auditory ossicles	28 bones, as follows: 8 14 6
Thoracic cage	**25 bones**
Appendicular skeleton: a. Upper extremity b. Lower extremity c. Pelvic girdle d. Pectoral girdle	126 bones, as follows: 60 60 2 4

Table 2-3

Vertebral column, or **spinal column:** The portion of the skeleton consisting of vertebrae (26 in the human adult) and intervertebral disks. There are four curvatures: cervical curve, thoracic curve, lumbar curve, and sacral curve.

Atlas: The first cervical vertebra. It articulates with the occipital bone and the axis.

Axis: The second cervical vertebra, with which the atlas bone articulates. This articulation allows the head to be turned (rotated), extended, and flexed.

Coccyx: The last bone at the base of the vertebral column. The coccyx, also called the tailbone, attaches to the end of the sacrum.

Sternum: The bone that forms the anterior portion of the thoracic cage. It consists of the manubrium, the body (or gladiolus), and the xiphoid process. It supports the clavicles and articulates directly with the first seven pairs of the ribs.

True ribs: Seven pairs of ribs, which attach to the sternum directly by their individual costal cartilages.

False ribs: Ribs in pairs 8 through 10, which attach to the sternum indirectly.

Floating ribs: Ribs in pairs 11 and 12, which do not attach to the sternum.

Pectoral girdle: The skeletal structure consisting of the two clavicles, or collarbones, and the two scapulae, or shoulder blades.

Clavicle: One of the pair of long bones that form the anterior part of the pectoral girdle. It is commonly called the collarbone.

Scapula: One of the pair of large, flat, triangular bones that form the dorsal part of the pectoral girdle. It is commonly called the shoulder blade.

Olecranon process: A projection on the ulna that forms the bony point of the elbow.

Styloid process: A projection on the temporal bone.

Pelvic girdle: The skeletal structure consisting of the ilium, the sacrum, and the coccyx.

Acetabulum: The deep depression on the lateral surface of the hipbone, on which the ball-shaped head of the femur articulates.

Obturator foramen: A large opening on each side of the lower part of the hipbone.

Patella: A flat, triangular bone at the front of the knee joint. It is also called the kneecap.

Muscular System

Muscle: Connective tissue made up of contractile cells or fibers that produce movement. There are three types of muscle: striated, skeletal, or voluntary; smooth, visceral, or involuntary; and cardiac. There are two types of proteins in muscle tissue: actin and myosin. For a list of some of the main muscles of the human body, see Figure 2-6 on p. 50.

Skeletal muscle: A muscle composed of cylindrical, multinucleated, and striated fibers that works together with bones to enable movement. Skeletal muscles are characterized by contractility, elasticity, excitability, and extensibility. There are more than 600 skeletal muscles in the human body. See Table 2-4 on p. 51 for examples of skeletal muscles and their actions. Skeletal muscles are also called striated or voluntary muscles.

Smooth muscle: A spindle-shaped muscle that causes the contraction of blood vessels and viscera such as the intestines and the stomach.

Cardiac muscle: A special striated muscle of the myocardium that pumps blood through the heart and blood vessels. Its contraction is not under voluntary control.

Muscle fiber: Any individual muscle cell.

Myofibril, or myofibrilla: A slender, striated strand of contractile fiber within skeletal and cardiac muscle cells.

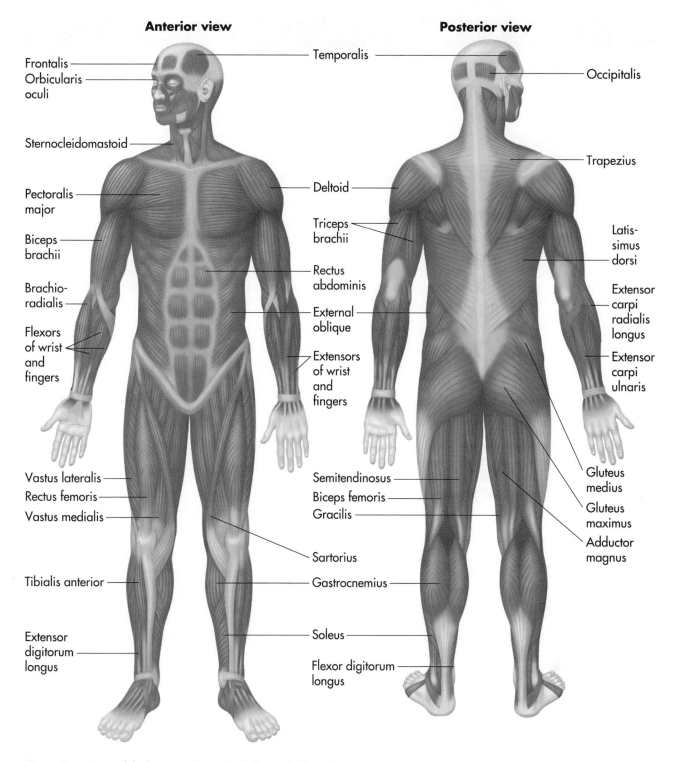

Anterior view

Frontalis
Orbicularis oculi
Sternocleidomastoid
Pectoralis major
Biceps brachii
Brachioradialis
Flexors of wrist and fingers
Vastus lateralis
Rectus femoris
Vastus medialis
Tibialis anterior
Extensor digitorum longus

Temporalis
Deltoid
Triceps brachii
Rectus abdominis
External oblique
Extensors of wrist and fingers
Semitendinosus
Biceps femoris
Gracilis
Sartorius
Gastrocnemius
Soleus
Flexor digitorum longus

Posterior view

Occipitalis
Trapezius
Latissimus dorsi
Extensor carpi radialis longus
Extensor carpi ulnaris
Gluteus medius
Gluteus maximus
Adductor magnus

Figure 2-6. *Many of the large muscles in the body are visible in these anterior and posterior views.*

Epimysium: The fibrous sheath that surrounds muscle tissue. It may also fuse with a fascia that attaches a muscle to a bone.

Endomysium: The fibrous sheath that surrounds each individual muscle cell.

Fascia: A sheet of fibrous connective tissue that covers, separates, or supports muscle.

Tendon: A band of dense fibrous connective tissue, generally white in color, that attaches muscle to bone.

Ligament: A band or sheet of fibrous tissue that connects two or more bones, cartilages, or other structures.

Sarcoplasm: The cytoplasm of muscle fiber.

Sarcolemma: The cell membrane of a muscle fiber.

Sarcomere: The smallest functional unit of a myofibril.

Neuromuscular junction: The region of contact between the ends of an axon and a skeletal muscle fiber.

Excitability: The ability of muscle tissue to react and respond to stimulation.

Skeletal Muscle	Action
Masseter	Closes the jaw
Temporalis	Closes the jaw
Sternocleidomastoid	Flexes and rotates the head
Trapezius	Extends the head and moves the scapula
Pectoralis major	Adducts and flexes the arm
Deltoid	Abducts the arm
Biceps	Flexes and supinates the forearm
Triceps	Extends the forearm
Brachioradialis	Flexes the forearm
Brachialis	Flexes the forearm
Gluteus maximus	Extends the thigh
Gluteus medius	Abducts and rotates the thigh
Quadriceps femoris	Extends the leg
Sartorius	Flexes the thigh; flexes and rotates the leg
Hamstring	Flexes the leg and extends the thigh
Gastrocnemius	Flexes the foot

Table 2-4

Contractility: The ability of muscle tissue to shorten, or contract, in response to a stimulus.

Elasticity: The capacity of tissues to return to their original shape and length after contraction or extension.

Contraction: A shortening or tightening of a muscle. Skeletal muscles need actin, myosin, calcium, ATP, and neurotransmitters to contract. All other muscles need only ATP and calcium.

Actin: A protein that forms the thin fibrils in muscle fibers.

Myosin: A skeletal and cardiac muscle protein that interacts with actin to cause muscle contraction.

Muscle tone: The continual state of slight contraction present in muscles. It is also called tonus.

Flexion: A bending that decreases the angle between two bones of a joint.

Extension: A straightening that increases the angle between two bones of a joint.

Nervous System

Nervous system: One of the body's regulatory systems. It controls all body activities by responding to internal and external stimuli and sending out signals or impulses to other nerves and various body organs. The brain, the spinal cord, and the nerves make up the nervous system, which is divided into two groups: the central nervous system and the peripheral nervous system. See Figure 2-7 on p. 52.

Nerve Cells and Neurotransmitters

Neuron: A nerve cell, the basic unit of the nervous system. It consists of a cell body, one or more dendrites, and a single axon. The two forms of neurons are sensory and motor.

Cell body of a neuron: The main part of the neuron. It is also called the soma.

Dendrite: A nerve cell process that conducts impulses to the cell body.

Axon: A nerve cell process that conducts impulses away from the cell body.

Sensory neuron: A neuron that carries impulses to the spinal cord and the brain. It is also known as an afferent neuron.

Motor neuron: A neuron that carries impulses from the central nervous system out to muscles and glands. It stimulates a muscle to contract or a gland to secrete. It is also known as an efferent neuron.

Myelin: A white, fatty substance, largely composed of phospholipids and protein, that surrounds many nerve fibers.

Synapse: The junction between two neurons.

Neuroglia cell: A type of nerve cell that supports, protects, and nourishes the neuron. There are four kinds:

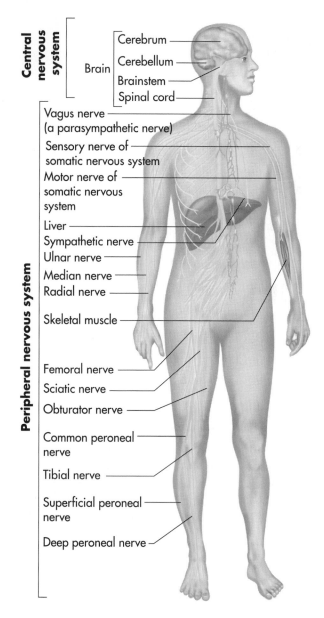

Central nervous system

Brain
- Cerebrum
- Cerebellum
- Brainstem

Spinal cord

Peripheral nervous system

Vagus nerve (a parasympathetic nerve)
Sensory nerve of somatic nervous system
Motor nerve of somatic nervous system
Liver
Sympathetic nerve
Ulnar nerve
Median nerve
Radial nerve
Skeletal muscle
Femoral nerve
Sciatic nerve
Obturator nerve
Common peroneal nerve
Tibial nerve
Superficial peroneal nerve
Deep peroneal nerve

Figure 2-7. *The main organs of the nervous system are the brain, the spinal cord, and the nerves. The spinal nerves originate in the spinal cord, whereas the cranial nerves (for example, the vagus nerve) originate in the brain.*

astrocytes, microglia, ependymal cells, and oligodendrocytes.

Astrocyte: A large, star-shaped cell that provides nutrition.

Microglion: One of many small interstitial cells in the brain and spinal cord that serve as phagocytic cells and respond to inflammation.

Ependymal cell: A columnar cell located in the brain that produces cerebrospinal fluid.

Oligodendrocyte: A type of neuroglial cell that produces myelin, the white matter of the nervous system.

Nerve impulse: The electrochemical process involved in neural transmission.

Action potential: The sudden electrical charge transmitted across the cell membrane of a nerve fiber.

Neurotransmitter: A chemical substance that is released from synaptic knobs into synaptic clefts. Neurotransmitters include acetylcholine, dopamine, norepinephrine, epinephrine, serotonin, histamine, and gamma-aminobutyric acid (GABA).

Central Nervous System

Central nervous system: The part of the nervous system consisting of the brain and the spinal cord.

The Brain

Brain: The part of the central nervous system contained within the cranium. The brain consists of three major parts: the cerebrum, the cerebellum, and the brainstem. See Figure 2-8.

Cerebrum: The largest and uppermost portion of the brain. The cerebrum is divided into two hemispheres, right and left, and five lobes: frontal, parietal, occipital, temporal, and insular.

Right hemisphere: The portion of the brain responsible for controlling the left side of the body. It also controls hearing and tactile and spatial perception.

Left hemisphere: The portion of the brain responsible for controlling the right side of the body. It is also responsible for verbal, analytical, and computational skills.

Frontal lobe: The part of the brain responsible for complex concentration, planning, and problem solving. It also contains the olfactory cortex, which interprets smells.

Parietal lobe: Responsible for the interpretation of sensory input other than sight, sound, and smell. It contains the gustatory area responsible for taste.

Occipital lobe: The part of the brain responsible for visual recognition.

Temporal lobe: The part of the brain responsible for the interpretation of sensory experiences such as hearing and smell. It is also said to be the center for emotion, memory, and personality.

Insular lobe, or central lobe: The part of the brain responsible for visceral or primitive emotions, drives, and reactions.

Broca's area: The part of the brain responsible for motor speech and for controlling the muscular actions of the mouth, tongue, and larynx.

Wernicke's area: The part of the brain responsible for language comprehension.

Corpus callosum: A large and transverse band of myelinated nerve fibers that connect the cerebral hemispheres. It is the largest commissure of the brain.

Basal ganglion: One of four islands of gray matter located in the white matter of the cerebrum: the lentiform nucleus, the caudate nucleus, the amygdaloid nucleus, and the claustrum. One function of the basal ganglia is to initiate and regulate muscular activity.

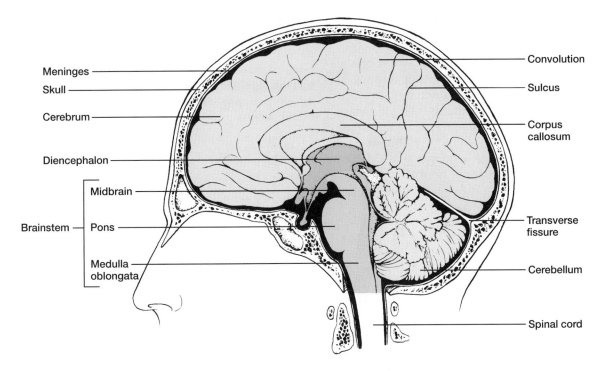

Mened
Skull
Cerebrum
Diencephalon
Midbrain
Brainstem
Pons
Medulla
oblongata

Convolution
Sulcus
Corpus
callosum
Transverse
fissure
Cerebellum
Spinal cord

Figure 2-8. *The major portions of the brain include the cerebrum, the cerebellum, and the brainstem.*

Diencephalon: The centrally located portion of the brain surrounded by the cerebrum that contains the thalamus and hypothalamus.

Thalamus: The subdivision of the diencephalon that sorts sensory impulses and directs them to the appropriate areas in the brain. It is basically a relay station for sensory impulses.

Hypothalamus: The subdivision of the diencephalon that assists in controlling body temperature, water balance, sleep, appetite, emotions of fear and pleasure, and involuntary functions.

Brainstem: The portion of the brain, located between the diencephalon and the spinal cord that controls vital visceral activities. It consists of the midbrain, the pons, and the medulla oblongata.

Midbrain: The section of the brainstem that controls visual and auditory reflexes, such as turning to listen to a loud noise.

Pons: The section of the brainstem that relays sensory impulses and regulates the rate and depth of breathing in coordination with the medulla oblongata.

Medulla oblongata: The section of the brainstem that contains the cardiac center (which controls heart rate), the vasomotor center (which controls blood pressure), and the respiratory center (which controls the rate, rhythm, and depth of breathing).

Cerebellum: The second largest portion of the brain, located below the occipital lobes of the cerebrum, which coordinates skeletal muscle activity. Damage to this area can result in tremors, loss of muscle tone, and loss of equilibrium.

Ventricle: One of four small interconnected cavities within the brain filled with cerebrospinal fluid.

The Spinal Cord

Spinal cord: A part of the central nervous system that conducts sensory and motor impulses, through nerves to the trunk and limbs, and serves as a center for reflex activities. Located in the vertebral canal, it extends from the foramen magnum at the base of the skull to the lumbar region.

Peripheral Nervous System

Peripheral nervous system: The portion of the nervous system outside the central nervous system, consisting of the cranial nerves, the spinal nerves, and ganglia. It can be subdivided into the somatic and the autonomic nervous systems.

Somatic Nervous System

Somatic nervous system: The part of the peripheral nervous system consisting of the cranial and spinal nerves that connect the central nervous system with the skin and skeletal muscles. The somatic nervous system is responsible for conscious activities.

Cranial nerves: Twelve pairs of nerves that emerge from the brainstem. Three pairs have only sensory fibers.

Spinal nerves: Thirty-one pairs of spinal nerves that emerge from the spinal cord. They provide two-way communication between the spinal cord and the body's extremities, limbs, neck, and trunk.

Autonomic Nervous System

Autonomic nervous system: The part of the peripheral nervous system that regulates the action of the glands, the heart muscle, and the smooth muscles of hollow organs and vessels. The autonomic nervous system controls unconscious activities such as reflexes. It consists of the sympathetic and the parasympathetic systems. See Table 2-5.

Fight-or-flight response: A reaction in which the sympathetic part of the autonomic nervous system acts as an accelerator for organs whose functions are needed to meet a stressful situation.

Sensory System

Sense: A general faculty of physical perception. In addition to the commonly recognized "five senses" (smell, taste, sight, hearing, and touch and pressure), important senses in human beings include position, equilibrium, proprioception, temperature, hunger and thirst, and pain. They are found throughout the body and are therefore referred to as somatic senses.

Smell

Olfaction: The sense of smell.
Nose: The organ of smell. It also moistens, warms, and filters air that passes through it.

Olfactory receptor: A receptor, located in the upper portions of the nose, that is sensitive to gases and dissolved chemicals. Olfactory receptors are easily fatigued; that is, they easily adapt to a particular smell and do not continuously inform the brain about an odor's presence. However, their sensitivity to other odors persists.

Taste

Gustatory sense, or **taste:** A chemical sense produced by stimulation of the taste buds. The taste buds are distributed on the surface of the tongue. There are four basic taste sensations: salty, sweet, sour, and bitter. The tip of the tongue contains sweet and salty receptors, the sides of the tongue contain sour receptors, and the back of the tongue contains bitter receptors.

Sight

Eye: A group of specialized tissues that permits sight. Tears, lashes, eyelids, muscle, and fatty tissue surround and protect the eye.
Eyeball: The globe of the eye. It is made up of concentric coats, or tunics. The outer layer is the fibrous tunic. The middle layer, or uvea, consists of the choroid, the

AT A GLANCE	Effects of the Sympathetic and Parasympathetic Systems on Selected Visceral Effectors	
Visceral Effector	**Sympathetic Action**	**Parasympathetic Action**
Pupil of the eye	Dilation	Constriction
Sweat glands	Stimulation	No effect
Heart	Increase in heart rate	Decrease in heart rate
Bronchi	Dilation	Constriction
Digestive gland	Decrease in secretion of enzymes	Increase in secretion of enzymes
Digestive tract	Decrease in peristalsis	Increase in peristalsis
Digestive tract sphincter	Stimulation (closing of sphincter)	Inhibition (opening of sphincter)
Urinary bladder	Closing of sphincter	Opening of sphincter
Penis	Ejaculation	Erection
Adrenal medulla	Stimulation	No effect
Liver	Increase in release of glucose	No effect

Table 2-5

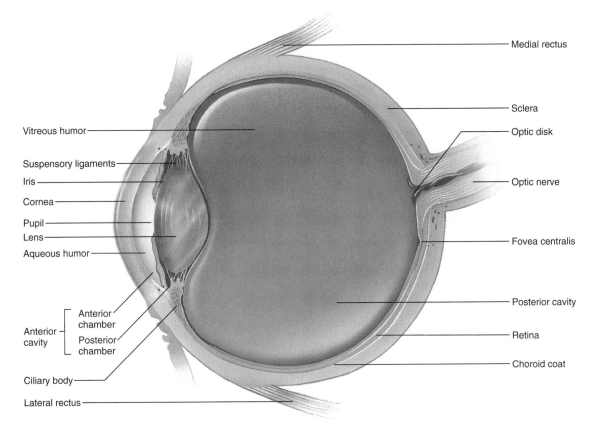

Figure 2-9. *Transverse section of the left eye (superior view).*

ciliary body, and the iris. The innermost coat of the eye is called the nervous tunic, or retina. The bulb of the eye is composed of two cavities separated by a crystalline lens. See Figure 2-9.

Fibrous tunic: The outermost, external protective layer of the eye. It consists of the white, opaque sclera and the transparent cornea.

Cornea: The transparent outer layer of the eye.

Sclera: The white outer layer of the eye.

Choroid: The part of the uvea that absorbs excess light rays.

Ciliary body: The part of the uvea that changes the shape of the lens.

Iris: The part of the uvea that regulates the size of the pupil and gives the eye its color.

Pupil: The dark opening of the eye, surrounded by the iris, through which light rays pass.

Retina: The light-sensitive nerve cell layer of the eye that contains the rods and cones.

Rod: A photoreceptor for black-and-white vision. Rods are essential for vision in dim light and for peripheral vision.

Cone: A photoreceptor for color vision and visual acuity. The three types distinguish blue, red, and green.

Aqueous humor: A clear, watery fluid that fills the anterior cavity of the eye and circulates in the anterior and posterior chambers.

Vitreous humor: A transparent jellylike substance that fills the posterior cavity of the eye, between the lens and the retina. It is the main component of the vitreous body; the two terms are used synonymously. It helps maintain sufficient intraocular pressure to prevent the eyeball from collapsing.

Accommodation: The adjustment of the eye for close or distant vision, which is primarily achieved through changing the curvature of the lens.

Hearing

Ear: The organ of hearing. It consists of three parts: the external, the middle, and the inner ear. This complex organ also aids in balance. See Figure 2-10 on p. 56.

External ear: The part of the ear consisting of the auricle and the external auditory meatus. It ends at the tympanic membrane.

Tympanic membrane: The eardrum, which separates the external from the middle ear, covers the auditory canal, and transmits sound vibrations to the inner ear by the auditory ossicles.

Middle ear: The part of the ear containing the auditory ossicles, the oval window, and the round window. It is also called the tympanic cavity.

Eustachian tube: A tube that joins the nasopharynx and the middle ear cavity.

Auditory ossicles: The three tiny bones in the middle ear: the malleus (hammer), the incus (anvil), and the stapes (stirrup). These bones transmit and amplify vibrations.

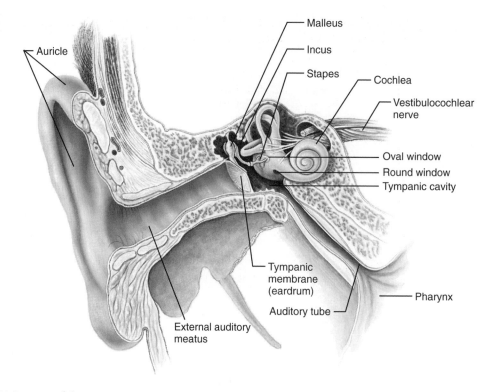

Figure 2-10. *Major parts of the ear.*

Inner ear: The part of the ear consisting of the vestibule, the semicircular canals, and the cochlea.

Vestibule: The middle part of the inner ear, involved in balance.

Semicircular canal: One of three curved passages in the inner ear that detect motion and govern balance.

Cochlea: The snail-shaped, spiral tube that contains the organ of Corti, the receptor for hearing.

Labyrinth: Those passages of the vestibule, the semicircular canals, and the cochlea that contain receptors for hearing and equilibrium. The term is loosely used as a synonym for the inner ear.

Cerumen: A waxy substance secreted by the external ear. It is also called ear wax.

Endocrine System

Endocrine system: A system of glands whose secretions coordinate many body functions. Its response to change is slower and more prolonged than that of the nervous system.

Endocrine gland: A ductless gland that secretes hormones directly into the bloodstream. See Figure 2-11 and Table 2-6.

Hormone: A protein or steroid carried through the blood to a target organ. Secretion is regulated by other hormones, through a negative feedback system, or by neurotransmitters.

Steroid hormone: A hormone derived from cholesterol. Steroid hormones include the adrenal cortex hormones, androgens, and estrogens.

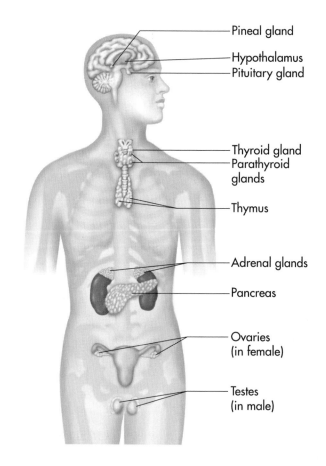

Figure 2-11. *The endocrine system produces hormones that affect activities such as growth, metabolism, and reproduction.*

Gland	Hormones	Major Functions
Hypothalamus	Releasing and inhibiting hormones (TRH, CRH, GnRH, GHRH)	These hormones control the release of anterior pituitary hormones.
Posterior pituitary (hormone storage site)	Vasopressin (antidiuretic hormone)	Vasopressin increases reabsorption of water in kidney tubules and stimulates smooth muscle tissue in blood vessels to constrict.
	Oxytocin	Oxytocin increases the contractility of the uterus and causes milk ejection.
Anterior pituitary	Thyroid-stimulating hormone (TSH)	TSH stimulates the thyroid gland to produce thyroid hormones (T_3 and T_4 secretion).
	Adrenocorticotropic hormone (ACTH)	ACTH stimulates the adrenal cortex to produce cortisol.
	Growth hormone (GH)	GH promotes growth of bone and soft tissue.
	Follicle-stimulating hormone (FSH)	FSH stimulates follicular growth and secretion of estrogen; it also stimulates growth of the testes and promotes development of sperm cells.
	Luteinizing hormone (LH; in males, called interstitial cell-stimulating hormone or ICSH)	LH causes development of a corpus luteum at the site of a ruptured ovarian follicle in females; also it can stimulate secretion of testosterone in males.
	Prolactin	Prolactin promotes breast development in females and stimulates milk secretion.
Thyroid	Thyroid hormone (thyroxine or T_4, and triiodothyronine or T_3)	Thyroxine increases metabolic rate; it is essential for normal growth and nerve development.
	Calcitonin	Calcitonin decreases plasma calcium concentrations.
Parathyroid	Parathyroid hormone	Parathyroid hormone regulates the exchange of calcium between the blood and bones, and it increases the calcium level in the blood.
Thymus	Thymosin	Thymosin enhances the proliferation and function of T lymphocytes.

Table 2-6

Gland	Hormones	Major Functions
Adrenal cortex	Aldosterone (a mineralocorticoid)	Aldosterone increases Na$^+$ reabsorption and K$^+$ secretion in kidney tubules.
	Cortisol (a glucocorticoid)	Cortisol increases blood glucose at the expense of protein and fat stores; it also contributes to stress adaptation.
	androgens	Androgens are responsible for stimulating development of secondary sex characteristics.
Adrenal medulla	Epinephrine Norepinephrine	Epinephrine increases blood pressure and heart rate. Norepinephrine reinforces the sympathetic nervous system.
Endocrine pancreas (islets of Langerhans)	Insulin (produced by beta cells)	Insulin promotes cellular uptake and is required for cellular metabolism of nutrients, especially glucose; it also decreases blood sugar levels.
	Glucagon (produced by alpha cells)	Glucagon stimulates the liver to release glucose and increase blood sugar levels.
Ovaries	Estrogens (e.g., estradiol)	Estrogens promote follicular development, which is responsible for development of secondary sex characteristics; it also stimulates uterine and breast growth.
	Progesterone	Progesterone prepares the uterus for pregnancy.
Testes	Testosterone	Testosterone stimulates the production of spermata and their maturation; it also is responsible for development of secondary sex characteristics.

Table 2-6, continued

Cardiovascular System

The Blood

Blood: A type of connective tissue that contains cellular and liquid components. The blood volume of the adult human is about 5 liters and accounts for 8% of body weight. About 55% of blood is plasma, and 45% is formed elements.

Arterial blood: Highly oxygenated, bright red blood that travels from the heart to the capillaries.

Venous blood: Dark red, carbon-dioxide-rich blood that travels from the capillaries to the heart.

Formed element: An erythrocyte, a leukocyte, or a thrombocyte.

Hemocytoblast: The stem cell from which all formed elements of the blood develop. It is found in bone marrow and in lymphatic tissue. See Figure 2-12.

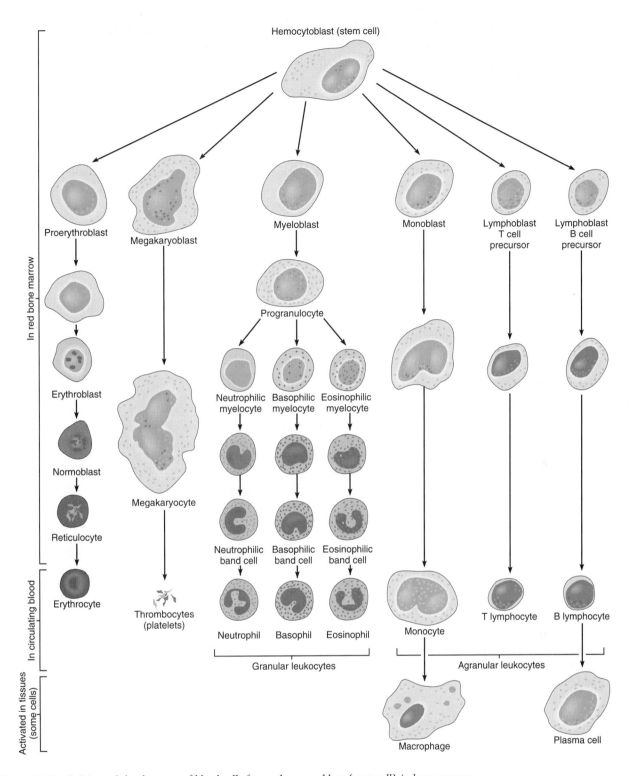

Figure 2-12. *Origin and development of blood cells from a hemocytoblast (stem cell) in bone marrow.*

Plasma: The liquid portion of blood, made up of 90% water and 10% solutes.

Albumin: The most abundant plasma protein, which maintains the osmotic pressure of the blood.

Globulin: One of a number of simple plasma proteins, which are classified in three groups: alpha, beta, and gamma.

Gamma globulin: An antibody obtained from pooled human plasma.

Fibrinogen: The smallest fraction of plasma protein, which functions to form blood clots.

Erythropoietin: A glycoprotein hormone released from the kidney that regulates the formation of red blood cells.

Fibrin: An insoluble fibrous protein formed by the action of thrombin on fibrinogen during blood coagulation.

Prothrombin: A plasma protein that leads to the formation of blood clots.

Embolus: A piece of thrombus or fragment of a clot that moves in a blood vessel.

Thrombus: A blood clot that remains at its formation site in a blood vessel.

Hemoglobin: A complex protein-iron compound in the blood that carries oxygen to the cells from the lungs and carbon dioxide away from the cells to the lungs.

Hemostasis: The stoppage of bleeding.

Hematocrit: A measure of the packed cell volume of red blood cells, expressed as a percentage of the total blood volume.

Agglutinin: An antibody in plasma.

Agglutination: The clumping of red blood cells.

Agglutinogen: A genetically determined antigen on the cell membrane of a red blood cell that determines blood types.

Blood typing: The identification of genetically determined specific antigens and antibodies related to red blood cells.

Blood group: A genetically determined pattern of antigen distribution on the surface of a red blood cell. In the ABO system, there are four blood groups: A, B, AB, and O. The ABO group is important in establishing compatibility in blood transfusions. The Rhesus (Rh) blood group system is important in obstetrics.

Type A blood: Blood that has the A antigen on the surface of red blood cells and B antibodies in plasma.

Type B blood: Blood that has the B antigen on the surface of red blood cells and A antibodies in plasma.

Type O blood: Blood that has neither A nor B antigens on the surface of red blood cells and has both A and B antibodies in plasma.

Type AB blood: Blood that has both A and B antigens on the surface of red cells and has neither A nor B antibodies in plasma.

Rh+ blood: Blood in which the Rh factor is present.

Rh- blood: Blood from which the Rh factor is absent. When a woman with Rh- blood is pregnant with a fetus with Rh+ blood, the interaction between the two blood types will create anti-Rh agglutinin in the woman's blood. In subsequent pregnancies, these Rh antibodies may cross the placenta and destroy fetal cells.

Universal donor: A person with blood type O, Rh-.

Universal recipient: A person with blood type AB, Rh+.

Blood Cell Types

Erythrocyte, or red blood cell (RBC): A type of blood cell that has no nucleus and usually survives for 120 days, after which it is destroyed by the liver and the spleen. Red blood cells contain hemoglobin, which contains iron and carries oxygen from the lungs to the body and carries carbon dioxide from the body tissues to the lungs.

Erythrocytosis: An increased number of red cells in the blood, also called polycythemia.

Anisocytosis: A condition in which there is excessive inequality in the size of blood cells.

Reticulocyte: An immature red blood cell.

Poikilocytosis: Variation in the shape of red blood cells (sickle cells, spherocytes, elliptocytes, etc.).

Leukocyte, or white blood cell (WBC): A part of the body's defense against infection. Leukocytes do not have hemoglobin, and they move through capillary walls by diapedesis. They are classified into two groups: granulocytes and agranulocytes.

Granulocyte, or granular leukocyte: A leukocyte that has large granules in its cytoplasm, which stain in different colors under a microscope. Granular leukocytes include neutrophils, basophils, and eosinophils.

Neutrophil: The most frequently occurring leukocyte (55% to 70% of all WBCs). Neutrophils are phagocytic in acute inflammatory response.

Basophil: A granulocyte that mediates allergic reactions. In the tissues, a basophil is called a mast cell.

Eosinophil: A granulocyte that functions as defense against helminthic and protozoan infections.

Phagocyte: A cell that ingests bacteria, foreign particles, and other cells.

Phagocytosis: The process by which special cells engulf and destroy cellular debris and microorganisms. It is also called cell eating.

Pinocytosis: The process by which extracellular fluid is taken into a cell. It is also known as cell drinking.

Agranulocyte: A leukocyte that lacks granules. Nongranular leukocytes include lymphocytes and monocytes.

Lymphocyte: The smallest white blood cell. These cells travel from the blood to the lymph and lymph nodes and back into circulation. They are the main means of providing the body with immunity. They recognize antigens, produce antibodies, prevent excess tissue damage, and become memory cells. **Type B lymphocytes** produce antibodies. **Type T lymphocytes** regulate type B lymphocytes and macrophages.

Monocyte: The largest of the white blood cells. Monocytes are largely phagocytic.

Macrophage: A monocyte that has left circulation and settled in tissue. Along with neutrophils, macrophages are the major phagocytic cells of the immune system. They recognize and digest all antigens and also process and present these antigens to T cells, activating the specific immune response.

Thrombocyte: A cell fragment and the smallest formed element of blood. It is also called a platelet. Thrombocytes are essential in blood coagulation.

The Heart and Blood Vessels

Heart: A muscular organ, about the size of a closed fist, that acts as the pump of the circulatory system. It is made up of 3 layers: the epicardium, the myocardium, and the endocardium. See Figure 2-13.

Endocardium: The innermost layer of the heart.

Myocardium: The middle layer of the heart and the most important structure of the heart. It contains the heart muscles that can regulate cardiac output.

Epicardium: The outermost layer of the heart.

Atrium: A thin-walled chamber that receives blood from the veins. There are two atria in the heart, the right and the left.

Right atrium: The chamber that receives deoxygenated blood from systemic veins.

Left atrium: The chamber that receives oxygenated blood from the pulmonary veins.

Ventricle: A thick-walled chamber that pumps blood out of the heart. There are two ventricles in the heart, the right and the left.

Right ventricle: The chamber that pumps blood to the lungs.

Left ventricle: The chamber that pumps blood to the tissues of the whole body.

Valve: A membranous structure that temporarily closes to permit the flow of fluid through a passage in only one direction. The four valves in the heart are the bicuspid (or mitral) valve, the tricuspid valve, the aortic valve, and the pulmonary valve.

Cardiac cycle: The contraction and relaxation of the ventricles, known as systole and diastole. At a normal heart rate, one cardiac cycle lasts 0.8 seconds.

Systole: The contraction phase.

Diastole: The relaxation phase.

Cardiac center: The control center of the heart located in the medulla oblongata. It has both sympathetic and parasympathetic components.

Cardiac conduction system: A system consisting of specialized cardiac muscle cells. Its components are the sinoatrial (SA) node, the atrioventricular (A-V) node, the atrioventricular bundle (bundle of His), bundle branches, and the Purkinje fibers.

Cardiac output: The volume of blood pumped per minute by the heart, which increases during exercise.

Stroke volume: The amount of blood that the ventricle discharges with each heartbeat.

Pulse pressure: The pressure exerted by the circulating volume of blood on the walls of the blood vessels. It is proportional to stroke volume.

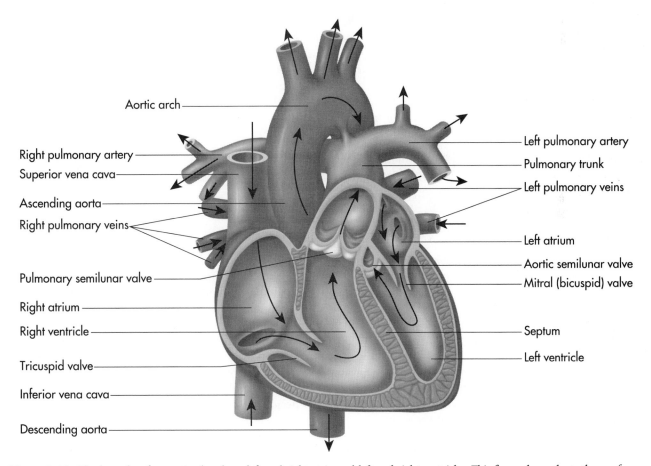

Figure 2-13. *The heart has four main chambers: left and right atria and left and right ventricles. This figure shows the pathway of blood through the heart.*

Myocardial oxygen demand: The demand for oxygen by the heart muscle. It is raised by increases in diastolic blood pressure, contractility, heart rate, and heart size.

Contractility: The force of left ventricular ejection.

Diastolic blood pressure: The blood pressure during diastole, the period of least pressure in the arterial vascular system.

Heart sound: A normal noise produced during the cardiac cycle by the closure of the mitral and tricuspid valves and of the aortic and pulmonic valves.

Murmur: Abnormal heart sound. The three types of murmurs are systolic, diastolic, and continuous murmurs.

Artery: A vessel that carries blood away from the heart.

Capillary: One of many very small vessels that connect arteries and veins.

Vein: A vessel that sends blood toward the heart. Its walls are thinner than those of arteries, and it contains valves.

Systemic artery: An artery that carries oxygenated blood.

Pulmonary artery: An artery that transfers low-oxygen blood to the lungs.

Aorta: The largest artery in the body. It consists of the ascending aorta, the aortic arch, and the descending aorta. The descending aorta consists of the thoracic aorta and the abdominal aorta.

Coronary artery: One of a pair of vessels that supply blood to the myocardium. The coronary arteries are the only vessels that branch from the ascending aorta.

Aortic arch: A part of the aorta from which three vessels branch: the brachiocephalic trunk (or innominate artery), the left common carotid artery, and the left subclavian artery.

External iliac artery: An artery that provides the blood supply for the lower extremities.

Internal iliac artery: An artery that supplies blood to the pelvic organs.

Internal carotid artery: One of the primary vessels that provide blood to the brain.

Vertebral artery: One of the primary vessels that provide blood to the brain.

Internal jugular vein: One of the primary vessels that drain blood from the brain.

Vertebral vein: One of the primary vessels that drain blood from the brain.

Azygous vein: One of the seven veins in the thorax. It drains blood from the thoracic and abdominal walls and empties into the superior vena cava.

Saphenous vein: A superficial vein of the lower extremity. It is the longest vein in the body.

Umbilical cord: The attachment connecting a fetus with the placenta. First formed during the fifth week of pregnancy, it contains two arteries and one vein.

Ductus venosus: The vascular channel in the fetus that is a continuation of the umbilical vein to the inferior vena cava. It becomes the ligamentum venosum of the liver.

Ductus arteriosus: A vascular channel in the fetus located between the pulmonary artery and the aorta. It becomes the ligamentum arteriosum.

Fetal circulation: The pathway of blood circulation in the fetus. Oxygenated blood from the placenta is carried through the umbilical vein to the fetal heart. See Table 2-7.

AT A GLANCE	Fetal Circulation	
Structure	**Location**	**Function**
Umbilical vein	In the umbilical cord	Transports oxygenated blood from the placenta to the fetus.
Umbilical arteries (2)	In the umbilical cord	Transports blood from the fetus to the placenta to obtain oxygen and nutrients and to get rid of carbon dioxide.
Ductus arteriosus	Between the pulmonary trunk and the aorta	Transports blood directly between the pulmonary artery and the aorta.
Ductus venosus	Continuation of the umbilical vein to the inferior vena cava	Carries blood directly from the umbilical vein to the inferior vena cava; bypasses the liver.
Foramen ovale	In the septum between the right and left atria	Transports blood directly from the right atrium into the left atrium to bypass pulmonary circulation.

Table 2-7

Lymphatic System

Lymphatic system: The body system that returns excess interstitial fluid to the blood and protects the body against disease.

Lymph: A thin, watery fluid in the lymphatic vessels that is filtered by the lymph nodes and contains chyle, red blood cells, and white blood cells, most of which are lymphocytes.

Chyle: A milklike alkaline fluid consisting of digestive products and absorbed fats.

Lymphatic vessel: A vessel that carries lymph. Lymphatic vessels resemble veins, but they have more valves, thinner walls, and lymph nodes, and they carry fluid away from the tissues.

Right lymphatic duct: The lymphatic vessel that drains lymph from the upper right quadrant of the body.

Thoracic duct: The lymphatic vessel that drains all the lymph not drained by the right lymphatic duct.

Lymph node: A small, oval structure that filters the lymph and fights infection. Lymph nodes are located along lymphatic vessels except in the nervous system. Superficial nodes are found in the neck, axilla, and groin.

Spleen: The lymph organ that filters, and also serves as a reservoir for blood.

Thymus: A gland essential to the maturation and development of the immune system. T-lymphocytes mature in this gland.

Respiratory System

Respiratory system: The body system that provides oxygen to cells and removes carbon dioxide from them. The organs of the respiratory system include the nose, the pharynx, the larynx, the trachea, the bronchi, and the lungs. The nose, pharynx, larynx, and upper trachea are collectively known as the upper respiratory tract. The lower respiratory tract consists of the lower trachea, the bronchi, and the lungs. See Figure 2-14.

Respiratory center: A group of nerve cells in the medulla oblongata and pons of the brain that control the rhythm of breathing in response to changes in oxygen and carbon dioxide levels in the blood and cerebrospinal fluid.

Nose: The projection that serves as the entrance to the nasal cavities. Hairs and cilia in the nose help trap dust, bacteria, and other particles and keep them from entering the body. The nose also warms and moistens the air, and it is involved with the sense of smell.

Larynx: The organ at the upper end of the trachea that contains the vocal cords, which vibrate to make speech.

Trachea: The tube that extends from the larynx and branches into two bronchi that lead to the lungs. It is also called the windpipe.

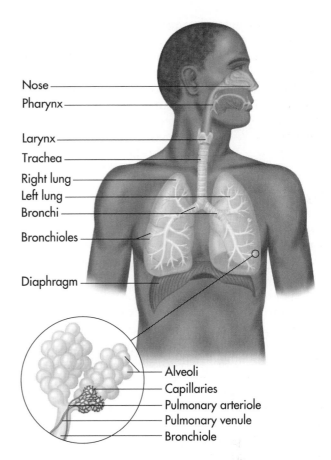

Figure 2-14. *The exchange of oxygen for carbon dioxide between the air and blood occurs within the lungs, where the alveoli and the capillaries are in intimate contact.*

Lung: A spongy organ in the thorax used for breathing. The two highly elastic lungs are the main component of the respiratory system. The left lung is divided into two lobes, and the right lung is divided into three lobes.

Alveolus: One of many clusters of air sacs at the end of the bronchioles in the lungs. The exchange of gases occurs in the alveoli.

Inspiration: The process of letting air into the lungs, also known as inhalation. The major muscle of inspiration is the diaphragm, the contraction of which creates a negative pressure in the chest.

Expiration: Breathing out, the process of letting air out of the lungs, which is normally a passive process. It is also called exhalation.

External respiration: The exchange of oxygen and carbon dioxide between the air in the lungs and the blood in the surrounding capillaries.

Internal respiration: The exchange of gases between the tissue cells and the blood in the tissue capillaries.

Carbon dioxide transport: A process that moves carbon dioxide from the tissues to the lungs in three forms: as bicarbonate, bound to hemoglobin, as carbaminohemoglobin, and as dissolved carbon dioxide.

Oxygen transport: The transfer of oxygen in the blood. Approximately 3% of oxygen is transported as a dissolved gas in the plasma; 97% is carried by hemoglobin molecules.

Surfactant: Any of certain lipoproteins that are produced by the lungs and that reduce the surface tension within the alveoli.

Spirometer: An instrument that measures and records the volume of air that moves in and out of the lungs.

Spirogram: A chart with recorded volumetric information.

Digestive System

Digestive system: The group of organs that change food so that it can be used by the body. The organs of the digestive system include the mouth, the pharynx, the esophagus, the stomach, and the small and large intestines. See Figure 2-15.

Digestive tract, or **alimentary canal:** The digestive tube, running from the mouth to the anus. The wall consists of four layers, or tunics: the mucosa, the submucosa, the muscular layer, and the serous layer, or serosa.

Serosa: The outermost layer of the digestive tract. It is composed of connective tissue. Above the diaphragm, it is known as the adventitia.

Mouth: The cavity where food is chewed into small pieces and is mixed with saliva to form a moist, soft lump called a bolus.

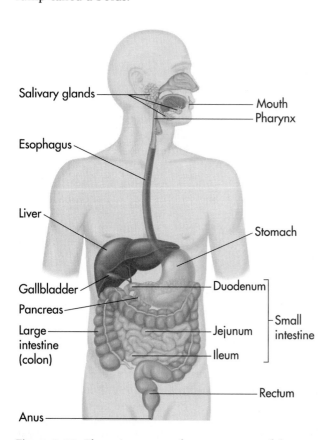

Figure 2-15. *The main organs and accessory organs of the digestive system change food into a form the body can use.*

Saliva: A fluid that moistens food and begins the chemical breakdown of carbohydrates. It is produced by the salivary glands located along the upper and lower jaws and under the tongue.

Salivary gland: A gland that secretes saliva. There are three pairs of glands secreting into the mouth: the parotid glands, the sublingual glands, and the submandibular glands.

Parotid gland: The largest salivary gland, which secretes serous fluid.

Sublingual gland: The smallest salivary gland, which secretes mucus.

Submandibular gland: A salivary gland located in the floor of the mouth. It secretes both mucus and serous fluid.

Uvula: A structure of soft tissue hanging down from the soft palate in the mouth.

Tooth: A dental structure that develops in the jaws, consisting of the crown (which projects above the gum), the neck (between the crown and the root), and the root.

Enamel: The hardest substance in the body, covering the crown and consisting mainly of calcium salts.

Dentin: The bulk of the tooth.

Pulp cavity: The interior part of a tooth, containing dental pulp, which consists of cells, nerves, and blood vessels or lymph vessels.

Deciduous dentition: The set of teeth that appear in the mouth first, also called deciduous or primary teeth.

Esophageal sphincter: The sphincter located in the lower portion of the esophagus. It is also called the cardiac sphincter.

Peristalsis: Rhythmic contractions that move food. This action occurs throughout the digestive tract.

Stomach: A muscular J-shaped organ that stores, churns, and further digests food. The stomach produces strong acids and enzymes that, combined with the churning action, begin the chemical breakdown of food.

Gastric gland: One of the glands in the stomach mucosa that secrete hydrochloric acid, mucin, and pepsinogen. Four different types of cells make up the gastric glands: mucous cells (goblet cells), parietal cells, chief cells, and endocrine cells.

Parietal cell: A gastric cell that secretes hydrochloric acid and intrinsic factor, which aids in the absorption of vitamin B_{12}.

Chief cell: A gastric cell that secretes pepsinogen, an active form of the enzyme pepsin.

Endocrine cell: A gastric cell that secretes the hormone gastrin, which regulates gastric activity. See Table 2-8.

Chyme: A mixture of partially digested food, water, and digestive juices that forms in the stomach and passes through the pylorus into the duodenum.

Intestine: One of two long, tubular organs distinguished by the difference in their diameters.

Small intestine: The longest part of the digestive tract. The chemical digestion of fats and the final breakdown

Secretion	Source
Gastrin	Stomach
Secretin	Small intestine
Cholecystokinin	Small intestine

Table 2-8

of carbohydrates and proteins take place here. Most of the nutrients in food are absorbed in the small intestine. The small intestine is divided into three parts: the duodenum, the jejunum, and the ileum.

Villus: One of many small, fingerlike projections, or villi, on the surface of the membrane in the small intestine through which digested food is absorbed.

Cholecystokinin: A hormone that is secreted from the mucosa of the upper small intestine and stimulates contraction of the gallbladder to release bile and pancreatic enzymes.

Large intestine: The intestine joined to the small intestine at the ileum and extending to the anus. It consists of the cecum, the colon, the rectum, and the anal canal. It is divided into ascending, transverse, descending, and sigmoid portions. The large intestine is responsible for making Vitamin K and some B vitamins, absorbing water and electrolytes, and storing and eliminating undigested waste.

Anal canal: The final portion of the digestive tract, between the rectum and the anus. Material that the body cannot use is excreted through the anus as feces. The internal anal sphincter is under involuntary control. The external anal sphincter can be controlled voluntarily.

Additional Organs and Processes Involved with Digestion

Kupffer cell: A cell in the liver responsible for cleansing the blood.

Hepatocyte: A liver cell responsible for storage, synthesis of bile salts, detoxification, synthesis of plasma proteins, and metabolism of carbohydrates, proteins, and lipids.

Liver: An organ of the digestive system whose main role is to produce bile.

Bile: The fluid responsible for excreting bile pigments and cholesterol from the breakdown of hemoglobin. Bile helps the body digest and absorb fat.

Pancreas: An organ that produces enzymes that digest fats, proteins, and carbohydrates. Pancreatic substances also neutralize the acids produced by the stomach.

Metabolism: The physical and chemical processes that take place in a living organism resulting in growth, production of energy, elimination of wastes, and other body functions. The fundamental metabolic processes are anabolism and catabolism.

Basal metabolism: The minimal energy that is necessary to maintain the body's functions at a low level.

Anabolism: The conversion of simple compounds into more complex substances needed by the body and living matter.

Catabolism: The breakdown of substances into simple compounds that liberates energy for use in work and heat production. It produces carbon dioxide, water, and energy.

Thermogenesis: The production of heat needed to utilize food, especially within the human body.

Core temperature: The temperature around the internal organs.

Shell temperature: The temperature near the body surface.

Urinary System

Urinary system: The system that removes waste products, salts, and excess water from the blood and eliminates them from the body. The organs of the urinary system are the kidneys, the ureters, the urinary bladder, and the urethra. See Figure 2-16 on p. 66.

Body Fluids

Body fluid: Any of several fluids, primarily intracellular and extracellular fluids, that make up 60% of the adult's body weight.

Extracellular fluid: Fluid outside a cell. Extracellular fluids are composed of intravascular and interstitial fluids.

Intracellular fluid: Fluid within cells. Intracellular fluids contain potassium and phosphates.

Organs and Function of the Urinary System

Kidney: One of a pair of organs that perform the main functions of the urinary system. They lie against the back muscles of the upper abdomen. The kidneys help

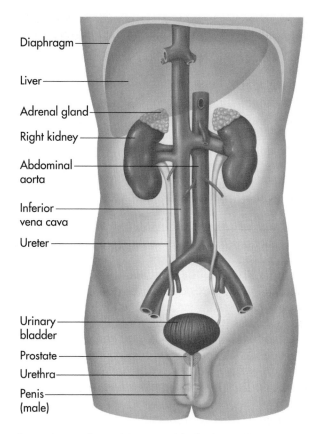

Diaphragm
Liver
Adrenal gland
Right kidney
Abdominal aorta
Inferior vena cava
Ureter
Urinary bladder
Prostate
Urethra
Penis (male)

Figure 2-16. *The urinary system, also known as the excretory system, removes waste products from the body and maintains the proper balance of body fluids and their chemistry.*

maintain balance in the volume of body fluid and in the levels of potassium, sodium, and chloride. The functions of the kidneys, which are governed by hormones, involve the processes of glomerular filtration, tubular reabsorption, and tubular secretion. See Table 2-9.

Glomerular filtration: A process in which plasma components cross the filtration membrane from the glomerulus into the glomerular capsule.

Tubular reabsorption: A process that moves substances from the filtrate into the blood. About 65% of the reabsorption takes place in the proximal convoluted tubule.

Tubular secretion: A process in which the kidney tubules selectively add some toxic waste products to the quantity already filtered by the process of tubular reabsorption.

Nephron: The functional unit of the kidney that consists of the renal corpuscle, the renal tubule, and the collecting tubule. Nephrons filter water and waste products from the blood and create urine.

Renal corpuscle: A part of the nephron, consisting of a glomerulus enclosed within Bowman's capsule.

Renal tubule: A structure that carries fluid away from the glomerular capsule; consisting of three regions: the proximal convoluted tubule, the nephron loop (Henle's loop), and the distal convoluted tubule.

Juxtaglomerular apparatus: A structure that monitors blood pressure and secretes renin.

Ureter: One of two long, slender tubes that extend from the kidneys to the urinary bladder.

Urinary bladder: The expandable organ that temporarily stores urine. Stretch receptors in the bladder create the urge to urinate. Urination is also called voiding urine or micturition.

Ruga: A ridge, wrinkle, or fold, as in a mucous membrane. Rugae line the urinary bladder and the stomach.

Detrusor muscle: The smooth muscle of the urinary bladder wall.

Trigone: A triangular area on the internal floor of the bladder between the opening of the two ureters and the internal urethral orifice.

Urethra: The tube through which urine leaves the body.

Buffer system: A physical or physiological system that tends to maintain constancy. For example, the kidneys act as a buffer system to help regulate blood pH.

Reproductive System

Genitalia: The reproductive organs of males and females.

Gonad: One of the two types of primary reproductive organ, the ovary and the testis, or testicle. Ovaries and testes produce gametes and hormones.

Follicle-stimulating hormone (FSH): The hormone produced by the anterior pituitary that stimulates development of ova in the ovary and spermatozoa in the testes.

AT A GLANCE	Hormonal Effects on the Kidneys
Hormone	**Stimulus**
Vasopressin (ADH)	Increases plasma osmolarity and decreases blood volume.
aldosterone	Decreases blood volume via angiotensin II and increases plasma potassium ions.
Angiotensin II	Decreases blood volume via renin.
Parathyroid hormone	Decreases plasma calcium ions.

Table 2-9

Male Reproductive System (Figure 2-17)

Testis: The male gonad. There are two testes, normally situated in the scrotum, which produce sperm cells and male sex hormones.

Lobule: One of two layers that surround each testis: an outer mesothelial layer (tunica vaginalis) and an inner white capsule (tunica albuginea).

Spermatogonium: A male germ cell that gives rise to spermatocyte early in spermatogenesis.

Spermatocyte: A male germ cell, or gamete, that arises from a spermatogonium.

Spermatozoon: A mature male gamete that develops in the seminiferous tubules of the testes, consisting of a head, a midpiece, and a tail.

Acrosome: A caplike structure over the head of the spermatozoon that helps the sperm to penetrate the ovum during fertilization. It is also called the acrosomal cap.

Ejaculatory duct: The passage formed by the junction of the duct of the seminal vesicles and ductus deferens through which semen enters the urethra.

Seminal vesicle: One of a pair of saclike accessory glands located posterior to the urinary bladder in the male that provide nourishment for sperm.

Prostate: A gland, located below the neck of the bladder in males, that surrounds the proximal portion of the urethra. It is a firm structure composed of muscular and glandular tissue that secretes alkaline phosphatase.

Cowper's gland: One of two pea-sized glands near the base of the penis in the male. It is also called a bulbourethral gland.

Semen, or **seminal fluid:** A thick, whitish secretion of the male reproductive organs discharged from the urethra on ejaculation.

Epididymis: One of the pair of long, tightly coiled tubules along the posterior margin of each testis that store and carry sperm from the testis to the vas deferens.

Glans penis: The bulbous end of the penis.

Prepuce, or **foreskin:** A fold of loose skin that covers the glans penis.

Emission: A discharge or release of seminal fluid into the urethra.

Tunica albuginea: A white capsule that surrounds each testis in the male.

Phimosis: A tightness and narrowing of the prepuce on the penis that prevents the retraction of the foreskin over the glans penis. It may obstruct urine flow and is usually congenital, although it may be caused by infection.

Impotence: The inability to achieve penile erection or to ejaculate after achieving an erection.

Circumcision: Surgical removal of the foreskin, or prepuce of the penis, commonly performed on newborn boys.

Vasectomy: Surgical removal of the bilateral part or all of the ductus (vas) deferens for male sterilization.

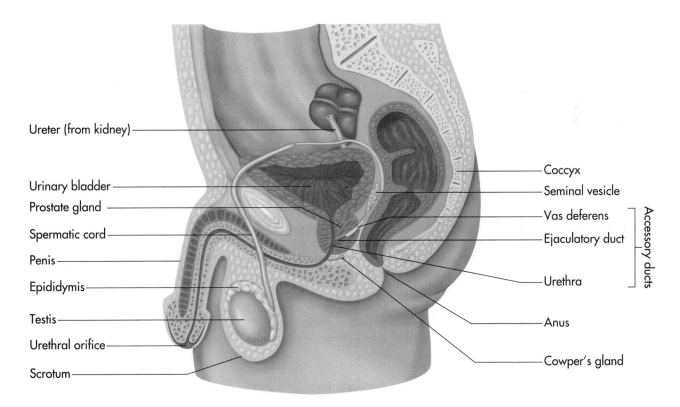

Figure 2-17. *The male reproductive system produces sperm and delivers them in a form that keeps them viable long enough to fertilize an egg.*

Female Reproductive System (Figure 2-18)

Ovary: The female gonad, located in the pelvis, in which the ova, or germ cells, are formed. There are two ovaries; each is covered with a single layer of epithelium. The ovarian follicle walls secrete estrogen.

Oogonium: A female germ cell that gives rise to an oocyte.

Oocyte: A female germ cell, or gamete, that arises from an oogonium.

Ovum: A mature female gamete.

Graafian follicle: A vesicular follicle of the ovary containing an oocyte.

Oogenesis: The process of cell division, growth, and maturation of the ova.

Ovulation: The expulsion and release of a mature ovum from a follicle in the ovary as a result of cyclic ovarian and pituitary endocrine function, usually about two weeks before the next menstrual period.

Corpus luteum: A yellow-bodied spheroid formed from an ovarian follicle after ovulation that secretes progesterone.

Progesterone: A hormone that maintains the uterine endometrium in the richly vascular state necessary for implantation and pregnancy.

Corpus albicans: A pale white scar tissue on the surface of the ovary that arises from the corpus luteum if conception does not occur.

Broad ligament: The largest peritoneal ligament that supports the uterus. It is also called the ligamentum latum uteri.

Mons pubis: A pad of fatty tissue that overlies the pubic symphysis in females. After puberty, it is covered with pubic hair.

Menstrual cycle: The recurring 28-day cycle of change in the endometrium during which the decidual layer of the endometrium is shed, then regrows, and proliferates. The uterine phases of the cycle are the proliferative phase, the secretory phase, and the menstrual phase. See Figure 2-19.

Menarche: The first menstruation in females, which usually occurs between the ages of 9 and 17.

Menopause: The cessation of the reproductive cycle. Menstrual cycles stop naturally with the decline of cyclic hormonal production between the ages of 35 and 60.

Fetus: The developing organism in the uterus. In humans, the term is applied after the eighth week of gestation.

Gestation: The period of development of the fetus from the time of fertilization to birth. It is another name for pregnancy.

Ante partum: Before delivery.

Parturition: The process of giving birth to a child, or delivery.

Neonatal: Pertaining to the first four weeks after birth.

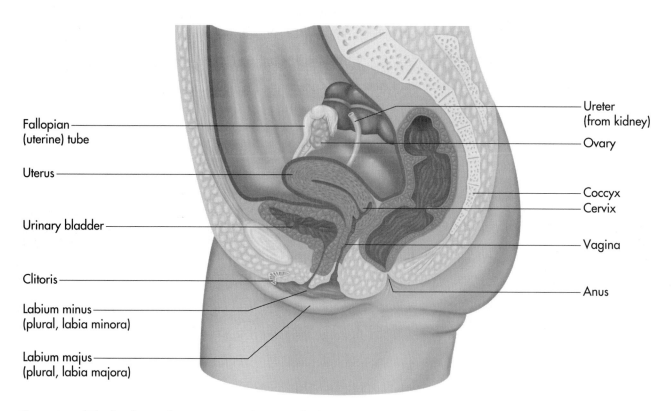

Figure 2-18. *The female reproductive system produces eggs for fertilization and provides the place and means for a fertilized egg to develop.*

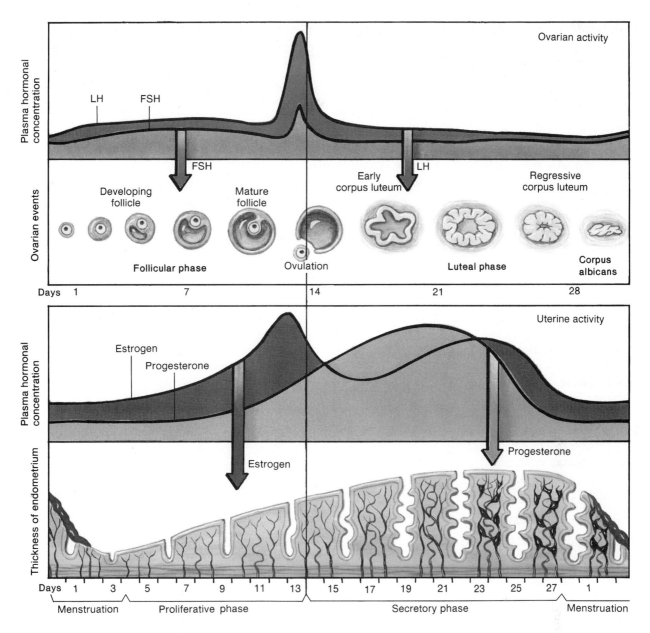

Figure 2-19. *Major events in the ovarian and menstrual cycles.*

CHAPTER 2 REVIEW

Instructions:

Answer the following questions. Check your answers in the *Answer Key* that follows this section.

1. The first period of menstrual bleeding is called
   - A. Menses
   - B. Menopause
   - C. Menstruation
   - D. Menarche
   - E. Mendacious

2. The energy that is necessary to keep the body functioning at a minimal level is known as
   - A. Thermogenesis
   - B. Catabolism
   - C. Metabolite
   - D. Metabolic reaction
   - E. Basal metabolism

3. The portion of the brain that coordinates skeletal muscle activity is the
   - A. Cerebellum
   - B. Pons
   - C. Medulla oblongata
   - D. Thalamus
   - E. Hypothalamus

4. The strands of DNA in the nucleus are called
   - A. Chromatin
   - B. Nucleolus
   - C. Network
   - D. Granules of RNA
   - E. Guanine

5. The part of the nervous system that governs conscious activities is the
   - A. Central
   - B. Autonomic
   - C. Somatic
   - D. Ventral
   - E. Myelin

6. A translucent band that is present in thick skin is called
   - A. Stratum corneum
   - B. Stratum granulosum
   - C. Stratum germinativum
   - D. Stratum spongiosum
   - E. Stratum lucidum

7. Which of the following endocrine glands releases glucagon?
   - A. Adrenal cortex
   - B. Thyroid gland
   - C. Pancreas
   - D. Hypothalamus
   - E. Anterior pituitary

8. Muscles are characterized by
   - A. Contractility
   - B. Elasticity
   - C. Extensibility
   - D. Excitability
   - E. All of the above

9. The part of the eye responsible for peripheral vision is the
   - A. Iris
   - B. Cone
   - C. Rod
   - D. Aqueous humor
   - E. Conjunctiva

10. The hypothalamus releases
    - A. Prolactin
    - B. Inhibiting hormones
    - C. Vasopressin
    - D. Testosterone
    - E. Gonadotropic hormones

11. All formed elements of blood originate from
    - A. Hemocytoblasts
    - B. Globulins
    - C. Myeloblasts
    - D. Plasma
    - E. Leukocytes

12. The muscle that flexes the foot is the
    A. Deltoid
    B. Gastrocnemius
    C. Gluteus maximus
    D. Quadriceps femoris
    E. Trapezius

13. The universal donor blood group is
    A. Type A
    B. Type O
    C. Type B
    D. Type AB
    E. Both B and D

14. The organs of the respiratory system include all of the following except
    A. Larynx
    B. Pharynx
    C. Trachea
    D. Bronchi
    E. Thoracic duct

15. A fold of loose skin that covers the penis is the
    A. Epididymis
    B. Cicumcision
    C. Prepuce
    D. Tunica albuginea
    E. Lobule

16. An expandable organ that stores urine is the
    A. Urinary bladder
    B. Kidney
    C. Urethra
    D. Ureter
    E. Nephron

17. The longest part of the digestive system is the
    A. Stomach
    B. Sphincter
    C. Large Intestine
    D. Anal canal
    E. Small intestine

18. Which of the following is not connective tissue?
    A. Bone
    B. Blood
    C. Nervous tissue
    D. Supportive tissue
    E. Loose tissue

19. Which of the following bones in the neck is U-shaped?
    A. Hyoid bone
    B. Atlas
    C. Axis
    D. Coccyx
    E. None of the above

20. Substances that are not chemically combined and that can be separated by physical means are
    A. Solutes
    B. Cultures
    C. Compounds
    D. Molecules
    E. Mixtures

21. All of the following are neurotransmitters except
    A. Histamine
    B. Dopamine
    C. Renin
    D. Serotonin
    E. Norepinephrine

22. Which of the following terms means "cell eating"?
    A. Pinocytosis
    B. Phagocytosis
    C. Exocytosis
    D. Endocytosis
    E. Cytokinesis

23. All of the following are major functions of the skin except

   A. Sensory reception
   B. Synthesis of vitamin A
   C. Protection
   D. Synthesis of vitamin D
   E. All of the above are major functions of the skin

24. Skeletal muscles need all of the following factors to contract except

   A. Actin
   B. Myosin
   C. Vitamin D
   D. ATP
   E. Calcium

25. Which of the following is not a glandular mode of secretion?

   A. Transitional
   B. Merocrine
   C. Holocrine
   D. Apocrine
   E. All of the above are glandular modes of secretion

26. Which of the following is not a body plane?

   A. Dorsal
   B. Frontal
   C. Sagittal
   D. Transverse
   E. They are all body planes

27. The first cervical vertebra is the

   A. Sternum
   B. Axis
   C. Scapula
   D. Atlas
   E. Clavicle

28. Which of the following is not a type of muscle tissue?

   A. Striated
   B. Visceral
   C. Skeletal
   D. Smooth
   E. Patella

29. The production of heat needed to utilize food is called

   A. Catabolism
   B. Thermogenesis
   C. Anabolism
   D. Metabolism
   E. Both A and D

30. Pulmonary arteries

   A. Send blood toward the heart
   B. Transfer oxygenated blood away from the heart
   C. Transfer low-oxygen blood away from the heart
   D. Are very small vessels that connect with veins
   E. Transfer blood to the brain

31. The three bones in the middle ear that amplify vibrations are called

   A. Auditory ossicles
   B. Cochlea
   C. Organs of Corti
   D. Vestibule
   E. Malleus

32. The part of the brain responsible for visual recognition is

   A. Occipital lobe
   B. Temporal lobe
   C. Parietal l lobe
   D. Broca's area
   E. Pons

33. Wernicke's area in the brain is involved with

   A. Emotion
   B. Taste
   C. Visceral emotions, drives, and reactions
   D. Language comprehension
   E. Muscle control

34. The thalamus
    A. Controls body temperature
    B. Acts as a relay station for sensory impulses
    C. Is the center of the brain for memory and visual recognition
    D. Connects the two hemispheres of the brain
    E. Has no known function

35. Bitter taste receptors are located on what part of the tongue?
    A. Tip
    B. Right side
    C. Left side
    D. Middle
    E. Back

36. The white and outermost layer of the eye is called
    A. Retina
    B. Iris
    C. Ciliary body
    D. Vitreous humor
    E. Sclera

37. The hormone epinephrine is produced by the
    A. Ovaries
    B. Adrenal medulla
    C. Thyroid
    D. Anterior pituitary
    E. Testes

38. Secretion of hormones is regulated by
    A. Other hormones
    B. Neurotransmitters
    C. Negative feedback system
    D. All of the above
    E. None of the above

39. All of the following are characteristics of the endocrine system except
    A. It is responsible for many conscious and unconscious activities.
    B. Its response is slow and prolonged when compared to that of the nervous system.
    C. Endocrine glands are ductless and release hormones into the bloodstream.
    D. It controls many body functions such as blood pressure, heart rate, and sexual characteristics.
    E. The endocrine system produces hormones that affect activities such as growth, metabolism, and reproduction.

40. Type A blood has
    A. A antigen on the red blood cells and A antibodies in plasma
    B. B antigen on the red blood cells and A antibodies in plasma
    C. A antigen on the red blood cells and B antibodies in plasma
    D. Both A and B antigens on red blood cells and no antibodies in plasma
    E. No antigens on red blood cells and both A and B antibodies in plasma

41. The sympathetic action of the pupil of the eye is
    A. Constriction
    B. Dilation
    C. Stimulation
    D. Maintaining a constant size
    E. None of the above

42. A synapse is
    A. The junction between two neurons
    B. The junction between two bones
    C. The main part of the neuron
    D. A type of nerve cell that supports, protects, and nourishes the neuron
    E. A type of bone cell that supports, protects, and nourishes the bone

ANSWER KEY

1.	D		22.	B
2.	E		23.	B
3.	A		24.	C
4.	A		25.	A
5.	C		26.	A
6.	E		27.	D
7.	C		28.	E
8.	E		29.	B
9.	C		30.	C
10.	B		31.	A
11.	A		32.	A
12.	B		33.	D
13.	B		34.	B
14.	E		35.	E
15.	C		36.	E
16.	A		37.	B
17.	E		38.	D
18.	C		39.	A
19.	A		40.	C
20.	E		41.	B
21.	C		42.	A

CHAPTER 3

Pathophysiology

CHAPTER OUTLINE

Mechanisms of Disease

Immunology

    Nonspecific Defense Mechanism
    Specific Immune Response
    Organs and Tissues of the Immune System

Hereditary and Congenital Diseases and Conditions

    Hereditary Diseases and Conditions
    Congenital Conditions

Neoplasia

Common Infectious Diseases

Major Diseases and Disorders

    Diseases and Disorders of the Integumentary System
    Diseases and Disorders of the Musculoskeletal System
    Diseases and Disorders of the Nervous System
    Diseases and Disorders of the Sensory System
    Diseases and Disorders of the Endocrine System
    Diseases and Disorders of the Cardiovascular System
    Diseases and Disorders of the Respiratory System
    Diseases and Disorders of the Digestive System
    Diseases and Disorders of the Urinary System
    Diseases and Disorders of the Reproductive System
    Diseases and Disorders Specific to Children

AAMA—ROLE DELINEATION STUDY AREAS OF COMPETENCE

General (Transdisciplinary)

Communication Skills

- Use medical terminology appropriately

AMT—RMA CERTIFICATION EXAM TOPICS

Anatomy and Physiology

- Disorders of the body

Medical Terminology

- Definitions
- Spelling

Mechanisms of Disease

Pathology: The study of the characteristics, causes, and effects of disease. Also, a condition produced by disease.

Etiology: The study of all factors that cause a disease. Also, the cause of a disease.

Idiopathic: Pertaining to a disease of unknown cause.

Necrosis: Localized cell or tissue death that occurs in response to disease or injury.

Nosocomial: Pertaining to an infection acquired in a hospital or other medical care facility at least 72 hours after admission.

Acute: Characterized by sudden onset and short duration, with marked intensity or sharpness.

Chronic: Developing gradually and persisting for a long period, often for the remainder of a person's lifetime.

Mortality: The condition of being subject to death. Also, the death rate, or the ratio of the number of deaths to a given population.

Morbidity: The state of being diseased. Also, the ratio of the number of cases of certain diseases to the population in which they occur.

Atresia: The absence or closure of a normal body opening, duct, or canal, such as the external ear canal or anus.

Aplastic: Lacking new development, or pertaining to the failure of a tissue to produce normal cell division.

Hypertrophy: An increase in the size of individual cells or an organ, resulting in an enlarged tissue mass. The cells of the heart, kidney, and prostate are particularly prone to hypertrophy.

Ischemia: Inadequate oxygenated blood supply to an organ or tissue, often marked by pain and organ dysfunction.

Infarction: An area of dead cells that results from a lack of oxygen.

Gangrene: An area of necrotic or dead tissue caused by an invasion of bacteria or loss of blood supply (ischemia). The extremities are most often affected, but it can occur in the intestines or gallbladder.

Immunology

Immunity: The quality of being resistant to a disease, often because of the presence of antibodies. Immunity can be acquired in a variety of different ways. See Table 3-1.

AT A GLANCE | Ways of Acquiring Immunity

ACTIVE IMMUNITY	PASSIVE IMMUNITY
The body produces its own antibodies. Provides long term immunity.	Antibodies produced outside the body are introduced into the body. Provides temporary immunity.
Natural Active Immunity	**Natural Passive Immunity**
Results from exposure to disease-causing organism.	Results when antibodies from the mother cross the placenta to the fetus.
Artificial Active Immunity	**Artificial Passive Immunity**
Results from the administration of a vaccine with killed or weakened organisms.	Results from immunization with antibodies to a disease-causing organism.

Table 3-1

Immune system: Includes two major components: nonspecific immune mechanisms and specific immune mechanisms.

Antigen: A marker on the surface of a cell that identifies the cell as self or non-self. A non-self (foreign) antigen stimulates an immune response.

Immunodeficiency disorders: Health conditions caused by a deficiency of the immune system in which individuals are more susceptible to infections and chronic diseases. These diseases may be congenital or acquired, or they may result from therapeutic intervention for transplants.

Nonspecific Defense Mechanism

Nonspecific defense mechanism: The body's initial response to any threat, whether it be trauma, organisms, or chemicals. It is also known as inflammation. It is characterized by heat, redness, swelling, and pain.

Phagocyte: A cell that has the ability to ingest and destroy pathogens such as bacteria and protozoa, as well as cells, cell debris, and dust particles.

Macrophages: The main phagocytic cells of the immune system. They have the ability to recognize and ingest all foreign antigens. These antigens are then destroyed by lysosomes. Macrophages also serve a vital role in processing antigens and presenting them to T cells, thereby activating a specific immune response. Macrophages are present in the lymph nodes, liver, spleen, lungs, bone marrow, and connective tissue and in the blood as monocytes.

Kupffer cells: The fixed macrophages of the liver.

Neutrophil: A granular leukocyte that is responsible for much of the body's protection against infection. Neutrophils destroy antigens by phagocytosis, and they play a vital role in inflammation and the nonspecific immune response.

Interferons: Antiviral, soluble glycoproteins produced by cells infected with viruses, chlamydiae, rickettsiae, and protozoa (e.g., malaria). They inhibit virus production within the cells and mark infected cells to be destroyed by T cells.

Specific Immune Response

Specific immune mechanisms: Required if the nonspecific immune response could not cope with the invasion or injury to the body. It is directed and controlled by T cells and B cells. These defenses are highly changed after exposure to a pathogen. They can "remember" pathogens such that the next time they invade the body, the specific immune response is quicker and specifically directed at the pathogen.

Cell-mediated immune response: Involves the production of lymphocytes by the thymus (T cells) in response to antigen exposure. This response is important in the rejection of transplants, malignant growths, hypersensitivity, and some infections.

Humoral immune response: Involves the production of plasma lymphocytes (B cells) leading to subsequent antibody formation. This response can produce immunity and hypersensitivity.

Antibody: An immunoglobulin produced by the lymphocytes in response to foreign antigens, such as those on bacteria and viruses.

Autoantibody: An antibody produced in response to a self-antigen. An autoantibody attacks the body's own cells. Autoantibodies are the basis for autoimmune diseases such as rheumatoid arthritis.

Eosinophils: White blood cells that participate in allergic response.

Hypersensitivity: An abnormal condition characterized by an exaggerated response of the immune system to an antigen. The four types of hypersensitivity are shown in Table 3-2 on the next page.

Type	Example
I	Hay fever, anaphylaxis, asthma, and eczema
II	Transfusion reactions, drug reactions, erythroblastosis fetalis, autoimmune disorders, glomerulonephritis
III	Serum sickness
IV	Tuberculin reaction, contact dermatitis, transplant rejection

Types of Hypersensitivity

Table 3-2

Organs and Tissues of the Immune System

Thymus: The gland located in the mediastinum. It is the site of the maturation and proliferation of the T lymphocytes.

Lymphatic tissue: Contains many lymphocytes that remove foreign matter.

Bone marrow: Soft material that fills the cavity of the bones. Bone marrow is the source of stem cells and lymphocytes, and it is the site where B lymphocytes mature.

Hereditary and Congenital Diseases and Conditions

Hereditary diseases: Diseases caused by an error in the individual's genetic or chromosomal makeup. These diseases may or may not be apparent at birth.

Congenital anomaly: Any abnormality present at birth, which may be inherited or acquired during gestation. It is also called a birth defect.

Hereditary Diseases and Conditions

Albinism: A genetic condition that results in the lack of melanin pigment in the body, increasing the chance of sunburn and skin cancer.

Classic hemophilia: A hereditary bleeding disorder caused by a deficiency of clotting factors. Hemophilia is an X-linked genetic disorder in males.

Color blindness: The hereditary inability to distinguish between certain colors, generally red and green. Color blindness is more common in males.

Galactosemia: An inherited disorder in which the patient lacks the enzyme that converts galactose to glucose. Galactose accumulates in the blood and interferes with development of the brain, liver, and eyes and can lead to anorexia, vomiting, diarrhea, and even death if it goes untreated. This condition is usually present at birth, so it is also congenital. The diagnosis is confirmed by testing the newborn's urine.

Phenylketonuria (PKU): A hereditary congenital disease in which the newborn child is unable to oxidize an amino acid because of a defective enzyme. If not treated early, this condition results in brain damage and severe mental retardation. Some states require that newborns be tested for this disease.

Sickle cell anemia: An inherited disorder that primarily affects Africans and African Americans. Red blood cells become crescent-shaped, rigid, sticky, and fragile and cause chronic anemia, tissue hypoxia, weakness, and fatigue.

Tay-Sachs disease: A hereditary congenital disease that primarily affects people of Ashkenazic (Eastern European) Jewish origin. This enzyme deficiency causes abnormal lipid metabolism in the brain, which leads to mental and physical retardation.

Congenital Conditions

Achondroplasia: Defective cartilage formation in the fetus. As a result, the long bones of the arm and legs are short, the trunk of the body is normal in size, and the head is large.

Down syndrome: A congenital condition caused by trisomy 21 (the presence of an extra autosomal chromosome 21). It results in varying degrees of mental retardation and distinctive physical features.

Klinefelter's syndrome: A congenital endocrine condition caused by the presence of an extra X chromosome, in which the individual appears to be male but has small testes and enlarged breasts.

Polydactyly: Congenital anomaly characterized by the presence of extra fingers or toes.

Turner's syndrome: A congenital endocrine disorder caused by the lack of a second X chromosome in females. The individual appears to be female, but the ovaries do not develop.

Ventricular septal defect: The most common congenital cardiac disease, in which a defect in the septum allows blood to be shunted between the left and right ventricles.

Coarctation of the aorta: Narrowing of the aortic arch, which creates increased left ventricular pressure and decreased blood pressure distal to the narrowing. Signs include left ventricular failure with pulmonary edema, dyspnea, and tachycardia.

Patent ductus arteriosus (PDA): A defect in which the ductus arteriosus, a fetal blood vessel, fails to close after birth. This condition often results in heart failure.

Tetralogy of Fallot: The most common cyanotic cardiac defect, in which there are four symptoms: ventricular septal defect, dextroposition of the aorta, pulmonary stenosis, and right ventricular hypertrophy.

Cyanosis: A bluish or grayish discoloration of the skin due to decreased amounts of hemoglobin in the blood.

Cerebral palsy: The name given to a group of motor impairment syndromes caused by lesions or anomalies in the brain in the early stages of development. Motor impairment generally occurs with secondary defects such as mental retardation or epilepsy. There are three major types: spastic (the most common), athetoid, and ataxic.

Spina bifida: The incomplete closure of the vertebral column. In cases that are not severe, surgery may be performed to close the defect and thus prevent damage to the spinal cord.

Myelomeningocele: Also known as spina bifida cystica, in which a congenital defect in the walls of the spinal canal allows the membranes of the spinal cord to push through and form a tumor. It usually occurs within the first 24 hours after birth, and surgical correction is necessary.

Hydrocephalus: A condition in which there is excessive fluid in or around the brain, an abnormal enlargement of the head, and abnormal muscle tone of the legs.

Muscular dystrophy: A progressive degeneration and weakening of the skeletal muscles.

Duchene's muscular dystrophy: The most common type of muscular dystrophy, which mostly affects males and involves the muscles of the shoulders, hips, and thighs.

Phimosis: A narrowing of the opening of the foreskin.

Congenital pyloric stenosis: A narrowing of the pyloric sphincter at the exit of the stomach. A symptom of this disease is projectile vomiting after feeding that starts at 2 to 3 weeks of age.

Hirschsprung's disease: Also called congenital aganglionic megacolon, an impairment of intestinal motility that causes obstruction of the distal colon. The newborn fails to pass meconium within 48 hours after birth.

Meconium: First feces of a newborn infant.

Congenital myxedema: A condition characterized by severe hypothyroidism and often associated with other endocrine abnormalities. Typical signs of myxedema include lack of growth, mental deficiency, puffy facial features, dry skin, and a large tongue. The condition is also referred to as cretinism.

Neoplasia

Neoplasia: The new and abnormal growth of cells, which may be benign or malignant.

Neoplasm: Literally, a new growth, commonly called a tumor.

Hyperplasia: An increase in the number of cells in a body part that results from an increased rate of cellular division that can cause the formation of a tumor.

Malignant: Invasive and capable of metastasis.

Benign: Not recurrent or progressive; nonmalignant.

Metastasis: Development of a tumor away from the site of origin. It occurs when tumor cells spread to distant parts of the body through lymphatic circulation or the bloodstream and implant in lymph nodes or other organs.

Cancer: A neoplasm characterized by the uncontrolled growth of abnormal cells that invade surrounding tissue and metastasize to distant body sites. As shown in Table 3-3, cancer is second only to heart disease as a cause of mortality in the United States. Possible causes of cancer include smoking; viruses; hormones; radiation; genetic predisposition; chemicals used in industry, food, cosmetics, and plastic; and air and water pollution. See Table 3-4 on p. 80 for the most common types of cancer in men, women, and children. See Table 3-5 on p. 80 for the most common types of cancer that result in death for men and women.

Carcinogen: A substance or agent that causes cancer or increases the incidence of cancer.

Carcinogenesis: The process by which normal cells are transformed into cancer cells.

Carcinoma: A malignant tumor of the epithelial cells. This neoplasm tends to infiltrate and metastasize through the lymphatic system or the blood stream. It develops most often in the skin, large intestine, lungs, stomach, prostate, cervix, or breast.

Sarcoma: A malignant neoplasm of the connective tissues such as bone or muscle. This type of cancer might affect the bones, bladder, kidneys, liver, lungs, or spleen.

Epidermoid carcinoma: A malignant tumor of epidermal cells of the skin.

Common Causes of Death in the United States
1. Heart disease
2. Cancer
3. Cerebrovascular diseases
4. Pulmonary diseases and conditions

Table 3-3

Most Common Cancers

Men	Women	Children
Prostate	Breast	Leukemia
Lung	Lung	Brain and other nervous system
Colon	Colon	

Table 3-4

Most Common Lethal Cancers

Male	Female
Lung	Lung
Prostate	Breast
Colon and rectum	Colon and rectum
Pancreas	Ovary

Table 3-5

Adenocarcinoma: A cancer of glandular epithelial cells.

Teratoma: A congenital tumor composed of different kinds of tissue, none of which normally occur together or at the site of the tumor. Most common in the ovaries or testes.

Dermoid cyst: A cyst containing elements of hair, teeth, or skin that commonly occurs in the ovaries or testes.

Leukemia: A primary cancer of the bone marrow with proliferating leukocyte precursors. Its cause is generally unknown, but environmental risk factors include exposure to radiation and to certain chemicals.

Lymphoma: A cancer of the lymph nodes and lymphoid tissue that usually responds to treatment. The two main kinds are Hodgkin's disease and non-Hodgkin's lymphoma.

Renal carcinoma: A cancer of the kidneys, also called hypernephroma. Painless hematuria is common with this condition. Metastasis to the lungs, liver, bones, and brain is possible.

Prostate cancer: A slowly progressive adenocarcinoma of the prostate that affects males after the age of 50. It is the second leading cause of cancer death among men in the United States. The cause is unknown, but it is believed to be hormone-related.

Bladder cancer: The most common cancer of the urinary tract, it occurs more often in men than in women. The risk of bladder cancer increases with cigarette smoking and exposure to aniline dyes and to materials used in the petroleum, paint, plastics, and timber industries.

Cancer of the mouth: May develop in the gums, cheeks, or on the roof of the mouth. In men, it is common to see a cancer of the lower lip, which may be related to pipe smoking.

Stomach cancer: A malignancy of the stomach that is declining in incidence in North America but is common in Japan. It often spreads to the liver.

Colorectal cancer: A malignant cancer of the large intestine, characterized by a change in bowel habits and the passing of blood. This cancer usually occurs among people older than 50. The risk of colorectal cancer is increased in patients with chronic ulcerative colitis, Crohn's disease, villous adenomas, and familial adenomatous polyposis of the colon.

Laryngeal cancer: A cancer of the larynx that occurs most frequently in those between 50 and 70 years of age. Persistent hoarseness or dysphonia are usually the only symptoms.

Lung cancer: A pulmonary malignancy attributable in the majority of cases to cigarette smoking. Other predisposing factors are exposure to arsenic, asbestos, coal products, ionizing radiation, mustard gas, and petroleum. It is the leading cause of cancer death in the United States. Metastasis is to the brain, bone, and skin.

Cervical cancer: A malignancy of the uterine cervix that can be detected in the early, curable stage by the Papanicolaou (Pap) test. Risk factors include coitus at an early age, relations with many sexual partners, genital herpes virus infections, multiparity, and poor obstetric and gynecological care.

Endometrial cancer: An adenocarcinoma of the endometrium of the uterus. It is the most prevalent malignancy of the female reproductive system, most often occurring in the fifth or sixth decade of life. Some of the risk factors include infertility; anovulation; late menopause; administration of exogenous estrogen; and a combination of diabetes, hypertension, and obesity.

Ovarian carcinoma: A malignant neoplasm of the ovaries rarely detected in the early stage. It occurs commonly in the fifth decade of life. Risk factors include infertility, nulliparity or low parity, delayed childbearing, repeated spontaneous abortion, endometriosis, and group A blood type.

Choriocarcinoma: An epithelial malignancy of fetal origin. The primary tumor usually appears in the uterus and may metastasize to the lungs, liver, and brain. This cancer is more common in older women.

Adenocarcinoma of the vagina: A small percentage of women whose mothers were given the synthetic hormone diethylstilbestrol (DES), used to prevent spontaneous abortion, have developed this form of cancer. Most cases are in women whose mothers did not take the hormone.

Breast cancer: This adenocarcinoma is the most common cancer in North American women and is the leading cause of death in females 35 to 54 years of age. Metastases are commonly to the lungs, liver, brain, and bone.

Testicular cancer: A malignant neoplastic disease of the testis occurring most frequently in men between 20 and 35 years of age. Patients with early testicular cancer are often asymptomatic, and metastases may be present in lymph nodes, the lungs, and the liver.

Common Infectious Diseases

Common cold: Acute viral inflammation of any or all parts of the respiratory tract marked by congestion of the nasal mucosa, sneezing, and malaise, among other symptoms. The contagious period begins before the onset of symptoms, and the incubation period is from 12 to 72 hours.

Influenza: Also known as the flu or grippe, an acute respiratory infection characterized by the sudden onset of fever, chills, headache, and muscle pain or tenderness. Inflammation of the nasal mucous membrane, cough, and sore throat are common. The incubation period is from 1 to 3 days.

Mumps (parotitis): The inflammation of one or both parotid glands caused by viral infection, with an incubation period of 2 to 3 weeks. Complications may include meningoencephalitis, pericarditis, deafness, arthritis, nephritis, and sterility in men.

Chickenpox (varicella): A highly contagious, acute viral infection characterized by spots and an elevated temperature. The incubation period is 2 to 3 weeks. Complications may include encephalitis, meningitis, Reye's syndrome, pneumonia, and conjunctival ulcer. The virus may reemerge later as shingles. Chickenpox can be severely damaging to a fetus.

Measles (rubeola): An acute, highly contagious viral disease. The incubation period is 7 to 14 days. The condition is characterized by spots and a rash. Complications may include otitis media, pneumonia, and encephalitis.

German measles (rubella): Also called three-day measles, a highly communicable viral disease that has an incubation period of 14 to 21 days. It is characterized by spots. Rubella poses great danger to the fetus.

Meningitis: Any infection or inflammation of the membranes covering the brain and spinal cord. The most common causes for different age groups are summarized in Table 3-6. Aseptic meningitis may be caused by nonbacterial agents such as chemical irritants, viruses, or neoplasms.

Infectious mononucleosis: An acute infectious disease that causes changes in the leukocytes. It is also called glandular fever and the "kissing disease." Mononucleosis is caused by the Epstein-Barr virus and is usually transmitted by direct oral contact. It is rare in those older than 35.

Epiglottiditis: An inflammation of the epiglottis that commonly occurs in children between 3 and 7 years old. The most common cause is *Haemophilus influenzae* type B bacteria.

Genital lesion: A symptom that usually accompanies a sexually transmitted disease such as herpes or syphilis. It is found in the genital region of either males or females.

Botulism: A severe form of food poisoning from botulinus toxins produced by the *Clostridium botulinum* bacterium.

Gatroenteritis: Stomach and intestinal inflammation caused by a food- or waterborne virus.

AT A GLANCE	Meningitis	
Age Group	**Most Common Infective Causes**
Neonates	*Streptococcus, Escherichia coli*
Infants	*Haemophilus influenzae*
Adults	*Neisseria meningitidis*
Elderly individuals	*Streptococcus pneumonia*
Overall	*Haemophilus influenzae*

Table 3-6

Tetanus: An infection of the central nervous system caused by the tetanus bacillus, *Clostridium tetani*. The symptoms include sudden, extremely painful muscle contractions and stiffness of certain muscles such as the neck and the jaw. It is commonly called lockjaw.

Tapeworm: A species of parasitic worm that can infect the intestines when ingested with uncooked meat containing the larvae. Symptoms are often absent, but too many tapeworms can cause intestinal obstruction.

Malaria: An acute and sometimes chronic infection of red blood cells, transmitted by the bite of an infected female mosquito. Symptoms include chills, shaking, discomfort, fatigue, fevers, and headaches.

Yellow fever: An acute infectious viral infection transmitted by mosquitoes. Symptoms include jaundice, abdominal tenderness, vomiting, and fevers.

Major Diseases and Disorders

Diseases and Disorders of the Integumentary System

Viral infections of the skin: Include chickenpox and shingles (varicella), measles (rubeola), German measles (rubella), and warts (condyloma acuminata).

Bacterial infections of the skin: Include scarlet fever (erysipelas), impetigo (a type of pyoderma), folliculitis (carbuncles), and anthrax (woolsorter's disease).

Fungal infections of the skin: Include ringworm, dermatophytosis, dermatomycosis, and tinea.

Shingles: A reactivation in adults of the varicella (chickenpox) provirus, *Herpes zoster*, marked by inflammation of segments of the spinal or cranial peripheral nerves and painful eruption along the course of the nerve.

Scarlet fever: A contagious disease characterized by sore throat, strawberry tongue, fever, rash, and rapid pulse.

Wart: Also known as condyloma acuminata, a fibrous, superficial papule of the skin and mucous membranes, including those of the genitalia. The incubation period is 1 to 20 months.

Impetigo: A type of pyoderma, its symptoms include skin lesions, caused by *Staphylococcus aureus* or *Streptococcus pyogenes* or both. The incubation period is 4 to 10 days.

Carbuncle: A circumscribed inflammation of the skin and deeper tissues that begins with a painful node covered by tight, red skin that later becomes thin and perforates, discharging pus.

Anthrax: Also called woolsorter's disease, its symptoms are cutaneous blackened lesions caused by necrotoxin. Pneumonia may also develop. Caused by *Bacillus anthracis*, a gram-positive, aerobic bacillus. The incubation period is 3 to 5 days.

Tinea: A fungal skin disease also known as cutaneous mycoses or ringworm.

Tinea corporis: Infects the skin.

Tinea capitis: Infects the scalp.

Tinea cruris: Infects the groin. It is also known as jock itch.

Tinea pedis: Athlete's foot.

Dermatophytosis: Fungal infection of the skin of the hands and feet, especially between the toes.

Dermatomycosis: Skin infection caused by certain fungi.

Acne: An inflammatory disease of the sebaceous glands and hair follicles of the skin.

Eczema: Acute or chronic inflammation of the skin.

Psoriasis: Chronic disease of the skin that forms lesions.

Diseases and Disorders of the Musculoskeletal System

Atrophy: A decrease in the size of cells, resulting in reduced tissue mass. A skeletal muscle may undergo atrophy as a result of lack of physical exercise or neurologic disease.

Crepitation: Grating sound made by movement of some joints or broken bones.

Exostosis: Projection arising from a bone that develops from cartilage.

Myalgia: Muscle pain.

Herniated disk: Protrusion of a degenerated or fragmented intervertebral disk that causes compression of the nerve root.

Arthritis: Inflammation of the joints characterized by swelling, redness, warmth, pain, and limited movement.

Osteoarthritis: The most common form of arthritis, it affects the weight-bearing joints.

Rheumatoid arthritis: The most crippling form of arthritis, characterized by chronic systemic inflammation of joints and synovial membranes.

Gout: Hereditary metabolic form of acute arthritis.

Tendinitis or **tendonitis:** Inflammation of a tendon.

Scoliosis: Abnormal sideways curvature of the spine.

Kyphosis: Abnormal outward curvature of the spine. This condition is also known as a humpback.

Lordosis: Abnormal inward curvature of the spine.

Fracture: A break or crack in a bone. Table 3-7 lists the types of fracture.

Battle sign: A feeling of bogginess in the temporal region of the head. It usually indicates a fracture of the basilar area of the skull.

Diseases and Disorders of the Nervous System

Dysphasia: Difficulty in speaking.

Coma: An abnormal state of unconsciousness from which the patient cannot be aroused by external stimuli. Frequent causes of coma include trauma to the head, circulatory accidents in the brain, and systemic infections of the brain or meninges.

Fracture	Description
Closed or simple	The bone has a fracture, but no external wound exists.
Comminuted	The bone has broken into pieces.
Greenstick	The bone is partially bent and partially broken. This type of fracture occurs in children.
Impacted	The bone is broken and one end is wedged into the interior of the other.
Incomplete	The line of fracture does not continue through the whole bone.
Oblique	The bone has a slanted fracture of the shaft on its long axis.
Open or compound	The broken bone creates an external wound that leads to the site of fracture; fragments of bone commonly open the skin.

Table 3-7

Delirium: A state of mental confusion due to disturbances in mental function.

Dementia: Impairment of intellectual function characterized by disorientation, confusion, and memory loss.

Encephalitis: Inflammation of the brain, commonly caused by a viral infection. Secondary encephalitis may develop from viral childhood diseases such as measles, mumps, or chickenpox.

Sleeping sickness: A type of encephalitis characterized by lethargy, oculomotor paralysis, delirium, stupor, coma, and reversal of sleep rhythm.

Poliomyelitis: An infectious disease of the brain and spinal cord caused by a small RNA enterovirus. Type 1, the most common, causes paralysis. Transmission is by direct contact or by the fecal-oral route in areas with poor sanitation. Types 2 and 3 are frequently vaccine-associated.

Rabies: An infectious, acute, fatal disease of the brain and spinal cord caused by an RNA virus that is transmitted by the saliva of an infected animal, often through a bite. The incubation period is long, 40 to 60 days or more. Rabies is also called hydrophobia (fear of water).

Multiple sclerosis (MS): A chronic, progressive inflammatory disease of unknown origin that usually affects young adults between the ages of 20 and 40. Symptoms include changes in vision and muscle weakness. It is difficult to diagnose and has no specific treatment.

Amyotrophic lateral sclerosis (ALS): Also known as Lou Gehrig's disease, a chronic, terminal neurological disease that causes progressive muscular atrophy. The cause is unknown. It occurs most commonly in people in their 50s and 60s, and it is slightly more common in males than females.

Alzheimer's disease: Diffuse cortical atrophy of the brain characterized by confusion, memory failure, disorientation, and hallucination. The most common form occurs in people older than 65, but a presenile form can begin earlier.

Parkinson's disease: A brain degeneration that appears gradually and progresses slowly. It is also known as shaking palsy. Signs of Parkinson's disease include slowness of movement, resting tremor, and rigidity. The degeneration occurs in the basal ganglia. There is dopamine depletion.

Cerebral hemorrhage: Hemorrhage in epidural, subdural, or subarachnoid spaces in the meninges. The major cause of this condition is hypertension.

Concussion: An immediate loss of consciousness caused by a violent blow to the head or neck. It may last from a few seconds to several minutes.

Contusion: Bruising of the brain, a more serious head injury than a concussion. Permanent damage to the brain may result. It is commonly associated with skull fracture.

Paraplegia: Paralysis of motor or sensory abilities of the lower trunk and lower extremities. The individual may lose bowel and bladder control, and sexual dysfunction is common.

Quadriplegia: Paralysis of the lower and upper extremities (the arms, legs, and trunk) that results from injury to the spinal cord at the fifth, sixth, or seventh cervical vertebra. A major cause of death is respiratory failure.

Hemiplegia: Paralysis on one side of the body.

Epilepsy: A chronic brain disorder, characterized by sudden and recurrent episodes of convulsive seizures. There are two major types of seizure: partial seizures and generalized. A simple partial seizure was originally called jacksonian epilepsy. Generalized seizures include absence (petit mal) and tonic–clonic (grand mal).

Bell's palsy: A paralysis of the facial nerve that results from trauma to the nerve, compression of the nerve by a tumor, or an unknown infection. It commonly occurs between 20 and 60 years of age. It is usually self-limiting (temporary paralysis).

Trigeminal neuralgia: Also called tic douloureux, it involves pain in the fifth cranial nerve. Paroxysmal episodes of the pain may last for hours.

Carpal tunnel syndrome: Pain or numbness in the median nerve of the hand, generally as a result of cumulative trauma to the wrist.

Migraine: A type of periodic headache, which may or may not be accompanied by aura or neurologic dysfunction. Pain is usually confined to one side, but it can be bilateral.

Diseases and Disorders of the Sensory System

Diseases and Disorders of the Eye

Myopia: A severe form of nearsightedness that results when light rays entering the eye focus in front of the retina. Myopia occurs when the eyeball is abnormally long.

Hyperopia: A severe form of farsightedness that occurs when light rays entering the eye focus behind the retina. The eyeball is abnormally short.

Presbyopia: The inability to focus with the lens because of loss of its elasticity. It commonly develops with advancing age, usually beginning in the mid 40s.

Nystagmus: Involuntary, rhythmic movement of the eyes. Brain tumors or cerebrovascular lesions may cause nystagmus.

Astigmatism: An irregular focusing of the light rays entering the eye. The cornea is not spherical, and vision is typically blurred.

Strabismus: A disorder in which the visual axes of the eyes are not directed at the same point. Hence, the eyes are crossed. The main symptom is diplopia.

Conjunctivitis: Inflammation of the conjunctiva, caused by bacterial or viral infection, allergy, or environmental factors. Red eyes, thick discharge, and sticky eyelids in the morning are the most common signs and symptoms.

Hordeolum: Also called stye, an infection of the hair follicles of the eyelids.

Cataract: A clouding of a normally clear lens of the eye. The most common cause is aging.

Glaucoma: One of the most common and severe ocular diseases, characterized by increased intraocular pressure, which can result in damage to the optic nerve. It is more common in people 60 and older.

Retinal detachment: An elevation of the retina from the choroid. Extremely nearsighted people are more susceptible to retinal detachments.

Uveitis: Inflammation of the uveal tract, including the iris, ciliary body, and choroid. It can be caused by autoimmune disorders or by infections such as tuberculosis, toxoplasmosis, syphilis, or histoplasmosis.

Diseases and Disorders of the Ear

Otalgia: Earache.

External otitis: Also known as swimmer's ear, an infection of the ear canal, commonly caused by *Escherichia coli*, *Pseudomonas aeruginosa*, *Proteus vulgaris*, *Staphylococcus aureus*, or *Aspergillus* (a genus of fungi).

Otitis media: An infection of the middle ear. It is most common in children younger than 8. The bacteria that most often cause otitis media are *Haemophilus influenzae*, *Streptococcus pneumoniae*, *Streptococcus pyogenes*, and *Staphylococcus aureus*.

Tympanitis: Inflammation of the eardrum.

Conductive hearing loss: Loss of hearing caused by an interruption in the transmission of sound waves to the inner ear.

Sensorineural hearing loss: Hearing loss caused by damage to the inner ear, to the nerve from the ear to the brain, or to the brain itself, so that the brain does not perceive sound waves as sound.

Anacusis: Total hearing loss.

Tinnitus: Ringing or buzzing in the ear.

Vertigo: Dizziness.

Diseases and Disorders of the Endocrine System

Hypoglycemia: Low blood sugar.

Hyperglycemia: High blood sugar.

Ketosis: The accumulation of ketone bodies in the blood and urine as a result of abnormal utilization of carbohydrates.

Gigantism: Excessive size and stature of the body, usually caused by the hypersecretion of growth hormone. It is usually the result of a tumor (adenoma) of the anterior pituitary and generally occurs before puberty.

Acromegaly: A disease caused by an excess of growth hormone in an adult. The bones of the hands, feet, and face can be enlarged. It is generally due to a tumor.

Dwarfism: A growth hormone deficiency that results in the abnormal underdevelopment of the body, or hypopituitarism, mainly in children. It causes extreme shortness of stature.

Hyperthyroidism: Hypersecretion of the thyroid gland that results in protrusion of the eyeballs, tachycardia, goiter, and tumor.

Hypothyroidism: Hyposecretion of the thyroid gland that results in sluggishness, slow pulse, and obesity.

Goiter: An enlargement of the thyroid gland, possibly due to a lack of iodine in the diet, thyroiditis, inflammation from infection, tumors, or hyperfunction or hypofunction of the thyroid gland.

Graves' disease: A condition of severe hyperthyroidism, possibly with an autoimmune base. A sudden exacerbation of symptoms may signal thyrotoxicosis.

Thyrotoxicosis: A toxic condition caused by hyperactivity of the thyroid gland and characterized by rapid heartbeat, tremors, nervous symptoms, and weight loss.

Hashimoto's disease: An inflammatory autoimmune disease that attacks the thyroid gland. It is more common in women and is the leading cause of non-simple goiter and hypothyroidism.

Myxedema: The acquired form of severe hypothyroidism. It is more common in females and occurs in adulthood.

Cushing's syndrome: Hyperactivity of the adrenal cortical gland that develops from an excess of the glucocorticoid hormone. The individual experiences fatigue, weakness, fat deposits in the scapular area (buffalo humps), protruding abdomen, hypertension, edema, and hyperlipidemia.

Addison's disease: A life-threatening condition resulting from chronic hypoadrenalism. Symptoms include weakness, nausea, abdominal discomfort, anorexia, and weight loss, among many others.

Diabetes insipidus: A metabolic disorder caused by injury to the neurohypophyseal system. The disease results from antidiuretic hormone deficiency.

Diabetes mellitus: A chronic disorder of carbohydrate, fat, and protein metabolism resulting from inadequate production of insulin by the pancreas. This disorder results in hyperglycemia.

Hyperinsulinism: A condition resulting from excessive insulin in the blood, causing hypoglycemia, fainting, and convulsions.

Diseases and Disorders of the Cardiovascular System

Arteriosclerosis: A disease of the arterial vessels characterized by thickening, hardening, and loss of elasticity in the arteries.

Atherosclerosis: The most common form of arteriosclerosis, marked by cholesterol, lipid, and calcium deposits in arterial linings.

Angina pectoris: A paroxysmal chest pain caused by a temporary oxygen insufficiency as a result of atherosclerosis, spasms of the coronary arteries, or thrombosis.

Myocardial infarction: Necrosis of the myocardium often as a result of the occlusion of a coronary artery by atherosclerotic plaque, myocardium spasm, or thrombus.

Coronary thrombosis: A blood clot in a coronary artery, the most common cause of myocardial infarction.

Myocarditis: Inflammation of the myocardium. It is commonly caused by viruses, bacteria, fungi, or protozoa.

Endocarditis: Inflammation of the lining and valves of the heart due to an invasion of microorganisms or an abnormal immunological reaction. There are several types of endocarditis.

Acute endocarditis: Caused by *Staphylococcus aureus* and group A beta-hemolytic streptococci.

Subacute endocarditis: Commonly caused by *Escherichia coli* or *Streptococcus viridans*.

Pericarditis: Inflammation of the pericardium. It may be caused by myocardial infarction, viral uremia, bacteria, fungi, parasites, or rheumatic fever. There are three types: fibrinous, serous, and suppurative.

Rheumatic fever: A systemic, inflammatory autoimmune disease involving the heart and the joints. There are two types: acute rheumatic fever and rheumatic heart disease.

Acute rheumatic fever: More common in children. It is caused by beta-hemolytic streptococci and is characterized by polyarthritis, erythema, subcutaneous nodules, chorea, and carditis.

Rheumatic heart disease: Causes stenosis or insufficiency of the mitral valve.

Shock: The collapse of the cardiovascular system—a dangerous reduction of blood flow throughout the body tissues. It is a life-threatening emergency that can be caused by sepsis, hemorrhage, heart failure, respiratory distress, or anaphylaxis.

Cardiac tamponade: Accumulation of fluid, such as blood, in the pericardial sac.

Cardiogenic shock: Shock resulting from extensive myocardial infarction.

Aneurysm: A dilation or saclike formation in a weakened blood vessel wall. A common cause is atherosclerotic plaque. Other causative agents include trauma, inflammation or infection, and congenital factors.

Abdominal aortic aneurysm: The most common form of aneurysm.

Thrombophlebitis: Also called phlebitis, the inflammation of a vein, often accompanied by the formation of a clot. It occurs most commonly in the lower legs.

Varicose vein: An enlarged, twisted superficial vein, usually in the lower leg, caused by incompetent valves. It is very common, especially in women.

Buerger's disease (thromboangiitis obliterans): An occlusion and inflammation of the peripheral vascular circulation, usually in the leg or foot. The primary cause is a long history of smoking tobacco.

Raynaud's disease: Episodic vasospasm of the small cutaneous arteries, usually occurring in the fingers. It is often aggravated by a cold.

Anemia: A reduction in the quantity of either red blood cells or hemoglobin in a measured volume of blood. There are several forms of anemia, including iron-deficiency anemia, pernicious anemia, and aplastic anemia.

Iron-deficiency anemia: The most common type of anemia. It results from greater demand on stored iron than can be supplied. Red blood cell count may be normal, but there is insufficient hemoglobin.

Pernicious anemia: Chronic anemia caused by decreased hydrochloric acid in the stomach, lack of intrinsic factor, and a vitamin B_{12} deficiency.

Aplastic anemia: A congenital form of anemia, also called Fanconi syndrome. The bone marrow stops producing erythrocytes, leukocytes, and platelets. It is caused by exposure to excessive radiation, certain drugs, and industrial toxins.

Polycythemia: An increase in the number of circulating erythrocytes and the amount of hemoglobin. There are three types: polycythemia vera, secondary polycythemia, and relative polycythemia. Complications may include thrombosis, cerebrovascular accident, peptic ulcers, leukemia, and hemorrhage.

Agranulocytosis: Also called neutropenia, a condition in which the number of leukocytes is very low.

Lymphedema: An abnormal collection of lymph, commonly in the extremities. Congenital lymphedema is known as Milroy's disease.

Lyme disease: A tickborne disease characterized by skin lesions, malaise, fatigue, arthritis, carditis, encephalitis, meningitis, loss of memory, numbness, and facial palsy. The incubation period is 3 to 33 days after a tick bite.

Plague: A highly fatal disease characterized by high fever, mental confusion, prostration, delirium, shock, and coma. There are three types: bubonic, septicemic, and pneumonic. Caused by *Yersinia pestis*, a gram-negative, nonmotile bacillus. The incubation period is 2 to 6 days.

Pneumonic plague: Characterized by extensive involvement of the lungs, it is very contagious and usually fatal.

Bubonic plague: An acute or severe infection characterized by the formation of buboes, which are inflamed and swollen lymph nodes. It is transmitted by infected rats and squirrels. In the Middle Ages, it was also known as the Black Death.

Toxoplasmosis: A systemic protozoan disease that results in fever, lymphadenopathy, lymphocytosis, pneumonia, rashes, myocarditis, and death. The primary infection may be asymptomatic.

Diseases and Disorders of the Respiratory System

Pharyngitis: Inflammation of the pharynx most often caused by a viral infection.

Anosmia: The loss or impairment of the sense of smell. Nasal polyps and allergic rhinitis are the most common cause.

Rhinitis: Inflammation of the nasal mucosa, causing nasal congestion, sneezing, and itching of the nose.

Allergic rhinitis: Hay fever.

Bronchiectasis: Chronic dilation and distention of the bronchial walls. It is irreversible. Complications are lung abscess, pneumonia, and empyema.

Atelectasis: A collapsed or airless state of the lung that results in hypoxia. Dyspnea may be the only symptom.

Pneumonia: Inflammation of the lungs. It is caused by viral or bacterial infection. Bacterial pneumonia is commonly caused by pneumococci, staphylococci, *Klebsiella pneumoniae*, or group A hemolytic streptococci. *Streptococcus pneumoniae* is the most common cause in all age groups. When a bacterial cause cannot be identified, it is called atypical pneumonia. It is the fifth leading cause of death in the U.S.

Emphysema: A chronic pulmonary disease characterized by an abnormal increase in the size of air spaces distal to the terminal bronchiole with destructive changes in their walls.

Asthma: A respiratory disorder characterized by recurring episodes of paroxysmal dyspnea, wheezing on expiration and inspiration caused by constriction of the bronchi, coughing, and viscous mucoid bronchial secretions. The episodes may occur as a result of inhalation of allergens or pollutants, infection, cold air, vigorous exercise, or emotional stress.

Cystic fibrosis: An inherited autosomal-recessive disorder of the exocrine glands, which causes the production of abnormally thick secretions of mucus, the elevation of sweat electrolytes, and an increase in the enzymes of saliva. The glands most affected are those in the pancreas and respiratory system, and the sweat glands. Cystic fibrosis is usually recognized in infancy or early childhood.

Hemoptysis: Coughing and spitting up of blood from the respiratory tract. In true hemoptysis, the sputum is bright red and frothy with air bubbles.

Hematemesis: Vomiting of blood, with red-and-black-colored sputum. It is a symptom of several diseases of the pulmonary system.

Legionnaires' disease: A type of pneumonia caused by *Legionella pneumophila*. Predisposing factors include smoking, alcoholism, and physical debilitation.

Histoplasmosis: A type of pneumonia that may become a systemic disease. It is caused by inhalation of dust containing spores of *Histoplasma capsulatum*, a fungus commonly seen in the Mississippi and Ohio River valleys. It is also called Darling's disease, and it clinically resembles tuberculosis.

Pneumoconiosis or **pneumonoconiosis:** Any disease of the lung caused by chronic inhalation of dust (mineral dust). It is of occupational origin and involves a chronic inflammation and infection in the lungs. It takes at least 10 years of continual daily exposure to develop these diseases. Forms of pneumoconiosis include anthracosis, asbestosis, and silicosis.

Anthracosis: A lung disease caused by inhalation of coal dust. It is also called coal-miner's lung or black lung.

Asbestosis: A form of pneumoconiosis caused by exposure to asbestos. It is the most common type of dust disease.

Silicosis: Long-term inhalation of the dust of an inorganic compound, silicon dioxide, which is found in sands, quartzes, and flints. It is also called grinder's disease.

Pleurisy: Inflammation of the pleural membranes.

Pneumothorax: Entrance of air or gas into the pleural space, resulting in a collapsed lung.

Hemothorax: Blood in the pleural cavity. It is caused by trauma to or erosion of a pulmonary vessel. It can also cause the lung to collapse.

Flail chest: A loss of stability in the chest wall, due to a multiple fracture of each affected rib, that produces a characteristic movement pattern during respiration.

Diphtheria: A potentially fatal childhood disease, caused by *Corynebacterium diphtheriae*, that begins with a sore throat and affects the mucous membranes of the respiratory tract. A gram-positive bacillus secretes a strong exotoxin, resulting in a grayish-white pseudomembrane on the skin. The incubation period is 1 to 4 days. Immunity or susceptibility can be determined by the Schick test. Complications may include myocarditis, heart failure, pneumonia, otitis media, and pulmonary emboli.

Tuberculosis: An infectious disease caused by *Mycobacterium tuberculosis*. Tuberculosis is transmitted through inhalation of airborne droplets, prolonged direct contact with infected individuals, consumption of contaminated milk, or contact with infected cattle. The incubation period is 4 to 12 weeks.

Whooping cough: Also called pertussis, an infectious disease caused by *Bordetella pertussis*, a gram-negative, encapsulated coccobacillus. It produces both an endotoxin and an exotoxin.

Diseases and Disorders of the Digestive System

Gingivitis: Inflammation and swelling of the gums, often the result of poor oral hygiene.

Oral leukoplakia: A precancerous disease that results in the thickening and hardening of a part of the mucous membranes in the mouth. It is more common in elderly individuals.

Esophagitis: Inflammation of the mucosal lining of the esophagus. Its·most common cause is a backflow of gastric juice from the stomach.

Gastritis: Inflammation of the lining of the stomach, caused by aspirin, excessive coffee, tobacco, or alcohol intake or by an infection. It can be acute or chronic.

Peptic ulcers: Ulcers of the stomach or duodenum. They are also called gastric ulcers, and they may be acute or chronic. *Helicobacter pylori* is a bacterium that may cause peptic ulcers.

Regional enteritis (Crohn's disease): A chronic, inflammatory bowel disease of unknown origin that affects the ileum or the colon. It more commonly affects young adults and females.

Ulcerative colitis: A chronic, episodic, inflammatory disease of the colon and rectum. The cause is unknown. It is also called inflammatory bowel disease. Complications can include perforation of the bowel, septicemia, and death. There is a high risk of a colon malignancy.

Intussusception: The prolapse of one segment of the intestine into the lumen of another segment, causing intestinal obstruction. The cause is usually unknown. It is one of the most common causes of intestinal obstruction in infants.

Volvulus: The torsion of a loop of intestine, causing intestinal obstruction with or without strangulation. It occurs most often in the ileum, the cecum, or the sigmoid colon in infants.

Diverticula: Abnormal pockets in the gastrointestinal tract.

Diverticulosis: The presence of diverticula in the colon. There is no inflammation, and the symptoms include a bloated sensation, episodes of pain in the lower abdomen, and changes in bowel habits such as constipation and diarrhea. It may lead to diverticulitis.

Diverticulitis: Inflammation and perforation of diverticula, which causes fever, pain, tenderness, and rigidity of the abdomen over the area of the intestine involved. Chronic diverticulitis can cause complications such as abscesses, fistulas, and adhesions.

Viral gastrointestinal infection: Also known as the 24-hour flu, a self-limiting viral infection of the lining in the gastrointestinal tract that is caused by different types of viruses.

Enteritis: Inflammation of the intestine, particularly the small intestine.

Food poisoning: Results from the ingestion of foods containing poisonous substances. Symptoms of poisoning include nausea, cramping, vomiting, and diarrhea.

Botulism: Food poisoning that results from eating improperly canned or preserved foods that have been contaminated by the *Clostridium botulinum* bacterium.

Enteric fevers: Systemic infections caused by pathogens that enter the gastrointestinal tract and are absorbed through the intestinal mucosa into the blood stream. These fevers are characterized by intestinal inflammation and dysfunction. Examples of causative pathogens include *Escherichia coli*, *Vibrio cholerae*, some *Salmonella*, and some *Shigella*.

Cholera: An acute enteric diarrheal disease marked by loose stools and copious amounts of mucous fluid resembling rice water. The bacterium is a gram-negative curved rod, C- or S-shaped, that secretes an enterotoxin called choleragin.

Giardiasis: Also called traveler's diarrhea, an infection of the small intestine caused by *Giardia lamblia*, a flagellate protozoon that produces cysts. The source of infection is usually untreated contaminated water.

Appendicitis: Inflammation of the appendix.

Hepatitis: Infectious inflammation of the liver most commonly caused by either the type A or type B hepatitis virus.

Hernia: Protrusion of a part from its normal location. See Table 3-8 for types of hernia.

Diseases and Disorders of the Urinary System

Dysuria: Painful urination.

Enuresis: Involuntary discharge of urine, most often due to a lack of bladder control.

Incontinence: Involuntary discharge of urine, feces, or semen.

Urethritis: Inflammation of the urethra.

Cystitis: Inflammation of the urinary bladder. It is more common in women.

Urinary tract infection (UTI): Bacteria or other organisms in the urethra and bladder, causing dysuria and malaise.

Renal failure: Acute cases are a sudden and severe reduction in renal function. Causes include complications from surgery, shock after an incompatible blood transfusion, severe dehydration, and trauma or kidney disease. Renal failure results in uremia.

Uremia: Excess of urea and other waste in the blood as a result of kidney failure.

Glomerulonephritis: Inflammation of the glomerulus in the kidney. There are three types: acute, chronic, and subacute.

Acute glomerulonephritis: A common disease, primarily affecting children and young adults, marked by protein and blood in the urine and edema with no pus formation. It is a type of allergic disease caused by an antigen-antibody reaction.

Chronic glomerulonephritis: A slowly progressive, noninfectious disease that may result in irreversible renal damage and renal failure. Uremia is common with this condition.

Nephrotic syndrome: Referred to as the protein-losing kidney. Symptoms include protein in the urine, hypoalbuminemia, hypertension, and hyperlipidemia.

Pyelonephritis: A diffuse pyogenic infection of the renal pelvis. It is the most common type of renal disease, and it may be acute or chronic. It is commonly caused by infection, calculi, pregnancy, tumors, or benign prostatic hypertrophy.

Hydronephrosis: Distention of the pelvis and calyces of the kidney by urine that cannot flow past an obstruction in the ureter. The obstruction may be a result of urinary calculi, a tumor, an enlarged prostate gland, or pregnancy.

Polycystic renal disease: A congenital anomaly that affects children and adults and results in kidney failure due to the presence of multiple cysts in the kidney tubules.

Renal calculus: Better known as a kidney stone. Kidney stones can block urine flow in the ureter, resulting in renal colic with chills, fever, hematuria, and a frequent need to urinate. They can be treated with smooth muscle relaxants that help pass the stones and offer some pain relief. If the stones don't pass and they continue to block urine flow, surgery must be performed, or the stones can be destroyed with ultrasound.

Diseases and Disorders of the Reproductive System

Gonorrhea: A contagious inflammation of the genital mucous membrane of both sexes caused by the gram negative gonococcus bacterium. It may also affect other parts of the body including the heart, rectum, and joints, and in women it may cause pelvic inflammatory disease.

AT A GLANCE	Types of Hernia
Type	**Description**
Hiatal	A part of the stomach protruding upward through the diaphragm
Incarcerated	A hernia that is swollen and fixed within a sac, creating an obstruction
Inguinal	A loop of the intestine protruding through the abdominal wall in the inguinal region
Strangulated	A hernia that is so constricted (cut off from circulation) that it may become gangrenous
Umbilical	A part of the intestine protruding through the abdominal wall around the umbilicus

Table 3-8

Genital warts: An infection caused by any of a group of human papillomaviruses (HPVs). In women, genital warts may be associated with cancer of the cervix.

Chlamydial infection: The most prevalent sexually transmitted disease in the U.S. It is a leading cause of pelvic inflammatory disease in women. In men, chlamydia may cause urethritis and penile discharge. Chlamydia is caused by the *Chlamydia trachomatis* bacterium, and it is sometimes called the silent STD because the symptoms may be very mild.

Syphilis: One of the most serious sexually transmitted diseases. The causative organism is a spirochete, *Treponema pallidum*. Infection in pregnant women can cause congenital defects in the fetus (such as mental retardation, physical deformities, deafness, and blindness), the death of the fetus, and spontaneous abortion.

Genital herpes: A very painful, recurring, incurable viral disease that involves the mucous membranes of the genital tracts. During pregnancy, it can cause spontaneous abortion, premature delivery, and transmission to the newborn. It can also develop into cervical cancer and spread to the lungs, brain, liver, and spleen.

HIV: The human immunodeficiency virus, which is transferable by direct sexual contact (homosexual or heterosexual), by contaminated intravenous needles and syringes, and by blood transfusion with contaminated blood or other blood products. It is also transplacental and can be transferred from mother to child. The first signs of infection include fever, malaise, rashes, arthralgia, and lymphadenopathy. As the disease progresses, there is a steady drop in the number of T cells in the blood. Diagnosis is determined by the detection of HIV antibodies in the blood.

AIDS: Acquired immunodeficiency syndrome, the ultimate result of infection with HIV. It is currently a fatal disease of the immune system. AIDS is marked by opportunistic infections that would otherwise be eliminated by a healthy individual's immune responses. These infections include candidiasis, herpes, Kaposi's sarcoma, recurrent pneumonia, and lymphoma. The incubation period is 6 months to 5 years, or longer. See Figure 3-1.

Diseases and Disorders of the Female Reproductive System

Pelvic inflammatory disease: Inflammation of organs in the pelvic cavity, including the fallopian tubes, ovaries, and endometrium.

Salpingitis: Inflammation of the fallopian tubes.

Vaginitis: Inflammation of the vagina.

Leukorrhea: Any vaginal discharge other than blood.

Puerperal sepsis: An infection of the endometrium after childbirth or an abortion.

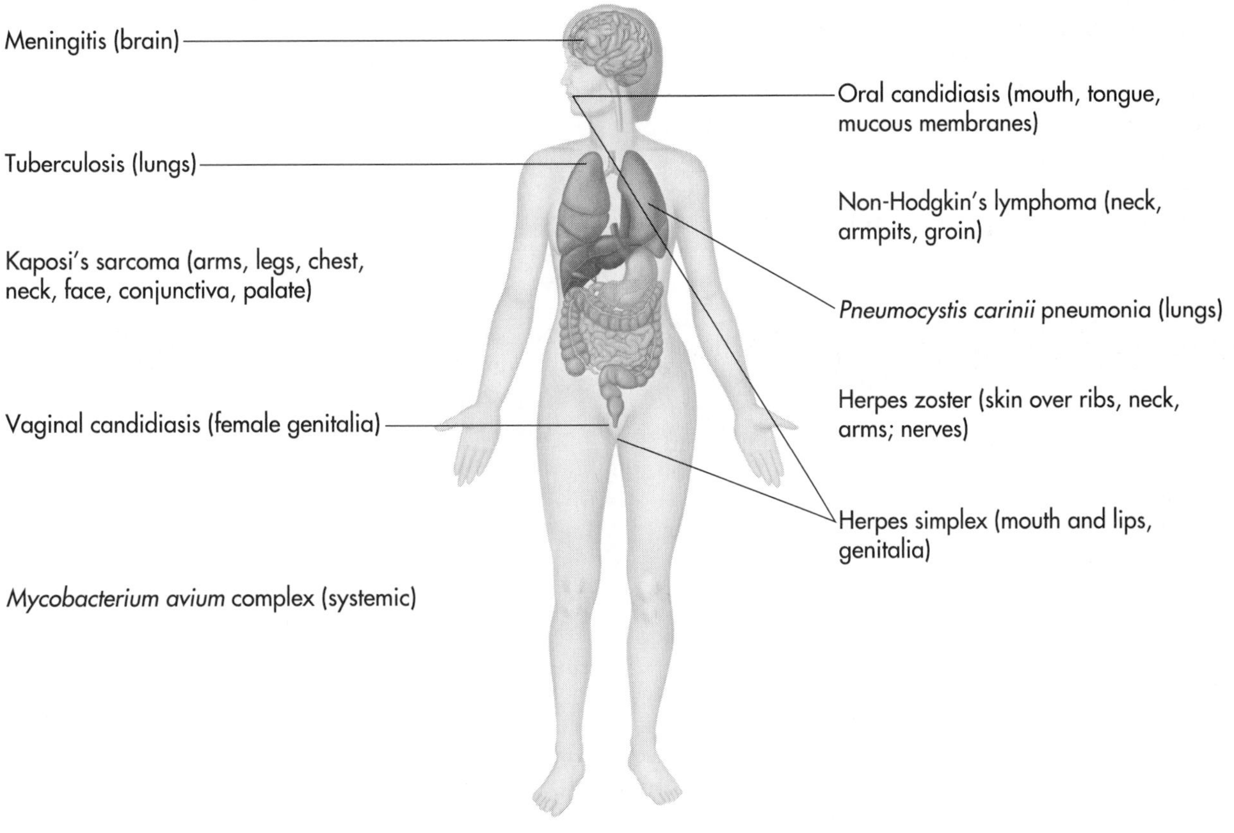

Meningitis (brain)

Tuberculosis (lungs)

Kaposi's sarcoma (arms, legs, chest, neck, face, conjunctiva, palate)

Vaginal candidiasis (female genitalia)

Mycobacterium avium complex (systemic)

Oral candidiasis (mouth, tongue, mucous membranes)

Non-Hodgkin's lymphoma (neck, armpits, groin)

Pneumocystis carinii pneumonia (lungs)

Herpes zoster (skin over ribs, neck, arms; nerves)

Herpes simplex (mouth and lips, genitalia)

Figure 3-1. *An individual with AIDS may contract a variety of opportunistic infections, which affect many different parts of the body.*

Fibroid tumors: Benign tumors of the smooth muscle of the uterus, also called leiomyomata. They are the most common tumors of the female reproductive system. Fibroid tumors are often multiple and vary greatly in size. Tumor growth is stimulated by estrogen.

Hydatidiform moles: Tumors of the uterine lining, most of which are benign, that develop after pregnancy or in association with an abnormal pregnancy. These tumors consist of multiple cysts that resemble a bunch of grapes.

Fibroadenoma: The most common benign tumor of the breast. It is a single, movable nodule that occurs at any age. It is painful at the time of the menstrual period.

Amenorrhea: The absence of the onset of menstruation at puberty or the cessation or interruption of menstruation in adulthood.

Menorrhagia: Excessive uterine bleeding that occurs between menstrual periods. Its causes include uterine tumors, pelvic inflammatory disease, and abnormal conditions of pregnancy.

Metrorrhagia: Uterine bleeding at any time other than during menstruation.

Endometriosis: Proliferation of endometrial tissue outside of the uterus. Endometriosis may cause dysmenorrhea, sterility, and dyspareunia.

Ectopic pregnancy: Implantation of the fertilized ovum outside of the uterus, most commonly in the fallopian tubes, rather than on the inside wall of the uterus. It is also called extrauterine pregnancy.

Miscarriage: A spontaneous abortion, commonly as a result of a genetic abnormality.

Preeclampsia: A pathologic condition of late pregnancy characterized by edema, protein in the urine, and hypertension. It is also known as the first phase of the toxemia of pregnancy.

Eclampsia: Toxemia of pregnancy resulting in convulsions and coma. It is a potentially life-threatening disorder characterized by severe hypertension, edema, and protein in the urine.

Placenta previa: Implantation of the placenta in the lower uterine segment on the internal cervical os, which causes painless bleeding.

Abruptio placentae: Separation of the placenta from the uterine wall too early during pregnancy.

Diseases and Disorders of the Male Reproductive System

Impotence: Failure to initiate or maintain an erection until ejaculation.

Peyronie's disease: Disorder characterized by the hardness of the corpus cavernosum in the penis.

Prostatitis: Inflammation of the prostate.

Benign prostatic hyperplasia: Enlargement of the prostate gland. It is common in men over 50.

Cryptorchidism: The failure of the testes to descend into the scrotum from the abdominal cavity. Undescended testes atrophy and may become the potential site of cancer.

Diseases and Disorders Specific to Children

Colic: Abdominal distress of unknown cause in newborns or young infants.

Reye's syndrome: A combination of encephalopathy and fatty infiltration of the internal organs that may follow acute viral infections, most commonly in children under 15 years of age. The condition sometimes arises following infection with influenza A or B viruses or chickenpox and has been linked to the use of aspirin during these infections.

Sudden infant death syndrome: SIDS, also called crib death. It occurs in infants younger than 1 year old. Death occurs within seconds during sleep. The cause is unknown.

Erythroblastosis fetalis: A type of hemolytic anemia in newborns that results from maternal fetal blood group incompatibility, specifically involving the Rh factor and the ABO blood groups. Common symptoms include anemia, jaundice, kernicterus, splenomegaly, and hepatomegaly. It is sometimes called hydrops fetalis.

STRATEGIES TO SUCCESS

▶ Test-Taking Skills

No tricks, just focus!
Always read all the responses to a question before answering. If you choose an answer too hastily, you might miss the best answer. Don't make any assumptions about the questions and how the writer of the question might be trying to trick you. Use only the information provided in the question and choose the best answer based on your knowledge of the subject matter.

Instructions:

Answer the following questions. Check your answers in the *Answer Key* that follows this section.

1. Chronic glomerulonephritis and renal failure may both result in
   A. Dehydration
   B. Cystitis
   C. Uremia
   D. An enlarged prostate
   E. Hirschsprung's disease

2. Which of the following definitions best explains encephalitis?
   A. Inflammation of the brain
   B. Inflammation of the meninges
   C. Inflammation of the spinal cord
   D. Inflammation of the brain and meninges
   E. Inflammation of the brain and spinal cord

3. What is the name of the condition caused by hypersecretion of growth hormone before puberty?
   A. Myxedema
   B. Acromegaly
   C. Dwarfism
   D. Gigantism
   E. Hyperthyroidism

4. Which of following sexually transmitted diseases is sometimes called the silent STD?
   A. Syphilis
   B. AIDS
   C. Genital warts
   D. Moles
   E. Chlamydial infection

5. Cancer in which of the following sites is the leading cause of cancer death in males?
   A. Prostate
   B. Pancreas
   C. Lung
   D. Colon
   E. Kidney

6. Chronic dilation and distention of the bronchial walls is called
   A. Hemoptysis
   B. Pneumoconiosis
   C. Bronchiectasis
   D. Atelectasis
   E. Bronchitis

7. Failure of the testes to descend into the scrotum from the abdominal cavity is called
   A. Orchitis
   B. Epididymitis
   C. Varicocele
   D. Cryptorchidism
   E. Peyronie's disease

8. Which of the following conditions may result in a lack of melanin pigment in the body?
   A. Color blindness
   B. Achondroplasia
   C. Albinism
   D. Galactosemia
   E. Rubella

9. Acute glomerulonephritis is marked by all of the following except
   A. Edema
   B. Hematuria
   C. Pus formation
   D. Protein in the urine
   E. Blood in the urine

10. The most common cyanotic cardiac defect is
    A. Patent ductus arteriosus
    B. Angina pectoris
    C. Ventricular septal defect
    D. Coarctation of the aorta
    E. Tetralogy of Fallot

11. Which of the following is the most common disease or condition of the urinary system?
    A. Hydronephrosis
    B. Renal failure
    C. Pyelonephritis
    D. Renal atrophy
    E. Nephrotic syndrome

CHAPTER 3 REVIEW

12. Diabetes insipidus results from the lack or deficiency of which of the following?

    A. Insulin
    B. Thyroxine
    C. Aldosterone
    D. Antidiuretic hormone
    E. Glucose

13. Diverticulosis occurs particularly in the

    A. Lungs
    B. Cecum
    C. Ileum
    D. Anus
    E. Colon

14. German measles is also called

    A. Rubeola
    B. Three-day measles
    C. Rubella
    D. B and C
    E. A and B

15. All of the following are causative factors for pernicious anemia except

    A. Vitamin B$_{12}$ deficiency
    B. Folic acid deficiency
    C. Lack of intrinsic factor
    D. Decreased hydrochloric acid in the stomach
    E. Regional entertitis (Crohn's disease)

16. The failure of bone marrow to produce erythrocytes, leukocytes, and platelets is called

    A. Leukemia
    B. Leukoplakia
    C. Hemolytic anemia
    D. Aplastic anemia
    E. Sickle cell anemia

17. Tetanus is commonly called

    A. Lockjaw
    B. Sleeping sickness
    C. Hydrophobia
    D. Hydronephrosis
    E. Both A and C

18. Which of the following is not an obvious sign of Parkinson's disease?

    A. Tremor
    B. Rigidity
    C. Seizure
    D. Slowness of movement
    E. They are all signs of the disease

19. Which of the following fractures of the bone may cause Battle sign?

    A. Basilar skull fracture
    B. Mandibular fracture
    C. Maxillary fracture
    D. Hyoid fracture
    E. Greenstick fracture

20. All of the following are symptoms of nephrotic syndrome except

    A. Hyperlipidemia
    B. Hypoalbuminemia
    C. Proteinuria
    D. Hypertension
    E. Hypotension

21. The absence of the onset of menstruation at puberty is called

    A. Metrorrhagia
    B. Amenorrhea
    C. Dysmenorrhea
    D. Miscarriage
    E. Eclampsia

22. Undescended testes may become the potential site of

    A. Infection
    B. Lymphedema
    C. Gangrene
    D. Polyposis
    E. Cancer

23. The cause of regional enteritis (Crohn's disease) is

    A. Unknown
    B. Viruses
    C. The use of artificial sweeteners
    D. Coffee drinking
    E. Bacteria

24. A prolapse of one section of the intestine into the lumen of another segment, causing intestinal blockage, is called

    A. Intussusception
    B. Diverticulosis
    C. Volvulus
    D. Crohn's disease
    E. Luminescence

25. Episodic vasospasm of the small cutaneous arteries, usually located in the finger, is known as

    A. Buerger's disease
    B. Raynaud's disease
    C. Phlebitis
    D. Varicose veins
    E. Thrombosis

26. The most common type of anemia in the U.S. is

    A. Sickle cell
    B. Pernicious
    C. Folic acid deficiency
    D. Iron-deficiency
    E. None of the above

27. Gangrene, which is necrotic tissue due to loss of blood supply, may occur in which of the following?

    A. Gallbladder
    B. Intestines
    C. Extremities
    D. All of the above
    E. None of the above

28. Which of the following cells can release histamine and heparin?

    A. Lymphocytes
    B. Kupffer cells
    C. Erythrocytes
    D. Neurons
    E. Mast cells

29. The most common causative organism of meningitis in adults is

    A. *Herpes zoster*
    B. *Streptococcus pneumoniae*
    C. Poliovirus
    D. *Neisseria meningitides*
    E. *Escherichia coli*

30. Trisomy 21 is also called

    A. Galactosemia
    B. Turner's syndrome
    C. Down syndrome
    D. Polydactyly
    E. Klinefelter's syndrome

31. Thrombophlebitis occurs most commonly in the

    A. Lower legs
    B. Lower arms
    C. Lower abdomen
    D. Neck
    E. Lungs

32. The sudden onset of a disease marked by intensity is described as

    A. Critical
    B. Aplastic
    C. Chronic
    D. Morbid
    E. Acute

33. The body's initial response to threat by trauma or an invading organism is

    A. Nonspecific immune response
    B. Specific immune mechanism
    C. Inflammation
    D. Both A and C
    E. Both B and C

34. Serum sickness is what type of hypersensitivity?

    A. I
    B. II
    C. III
    D. IV
    E. V

35. An area of dead cells due to lack of oxygen is called

A. Ischemia
B. Infarction
C. Atresia
D. Gangrene
E. Placenta previa

36. The condition in which one of the sex chromosomes is missing is called

A. Klinefelter's syndrome
B. Turner's syndrome
C. Down syndrome
D. Tetralogy of Fallot
E. Peyronie's disease

37. A cancer of the epithelial cells is called

A. Carcinoma
B. Sarcoma
C. Carcinogen
D. Metastasis
E. Endometriosis

38. Athlete's foot is otherwise known as

A. Tinea cruris
B. Tinea capitis
C. Tinea epidermis
D. Tinea corporis
E. Tinea pedis

ANSWER KEY

1.	C	20.	E
2.	A	21.	B
3.	D	22.	E
4.	E	23.	A
5.	C	24.	A
6.	C	25.	B
7.	D	26.	D
8.	C	27.	D
9.	C	28.	E
10.	E	29.	D
11.	C	30.	C
12.	D	31.	A
13.	E	32.	E
14.	D	33.	D
15.	B	34.	C
16.	D	35.	B
17.	A	36.	B
18.	C	37.	A
19.	A	38.	E

Microbiology

AREAS OF COMPETENCE

AAMA—ROLE DELINEATION AREAS OF COMPETENCE

Clinical

Fundamental Principles

- Apply principles of aseptic technique and infection control

General (Transdisciplinary)

Communication Skills

- Use medical terminology appropriately

AMT—RMA CERTIFICATION EXAM TOPICS

Medical Terminology

- Definitions
- Spelling

(Chart continued on next page.)

Asepsis

- Terminology
- Medical Asepsis
- Surgical Asepsis

Sterilization

- Terminology

Microorganisms

Microbiology: The study of very small living organisms, including bacteria, algae, fungi, protozoa, and viruses; often called microbes, germs, or single-celled organisms.

Microscope: An instrument used to obtain an enlarged image of small object and reveal details of a structure otherwise not distinguishable. Microscopes are routinely used in a modern medical laboratory and magnify anywhere from 10× up to 1000×.

Microorganisms: Tiny microscopic entities that are able to carry on all the processes of life, including metabolism, reproduction, and motility. Some microorganisms are pathogenic, and others are either beneficial or neutral in relationship to human beings. There are two main types of microorganisms: eukaryotes and prokaryotes.

Prokaryote: A simple, single-celled organism that lacks a nucleus and organelles. Most prokaryotes have only a cell membrane, cytoplasm, ribosomes, and chromatin bodies. Bacteria are considered prokaryotes.

Eukaryote: Has a more complex cell structure than prokaryotes. It has a nucleus and several other specialized structures called organelles. Eukaryotic cells contain mitochondria, lysosomes, chloroplasts, and the Golgi apparatus. Protozoa, fungi, algae, plants, and animals are considered eukaryotes.

Saprophyte: An organism that obtains its nutrients from dead organic matter. Many bacteria and fungi are saprophytes.

Bacteria

Bacteria: Prokaryotic cells, the majority of which are harmless. They vary widely in size, shape, and cell arrangement and include bacilli, cocci, spirilla, diplobacilli, streptobacilli, coccobacilli, and those that appear curved and comma-like. See Figure 4-1. There are three basic forms of bacteria: bacilli, cocci, and spirilla.

Bacilli: Rod-shaped bacteria, such as *Bacillus anthracis*, coliform bacilli, tubercle bacilli, and typhoid bacilli.

Cocci: Spherical bacteria. Pathogenic cocci are staphylococci, streptococci, and diplococci. See Table 4-1.

Spirilla: Spiral-shaped bacteria.

Diplococci: Any of the spherical or coffee bean-shaped bacteria that usually appear in pairs.

Streptobacilli: Bacteria in which the rods or filaments tend to fragment into chains.

Coccobacilli: Short bacilli that are thick and somewhat ovoid.

Characteristics of bacteria: Bacteria are classified according to morphology, motility, growth, staining reactions, metabolic activities, pathogenicity, antigen-antibody reactions, and genetic composition.

Stain: A substance used to impart color to tissue or cells in order to study and identify microscopic organisms.

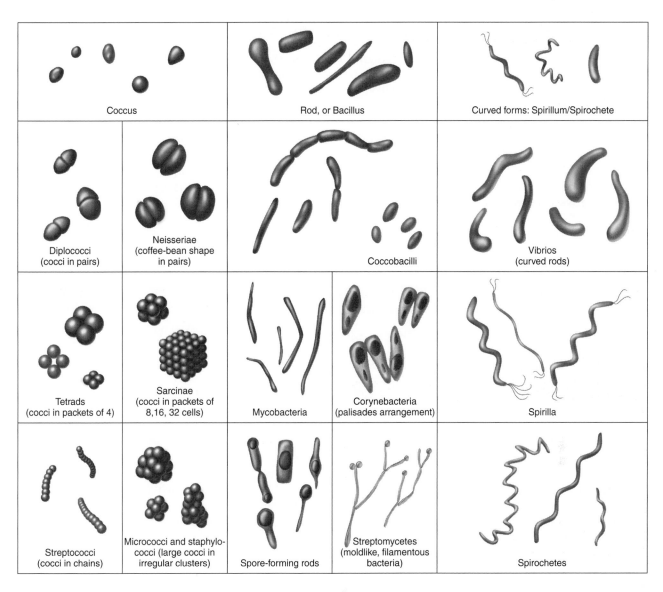

| Coccus | Rod, or Bacillus | Curved forms: Spirillum/Spirochete |

| Diplococci (cocci in pairs) | Neisseriae (coffee-bean shape in pairs) | Coccobacilli | Vibrios (curved rods) |

| Tetrads (cocci in packets of 4) | Sarcinae (cocci in packets of 8,16, 32 cells) | Mycobacteria | Corynebacteria (palisades arrangement) | Spirilla |

| Streptococci (cocci in chains) | Micrococci and staphylococci (large cocci in irregular clusters) | Spore-forming rods | Streptomycetes (moldlike, filamentous bacteria) | Spirochetes |

Figure 4-1. *Bacterial shapes and arrangements (not necessarily shown to exact scale).*

AT A GLANCE — Arrangement of Cocci

Arrangement	Description	Pathogenic Form
Diplococci	Pairs	*Neisseria gonorrhoeae*
Streptococci	Chains	*Streptococcus pyogenes*
Staphylococci	Clusters	*Staphylococcus aureus*

Table 4-1

Gram's stain: A staining procedure in which bacteria are stained with crystal violet, treated with strong iodine solution, and decolorized with ethanol. Microorganisms that retain the stain are said to be gram-positive, and those that lose the crystal violet stain by decolorization but stain with a counterstain are said to be gram-negative.

Gram-positive bacteria: Bacteria with cell walls that are composed of peptidoglycan and teichoic acid. Some of the most important pathogenic gram-positive bacteria are listed in Table 4-2.

Gram-negative bacteria: Bacteria with cell walls that are composed of a thin layer of peptidoglycan covered by an outer membrane of lipoprotein and lipopolysaccharide. Table 4-3 is a summary of some gram-negative bacteria.

Gram stain limitations: The following organisms do not Gram stain well: rickettsia, mycoplasma, treponema, chlamydia, mycobacteria, and Legionella pneumophila.

Streptococci: A genus of gram-positive bacteria that occurs in chains. They are classified in four types: the pyogenic group, the viridans group, the enterococcus group, and the lactic group.

Staphylococci: A genus of gram-positive bacteria made up of spherical microorganisms and grapelike clusters. See Table 4-4.

AT A GLANCE	Some Important Pathogenic Gram-Positive Bacteria	
Bacterium	**Type**	**Diseases Caused**
Corynebacterium diphtheriae	Rod, nonmotile	Diphtheria
Staphylococcus aureus	Cocci in clusters	Carbuncles, septicemia, pneumonia, boils
Streptococcus pyogenes	Cocci in chains	Strep throat, rheumatic fever, septicemia, scarlet fever
Streptococcus pneumoniae	Diplococcus	Pneumonia
Mycobacterium tuberculosis	Rod	Tuberculosis
Mycobacterium leprae	Rod	Leprosy
Clostridium tetani	Noncapsulate, sporing, motile	Tetanus
Clostridium botulinum	Spore-forming rod, noncapsulate, motile	Botulism (food poisoning)
Clostridium perfringens	Spore-forming rod, nonmotile, noncapsulate	Gas gangrene, wound infections

Table 4-2

AT A GLANCE	Some Important Pathogenic Gram-Negative Bacteria	
Bacterium	**Type**	**Diseases Caused**
Escherichia coli	Rod	Urinary infections
Haemophilus influenzae	Rod	Meningitis or pneumonia
Haemophilus ducreyi	Rod	Chancroid

Table 4-3

AT A GLANCE	Some Important Pathogenic Gram-Negative Bacteria	
Bacterium	**Type**	**Diseases Caused**
Klebsiella pneumoniae	Rod	Pneumonia
Neisseria gonorrhoeae	Diplococci	Gonorrhea
Neisseria meningitidis	Diplococci	Meningitis
Rickettsia rickettsii	Rod	Rocky mountain spotted fever
Salmonella typhi	Rod	Typhoid fever
Shigella species	Rod	Shigellosis (bacillary dysentery)
Treponema pallidum	Spirochete	Syphilis
Vibrio cholerae	Curved rod	Cholera

Table 4-3, continued

AT A GLANCE	Staphylococci
Type	**Diseases Caused**
S. aureus	Skin infections Osteopyelitis Food poisoning Endocarditis Toxic shock syndrome
S. epidermidis	Infections following instrumentation or implantation
S. saprophyticus	Urinary tract infection

Table 4-4

Intermediate organisms: Obligate intracellular parasites, which can reproduce only in living cells. There are three groups: rickettsia, chlamydia, and mycoplasma.

Rickettsia: Any of several small intracellular parasites of the genus *Rickettsia* that require a vector (such as fleas, ticks, or lice) to spread disease.

Chlamydia: A gram-negative nonmotile obligate intracellular parasite that is totally dependent on the host cell for energy. The genus *Chlamydia* comprises three species: *C. trachomatis*, *C. psittaci*, and *C. pneumoniae*. See Table 4-5 on p. 100.

Mycoplasma: A group of bacteria considered to be the smallest free-living organisms. Unlike most other bacteria, they lack a cell wall. Some are saprophytes, some are parasites, and many are pathogens. They cause primary atypical pneumonia and many secondary infections.

Mycobacterium: A genus of bacteria distinguished by a high lipid content that produces resistance to drying, acids, and various germicides. In form, mycobacteria are long, slender, straight or curved rods. Several are highly significant human pathogens that cause tuberculosis, leprosy, granuloma, and skin ulcers.

Legionella pneumophila: The bacterium that causes Legionnaires' disease. Primarily intracellular, it stains by silver stain.

AT A GLANCE	Chlamydia	
Type	**Diseases Caused**	**Treatment**
C. trachomatis	Urethritis	Tetracycline; ophthalmic antibiotic solution for newborns
C. psittaci (found in bird feces)	Psittacosis	Tetracycline or doxycycline
C. pneumoniae	Pneumonia, bronchitis, sinusitis	Tetracycline or erythromycin

Table 4-5

Viruses

Viruses: Infectious agents that are even simpler in nature than the prokaryotes. They are usually not considered cellular. Viruses are composed of a small amount of DNA or RNA wrapped in a protein covering. A virus is visible only with an electron microscope.
Viron: A virus that exists outside a host cell.
Bacteriophage or **phage:** A virus that has a bacterial host.

Fungi

Fungi: Eukaryotic organisms with cellulose or chitin cell walls that include mushrooms, molds, and yeasts. Spores, the means of reproduction for fungi, can be carried great distances by the wind and are resistant to heat, cold, acids, bases, and other chemicals.
Mushrooms: A class of true fungi.
Mycelium: A network of filaments or strands in mushrooms.
Molds: Multicellular fungi that are the main source of antibiotics. Some are used to produce large quantities of enzymes (amylases) and citric acid. Molds can also be harmful, and some are toxic.
Aflatoxin: A toxin produced by *Aspergillus* mold on peanuts and cottonseed. Aflatoxin is extremely toxic to humans and farm animals, and it is also carcinogenic.
Yeasts: Single-celled microscopic eukaryotes that produce vitamins and proteins.
Candida albicans: A type of pathogenic yeast that is dimorphous.
Dimorphism: The ability to live in two different forms, such as the few fungi, usually pathogens, that can live either as molds or as yeasts depending on growth conditions.

Protozoa

Protozoa: The lowest forms of animal life. Protozoa have the ability to move, and they are found in water and soil. Most protozoa are saprophytes, living in the soil and feeding off decaying organic material. Some protozoa are pathogenic; these pathogens are summarized in Table 4-6. (The singular form is *protozoon*.)

AT A GLANCE	Protozoal Pathogens and Infections
Pathogen	**Diseases Caused**
Entamoeba histolytica	Amebic dysentery
Dientamoeba fragilis	Diarrhea, fever
Trypanosoma gambiense	Sleeping sickness
Trichomonas vaginalis	Infections of the male and female genital tracts
Giardia lamblia	Gastroenteritis (intestinal infection)
Plasmodium species	Malaria
Pneumocystis carinii	Severe secondary infections in persons with suppressed immune systems (such as those who have AIDS)

Table 4-6

Microbial Growth

Microbial growth: Dependent on a source of energy and nutrient chemicals and influenced by temperature, pH (acidity), moisture content, and available nutrients. There are three types of microbial metabolism: fermentation, respiration, and photosynthesis.

Fermentation: The decomposition of complex substances through the action of enzymes produced by microorganisms.

Respiration: The interchange of gases between an organism and the medium in which it lives.

Photosynthesis: A process by which the energy of light is used to produce organic molecules. This process is most often used by plants to manufacture carbohydrates, but some bacteria are also capable of photosynthesis.

Aerobe: A microorganism that lives and grows in the presence of free oxygen. The majority of microbes are aerobes.

Facultative aerobe: An organism that is able to grow under anaerobic conditions but grows most rapidly in an aerobic environment.

Anaerobe: A microbe that grows and lives in the absence of oxygen.

Facultative anaerobe: A microbe that can grow either with or without oxygen but develops most rapidly in an anaerobic environment.

Obligate anaerobe: A microbe that lives only in the absence of oxygen.

Nutritional types: There are two types of organisms: heterotrophs and autotrophs.

Heterotrophs: Organisms that obtain carbon from organic material.

Autotrophs: Organisms that use inorganic carbon dioxide (CO_2) as their basic carbon source.

Chemotrophs: Organisms that use chemical substances as a source of energy.

Phototrophs: Organisms that use light as a source of energy.

Binary fission: Also called simple fission, the common form of asexual reproduction of bacteria in which each bacterium splits into two similar cells.

Optimum pH: The level of acidity or alkalinity most conducive to functioning. Each microorganism has an optimum pH for growth.

Acidophile: A bacterial organism that grows well in an acid medium.

Exotoxin: A potent toxin that is secreted or excreted by living microorganisms as the result of bacterial metabolism. Exotoxins are the most poisonous substances known to human beings. Bacteria of the genus *Clostridium* are the most frequent producers of exotoxins.

Enterotoxin: An exotoxin that affects cells of the intestinal mucosa, causing vomiting and diarrhea.

Microbes and the Human Body

Medical microbiology: The study of pathogens and the disease process, including epidemiology, diagnosis, treatment, infection control, and immunology.

Normal flora: Bacteria that are permanent and beneficial residents in the human body. The most common normal flora of the body are presented in Table 4-7 on p. 102.

Host: An organism in which another, usually parasitic, organism is nourished and harbored.

Symbiosis: The living together of two organisms of different species. Four major types of symbiotic relationships exist between humans and their flora: mutualism, commensalism, parasitism, and opportunism.

Mutualism: A relationship in which both organisms benefit. For example, certain normal flora living in the human intestine synthesize vitamin K, biotin, riboflavin, pantothenate, and pyridoxine.

Commensalism: A one-sided relationship in which one member benefits and neither is harmed. Yeast, *Candida albicans,* is one of the normal flora that has a commensal relationship with the skin.

Parasitism: A one-sided relationship between a host and a parasite.

Parasite: An organism that lives in, on, or at the expense of another organism without contributing to the host's survival.

Obligate intracellular parasite: A parasite that is completely dependent on its host and must be in a living cell in order to reproduce.

Opportunism: A relationship in which a usually harmless organism becomes pathogenic when the host's resistance is impaired.

Opportunistic microbe: A harmless microorganism that causes disease only if it invades the body when the immune system is weakened and unable to defend against it.

Pathogens: Disease-causing microorganisms. Only a small percentage of microbes are pathogenic; the others are considered harmless or beneficial.

Pathogenicity: The ability of a pathogenic agent to cause a disease.

Virulence: The degree of pathogenicity or relative power of an organism to produce a disease.

Infective dose: The number of organisms required to cause a disease in a susceptible host.

Contagious disease: A disease that is transmitted from one person to another. The following factors influence the cycle involved in the spread of infectious disease: means of transmission, means of entrance, susceptible host, reservoir host, and means of exit. See Figure 4-2 on p. 102.

Common Normal Flora of the Body

Body Part	Normal Flora
Skin	*Staphylococcus epidermidis*
Nose	*Staphylococcus aureus, S. epidermidis*
Nasopharynx (upper respiratory tract)	*Streptococcus pneumoniae, Neisseria meningitidis, Haemophilus influenzae*
Eye	*Staphylococcus epidermidis*
Stomach	Because of the stomach's acidic pH, it contains very few microorganisms.
Intestine	The distal portion of the small intestine and the entire large intestine have the largest microbial population in the body. The most common microbes in the large intestine are *Bacteroides fragilis, Escherichia coli, Proteus mirabilis,* and *Candida albicans.*
Genital tract	*Lactobacillus*

Table 4-7

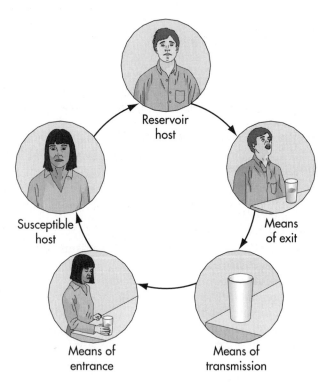

Figure 4-2. *The cycle of infection must be broken at some point to prevent the spread of disease.*

Breaking the cycle of infection: Medical assistants can help break the cycle of infection by maintaining strict housekeeping standards, adhering to government guidelines to protect against diseases, and educating patients about hygiene, health promotion, and disease prevention.

Vector: A carrier of pathogenic organisms, especially one that can transmit a disease. See Table 4-8.

Biological vector: An animal in which the infecting organism multiplies or develops prior to becoming infectious.

Resistance: The body mechanisms that oppose infection. The host's state of health and other factors, including race, age, sex, and occupation, affect the ability of a pathogen to cause disease. Also, the ability of a microorganism to live in the presence of antibiotics, antimicrobial agents, and phages.

AT A GLANCE	**Vectors**
Carrier	**Diseases**
Dogs, raccoons	Rabies
Mosquitoes	Malaria, encephalitis
Ticks	Rocky Mountain spotted fever, Lyme disease

Table 4-8

Microbial Control and Asepsis

Microbial control: The prevention of infectious diseases using heat, steam, fire, and chemicals to control the growth of microbes.

Asepsis: Freedom from infection or infectious material.

Medical asepsis: Destruction of organisms after they leave the body.

Office asepsis procedures: Can include cleaning the office regularly, enforcing a strict no-eating and no-drinking policy, emptying the trash often, and asking patients to use tissues for coughs and sneezes.

Aseptic hand washing: The most important aseptic procedure for a medical assistant. Wash hands regularly, including at the beginning of the day; before and after lunch; before using gloves, handling specimens or waste, seeing each patient, and handling clean and sterile supplies; after blowing your nose and coughing; after breaks; and before leaving for the day. Remove all jewelry, use warm water and liquid soap, and scrub vigorously for at least 2 minutes. Make sure that you clean all surfaces of your hands, including under the nails and cuticles (use a nailbrush). Rinse well and make sure that your hands don't touch the sink or faucet. Dry with a clean paper towel, and turn off the faucets using a paper towel, not your hands.

Surgical asepsis: Destruction of organisms before they enter the body.

Sterilization: Complete destruction of all microorganisms.

Sterile or surgical scrub: A procedure that differs from aseptic hand washing in several important respects: A sterile scrub brush is used instead of a nailbrush, both the hands and the forearms are washed, hands are kept above the elbows to prevent water from running from the arms onto washed areas, sterile towels are used instead of paper towels, and sterile gloves are put on immediately after the hands are dried.

Sanitization: Reduction of the number of microorganisms on an object to a fairly small and safe level.

Disinfection: The process of removing or killing pathogens. Common disinfectants include various chemicals, boiling water, and steam.

Antiseptic: A substance, such as hydrogen peroxide, used externally to prevent or inhibit the growth and reproduction of microorganisms.

Bactericidal or **bacteriocidal:** Destructive to or destroying bacteria.

Bacteriostatic: Inhibiting the growth of bacteria.

Antisepsis: Inhibition, usually through a topical application, of the growth and multiplication of microorganisms.

Biohazardous waste containers: Leakproof, puncture-resistant containers that are color-coded or labeled with special symbols to show that they contain biohazardous materials such as blood and other body fluids, human tissue, or equipment that is no longer sterile. These containers are used to store and dispose of contaminated supplies and equipment.

Instructions:

Answer the following questions. Check your answers in the *Answer Key* that follows this section.

1. An organism that obtains its nutrients from dead organic matter is called
   A. Diplococcus
   B. Chlamydia
   C. Saprophyte
   D. Mycoplasma
   E. Protozoon

2. Eukaryotes are characterized by
   A. Bacteria
   B. Viruses
   C. Lack of organelles
   D. Lack of a nucleus
   E. The presence of a true nucleus

3. Which of the following organisms requires a vector?
   A. Chlamydia
   B. Mycoplasma
   C. Rickettsia
   D. All of the above
   E. None of the above

4. Bacteria that are permanent and beneficial residents in the human body are called
   A. Pathogens
   B. Hosts
   C. Normal flora
   D. Parasites
   E. Normal fauna

5. Simple, single-celled organisms that lack a nucleus and organelles are called
   A. Prokaryotes
   B. Eukaryotes
   C. Viruses
   D. Acidophiles
   E. Bacteria

6. Aseptic hand washing techniques include all of the following <u>except</u>
   A. Removing all jewelry
   B. Using a nailbrush to scrub under the nails and cuticles
   C. Using liquid soap
   D. Turning off the faucet with the hands
   E. Scrubbing vigorously

7. If a virus has a bacterial host, it is called
   A. A bacteriophage
   B. Bacteriostatic
   C. Bactericidal
   D. Either B or C
   E. None of the above

8. Microbes that can grow either with or without oxygen are called
   A. Anaerobes
   B. Facultative anaerobes
   C. Aerobes
   D. Obligate anaerobes
   E. Aerobic

9. Hydrogen peroxide is an example of a(n)
   A. Sepsis
   B. Aseptic
   C. Antisepsis
   D. Antiseptic
   E. Bacteriostatic agent

10. Any close relationship that exists between two different species is known as
    A. Sebum
    B. Symbionts
    C. Syncope
    D. Synergism
    E. Symbiosis

11. All of the following factors may influence the cycle involved in the spread of infectious disease <u>except</u>

    A. Means of transmission
    B. Susceptible host
    C. Interferons
    D. Means of entrance
    E. All of these factors may influence the cycle of infection

12. The degree to which an organism is pathogenic is known as

    A. Infective dose
    B. Pathogen
    C. Tetany
    D. Resistance
    E. Virulence

13. A substance that inhibits the growth of bacteria is said to be

    A. Sterile
    B. Anaerobic
    C. Bactericidal
    D. Bacteriostatic
    E. Symbiotic

14. Which of the following is <u>not</u> true of the Gram staining procedure?

    A. It works for all bacteria
    B. The stain used is crystal violet
    C. It differentiates between gram-positive and gram-negative bacteria
    D. Some bacteria lose the stain by decolorization
    E. They are all true

15. Sterilization is

    A. The process of preventing infectious disease
    B. A substance that destroys or kills bacteria
    C. A technique for destroying microorganisms
    D. A substance for inhibiting the growth of microorganisms
    E. None of the above

16. Biohazardous waste containers

    A. Are color-coded or labeled
    B. Are leakproof
    C. Are puncture-resistant
    D. Can contain blood and other body fluids
    E. Are all of the above

17. Disinfection is

    A. The process of removing or killing pathogens
    B. The process of reducing the number of microorganisms to a safe level
    C. Complete destruction of all microorganisms
    D. Both A and C
    E. All of the above

18. Spiral-shaped bacteria are called

    A. Cocci
    B. Spirilla
    C. Bacilli
    D. Diplococci
    E. Sarcinae

19. Streptococci appear in

    A. Clusters of cocci
    B. Pairs of cocci
    C. Chains of cocci
    D. Either B or C
    E. None of the above

20. The bacterium *Escherichia coli* can cause

    A. Urinary infections
    B. Pneumonia
    C. Gonorrhea
    D. Chancroid
    E. Arthritis

21. A carrier of causative organisms that can transmit diseases to noninfected individuals is called a

    A. Viron
    B. Bacterium
    C. Virus
    D. Vector
    E. Protozoon

22. Viruses are
    A. Simpler than prokaryotes
    B. Visible to the naked eye
    C. Complex disease-causing organisms
    D. The same thing as bacteria
    E. The same thing as fungus

23. Which of the following words is misspelled?
    A. Chlamydia
    B. Myecobacteria
    C. Staphylococci
    D. Eukaryote
    E. Rickettsia

24. A medical assistant needs to wash his or her hands
    A. Before seeing each patient
    B. After handling waste
    C. After using gloves
    D. Before leaving for the day
    E. All of the above

ANSWER KEY

1.	C	13.	D
2.	E	14.	A
3.	C	15.	C
4.	C	16.	E
5.	A	17.	A
6.	D	18.	B
7.	A	19.	C
8.	B	20.	A
9.	D	21.	D
10.	E	22.	A
11.	C	23.	B
12.	E	24.	E

CHAPTER 5

Pharmacology

Antiarrhythmic Drugs
Anticoagulant Drugs
Hypolipidemic Drugs

Pharmacology of the Respiratory System

Antihistamines
Antiallergic Drugs
Asthma Drugs

Pharmacology of the Digestive System

Pharmacology of the Urinary System

Organic Acid or Loop Diuretics
Thiazide and Thiazide-like Diuretics
Potassium-Sparing Diuretics

Pharmacology of the Reproductive System

Use of Gonadal Hormones
Impotence

AREAS OF COMPETENCE

AAMA—ROLE DELINEATION STUDY AREAS OF COMPETENCE

Clinical

Patient Care

- Maintain medication and immunization records

General (Transdisciplinary)

Communication Skills

- Use medical terminology appropriately

Legal Concepts

- Document accurately
- Follow federal, state, and local legal guidelines
- Maintain awareness of federal and state health care legislation and regulations
- Maintain and dispose of regulated substances in compliance with government guidelines

AMT—RMA CERTIFICATION EXAM TOPICS

Medical Terminology

- Definitions
- Spelling

(Chart continued on next page.)

Clinical Pharmacology

- Terminology
- Prescriptions
- Drugs

Medical Law

- Medical law

STRATEGIES TO SUCCESS

▶ Study Skills

Ask questions!

When you have trouble understanding a concept, don't be afraid to ask your instructor to explain it to you. If you are still unclear about something, go to your local library and try to find the answer in a reference book or check the internet. The job of a medical assistant is complex, and it's easy to feel overwhelmed. Take control of your own education and success, and seek out the answers you need.

General Pharmacology Terms and Concepts

Pharmacology: The study of the origin, nature, chemistry, effects, and uses of drugs.

Drug: Any substance that may modify one or more of the functions of a living organism. Drugs have several uses including therapeutic, palliative, preventive, replacement, and diagnostic. See Table 5-1 on p. 110.

Pharmacy: The art of compounding, preparing, dispensing, and correctly utilizing drugs for medicinal use. Also, a drugstore.

Pharmacognosy: The branch of pharmacology dealing with natural drugs or natural products chemistry.

Pharmacodynamics: The study of the mechanisms of actions of drugs on living organisms.

Pharmacokinetics: The study of the movement of drugs, metabolism, and action of drugs within the body, especially the processes of absorption, distribution, biotransformation, localization in tissue, and excretion.

Toxicology: The science that deals with poisons.

Prophylactic: An agent used to prevent disease.

Drugs and Their Effects

Drug process: There are four basic stages a drug must pass through: absorption, distribution, metabolism, and excretion.

Absorption: The process by which a drug is absorbed into circulation.

Distribution: The process by which the circulatory system transports drugs to the affected body parts.

Metabolism: The process by which drugs are broken down into useful byproducts by enzymes in the liver. It is also known as biotransformation. The liver is the main body organ involved in the metabolism of drugs.

Excretion: The kidney is responsible for filtering out drugs from the blood. Drugs are also excreted through the lungs, sweat glands, and intestines.

Mechanism of action: The way in which a drug produces its effects.

Drug classification: Drugs are classified according to their effect on the body. See Table 5-2 on p. 110.

Synergism: The joint action of agents in which their combined effect is more intense than the sum of their individual effects.

Cumulation: The compound effect of an agent taken over time in individual small amounts.

Allergic reaction: An acquired, abnormal immune response to a substance that does not normally cause a reaction. It may develop within 30 minutes of administration of therapy. Symptoms of a mild allergic reaction include skin rashes, swelling, itchy eyes and

Drugs and Their Uses

Type of Use	Purpose of Use
Therapeutic	To cure disease
Palliative	To relieve symptoms
Preventive	To prevent certain conditions
Replacement	To replace substances that the body is not producing sufficiently
Diagnostic	To diagnose disease

Table 5-1

Common Drug Classifications and Actions

Classification	Action
General	
Analgesic	Relieves pain
Antibiotic	Destroys or inhibits bacterial growth
Integumentary System	
Antifungal	Treats fungal infections
Antihidrotic	Prevents or decreases perspiration
Antipruritic	Relieves itches
Musculoskeletal System	
Muscle relaxant	Relaxes muscles on a short-term basis
Nonsteroidal anti-inflammatory drug (NSAID)	Reduces pain, inflammation, and fever
Nervous System	
Antianxiety	Depresses the central nervous system (CNS)
Anticonvulsant	Prevents or relieves convulsions
Antidepressant	Prevents or treats mental depression
Antiepileptic	Treats epilepsy
Antihypnotic	Prevents or inhibits sleep
Antiparkinsonian	Treats Parkinson's disease
Antipsychotic	Treats psychosis
Sedative	Creates tranquilizing, soothing effects
Endocrine System	
Antisecretory	Inhibits secretion
Insulin	Treats diabetes
Thyroid agent	Replaces thyroid function

Table 5-2 (table continued on the next page)

Classification	Action
Cardiovascular System	
Antiarrhythmic	Regulates the heartbeat
Anticoagulant	Slows the coagulation process
Antihypercholesterolemic	Prevents or controls high cholesterol
Antihypertensive	Prevents or controls high blood pressure
Vasodilator	Relaxes or dilates blood vessels
Respiratory System	
Antihistamine	Relieves allergies
Antitussive	Relieves or prevents coughs
Decongestant	Reduces mucus production
Digestive System	
Antacid	Neutralizes gastric acids
Antiemetic	Controls nausea, vomiting, and motion sickness
Laxative	Promotes evacuation of the intestines
Urinary System	
Diuretic	Increases urine excretion
Reproductive System	
Androgen	Replaces male hormones
Antivenereal	Prevents or controls sexually transmitted (venereal) diseases
Contraceptive	Prevents conception
Estrogen	Replaces female hormones

Table 5-2, continued

skin, wheezing, and fever. Severe allergic reactions include extreme weakness, nausea, vomiting, cyanosis, dyspnea, hypotension, shock, and cardiac arrest.

Adverse effect: A general term for an undesirable and potentially harmful drug effect.

Anaphylaxis: A severe allergic response to medication, involving respiratory distress.

Side effect: An adverse effect of a drug on another organ system that is not related to the main target of the drug.

Toxic effect: An adverse drug effect that can be harmful or life-threatening.

Antagonism: The combined effect of two drugs that is less than the effect of either drug taken alone.

Tolerance: Increasing resistance to the usual effects of an established dosage of a drug as a result of continued use.

Dependence: A state of reliance on a drug, either psychological or physiological, that may result in withdrawal symptoms if drug use is discontinued.

Idiosyncrasy: An abnormal sensitivity to a drug. It usually refers to an individual patient's unique response to medication.

Factors that affect individual variation in a drug's effect: Age, weight, sex and percentage of body fat, time of day, tolerance, genetic variation, emotional state, placebo effect, presence of a disease, and patient compliance.

Drug indications: Intended uses of any drug.

Contraindications: Situations or conditions under which a certain drug should not be administered.

Drug abuse: The use or overuse of any drug in a manner that deviates from the prescribed pattern.

Prophylaxis: A procedure or medication used to prevent a disease rather than to treat an existing disease.

Half-life: The amount of time required for 50% of the drug to be eliminated from the body.

Teratogen: A drug that causes birth defects. These drugs affect the X chromosome and therefore should not be given to pregnant women.

Placebo: A drug dosage form that has no pharmacological effect because it contains no active ingredients. Placebos are used in controlled clinical trials of new drugs.

Efficacy: A drug's therapeutic value.

Potency: A measure of the strength or concentration of a drug required to produce the desired effect.

Posology: The study of the amount of drug that is required to produce therapeutic effects.

Polypharmacy: Multiple drug prescriptions. This situation is very common for elderly individuals, and it often increases confusion, forgetfulness, and noncompliance. Minimizing polypharmacy should also be an important consideration when trying to avoid harmful drug interactions.

Dosage: The amount of a drug prescribed for a given patient.

Dose: The measured portion of medication to be taken at one time.

Dispense: To distribute a drug in properly labeled containers to a patient.

Administer: To give a drug directly to a patient by injection, by mouth, or by any route that introduces the drug directly into the patient's body.

Lethal dose 50 (LD_{50}): The dose that will kill 50% of the subjects tested.

Effective dose 50 (ED_{50}): The dose that will produce an effect in 50% of the subjects tested.

Therapeutic index (TI): The ratio of the LD_{50} to the ED_{50}. $TI = LD_{50}/ED_{50}$. The ratio gives an estimate of the relative safety of a drug.

Drug names: There are three types of names for any drug: chemical, generic or official, and trade name or brand name.

Chemical name: The chemical structure of a drug that explains the composition of a drug.

Generic name: The official and nonproprietary name of a drug assigned by the United States Adopted Names (USAN) council.

Trade name or **brand name:** A word, symbol, or device assigned to a drug (or other product) by its manufacturer, registered by the United States Patent Office, and approved by the United States Food and Drug Administration.

Prescription: An order written by a physician to be filled by a pharmacist. Physicians must sign their name and title to every prescription. Most prescriptions also contain the DEA number of the item.

Superscription: The part of a prescription that includes the patient's name, address, date, and the symbol *Rx*, which means "take."

Inscription: The part of a prescription containing the names and quantities of the ingredients.

Subscription: The part of a drug prescription that gives directions to the pharmacist about how to prepare the drug.

Signature: The part of a prescription that gives instructions to patients. A signature tells the patient how to take the drug, when to take it, and how much to take.

Over-the-counter (OTC): Available without a prescription.

Drug Forms

Water-Based Solutions

Syrup (syr.): A solution of water and sugar to which a drug is added. Adding flavors can also eliminate the bitter taste of certain drugs. Example: *Robitussin®*, a cough syrup.

Emulsion: Liquid medication that contains fats or oils suspended in water. They must be shaken before use. Cod liver oil used as a laxative is an emulsion.

Magma: Heavy particles mixed with water to form a milky liquid. Magmas must be shaken before administration. Example: milk of magnesia.

Lotion: A suspension of drugs in a water base for external use. Lotions must be patted on the skin for protective, emollient, or antipruritic purposes. **Example:** calamine lotion used as an antipruritic for poison ivy.

Liniment: A liquid suspension that is rubbed onto the skin. Liniments relieve pain and swelling. Example: *Ben-Gay®*.

Aerosol: A liquid or semiliquid delivered as mist by pressurized gas, for example with oral inhalers or nebulizers, which allows rapid absorption into the bloodstream. Example: *Proventil®*, a bronchodilator used for asthma.

Alcoholic Solutions

Elixir (elix.): A fluid extract of drugs that are dissolved in various concentrations of alcohol, usually between 10 and 20 percent. Examples: phenobarbital elixir, an anticonvulsant; and *Benadryl®* elixir, an antihistamine.

Tincture: A potent solution made with alcohol. Examples: iodine, a strong antiseptic; belladonna tincture, an anticholinergic; and camphorated opium tincture, a laxative.

Injectible Forms

Ampule: A single dose of sterile solution contained in a glass bottle whose seal must be broken to draw up medication.

Vial: A bottle with a rubber stopper or other nonsterile seal. Vials provide multiple doses of medication.

Solids and Semisolids

Ointment: Drugs mixed with lanolin or petrolatum.

Powder: Drugs dried and ground into fine particles. Example: potassium chloride (*Kato Powder®*).

Tablet (tab.): Drug powders compressed into a convenient form for swallowing.

Troche or **lozenge:** A flattened tablet that is dissolved in the mouth. These medications are often used for colds and sore throats.

Capsule (cap.): A small gelatin enclosure containing powder or liquid drugs. The capsule dissolves in the stomach, releasing the drugs.

Delayed-release: Certain tablets and capsules are treated with special coatings so that various portions of the drug dissolve at different rates. In this way, drug effects can be extended over time.

Enteric-coated: Certain tablets and capsules are coated with an acid-resistant substance so that the drug will be absorbed only in the less acidic portions of the intestine. Enteric-coated products need to be taken on an empty stomach with water, either 1 hour before or 2 hours after a meal.

Spheroidal Oral Drug Absorption System (SODAS): Pellets covered in a gelatin capsule that slowly release the drug, unaffected by food or the acid in the GI tract.

Gastrointestinal Therapeutic System (GITS): A two-compartment tablet. In the GI tract, water is drawn into the tablet forcing the drug out. This system delivers drugs at a constant rate over extended periods of time.

Suppository (supp.): Drugs mixed with a substance (cocoa butter) that will melt at body temperature. Suppositories are inserted into the rectum, urethra, or vagina.

Ointment or **unguent (oint., ung.):** A salve of soft, oily substances to which a drug has been added. It is applied to the skin.

Cream: A thick, smooth, water-based topical medication.

Transdermal: Administered through the skin with a bandage or a patch system. Patches are easy to apply and cause little or no discomfort, and they provide a continuous source of the drug over 24 hours or more.

Sources of Drug Information

***Physicians' Desk Reference* (PDR):** The most widely used drug reference publication. It contains an index of manufacturers, a brand name and generic name index, a product category index, and a product identification guide. The brand name and generic name index makes up the pink section, the product classification or category index is the blue section, an alphabetical index by manufacturers is featured in the white section, a generic and chemical name index constitutes the yellow section, and diagnostic product information is found in the green section. The PDR is revised annually.

***United States Pharmacopeia Dispensing Information* (USPDI):** Published in three volumes with monthly updates. Volume I provides in-depth information about prescription and over-the-counter medications and nutritional supplements. Volume II contains advice for the patient. Volume III contains state and federal requirements for prescribing and dispensing drugs.

Drug Regulation

Controlled Substance Act of 1970: A law that controls the distribution and use of all drugs of abuse or potential abuse as designated by the Drug Enforcement Administration (DEA). It divides narcotics, stimulants, and some sedatives into five classes, called schedules. See Table 5-3 on p. 114 for examples.

Drug Regulation and Reform Act of 1978: Permits briefer investigation of new drugs, allowing consumers earlier access.

Orphan Drug Act of 1983: Speeds up the availability of drugs for patients with rare diseases.

Record keeping: A doctor's office must maintain two types of records: dispensing and inventory. Dispensing records must indicate to whom, when, and how much of the drug was administered or dispensed. Inventory records involve counting the amount of each drug on hand. The controlled drug inventory must be completed every 2 years with all the invoice copies from the drug suppliers included.

Registration: Doctor's offices that dispense or administer drugs must register with the DEA with a form called the "Application for Registration Under the Controlled Substances Act of 1970."

Storage: Some medications such as antibiotics may need to be refrigerated. All medications should be left in their original containers. Read drug labels and inserts for specific storage directions for each type of drug.

Security: Store controlled substances and prescription pads in a locked area. Be aware of and follow state guidelines and laws about keeping controlled substances secure.

Discarding drugs: Any medication that is out of date or without a label should be discarded. These drugs should be poured down a sink so that no one will be able to take them.

Patient Education

Patient education: Advise patients to provide your medical office with a complete list of drugs they use regularly or periodically—including alcohol and recreational drugs, as well as herbal medicines. Explain to patients how and when to take each drug to ensure safety and effectiveness. Explain how to identify possible adverse effects, and be prepared to answer any questions.

Poisons

Poisons: All drugs will act as poisons if taken in excess. Only the dose separates the therapeutic effect from a toxic effect.

Antidote: An agent that counteracts a poison. There are four types: chemical, mechanical, physiological, and universal. Antidotes for some of the most common poisons are shown in Table 5-4 on p. 114.

Chemical antidotes: Neutralize the poison by changing its chemical nature.

Physiological antidotes: Counteract the effects of the poison by releasing opposing effects.

Mechanical antidotes: Prevent absorption of the poison.

Universal antidotes: Were supposedly effective against a wide range of toxins. These mixtures were formerly recommended as antidotes when the exact poison was not known. There is, in fact, no known universal antidote.

Schedule	Abuse Potential	Prescription Requirement	Examples
I	High abuse potential; no accepted medical use	No prescription permitted	Heroin, hallucinogens, marijuana, fenethylline, hashish, lysergic acid diethylamide (LSD), methaqualone (*Quaalude®*), peyote
II	High abuse potential; an accepted medical use	Prescription required; no refills permitted without a new written prescription	Narcotics, cocaine, morphine, opium, anabolic steroids, hydromorphone hydrochloride (*Dilaudid®*), amphetamines, short-acting barbiturates
III	Moderate abuse potential; an accepted medical use	Prescription required; 5 refills permitted in 6 months	Moderate acting barbiturates, butabarbital (*Butisol®*), secobarbital (*Seconal®*), glutethimide, most preparations that include codeine combined with something else
IV	Low abuse potential; an accepted medical use	Prescription required; 5 refills permitted in 6 months	Chloral hydrate (*Noctec®*), diazepam (*Valium®*), alprazolam (*Xanax®*), pentazocine HCl (*Talwin®*)
V	Low abuse potential; an accepted medical use	No prescription required for individuals 18 or older	Cough syrups with codeine (*Cheracol®* with codeine), guaifenesin (*Naldecon Dx®*), *Lomotil®*, *Parepectolin®*

Table 5-3

Poison	Antidote
Acetaminophen	N-acetylcysteine
Benzodiazepines	Flumazenil
Carbon monoxide	Oxygen
Cyanide	Amyl nitrite
Iron	Deferoxamine
Methanol	Ethanol
Opiates	Naloxone
Organophosphates	Atropine or pralidoxime

Table 5-4

Drug Administration

Oral route: The drug is swallowed. This is the safest and most convenient route used for most medications. Oral medications may cause nausea and stomach irritation. They also have a slow absorption rate that can be affected by food. Examples include aspirin, sedatives, hypnotics, and antibiotics.

Buccal route (buc): The drug is placed between the gum and cheek and left there until it is dissolved. Examples include *Oxytocin®*, which induces labor.

Sublingual route (subling, subl, SL): The drug is placed under the tongue and left there until it is dissolved. These drugs are used when rapid effects are needed; for example, nitroglycerin for angina pectoris and ergotamine tartate (*Ergostat®*) for migraines.

Topical route(T): The drug is rubbed into, patted on, sprayed on, swabbed on, or rinsed on skin. These drugs are used to soothe irritated areas or to cure local infections. Examples include most creams and ointments.

Transdermal route: A patch is applied to clean, dry, non-hairy skin. This is a convenient form that provides continuous absorption and effects that last over many hours. Estrogen and nitroglycerin can be administered in this way.

Inhalation route, inhalation therapy: The drug is inhaled to achieve local effects within the respiratory tract. Antiasthmatic medications such as epinephrine are administered in this way.

Ophthalmic: Drops are placed into the eye.

Otic route: Drops are placed into the ear.

Rectal route (R): A suppository is inserted into the rectum, or a solution is administered as an enema. This method is used when a patient cannot take oral medications or when local effects are desired. Analgesics and laxatives can be administered in this way.

Urethral route: A solution is instilled into the bladder using a catheter.

Vaginal route (p.v., vag): A solution is administered as a douche. Other forms are inserted into the vagina with an applicator. Example: *Mycostatin®*.

Parenteral route: The drug is injected into the body with a needle and syringe for rapid absorption and controlled dosage. Parenteral administration is divided into four main categories according to the location of the injection: intradermal, subcutaneous, intramuscular, and intravenous.

Intradermal route: The drug is injected into the upper layers of the skin.

Subcutaneous route (SUBQ, SC): The drug is injected into the subcutaneous layer of the skin.

Intramuscular route (IM): The drug is injected into a muscle. This method is used when a drug has poor oral absorption, when high blood levels are required, or when rapid effects are desired. Narcotic analgesics and antibiotics are administered in this way.

Intravenous route (IV): The drug is injected or infused into a vein. This method is used when an emergency situation exists, when immediate effects are required, and also when other medications are being administered by infusion. Examples include IV fluids (e.g., dextrose solution), nutrient supplementation, and antibiotics.

Antibiotics

Antibiotic: A chemical substance that destroys or interferes with the development of bacterial microorganisms. Antibiotics are derived from other living microorganisms. These agents are sufficiently nontoxic to the host and are used in the treatment of infectious diseases. They are divided into two groups: bactericidal and bacteriostatic. Some examples of both are shown in Table 5-5.

Bactericidal: Destructive to or killing bacteria.

Bacteriostatic: Inhibiting the growth of bacteria.

Antimicrobial: Killing or inhibiting the growth of microorganisms.

Broad-spectrum: Effective against a wide variety of both gram-positive and gram-negative pathogenic bacteria.

AT A GLANCE	Examples of the Two Different Types of Antibiotics	
Bactericidal	**Bacteriostatic**
Penicillins	Sulfonamides
Cephalosporins	Tetracyclines
Aminoglycosides	Chloramphenicol
Vancomycin	Clindamycin
	Spetinomycin

Table 5-5

Bacterial resistance: The ability of some bacteria to resist the actions of antibiotics.

Chemotherapy: The use of drugs to kill or to inhibit the growth of infectious organisms or cancerous cells.

Bactericidal Antibiotics

Penicillin: A large group of natural or synthetic antibacterial agents derived from fungi of the genus *Penicillum*. Penicillins were the first true antibiotics, and they are the most widely used class of antibiotics. They interfere with the synthesis of bacterial cell walls. Classifications of penicillin and examples (with generic names and brand names) are seen in Table 5-6 on p. 116. Common uses of penicillin: treatment of otitis media, pneumonia, gonorrhea, syphilis, rheumatic fever, and meningitis. Common side effects of penicillin: diarrhea, nausea, rashes, thrombophlebitis, hyperkalemia, and hypernatremia. When used in high doses, penicillins may cause central nervous system disturbances, including convulsions. As a drug class, penicillins also cause the highest incidence of drug allergy. Patients must be questioned about the possibility of a penicillin allergy.

Beta-lactamases: Bacterial enzymes that inactivate penicillin and cephalosporin antibiotics.

Penicillinase: An enzyme produced by some bacteria that inactivates penicillin, thus increasing resistance to the antibiotic. It is used in the treatment of reactions to penicillin.

Cephalosporin: One of a large group of broad-spectrum antibiotics from *Cephalosporium*, a genus of soil-inhabiting fungi. They are similar in structure and action to penicillin. Like penicillins, the cephalosporins are classified into four generations. They inhibit cell wall synthesis in bacteria. Common uses of cephalosporins: administration in patients allergic to the penicillins, treatment of certain urinary and respi-

Classification	Example Generic Name (*Brand Name*)	Effectiveness
First Generation		
Narrow-spectrum	Penicillin G (*Pentids*)	Gram positive streptococci
Beta-lactamase sensitive	Penicillin V (*Pen-Vee K®*)	Gram positive streptococci
Beta-lactamase resistant	Oxacillin (*Prostaphlin®*) Cloxacillin (*Tegopen®*) Methicillin (*Staphcillin®*) Nafcillin (*Unipen®*) Dicloxacillin (*Dynapen®*)	Gram positive streptococci
Second Generation		
Broad-spectrum	Ampicillin (*Omnipen®*) Amoxicillin (*Amoxil®*)	*Hemophilus* *Escherichia coli* *Neisseria*
Third Generation		
Extended spectrum	Carbenicillin (*Geocillin®*)	*Pseudomonas*
Fourth Generation		
Widest spectrum, potent	Mezlocillin (*Mezlin®*) Piperacillin (*Pipracil®*)	Serious infections, *Pseudomonas aeruginosa, Proteus vulgaris, Klebsiella pneumoniae*

Table 5-6

ratory tract infections. Side effects of cephalosporins: oral thrush, diarrhea, rashes, vaginitis, thrombophlebitis, and sometimes electrolyte imbalance. Intramuscular injections of cephalosporins are usually painful and may cause inflammation.

First-generation cephalosporins: Used to treat common gram-positive and gram-negative infections. Examples: cefazolin (*Kefzol®*), cephalothin (*Keflin®*), and cephradine (*Velosef®*).

Second-generation cephalosporins: Used for gram-negative infections. They are more resistant to the actions of penicillinase and cephalosporinase. Examples: cefamamandole (*Mandol®*), cefotetan (*Cefotan®*), and cefotixin (*Mefoxin®*).

Third-generation cephalosporins: Used for serious gram-negative infections. They have longer duration of action and are more potent than the first- or second-generation cephalosporins. Examples: cefotaxime (*Claforan®*) and ceftriaxone (*Rocephin®*).

Fourth-generation cephalosporins: Similar in spectrum to third-generation drugs. They have a greater resistance to beta-lactamase inactivating enzymes. Example: cefepime (*Maxapime®*).

Aminoglycoside: One of a group of bacterial antibiotics derived from the genus *Streptomyces* that irreversibly inhibit protein synthesis. All of the aminoglycosides are highly toxic. Types of aminoglycosides: amikacin (*Amikin®*), gentamicin (*Garamycin®*), kanamycin (*Kantrex®*), neomycin (*Neobiotic®*), streptomycin, tobramycin (*Nebcin®*). Uses of aminoglycosides: to treat infections caused by gram-negative organisms. They are often given in large doses before abdominal surgery to "sterilize" the bowel. They are also used for the treatment of resistant urinary tract infections. Streptomycin is used to treat tuberculosis, plague, and tularemia. Side effects: nausea, vomiting, diarrhea, ototoxicity (which can result in deafness), and nephrotoxicity. Aminoglycosides may interfere with normal renal function. Contraindications: Aminoglycosides should not be used during pregnancy.

Quinolone: A general class of broad-spectrum antibiotics that interrupt the replication of DNA molecules in bacteria. They are well absorbed in the GI tract after oral administration. Examples: ciprofloxacin (*Cipro®*) and nalidixic acid. Common uses: treatment of urinary, GI, respiratory, bone and joint, and soft tissue infections. Common side effects: headache, dizziness, GI disturbances, and rash. Contraindications: Quinolones are not recommended for pediatric therapy because they cause permanent cartilage damage. Quinolones are also not recommended during pregnancy. Fluoroquinolones are synthetic quinolones.

Vancomycin (*Vancocin®*): A miscellaneous antibacterial agent that does not fit into any of the preceding categories. Vancomycin interferes with cell wall synthesis and is bactericidal. It is effective only on gram-positive bacteria, particularly staphylococcal infections that are resistant to other antibiotics. It also is prescribed in the treatment of infectious diseases such as pneumonia, meningitis, endocarditis, septicemia, and osteomyelitis. Common side effects: ototoxicity, nephrotoxicity, and a flushing redness of the neck and trunk caused by histamines.

Bacteriostatic Antibiotics

Sulfonamides: Synthetic antibiotics that now have limited uses because of bacterial resistance. They block the synthesis of folic acid, creating a bacteriostatic effect. Examples: mafenide (*Sulfamylon®*), sulfacetamide (*Sulamyd®*), and sulfamethizole (*Thiosulfil®*). Common uses: topical treatment of burns and treatment of urinary and GI tract infections. Common side effects: nausea, vomiting, diarrhea, crystalluria, anemia, leukopenia, and rashes.

Tetracycline: A broad-spectrum antibiotic that is effective against both gram-negative and gram-positive microorganisms. Tetracycline inhibits protein synthesis by bacterial cells. Foods containing calcium, mineral supplements, and antacids interfere with absorption of the tetracyclines. Examples: chlortetracycline (*Aureomycin®*), doxycycline (*Vibramycin®*), and tetracycline (*Achromycin®*). Common uses: treatment of urethritis, cholera, lower respiratory tract infections, meningitis, rickettsiae, and Lyme disease. Common side effects: nausea, vomiting, abdominal cramps, anorexia, and diarrhea. It should not be administered in the last half of pregnancy and to children under 8 years of age (because it discolors teeth). It is also secreted in breast milk. The use of outdated tetracycline may cause Fanconi's syndrome.

Chloramphenicol (*Chloromycetin®*): A broad-spectrum antibiotic with specific therapeutic action against rickettsiae. It is a miscellaneous bacteriostatic antibiotic that does not fit into any of the preceding categories. Chloramphenicol inhibits bacterial protein synthesis, creating a bacteriostatic effect. Common uses: treatment of rickettsial infections, typhoid fever, and meningitis. It is reserved for serious or life-threatening infections. Side effects: aplastic anemia (bone marrow depression), oral thrush, and genital/anal pruritus (itching). Chloramphenicol is potentially a very toxic drug. In most cases, its effects are irreversible. It should not be administered to a newborn less than 2 weeks old because it can result in a condition known as the gray baby syndrome involving circulatory collapse, abdominal distention, and respiratory failure.

Clindamycin (*Cleocin®*): A miscellaneous bacteriostatic antibacterial agent that inhibits protein synthesis. It is used for the treatment of a variety of gram-negative aerobic and gram-positive and gram-negative anaerobic organisms. Common uses: treatment especially against anaerobic organisms. Side effects: psuedomembranous colitis, severe gastrointestinal disturbances, and hypersensitivity.

Spectinomycin: An antibiotic that is often called by the trademark *Trobicin®*. It inhibits protein synthesis and is used in the treatment of gonorrhea and certain other infections and in penicillin-allergic patients. Side effects include pain at the injection site and hypersensitivity to this drug.

Both Bactericidal and Bacteriostatic Antibiotics

Macrolid: An antibiotic with molecules that have many-membered lacton rings. Macrolids inhibit protein-synthesis in some bacteria. They are bactericidal and bacteriostatic. Examples: erythromycin (*E-mycin®*), azithromycin (*Zithromax®*), and clarithromycin (*Biaxin®*). Common uses: treatment of diseases of the gastrointestinal tract, skin, and respiratory system and of sexually transmitted diseases. Side effects: thrombophlebitis, diarrhea, nausea, vomiting, and abnormal tastes in the mouth.

Antitubercular Agents

Antitubercular agents: A group of drugs used to treat tuberculosis. At least two drugs, and usually three, are required in various combinations in pulmonary tuberculosis therapy. Examples: isoniazid (*INH®*), rifampin (*Rifadin®*), ethambutol (*Myambutol®*), and streptomycin.

Isoniazid (*INH®*): A synthetic bactericidal drug used to treat tuberculosis. The drug inhibits the production of mycolic acid and thus prevents cell wall synthesis. Common uses: prophylaxis and treatment of tuberculosis. Side effects: peripheral neuritis, hepatitis, numbness, nausea, vomiting, dizziness, ataxia, and hepatotoxicity.

Rifampin (*Rifadin®*): An antibiotic that prevents RNA synthesis. Common uses: treatment of tuberculosis and prevention of meningococci outbreaks. Common side effect: reddish-orange color in urine, saliva, feces, sputum, sweat, and tears. It can permanently discolor soft contact lenses.

Ethambutol (*Myambutol®*): A bacteriostatic synthetic compound that inhibits the incorporation of mycolic acid into the bacterial cell wall. Side effects: confusion, fever, hallucinations, blurred vision (red-green color changes).

Antifungal Agents

Antifungal: Destructive to fungi or inhibiting their growth. An antifungal drug is also called antimycotic. See Table 5-7 on p. 118 for a list of antifungal drugs.

Antiviral Agents

Amantadine (*Symmetrel®*): Prevents the virus that causes Asian influenza from penetrating human cells and releasing viral DNA into the cell. After exposure to the flu, it also reduces the severity of the infection. It is recommended for high-risk patients only.

Generic Name	Trade Name	Uses
Amphoterian B	*Fungizone®*	Systemic fungal infections, severe progressive fungal infections, cryptococcosis
Fluconazole	*Diflucan®*	Systemic infection, oroesophageal candidiasis
Ketoconazole	*Nizoral®*	Systemic infection
Nystatin	*Mycostatin®*	Candidiasis, skin infections, GI infections
Griseofulvin	*Grifulvin®*	Superficial fungal (dermatophytic) infections
Butenafine	*Mentax®*	Athlete's foot
Terconazole	*Terazol-3®, Terazol-7®*	Vulvovaginal candidiasis

Table 5-7

Acyclovir (*Zovirax®*): Inhibits viral DNA replication. It is used in the treatment of genital herpes and chickenpox. Side effects: kidney damage, headache, confusion, irritability, nausea, and vomiting.

Idoxuridine (*Herplex®*): Inhibits viral DNA synthesis by blocking incorporation of thymidine. It is used to treat herpes simplex keratitis.

Drugs used against HIV: Didanosine (*Videx®*), indinavir (*Crixivan®*), nelfinavir (*Viracept®*), saquinavir (*Invirase®*), zalcitabine (*Hivid®*), and zidovudine (*Retrovir®*). The frequency of HIV mutation and drug resistance results in poor clinical response.

Pharmacology of the Integumentary System

Anti-inflammatory drugs: Suppress inflammation and relieve itching (pruritus) and swelling (edema). Examples: betamethasone valerate (*Valosine®*) and hydrocortisone.

Astringents: Relieve itching, soothe mild sunburns, and dry the skin. They are used for poison ivy, insect bites, and mild sunburn. Examples: calamine and diphenhydramine (*Caladryl®*).

Antipruritics: Relieve itching. They also have an antihistamine, sedative, and drying effect. Example: trimeprazine tartrate (*Temaril®*).

Erythema: Redness caused by an expansion of the capillaries at the skin's surface.

Vasoconstrictors: Reduce swelling and edema (caused by buildup of fluid in the tissues) and increase venous flow. They are used to treat dermal ulcers. Examples: *Debrisan®* and *DuoDERM®* hydroactive.

Antiseptics: Kill germs and are used to treat surface infections, burns, minor wounds, and vaginitis. Example: povidone-iodine (*Betadine®*).

Keratolytics: Swell and soften excess keratin for easy removal and shedding. They are used for warts, corns, calluses, psoriasis, and seborrheic dermatitis. Example: salicylic acid.

Pharmacology of the Musculoskeletal System

Centrally acting skeletal muscle relaxant: Inhibits skeletal muscle contraction by blocking conduction within the spinal cord. Examples: baclofen (*Lioresal®*), carisoprodol (*Rela®*, *Soma®*), and tizandine (*Zanaflex®*). Common uses: therapy for muscle strain and multiple sclerosis. Side effects: blurred vision, dizziness, lethargy, and decreased mental alertness.

Peripheral skeletal muscle relaxant: Inhibits muscle contraction at the neuromuscular junction or within the contractile process. Example: dantrolene (*Dantrium®*). Common uses: during surgical procedures to relax the abdominal muscle, during shock therapy, and during tetanus. Side effects: toxicity-induced paralysis of the respiratory muscles.

Pharmacology of the Nervous System

Central Nervous System

Sedatives and Hypnotic Drugs

Hypnotic: A drug that causes insensitivity to pain by inhibiting the reception of sensory impressions in the brain, causing partial or complete unconsciousness. Sedative and hypnotic drugs produce their effects by increasing the inhibitory activity of gamma-aminobutyric acid (GABA), a neurotransmitter in the central nervous system (CNS).

Sedative: A hypnotic drug that exerts a quieting or tranquilizing effect. The most common sedatives and hypnotics are summarized in Table 5-8.

Barbiturate: A sedative drug that reduces brain activity and promotes sleep. The main sites of action of barbiturates are the reticular formation and the cerebral cortex. Barbiturates are used as sleep aids and as treatment for convulsions or seizures. Common side effects: drowsiness, dry mouth, lethargy, and lack of coordination. An overdose can result in extensive cardiovascular and CNS depression leading to coma, respiratory depression, and death. Prolonged and excessive use of barbiturates can result in tolerance and physical dependence. Contraindications: Patients who have acute intermittent porphyria should not take barbiturates because they may cause nerve damage, pain, and paralysis. Barbiturates should not be taken during pregnancy.

Nonbarbiturate: Any of a diverse group of drugs that produce effects similar to those of barbiturates. Some of these agents were developed with the hope that they would not produce addictions and dependence. Unfortunately, prolonged abuse of these drugs will still result in physical dependence and tolerance. Chloral hydrate is a good example of a nonbarbiturate drug. Its mechanism of action is similar to alcohol, and it is used as a hypnotic, particularly in elderly individuals. Side effects involve excessive CNS depression and gastric irritation.

Benzodiazepines: A class of drugs used in the treatment of anxiety. They are commonly referred to as antianxiety drugs. They depress the reticular activating system to produce sedation and hypnosis. Benzodiazepines are well tolerated and produce few side effects. They do not interfere with REM sleep and produce less tolerance than barbiturates. Flurazepam, a type of benzodiazepine, may cause sedation or a "hangover effect" the following day after use. Contraindication: pregnancy.

AT A GLANCE	Sedatives and Hypnotic Drugs		
Classification	**Uses**	**Side Effects**	**Contraindications**
• Drug			
Sedative-Hypnotic Barbiturates			
• Pentobarbital (*Nembutal®, Luminal®*) • Secobarbital (*Seconal®*)	Sedation in smaller doses, promotion of sleep in larger doses; treatment of seizure disorders; control of epilepsy	Drowsiness, dry mouth, confusion, incoordination, respiratory depression, coma	Acute intermittent porphyria, pregnancy, suicidal tendencies
Sedative-Hypnotic Nonbarbiturates			
• Chloral hydrate (*Noctec®, SK-chloral®*) • Zolpidem (*Ambien®*)	Treatment of insomnia; sedation in elderly individuals	Nausea, vomiting, diarrhea, gastric irritation, dizziness	
Benzodiazepines			
• Flurazepam (*Dalmane®*) • Temazepam (*Restoril®*) • Triazolam (*Halcion®*)	Treatment of anxiety	Flurazepam: hangover effect after use Triazolam: rebound insomnia and increased daytime anxiety after use	Pregnancy

Table 5-8

Antipsychotics

Antipsychotic drugs: Drugs that are used to treat schizophrenia and other psychotic mental disorders characterized by gross impairment in reality testing. Antipsychotic drugs are also referred to as neuroleptics. These drugs are not a cure but a method to control irrational and bizarre behavior and thought associated with psychoses. Most antipsychotics block dopamine D2 receptors. The most important types of antipsychotic drugs are phenothiazines, butyrophenones, and thioxanthenes. See Table 5-9. Common side effects: sedation; dry mouth; constipation; visual disturbances; dystonic reactions with muscle spasms; akathisia with continuous body movement and restlessness; parkinsonism with muscular rigidity and tremors; tardive dyskinesia involving involuntary movements of the lips, jaw, tongue, and extremities; and neuroleptic malignant syndrome with hyperthermia, muscular rigidity, catatonia, and autonomic nervous system instability. Contraindication: pregnancy.

Clozapine: Atypically blocks both dopamine (D4) and serotonin receptors. It is the second-line drug used for the treatment of schizophrenia and psychosis. Common side effects include a reduction in the number of granulocytes.

AT A GLANCE	Common Antipsychotic Drugs		
Classification	**Uses**	**Side Effects**	**Contraindications**
• Drug			
Phenothiazines			
• Chlorpromazine (*Thorazine®*) • Triflupromazine (*Vesprin®*)	Antipsychotic; also antihistaminic, anticholinergic, alpha-adrenergic blocking, and antiemetic	Sedation, dry mouth, constipation, visual disturbances, dystonic reactions, akathisia, parkinsonism, tardive dyskinesia, neuroleptic malignant syndrome	Pregnancy
Butyrophenones			
• Haloperidol (*Haldol®*)	Treatment of highly agitated and manic patients (more potent than the phenothiazines)	Fewer peripheral (antihistaminic, anticholinergic, etc.) effects but greater movement disturbances	Pregnancy
Thioxanthenes			
• Thiothixene (*Navane®*)	Treatment of psychosis; few other pharmacological effects (more selective action than other antipsychotic drugs)	Drowsiness, postural hypotension, disturbances in movement	Pregnancy
Other Antipsychotic Drugs			
• Clozapine (*Clozaril®*)	Sedation, hypotension, and anticholinergic effects (atypical in that it blocks serotonin receptors in addition to dopamine receptors)	Reduction in granulocyte count in blood, no extra-pyramidal effects such as parkinsonism or tardive dyskinesia	Pregnancy

Table 5-9

Antidepressants, Psychomotor Stimulants, and Lithium

Antidepressant: A drug that prevents or relieves depression. Low levels of norepinephrine and serotonin are associated with mental depression, whereas high levels of norepinephrine and serotonin are involved in mania. Antidepressants increase the level of norepinephrine and serotonin in the brain. There are three major classes of antidepressants: monoamine oxidase (MAO) inhibitors, tricyclic antidepressants (TCAs), and selective serotonin reuptake inhibitors (SSRIs).

Monoamine oxidase (MAO) inhibitors: Increase the concentration of epinephrine, norepinephrine, and serotonin in storage sites in the nervous system. After 2 to 4 weeks of treatment, patients feel an increase in appetite and sleep and an elevation of mood. One of the disadvantages of MAO inhibitors is the dietary restriction of foods containing tyramine (wine, beer, herring, and certain cheeses). A combination of tyramine and MAO inhibitors may cause a hypertensive crisis or cerebral stroke. Other common side effects: postural hypotension, dry mouth, constipation, urinary retention, blurred vision, insomnia, tremors, convulsions, liver damage, and impotency in males. Examples: isocarboxazid (*Marplan*®), phenylzine (*Nardil*®), and tranylcypromine (*Parnate*®).

Tricyclic antidepressant drugs: Block the reuptake of norepinephrine and serotonin into the neuronal nerve endings. These drugs get their name from their characteristic triple-ring structure. In addition to the antidepressant effect, they also produce varying degrees of sedation, anticholinergic effects, and alpha-adrenergic blockade. Common side effects: dry mouth, weight gain, constipation, urinary retention, rapid heartbeat, postural hypotension, blurred vision, drowsiness, restlessness, tremors, convulsion, mania, cardiac arrhythmias, and jaundice. Examples: imipramine (*Tofranil*®), doxepin (*Sinequan*®), desipramine (*Petrofrane*®), and amoxapine (*Asendin*®).

Selective serotonin reuptake inhibitors: Newer antidepressant drugs that block the reuptake and inactivation of serotonin in the brain. They are the most widely used antidepressants. Fluoxetine (*Prozac*®) was the first drug of this class to be introduced. Fluoxetine is effective against depression and also obsessive-compulsive disorders. Other examples: fluvoxamine (*Luvox*®) and sertraline (*Zoloft*®). Common side effects: headache, nervousness, insomnia, tremors, nausea, diarrhea, dry mouth, weight loss, and anorexia.

Psychomotor stimulants: Include amphetamines and other closely related drugs. They are often used during the first few weeks of depression treatment until other antidepressants such as the MAO inhibitors or tricyclics begin their therapeutic effect. They are also used to treat narcolepsy and hyperkinesis. Amphetamines increase the activity of norepinephrine and dopamine in the brain. Common side effects: dry mouth, rapid heartbeat, increased blood pressure, restlessness, and insomnia. Examples: dextroamphetamine (*Dexedrine*®) and methylphenidate (*Ritalin*®).

Lithium: An antimanic drug prescribed in the treatment of manic episodes. Lithium decreases the excitability of nerve tissue, increases the reuptake of norepinephrine and dopamine, and decreases the release of neurotransmitters. Clinical use includes the treatment of bipolar affective disorder and acute manic conditions. Lithium also blocks relapse. Common side effects: hypothyroidism, polyuria, polydipsia, tremor, and teratogenesis. Other side effects: nausea, tremors, cardiac arrhythmias, and nephritis. Contraindication: pregnancy.

Antiepileptic Drugs

Antiepileptic drugs: Reduce or prevent the severity of epileptic or other convulsive seizures. Antiepileptic drugs decrease the excitability of brain cells. The drug of choice for each type of seizure is shown in Table 5-10. Side effects of antiepileptic drugs are summarized in Table 5-11 on p. 122.

AT A GLANCE	Antiepileptic Drugs
Type of Seizure	**Drugs of Choice**
Grand mal (tonic-clonic)	Phenytoin (*Dilantin*®), carbamazepine (*Tegretol*®), phenobarbital (*Luminal*®)
Status epilepticus	Diazepam (*Valium*®), phenytoin (*Dilantin*®), phenobarbital (*Luminal*®)
Complex partial (temporal lobe)	Carbamazepine (*Tegretol*®), phenytoin (*Dilantin*®), primidone
Petit mal	Ethosuximide (*Zarontin*®), valproic acid (*Depakene*®), clonazepam (*Klonopin*®)

Table 5-10

Antiepileptic Drug Toxicities

Drug	Side Effects
Phenobarbital	Sedation, tolerance, dependence
Valproic acid	Nausea, vomiting, diarrhea, tremors, liver toxicity in young patients
Benzodiazepines	Sedation, dependence, tolerance
Phenytoin	Birth defects, gingival hyperplasia, nystagmus, anemias, hirsutism
Carbamazepine	Blood dyscrasias, diplopia, ataxia

Table 5-11

Valproic acid (*Depakene*®): One of the few drugs that can be used in all types of epilepsy. Its mechanism of action is related to its ability to increase levels of GABA, the inhibitory neurotransmitter in the CNS. Common side effects: nausea, vomiting, diarrhea, tremors, and liver toxicity.

Antiparkinsonian Drugs

Levodopa (*Dopar*®, *Larodopa*®): The most effective drug available for Parkinson's disease. In the basal ganglia, levodopa is converted to dopamine, and increased levels of dopamine lessen parkinsonian symptoms. Common side effects: nausea, vomiting, anorexia, orthostatic hypotension or fainting, irregular heartbeat, dystonias, and dyskinesias.

Selegiline (*Eldepryl*®): Inhibits the metabolism of dopamine in the brain. It slows the progression of Parkinson's disease.

Amantadine (*Symmetrel*®): An antiviral agent that is often effective in the treatment of Parkinson's disease. Common side effects: dry mouth, GI disturbances, visual disturbances, dizziness, skin discoloration, and confusion.

Atropine and scopolamine: Anticholinergic drugs that relieve some of the symptoms of Parkinson's disease because they decrease the level of cholinergic activity and thus reduce tremors, muscle rigidity, and postural disturbances. Side effects: dry mouth, constipation, urinary retention, rapid heartbeat, and pupillary dilation.

Anesthetics and Analgesics

Anesthetic: A substance that depresses all nervous tissue, inhibits voluntary and involuntary systems, and depresses respiratory function.

General anesthetics: Administered by inhalation or intravenous injection. Inhalation anesthetics include chloroform, ether, and nitrous oxide. Injectable anesthetics include barbiturates, etomidate, ketamine, midazolam, and propofol; they are usually administered intravenously. In addition to anesthetic agents, a variety of preanesthetic and postanesthetic medications are used to aid induction of general anesthesia, to counteract side effects, or to make recovery more comfortable. Side effects: dizziness, nausea, mental disorientation, lack of coordination.

Narcotic (opioid) analgesics: Derivatives of opium or synthetic chemicals that relieve severe pain. Certain narcotic analgesics (codeine and dextromethorphan) are also antitussive. All narcotic analgesics produce tolerance and physical dependency with chronic use. Morphine and other narcotic analgesics mimic the effects of endorphins by blocking pain transmission to the brain. For a list of narcotic analgesics, see Table 5-12.

Nonopioid analgesics: The most common drugs used for relieving pain. See Table 5-13.

Autonomic Nervous System

Autonomic nervous system drugs: Drugs that treat the body systems regulated by the autonomic nervous system. They are classified into four groups: adrenergics, adrenergic blockers, cholinergics, and cholinergic blockers. See Table 5-14 on p. 124.

Sympathetic Nervous System

Adrenergic drugs: Also called sympathomimetic agents, these drugs mimic or stimulate the sympathetic nervous system. They include epinephrine, dopamine, dolutamine, and ephedrine. Adrenergic drugs have two effects: alpha and beta.

Alpha-adrenergic drugs: Cause the contraction of smooth muscle, thereby increasing blood pressure. The prototype alpha-adrenergic drug is norepinephrine. Common uses: to increase blood pressure in hypotensive states (such as after surgery) and to reduce congestion of nasal and ocular mucosa. Side effects: excessive vasoconstriction of blood vessels, heart

Drug	Uses	Side Effects	Contraindications
• Codeine • Meperidine (*Demerol®*) • Morphine • Pentazocine (*Talwin®*) • Propoxyphene (*Darvon®, Dolene®*)	Relief of severe acute and chronic pain; relief of pain associated with myocardial infarction, posttrauma, cancer, and chronic inflammatory conditions; suppression of coughing (codeine)	Sedation, confusion, euphoria, agitation, headache and dizziness, hypotension, bradycardia, nausea, vomiting, urinary retention, respiratory depression, physical and emotional dependence, convulsions with large doses	Bronchia asthma, heavy pulmonary secretions, convulsive disorders, biliary obstruction, head injuries, pregnancy

Table 5-12

Classification • Drug	Uses	Side Effects	Contraindications
Salicylates			
Aspirin (*Bayer® aspirin, Bufferin®, Anacin®*)	Relief of mild to moderate pain and fever; treatment of inflammation; possible reduction in the risk of reinfarction and death following a myocardial infarction	Prolonged bleeding time, bleeding, gastric ulcer and bleeding, tinnitus, renal insufficiency, rash, hepatic dysfunction, stomach irritation, and nausea	GI ulcer and bleeding, asthma, bleeding disorders, influenza-like syndrome in children, pregnancy, vitamin K deficiency
N-Acetyl-P-Aminophenol			
Acetaminophen (*Tylenol®*)	Relief of fever, pain, and discomfort associated with the common cold and flu	Coma, respiratory failure, severe liver toxicity, renal insufficiency, rash	Renal or hepatic disease, anemia, cardiac or pulmonary disease
Synthetic Nonsteroidal Antiinflammatory Drugs (NSAIDs)			
Ibuprofen (*Advil®, Motrin®, Nuprin®*)	Relief of mild to moderate pain (headache, dental extraction, soft tissue injury, sunburn); treatment of chronic osteoarthritis and rheumatoid arthritis	Nausea, GI distress, ulceration, vertigo, confusion	

Table 5-13

Adrenergics	Adrenergic Blockers	Cholinergics	Cholinergic Blockers
• Epinephrine (*Adrenalin*®) • Ephedrine	Methyldopa (*Aldomet*®)	Neostigmine	Atropine
• Dopamine	Guanethidine (*Ismelin*®)	*Prostigmim*®	Scopolamine
• Norepinephrine	Reserpine (*Serpasil*®)	Pilocarpine (*Pilomiotin*®, *Ocusert*®) Bethanechol (*Urecholine*®)	Homatropine Methantheline (*Banthine*®)
• Isoproterenol			

Table 5-14

palpitations, hypertension, and tissue necrosis. Contraindications: hypertension and cardiac arrhythmias.

Beta-adrenergic drugs: Stimulate the heartbeat and act as bronchodilators. Isoproterenol is the most potent of these drugs; it acts as both as a cardiac stimulant and as a bronchodilator. Common use: treatment of acute allergic reactions, such as anaphylaxis. Common side effects: restlessness, tremors, anxiety, overstimulation of the heart, palpitation, arrhythmias. Contraindications: Use with caution in patients with existing heart disease.

Alpha-adrenergic blocking agents: Prevent norepinephrine from producing sympathetic responses resulting in vasodilation and lowered blood pressure. Doxazosin, phentolamine, and prazosin are common alpha-adrenergic blocking drugs. Common uses: treatment of hypertension, treatment of vascular disease, and diagnosis of pheochromocytoma. Common side effects: nasal congestion, increased GI activity, low blood pressure, fainting.

Beta-adrenergic blocking agents (beta-blockers): Decrease the activity of the heart. Propranolol is a common beta-adrenergic drug administered for cardiac arrhythmias, angina pectoris, and hypertension. Side effects: nausea, vomiting, diarrhea, bradycardia, cardiac arrest. Contraindications: Antiadrenergic drugs should not be used in patients with asthma or other respiratory conditions.

Parasympathetic Nervous System

Cholinergic: An agent that allows the parasympathetic nerve fibers to liberate acetylcholine. Cholinergics are also called parasympathomimetic drugs. Examples: neostigmine, pilocarpine, and bethanechol. Common uses: treatment of myasthenia gravis (neostigmine), glaucoma (pilocarpine), and nonobstructive urinary

retention (bethanechol). Side effects: nausea, vomiting, diarrhea, blurred vision, excessive sweating, weakness, hypotension, bronchospasm, and respiratory depression. Contraindications: asthma, cardiac disorders, peptic ulcer, and benign prostatic hypertrophy.

Cholinergic blocking agents: Drugs that block the action of acetylcholine. These agents, also called anticholinergics or parasympatholytics, may be used by patients who have bradycardia. Examples: atropine, scopolamine, and homatropine. Common uses: as antispasmodics, as preanesthetics, and as antidotes for insecticide poisoning. Common side effects: fever or flushing, blurred vision, dry mouth, urinary retention, and tachycardia. Contraindications: asthma, chronic obstructive pulmonary disease, angle-closure glaucoma, gastrointestinal or genitourinary obstruction, hypertension, hypothyroidism, and hepatic or renal disease.

Pharmacology of the Sensory System

Eye Medications

Pilocarpine HCl (*Isopto Carpine*®): A topical medication that causes pupil constriction and reduces intraocular pressure. It is used in the treatment of glaucoma. Side effects: blurred vision, brow pain, eye irritation, myopia.

Acetazolamide (*Diamox*®): Decreases the production of aqueous humor and is used to treat glaucoma. It is a carbonic anhydrase inhibitor (a diuretic). Side effects: myopia, paresthesia, drowsiness, nausea, vomiting.

Betaxolol (*Betoptic*®): A beta-adrenergic blocking agent that reduces the production of aqueous humor. It is used to treat glaucoma. Side effects: photophobia, overproduction of tears.

Atropine sulfate (*Isopto Atropine®*): Used for refraction during an eye exam. It dilates the pupil and causes the paralysis of muscles. Side effects: blurred vision, photophobia.

Ear Medications

Triethanolamine polypeptide oleate-condensate (*Cerumenex®*): Use to soften ear wax (cerumen). Side effects: ear redness and itching.

Pharmacology of the Endocrine System

Adrenal steroids: Corticosteroids produced by the adrenal cortex. They are prescribed as treatment for Addison's disease when there is a hormone deficiency. This type of treatment is called replacement therapy. Examples: cortisone (*Cortone®*), prednisone (*Deltasone®*), and dexamethasone (*Decadron®*).

Anti-inflammatory effects of adrenal steroids: Steroids are also used in acute and chronic inflammatory conditions such as rheumatoid arthritis. Synthetic versions of glucocorticoids, which are adrenal steroids, are commonly used to treat inflammatory and allergic reactions. Side effects with long-term use: steroid addiction, mood changes, insomnia, personality changes, and psychological dependency.

Thyroid agents: Used in the treatment of two conditions: hyposecretion of the thyroid hormone (hypothyroidism) and hypersecretion of the thyroid hormone (hyperthyroidism). Thyroid hormone replacement therapy is used to treat hypothyroidism, and antithyroid drugs (iodide and iodine) are used for hyperthyroidism, which is often caused by a tumor. Examples: liothyroine sodium (*Cytomel®*), thyroglobulin (*Prolid®*), and liotrix (*Euthroid®*).

Insulin: Seven types of insulin are available for subcutaneous and intramuscular injection. Insulin is used to treat type I diabetes mellitus and type II diabetes mellitus that cannot be controlled by diet and exercise. Insulins can also reduce hyperkalemia. Side effects: blurred vision, hypoglycemia, headaches, fatigue, anxiety, nervousness, fainting, and convulsions.

Pharmacology of the Cardiovascular System

Cardiac Glycosides

Cardiac glycosides: Used in the treatment of congestive heart failure (CHF), atrial fibrillation, and atrial tachycardia to increase the force of myocardial contractions. Glycosides slow and strengthen the heartbeat and increase cardiac output. Major side effects of overdose: arrhythmia, headache, visual disturbances, nausea, vomiting, and diarrhea. Examples: deslanoside (*Cedilanid-D®*), digitoxin (*Puradigin®*), and digoxin (*Lanoxin®*).

Antianginal Drugs

Nitroglycerin: The most common and widely used drug for angina pectoris. Nitroglycerin produces general vasodilation of systemic veins and arteries and decreases the preload and afterload of the heart, thereby reducing cardiac work and oxygen consumption. See Table 5-15.

Antihypertensive Drugs

Antihypertensive agents: Agents that are effective against hypertension. Some antihypertensives such as calcium antagonists and sympathetic beta-blockers are also antianginal agents. Some antihypertensive drugs and their side effects are listed in Table 5-16. Other

AT A GLANCE	Antianginal Drugs (Vasodilators)
Drug	**Effects**
Nitroglycerin (*Nitrol®*, *Nitrostat®*, *Nitrong®*)	Dilates veins in low doses. In high doses, it also dilates arterioles, so angina may get worse. It increases blood flow in the coronary arteries and thereby decreases angina and hypertension.
Isosorbide dinitrate (*Isordil®*)	Dilates vessels; it is orally active but less potent than nitroglycerin.
Nifedipine (*Procardia®*)	Relaxes arterioles; it is best for coronary artery spasm.
Verapamil (*Calan®*, *Isoptin®*)	Slows the heart rate; its effect is partially overcome by reflex tachycardia. This drug is also widely used to treat supraventricular arrhythmias.

Table 5-15

Drug	Side Effects
Thiazide and Thiazide-like Diuretics	
• Hydrochlorothiazide (*HydroDIURIL®*)	Hypokalemia, hyperuricemia, depression, slight hyperlipidemia
Sympathetic Blocking Drugs	
• Methyldopa (*Aldomet®*)	Positive Coombs' test, sedation
• Clonidine (*Catapres®*)	Dry mouth, sedation
• Propranolol (*Inderal®*)	Hypotension, palpitations, bradycardia
Angiotensin-Converting Enzyme (ACE) Inhibitors	
• Benazepril (*Lotensin®*)	Headache, dizziness, GI disturbances
• Captopril (*Capoten®*)	Leukocytopenia, tachycardia, hypotension
Calcium Antagonists	
• Diltiazem (*Cardizem®*)	Lethargy, arrhythmias, bradycardia, hypotension, photosensitivity
• Verapamil (*Calan®*)	Dizziness, hypotension, bradycardia
Vasodilator Drugs	
• Hydralazine (*Apresoline®*)	Nausea, vomiting, reflex tachycardia, rheumatoid arthritis, systemic lupus erythematosus
• Minoxidil (*Rogaine®*)	Myocardial ischemia, pericardial effusion, hirsutism (growth of hair)

Table 5-16

antihypertensive drugs, indications, and contraindications are summarized in Table 5-17.

Antiarrhythmic Drugs

Antiarrhythmic drug: An agent that prevents or alleviates cardiac arrhythmias. Some of these agents are useful in several types of cardiac diseases. There are four classes, which are listed in Table 5-18.

Anticoagulant Drugs

Anticoagulants: The two classes of anticoagulants used most frequently today are coumarin derivatives and heparin. They are employed to prevent venous thrombosis, especially pulmonary embolism. Anticoagulants such as heparin inhibit the function of clotting factors, and anticoagulants such as coumarin derivatives prevent the synthesis of normal clotting factors. They are used in the treatment of myocardial infarction, thrombophlebitis, and stroke. Heparin is the preferred drug to be given to pregnant women because it does not cross the placenta and affect the fetus. Examples: adeparin (*Normiflo®*), baltepatin (*Fragmin®*), and heparin.

Hypolipidemic Drugs

Hypolipidemic drug: Used as a dietary control and as a means to reduce cholesterol in the body. There are three main types of hypolipidemic drugs: bile acid sequestrants, HMG-CoA enzyme inhibitors, and drugs that alter lipid and lipoprotein metabolism. Examples: cholestyramine (*Questran®*), simastatin (*Zocor®*), and dextrothyroxine (*Choloxin®*).

Anti-Hypertensive Drugs and Their Indications and Contraindications

Drug	Indications	Contraindications
Beta-blockers	Angina pectoris, postmyocardial infarction	Diabetes, asthma, peripheral vascular disease
Diuretics	Congestive heart failure, chronic renal failure	Diabetes, hyperlipidemia
Calcium channel blockers	Angina, hypertension, supraventricular tachycardia	Congestive heart failure

Table 5-17

Antiarrhythmic Drugs

Drug	Mechanism of Action	Uses	Side Effects
Class 1 • Quinididine (*Cardioquin®*, *Quinidex®*)	Depresses the myocardium and the conduction system. Slows the heart rate.	Ventricular arrhythmias, supraventricular tachycardia	Nausea, vomiting, diarrhea, cinchonism due to drug sensitivity or an overdose, hypotension, fatigue
• Procainamide (*Procanbid®*)	Depresses the myocardium and the conduction system. Slows the heart rate.	Superventricular arrhythmias, supraventricular tachycardia	Nausea, vomiting, anorexia, skin rashes
• Lidocaine (*Xylocaine®*)	Suppresses ectopic foci but does not depress normal impulse conduction. Depresses automaticity.	Ventricular arrhythmias (especially from a myocardial infarction or from surgery); as a local anesthetic	Impaired liver function, convulsions due to stimulation of CNS
• Phenytoin (*Dilantin®*)	Appears to increase AV conduction and may eliminate AV blockage.	Ventricular arrhythmias induced by digitalis, epileptic seizure	Blurred vision, vertigo, nystagmus, hyperglycemia, gingival hyperplasia
Class 2 • Propranolol (*Inderal®*)	Beta-blocker. Depresses cardiac membranes. Slows the heart rate, decreases AV conduction, and prolongs the refractory period.	Supraventricular and ventricular tachycardia	Hypotension, bradycardia, possible cardiac arrest, skin rashes, mental confusion, visual disturbances
• Esmolol (*Brevibloc®*)	Selective beta-blocker.	Supraventricular and ventricular tachycardia	(With overdose): excessive bradycardia, delayed AV conduction, hypotension

Table 5-18

Drug	Mechanism of Action	Uses	Side Effects
Class 3			
• Amiodarone (*Cordarone®*)	Very potent local anesthetic. Blocks alpha-adrenergic, beta-adrenergic, and calcium receptors, and prolongs the refractory period.	Ventricular tachycardia	Corneal deposits, visual disturbances, dermatitis, skin discoloration, pulmonary fibrosis, liver dysfunction Contraindications: pregnancy, nursing
• Bretylium (*Bretylol®*)	Adrenergic neuronal blocker. Prolongs the refractory period of the ventricles	Ventricular tachycardia and ventricular fibrillation	GI disturbances, nausea, diarrhea, hypotension
Class 4			
• Verapamil (*Calan®*)	Affects pacemaker cells of the heart. Decreases SA node activity and AV node conduction.	Supraventricular tachycardia	Headache, dizziness, minor GI disturbances, constipation, hypotension

Table 5-18, continued

Pharmacology of the Respiratory System

Antihistamines

Histamine: A substance that creates a pharmacological reaction when it is released from an injured cell.

Antihistamine: A drug that counteracts the effects of histamine. Antihistamines are used to relieve the symptoms of allergic reactions such as hay fever and other allergic disorders of the nasal passages. Sometimes antihistamines are also useful in the relief of motion sickness. Others have a sedative and hypnotic action and may be used as tranquilizers. Examples: cetirizine (*Zyrtec®*), clemastine (*Tavist®*), dimenhydrinate (*Dramamine®*), fexofenadine (*Allegra®*), and loratadine (*Claritin®*).

Antiallergic Drugs

Antiallergic drug: Prevents mast cells from releasing histamine and other vasoactive substances.

Prophylactic drug: Prevents the onset of exposure-induced symptoms before the reactive process can take place. Cromolyn sodium is such an antiallergic agent.

Asthma Drugs

Asthma drugs: The drug of choice for asthma depends on the severity of the condition. See Table 5-19.

Pharmacology of the Digestive System

Healing ulcers: There are two primary mechanisms involved in medication therapy for ulcers: reduction of gastric acidity and enhancement of mucosal barrier defenses. Antihistaminics, prostaglandins, proton pump inhibitors, and anticholinergic drugs reduce the volume and concentration of gastric acid. These drugs are known as antisecretory drugs.

Antisecretory drugs: Inhibit the secretion of digestive enzymes, hormones, or acid. Examples: famotidine (*Pepcid®*) and cimetidine (*Tagamet®*).

Antacids: Neutralize the acid present in the digestive system. Antacids react with hydrochloric acid (HCl) to form water and salts. Examples: *Alka-Seltzer®*, *Maalox®*, and *Rolaids®*.

Laxatives and cathartics: Agents that stimulate defecation. Laxatives produce a mild, gentle stimulus for

Indication	Drug of Choice
Mild, intermittent symptoms	Metaproterenol (*Alupent*®), albuterol (*Proventil*®, *Ventolin*®), terbutaline (*Brethine*®)
More severe symptoms	Theophylline
Prophylaxis	Cromolyn
Chronic; *status asthmaticus*	Corticosteroids

Table 5-19

defecation, and cathartics produce a more intense action on the bowel. They act directly on the intestine to alter stool formation. These drugs are used to relieve constipation and to evacuate the intestine prior to surgery or diagnostic examination.

Pharmacology of the Urinary System

Diuretics: Help the body eliminate excess fluids through urinary excretion. They decrease the reabsorption of salts and water from the kidney tubules, which results in more urine production. Some also help to dilate blood vessels and sometimes are given along with antihypertensive drugs to reduce high blood pressure.

Organic Acid or Loop Diuretics

Furosemide (*Lasix*): A sulfonamide loop diuretic that prevents sodium and chloride ion transport in the loop of Henle, resulting in a greater loss of sodium, chloride, and water. Common uses: treatment of congestive heart failure, cirrhosis, nephrotic syndrome, and hypercalcemia. Side effects: ototoxicity, nephritis, gout, hypokalemia, and dehydration.

Thiazide and Thiazide-Like Diuretics

Hydrochlorothiazide (*Diucardin*®, *Esidrix*®, *Hydro-DIURIL*®): The most frequently prescribed diuretic because it is moderately potent and has relatively few side effects. It inhibits sodium transport in the distal portion of the nephron and increases chloride and potassium excretion. Common uses: treatment of hypertension, congestive heart failure, calcium stone formation, and diabetes insipidus. Side effects: hyponatremia, hypokalemic metabolic alkalosis, hyperglycemia, hyperlipidemia, hyperuricemia, and hypercalcemia.

Potassium-Sparing Diuretics

Potassium-sparing diuretics: Produce diuresis by blocking aldosterone receptors, thus inhibiting potassium secretion in the distal convoluted tubules. They do present a potential problem of hyperkalemia. Examples: spironolactone, triamterene, and amiloride. Common uses: treatment of hyperaldosteronism and K+ depletion. Side effects: hyperkalemia and gynecomastia.

Pharmacology of the Reproductive System

Use of Gonadal Hormones

Gonadal hormones: Sex hormones, produced by the ovaries in females and by the testes in males, which are under control of the anterior pituitary gland.
Androgen: Male sex hormone.
Estrogen and progesterone: Female sex hormones.
Common uses of female gonadal hormones: Hormone replacement therapy (HRT), oral contraception, fertility enhancement, treatment of breast cancers, and treatment after ovarectomy between ages 20 and 45 or at menopause. Hormone replacement therapy in females may cause some side effects. For side effects of gonadal hormone therapies, see Table 5-20.
Hormone replacement therapy: Required in children with hypogonadism, primary ovarian failure, or incomplete puberty with resulting inadequate bone growth. In adults, the need for replacement therapy arises from the removal of the ovaries or the cessation of ovarian activity at menopause. Estrogens are now also clinically indicated for the prevention and treatment of osteoporosis.
Oral contraceptives: Pills containing chemicals that are similar to natural estrogen and progesterone that prevent ovulation and thus prevent pregnancy. There

Sex Hormones and Their Side Effects	
Estrogens	**Progesterones**
Nausea	Weight gain
Vomiting	Depression
Breast tenderness	Hirsutism
Skin pigmentation	
Hypertension	
Breakthrough bleeding	

Table 5-20

are three main types: combined pill, phased pill, and mini pill.

Combined pill: Contains estrogen and progesterone in fixed doses.

Phased pill: Alternates pure estrogen and a combination of estrogen and progesterone.

Mini pill: Contains a fixed dose of progesterone only.

Morning-after pill: A contraceptive used after the fact. It contains only progesterone and is used as emergency contraception.

Side effects of oral contraceptives: Thromboemboli, benign adenoma of the liver, and vaginal cancers in daughters of a mother who received diethylstilbestrol (DES).

Spermicide: A foam, cream, jelly, or sponge that protects against pregnancy by killing the sperm.

Fertility drugs: Drugs that bring about ovulation. There are currently two types: one is synthetic and the other is a combination of three protein hormones extracted from human fluids. These drugs are prescribed for patients who desire to become pregnant but for some reason cannot ovulate or release an egg.

Cancer therapy: Certain cancers involving the breast, uterus, and prostate gland appear to be dependent on the presence of sex hormones. In some cases, the use of sex hormones seems to decrease tumor growth, whereas in others the removal of the ovaries or testes can produce beneficial results. Megestrol is specifically used in the treatment of breast cancer.

Androgens: Administered as replacement therapy to maintain male sex characteristics and organ function. Androgen replacement therapy is used for primary hypogonadism, hypogonadotropic hypogonadism, delayed puberty, and impotence that is the result of androgen deficiency. In women, androgens are used to treat metastatic inoperable breast cancer and postpartum breast engorgement.

Impotence

Sildenagil (*Viagra*®): An oral phosphodiesterase inhibitor indicated for erectile dysfunction in men. Common side effects: headache, flushing of the skin, upset stomach, nasal congestion, diarrhea, visual disturbances, and rash.

STRATEGIES TO SUCCESS

▶ *Test-Taking Skills*

Know where you're going!

After you register for the exam, find out where it's located and make sure that you can easily find your way there. On the day of the exam, leave early to account for any unforeseen problems and, if possible, try to arrive early. This approach will allow you to catch your breath and relax before the exam.

CHAPTER 5 REVIEW

Instructions:

Answer the following questions. Check your answers in the *Answer Key* that follows this section.

1. The study of natural drugs is called
   - A. Pharmacology
   - B. Toxicology
   - C. Posology
   - D. Pharmacognosy
   - E. Pharmacokinetics

2. The formula that explains the composition of the drug is known as its
   - A. Generic name
   - B. Chemical name
   - C. Trade name
   - D. Brand name
   - E. Biological name

3. Drugs with high abuse potential and no accepted medical use are classified in Schedule
   - A. I
   - B. II
   - C. III
   - D. IV
   - E. V

4. Which route is involved in administering a drug by placing it under the patient's tongue and leaving it there until it is dissolved?
   - A. Buccal route
   - B. Sublingual route
   - C. Subcutaneous route
   - D. Lozenge route
   - E. Transdermal route

5. The combined effect of two drugs that is less than the effect of either drug taken alone is called
   - A. Synergism
   - B. Dependence
   - C. Antagonism
   - D. Adverse effect
   - E. Idiosyncrasy

6. Which part of a prescription contains the patient's name, address, date, and the symbol *Rx*?
   - A. Inscription
   - B. Embossment
   - C. Subscription
   - D. Signature
   - E. Superscription

7. Which of the following is <u>not</u> a bacteriostatic antibiotic?
   - A. Sulfonamide
   - B. Tetracycline
   - C. Penicillin
   - D. Chloramphenicol
   - E. Clindamycin

8. Which of the following is a main use of rifampin?
   - A. Treatment of tuberculosis
   - B. Prevention of meningococci outbreaks
   - C. Elimination of type B influenzas
   - D. Both A and B
   - E. All of the above

9. Which of the following is a sedative?
   - A. Phenothiazine
   - B. Barbiturate
   - C. Monoamine oxidase inhibitor
   - D. Lithium
   - E. Levodopa

10. Which of the following is <u>not</u> an adrenergic drug?
    - A. Epinephrine
    - B. Isoproterenol
    - C. Dopamine
    - D. Norepinephrine
    - E. Neostigmine

11. Estrogen is often prescribed to treat
    - A. Osteoporosis
    - B. Menopause
    - C. Ovarian failure
    - D. Both A and B
    - E. All of the above

12. *Cytomel®* is a type of
    A. Insulin
    B. Antidepressant
    C. Thyroid agent
    D. Cardiac glycoside
    E. Narcotic analgesic

13. Codeine is an example of what kind of drug?
    A. Antidepressant
    B. Narcotic analgesic
    C. Sedative
    D. Nonnarcotic analgesic
    E. Antiepileptic drug

14. A chemical substance that interferes with the development of bacterial organisms is
    A. Antiinflammatory
    B. Antiviral
    C. Antisecretory
    D. Antiepileptic
    E. Antibiotic

15. Cefazolin is a type of
    A. Penicillin
    B. Cephalosporin
    C. Quinolone
    D. Aminoglycoside
    E. Vasodilator

16. A controlled drug inventory must be completed every
    A. 1 year
    B. 4 years
    C. 3 years
    D. 2 years
    E. 6 months

17. A solution of water, sugar, and a drug is called
    A. Emulsion
    B. Elixir
    C. Ointment
    D. Syrup
    E. Liniment

18. The amount of time required for 50% of a drug to be eliminated from the body is called
    A. Half-life
    B. Effective dose 50 (ED_{50})
    C. Lethal dose 50 (LD_{50})
    D. Dosage
    E. Half dosage

19. A drug that induces birth defects is known as a(n)
    A. Allergic reaction
    B. Prophylactic
    C. Teratogen
    D. Idiosyncrasy
    E. Palliative

20. In the *Physicians' Desk Reference,* the index of brand names and generic names for drugs is found in which section?
    A. White
    B. Blue
    C. Pink
    D. All of the above
    E. None of the above

21. Amantadine is classified as
    A. Antiviral
    B. Antibiotic
    C. Antiinflammatory
    D. Antiepileptic
    E. Antifungal

22. A medical assistant might be required to collect information about a patient's
    A. Alcohol and recreational drug use
    B. Herbal medicines
    C. Allergies
    D. All of the above
    E. None of the above

23. Heroin is an example of a drug from which schedule?
    A. Schedule II
    B. Schedule I
    C. Schedule IV
    D. Schedule V
    E. Schedule III

24. Pentobarbital is a type of
    A. Antidepressant
    B. Hypolipidemic
    C. Anabolic steroid
    D. Nonbarbiturate
    E. Barbiturate

25. What drug is prescribed for the treatment of manic episodes?
    A. Idoxuridine
    B. Lithium
    C. Baclofen
    D. Zolpidem
    E. Ampicillin

26. Drugs that increase urine secretion are
    A. Laxatives
    B. Diuretics
    C. Hypolipidemics
    D. Cromolyns
    E. Uremics

27. Epinephrine is a(n)
    A. Adrenergic
    B. Adrenergic blocker
    C. Cholinergic
    D. Cholinergic blocker
    E. None of the above

28. Fluoxetine is a type of
    A. Antipsychotic
    B. Antihypertensive
    C. Analgesic
    D. Antidepressant
    E. Hypolipidemic

29. *Depakene*® is a type of
    A. Antipsychotic
    B. Antidepressant
    C. Antiepileptic
    D. Antibiotic
    E. Antivenereal

30. Butenafine is prescribed to treat
    A. Depression
    B. Constipation
    C. Osteoporosis
    D. Athlete's foot
    E. Obesity

31. Lidocaine is a type of
    A. Antibiotic
    B. Antiarrhythmic
    C. Diuretic
    D. Anesthetic
    E. Antihypnotic

32. Cromolyn is used to treat
    A. Asthma
    B. Allergies
    C. Viral infections
    D. Tuberculosis
    E. Pneumonia

33. Furosemide is prescribed for
    A. Congestive heart failure
    B. Nephrotic syndrome
    C. Hypercalcemia
    D. Both B and C
    E. All of the above

34. The main body part involved in the metabolism of drugs is the
    A. Stomach
    B. Kidney
    C. Small intestine
    D. Large intestine
    E. Liver

35. A substance that is released from an injured cell is called a(n)
    A. Antihistamine
    B. Histamine
    C. Antibiotic
    D. Anticoagulant
    E. Ampule

36. Which of the following is a mechanism involved in healing ulcers?

   A. Reduction of gastric acidity
   B. Enhancement of mucosal defenses
   C. Increase of gastric acidity
   D. Both A and B
   E. None of the above

37. The combined contraceptive pill contains

   A. Estrogen only
   B. Progesterone only
   C. Both estrogen and progesterone
   D. Progesterone and testosterone
   E. None of the above

38. Which of the following drug types is used to reduce cholesterol?

   A. Hypolipidemic
   B. Anticoagulant
   C. Antiarrhythmic
   D. Cholinergic
   E. Antisecretory

ANSWER KEY

1.	D	20.	C
2.	B	21.	A
3.	A	22.	D
4.	B	23.	B
5.	C	24.	E
6.	E	25.	B
7.	C	26.	B
8.	D	27.	A
9.	B	28.	D
10.	E	29.	C
11.	E	30.	D
12.	C	31.	B
13.	B	32.	A
14.	E	33.	E
15.	B	34.	E
16.	D	35.	B
17.	D	36.	D
18.	A	37.	C
19.	C	38.	A

Nutrition

CHAPTER OUTLINE

AREAS OF COMPETENCE

AAMA—ROLE DELINEATION STUDY AREAS OF COMPETENCE

General (Transdisciplinary)

Communication Skills

- Treat all patients with compassion and empathy
- Recognize and respect cultural diversity
- Adapt communications to individual's ability to understand
- Use medical terminology appropriately

(Chart continued on next page.)

Instruction
- Teach methods of health promotion and disease prevention

AMT—RMA CERTIFICATION EXAM TOPICS

Anatomy and Physiology
- Disorders of the body

Medical Terminology
- Definitions
- Spelling

Patient Education
- Patient instruction

STRATEGIES TO SUCCESS

▶ Study Skills

Practice!

As part of your studies, take a number of practice exams and practice answering questions before the real exam. Use these practice exams to help determine your strengths and weaknesses. When you get a question wrong, go back and review the material that you don't understand.

Nutrition

Nutrients: Chemical substances that are necessary for growth, normal functioning, and maintaining life. These substances cannot be synthesized by the body and must be supplied by food. There are six basic groups of nutrients: carbohydrates, fats, proteins, vitamins, minerals, and water. Of these, only carbohydrates, fats, and proteins contain calories that provide the body with energy.

Nourish: To supply the essential food for maintaining life.

Nutritious: Containing substantial amounts of essential nutrients.

Nutritional value: The nutrient content of foods or beverages.

Nutritional status: An individual's physical condition as determined by diet.

Overweight: Having a body weight that is 10 percent greater than the standard for the person's age, height, and body type.

Obesity: Excessive accumulation of fat in the body. Also, weight 20 percent higher than that considered desirable for the person's age, height, and bone structure.

Skinfold test: A procedure that determines fat as a percentage of body weight, in which the thickness of a fold of skin measured with a caliper indicates the total percentage of fat. See Figure 6-1.

Malnutrition: Poor nutrition caused by poor diet or by poor utilization of food that may result from an unbalanced, insufficient, or excessive diet.

Metabolism: The use of food as fuel, resulting in the generation of energy and growth, and the elimination of waste.

Kilocalorie (Kcal): Commonly known as a calorie and also referred to as a "large calorie," which is equivalent to 1000 "small calories." One kilocalorie is the amount of energy needed to raise the temperature of 1 kg of water by 1°C. Calories measure the amount of energy a food produces in the body.

Energy value: Also called caloric density, the number of calories in food. Energy value is determined by the types and amounts of nutrients each food contains.

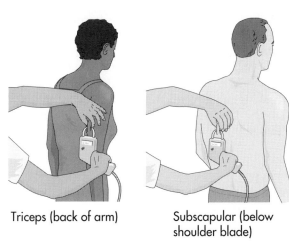

Triceps (back of arm)

Subscapular (below shoulder blade)

Suprailiac (above hipbone)

Thigh (front)

Figure 6-1. *To estimate an individual's body fat percentage, a professional uses a tool called a caliper to measure the thickness of a fold of skin at one or more points on the body.*

Water

Water: Has no caloric value, contributes about 65% of an individual's body weight, helps maintain fluid balance, dissolves chemicals and nutrients, transports nutrients, lubricates, aids in digestion, flushes out wastes, and regulates body temperature through perspiration.

Amount of water in human cells: Water is the largest single component of the body. Metabolically active cells of the muscle and viscera have the highest concentration, and calcified tissue cells the lowest. Total body water is higher in athletes than in nonathletes and decreases significantly with age because of diminished muscle mass.

Amount of water needed: On average, people should drink 6 to 8 glasses (48 to 64 ounces, or 3 to 4 pints) of water a day to maintain a healthy water balance.

Thirst: Water intake is controlled mainly by thirst. Thirst control centers are located in the hypothalamus.

Absorption of water: Water is ingested as fluid and also as part of ingested food. Water is absorbed rapidly because it moves freely through membranes, mainly by diffusion.

Water loss: Water loss normally occurs through the kidneys in urine, through the gastrointestinal tract in the feces, through the lungs in expired air and through the skin in sweat that evaporates from the skin. The amount of water taken in daily is approximately equivalent to the amount lost.

Effects of water loss: The loss of 20% of body water may cause death, and the loss of only 10% causes severe disorders. In moderate weather, adults can live up to 10 days without water; children can live up to 5 days. By contrast, it is possible to survive without food for several weeks.

Dehydration: Excessive loss of body water that usually is accompanied by electrolyte balance changes.

Water intoxication: The presence of excess water that causes cells, particularly brain cells, to swell, leading to headache, nausea, vomiting, convulsion, and death. Water intoxication may result from the excessive administration of water when the antidiuretic hormone and the kidney cannot respond, such as after surgery, trauma, or another condition that causes salt and water loss.

Carbohydrates

Carbohydrate: The body's primary source of energy. They provide heat, help metabolize fat, and help reserve protein for uses other than supplying energy. One gram of carbohydrate yields 4 calories. Excess carbohydrates are stored in the liver and muscles as glycogen. According to the current dietary recommendations, carbohydrates should provide 55% to 60% of an individual's total calorie intake. Carbohydrates are classified according to their complexity, from simple sugars to complex saccharides. Fruits, vegetables, pasta, cereal, potatoes, and sugary foods are good sources of carbohydrates.

Starch: A complex carbohydrate that is a major source of energy from plant foods.

Dietary fiber: A nondigestible carbohydrate found in plant cells. It provides bulk and stimulation for the intestines. The main dietary fiber components are cellulose, pectin, lignin, and gums. Some forms are soluble in water; others are not. Dietary fiber is used to treat and prevent constipation, hemorrhoids, diverticular disease, and irritable bowel syndrome. Studies have linked it to reduced levels of blood cholesterol, reduced formation of gallstones, and control of diabetes. Sources of dietary fiber: oats, dry beans, barley, some fruits and vegetables, whole wheat bread, and brown rice.

Lipids

Fats: Also called lipids, fats are not soluble in water but are soluble in some solvents such as alcohol. They provide energy and heat, carry fat-soluble vitamins, protect and support organs and bones, insulate from cold, and supply essential fatty acids. Each gram of fat provides 9 calories. Fats are classified as saturated or unsaturated; unsaturated fats are either monounsaturated or polyunsaturated.

Saturated fats: Generally derived from animal sources and usually solid at room temperature. Found in meat, butter, egg yolks, whole milk, and coconut and palm oil, they tend to raise blood cholesterol levels.

Unsaturated fats: Usually liquid at room temperature, they can be monounsaturated or polyunsaturated. They tend to lower blood cholesterol levels.

Monounsaturated fats: Examples include oil from olives, avocados, or cashew nuts.

Polyunsaturated fats: Examples include cooking oils made from sunflower seeds, peanuts, or safflower seeds.

Ketones: Chemical substances that are broken down by fatty acids in the liver.

Ketosis: The abnormal collection of ketones in the blood as a result of excessive breakdown of fats caused by an insufficiency of glucose available for energy.

Cholesterol: A waxy lipid found almost exclusively in foods of animal origin and continuously synthesized in the body. Produced by the liver, cholesterol is essential for the production of vitamin D and bile acid. Because the body produces cholesterol, it is not essential in the diet. Cholesterol is measured by means of a blood test. See Table 6-1.

High-density lipoprotein (HDL): Called "good" cholesterol. It helps transport cholesterol to the liver where it is disposed. It may serve to stabilize very low-density lipoprotein.

Low-density lipoprotein (LDL): Called "bad" cholesterol. A high concentration may result in atherosclerosis and thus puts patients at risk of heart disease.

Cholesterolemia: The presence of an excessive amount of cholesterol in the blood. To reduce cholesterol level, individuals should reduce fat consumption to less than 30 percent of total caloric intake, with saturated fats providing less than 10 percent of caloric intake, and should increase consumption of soluble fiber.

Triglyceride: One of several combinations of fatty acids and glycerol that circulate in the blood with HDL and LDL. High levels are associated with atherosclerosis.

Protein

Protein: The primary function of protein is to build and repair body tissues. It is the only substance that can make new cells and rebuild tissue. Proteins are also important components of hormones and enzymes. They maintain fluid balance, are essential for the development of antibodies, and can provide energy. Each gram of protein provides 4 calories of energy. Proteins are not as efficient as carbohydrates and fats in providing energy.

Amino acids: Nitrogen-containing compounds that make up proteins, they are also called the building blocks of protein.

Classification of amino acids: There are about 80 amino acids, of which 20 are necessary for human metabolism and growth. The adult body does not produce 9 of them, which must be provided in the diet and are known as essential amino acids. See Table 6-2 for a list of the essential and nonessential amino acids.

AT A GLANCE	Common Nutrition-Related Blood Tests
Test	**Normal Range in Adults**
Cholesterol	Total: 150–200 mg/dl HDL: 25–90 mg/dl LDL: 85–200 mg/dl
Glucose	90–120 mg/dl
Iron	50–175 µg/dl
Triglycerides	200–300 mg/dl

Table 6-1

AT A GLANCE	Amino Acids
Essential	**Nonessential**
Arginine (in young children)	Alanine
Histidine	Arginine (in adults)
Isoleucine	Asparagine
Leucine	Aspartic acid
Lysine	Cysteine
Methionine	Glutamic acid
Phenylalanine	Glutamine
Threonine	Glycine
Tryptophan	Proline
Valine	Serine
	Tyrosine

Table 6-2

Complete protein: A protein that contains all the essential amino acids and consequently is of high biological value. Casein (milk protein) and egg whites are examples of complete proteins.

Sources of protein: Meat, fish, poultry, eggs, and milk, which are complete proteins; and nuts, dry beans, grains, and vegetables, which are incomplete proteins.

Adequate protein intake: Learning to combine foods containing incomplete proteins in order to obtain all 9 essential amino acids is especially important for people who follow vegetarian diets.

Vitamins

Vitamin: An organic compound that does not provide energy but helps in the metabolism of protein, carbohydrates, and fat. Vitamins act as catalysts and body regulators for the bones, skins, glands, nerves, brain, and blood, and they protect against diseases caused by nutritional deficiencies. With a few exceptions, vitamins cannot be produced by the body and must be supplied in the diet. Although they are essential, they should not be overused. There are two types of vitamins: water-soluble and fat-soluble. See Table 6-3.

Water-Soluble Vitamins

Vitamin B_1 (thiamine): Plays a role in carbohydrate metabolism and is essential for normal metabolism of the nervous system, heart, and muscles. Thiamine also promotes good appetite. It is not stored in the body and must be supplied daily. Sources: lean pork, wheat germ, lean meat, egg yolk, and fish. Deficiency causes loss of appetite, irritability, tiredness, sleep disturbance, nervous disorders, beriberi, loss of coordination, paralysis, and Wernicke-Korsakoff syndrome in people severely dependent on alcohol. Deficiency is often associated with alcoholism.

Vitamin B_2 (riboflavin): Essential for certain enzyme systems in the metabolism of fats and proteins. It can be sensitive to light. Sources: milk, cheddar cheese, cottage cheese, organ meats, and eggs. Deficiency causes impaired growth, weakness, lip sores and cracks at the corners of the mouth, cheilosis, photophobia, cataracts, anemia, and glossitis.

Vitamin B_3 (niacin): Part of two enzymes that regulate energy metabolism. Also called nicotinic acid and nicotinamide, it maintains the health of the skin, tongue, and digestive system. Sources: lean meats, poultry, fish, and peanuts. Deficiency causes pellagra, gastrointestinal disturbance, and mental disturbances.

Vitamin B_6 (pyridoxine): Aids enzymes in the synthesis of amino acids and is essential for proper growth and maintenance of body functions. Sources: yeast, wheat germ, pork, bananas, and oatmeal. Deficiency causes anemia, neuritis, anorexia, nausea, depressed immunity, and dermatitis.

Vitamin B_9 (folic acid): Essential for cell growth and the reproduction of red blood cells. Also called folacin, it functions in the formation of hemoglobin and aids in metabolism of protein. It is also essential for fetal development, particularly of the neural tube. Sources: liver, kidney beans, lima beans, and fresh dark green leafy vegetables. Deficiency causes anemia and may cause spina bifida in a fetus.

Vitamin B_{12} (cyanocobalamin): Aids in hemoglobin synthesis, is essential for normal functioning of all cells, and is important in energy metabolism. Sources: liver, kidney, milk, eggs, fish, and cheese. Deficiency causes pernicious anemia and neurological disorders.

Pantothenic acid: A part of the vitamin B complex that is essential for fatty acid metabolism, the

AT A GLANCE	Classification of VItamins
Water-Soluble Vitamins	**Fat-Soluble Vitamins**

Vitamin B complex:
    Thiamine (vitamin B_1)
    Riboflavin (vitamin B_2)
    Niacin (vitamin B_3)
    Pyridoxine (vitamin B_6)
    Folic acid (vitamin B_9)
    Cyanocobalamin (vitamin B_{12})
    Pantothenic acid
    Biotin (formerly vitamin H)
 	
 Vitamin C
	Vitamin A
	
	 Vitamin D
	
	 Vitamin E
	
	 Vitamin K

Table 6-3

manufacture of sex hormones, the utilization of other vitamins, the functioning of the nervous system and the adrenal glands, and normal growth and development. Sources: egg yolks, kidney, liver, and yeast. Deficiency causes fatigue, headaches, nausea, abdominal pain, numbness, tingling, muscle cramps, and susceptibility to respiratory infections and peptic ulcers.

Biotin (formerly vitamin H): A water-soluble B-complex vitamin essential for the breakdown of fatty acids and carbohydrates and for the excretion of the waste products of protein breakdown. Good sources: kidney, liver, egg yolks, soybeans, and yeast.

Vitamin C: Also called ascorbic acid, it protects the body against infections and helps heal wounds. Best sources: fruits and vegetables, especially citrus fruits and tomatoes. Deficiency causes scurvy, lowered resistance to infections, joint tenderness, dental caries, bleeding gums, delayed wound healing, bruising, hemorrhage, and anemia. Vitamin C is lost in cooking fresh foods but not in cooking frozen foods.

Fat-Soluble Vitamins

Vitamin A (retinol, carotene): Contributes to the maintenance of epithelial cells and mucous membranes and is important for night vision. Retinol is also necessary for normal growth, development, and reproduction as well as an adequate immune response. Sources: liver, beef, sweet potato, spinach, milk, and egg yolks. Deficiency causes retarded growth, susceptibility to infection, dry skin, night blindness, xeropthalmia, abnormal gastrointestinal function, dry mucous membranes, and degeneration of the spinal cord and peripheral nerves.

Vitamin D: Essential for the normal formation of bones and teeth. It aids in the reabsorption of calcium and phosphorus and regulates blood levels of calcium. There are two major forms of vitamin D: vitamin D_2, formed in plants, and vitamin D_3, formed in humans from cholesterol in the skin exposed to sunlight or other ultraviolet radiation. Best sources: butter, cream, egg yolks, liver, and fish liver oils. Deficiency causes rickets and osteomalacia.

Vitamin E: An antioxidant, also called tocopherol. It prevents oxidative destruction of vitamin A in the intestine, and it is essential for normal reproduction, muscle development, and resistance of red blood cells to hemolysis. Vitamin E also helps maintain normal cell membranes. Sources: seed oil, fruits, vegetables, and animal fats.

Vitamin K: Essential to blood clotting. There are several fat-soluble compounds of vitamin K. Vitamin K_2 is synthesized in the intestine by bacteria and is also found in animal foods. Vitamin K is found in large amounts in green leafy vegetables (especially broccoli, cabbage, and lettuce) and in fruits. Vitamin K can be used as an antidote for an overdose of an anticoagulant. Deficiency causes hemorrhage.

Conditions Associated with Vitamins

Avitaminosis: Deficiency of vitamins in the diet that causes a disease such as scurvy, rickets, or beriberi. See Table 6-4 for symptoms and diseases caused by vitamin deficiency.

Hypervitaminosis: A condition caused by an overdose of vitamins, especially fat-soluble vitamins. The main symptoms are loss of hair, severe itching, skin lesions, and abnormal tissue growth.

Excessive intake of vitamin A: Can result in a condition called hypervitaminosis A, the symptoms of which include headache, tiredness, nausea, loss of appetite, diarrhea, dry and itchy skin, hair loss, a yellow discoloration, and irregular menstrual periods. Excessive intake during pregnancy may cause birth defects.

Excessive intake of vitamin B_6: May cause neuritis.

Minerals

Minerals: Natural, inorganic substances that the body needs to help build and maintain body tissues and to carry on life functions. There are two separate classes of minerals: major minerals and trace elements. Diseases and symptoms associated with mineral deficiencies are listed in Table 6-5. Deficiencies of calcium, iron, and iodine are the three most common mineral deficiencies.

Electrolytes: Compounds, particularly salts, that break up into their separate component particles in water. The particles are called ions, which are electrically charged atoms. Sodium, potassium, and chloride are commonly called electrolytes. Minerals help keep the body's water and electrolytes in balance.

Major Minerals

Calcium (Ca): The body requires calcium for the transmission of nerve impulses, muscle contraction, blood coagulation, and cardiac functions. Calcium also helps build strong bones and teeth and may prevent hypertension. Normal daily requirement: 800–1200 mg. The following factors enhance the absorption of calcium: adequate vitamin D, large quantities of calcium and phosphorus in diet, and the presence of lactose. A lack of physical activity reduces the amount of calcium absorption.

Vitamin	Symptoms and Diseases
Vitamin A	Retarded growth, susceptibility to infection, dry skin, night blindness, xeropthalmia, abnormal gastrointestinal function, dry mucous membranes, degeneration of the spinal cord and peripheral nerves
Vitamin B_1	Loss of appetite, irritability, tiredness, nervous disorders, sleep disturbance, beriberi, loss of coordination, paralysis, and Wernicke-Korsakoff syndrome
Vitamin B_2	Impaired growth, weakness, lip sores and cracks at the corners of the mouth, cheilosis, photophobia, cataracts, anemia, and glossitis (Riboflavin deficiency is believed to be the most common vitamin deficiency in the United States.)
Vitamin B_3	Pellagra, characterized by dermatitis, diarrhea, dementia, and death; gastrointestinal and mental disturbances
Vitamin B_6	Anemia, neuritis, anorexia, nausea, depressed immunity, dermatitis
Viramin B_9 (folic acid)	Anemia, spina bifida in fetal development
Vitamin B_{12}	Pernicious anemia, neurological disorders
Pantothenic acid	Fatigue, headaches, nausea, abdominal pain, numbness, tingling, muscle cramps, susceptibility to respiratory infections and peptic ulcers
Vitamin C	Scurvy, characterized by gingivitis, loose teeth, and slow healing of wounds; lowered resistance to infections; joint tenderness; dental caries; bleeding gums; delayed wound healing; bruising; hemorrhage; and anemia
Vitamin D	Rickets and osteomalacia
Vitamin K	Hemorrhage (Extensive oral antibiotic therapy may cause vitamin K_2 deficiency.)

Table 6-4

Phosphorus (P): Essential for the metabolism of protein, calcium, and glucose. It helps to build strong bones and teeth and aids in maintaining the body's acid-base balance. Phosphorus is found in dairy foods, animal foods, fish, cereals, nuts, and legumes.

Chloride (Cl): Involved in the maintenance of fluid and the body's acid-base balance. Disturbances in the acid-base balance can result in possible growth retardation and memory loss.

Sodium (Na): Plays a key role in the maintenance of the body's acid-base balance. It transmits nerve impulses and helps control muscle contractions. Toxic levels may cause hypertension and renal disease. The kidney is the chief regulator of sodium levels in body fluids.

Potassium (K): Important in protein synthesis, correction of imbalance in acid-base metabolism, and glycogen formation. It transmits nerve impulses and helps control them. It also promotes regular heartbeat and is needed for enzyme reactions.

Magnesium (Mg): Helps build strong bones and teeth and activates many enzymes. It helps regulate heartbeat and is essential for metabolism and many enzyme activities. It is stored in bone and is excreted mainly by the kidneys.

Mineral	Symptoms and Diseases
Calcium	Rickets, osteomalacia (adult rickets), tetany, osteoporosis
Copper	Anemia, bone disease (Copper deficiency is very rare in adults.)
Fluoride	Tooth decay, possibly osteoporosis
Iodine	Goiter, cretinism (congenital myxedema) (Goiter is more common among women. A thyroid gland dysfunction can cause acquired myxedema, commonly known as hypothyroidism, in adults.)
Iron	Iron-deficiency anemia, nutritional anemia
Phosphorus	Weight loss, anemia, anorexia, fatigue, abnormal growth, bone demineralization (mineral loss)
Potassium	Impaired growth, hypertension, bone fragility, renal hypertrophy, bradycardia, death
Zinc	Dwarfism, delayed growth, hypogonadism, anemia, decreased appetite

Table 6-5

Trace Elements

Iodine (I): A component of the thyroid hormone thyroxine. Iodine is also used as a contrast medium for blood vessels in CT scans.

Zinc (Zn): Essential for several enzymes, growth, glucose tolerance, wound healing, and taste acuity. Best sources: protein foods.

Iron (Fe): A component of hemoglobin and myoglobin. The major role of iron is to deliver oxygen to the body tissues.

Ferrous sulfate (*Feosol*): The most inexpensive and most commonly used form of iron supplement.

Iron dextran (*Imferon*): An injectable form of iron supplement.

Hemochromatosis: Excessive absorption of iron.

Copper (Cu): Most concentrated in the liver, heart, brain, and kidneys. It is essential for several important enzymes and for good health. It aids in the formation of hemoglobin. Copper helps in the transportation of iron to bone marrow.

Wilson's disease: A hereditary disease that causes copper accumulation in various organs and can result in degeneration of the brain, cirrhosis of the liver, psychic disturbances, and progressive weakness.

Fluoride: Increases resistance to tooth decay. It protects against osteoporosis and periodontal (gum) disease. Excessive amounts of fluoride in drinking water may cause the discoloration of teeth.

Nutrition and Diet Needs

Dietary guidelines: Developed by the U.S. Department of Agriculture and the U.S. Department of Health and Human Services, recommendations to encourage people to eat a balanced diet. Table 6-6 lists the guidelines.

Food pyramid: A diagram introduced by the U.S. Department of Agriculture to show the quantities of food people should consume daily from each of the basic food groups. See Figure 6-2.

Therapeutic nutrition: Also referred to as medical nutrition therapy or a therapeutic diet. It may be necessary in order to maintain or improve nutritional status; to correct nutritional deficiencies; to maintain, decrease, or increase body weight; or to eliminate particular foods that may cause allergies.

Nutrition during pregnancy: The protein requirement is increased by 20 percent for pregnant women. An increase is also recommended in calcium, iron, and folic acid intake. The average energy allowance during the first trimester is 2200 Kcal per day. Lactating women during the first 6 months need 2700 Kcal per day. Doctors recommend that pregnant women gain from 24 to 35 pounds during their pregnancy.

Breastfeeding: The mother's milk provides the infant with temporary immunity to many infectious diseases. It is free from germs and is easy to digest. It usually

Eat a variety of foods to get the energy, protein, vitamins, minerals, and fiber you need for good health.

Balance the food you eat with physical activity.

Choose a diet with plenty of grain products, vegetables, and fruits.

Choose a diet low in fat, saturated fat, and cholesterol.

Choose a diet moderate in sugars.

Choose a diet moderate in salt and sodium.

If you drink alcoholic beverages, do so in moderation.

Table 6-6

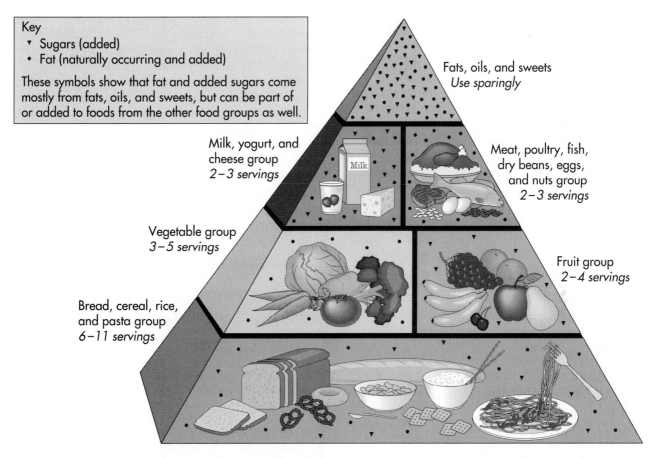

Key
- ▼ Sugars (added)
- • Fat (naturally occurring and added)

These symbols show that fat and added sugars come mostly from fats, oils, and sweets, but can be part of or added to foods from the other food groups as well.

Fats, oils, and sweets
Use sparingly

Milk, yogurt, and cheese group
2–3 servings

Meat, poultry, fish, dry beans, eggs, and nuts group
2–3 servings

Vegetable group
3–5 servings

Fruit group
2–4 servings

Bread, cereal, rice, and pasta group
6–11 servings

Figure 6-2. *The U.S. Department of Agriculture's Food Guide Pyramid can be used to plan a nutritious, well-balanced diet.*

does not cause allergic reactions. Breastfeeding also stimulates an emotional bond between mother and infant.

Mechanical soft diet: Consists of soft but otherwise normal foods. It is used by individuals who have difficulty chewing because of a lack of dentures or teeth, inflammation of the oral cavity, or severe dental decay that may cause pain in chewing.

Liquid diet: Used by individuals who cannot tolerate solid foods or by patients whose gastrointestinal tract must be free of solid foods. The diet consists of tea, coffee, cream soups, fruit juices, clear broths, and eggnog.

Tube feeding: Used for patients with indications such as esophageal obstruction, burns, gastric surgery, or anorexia nervosa.

Bland diet: A diet that is nonirritating to the gastrointestinal tract. It is often prescribed in the treatment of peptic ulcer, ulcerative colitis, gallbladder disease, diverticulitis, and gastritis. This diet consists of milk, cream, mashed potatoes, and hot cereal.

High-fiber diet: May be prescribed for atonic constipation, diverticulosis, therapy of gastric ulcers, cancer of the colon, hypercholesterolemia, diabetes, or obesity.

Diabetic diet: A diet prescribed in the treatment of diabetes mellitus. It usually contains limited amounts of simple sugars and increased amounts of proteins, complex carbohydrates, and unsaturated fats. This diet is carefully calculated for each patient to minimize the occurrence of hyperglycemia and hypoglycemia, to maintain body weight, and to promote good health.

Dumping syndrome diet: Used for patients who have had a partial gastrectomy or gastric bypass surgery. This diet is low in concentrated sweets and limits fluids at mealtimes to avoid dumping the stomach contents into the small intestine, which results in diarrhea.

Restricted-fat diet: Used for patients with diseases of the liver, gallbladder, and pancreas. Generally 40 to 50 grams of fat per day is an adequate and realistic restriction.

Low-cholesterol diet: Often recommended for patients with elevated blood cholesterol levels, those with atherosclerosis, and those with elevated triglycerides and low HDL-cholesterol.

High-fat diet: This diet may be indicated for purposes of weight gain. Ideally, the fat should be monounsaturated. The maximum fat intake is generally 35 to 40 percent of kilocalories.

Restricted-sodium diet: This type of diet is very common for patients with hypertension, renal disease with edema, congestive heart failure, and cirrhosis of the liver with ascites.

Increased-sodium diet: May be useful in treating Addison's disease.

Restricted-potassium diet: May be necessary for patients with renal disease.

Increased-potassium diet: Used for patients who are on diuretics.

High-iron diet: A diet to treat iron-deficiency anemia.

High-calcium and high-phosphorus diets: An increase in calcium and phosphorus intake is desirable in a patient with rickets, osteomalacia, tetany, dental caries, or acute lead poisoning.

Restricted-copper diet: A diet to treat Wilson's disease, oliguria, and anuria.

Food-Related Diseases

Food poisoning: Usually caused by human ignorance or carelessness. Food is generally contaminated with harmful microorganisms or chemical poisons. The most common food illnesses are caused by *Salmonella* bacteria, *Clostridium perfringens*, *Staphylococcus aureus*, botulism, trichinosis, and protozoa.

Trichinosis: Infestation with the parasitic roundworm *Trichinella spiralis*. It is transmitted by eating raw or undercooked pork from infected pigs.

Botulism: Caused by the toxin produced by the spores of the *Clostridium botulinum* bacterium. It is the most deadly of all food poisonings. Home-canned foods are generally the source of botulism. It is characterized by fatigue and muscle weakness, visual disturbances, and dysphagia. The antitoxin must be administered as soon as possible.

Food allergies: Usually develop as a reaction to proteins. Allergies to specific substances are not inherited, but the tendency to develop allergies is inherited. Allergic individuals seem most prone to allergic reactions during periods of stress.

Anorexia nervosa: An eating disorder in which people starve themselves because they fear that otherwise they will become grossly overweight. It is most common among women in their teens and early 20s.

Bulimia: An eating disorder in which people eat a large amount of food in a short time, then attempt to counter the effects by self-induced vomiting, the use of laxatives or diuretics, and/or excessive exercise.

Binge eating: Eating a large amount of food in a short time without subsequent purging.

CHAPTER 6 REVIEW

Instructions:

Answer the following questions. Check your answers in the *Answer Key* that follows this section.

1. In obesity, body weight exceeds normal by at least
   A. 10 percent
   B. 20 percent
   C. 30 percent
   D. 40 percent
   E. 50 percent

2. Which of the following nutrients are the body's primary source of energy?
   A. Proteins
   B. Vitamins
   C. Amino acids
   D. Fats
   E. Carbohydrates

3. Phosphorus is essential for the metabolism of all of the following except
   A. Calcium
   B. Glucose
   C. Protein
   D. Cholesterol
   E. Bones

4. One gram of carbohydrate yields
   A. 4 kilocalories
   B. 6 kilocalories
   C. 8 kilocalories
   D. 9 kilocalories
   E. 10 kilocalories

5. Botulism
   A. Is a food allergy
   B. Is a symptom of anorexia nervosa
   C. Can be treated with a restricted-potassium diet
   D. Is caused by a roundworm
   E. Is a form of food poisoning often caused by poorly canned foods

6. Which of the following is called "good" cholesterol?
   A. HDL
   B. LDL
   C. VLDL
   D. Triglycerides
   E. None of the above

7. How many amino acids are essential to include in a person's diet because they cannot be produced by the adult human body?
   A. 9
   B. 11
   C. 20
   D. 22
   E. 30

8. Olive oil is an example of a
   A. Polyunsaturated fat
   B. Protein
   C. Saturated fat
   D. Vitamin
   E. Monounsaturated fat

9. Potassium deficiency may cause all of the following except
   A. Bradycardia
   B. Hypertension
   C. Hypothyroidism
   D. Bone fragility
   E. Impaired growth

10. The best source of vitamin C (ascorbic acid) is
    A. Liver
    B. Fruits
    C. Sweet potato
    D. Egg yolk
    E. Lettuce

11. Zinc deficiency may result in all of the following except
    A. Dwarfism
    B. Delayed growth
    C. Hypogonadism
    D. Anemia
    E. Acromegaly

12. A deficiency of which of the following vitamins may result in pernicious anemia?

A. Vitamin B_2
B. Vitamin B_3
C. Vitamin B_6
D. Vitamin B_{12}
E. Vitamin B_9

13. Weight gain during pregnancy

A. Should be avoided
B. Is treated with a low-fat diet
C. Should not exceed 10 pounds
D. Is recommended to be anywhere between 24 and 35 pounds
E. Both A and B

14. Calcium deficiency may result in all of the following disorders except

A. Tetany
B. Rickets
C. Renal hypertrophy
D. Osteomalacia
E. Osteoporosis

15. Excessive amounts of fluoride in drinking water may cause discoloration of the

A. Skin
B. Teeth
C. Nails
D. Hair
E. Tongue

16. Which of the following is the most deadly of all food poisonings?

A. Trichinosis
B. Salmonellosis
C. Shigellosis
D. Botulism
E. Tinnitus

17. Water intoxication may result in which of the following conditions?

A. Stroke
B. Fatigue
C. Hypotension
D. Insomnia
E. Swelling of the brain cells

18. A bland diet is often prescribed in the treatment of all of the following except

A. Ulcerative colitis
B. Gastritis
C. Gallbladder disease
D. Heart failure
E. Peptic ulcer

19. According to the food pyramid, people should eat the most servings of which category of food?

A. Vegetable group
B. Fruit group
C. Bread, cereal, rice, and pasta group
D. Milk, yogurt, and cheese group
E. Meat, poultry, fish, dry beans, eggs, and nuts group

20. Iodine deficiency may cause

A. Cretinism (congenital myxedema)
B. Anemia
C. Rickets
D. Osteoporosis
E. Hypertension

21. Vitamin B_9 is also known as

A. Cyanocobalamin
B. Niacin
C. Riboflavin
D. Folic acid
E. Thiamine

22. Vitamin D deficiency can cause

A. Dry skin
B. Rickets
C. Night blindness
D. Osteomalacia
E. Both B and D

23. How many glasses of water a day should people drink on average?

   A. 3 to 5
   B. 6 to 8
   C. 10 to 12
   D. 9 to 11
   E. 48 to 64

24. Vitamin C

   A. Is important for night vision
   B. Is essential for normal formation of bones and teeth
   C. Helps heal wounds and protect against infections
   D. Is important for muscle development
   E. Helps prevent spina bifida

25. A condition caused by an overdose of vitamins is

   A. Hypervitaminosis
   B. Beriberi
   C. Wernicke-Korsakoff syndrome
   D. Avitaminosis
   E. Anemia

ANSWER KEY

1.	B	14.	C
2.	E	15.	B
3.	D	16.	D
4.	A	17.	E
5.	E	18.	D
6.	A	19.	C
7.	A	20.	A
8.	E	21.	D
9.	C	22.	E
10.	B	23.	B
11.	E	24.	C
12.	D	25.	A
13.	D		

Medical Law and Ethics

AREAS OF COMPETENCE

AAMA—ROLE DELINEATION STUDY AREAS OF COMPETENCE

General (Transdisciplinary)

Professionalism

- Project a professional manner and image
- Adhere to ethical principles
- Promote the CMA credential
- Enhance skills through continuing education

(Chart continued on next page.)

Communication Skills

- Treat all patients with compassion and empathy
- Recognize and respect cultural diversity
- Use a professional telephone technique
- Promote the practice through positive public relations

Legal Concepts

- Maintain confidentiality
- Practice within the scope of education, training, and personal capabilities
- Prepare and maintain medical records
- Document accurately
- Use appropriate guidelines when releasing information
- Follow employer's established policies dealing with the health care contract
- Follow federal, state, and local legal guidelines
- Maintain awareness of federal and state health care legislation and regulations
- Recognize professional credentialing criteria
- Participate in the development and maintenance of personnel, policy, and procedure manuals

AMT—RMA CERTIFICATION EXAM TOPICS

Medical Law

- Medical law
- Licensure, certification, and registration

Medical Ethics

- Principles of medical ethics
- Ethical conduct

Human Relations

- Patient relations
- Other interpersonal relations

Medical Secretarial-Receptionist

- Oral and written communications
- Records management

▶ Study Skills

Set goals!

The CMA and RMA exams cover a lot of material, and it's not uncommon to feel stressed in trying to review it all. Try to make your workload easier by prioritizing and setting goals. Create a schedule to review material and set aside time to practice answering exam questions. If there is a certain topic you know you have difficulty with, make sure that you devote more time to review it and less time to something you know you already understand.

Law

Law: A body of regulations that govern society and that people are obligated to observe.

Sources of law: The U.S. Constitution divides the federal government into three equal branches: the Legislative Branch, which passes laws; the Executive Branch, which implements laws; and the Judicial Branch, which interprets laws.

Types of Law

Common law: Law that derives authority from ancient usages and customs affirmed by court judgments and decrees. It is created by the judicial branch through decisions in court cases.

Criminal law: Law dealing with criminal offenses and their punishments.

Private law: The legal rights defining the relationship between private entities.

Public law: The legal rights defining the relationship between the government and the governed.

Case law: Law established by judicial decision in legal cases and used as legal precedent.

The Legal System

Defendant: The person or group accused in a court action.

Plaintiff: A person who files a lawsuit initiating a civil legal action. In criminal actions, the prosecution is the plaintiff, acting on behalf of the people.

Litigant: A party to a lawsuit.

Litigation: A lawsuit or a contest in court.

Jurisdiction: The power, right, and authority given to a court to hear a case and to make a judgment.

Layperson: An individual who does not have training in a specific profession.

Violations of the Law

Crime: An act that violates a criminal law.

Criminal: A person who has committed a crime or who has been proven guilty of a crime.

Accessory: A person who contributes to or aids in the commission of a crime, either by a direct or an indirect act.

Felony: A serious crime, such as murder, kidnapping, assault, or rape. Punishment is usually severe: a prison sentence for more than one year or, in some cases, death.

Misdemeanor: A crime that is less serious than a felony and consequently carries a lesser penalty. It is punishable by fine or by imprisonment in a facility other than a prison for less than one year.

Tort: A civil wrong committed against a person or property, excluding a breach of contract. A tort is the most common civil claim in medical law. When one person intentionally harms another, the law allows the injured party to seek remedy in a civil suit. If the conduct is judged to be malicious, punitive damages may also be awarded.

Intentional torts: Assault, battery, defamation of character, false imprisonment, fraud, invasion of privacy, trespass, and infliction of emotional distress.

Assault: A willful attempt or threat by one person to injure another person with the apparent ability to do so.

Defamation: Spoken or written words about a person that are both false and malicious and that injure that person's reputation or means of livelihood and for which damages can be recovered. Defamation can take the form of libel or slander.

Libel: Defamatory writing, such as published material or pictures.

Slander: Defamatory spoken words.

False imprisonment: The intentional, unlawful restraint or confinement of a person. Refusing to dismiss a patient from a health care facility upon his or her request or preventing a patient from leaving the facility may be seen as false imprisonment.

Fraud: Dishonest and deceitful practices undertaken in order to induce someone to part with something of value or a legal right.

Invasion of privacy: Intrusion into a person's private affairs and public disclosure of private facts about a person. Improper use of or breaching the confidentiality of medical records may be seen as an invasion of privacy.

Infliction of emotional distress: Intentionally or recklessly causing emotional or mental suffering to others.

Battery: The unlawful use of force on a person. Also, nonconsensual or illegal touching of another person.

Trespass: Wrongful injury or interference with the property of another.

Burglary: The act of breaking and entering into a building with intent to commit a felony, especially in order to steal. In a medical building, most burglary attempts are made to steal narcotics.

Misuse of legal procedure: Bringing legal action with malice and without probable cause.

Unintentional torts: Acts that are not intended to cause harm but are committed unreasonably or with disregard for the consequences. The legal term for the commission of an unintentional tort is negligence. Negligence is charged when a health care practitioner fails to exercise ordinary care and a patient is injured as a result.

Tortfeasor: A person who commits a tort either intentionally or unintentionally.

The Court System

Court system: There are both federal and state court systems, and each system has two types of court: lower and higher, or inferior and superior. See Figure 7-1.

Supreme court: There are both state and federal supreme courts. A state supreme court is the highest state court. Its decisions are generally final in matters of state law. The federal Supreme Court is the final court of appeal, the highest court in the United States, sometimes also referred to as the court of last resort.

Appeal: A legal proceeding by which a case is transferred from a lower to a higher court for rehearing.

Motion: An application made to a court or judge to obtain an order, ruling, or direction.

Arbitration: The hearing and determination of a case in controversy, without litigation, by a person chosen by the parties involved or appointed under statutory authority.

Summons: Issued by the clerk of the court and delivered with a copy of the complaint to the defendant, directing him or her to respond to the charges.

Subpoena: An official paper ordering a person to appear in court under penalty for failure to do so.

Subpoena _duces tecum_: A legal document requiring the recipient to bring certain records to court to be used as evidence in a lawsuit.

Witness: A person who can testify under oath to events he or she has heard or observed, such as the signing of a will or a consent form.

Testimony: Statements sworn to under oath by witnesses testifying in court and giving depositions.

Deposition: Sworn pretrial testimony given by a witness in response to written or oral questions and cross-examination. It is made before a public officer for use in a lawsuit, and it may also be presented at the trial if the witness cannot be present.

Perjury: The voluntary violation of an oath to tell the truth. Also, a false statement made under oath.

Interrogatory: Formal written questions about a case, addressed to one party by another, which are required to be answered under direction of a court.

Credibility: The quality or power of a witness to inspire belief.

Disposition: The final settlement of a case in criminal law.

Verdict: The finding or decision reached by a jury or judge on the matter submitted to trial.

Bench trial: A trial in which a judge serves without a jury and rules on the law as well as the facts.

Assumption of risk: A legal defense that holds that the defendant is not guilty of a negligent act because the plaintiff knew of and accepted beforehand any risk involved.

Burden of proof: The task of presenting testimony to prove guilt or innocence at a trial.

Statute of limitations: The period of time established by state law during which a lawsuit may be filed.

The Law and Medicine

Confidentiality: The principle and practice of treating something as a private matter not intended for public knowledge. Confidentiality protects information so that it is not released to anyone unless such release is required by law. Confidentiality is important because it builds trust and maintains patient dignity. Care should also be taken that any information about a patient cannot be overheard by others. Tables 7-1 and 7-2 on p. 154 present principles for preventing the improper release of information.

Releasing medical records: Permitted only when authorized in writing by the patient or the patient's legal guardian, when ordered by subpoena, or when dictated by statute to protect public health or welfare. The patient or guardian must sign a legal release form before records can be released to another physician or to an insurance company. The unauthorized disclosure of client information can be considered an invasion of privacy.

Maintaining patients' privacy: Keep these considerations in mind when handling sensitive information about patients:

- Do not leave confidential papers anywhere on the copier.

- Do not discard copies in shared trash containers. Always shred them.

- Always verify the telephone number of the receiving location before faxing confidential material.

- Never fax confidential material to an unauthorized person or in a room where others can observe the material. Use a fax cover sheet with a cautionary statement, "Confidential: To addressee only. Please return by mail if received in error."

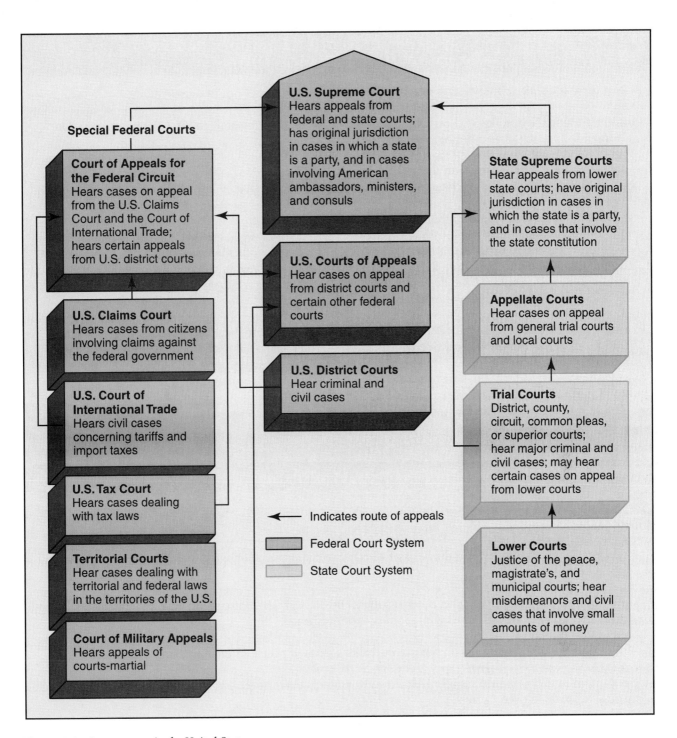

Figure 7-1. *Court systems in the United States.*

- Do not leave a computer monitor unattended if confidential material is displayed on it.
- It is recommended that you not send confidential materials via e-mail.
- Do not print confidential material on a printer shared by other departments or in an area where others can see the printed output.
- Do not leave a printer unattended while printing confidential material.

Privilege: Authority granted to a physician by a hospital governing board to provide patient care in the hospital.

Privileged communication: Information held confidential within a protected relationship, such as attorney-client and physician-patient. Physicians are prohibited from revealing information about clients in court.

Consent: Approval and permission from a patient to allow touching, examination, or treatment by

Principles for Preventing Improper Release of Information from a Medical Office

When there is doubt about whether to release information, it is better not to release it.
It is the patient's right to keep information confidential. If the patient wants to disclose the information, it is unethical for the physician not to do so.
All patients should be treated with the same degree of confidentiality, whatever the health care professional's personal opinion of the patient might be.
Be aware of all applicable laws and of the regulations of agencies such as public health departments.
When it is necessary to break confidentiality, and when there is a conflict between ethics and confidentiality, discuss the matter with the patient. If the law does not dictate what to do in the situation, the attending physician should make the judgment based on the urgency of the situation and any danger that might be posed to the patient or others.
Legally required disclosures include those ordered by subpoena, those dictated by statute to protect public health or welfare, and those considered necessary to protect the welfare of a patient or third party.
Get written approval from the patient before releasing information. For common situations, the patient should sign a standard release of records form.

Table 7-1

Guarding the Privacy of Patients

Do not disclose information, including whether the person is a patient, to any third party without the patient's signed consent.
Do not decide confidentiality on the basis of whether you approve of or agree with the views or morals of the patient.
Do not reveal financial information about a patient. Be discreet when discussing a patient's account balance so that others in the office waiting room do not overhear.
When talking on the telephone, do not use the caller's name if others in the room might overhear.
Use caution in giving the results of medical tests to patients over the telephone to prevent others in the medical office from overhearing.
When leaving a message at a patient's home or place of employment, simply ask the patient to return a call regarding a recent visit or appointment on a specific date. Do not mention the nature of the call.
It is preferable not to leave a message for a patient to call an oncologist, OB-GYN physician, or other specialist. If test results are abnormal, the physician generally speaks directly to the patient and an appointment is made to discuss the results.
Do not leave medical charts, insurance reports, or patient sign-in sheets where patients or office visitors can see them.
Make sure that the confidentiality protocol is noted in the office procedures manual and that new employees learn it.

Table 7-2

medically authorized personnel. Consent is unnecessary in emergency situations.

Doctrine of informed consent: A legal precept that is usually outlined in a state's medical practice acts. Informed consent implies that the patient understands the proposed modes of treatment, why the treatment is necessary, the risks involved in the proposed treatment, available alternative modes of treatment, the risks of alternative modes of treatment, and the risks involved if treatment is refused. After the patient signs an informed consent form, the medical assistant should document that fact in the patient's chart and note that the patient's questions were answered and that risks and alternative treatments were discussed.

Good Samaritan Act: Provides immunity from liability to volunteers at the scene of an accident who render emergency care. Today all 50 states have Good Samaritan statutes. They provide a measure of protection to physicians who might otherwise be discouraged by the possibility of a lawsuit from intervening at accident sites.

Mandatory reports: Physicians are required to submit statutory reports on a regular basis to various governmental agencies. Certain reports are required from all practicing physicians, including reports of births, deaths, and cases of food poisoning and communicable diseases (AIDS, hepatitis, neonatal herpes, Lyme disease, rabies, and sexually transmitted diseases). Physicians also need to report known or suspected abuse of any individual (child, elderly adult, or battered woman), drug abuse, and criminal acts (indicated by injuries resulting from violence, such as gunshot or stab wounds).

Birth certificate: A legal document that records information about a birth. It is used throughout a person's life to prove age, parentage, and citizenship. It also tells whether a certified midwife was present at birth.

Minor: A person who has not reached the age of majority, or legal age. The age of majority is 18 years in most jurisdictions, 21 in some. Minors usually cannot consent to their own medical treatment unless they are substantially independent of their parents, are married, or are in other ways self-sufficient.

Standard of care: The degree of care that a reasonably prudent person should exercise under the same or similar circumstances.

Medical practice acts: State laws that govern the practice of medicine. Health professionals must practice within the scope of their training and not beyond the limits of the state's medical practice acts.

Medical boards: Established by each state's medical practice act to protect the health, safety, and welfare of health care consumers by licensing health care practitioners.

Protocol: A written plan specifying the procedures to be followed in giving a particular examination. It is also the rules or standards of behavior applicable to one's place of employment.

Patient's Bill of Rights: A statement by the American Hospital Association that guarantees patients certain rights, as shown in Table 7-3.

Defensive medicine: The practice of performing medical tests and procedures in order to protect against future liability and to document the health care provider's judgment.

Forensic medicine: A division of medicine that involves medical issues or medical proof at trials having to do with malpractice, crimes, and accidents.

Malpractice

Medical malpractice: Medical professional misconduct, also called professional negligence. It stems from a lack of the professional knowledge, experience, or

---

AT A GLANCE | **Patient's Bill of Rights**

The patient has a right to
- Receive considerate and respectful care.
- Receive complete, current information concerning his or her diagnosis, treatment, and prognosis.
- Receive information necessary to give informed consent prior to the start of any procedure and/or treatment.
- Refuse treatment to the extent permitted by law.
- Receive every consideration of his or her privacy.
- Be assured of confidentiality.
- Obtain reasonable responses to requests for service.
- Obtain information about his or her health care.
- Know whether treatment is experimental.
- Expect reasonable continuity of care.
- Examine his or her bill and have it explained.
- Know which hospital rules and regulations apply to patient conduct.

Table 7-3

skill that is expected from practitioners and results in injury or harm to the patient.

Negligence: Elements necessary to prove negligence: duty, dereliction, direct cause, and damage. These elements are often called the four *Ds* of negligence.

Res ipsa loquitur: A Latin phrase meaning "the matter speaks for itself," also known as the doctrine of common knowledge. This doctrine applies if a result could not have occurred without someone's being negligent. Negligence cases chiefly involve acts such as unintentionally leaving foreign bodies inside a patient during surgery, accidentally injuring a patient in surgical procedures, and injuring a portion of the patient's body outside the field of treatment. In these cases, the physician has the burden of proving innocence and nonnegligence. If a malpractice case is not tried under this doctrine and general law of negligence, the patient has the burden of proving that the physician was at fault and negligent.

Contributing negligence: A legal term defining a situation in which both the plaintiff and the defendant share in the negligence that caused injury to the plaintiff.

Quid pro quo: A Latin phrase that means "something for something"—that is, giving something in return for something else.

Abuse: The improper use of equipment, a substance (such as a drug), or a service (such as a program), either intentionally or unintentionally.

Respondeat superior: A Latin phrase meaning "let the higher-up answer"—that is, that the physician is responsible for employee acts.

Scope of education and training: Often, laws dictate what medical assistants may or may not do. For example, in some states it is illegal for medical assistants to draw blood. It is illegal in all states for a medical assistant to diagnose a condition, prescribe treatment, and engage in deception about certification, title, or level of education.

Res judicata: A Latin phrase meaning "the matter has been decided." It signifies that a claim cannot be retried between the same parties if it has already been legally resolved.

Criminal Law

Child abuse: The physical, sexual, or emotional maltreatment of a child.

Child Abuse Prevention and Treatment Act: A law passed by Congress mandating the reporting of cases of child abuse. In all states, teachers, physicians, and other licensed health care practitioners are responsible for reporting such cases in person or by telephone and for following up with a written report within a specific time frame, such as 72 hours.

Elder abuse: The physical abuse, neglect, intimidation, or cruel punishment of an elderly individual.

Amendments to the Older Americans Act: A law passed by Congress that defines elder abuse, neglect,

and exploitation but that does not deal with enforcement. In 42 states, however, reporting suspected elder abuse is mandatory for physicians; such reporting is voluntary in the other 8 states.

Rape: A sexual assault involving intercourse without consent. Rape is a crime of violence, and the victims are treated for medical and psychological trauma. Rapes are criminal acts that should be reported to local law enforcement officials.

Drug Enforcement Administration (DEA): The agency responsible for enforcing the Comprehensive Drug Abuse Prevention and Control Act of 1970. Requirements for physicians include registration (renewed every three years), keeping of records (maintained for two years and specifying the patient, the drug, the dosage, the date, and reason for use), inventory (taken on the date of registration and every two years following), disposal of drugs (recorded in a log and witnessed), and proper security especially for controlled substances, all of which are major responsibilities of medical assistants.

Business Law

Contracts: Voluntary agreements between two or more parties in which specific promises are made for a consideration. There are three parts to any contract: the offer, the acceptance, and the consideration.

Offer: The contract process begins when one party makes an offer to another. The offer must be communicated effectively and must be made in good faith and not under duress or as a joke. The offer must also be clear enough to be understood by both parties, and it must define what both parties will do if the offer is accepted.

Acceptance: A patient indicates acceptance of the physician's offer of practicing medicine by scheduling appointments, submitting to physical examinations, and allowing the physician to prescribe or perform medical treatment. Acceptance must be absolute and made according to the terms of the offer. If acceptance includes conditions or terms other than the ones made in the original offer, then acceptance actually constitutes a counteroffer for a different contract.

Consideration: Something of value that is bargained for as part of a contract. It is what each party agrees to provide for the other.

Breach of contract: Failure of a party to comply with the terms of a legally valid contract.

Void: Without legal force or effect.

Implied contract: An unwritten and unspoken agreement, the terms of which result from the actions of the parties involved.

Termination of contract: Generally takes place when all treatment has been completed and all bills have been fully paid.

Premature termination of contract: May occur as a result of failure to pay for services, missed appointments, failure to follow the physician's instructions, or obtaining the services of another physician. Figure 7-2 is a sample of a letter sent by a physician who is withdrawing from a case as a result of a patient's failure to follow medical advice.

Liable: Accountable under the law.

Bonding: Insurance against embezzlement for employees who handle financial matters in the medical office.

Licensure: The granting of permission by a competent authority to an individual or organization to engage in a practice or activity that would otherwise be illegal. Licensure is a mandatory credential process established by law. It is the strongest form of regulation. It gives legal permission, granted by state statutes, to perform specific acts.

Registration: The recording of professional qualification information relevant to government licensing regulations.

Certification: A voluntary credential process usually made by a nongovernmental agency. The purpose of certification is to ensure that the standards met are those necessary for safe and ethical practice of the profession.

Reciprocity: The policy under which a professional license obtained in one state may be accepted as valid in other states by prior agreement.

Telemedicine: Remote consultation by patients with physicians or other health professionals via telephone, the Internet, or closed-circuit television. Legal concerns over telemedicine involve matters such as state licenses, reimbursement, confidentiality, and informed consent.

Business structures: Legally, business structures include sole proprietorships, partnerships, and corporations.

Sole proprietorship: A type of medical practice management in which a physician practices alone and is responsible for all profits and liabilities of the business. It is the oldest form of business and is the easiest to start, operate, and dissolve. The advantages are simplicity of organization, being one's own boss, being the sole receiver of all profits, and having fewer government regulations to follow.

Partnership: A type of medical practice management involving the association of two or more individuals practicing together under a written agreement specifying the rights, obligations, and responsibilities of each partner. A partnership has more financial strength than a sole proprietorship, but its organization remains relatively simple. There is no limit to the number of partners. The partnership agreement should be written and reviewed by an attorney. A disadvantage of a partnership is that two or more people make the decisions. Each partner is responsible or liable for the business.

LETTER OF WITHDRAWAL FROM CASE

Dear _____:

I find it necessary to inform you that I am withdrawing from further professional attendance upon you for the reason that you have persisted in refusing to follow my medical advice and treatment. Since your condition requires medical attention, I suggest that you place yourself under the care of another physician without delay. If you so desire, I shall be available to attend you for a reasonable time after you have received this letter, but in no event for more than five days.

This should give you ample time to select a physician of your choice from the many competent practitioners in this city. With your approval, I will make available to this physician your case history and information regarding the diagnosis and treatment which you have received from me.

Very truly yours,

_____, MD

Figure 7-2. *Physicians are required to inform patients in writing if they wish to withdraw from a case.* Source: *Medicolegal Forms With Legal Analysis, American Medical Association, © 1991.*

Corporation: A body formed by a group of people who are authorized by law to act as a single person. Corporations are governed by state law. There are income and tax advantages to incorporating.

Professional corporation: Designed for professionals such as physicians, dentists, lawyers, and accountants.

Group practice: A medical management system in which a group of three or more licensed physicians share their collective income, expenses, facilities, equipment, records, and personnel. There are single-specialty, multispecialty, and primary care group practices.

Indemnity: A security against loss, hurt, or damage. Indemnity is a traditional form of health insurance that covers the insured against a potential loss of money from medical expenses for an illness or accident.

Managed care: A system in which the financing, administration, and delivery of health care are combined to provide medical services to subscribers for a prepaid fee.

Capitation: A payment method for health care services in which a fixed amount of money is paid per month or other period to an HMO, medical group, or individual health provider for full medical care of subscribers. The contractual rates are usually adjusted for age, gender, illness, and regional differences.

Liability insurance: Contract coverage for potential damages incurred as a result of a negligent act. Doctors are often required to show proof of coverage up to a predetermined amount before hospitals will grant privileges or before managed care organizations will enter into a contractual agreement.

Workplace Legalities

Employment-at-will: A concept of employment whereby either the employer or the employee can terminate employment at any time and for any reason.

Wrongful discharge: A concept established by precedent whereby an employer risks litigation if he or she does not have just cause for firing an employee.

Legal protections: Laws against wrongful discharge prevent employers from firing someone for refusing to commit an illegal act, whistleblowing, performing a legal duty, or exercising a private right.

Wagner Act of 1935: Makes it illegal to discriminate in hiring or firing because of union membership or organizing activities.

Fair Labor Standards Act of 1938: Prohibits child labor and the firing of employees for exercising their rights under the act's wage and hour standards. It also provides for overtime pay and a minimum wage.

Equal Pay Act of 1963: Requires equal pay for men and women doing equal work.

Title VII of the Civil Rights Act of 1964: Applies to businesses with 15 or more employees working at least 20 weeks of the year. The act prevents employers from discriminating in hiring or firing on the basis of race, color, religion, sex, or national origin. Some states have laws that also prohibit discrimination based on marital status, parenthood, mental health status, mental retardation, other disabilities, sexual orientation, personal appearance, or political affiliation.

Right-to-know laws: State laws that allow employees access to information about toxic or hazardous substances, employer duties, employee rights, and other workplace health and safety issues.

Documentation and Records Management

SOAP: An approach to documentation that provides an orderly series of steps for dealing with a medical case, which lists (1) the patient's symptoms (*subjective* data), (2) the diagnosis (*objective* data), (3) an *assessment*, and (4) a *plan* of action.

POMR or POR: A system of *problem-oriented medical records* based on client problems—conditions or behaviors that results in physical or emotional distress or interfere with functioning.

Ownership of medical records: Physicians are considered the owners of the medical records they have written. These medical records should not be released unless the patient or legal guardian has signed legal release forms, a court has subpoenaed the records, an act or law mandates that the records be released to protect public welfare and safety, or the physician determines that the release is necessary to protect the patient or a third party.

Transferring medical records: Clients who request that their medical records be transferred to another physician should do so in writing. The original record may be retained in the office. No information should be released from the medical record without the approval of the physician and the written permission of the patient. If the client is incompetent, the court-appointed guardian signs the release form.

Children's medical records: The parent or legal guardian may sign the release forms. If the parents are legally separated or divorced, release forms must be signed by the parent who has legal custody.

Ethics

Ethics: The study of values or principles governing personal relationships, including ideals of autonomy, justice, and conduct. The code of ethics for the profession of medical assisting is reproduced in Table 7-4.

Bioethics: A discipline dealing with the ethical and moral implications of biological research and applications, especially as they relate to life and death.

Moral: Conforming to a standard of right behavior or a rule of conduct based on standards of right and wrong. Moral beliefs are usually formed through the influence of family, culture, and society, and they serve as a guide for personal ethical conduct.

The Code of Ethics of the AAMA shall set forth principles of ethical and moral conduct as they relate to the medical profession and the particular practice of medical assisting.

Members of the AAMA dedicated to the conscientious pursuit of their profession, and thus desiring to merit the high regard of the entire medical profession and the respect of the general public which they serve, do pledge themselves to strive always to:

A. render service with full respect for the dignity of humanity;

B. respect confidential information obtained through employment unless legally authorized or required by responsible performance of duty to divulge such information;

C. uphold the honor and high principles of the profession and accept its disciplines;

D. seek to continually improve the knowledge and skills of medical assistants for the benefit of patients and professional colleagues;

E. participate in additional service activities aimed toward improving the health and well-being of the community.

Source: American Association of Medical Assistants.

Table 7-4

Philosophy: A basic viewpoint or system of values, general beliefs, concepts, and attitudes.

Etiquette: Standards of behavior considered appropriate within a profession. Etiquette describes a body of courtesies and manners to be observed in social situations.

Beneficence: Active goodness or kindness.

Nonmaleficence: Abstinence from committing any harm. As human beings, we have an obligation not to harm others.

Duty to improve oneself: As a medical assistant you should always continue your education, learn new competencies and skills, learn from your own mistakes, learn from others you work with, and strive to be a good role model.

Genetics

Genetic: Pertaining to reproduction, birth, or origin or to being produced by genes or attributable to them.

Genetic diseases: There are as many as 4,000 human genetic diseases. Approximately 500 of them are linked to a defect in a single gene.

Genetic screening: Requires a DNA sample from solid tissues, saliva, or blood. Genetic testing is appropriate for prospective parents whose genetic histories indicate an elevated risk for genetic disorders. When a genetic defect is found in the fetus, parents may have to make an ethical decision to request or refuse an abortion. Other ethical concerns include genetic testing by employers and the release of genetic information to insurance companies.

Genetic engineering: Gene splitting, recombinant DNA research, chemical synthesis of DNA, and other technology. It involves numerous ethical issues and requires following stringent ethical guidelines.

Gene therapy: The insertion of a normally functioning gene into cells in which an abnormal or absent element of the gene has caused disease. The goal of gene therapy is to alleviate suffering and disease, not to enhance desirable characteristics or to diminish undesirable characteristics not related to disease.

Cloning: A procedure for producing multiple copies of genetically identical organisms or individual genes.

Eugenics: The study of hereditary improvement achieved by controlling the characteristics of genes.

Pregnancy and Termination of Pregnancy

Artificial insemination: The mechanical injection of viable semen into the vagina. If the donor and the recipient are not married, the recipient will be considered the sole parent of the child except in cases in which both the donor and the recipient agree to recognize a paternity right. Selecting sperm to manipulate the gender of a resulting child is ethical only to avoid a sex-linked inheritable disease.

In vitro fertilization (IVF): Takes place outside a woman's body, usually in a test tube. Because of ethical concerns, fertilized human eggs should not be subjected to laboratory research.

Gestation: The length of time after conception during which developing offspring are carried in the uterus. In humans, the duration is approximately 280 days, or 40 weeks. Live birth with a gestation time of less than 37 weeks is considered premature. Beyond 42 weeks, the fetus is considered postmature.

Amniocentesis: An obstetric procedure in which a small amount of amniotic fluid is aspirated for the purpose of analyzing whether a fetus is developing normally.

Amniotomy: The artificial rupture of the fetal membranes. It is performed to stimulate or accelerate the onset of labor. The procedure is painless.

Anencephaly: A congenital deformity in newborns characterized by absence of the brain and spinal cord.

Stillbirth: The death of a fetus before or during delivery. It is known as fetal death if the weight of the fetus is more than 1000g. Stillbirths may require neither birth nor death certificates.

Abortion: The voluntary termination of pregnancy before gestation is complete and in most cases before the fetus is viable. Methods include uterine aspiration, dilation and curettage, saline injection, and cesarean section. Its legality as a medical procedure was affirmed by the U.S. Supreme Court in a 1973 case known as *Roe v. Wade* and in several subsequent cases. People's opinions on the controversial subject are based on their own personal ethical and moral values as well as on the law.

Organ and Tissue Donation and Transplantation

Uniform Anatomical Gift Act: All states have adopted this law. Its provisions are that (1) any person over 18 years may give all or any part of his or her body after death for research, transplantation, or placement in a tissue bank; (2) physicians who accept organs or tissue, relying in good faith on the documents, are protected from lawsuits; and (3) the time of death must be determined by a physician. A uniform donor card is shown in Figure 7-3.

Transplant: The transfer of an organ or tissue from one person to another or from one part of the body to another. Medical transplants are divided into four categories, depending on the source of the tissue used: autograft, homograft, heterograft, and isograft.

Autograft: Surgical transplantation of a person's own tissue from one part of the body to another location. Autografts are used in several kinds of plastic surgery, most commonly to replace skin lost in severe burns. The term can also be applied to transplants between identical twins.

Heterograft: The transplant of animal tissue into a human. It is also called a xenograft.

Homograft: The nonpermanent transplant of tissue from one body to another (in the same species), such as a tissue transplant between two humans who are not identical twins. It is also called an allograft.

Isograft: Surgical transplantation from genetically identical individuals, such as identical twins.

UNIFORM DONOR CARD

Of _____
                Print or type name of donor

in the hope that I may help others, I hereby make this anatomical gift, if medically acceptable, to take effect upon my death. The words and marks below indicate my desires.

I give: (a) ❏ any needed organs or parts
      (b) ❏ only the following organs or parts

_____
Specify the organ(s) or part(s)

for the purposes of transplantation, therapy, medical research or education:
      (c) ❏ my body for anatomical study if needed.
Limitations or special wishes, if any: _____
_____

Front of card

Signed by the donor and the following two witnesses in the presence of each other:

Signature of Donor _____
Date of Birth of Donor _____
Date Signed _____
City and State _____
Witness _____
Witness _____

THIS IS A LEGAL DOCUMENT UNDER THE UNIFORM ANATOMICAL GIFT ACT OR SIMILAR LAWS.

Back of card

Figure 7-3. *A sample uniform donor card.*

Death and Dying

Patient Self-Determination Act: A federal law that requires health care providers to provide written information to patients about their rights under state law to make medical decisions and to execute advance directives. It requires that medical care facilities ask patients whether they have prepared an advance directive for guidance in the event that they are terminally ill.

Advance directives: Documents that make wishes known in the event that individuals are unable to speak for themselves. Examples are living wills, durable powers of attorney, and health care proxies.

Living will: A document in which an individual expresses his or her wishes regarding medical treatment. It may detail circumstances under which treatment should be discontinued, which treatments to suspend, and which to maintain. A living will is legal only if the person is competent to create such a document and if two witnesses have attested to its accuracy by signing it. Figure 7-4 is a sample living will.

Durable power of attorney: A document that gives a designated person the authority to make legal decisions

Figure 7-4. *A sample living will.*

If the time comes when I am incapacitated to the point when I can no longer actively take part in decisions for my own life, and am unable to direct my physician as to my own medical care, I wish this statement to stand as a testament of my wishes. I _____ (name) request that I be allowed to die and not be kept alive through life-support systems if my condition is deemed terminal. I do not intend any direct taking of my life, but only that my dying not be unreasonably prolonged. This request is made, after careful reflection, while I am of sound mind.

_____
(Signature)

_____
(Date)

_____
(Witness)

_____
(Witness)

on behalf of the grantor, usually including health care decisions.

Health care proxy: A durable power of attorney issued for purposes of making health care decisions only. See Figure 7-5 on p. 162 for a sample health care proxy.

Do-not-resuscitate (DNR) order: Written at the request of patients or their authorized representatives stating that cardiopulmonary resuscitation should not be used to sustain life in a medical crisis.

Geriatrics: The branch of medicine pertaining to elderly individuals and the treatment of diseases affecting them.

Termination phase: The period of life of persons who are expected to die within six months. It is the last stage of therapy for patients.

Curative care: Treatment to cure a patient's disease.

Palliative care: Treatment of symptoms to make a dying person more comfortable. It is also called comfort care. Patients should never be abandoned when cure or recovery is impossible. They should continue to receive emotional support, adequate pain control, respect for their autonomy, and effective communication.

Euthanasia: The administration of a lethal agent by another person to a patient with an incurable disease or condition.

Physician-assisted suicide: Euthanasia by a physician at the request of a person who wishes to die.

Brain death: An irreversible cessation of all function in the entire brain, including the brain stem, while the heart continues to beat. Brain death or irreversible coma is declared when electrical activity is absent on two electroencephalograms performed 12 to 24 hours apart.

Signs of death: There are six signs for pronouncing a comatose patient dead: no breathing without assis-

tance, no coughing or gagging reflex, no blinking reflex when the cornea is touched, no pupil response to light, no response to pain, and no grimace reflex when the head is rotated or ears are flushed with ice water.

Thanatology: The study of death, dying, and psychological methods of coping with death and dying.

Autopsy: A postmortem examination of a body performed by a specially trained medical person to confirm or determine the cause of death.

Grief: A normal reaction to loss, such as the loss of a job, the loss of a close friend or family member, death, or a diagnosis of a terminal illness.

Stages of grief: A pattern of emotional and physical responses to separation and loss. Elisabeth Kübler-Ross defines five stages or responses of dying patients:

Stage 1 denial and isolation;

Stage 2 anger, asking "why me?";

Stage 3 bargaining and guilt;

Stage 4 depression;

Stage 5 acceptance.

STRATEGIES TO SUCCESS

▶ Test-Taking Skills

Don't leave any questions blank!
Make an educated guess for every question even when you don't know the right answer. There is no penalty for guessing, and you might get a few extra points just by filling in every bubble.

I, _____ , designate and appoint:

Name: _____

Address: _____

Telephone Number: _____

to be my agent for health care decisions and pursuant to the language stated below, on my behalf to:

(1) consent, refuse consent, or withdraw consent to any care, treatment, service or procedure to maintain, diagnose or treat a physical or mental condition, and to make decisions about organ donation, autopsy and disposition of the body;

(2) make all necessary arrangements at any hospital, psychiatric hospital or psychiatric treatment facility, hospice, nursing home or similar institution; to employ or discharge health care personnel to include physicians, psychiatrists, psychologists, dentists, nurses, therapists or any other person who is licensed, certified or otherwise authorized or permitted by the laws of this state to administer health care as the agent shall deem necessary for my physical, mental and emotional well-being; and

(3) request, receive and review any information, verbal or written, regarding my personal affairs or physical or mental health including medical and hospital records and to execute any releases of other documents that may be required in order to obtain such information.

In exercising the grant of authority set forth above my agent for health care decisions shall:

_____

The powers of the agent herein shall be limited to the extent set out in writing in this durable power of attorney for health care decisions, and shall not include the power to revoke or invalidate any previously existing declaration made in accordance with the natural death act.

The agent shall be prohibited from authorizing consent for the following items:

_____

The durable power of attorney for health care decisions shall be subject to these additional limitations:

_____

This power of attorney for health care decisions shall become effective immediately and shall not be affected by my subsequent disability or incapacity or upon the occurrence of my disability or incapacity.

Any durable power of attorney for health care decisions I have previously made is hereby revoked. This durable power of attorney for health care decisions shall be revoked in writing, executed and witnessed or acknowledged in the same manner as required herein.

Executed this _____ , at _____

_____
(Signature of principal)

State _____ County _____ S.S. No. _____

This instrument was acknowledged before me _____ (date) by _____ (name)

_____
(Signature of notary public)

Figure 7-5. *A sample health care proxy.*

CHAPTER 7 REVIEW

Instructions:
Answer the following questions. Check your answers in the *Answer Key* that follows this section.

1. *Liable* means
   A. Without legal force or effect
   B. A moral code
   C. Accountable under law
   D. False, defamatory writing
   E. A crime that is less serious than a felony and consequently carries a lesser penalty

2. A partnership is
   A. A consultation with physicians and patients via the telephone or the Internet
   B. An association in which two or more individuals practice together and each assumes liability
   C. A group of people authorized by law to act as a single person
   D. A security against loss, hurt, or damage
   E. The physicians and employees working in a practice

3. The power and authority given to a court to hear a case and to make a judgment is called
   A. Jurisdiction
   B. Judiciary
   C. Judging
   D. Judicial
   E. Litigation

4. A physician is required to report
   A. Births
   B. Deaths
   C. Abuse
   D. Communicable diseases
   E. All of the above

5. A crime punishable by a fine or imprisonment for less than one year is known as a
   A. Misdemeanor
   B. Felony
   C. Mitigation
   D. Mutual assent
   E. Arbitration

6. Professional negligence is also called
   A. Malpractice
   B. Malfunction
   C. Malice
   D. All of the above
   E. None of the above

7. All of the following are the *Ds* of negligence except
   A. Dereliction
   B. Damages
   C. Duty
   D. Debts
   E. Direct cause

8. In which case can a minor's medical records be released?
   A. The patient has given verbal permission to release the records
   B. A parent with legal custody has signed the release forms
   C. The patient has signed the legal release forms
   D. A fellow physician has called the office and requested their release
   E. The insurance company has requested their release

9. In order to protect the confidentiality and privacy of patients, medical assistants should not
   A. Discuss confidential matters such as test results and finances over the telephone
   B. Leave messages with someone other than the patient about test results or finances
   C. Release medical records without the signed consent of the patient or legal guardian
   D. Both B and C
   E. All of the above

10. A contract
   A. Is a voluntary agreement
   B. Is made for a consideration
   C. Involves a specific promise made
   D. Involves two or more parties
   E. All of the above

11. Consent is unnecessary

    A. In emergency situations
    B. If the patient is an emancipated minor
    C. If the patient is mentally incompetent
    D. If the situation involves minors in foster homes
    E. Under no circumstances; it is always necessary, without exception

12. The transplant of animal tissue into a human is known as

    A. A homograft
    B. An autograft
    C. A heterograft
    D. A tissue graft
    E. Cloning

13. All of the following are stages of grief identified by Kübler-Ross except

    A. Depression
    B. Isolation
    C. Death
    D. Bargaining
    E. Anger

14. The age of majority in most jurisdictions is

    A. 21 years
    B. 19 years
    C. 16 years
    D. 17 years
    E. 18 years

15. It is permissible to release private and confidential information about a patient

    A. When you disagree with the patient's choices
    B. When the patient has signed a release form
    C. To a friend of the patient who is concerned about the patient's well-being
    D. Over the telephone when others can overhear
    E. Never; it is always inappropriate to release private or confidential information about a patient

16. Good Samaritan laws

    A. Encourage physicians to render emergency first aid
    B. Exist in all 50 states
    C. Protect physicians against liability for negligence in certain circumstances
    D. Deal with the treatment of accident victims
    E. All of the above

17. *Res ipsa loquitur* is a Latin phrase that refers to

    A. The responsibility of the physician for employee acts
    B. Something that is common knowledge or that speaks for itself
    C. The failure to do something that should have been done
    D. Getting something as a result of doing something
    E. Doing something in order to get something in return

18. All of the following are part of the Patient's Bill of Rights except

    A. Privacy
    B. Confidentiality
    C. Refusing discharge from the hospital
    D. Refusing treatment
    E. Expecting continuity of care

19. Which of the following means "let the higher-up answer"?

    A. Malfeasance
    B. Good Samaritan
    C. *Res ipsa loquitur*
    D. *Respondeat superior*
    E. *Novus Ordo Seclorum*

20. Which of the following items is the most important for medical assistants to keep in mind during their daily work routine in medical offices?

    A. Burglary
    B. Confidentiality
    C. Privilege granted to a physician
    D. Consent
    E. Good Samaritan laws

CHAPTER 7 REVIEW

21. In which of the following situations is it permissible to release information from a patient's records?

A. When an attorney requests it
B. When the patient's employer requests it
C. When the patient's best friend requests it
D. When a court requests it by means of a subpoena
E. When the patient's father requests it

22. Under which of the following circumstances is it permissible to release information from a patient's records?

A. When the patient signs a release
B. When a physician calls to request it
C. When the insurance company signs a release
D. When the patient has signed a living will
E. When the patient is in an accident

23. The fact that an individual is a patient of the practice is

A. Common knowledge
B. Part of the Patient's Bill of Rights
C. Confidential information
D. Privileged communication
E. Both B and C

24. In cases of malpractice involving *res ipsa loquitur,*

A. The patient has the burden of proving the physician's negligence
B. The physician has the burden of proving his or her innocence
C. The physician is not bound by physician-patient confidentiality
D. All of the above
E. None of the above

25. The Uniform Anatomical Gift Act includes the provision that

A. Physicians who accept organs and tissue in good faith, relying on apparently valid documents, are protected from lawsuits
B. The time of death must be determined by a physician
C. Any person over 18 years of age may give all or any part of his or her body up after death for research or transplantation
D. Both A and C
E. All of the above

ANSWER KEY

1.	C	14.	E
2.	B	15.	B
3.	A	16.	E
4.	E	17.	B
5.	A	18.	C
6.	A	19.	D
7.	D	20.	B
8.	B	21.	D
9.	E	22.	A
10.	E	23.	C
11.	A	24.	B
12.	C	25.	E
13.	C		

ADMINISTRATIVE

MEDICAL ASSISTING KNOWLEDGE

Theory Review

SECTION OUTLINE

CHAPTER 8

General Office Duties

Medical Records and Filing

Transcription and Dictation
Filing Systems
Filing Procedures
Filing Equipment

Computers

Hardware
Software
Networks and the Internet
Computers and Security

Policies and Procedures

AREAS OF COMPETENCE

AAMA—ROLE DELINEATION STUDY AREAS OF COMPETENCE

Administrative

Administrative Procedures

- Perform basic clerical functions
- Schedule, coordinate, and monitor appointments
- Schedule inpatient/outpatient admissions and procedures
- Perform medical transcription

General (Transdisciplinary)

Professionalism

- Project a professional manner and image
- Adhere to ethical principles
- Demonstrate initiative and responsibility
- Work as a team member
- Manage time effectively
- Prioritize and perform multiple tasks
- Adapt to change

Communication Skills

- Treat all patients with compassion and empathy
- Recognize and respect cultural diversity
- Adapt communications to individual's ability to understand
- Use professional telephone technique
- Use effective and correct verbal and written communications
- Recognize and respond to verbal and nonverbal communications
- Receive, organize, prioritize, and transmit information
- Serve as a liaison
- Promote the practice through positive public relations

(Chart continued on next page.)

AREAS OF COMPETENCE (cont.)

Legal Concepts
- Maintain confidentiality
- Prepare and maintain medical records
- Document accurately
- Use appropriate guidelines when releasing information
- Participate in the development and maintenance of personnel, policy, and procedure manuals

Instruction
- Instruct individuals according to their needs
- Explain office policies and procedures
- Locate community resources and disseminate information

Operational Functions
- Apply computer techniques to support office operations

AMT—RMA CERTIFICATION EXAM TOPICS

Human Relations
- Patient relations
- Other interpersonal relations

Patient Education
- Patient instruction
- Patient resource materials

Medical Secretarial–Receptionist
- Reception
- Scheduling
- Oral and written communications
- Records management
- Charts
- Transcription and dictation
- Computers for medical office applications

Manage your time!

It's easy to develop good study habits if you manage your time effectively. Every day, set aside a time when you can study without interruption. Don't let anything else intrude on this time—not shopping, not paying bills, not running errands, not socializing with friends, not even family (except in the direst emergencies). In this way you will have study time and still be able to get everything else done you want to. Write a daily to-do list and check tasks off as you complete them.

Communicating as a Health Care Professional

Communication cycle: Formed as the sender, or source, communicates a message to the receiver through a chosen channel of communication and the receiver responds with feedback. As the message is transmitted from the source to the receiver, it travels through noise, which can interfere with effective communication. See Figure 8-1. The five basic elements of the communication cycle are:

- The sender or source
- The message
- The channel or mode of communication
- The receiver
- Feedback

Feedback: Verbal and nonverbal evidence that a message was received and understood.

Noise: Anything that distorts the message in any way or interferes with the communication process.

The 5 Cs of communication:

- Complete—The message must contain all necessary information.
- Clear—The message must be free from obscurity and ambiguity.
- Concise—The message must not include any unnecessary information.
- Courteous—The message must be respectful and considerate of others.
- Cohesive—The message must be organized and logical.

Nonverbal communication: Includes facial expressions, hand gestures, personal space, eye contact, posture, and touch. It is also called body language. In many cases, body language conveys true feelings when words may not. Be aware of your body language and note the body language of others. Adjust your style of communicating to the preferences of the particular patient or colleague you are dealing with.

Facial expressions: Should be nonjudgmental and correspond with what you say.

Eye contact: Important to show interest, attention, and sensitivity.

Touch: Can show sensitivity and empathy. Not everyone, however, will be accepting of being touched. In general, a touch on the shoulder, back, or hand is acceptable, but beware of cultural and personal differences and adjust your style to the preferences of others.

Nodding: Acknowledges the information communicated and encourages the speaker to continue.

Posture: Turning and leaning your body toward a person usually shows interest and focuses your attention. An open posture, in which your arms lie comfortably at your sides or in your lap, is a positive form of communication. A closed posture such as folding your arms across your chest, leaning and turning away, or avoiding eye contact usually conveys anger or lack of caring.

Maslow's hierarchy: Part of a systematized theory of human behavior developed by Abraham Maslow. According to this theory, all human needs can be organized into five successive categories or levels. The first level includes basic needs, such as for food, water, shelter, and clothing. The second level includes needs for safety and security. The third level includes needs for human companionship and a sense of belonging to a group. The fourth level includes needs for respect and self-esteem. The fifth level includes the need to achieve one's highest level of potential, a concept referred to as self-actualization.

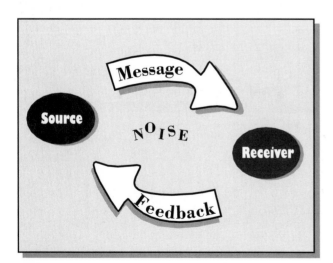

Figure 8-1. *The process of communication involves an exchange of messages through verbal and nonverbal means.*

Developing Good Communication Skills

Attitude: Your confidence and self-esteem can positively affect your success in the medical field. The way you represent yourself is the way others will see you. Steps toward having a positive attitude include:

- Smiling instead of frowning
- Saying something pleasant instead of complaining
- Using positive statements instead of negative statements

Stress: Can be a barrier to communication. Minimize stress by exercising, by eating a healthy diet, and by maintaining a balance between work, family, and leisure activities.

Communication skills: Good communication techniques include:

- Using tact and sensitivity
- Showing empathy
- Demonstrating respect
- Being genuine
- Displaying openness and friendliness
- Exhibiting a willingness to consider other viewpoints and concerns
- Refraining from passing judgment or stereotyping others
- Being supportive
- Asking for clarification and feedback
- Paraphrasing to make sure that you understand what others are saying
- Maintaining good eye contact
- Communicating honestly and straightforwardly but with tact and respect
- Being receptive to patients' needs
- Knowing when to speak and when to listen
- Knowing when to use active and passive listening techniques
- Paying close attention to your own and others' body language
- Being aware of cultural differences in nonverbal communication, including eye contact, touch, and personal space preferences
- Watching others' reaction to your personal style and adjusting it accordingly

Silence: Periods in which there is no verbal communication. Silence can allow the patient to think without pressure to speak.

Restating: Repeating to a patient what you believe is the main thought or idea expressed. It will also help to paraphrase ideas rather than repeating statements verbatim. In this way you can make sure that you understand what is being communicated.

Reflecting: Encouraging patients to think through and answer their own questions and concerns.

Open-ended questions: General questions that allow patients to elaborate on their answers, providing as much information as they wish to. They lead to better communication.

Focusing: Helping the patient stay on a particular topic with directing questions and statements.

Assertiveness: Being firm and standing up for oneself while showing respect for others. Being assertive is different from being aggressive. When people are aggressive, they try to impose their position on others.

Rapport: A positive and harmonious relationship, for example, a positive relationship between a patient and a medical assistant. You can build rapport with good communication skills.

Listening

Listening: The act of receiving a message. There are three different listening patterns used in a medical office: active, passive, and evaluative.

Active listening: Asking questions and offering feedback. See Figure 8-2.

Passive listening: Listening without answering or offering feedback.

Evaluative listening: Providing immediate response and opinion. It is very important to listen to everything a patient says; avoid "selective hearing."

Common Communication Problems

Passive voice: A grammatical sentence structure that emphasizes the receiver rather than the doer of an

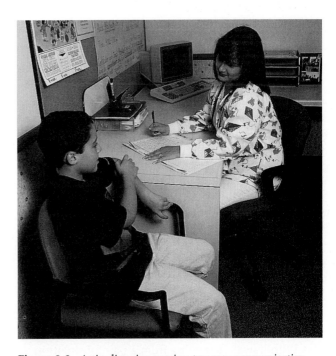

Figure 8-2. *Active listening requires two-way communication and positive body language.*

action, or agent. (Example: The paperwork has been completed.) The passive voice allows you to withhold information about the agent if you feel that this information is not important or necessary. However, using an active sentence structure conveys a more personal message. (Example: The medical assistant has completed the paperwork.)

Prejudice and bias: Personal preferences, biases, and prejudices can affect many relationships at work, both among coworkers and among patients and health care professionals. Such biases can often inadvertently provoke hostility in others, especially when individuals are not aware of their biases or prejudices. Medical assistants must recognize such attitudes and ensure that their own cultural biases do not prevent them from responding therapeutically and constructively in communications with patients and coworkers.

Gender bias: An attitude, reflected in action or language, that unjustly favors one gender over another.

Discrimination: Action that is based on group, characteristic, or class rather than on merit. Discrimination usually refers to the unfair treatment of others based on such factors as race, gender, religious affiliation, or disability. Discrimination is not just unethical; it is also illegal.

Negative communication: Some communication practices have a negative effect on others:

- Mumbling
- Interrupting
- Showing boredom
- Bragging and confronting
- Forgetting common courtesies such as saying "please" and "thank you"
- Speaking too quickly or sharply
- Using negative body language such as frowning, slouching, and crossing one's arms
- Avoiding eye contact

Defense mechanisms: Practices an individual might employ to avoid an uncomfortable situation. You should be aware of these mechanisms and avoid using them yourself, because they do not lead to effective communication. You may come across patients who use some of them. Some common defense mechanisms include:

- Repression: Pushing unpleasant thoughts or problems into the unconscious to avoid dealing with them.
- Projection: Blaming one's problems on others.
- Rationalization: Justifying problems or unacceptable behavior by giving acceptable reasons rather than real ones.
- Withdrawal: Retreating from a painful situation in order to avoid dealing with it.

Sexual harassment: Persistent, unwanted advances, attention, or communication of a sexual nature. It is prohibited in the workplace. Sexual harassment can be physical or verbal, expressed in gestures or images or in written or spoken words. It can occur at any level of the hierarchy within a workplace and can result in personal distress and legal implications for the medical facility.

Communicating with Patients as Individuals

Diversity: Patients in the medical office will come from a variety of personal, ethnic, and cultural backgrounds. You should be ready to interact with all patients according to their needs and circumstances.

Fearful patient: Perhaps fearful of an upcoming procedure, some patients may be anxious and nervous about their visit. You should be able to recognize the source of their fear and communicate understanding, empathy, and reassurance.

Angry patient: Some patients may be angry about their illness or injury, or they may be angered by the loss of a loved one. Anger can also stem from patients feeling that they are being unfairly or rudely treated. As a medical assistant, you must learn how to remain calm and help the patient express anger in a constructive manner. Allow the patient to talk, and genuinely listen to the complaints. Do everything you can to avoid a breakdown in communication.

Patients with a visual impairment: When communicating with a patient who has a visual impairment:

- Use large-print materials when appropriate.
- Make sure that there is adequate lighting in the room.
- Talk directly and honestly.

Patients with a hearing impairment: Here are a few suggestions to help you communicate effectively with an individual who has a hearing impairment:

- Minimize background noise.
- Position yourself close to the patient and face him or her.
- Let body language and facial expression supplement your voice.
- Speak slowly, but do not exaggerate pronunciation.
- Use written materials to reinforce verbal communication.

Elderly patients: Do not assume that all elderly patients are hard of hearing or are losing their memory. If you have reason to believe that an elderly patient is confused, these suggestions can help you communicate effectively:

- Act as if you expect the patient to understand.
- Respond calmly, tell the truth, and use facts.
- Use simple language, but do not speak as if the patient were a child.

- Explain slowly and clearly, using concrete terms.
- Ask the patient to relax and speak slowly.
- Ask the patient to explain anything you don't understand.

Children: To maximize communication with children:

- Work directly with them rather than communicating through their parents.
- Take their feelings seriously.
- Explain all procedures, even basic ones, in simple terms.
- Let them examine instruments.
- Use praise.
- Be truthful.
- Do not talk down to children.

Seriously ill patients: When dealing with a patient who is seriously ill:

- Do not trivialize the patient's feelings.
- Listen without judging.
- Avoid empty promises.
- Allow the patient to be alone when appropriate, but do not avoid the patient.

Patients with HIV/AIDS: Educate yourself about these conditions so that you can answer questions and so that you do not unnecessarily stigmatize patients affected by this disease. Remember that HIV cannot be transmitted by casual contact, so do not be afraid to be near patients or to touch them.

Communicating with Coworkers

Cooperation: The ability to work with others effectively.

Dependability: Teamwork is based on the ability of one worker to depend on another. To be dependable, follow these rules:

- Report to work on time.
- Do your fair share of work.
- Keep your promises.
- Don't gossip.

Politeness: A kind word or a friendly phrase goes a long way in establishing effective communication. Use the phrases "thank you" and "please" as often as appropriate.

Patience: The ability to remain calm and composed. Working in a medical office can be very confining and stressful, and it is essential to have patience when dealing with others.

Communicating with supervisors: Effective communication with supervisors and other superiors depends on following these recommendations:

- Keep superiors informed.
- Ask questions.
- Minimize interruptions.
- Show initiative.

Teamwork: Medical assistants are part of a health care professional team. In order to be a good team player, you should:

- Be ready to compromise and admit that you are wrong.
- Treat others with respect.
- Listen to everyone equally.
- Know that changing your position is not a sign of weakness but of strength.
- Avoid putting others on the defensive.
- Always think about what you say and how it might affect others.
- Don't rush to judgment about others, and don't rely on bias and stereotypes when dealing with coworkers and patients.
- Do not reinforce or adopt negative attitudes.
- Be a problem-solver and offer solutions, not just criticism.
- Learn from others.
- Remember your common goal of providing excellent health care to patients.

Reception

Receptionist: An employee, often a multi-skilled medical assistant, who greets patients as they come into the office. The receptionist is the first person who will have contact with the patient and help the patient form a first impression about the facility and its employees. He or she will usually sit in an area where the waiting patients can be observed.

First impression: Both the receptionist and the reception area help the patient form a first impression about the medical facility and its employees. This first impression should be of a positive, comfortable, safe, and clean environment.

Receptionist Duties

Receptionist duties: Receptionists should be professional, confident, and caring. They are responsible for ensuring patient safety and confidentiality at all times. Other duties vary depending on the facility. Some medical practices require different, specific tasks to be done each day. These tasks also differ between medical specialties. Generally, a receptionist's duties include:

- Opening and closing the office
- Replenishing supplies
- Greeting patients
- Signing in patients
- Registering new patients
- Answering patients' questions

- Assisting with patient forms
- Collating records
- Answering the phone
- Writing charge slips
- Inputting no-shows
- Preparing for patients to come in
- Escorting and instructing patients
- Making sure that the reception area is safe and clean
- Handling patients' complaints

Scheduling: Setting up appointments according to the method used by the physician to provide efficient services.

Opening the office: The receptionist responsible for opening the office should arrive 15 to 20 minutes before office hours begin.

Registering new patients: New patients need to fill out a complete patient registration form containing demographic information. Assist patients who are unable to read or write.

Collating records: Collect all records, test results, and information pertaining to the patient who is scheduled to be seen by the physician. Collation is usually done the day before the patient is seen.

Greeting: Although it is often overlooked, one of the very important tasks of a medical assistant is greeting patients. What you say and how you present yourself to patients the first time they enter the medical facility makes a difference in the way patients respond to you and in what they think of the facility. Greet patients by name, don't ask potentially personal or embarrassing questions, and make eye contact.

Dress code: Appearance is very important. The way you look, speak, and act reflects on who you are. Everything you do in the office is a reflection on the facility, the physician, and your coworkers. Each medical facility has its own dress code. General rules include:

- Attire should be clean, neat, and fresh.
- Shoes should be clean, neat, comfortable, and appropriate for the job.
- Hosiery (socks and stockings) should be of a neutral shade or a color that coordinates with the uniform.
- An identification tag or pin should be placed on the uniform where it can be seen and worn at all times during work hours.
- Hair should be clean, neat, and off the shoulders or collar.
- Nails should be cut to an appropriate length to ensure safety to patients. Nail polish, if used, should be of a natural color.
- Assistants should not have visible tattoos or body-piercing jewelry other than earrings worn in the earlobes.
- Makeup should be applied conservatively.
- No cologne or perfume should be worn.
- Facial hair should be clean and appropriately trimmed.

Professionalism: Always be professional. Get to know your patients, but only on a professional level, not on a personal level. Call your patients by name. Be polite, tactful, and respectful.

Reception Area

Reception area: When the receptionist arrives at the office, one of his or her first duties is to take a look at the reception area. This area should be clean and neat and should have proper lighting, so that patients may read if they desire. The area should be designed and arranged with patient comfort and safety in mind. See Figure 8-3.

Access: The way patients enter and exit a medical office. Patients should have easy, clear access from the parking lot to the medical office entrance. The entrance of the office should be clearly marked, noting the name of the practice and doctors associated with the practice. Doorways must be wide enough to accommodate patients using wheelchairs and walkers. Hallways should also be wide and without obstructions.

Reading material: Appropriate reading material should be placed on the tables in the reception area. The material should not be frightening, disturbing, or otherwise inappropriate.

Television: More and more medical practices have televisions in the reception area. Monitor this area to make sure that the program selected is appropriate for all viewers and that the sound level is acceptable.

Playroom: Make sure that the toys, games, videos, and books are safe for children to play with. Toys and any

Figure 8-3. *Specialty items—such as plants, paintings, and coatracks—enhance the reception area.*

toy parts should be free of sharp edges, too large to accidentally swallow, and easy to clean.

Beverages: Some medical facilities make coffee and drinking water available to patients. Make sure that these items are fresh each morning and that necessary supplies such as cream and sugar are available. The storage area should be safe and clean.

Interim room: A room in which people can talk or meet without being seen or heard from the patient reception area. This room provides an ideal location for medical staff to confer privately with patients about appointments or bills. An interim room also allows patients privacy to make telephone calls or to feed or diaper babies.

Managing Correspondence and Mail

Classification: Mail can be classified according to type, weight, and destination. The measurement units are the ounce and pound. The United States Postal Service has recently updated its classification system. Because the exam could contain questions about either the old or the new system, both are included and explained here. The following classifications of mail were used under the old system:

- First-Class Mail
- Priority Mail
- Second-Class Mail
- Third-Class Mail
- Fourth-Class Mail
- Express Mail

The following classifications of mail are used under the new system:

- First-Class Mail
- Priority Mail
- Periodicals
- Standard Mail (A)
- Standard Mail (B)
- Express Mail

As you can see, the classifications First-Class, Priority, and Express Mail were retained. However, Second-Class, Third-Class, and Fourth-Class Mail are no longer used. To get the most current information on classifications and rates or to order supplies, call the USPS or visit http://new.usps.com.

Types of Mail
Current Classifications

First-Class Mail: Only items that weigh 13 ounces or less may be sent as First-Class Mail. Items that weigh more than 13 ounces must be sent as Priority Mail rather than First-Class Mail. Anything the post office accepts for mailing can be sent as First-Class or Priority Mail; however, some things *must* be sent as First-Class Mail (or Priority Mail), such as handwritten or typewritten material, bills, statements of account or invoices, and credit cards. Nonstandard envelopes that are termed nonmachinable by the post office are subject to a surcharge. If you mail envelopes larger than the standard No. 10 size, the envelope should have a green diamond border to expedite First-Class delivery. If you mail 500 or more items, you can get a discounted bulk rate from the post office.

Priority Mail: Provides First-Class handling for all items that weigh 70 pounds or less. First-Class Mail that weighs more than 13 ounces *must* be sent as Priority Mail. Priority Mail provides second-day service between all major business markets and three-day service everywhere else within the United States. (Delivery within the stated period, however, is not guaranteed.) There is a basic rate for packages weighing up to 2 pounds. Larger packages can be sent as Priority Mail at higher rates according to weight.

Periodicals: Formerly called Second-Class Mail. This classification is designed for newspapers, magazines, and other periodical publications whose primary purpose is transmitting information to an established list of subscribers or requesters. Periodicals must be published at regular intervals at least four times a year from a known office of publication and must be formed of printed sheets. There are specific standards for, among other things, circulation, record keeping, and advertising limits. There is a nonrefundable application fee to become authorized for Periodicals mailing privileges.

Standard Mail (A): A mail classification designed for printed matter, flyers, circulars, advertising, newsletters, bulletins, catalogs, and small parcels. All Standard Mail (A) must be mailed in bulk. There must be at least 200 pieces of mail or 50 pounds of mail to get this lower rate. Automatic forwarding and return services are available at an additional cost; very few other special services are available for this classification.

Standard Mail (B): There are four subclasses within this classification: Parcel Post, Bound Printed Matter, Special Standard Mail, and Library Mail. Automatic forwarding and return services are available at an additional cost.

Parcel Post: A type of Standard Mail (B) used for mailing books, circulars, catalogs, and other printed merchandise.

Bound Printed Matter: Consists of advertising, promotional, directory, or editorial material. It must be securely bound by permanent fastenings such as staples, spiral binding, glue, or stitching. It must also contain material that is mostly typed not handwritten, and it should not be personal correspondence or stationery (including pads of blank printed forms).

Special Standard Mail: Generally used for books (at least 8 pages long), film (16mm or narrower), printed music, printed test materials, sound recordings, play scripts, educational charts, loose-leaf pages, binders consisting of medical information, and computer-readable material.

Library Mail: Used by qualifying institutions such as libraries, universities, zoos, and research institutions to mail educational and research material.

Express Mail: The fastest mail service offered by the Postal Service. It provides guaranteed expedited service for any mailable matter. Express mail is available seven days a week including holidays. Express Mail packaging supplies are available at no charge from your local post office. Express mail should be used for urgent business documents, such as contracts and sales orders. A flat rate is charged for anything mailed in the special USPS flat-rate envelope, regardless of weight. Overnight delivery is guaranteed. Federal Express and United Parcel Service (UPS) also offer next-day delivery service.

International mail: The majority of letters to distant foreign countries, as well as to Mexico and Canada, are sent by air mail at international rates determined by the U.S. Postal Service. Window envelopes cannot be used for international mail. Parcel Post is handled according to an agreement with countries that place restrictions on materials that enter their borders.

Combination mailing: A package with an accompanying letter is called combination mail. The letter should be attached to the outside of the package, or the letter should be placed inside the package and the package marked *Letter enclosed* just below the space for the postage. Separate postage is paid for the parcel and the letter. This method is commonly used to send X-rays with an accompanying report.

Old Classifications

Second-Class Mail: Publications such as newspapers, magazines, and journals were required to obtain Second-Class mailing privileges from the post office in order to use this special rate.

Third-Class Mail: Included books and catalogues of 24 or fewer bound pages, manuscript copies, identification cards, circulars, and other printed materials, as well as all other matter weighing less than 16 ounces that was not sent as First- or Second-Class Mail.

Fourth-Class Mail: This classification was reserved for all merchandise and materials not included in the other classifications, such as films and books of more than 24 pages. There were size limitations on Fourth-Class Mail. The items had to weigh at least 16 ounces and not more than 70 pounds.

Mail Characteristics

Prohibited items: The United States Postal Service prohibits the mailing of fraudulent or pornographic materials. The responsibility for mailing any materials, whether or not they are prohibited or hazardous, rests with the mailer.

Hazardous materials: Materials designated by the U.S. Department of Transportation (DOT) as being capable of posing unreasonable risk to health, safety, and property during transportation. Certain drugs and medicines can be classified as hazardous material. Before mailing anything that might be considered hazardous, check with the post office for appropriate labeling procedures.

Minimum size: The post office prescribes minimum sizes for mail to prevent individuals from mailing items so small that they might be lost. If a mailpiece is $\frac{1}{4}$ inch thick or less, it must be at least $3\frac{1}{2}$ inches high by 5 inches long. All mailable matter must be at least .007 inch thick.

Maximum size: The maximum size for mailpieces is 108 inches in combined length and girth. The maximum mailable weight of any mailpiece is 70 pounds. Items mailed as Parcel Post can have a maximum combined length and girth of 130 inches.

Shape: The shape of your mail can determine the rate you pay. In some instances, certain shapes such as squares and tubes are charged a higher rate or a special surcharge because those pieces must be processed manually. Generally, mail that is $\frac{1}{4}$ inch thick or less must be rectangular. Pieces more than $\frac{1}{4}$ inch thick do not have to be rectangular. The post office separates mail into four size and shape categories: cards, letters, flats/nonletters, and parcels.

Cards: Eligible for First-Class services such as forwarding and return. Cards must be at least $3\frac{1}{2}$ inches high by 5 inches long by .007 inch thick and no more than $4\frac{1}{4}$ inches high by 6 inches long by .016 inch thick.

Letters: Nonstandard envelopes must be at least $3\frac{1}{2}$ inches high by 5 inches long by .007 inch thick and no more than $6\frac{1}{8}$ inches high by $11\frac{1}{2}$ inches long by $\frac{1}{4}$ inch thick.

Flats: A category for large envelopes, newsletters, and magazines. To be considered a flat, a mailpiece must be at least $6\frac{1}{8}$ inches high *or* $11\frac{1}{2}$ inches long *or* $\frac{1}{4}$ inch thick. It should not be more than 12 inches high by 15 inches long by $\frac{3}{4}$ inch thick.

Parcels: Fall into two categories: machinable and nonmachinable. Machinable parcels (those that can fit through the post office's automated parcel sorting machines) should be at least 3 inches high by 6 inches long by $\frac{1}{4}$ inch thick and weigh at least 8 ounces (6 ounces for regular rectangular shapes); they should be no more than 17 inches high by 34 inches long by 17 inches thick and weigh no more than 35 pounds (25 pounds for bound printed matter).

Special Mail Services

Service endorsements: Used by mailers to notify the U.S. Postal Service about what to do with mail that is undeliverable as addressed. These endorsements consist of the keywords *Address, Forwarding, Return,* and *Change* followed by two words *Service Requested.* The endorsements are the same for all classes of mail, but the treatment and the cost differ by the class of mail. You must write these endorsements legibly and in the proper area. The endorsement must read in the same direction as the delivery and return address. It should be printed in no smaller than 8-point type, and it must stand out clearly against its background. There must be a $\frac{1}{4}$-inch clear space around the endorsement. The endorsement must be placed in one of these four positions: directly below the return address, directly above the delivery address area, directly to the left of the postage area and below any rate marking, or directly below the postage area and below any rate marking.

Address Service Requested: A special service endorsement that allows mail either (1) to be forwarded if the addressee left a change of address with the post office or (2) to be returned to the mailer if the mail is undeliverable. This service also provides the mailer with the new address. Forwarding is offered free of charge for Priority, First-Class, and Standard Mail (A). Only local Standard Mail (B) is forwarded at no charge; if it is going out of town, extra postage will be due. First-Class and Priority Mail is returned at no charge, Standard Mail (A) is returned for a charge based on weight, and Standard Mail (B) return is charged at the appropriate single-piece rate.

Return Service Requested: Provides no forwarding service, only return with a new address notification. This service is free for First-Class and Priority Mail; Standard Mail (A) is charged First-Class or Priority Mail rates for the return.

Forwarding Service Requested: Provides forwarding and return, but new address notification is provided only for returned items. (With an Address Service Requested endorsement, you would get a new address notification even if the mail was forwarded.) First-Class Mail, Priority Mail, and Express Mail automatically get this service without any endorsement and free of charge. Periodicals are forwarded without charge for 60 days when postage is fully prepaid by the sender. Standard Mail (B) also automatically gets this service, but the addressee is responsible to pay any applicable forwarding charges.

Special delivery: A service that was used to ensure that mail got delivered as soon as it reached the recipient's post office. Special delivery stamps could be purchased at the post office. Special delivery could be used for regular First-Class, Second-Class, and insured mail. It could not be used for mail addressed to a post office box or military installation. Although special delivery may no longer be available, please note that questions about this service may still appear on the certification exams.

Special handling: Required for parcels whose unusual contents require additional care in transit and handling. Special handling is not required for those parcels sent by First-Class, Express, or Priority Mail. Special handling is available for Standard Mail only, including insured and COD mail. Special handling service is not necessary for sending ordinary parcels even when they contain fragile items. Breakable items will receive adequate protection if they are packed with sufficient cushioning and are clearly marked *FRAGILE.* If special handling is required, the words *SPECIAL HANDLING* should be printed in capital letters (and similarly, other mailing notations such as *Certified, Hand Cancel,* and *Registered*) two lines (at least $\frac{1}{4}$ inch) below the postage. Special Handling can be used on Standard Mail to speed up delivery for an extra fee. Special Handling is not the same as Special Delivery. While it was available, Special Delivery could be used on top of Special Handling to ensure that mail was delivered as soon as it arrived at the destination post office.

Certificate of mailing: Can be purchased at the time of mailing. The certificate does not provide coverage for loss or damage, nor does it provide proof of delivery.

Certified mail: Offers a guarantee that the item has been mailed and received by the correct party by requiring the mail carrier to obtain a signature on delivery. It provides proof of mailing and delivery of mail. The sender receives a mailing receipt at the time of mailing, and a record of delivery is kept at the recipient's post office. A return receipt to provide the sender with proof of delivery can also be purchased for an additional fee. Certified mail service is available only for First-Class and Priority Mail. It the best way to send documents, contracts, mortgages, or bank books that are not valuable intrinsically but would be hard to duplicate if lost. Certified mail is the cheapest way to receive proof of mailing.

Insurance: You may insure any piece of domestic mail for damage or loss. Insurance is available for Priority Mail, First-Class, and Standard Mail. The post office must reimburse you for an insured item that is lost or damaged.

Registered mail: The most secure service offered by the post office is registered mail. Registered mail provides insurance coverage for valuable items and is controlled from the point of mailing to the point of delivery. This service should be reserved for mailing items of tangible value, such as gifts or items that cannot be replaced in case of loss or damage. Both First-Class Mail and Priority Mail can be registered.

Restricted delivery: Mail is delivered only to a specific addressee or to someone authorized in writing to receive mail for the addressee. Restricted delivery is available only for registered mail, certified mail, COD mail, and mail insured for more than $50.

Return receipt: A receipt that will be returned to the sender to prove that the item was delivered. For a small fee, this signed receipt may be obtained on Express Mail and on COD, registered, certified, and most insured mail.

Collect on delivery (COD): Used when the mailer wants to collect payment for merchandise or postage from the recipient when the mail is delivered. COD service can be used for merchandise sent as First-Class Mail, Express Mail, Priority Mail, and Standard Mail or as registered mail.

Tracing mail: If a piece of registered or certified mail is lost, you may ask the post office to trace it. You should bring any receipts associated with the item.

Recalling mail: You can recall mail by filling out a written application at the post office and submitting it along with an envelope that is addressed identically to the one you want to recall. A mail carrier is not permitted to simply give mail back to you.

Postal money orders: You should never send cash through the mail. Postal money orders are a safe way to send money. You can purchase one or multiple money orders at your local post office. If your money order is lost or stolen, you must present your customer receipt to apply for a replacement. For a small fee, you can obtain a copy of a paid money order up to 2 years after the date on which it is cashed.

Mailgram: An electronic message service offered by Western Union that provides next-day Postal Service delivery for messages sent to any address in the United States. The messages are transmitted electronically, printed, and processed for delivery with the next business day's mail. Mailgram service is also available for Canadian addresses. You can send Mailgram messages by calling Western Union and dictating your message to the operator; or you can use your office Telex or TWX.

Private delivery services: There are many private services that offer various delivery options and also deliver mail overnight. They include Federal Express (FedEx), United Parcel Service (UPS), Emery, and DHL.

Mail Processing

Opening mail: In general, mail processing involves sorting, opening, recording, annotating, and distributing. Some physicians prefer to open letters from attorneys or accountants. Mail such as routine office expense bills, insurance forms, and checks for deposit may not need to be opened by the physician. In general, when you transmit letters to the physician, place the most important letters on the top and the least important ones on the bottom. Usually something marked *Special Delivery* is considered important mail. After opening the mail, medical assistants usually need to date-stamp the letters, check for enclosures, and in some cases annotate the letter. You should not open mail marked *Personal* or *Confidential* unless you have the addressee's explicit permission.

Annotate: To furnish with notes, which are usually critical or explanatory. You must highlight key points of the letter or write reminders and comments in the margins of the letter.

Outgoing mail: In order to complete tasks connected with outgoing mail, you need the following supplies and equipment:

- Letterhead
- Envelopes
- Labels
- Invoices and statements
- A computer with word processing capabilities and a printer
- A typewriter

Postage meter: Most medical offices use a postage meter that automatically stamps large mailings. The meter can print postage directly onto an envelope or a special gummed label. The cost of a postage meter must be weighed against the expense and inconvenience of making trips to the post office and keeping several different denominations of stamps on hand. Remember to change the date daily on the postage meter.

Business Letter Components

Components: Business letters consist of letterhead on which are printed a dateline, an inside address, a salutation, a subject line, the body of the letter, a complimentary closing, a signature block, an identification line, and notations. See Figure 8-4.

Dateline: Usually keyed $2\frac{1}{2}$ inches below the top edge or $\frac{1}{2}$ inch below the letterhead. (Most word processors and typewriters are set to print six lines to the inch, so $2\frac{1}{2}$ inches is 15 lines and $\frac{1}{2}$ inch is 3 lines.) The date should be completely written out, as in *December 15, 2001*.

Inside address: States the title and address of the person for whom the letter is intended. Degree designations should always be abbreviated, and when a professional degree is used, no other title should be placed in front of the name. For a physician, therefore, the title should read either *Dr. John Smith* or *John Smith, M.D.* The form *Dr. John Smith, M.D.* is incorrect. If there is a choice, it is preferable to use a professional degree such as *M.D.* rather than an academic title such as *Dr.* Spell out numerical names of streets. Use numerals for the building number unless it is a single digit, which should be spelled out: *Three Broadway Place*. Also spell out the words *Street, Drive, Boulevard, Place*, and so on.

Salutation: Keyed flush with the left margin on the second line below the inside address. The formal salutation should refer to the receiver of the letter using a title and surname (last name): *Dear Mrs. Brown*. If the receiver and sender know each other well, the receiver's given name (first name) may be used. In formal correspondence, the salutation is followed by a colon (:); a comma should be used only in informal letters. No salutation is necessary in a memorandum.

Subject: The subject line is sometimes used to bring the subject of the letter to the reader's attention. It should be typed two lines below the salutation and two lines above the body of the letter.

Body: Begins two lines below the salutation or subject line. It is single-spaced with a blank line between

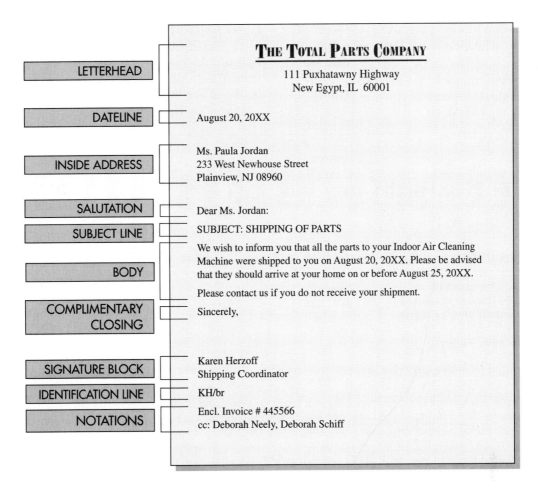

LETTERHEAD

THE TOTAL PARTS COMPANY

111 Puxhatawny Highway
New Egypt, IL 60001

DATELINE

August 20, 20XX

INSIDE ADDRESS

Ms. Paula Jordan
233 West Newhouse Street
Plainview, NJ 08960

SALUTATION

Dear Ms. Jordan:

SUBJECT LINE

SUBJECT: SHIPPING OF PARTS

BODY

We wish to inform you that all the parts to your Indoor Air Cleaning Machine were shipped to you on August 20, 20XX. Please be advised that they should arrive at your home on or before August 25, 20XX.

Please contact us if you do not receive your shipment.

COMPLIMENTARY CLOSING

Sincerely,

SIGNATURE BLOCK

Karen Herzoff
Shipping Coordinator

IDENTIFICATION LINE

KH/br

NOTATIONS

Encl. Invoice # 445566
cc: Deborah Neely, Deborah Schiff

Figure 8-4. *Knowing the parts of a typical business letter enables medical assistants to create written communications that reflect well on the office.*

paragraphs. Leave a blank line above and below a list, and indent each item on the list $\frac{1}{2}$ inch to 1 inch from the left margin.

Complimentary closing: Placed two lines below the last line of the body: *Sincerely, Yours truly, Best regards.* It is followed by a comma. Only the first letter of the first word is capitalized.

Signature: The signature block contains the sender's name on the first line and title on the second line. The block should be aligned with the closing and should be typed four lines below it to allow for the signature. Correspondence of a routine business nature, such as a supply order, is often signed by the medical assistant; however, medical reports, letters to insurance companies, consultation or referral letters, and letters clinical in nature should be signed by the physician.

Identification line: The typist's initials are sometimes included two lines below the signature block. These initials are often preceded by a colon or a slash. The traditional full form includes the initials of the person responsible for creating the letter followed by a colon or a slash and then the typist's initials.

Notations: Include information such as the number and type of enclosures and the names of other people who receive copies of the letter (referred to as carbon

copies or courtesy copies, abbreviated *cc*). The word *enclosure(s)* can be abbreviated as *Enc, Encl,* or *Encs.* The notation is typed two lines below the signature block or identification line.

Correspondence Style and Format

Format: The physical presentation of the message is as important as the written content. The guidelines for formatting letters are as follows:

- For most letters, your margins should be 1 inch wide.
- For shorter letters, you can use wider margins and start the address farther down the page.
- The body of the letter should be single-spaced. Between paragraphs, use double spacing.
- Use short sentences (fewer than 20 words).
- Use short paragraphs. Most of your business correspondence should be no more than a page long.
- For multi-page letters, use letterhead for the first page and blank paper for the other pages. This paper should be of the same bond and quality as the letterhead. On the second and subsequent

pages, insert a header that contains the name of the addressee, page number, date, and subject (if needed).

- Sign letters of routine business (such as ordering office supplies). Most other letters should be signed by the physician.

Letter styles: There are four major styles of letters: full-block, modified-block, indented, and simplified.

Full-block: Typed with all lines in standard letter format, flush left. It is quick and easy to write. This style is one of the most common formats used in medical practices. See Figure 8-5.

ABC PUBLISHERS, INC.

July 10, 20XX

Ms. Lara Erickson
2594 Hughes Boulevard
Hamilton City, NJ 08999

Dear Ms. Erickson:

SUBJECT: SHIPMENT DELAY

Thank you for contacting us regarding your order for *Smith and Doe's New Medical Dictionary*. Due to an unexpectedly heavy demand for the book, we are experiencing delays in processing and shipping orders.

We expect to ship your book in four weeks, around August 15. Because of this delay, we offer you the option of canceling your order with a full refund. If you would like to cancel at this point, please fill out and return the enclosed postcard. If we do not hear from you, your order will be shipped when ready.

We are sorry for any inconvenience this delay may cause you. Please be assured that ABC Publishers values its customers and always endeavors to fulfill orders in a timely fashion.

Sincerely yours,

Andrew Williams

Andrew Williams
Customer Service Manager

AW/cjc
Enclosure

117 New Avenue New York, NY 10000

Figure 8-5. *The full-block letter style is quicker and easier to type than other styles.*

Modified-block: All lines begin at the left margin, with the exception of the date line, complimentary closing, and keyed signature, which usually begin at the center position.

Simplified: Omits the salutation and the complimentary closing. All lines are keyed flush with the left margin. It is the most modern letter style. However, in most situations in a medical office, the simplified letter style may be too informal. See Figure 8-6.

Letterhead: Formal business stationery on which the name and address of the office or the physician are printed. Letterhead is usually printed on high-quality

---

ABC PUBLISHERS, INC.

July 10, 20XX

Ms. Lara Erickson
2594 Hughes Boulevard
Hamilton City, NJ 08999

SHIPMENT DELAY

Thank you for contacting us regarding your order for *Smith and Doe's New Medical Dictionary*. Due to an unexpectedly heavy demand for the book, we are experiencing delays in processing and shipping orders.

We expect to ship your book in four weeks, around August 15. Because of this delay, we offer you the option of canceling your order with a full refund. If you would like to cancel at this point, please fill out and return the enclosed postcard. If we do not hear from you, your order will be shipped when ready.

We are sorry for any inconvenience this delay may cause you. Please be assured that ABC Publishers values its customers and always endeavors to fulfill orders in a timely fashion.

Andrew Williams

ANDREW WILLIAMS, CUSTOMER SERVICE MANAGER

AW/cjc
Enclosure

117 New Avenue New York, NY 10000

Figure 8-6. *An example of the simplified letter style.*

paper of various fiber content (such as cotton bond) that usually bears a watermark. The quality is often described in terms of weight, which is based on 500 sheets of 17- by 22-inch paper. For letterhead, this weight is often 20 or 24 pounds, also referred to as Sub 20 and Sub 24. Letterhead paper is available in three sizes: standard, monarch or executive, and baronial.

Standard letterhead: Letterhead that is $8\frac{1}{2}$ by 11 inches in size and is used in professional correspondence and letters that discuss general business.

Executive letterhead: Letterhead that is $7\frac{1}{4}$ by $10\frac{1}{2}$ inches in size and is used for social and informal correspondence.

Baronial letterhead: Letterhead that is $5\frac{1}{2}$ by $8\frac{1}{2}$ inches in size and is used for short letters and memos.

Felt side of letterhead: The side from which the watermark is readable and the side on which printing and typing should be done.

Memorandum: Usually intended for interoffice correspondence. The purpose is to expedite the communication of a message in a manner that provides a record without becoming cumbersome. Interoffice memoranda are also called memos. They are used to inform personnel about meetings and general changes that affect everyone. You should not use salutations and complimentary closings in memos. The standard format for a memorandum begins with four lines specifying the recipient (the "to" line), the sender (the "from" line), the date, and the subject. The body of the memo starts two blank lines after the subject line and has no paragraph indentations.

Writing style: Good writing style demands accuracy, clarity, simplicity, and courtesy.

Proofreading: All letters must be checked for errors before mailing. Proofreading requires concentration and attention. Common mistakes involve content,

punctuation (including the use of apostrophes, hyphens, and parentheses), grammar, spelling, and spacing. You should use standard proofreader's marks to indicate changes that are required. See Figure 8-7. For the basic rules of writing, see Table 8-1.

Editing: The editing process ensures that the content of all documents is accurate, clear, complete, and organized logically. The writing style must be appropriate, and there must be no grammatical errors.

Abbreviations: Abbreviations recommended by the U.S. Postal Service (USPS) do not use punctuation marks. See Table 8-2 on p. 184. States and U.S. territories are designated by two-letter abbreviations.

ZIP Codes: Five-digit codes that identify the city, the individual post office, and the zone within the city.

ZIP+4 Code: Consists of the original five-digit code plus a four-digit add-on code. The add-on code specifies the geographic segment within the five-digit delivery area. This additional information helps the post office direct mail more efficiently and accurately. Your medical office may receive a discount on presorted First-Class Mail bearing ZIP+4 Codes if there are at least 500 pieces. A discount also applies to nonpresorted ZIP+4 mail of at least 250 pieces.

Envelopes: There are three commonly used sizes: Number $6\frac{3}{4}$ Number 7, and Number 10 (also called business size). Most common in the medical office are Number $6\frac{3}{4}$ and Number 10. The Number $6\frac{3}{4}$ size with a window is often used for mailing statements.

Folding letters: For standard letters that fit into a Number 10 envelope, fold the bottom third of the letter up and make a crease, then fold the top edge of the letter down to within about 3/8" of the first crease and make a second crease. Folding the top third toward you produces a D-fold; folding it away from you produces a Z-fold. For a Number $6\frac{3}{4}$ envelope, fold an $8\frac{1}{2}$ by 11-inch sheet in

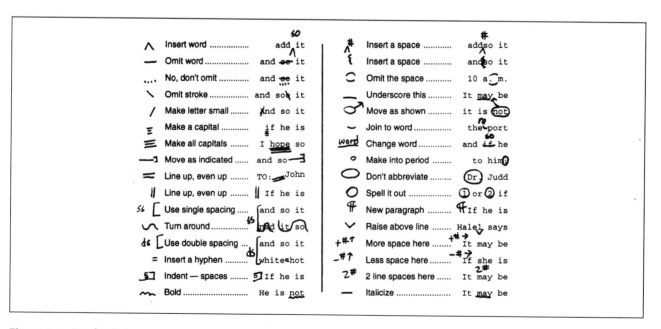

Figure 8-7. *Proofreader's marks.*

Word Division

Divide:
- According to pronunciation.
- Compound words between the two words from which they are derived.
- Hyphenated compound words at the hyphen.
- After a prefix.
- Before a suffix.
- Between two consonants that appear between vowels.
- Before *–ing* unless the last consonant is doubled, in which case, divide before the second consonant.

Do not divide:
- Such suffixes as *–sion*, *–tial*, and *–tion*.
- A word so that only one letter is left on a line.

Capitalization

Capitalize:
- All proper names.
- All titles, positions, or indications of family relation when preceding a proper name or in place of a proper noun. (Do not capitalize when the word is used alone or with possessive pronouns or articles.)
- Days of the week, months, and holidays.
- Names of organizations and membership designations.
- Racial, religious, and political designations.
- Adjectives, nouns, and verbs that are derived from proper nouns (including currently copyrighted trade names).
- Specific addresses and geographic locations.
- Sums of money written in legal or business documents.
- Titles or headings of books, magazines, and newspapers.

Plurals

- Add *s* or *es* to most singular nouns. (Plural forms of most medical terms do not follow this rule.)
  With medical terms ending in *is*, drop the *is* and add *es*: metastasis/metastases
  With terms ending in *um*, drop the *um* and add *a*: diverticulum/diverticula
  With terms ending in *us*, drop the *us* and add *i*: calculus/calculi
- Exception: The plural forms of some words, mainly from Latin, involve other changes: corpus/corpora, genus/genera, sinus/sinuses, virus/viruses
- With most terms ending in *ma*, add *ta*: stoma/stomata.
  With terms otherwise ending in *a*, drop the *a* and add *ae*: vertebra/vertebrae

Possessives

To show ownership or relation to another noun:
- For singular nouns, add an apostrophe and an *s*.
- For plural nouns that do not end in an *s*, add an apostrophe and an *s*.
- For plural nouns that end in an *s*, add just an apostrophe.

Numbers

Use numerals:
- In general writing, when the number is 11 or greater.
- With abbreviations and symbols.
- When discussing laboratory results or statistics.

Table 8-1 (table continued on the next page)

- When referring to specific sums of money.
- When using a series of numbers in a sentence.

Tips:
- Use commas when numerals have more than three digits.
- Do not use commas when referring to account numbers, page numbers, or policy numbers.
- Use a hyphen (or an en dash if possible) with numerals to indicate a range.

Table 8-1, continued

AT A GLANCE   USPS Abbreviations

Word	Abbreviation	Word	Abbreviation
Apartment	APT	Lane	LN
Avenue	AVE	North	N
Boulevard	BLVD	Parkway	PKY
Center	CTR	Place	PL
Circle	CIR	Plaza	PLZ
Corner	COR	Road	RD
Court	CT	Room	RM
Drive	DR	South	S
East	E	Street	ST
Expressway	EXPY	Suite	STE
Highway	HWY	West	W
Junction	JCT		

Table 8-2

half, fold the right third to the left, and fold the left third to the right. For window envelopes, make sure that when you make the final crease, the address faces outward and will show through the window correctly.

Sealing envelopes: Use a damp sponge and seal many envelopes at one time.

Address: Individual First-Class letters must be addressed clearly and legibly. To qualify for bulk or presort discounts, mail must be addressed according to certain conventions established by the USPS. The recipient address must be printed single-spaced on the envelope in all capital letters with no punctuation. Put the addressee's name on the first line, the department on the second line, and the company name on the third line. If the letter is being sent to someone's attention at a company, put the company name first and *ATTENTION: [NAME]* on the second line. The last line in the address must include the city, the two-letter state abbreviation, and the ZIP Code. See Figure 8-8.

Return address: A return address for the sender should always be placed in the upper left corner.

Handling instructions: Instructions, such as the words *Personal* or *Confidential,* should be placed three lines below the return address.

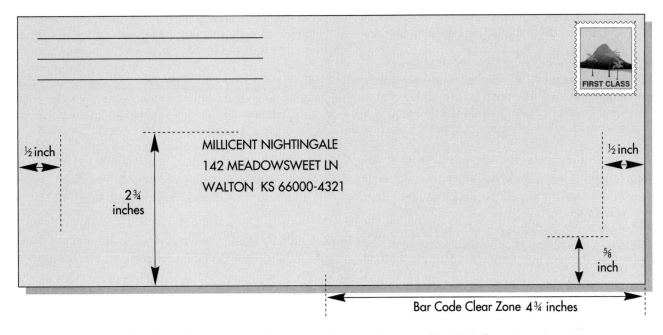

Figure 8-8. *Following this format for typing an envelope assures that it can be processed by USPS electronic equipment.*

In the figure:

½ inch

MILLICENT NIGHTINGALE
142 MEADOWSWEET LN
WALTON KS 66000-4321

2¾ inches

½ inch

⅝ inch

FIRST CLASS

Bar Code Clear Zone 4¾ inches

Telephone Techniques

Telephone calls: Classified as incoming, outgoing, and interoffice. Medical assistants can communicate with patients, pharmacies, laboratories, and other medical offices via telephone. First impressions matter in telephone communications. Because you are usually the first contact most people have with a medical office, you should convey a professional and positive attitude by what you say and how you sound to the caller. You also need to take care to maintain patient confidentiality. Always be aware of who is in hearing range of your conversation and use discretion in the type of information you discuss over the phone.

Volume: Should be the same as when speaking to someone in the same room, just loud enough for them to hear clearly. Bear in mind that some patients may be hard of hearing.

Enunciation: Speak clearly and articulate carefully. Don't slur your speech.

Pronunciation: Adopt a speech pattern that is considered standard. Make sure that you use terminology you are comfortable with so that all of your pronunciation is correct.

Speed: Should be at a normal rate, neither too fast nor too slow.

Answering system: May be an automated voice mail system, an answering machine, or an answering service.

Answering service: Answering services employ people rather than machines to answer the telephone. They take messages and communicate them to the doctor on call (the doctor who is responsible for handling emergencies that may occur when the office is closed). Answering machines sometimes are programmed to refer callers to an answering service in case of emergencies, or the answering service may directly answer the phone after a certain number of rings during specific hours. It is best to set a regular schedule to retrieve messages from the answering service. This way you are less likely to miss any messages.

Incoming Calls

Incoming calls: Handle incoming calls as follows:

- Answer telephone calls promptly, by the second or third ring.
- Hold the phone's mouthpiece about an inch away from your mouth, and leave at least one hand free to write with.
- Greet callers first with the name of the office and then with your name. Do not answer the phone by simply giving the number of your office or by saying "hello."
- Identify the caller. Demonstrate your willingness to assist the caller by asking, "How may I help you?"
- Be courteous, calm, and pleasant, using phrases such as "please" and "thank you."
- Pay full attention to the caller, and listen carefully. Identify the nature of the call.
- Use words appropriate to the situation, but avoid using technical terms.
- Avoid unnecessarily long conversations. Keep any personal conversations to a minimum.
- If you get interrupted by a second call, excuse yourself to the first caller and answer the second

call. Determine the identity of the second caller and the nature of the call. Return to the first call as soon as possible. Minimize waiting for all callers. In fact, if callers are on hold, return to them occasionally to reassure them that you have not forgotten about them and to update them on what is going on. For example, if someone is waiting to talk to the physician but the physician is still busy, offer the caller an opportunity to leave a message or have the physician return the call as soon as possible.

- At the end of the call, say "goodbye" and use the caller's name.

Calls for the physician(s): Some calls will require the physician's personal attention, such as:

- Emergency calls
- Calls from other doctors and physicians
- Calls from patients who want to discuss test results, particularly abnormal results
- Calls from patients who want to discuss symptoms with the physician
- Reports from patients concerning unsatisfactory progress
- Requests for prescription renewals when they have not been previously authorized by the physician
- Personal calls

Most medical offices have a routing procedure for various types of calls. In general, all emergencies should be routed to the physician immediately. Calls from other physicians should also be routed to the doctor immediately if possible. If a patient calls and the physician is not in, tell the patient right away; then find out the identity of the caller and the nature of the call and offer to take a message, or inform the patient of a better time to call back.

Transferring calls: When you transfer calls, identify the person calling to the physician and give a brief description of the nature of the call. If possible, try to get the patient's chart to the physician before transferring the call. If a caller refuses to be identified, you should not put the call through to the physician. Ask callers who cannot identify themselves on the phone to write a letter to the physician and mark it *Personal*.

Administrative-issue calls: Common calls to a physician's office that a medical assistant can handle. These calls include:

- Appointment scheduling, rescheduling, and canceling
- Insurance questions
- Inquiries about bills
- X-ray and laboratory reports
- Routine reports from hospitals regarding a patient's progress
- Satisfactory progress reports from patients
- Requests for referrals to other doctors
- Questions concerning office policies, fees, and hours and other such items
- Administrative calls such as complaints about administrative matters
- Prescription refills when they have been previously authorized by the physician

Emergency triage: The screening and sorting of emergency situations. It is used as a process of evaluating the urgency of a medical condition and deciding what necessary action to take. Depending on the medical facility, some medical assistants might be required to perform triage; therefore, you should be familiar with this concept. See Table 8-3 for information on which symptoms and conditions require immediate medical help.

AT A GLANCE	Symptoms and Conditions that Require Immediate Medical Help
Unconsciousness	
Lack of breathing or trouble breathing	
Severe bleeding	
Pressure or pain in the abdomen that will not go away	
Severe vomiting	
Bloody stools	

Table 8-3 (table continued on the next page)

Poisoning
Injuries to the head, neck, or back
Choking
Drowning
Electrical shock
Snakebites
Vehicle collisions
Allergic reactions to foods or insect stings
Chemicals or foreign objects in the eye
Fires, severe burns, or injuries from explosion
Human bites or any deep animal bites
Heart attack (Symptoms: chest pain or pressure; pain radiating from the chest to the arm, shoulder, neck, jaw, back, or stomach; nausea or vomiting; weakness; shortness of breath; pale or gray skin color)
Stroke (Symptoms: seizures, severe headache, slurred speech)
Broken bones (Symptoms: inability to move or put weight on the injured body part, misshapen appearance of body part)
Shock (Symptoms: paleness, feeling faint and sweaty, weak and rapid pulse, cold and moist skin, confusion or drowsiness)
Heatstroke (Symptoms: confusion, loss of consciousness, flushed skin that is hot and dry, strong and rapid pulse)
Hypothermia (Symptoms: increasing clumsiness; unreasonable behavior; irritability; confusion; sleepy, slurred speech; slipping into a coma with slow, weak breathing and heartbeat)

Table 8-3, continued

Documenting calls: Proper documentation protects the physician if the caller takes legal action. It is essential in a medical office. This documentation provides an accurate record and helps guard against lawsuits.

Taking messages: Use a standard self-duplicating telephone pad so that you have a record of all incoming calls. Record the date and time of the call, the name of the person being called, the name of the caller, the caller's telephone number, a description of needed action, a complete message, and your name or initials.

Problem calls: The receptionist occasionally has to speak with callers who are angry or upset. These situations must be handled in a calm and constructive manner at all times. Try not to interrupt the caller. Avoid putting the caller on hold. Express regret that the caller has a complaint, but do not necessarily admit an error or apologize for an error. Avoid blaming another staff member. Only if it is necessary, refer the caller to the office manager or to the physician.

Telecommunication

ARU telephone systems: Used in many hospitals and larger ambulatory care settings. When a call is answered, and a recorded voice identifies departments or services the caller can reach by pressing a specified number on the telephone keypad.

Fax (facsimile) machines: Very common in the physician's office. They are used to send reports, referrals, insurance approvals, and informal correspondence. A fax is sent over telephone lines from one fax machine (or fax modem) to another. As with the handling of most documents, a patient's confidentiality must be protected when sensitive information is faxed. The fax machine must be in a secure location where only authorized personnel have access to it.

Electronic mail: The process of sending, receiving, storing, and forwarding messages in digital form through telephone lines or via dedicated Internet connections. Messages are transmitted from computer to computer. The messages are stored until the receiver retrieves them. Both the sender and the receiver may print messages or forward them to another electronic mailbox. E-mail can save time and money.

Intercom: A direct line of an intercommunication system within the facility.

Medical Meetings

Agenda: The order of business for a meeting.

Preparing for a meeting: Requires the following arrangements:

- Select and reserve a room. You must know how many people are going to attend and the scheduled length of the meeting.

- Invite the speaker and confirm the speaker's acceptance of the invitation. You should also obtain the speaker's credentials for use during the introduction.

- Invite everyone to the meeting and confirm the acceptance of the invitation.

- Arrange for a luncheon, dinner, or other refreshments.

- Note the date and time of the meeting on the appointment calendar.

- Prepare and mail the meeting agenda to everyone who plans to attend.

- Make sure that the room has an adequate number of chairs, a writing board with marking pens or a chalkboard with chalk and an eraser, necessary multimedia equipment already set up, and fresh water.

Minutes: The official record of the proceedings of a meeting. It is not necessary to write everything down word for word, but all pertinent information discussed at the meeting should be noted. Note the following facts about the meeting:

- Date, location, time, and purpose of the meeting
- Name of the presiding officer

- Names of members in attendance
- Order of business from the agenda and any changes made in the order
- Motions made, whether approved or rejected
- Summaries of discussions

Travel Arrangements

Preparations for a trip: In preparing for a trip, the medical assistant should consult with the person traveling, carefully noting the date and time of departure, destinations, length of stay at each destination, and times of arrival at and departure from each destination. The best resource for travel information is a skilled agent at a reputable travel agency.

Reservations: Should be made at the earliest possible time to allow the travel agent an opportunity to secure the best rates. Request confirmations in writing if time permits, and make sure that the person traveling has all the relevant confirmation numbers.

Itinerary: A list that specifies each place the traveler will visit, the name and address of the hotel, the date and time of arrival and departure, and the schedule of the convention if relevant.

Duties during the physician's absence: Make sure that adequate arrangements are made with the physician before he or she leaves about how to handle bills, telephone calls, appointments, and mail. As soon as you know the dates for the physician's trip, you should block off this time in the appointment book so that no new patients are scheduled. If patients have regular appointments scheduled for this time already, they should be notified about the physician's planned absence, and you should make arrangements for new appointments. Also keep a daily log of all telephone calls and what action if any was taken.

Patient Education

Forms of patient education: Materials can be as simple as a single sheet of paper, or longer and more complex. Among the formats are brochures, booklets, fact sheets, educational newsletters, and community directories.

Visual materials: May be easier for many patients to understand. Videotapes are common, as are seminars and classes. See Figure 8-9.

Patient information packet: Material specific to the practice to help patients feel more comfortable with it. The packet normally contains the following information:

- Introduction to the office
- Physicians' qualifications
- Description of the practice

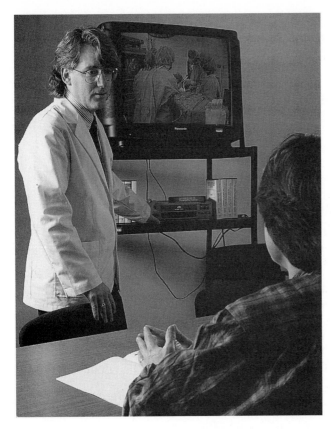

Figure 8-9. *Videotapes are an excellent educational aid for the medical office because of their visual format.*

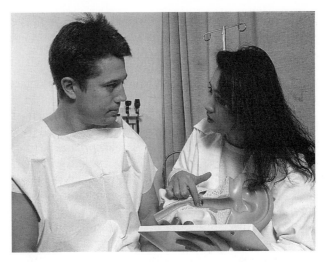

Figure 8-10. *An anatomical model can help patients visualize what will happen during surgery.*

- Introduction to the office staff
- Office hours
- Appointment scheduling policy and procedure
- Telephone policy
- Payment policy
- Insurance policies
- Patient confidentiality statement

Preoperative education: Instruction given to patients prior to surgery. It informs them about the details of the procedure and about diet and activity restrictions, among other things.

Anatomical model: A lifelike model of body parts or structures used to help patients visualize conditions or surgeries. See Figure 8-10.

Sources of materials: Libraries, the Internet, CD-ROMs, social service agencies, and health care organizations and associations.

Promoting patient health and preventing injury: One of the goals of patient education is to promote good health behaviors and to teach patients how to prevent common injuries. As a medical assistant, you can help patients develop healthy practices and habits. Encourage patients to eat well, exercise regularly, get adequate rest, limit alcohol consumption, stop smoking, and balance work and leisure to avoid stress. Also advise patients on how they can avoid common

injuries at home and in the workplace. For a list of tips on avoiding injury, see Table 8-4 on p. 190.

Appointments and Schedules

Appointment scheduling: The process that determines which patients will be seen by the physician, how soon they will be seen, and how much time will be allotted to each patient, based on the patient's complaint and the physician's availability. Although patient appointment scheduling may seem like a routine function, a smooth patient flow often determines the success of a day in the medical office.

Appointment book: A book in which medical facilities can keep track of appointments. The basic format of appointment books is the matrix, which requires blocking off times on the schedule during which the doctor is not available to see patients. These times include:

- Lunch
- Consultations
- Visits with drug company representatives
- Catch-up time
- Emergencies
- Hospital rounds
- Surgery
- Days off
- Holidays

See Figure 8-11 on p. 191 for a sample page from an appointment book.

Legal record: The appointment book is a legal record. Some experts advise holding on to old appointment books for at least 3 years.

Scheduling abbreviations: The receptionist who maintains the appointment book should be familiar

At Home

- Install smoke detectors, carbon monoxide detectors, and fire extinguishers.
- Keep all medicines, chemicals, and household cleaning solutions out of the reach of children. Purchase products in childproof containers. Lock or attach childproof latches to all cabinets, medicine chests, and drawers that contain poisonous items.
- Keep chemicals in their original containers, and store them out of children's reach.
- Install adequate lighting in rooms and hallways.
- Install railings on stairs.
- Use nonskid backing on rugs and bathroom mats to help prevent falls.
- Avoid plugging too many electrical appliances into the same outlet.
- Never use appliances in the bathtub or near a sink filled with water.

At Work

- Use appropriate safety equipment and protective gear.
- Lift heavy objects appropriately. Bend at the knees, not at the waist. Never attempt to move furniture on your own.
- Use surge protectors on computer equipment.
- Make sure that hallways, entrance areas, work areas, and parking lots are well lit.
- Practice proper posture when sitting. Do not sit for long periods of time. Get up and stretch, or walk down the hall and back.

Table 8-4

with the abbreviations in Table 8-5 to save space and time when entering information.

Types of Appointments

Types of appointments: A medical assistant may schedule appointments for any one of the following purposes:

- New patients
- Follow-up
- Admissions
- Surgery
- Physician referrals
- Salespersons, including pharmaceutical sales representatives
- Returning patients
- Specialists
- Buffer time

New patient: A patient who is not established at the medical practice and is scheduling the first visit. When you schedule appointments for new patients, make sure to allow enough time for filling out forms and making files.

Pharmaceutical sales representatives: Some doctors may be willing to schedule a short appointment with sales reps to take a look at products that might be useful in their medical practice.

Abbreviation	Meaning
can	Cancellation
cons	Consultation
CPE	Complete physical examination
FU	Follow-up appointment
NP	New patient
NS	No-show
PT	Physical therapy
re ✓	Recheck
ref	Referral
RS	Reschedule
surg	Surgery

Table 8-5

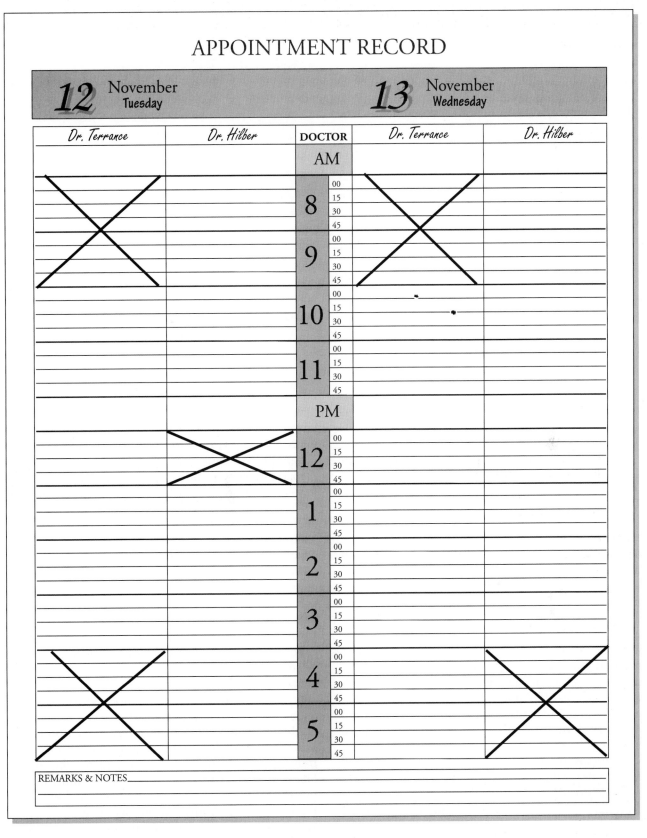

Figure 8-11. *It is important to establish a matrix in the appointment book so that appointments are not scheduled for times when the doctor will be out of the office.*

Buffer time: Appointment slots held open in case of emergencies. Every medical practice should have at least one or two slots open for buffer time each day.

Scheduling Process

Office hours: The physician or a group of physicians in the medical office usually determines office hours. By effectively scheduling patients to fit a particular practice, it is possible to make profitable use of physician and staff time. There are medical facilities, such as freestanding urgent care centers, that offer extended evening hours and may be open 24 hours a day.

Matrix: The schedule matrix contains the times already allotted, which therefore are not available for scheduling patients. The first step in preparing an appointment book is to block off these times and establish a matrix.

Scheduling guidelines: Once the matrix has been established, you can schedule patient appointments based on:

- Patient needs and preferences
- Physician preferences and habits
- Degree of illness and/or contagion
- Available facilities

Considerations: When scheduling appointments, you should consider:

- Legal issues
- Tailoring the scheduling system
- Analyzing patient flow
- Waiting time
- Flexibility

Appointment cards: On reminders given to patients the medical assistant should write the date and time when they are scheduled to return to the office for another appointment. The card is sent through the mail or handed to the patient if the appointment is made in person. See Figure 8-12.

Phone: You may be required to call the patient to schedule a follow-up appointment or to remind the patient about an upcoming appointment. These calls will depend on office policy, but it's common for many practices to call patients 1 or 2 days before an appointment to remind them of and to confirm the scheduled time.

Special problems: There will be times when you will have to deal with patients who are late for appointments or do not show up at all. For legal purposes, you must have careful and accurate documentation of these incidents.

Cancellations: When a patient calls to cancel an appointment, thank the patient for calling and offer to reschedule the appointment immediately. If the patient will call back later to reschedule, make a note of that fact. Also note the canceled appointment in the appointment book as well as the patient's medical record.

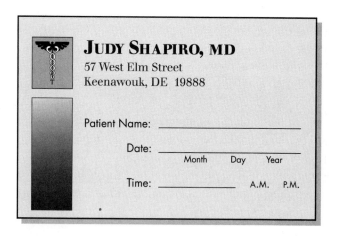

Figure 8-12. *Before patients leave the office, be sure to give them an appointment card if they are scheduled to return to the office.*

Rescheduling: Appointments are often rescheduled because of illness, emergencies, or other unforeseen problems.

Types of Scheduling Systems

Open hours: Some providers do not schedule appointments, and they conduct their practices with open office hours. This system is the least structured of all the scheduling systems. Patients come in during given hours of the day, sign in, and are seen on a first-come, first-served basis, unless there is an extreme emergency. One of the main disadvantages of this system is the inefficient use of the staff's time that results from uneven patient flow.

Double booking: The scheduling of two or more patients in the same time slot. This method is limited to practices in which more than one patient can be attended to at a time. In all other practices, you should not schedule multiple patients in the same time slot unless they can be seen in a fairly short amount of time (about 5 minutes). Patients will become inpatient and angry with long waits.

Wave scheduling: A method that can be used effectively in medical facilities that have several procedure rooms and adequate personnel to staff them. This method provides built-in flexibility to accommodate unforeseen situations, such as a patient who requires more time with the physician, a patient who arrives late, or a patient who fails to keep an appointment. The purpose of wave scheduling is to begin and end each hour on time, and medical practices that employ this system assume that the actual time needed for any particular patient will average out. For example, if the average amount of time needed for any one patient is 15 minutes, appointments can be made at 10:00, 10:15, 10:30, and 10:45.

Modified wave scheduling: Wave scheduling can be modified to prevent long waits by patients. In the modified wave method, appointments for two or more patients are scheduled at the beginning of each hour, followed by single appointments every 10 to 20 minutes for the remainder of the hour.

Advance scheduling: In some specialties, appointments may be made weeks or even months in advance.

Grouping: Reserving certain times such as a day of the week or time of the day to perform a number of similar procedures.

Exceptions: There are a few types of patients who cannot be fit neatly into a regular schedule:

- Emergency patients
- Acutely ill patients
- Patients who have a physician referral

Computerized scheduling: Becoming more common in medical offices because it has several advantages over handwritten systems (see Figure 8-13). One of the main advantages of a computerized system is that the scheduling information can be accessed from all terminals.

Medical Records and Filing

Medical records: Accurate medical records are essential to proper patient care. Medical records provide a continuous story of a patient's progress from the first visit to the last with all the important information, observations, illnesses, treatments, and outcomes carefully documented. These records are important communication and research tools as well as legal documents.

Reasons for medical records: Good reasons for carefully recording medical information include:

- To provide the best medical care to patients. Good medical records help a physician provide continuity in a patient's medical care.

- To supply statistical information. Properly conducted studies based on objective measurements can lead to revised techniques and treatments.

- To be used in lawsuits and malpractice cases either to support a patient's claim or to support the physician's defense against such a claim.

- To evaluate the quality of treatment a doctor's office provides.

- To facilitate reimbursement. Medical records provide documentation for insurance billing and the basis for defending audits by managed care and government (Medicare and Medicaid) regulatory agencies.

Documentation: The recording of information in a patient's medical record. The term also refers to information recorded.

Standard information to include in medical records: Each new patient who comes to the office will need a medical record. Each medical facility has its

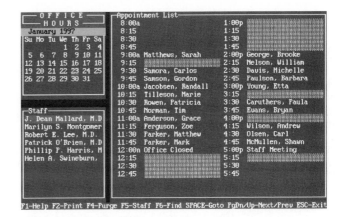

Figure 8-13. *Many medical offices are now using computerized scheduling instead of or in addition to a traditional appointment book.*

own forms and charts, but all records must contain certain standard information. For adequate legal protection, a patient's medical record should include the following items:

- Patient registration form (see Figure 8-14)
- Patient medical history
- Physical examination results
- Results of laboratory tests
- Copies of prescriptions and notes on refill authorizations
- Diagnosis and treatment plan
- Patient progress reports, documentation of follow-up visits, and notes on telephone calls
- Informed consent forms
- Discharge summary
- Correspondence with and about the patient

Make sure that you date and initial all entries. Always record all signs, symptoms, and other information the patient wishes to share with you. Use the patient's own words, not your interpretation of them. Make sure that any interviews are conducted in a private room where others cannot hear.

Six Cs of charting: In order to maintain accurate patient records, keep these six concepts in mind:

Client's words—Do not interpret the patient's words.

Clarity—Use precise and accurate medical terminology. Write legibly and neatly.

Completeness—Fill out all forms. All information should be complete and accurate.

Conciseness—Use abbreviations where appropriate.

Chronological order—Date all entries, and keep medical records up to date by entering all current reports and information.

Community Health Center • 6508 South Street • Kokomo, IN 46902
(317) 555-1234 • Fax: (317) 555-1245

Patient Registration
Patient Information

Name:_____ Today's Date:_____

Address:_____

City:_____ State:_____ Zip Code:_____

Telephone (Home):_____ (Work):_____

Birthdate:_____ Age:_____ Sex: M F No. of Children_____ Marital Status: M S W D

Social Security Number:_____ Employer:_____ Occupation:_____

Primary Physician:_____

Referred by:_____

Person to Contact in Emergency:_____

Emergency Telephone:_____

Special Needs:_____

Responsible Party

Party Responsible for Payment: Self   Spouse   Parent   Other

Name (If Other Than Self):_____

Address:_____

City:_____ State:_____ Zip Code:_____

Primary Insurance

Primary Medical Insurance:_____

Insured party: Self   Spouse   Parent   Other

ID#/Social Security No.:_____ Group/Plan No.:_____

Name (If Other Than Self):_____

Address:_____

City:_____ State:_____ Zip Code:_____

Secondary Insurance

Secondary Medical Insurance:_____

Insured party: Self   Spouse   Parent   Other

ID#/Social Security No.:_____ Group/Plan No.:_____

Name (If Other Than Self):_____

Address:_____

City:_____ State:_____ Zip Code:_____

Figure 8-14. *The patient registration form is often the first document used in initiating a patient record.*

Confidentiality—Protect the patient's privacy. Only the patient, the attending physician, and the medical assistant are allowed to see the charts without the patient's written consent or a court order.

Items to exclude: The following items should not be included in a patient's medical records:

- Reports from consulting physicians should not be placed in the record until carefully reviewed.
- Financial information is not included.
- Transferred records from the patient's previous physician are never added to the patient's record.
- Prejudicial, personal, or flippant comments are never entered into the record.

Records management: Records management includes assembling the medical record for each patient and having an efficient filing system for retrieval, transfer, protection, retention, storage, and destruction of these files. Some of the objectives of good records management include:

- Saving space
- Reducing filing equipment expenditures
- Preventing the creation of unnecessary records
- Retrieving information faster
- Reducing misfiles
- Complying with legal safeguards
- Saving the physicians' and patients' time

SOAP: An approach to documentation that provides an orderly series of steps for dealing with a medical case, which lists (1) the patient's symptoms (*s*ubjective data), (2) the diagnosis (*o*bjective data), (3) *a*ssessment, and (4) *p*lan of action.

POMR or POR: A system of *p*roblem-*o*riented *m*edical *r*ecords based on client problems—conditions or behaviors that result in physical or emotional distress or interfere with functioning.

Transcription and Dictation

Medical transcription: The transformation of spoken words into accurate written form. These written notes are then entered into the patient's record. Transcribed material must be accurate and complete, with correct grammar, spelling, medical abbreviations, medical codes, and terminology. Dictated materials are confidential and should be regarded as potential legal documents.

Ensuring accurate transcription: Fast, accurate transcription is achieved by following these recommendations:

- Have needed materials at hand.
- Adjust the transcribing equipment's speed, tone, and volume.
- Listen all the way through before starting to transcribe.

- If problems with the recorded material arise, write down the time on the digital counter so that you can find them quickly when requesting clarification.
- Listen carefully.

Dictation: Medical assistants may be required to take dictation directly from the physician. In order to take dictation properly, follow these guidelines:

- Use a writing pad with a stiff back or a clipboard.
- Use incomplete sentences to keep up with the speed of speech.
- Use abbreviations when you can.
- When something is unclear, ask for clarification right away.
- Read the dictation back to the physician to verify accuracy.

Confidentiality: The principle of treating something as a private matter not intended for public knowledge. Confidentiality protects information so that it is not released to anyone unless required by law. When children reach the age of 18, most states consider them adults with the right to privacy. No one, not even their parents, may see their medical records without their written consent or a court order.

Filing Systems

Alphabetical filing: Strict alphabetical filing is one of the simplest filing methods. It involves alphabetizing the files from A to Z. Files are labeled with the patient's surname (last name) first, followed by the given name (first name), and the middle initial.

Alphanumeric filing: A filing system based on combinations of letters and numbers.

Subject filing: Arranging records alphabetically by names of topics or things rather than by names of individuals. It can be either alphabetical or alphanumeric, such as: A1–5, B1–2, etc. It is the most widely used filing system for medical practices.

Chronological filing: A filing system based on time.

Numeric filing: The filing of records, correspondence, or cards by number. Such a system is often used when patient information is highly confidential. Numeric filing is used by practically every large clinic or hospital serving more than 5,000 patients.

Color-coding system: A filing system based on color. One commonly used system breaks the alphabet up into five different colors: red, yellow, green, blue, and purple. Red is for A through D, yellow for E through H, green for I through N, blue for O through Q, and purple for R through Z.

Computer records: Some medical practices use computer software to create and store patient records. One of the main advantages to computerization is that a physician can call up the record whenever it is needed, review or update the file, and save it to the central computer again.

Tickler file: A chronological file used as a reminder that something needs to be done on a certain date.

Filing Procedures

Filing procedures: There are five steps involved in filing:

- Inspecting
- Indexing
- Coding
- Sorting
- Storing and filing

Indexing: An organized method of identifying and separating items to be filed, such as letters or papers, by assigning essential pieces of information to numbered units (sometimes called fields). The key unit, unit 1, is generally the surname (last name). Unit 2 is the given name (first name). Unit 3 is the middle initial. Unit 4 is a title or special designation (Ms., Dr., Jr., Sr., etc.).

Coding: Placing some indication of the index on the material to be filed. Coding may be done by underlining the name or the subject. Every paper placed in a patient's medical record should have the date and the name of the patient on it, usually in the upper right corner.

Sorting: Arranging items to be filed in a sequence before going to the file cabinet or shelf.

Active files: Files that you use frequently.

Inactive files: Files that you use infrequently. Each practice develops guidelines for determining the point at which a file becomes inactive. In some practices, the file of a patient who has not been seen for a year may be considered inactive, whereas in others the amount of time may be 2 or 3 years.

Closed files: Files of patients who have died or moved away.

Transfer: Removing inactive records from the active files.

Retention period: The amount of time to keep different types of patient records in the office after files have become inactive or closed. Some legal requirements for retaining certain types of information are listed in Table 8-6.

Identical names: When filing identical names, use date of birth, patient identification number, or some other form of identification in order to distinguish between the two patients.

Business and organization records: File business and organization records according to subject and topic.

Filing Equipment

File shelves: An advantage of keeping files on shelves is that it allows several people to retrieve and return files at one time.

File cabinets: There are three types of file cabinets used in the medical office: vertical, lateral, and movable.

AT A GLANCE — Requirements for Retaining Records

Source	Type of Record	Retention Period
National Childhood Vaccine Injury Act of 1986	Immunization records	Permanently
Labor Standards Act	Employee health records	3 years
Statute of limitations	Records needed for civil suits	Varies by state, most commonly 2 years
Legal consultants	Patient records	At least 7 years
Internal Revenue Service	Financial records	10 years
State laws	Records of minors	From 2 to 7 years after the child reaches legal age, depending on the state
American Medical Association, American Hospital Association, other medical groups	Patient records	10 years after patient's final visit or contact

Table 8-6

Vertical file cabinets: Have from two to five drawers. They are the least efficient type of cabinet because half of the filing time goes into opening and closing drawers. Also, bending, squatting, and stretching to reach files makes these cabinets that much more inefficient.

Open-shelf file cabinets: Take up 50% less space, permit quick access, and have no drawers to open or close. They have the disadvantage of collecting dust.

Movable file units: Allow easy access to large record systems and require less space than vertical or lateral files.

Supplies: Supplies needed for file cabinets are:

File folders designed for the type of cabinet in use.

Identification labels, affixed either along the top of the file folder or along the side of the file folder in open-shelf file cabinets.

Guides and captions: Guides are used to separate the file folders. Captions are used to identify major sections of file folders by more manageable subunits.

Out guide: A cardboard or plastic sheet kept in place of the patient's chart when the chart is removed from filing storage.

Computers

Computer systems: Consist of hardware, software, data, and users (people). See Figure 8-15. As a medical assistant you should be familiar with the components and uses of a computer.

Hardware

Computer hardware: Can be broken down into four types of physical components: the processor (the central processing unit, or CPU), memory, storage, and input/output devices (peripherals). See Figure 8-16.

Processing

Processor: This single chip is the brain of a computer. Processors differ by manufacturer, type, and clock speed. The processor is a mathematical machine that controls the flow of and access to data and manages the use of all other computer components. The CPU and the memory are located on the computer's main system board, or motherboard. Every CPU has at least two basic parts: the control unit and the arithmetic-logic unit.

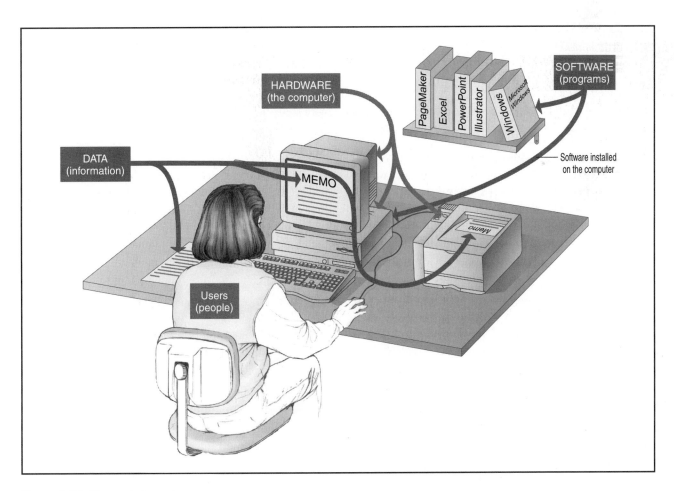

Figure 8-15. *The computer system.*

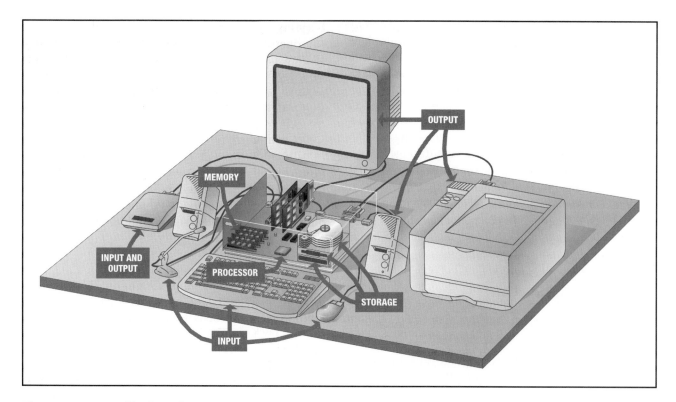

Figure 8-16. *Types of hardware devices.*

Control unit: Extracts instructions from memory, decodes, and executes them, calling on the arithmetic-logic unit as necessary.

Memory

Memory: Used to hold data and instructions (software programs) while they are being processed. There are three main types of memory: random-access memory (RAM), read-only memory (ROM), and virtual memory. Memory is usually measured in bytes, and the amount is generally expressed in units of 1 million bytes (megabytes).

Bit: The smallest piece of data available, stored by a computer essentially as either a *1 (on)* or a *0 (off)*. One byte is composed of eight bits. For common conversion formulas, see Table 8-7.

ROM: *R*ead-*o*nly *m*emory. It stores permanent, basic information such as instructions for starting up the computer. The data in the ROM portion of memory, usually installed at the factory where the computer was made, cannot generally be changed.

RAM: *R*andom-*a*ccess *m*emory is the temporary, programmable section of memory. RAM is volatile, meaning that it requires a steady flow of electricity to maintain its contents, whereas ROM does not. RAM can be separated into two subcategories: main memory and cache memory.

Cache memory: A type of RAM memory that is much faster and much smaller in size than main memory. The computer tries to keep frequently used data and

program instructions in cache memory, where they can be accessed faster than from main memory. Cache memory is often located on the CPU or in between the CPU and the main RAM memory.

Virtual memory: Uses the hard disk to store programs and data temporarily when all the RAM is in use. It is very slow.

Storage

Hard drive: The nonremovable magnetic medium inside the computer where information is stored for later retrieval. Most software programs and important

Memory Conversions		
8 bits	=	1 byte
1000 bytes	=	1 kilobyte (KB)
1000 KB	=	1 megabyte (MB)
1000 MB	=	1 gigabyte (GB)
1000 GB	=	1 terabyte (TB)
1000 TB	=	1 petabyte (PB)

Table 8-7

files are usually stored on the hard drive for quick and easy access. For examples of common storage devices, see Figure 8-17.

Disk drive: Can read and write to floppy disks or Zip® disks, which store information. Disks are portable and make it easy to transfer information from one computer to another. (Zip® is a registered trademark of Iomega Corporation.)

CD-ROM drive: Can read, but not record on, compact disks (CDs), which can store much more information than floppy disks. A single CD can hold about as much information as 460 floppy disks. Most software programs are released on compact disks that are read-only (CD-ROMs).

CD-R: Stands for *CD-recordable*. This type of CD will allow information and data to be recorded on (written to) it once.

CD-RW: Stands for *CD-rewritable*. This type of CD can be written to and overwritten multiple times.

CD-RW drive: Reads all CDs and writes to CD-R or CD-RW disks.

DVD drive: Can read DVDs and information stored in the DVD format.

DVD: Stands for *digital versatile disk*. A DVD looks like a CD, but it has a much higher storage capacity. Depending on the formatting, it can store anywhere between 4.7 GB and 17 GB of information. DVDs are commonly used to store multimedia applications and movies, but they can store any other type of digital information as well.

Input and Output Devices

Keyboard: The most common device used to input information into the computer. It resembles a typewriter, but in addition to standard typewriter keys, it has keys such as the arrow keys that allow you to move the cursor, function keys, and a numerical keypad for entering numbers more easily.

Avoiding typing injuries: If you use the keyboard improperly for extended periods of time, you may develop carpal tunnel syndrome, in which tendons around your wrist swell and may require medication or surgery. Proper posture and hand position, using a wrist rest, and taking breaks from long typing sessions can help you avoid injury. While typing on the keyboard, your wrist should be in a neutral position.

Monitor: A device that resembles a television screen and is used by the computer to display information. Using a higher-resolution monitor with a higher refresh rate will put less strain on your eyes. A low refresh rate especially strains the eyes because it makes the monitor image flicker.

Mouse: A device that enables the user to move a pointer around on the monitor to make selections or to place information. A mouse is equipped with at least one button; pressing and releasing a mouse button is called clicking. There is an important difference between clicking once (also called single-clicking) and rapidly clicking twice (double-clicking). Single-clicking is generally used to make an on-screen selection (e.g., an icon such as an *OK* button, a menu item, or a position for the cursor). Double-clicking activates an underlying function, such as starting up a program that is associated with the item selected.

Touch screen: A monitor with a touch-sensitive surface, on which the touch of a finger makes a selection as a mouse pointer does. Many surgical or X-ray systems have touch screens.

Scanner: A device that can convert printed matter and images to information that can be interpreted by the computer. Using a scanner can be much faster than inputting the same information with the keyboard.

Modem: A device used to transfer information from one computer to another using telephone lines and servers. Modems allow you to access the Internet and to use e-mail.

Printer: A device used to produce a paper copy of information to be sent to patients, vendors, other physicians, and insurance companies.

Software

Computer software: Can be classified into three groups: data, operating systems, and applications. All three are built from the same elements, electronic instructions to the processor. When a computer is running, or executing, a program, it is carrying out these instructions.

Operating system: The computer program that tells the processor how to interact with its internal and external environment. The operating system is the interface (means of communication) between application programs and the system's resources. Common operating systems include DOS (Disk Operating System), Windows (Windows 3.1, 95, 98, NT, 2000), UNIX, and MacOS.

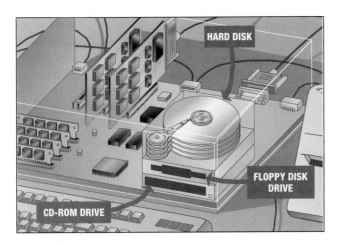

Figure 8-17. *Storage devices.*

Graphical user interface (GUI): A type of interface employed by most modern operating systems. It uses a mouse or another pointing device to aid input. This interface provides the user with on-screen icons, dialog boxes, and menus from which to select the desired options.

Pointer: The on-screen object, usually an arrow, that is used to select menus, icons, and text and to interact with programs, files, and data represented graphically.

Dialog box: A window that appears when a user issues certain commands in a program or a graphical user interface. A dialog box is used to seek information from the user that the program or operating system needs in order to perform a task.

Dragging and dropping: A common way to move text or graphics in a graphical user interface. The user must point to the desired information or object, hold down the mouse button, drag the selection to its new location, and place the selection by releasing the mouse button. See Figure 8-18.

Data

Data: Raw facts, numbers, letters, or symbols that the computer processes into meaningful information. Also, any type of information stored in a database, such as addresses, medical records, insurance claims, and so on.

Database: A collection of related data organized within a specific structure. For a list of information commonly stored in medical databases, see Table 8-8.

Applications

Application software: Makes the computer a useful tool. Most application software falls into one or more of the following categories:

- Word processing
- Graphics
- Database
- Spreadsheet

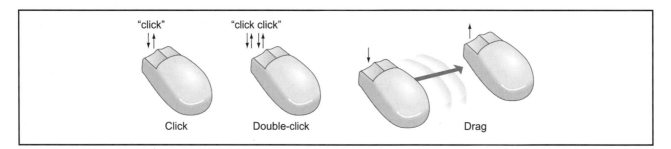

"click"   "click click"

Click   Double-click   Drag

Figure 8-18. *Three mouse techniques.*

AT A GLANCE	Information Stored in Medical Databases
Types of Data	**Information Contained in Database**
Provider	Name, address, phone number, tax and medical identifier numbers, and other information about the physician and the practice
Patients	Each patient's unique chart number and personal information
Insurance carriers	Names, addresses, other data about each insurance carrier and type of plan, and records about each carrier's electronic media claim submission
Diagnosis codes	Usually the codes from *International Classification of Diseases, 9th Edition, Clinical Modification* (ICD-9-CM), which indicate the reason why a service is provided
Procedure codes	Data needed to create charges, such as entries from the *Physicians' Current Procedural Terminology* (CPT) place of service (POS) designations, and charge for each procedure (information that appears on the patient superbill)
Transactions	Information about the patient's visits, diagnoses, procedures, and received and outstanding payments, recorded in the form of charges, payments, and adjustments

Table 8-8

- Presentation
- Utilities
- Communication

Word processing software: Used to produce doctors' notes, transcripts, reports, memos, and letters.

Graphics software: Used to produce information in the form of pictures. It can be used in training personnel or patients about upcoming procedures, and it is also used in visual displays of data, such as a CT scan, on computer screens.

Database software: Stores data such as patient records and drug libraries that are compiled and can be sorted.

Presentation software: Used to create slides or overheads to illustrate talks and other presentations.

Spreadsheet software: Simulates, in computer form, a business or scientific worksheet and performs the necessary calculations when pieces of data are changed. It is used most often in bookkeeping or accounting procedures.

Utilities software: Used to maintain the system or to provide additional features to the system. For example, there are common utility programs that protect against computer viruses.

Communication software: Used to communicate with others either within the medical office or in the outside world. Such software includes e-mail applications, web browsers, gophers, and telnet.

Telnet: An Internet tool used to access a host computer's data and to transmit, read, and copy files.

Gopher: An Internet tool that follows a simple protocol for organizing resources into multilevel menus to make finding information easier.

Server: A single computer that can be accessed by other computers over a network. In most cases, a central database of patients resides on a server.

Networks and the Internet

Local area network (LAN) connection: An interconnected system within a small area, such as one or two buildings. A LAN can have shared printers, scanners, storage devices, and communications devices. Computers today are easily and inexpensively interconnected to enable communication between systems. Larger, city-wide systems are known as metropolitan area networks (MANs). And still larger systems between cities are known as wide area networks (WANs).

Intranet: A local area network internal to a company but with links to an outside system such as the Internet.

Internet: A wide area network developed by the U.S. government that has become a global network of millions of computers.

World Wide Web (WWW, or the Web): A well-known and integral part of the Internet, which supports and displays documents specially formatted in hypertext markup language (HTML). HTML is the format of most documents displayed on the World Wide Web.

Server-centric applications: Types of applications loaded on a centralized high-speed machine that can have multiple users accessing them simultaneously.

Computers and Security

Passwords: In order to protect confidential information and applications from being accessed by unauthorized personnel, many medical offices will use passwords that are unique to each employee and are required to access applications and files on the computer.

Monitoring systems: Some health care facilities will also monitor the activity on each computer. Whenever someone accesses records and files, the system keeps track of the user's name and which files the user has modified or viewed. Security breaches then can be traced back to specific employees and computers.

Backup files: In order to protect essential information, it is important to make regular backups of files onto floppy disks, Zip® disks, CDs, or other media. Having a current backup provides a way to restore lost or damaged information in case of fire, a computer virus, or burglary. It is also important to store backup files off-premises.

Computer viruses: Programs written to infect and damage certain files and applications on your computer. They can be passed to your computer through shared infected disks or CDs as well as through the Internet and e-mail. In general, do not open an e-mail attachment you did not expect to receive even if it is from someone you know. Check with the person who sent you the e-mail message if you are unsure about the nature of its attachment. Do not open attachments from people you don't know. Another way to protect computers from viruses is to purchase one of the many computer virus detection and protection programs available. These programs provide an invaluable service, and they offer frequent updates and alerts about new viruses.

Policies and Procedures

Policy and procedures manual: A written document that covers all office policies and clinical procedures, developed by the physicians and the staff (particularly the medical assistant) for use by permanent and temporary employees.

Policies: Rules or guidelines that dictate the day-to-day workings of an office. Most manuals cover the following policy areas:

- Office purposes, objectives, and goals
- Rules and regulations
- Job descriptions and duties

MILLSTONE MEDICAL ASSOCIATES

Policy and Procedures Manual

Procedure for Creating a Medical File for a New Patient

GOAL: To create a complete medical record for each new patient containing all necessary personal and medical information.

PROCEDURE:

1. Establish that the patient is new to the doctor's office.

2. Ask the patient for all necessary insurance information. If the patient has an insurance card, make a photocopy of it for his or her file.

3. Ask the patient to fill out the patient information form. Keyboard the information onto a new patient information form, for legibility.

4. Review all information with the patient, to check for accuracy.

5. Label the new patient's folder according to office procedure. Type either the patient's name (for an alphabetic file) or the correct number (for a numerical file).

6. If filing is done numerically, fill out a cross-reference form on the computer, along with a patient ID card to be stored in a secure location.

7. Add the patient's name to the necessary financial records, including the office ledger, whether on paper or on the computer.

8. After completing the folder label information, place the new patient information form inside the folder, along with any other personal or medical information that pertains to the patient.

9. On the outside of patient's folder, clip a routing slip.

Figure 8-19. *This page from a policy and procedures manual provides the office staff with information about creating a medical file for a new patient.*

- Office hours
- Dress code
- Insurance and other benefits
- Vacation, sick leave, and other time away from the office
- Performance evaluations and salary
- Maintenance of equipment and supplies
- Mailings
- Bookkeeping
- Scheduling appointments
- Maintaining patient records
- Health and safety guidelines
- Organizational chart

Procedures: Detailed instructions for maintaining clinical and quality assurance.

Developing a manual: Begins with planning the format and outline, which should be approved by the office manager and physicians. Sources for developing and updating material include journals, product literature, textbooks, and standards publications, among others.

Manual format: Many offices prefer a loose-leaf binder in which pages can be replaced when necessary. Figure 8-19 shows a sample manual page.

STRATEGIES TO SUCCESS

▶ Test-Taking Skills

Eliminate wrong answers!

When answering multiple-choice questions, you can increase your chances of answering correctly by eliminating answers that you know are wrong. As you read the possible answers, put an *X* next to ones you know are incorrect, or cross them out completely. Once you have narrowed down your possible choices, you have a better chance of making an educated guess about the correct answer.

Instructions:

Answer the following questions. Check your answers in the *Answer Key* that follows this section.

1. Which of the following is the most widely used filing system for medical practices?

    A. Numeric
    B. Subject
    C. Alphabetical
    D. Chronological
    E. Alphanumeric

2. In appointment scheduling, the matrix indicates

    A. Time available to schedule patients
    B. Time not available to schedule patients
    C. Time open for pharmaceutical representatives
    D. Time open for surgery
    E. Time not available for surgery

3. Financial information

    A. Should always be included in the patient's medical records
    B. Should be included in the patient's medical record if the patient has been delinquent in payments
    C. Should not be included in the patient's medical records
    D. Should be included in the patient's medical record if the patient requests it
    E. Should be included in the patient's medical record if the patient's insurance provider requires it

4. Which of the following is not a way to communicate with a patient who has a hearing impairment?

    A. Minimize background disturbance
    B. Speak slowly
    C. Sit close and face the patient
    D. Use body language
    E. Shout at the patient

5. A chronological file used as a reminder is called a(n)

    A. Index file
    B. Tickler file
    C. Active file
    D. Closed file
    E. Timer file

6. The screening and sorting of emergency situations is called

    A. Emergency reception
    B. Documenting emergencies
    C. Telephone emergencies
    D. Incoming emergencies
    E. Emergency triage

7. Scheduling patients so that two come in at the beginning of each hour and the others are scheduled every 10 to 20 minutes is called

    A. Wave scheduling
    B. Appointment time pattern
    C. Modified wave scheduling
    D. Double booking
    E. Advance scheduling

8. Account statements for a medical practice should be sent as

    A. First-Class Mail
    B. Standard Mail (A)
    C. Standard Mail (B)
    D. Special Standard Mail
    E. Express Mail

9. Patients who want to talk about abnormal test results should speak with which of the following medical personnel?

    A. Laboratory technologists
    B. Nurses
    C. Medical assistants
    D. Physicians
    E. Any of the above

10. Which of the following is the most secure service offered by the United States Postal Service?

    A. Priority Mail
    B. First-Class Mail
    C. Express Mail
    D. Mail tracing
    E. Registered mail

11. If a patient calls about insurance coverage, the call should be handled by

    A. The physician who performed the test or procedure in question
    B. The medical assistant
    C. The next available physician
    D. The insurance company
    E. An insurance specialist only

12. Which of the following should be included in the patient's medical records?

    A. Physical examination results
    B. Correspondence with and about the patient
    C. Diagnosis and treatment plans
    D. Informed consent forms
    E. All of the above

13. You can protect your computer files against a computer virus by

    A. Not opening e-mail attachments from people you don't know
    B. Purchasing anti-virus software
    C. Making frequent backups of your files
    D. Both B and C
    E. All of the above

14. SOAP pertains to

    A. Malpractice
    B. Computer code
    C. Dictation equipment
    D. Asepsis
    E. Patient records

15. According to the Internal Revenue Service, financial records need to be retained for how long?

    A. 2 to 7 years
    B. 10 years
    C. 7 years
    D. 15 years
    E. Permanently

16. Which of the following is a way to store information on a computer?

    A. Hard drive
    B. CD-ROM drive
    C. Zip® drive
    D. All of the above
    E. None of the above

17. It is important to leave time to complete forms for patients who are

    A. Late for their appointment
    B. New
    C. Poor
    D. Rich
    E. Minors

18. Which one of these is a correct complimentary closing?

    A. Yours Truly,
    B. Very Best,
    C. Best regards,
    D. Yours Sincerely,
    E. Sincerely:

19. Which of the following mail is available seven days per week?

    A. Priority Mail
    B. First-Class Mail
    C. International mail
    D. Express Mail
    E. Standard Mail (A)

20. When an incoming call is received, the telephone should be answered

    A. Within one minute
    B. By the second or third ring
    C. By the third or fourth ring
    D. When there is no patient nearby
    E. After the doctor has been helped

21. If the patient calls in to report that he or she is doing well after surgery, the medical assistant should

    A. Transfer the call to the physician or surgeon
    B. Transfer the call to the attending nurse
    C. Handle the call and make note of the patient's report in his or her medical records
    D. Thank the patient for calling and hang up
    E. Explain to the patient that he or she needs to call only if things are not going well

22. An appointment book is considered

    A. An interpersonal skill
    B. A patient analysis
    C. The doctor's domain
    D. A scheduling system
    E. A legal document

23. The physician should handle calls from patients about which of the following?

    A. Insurance questions
    B. X-ray and laboratory reports
    C. Unsatisfactory progress
    D. Prescription refills previously authorized
    E. Scheduling appointments

24. The words *SPECIAL HANDLING* should appear where on an envelope?

    A. Above the *Attention* line
    B. Above the recipient's address
    C. Below the return address
    D. Below the recipient's address
    E. Below the postage

25. Open-ended questions

    A. Should never be asked of patients
    B. Should be asked of children, but not of adults
    C. Should be asked of adults, but not of children
    D. Should be asked of all patients
    E. Should help communication with patients who are hard of hearing

26. The receptionist who is responsible for opening the medical office must arrive how long before office hours begin?

    A. 45 to 60 minutes
    B. 30 to 45 minutes
    C. 15 to 20 minutes
    D. 5 to 10 minutes
    E. More than 60 minutes

27. What action should a medical assistant take if a caller wants to talk to a physician but refuses to identify himself or herself?

    A. Hang up
    B. Transfer the call to the physician anyway
    C. Advise the person that the physician is not in the office and tell him or her to call back
    D. Ask the person to write a letter to the physician and mark it *Personal*
    E. Transfer the call to another medical assistant

28. Certified mail is used to send

    A. All office mailings
    B. Hazardous materials
    C. Documents, contracts, and bank books
    D. Appointment reminders
    E. Results of medical tests

29. A medical assistant should do all of the following when answering the telephone <u>except</u>
    A. Give the caller the medical assistant's name first and then the name of the office
    B. Identify the caller
    C. Ask "How may I help you?"
    D. Hold the phone's mouthpiece an inch away from the mouth
    E. Use words appropriate to the situation, but avoid using technical terms

30. When greeting patients, a medical assistant should
    A. Make eye contact
    B. Avoid using their name to preserve their privacy
    C. Ask personal questions
    D. Tease them about the time they forgot an appointment
    E. Set up their next appointment

31. Through the U.S. Postal Service, a package of books that weighs 90 pounds
    A. Can be sent as Standard Mail (B)
    B. Can be sent as Priority Mail
    C. Cannot be sent because it exceeds weight limits
    D. Can be sent as Express Mail
    E. Can be sent Standard Mail (A)

32. Medical assistants should not take which of these actions when opening mail?
    A. Annotate mail with comments in the margin
    B. Open the physician's personal mail
    C. Date all opened mail
    D. Transmit letters to the physician with the most important ones on the top
    E. Check for enclosures

33. Standard letterhead is
    A. Used in general business correspondence
    B. $5\frac{1}{2}$ inch x $8\frac{1}{2}$ inch in size
    C. Used for social correspondence
    D. Not used in the medical office
    E. Both B and C

34. The subject line of a letter appears
    A. Two lines below the last line of the body
    B. Two lines below the salutation
    C. One line above the outside address
    D. One line above the inside address
    E. One line below the date

35. In the matrix scheduling system, medical assistants should block off
    A. Physicians' lunch hours
    B. Visits with drug company representatives
    C. Time for performing hospital rounds
    D. Both B and C
    E. All of the above

36. The abbreviation *NP* stands for
    A. Neurological performance
    B. No–show patient
    C. New practice
    D. New physical
    E. New patient

37. Scheduling two or more patients in the same slot is known as
    A. Wave scheduling
    B. Open hours
    C. Modified wave scheduling
    D. Double booking
    E. Either A or C

38. The 5 *Cs* of communication include
    A. Cyclic
    B. Cohesive
    C. Channeled
    D. Contact
    E. Closing

39. When dealing with a seriously ill patient, you should
    A. Trivialize the patient's feelings
    B. Judge the patient's statements
    C. Avoid empty promises
    D. Abandon the patient
    E. Isolate the patient

40. Publications and journals are usually sent as
    A. First-Class Mail
    B. Periodicals
    C. Standard Mail (A)
    D. Standard Mail (B)
    E. Priority Mail

ANSWER KEY

1.	B		21.	C
2.	B		22.	E
3.	C		23.	C
4.	E		24.	E
5.	B		25.	D
6.	E		26.	C
7.	C		27.	D
8.	A		28.	C
9.	D		29.	A
10.	E		30.	A
11.	B		31.	C
12.	E		32.	B
13.	E		33.	A
14.	E		34.	B
15.	B		35.	E
16.	D		36.	E
17.	B		37.	D
18.	C		38.	B
19.	D		39.	C
20.	B		40.	B

CHAPTER 9

Financial Management

CHAPTER OUTLINE

Purchasing

    Types of Supplies
    Ordering and Receiving Supplies
    Storage of Supplies
    Payment

Accounting

    Bookkeeping Systems
    Posting to Records
    Account Balances

Banking

    Types of Bank Accounts
    Checks
    Deposits
    Bill Payment

Billing and Collections

    Medical Billing
    Collection Policies and Procedures

Accounts Payable

    Payroll
    Tax

AAMA—ROLE DELINEATION STUDY AREAS OF COMPETENCE

Administrative

Practice Finances

- Apply bookkeeping principles
- Document and maintain accounting and banking records
- Manage accounts receivable
- Manage accounts payable
- Process payroll

General (Transdisciplinary)

Operational Functions

- Maintain supply inventory
- Evaluate and recommend equipment and supplies
- Apply computer techniques to support office operations

AMT—RMA CERTIFICATION EXAM TOPICS

Financial Bookkeeping

- Terminology
- Patient billing
- Collections
- Fundamental medical office accounting procedures
- Banking
- Employee payroll
- Financial mathematics

Purchasing

Medical office supplies: Purchasing and maintaining supplies for medical practices is essential. The medical assistant is usually responsible for taking inventory of equipment and supplies and for ordering anything that is needed.

Types of Supplies

Expendable items: Items that are used and then must be restocked, also known as consumables. Expendable items are used up within a short period of time, and they are relatively inexpensive. There are five categories of expendable supplies: general, administrative, clinical, vital, and incidental.

General supplies: Items used by both patients and staff, such as paper towels, soap, and toilet tissue.

Administrative supplies: Items used to keep the office running, such as stationery, typing paper, photocopy paper, medical record forms, appointment books, pens, colored highlighters, correcting tape, and toner.

Clinical supplies: Medically related items, such as towels, drapes, gowns, table paper, disposable vaginal speculas, lubricants, tongue blades, syringes, suture material, laboratory reagents, and elastic bandages.

Vital supplies: Can be both clinical and administrative in nature. These items are absolutely essential to ensure the smooth running of the practice. Examples include prescription pads and paper for examinations. To help keep track of supplies, categorize them according to the urgency of need, making sure that vital supplies are readily available.

Incidental supplies: Can be clinical, administrative, or general in nature. The efficiency of the office is not threatened if the supplies run low. Incidental supplies include rubber bands and staples.

Durable items: Pieces of equipment that are used indefinitely, such as telephones or computers, that are not considered supplies.

Capital equipment: Items that are considered major and involve expenditures above a predetermined dollar value. Capital equipment includes general equipment, large lab equipment, administrative equipment, and clinical equipment. Table 9-1 lists some examples of general, administrative, and clinical equipment.

Ordering and Receiving Supplies

Vendors: Obtain recommendations from other medical offices, gather competitive prices, and compare vendors on the basis of price, quality, service, and payment policies. It takes multiple vendors to provide all the supplies for a medical practice.

Local vendors: It is a good idea to establish good credit and business relationships with local vendors, even if they cost a little more. Local vendors may offer special discounts, emergency service, information about sales and specials, and personal assistance.

Catalog services: Can provide ease of availability, competitive pricing, and fast delivery. Many vendors accept telephone, fax, and e-mail orders as well as traditional order forms.

Ordering supplies: Expendable supplies and equipment must be replaced and reordered in time. A copy of the order form should be retained to check against the order when it arrives.

Purchase requisitions: Some practices require approval of a formal request before supplies can be ordered.

Receiving supplies: Check orders for completeness. One person should be responsible for receiving and signing for deliveries. This person must check invoices and/or packing slips against the items delivered, initial and date the invoices as items are received, and distribute goods to the storage room.

Packing slip: A list of supplies packed and shipped, supplied by the vendor in the package with the supplies.

Statement: The monthly bill summarizing invoices. It is a request for payment.

Supply budget: The average medical practice spends from 4% to 6% of its annual gross income on supplies. If costs exceed 6%, you might be required to reevaluate the office's spending practices.

Storage of Supplies

Storage room: Should be arranged with the most commonly used items within easiest reach. Place new stock in the back of the storage area, and move the old supplies up front so that they will be used first. This practice is referred to as rotating stock. You must know the storage requirements for various kinds of supplies. You must maintain an adequate quantity of supplies in a well-organized storage space to run the office smoothly.

Inventory: A list of articles in stock, with the description and quantity of each. Inventory control requires constant supervision, because a medical office cannot afford to run out of supplies. Most offices maintain an ongoing inventory system, which helps determine when to reorder supplies.

Reminder cards: Many offices develop color-coded reorder reminder cards, which are inserted into the

Examples of Capital Equipment		
General	**Administrative**	**Clinical**
• Office furnishings	Computers	Examination room furnishings
• Carpeting	Copy machines	Examination equipment such as microscopes, autoclaves, and ultrasound machines

Table 9-1

stack of inventory items. When the card comes to the top of the stack, it is time to reorder.

Payment

Invoice: A paper describing a purchase and the amount due. Check the invoice against the original order and the packing slip, mark it to confirm that the order was received, and pay it. The check number, date, and payment amount should then be recorded on the invoice. Invoices should be placed in a special folder until paid.

Payment terms: Many vendors do not charge a handling fee if an order is prepaid. Others offer a discount for enclosing a check with an order. Some delay billing for 30 to 90 days. The vendor's invoice usually describes payment terms.

Records: Copies of all bills and order forms for supplies should be kept on file for 10 years in case the practice is audited by the Internal Revenue Service (IRS).

Disbursement: Payment of funds, whether in cash or by check. Usually, you will write a check to the vendor and have the physician sign it. At the time of payment, write the date and check number on the statement, and place it in the paid file. Disbursements can be entered into the accounting records in several ways, depending on the accounting system used.

Purchasing procedure: The purchasing procedure should follow certain standard practices:

- An authorized person should be in charge of purchasing.
- High-quality goods and services should be ordered at the lowest possible prices.
- Receipts of goods should be recorded.
- Shipments received should be checked against packing slips to verify that all goods have been received.
- Invoices should be paid in a timely manner.
- Paid invoices should be kept on file.

Accounting

Accounting: A system of recording, classifying, and summarizing financial transactions.

Account: In bookkeeping terms, a single financial record category or division. It is used to track debit and credit changes, by date, in reference to a specific matter. For example, when a practice accepts a new patient, the patient is assigned an account. As the patient is charged for services and the patient (or third-party payer, such as an insurance company) pays those charges, entries are made in the patient's account.

Account balance: The debit or credit balance remaining in an account.

Accounts payable: Amounts charged with suppliers or creditors that remain unpaid.

Accounts receivable: Amounts owed to a business for services or goods supplied.

Assets: Possessions of value, which in a medical office are inventory, equipment, prepaid rent, and the amounts due from patients.

Liabilities: Amounts owed to creditors, such as a mortgage on the medical building and the accounts payable.

Balance sheet: A financial statement for a specific date or period that indicates the total assets, liabilities, and capital of the business.

Auditing: The review of financial data to verify accuracy and completeness. Medical assistants responsible for bookkeeping must provide required financial records and answer questions about accounting systems used.

Bookkeeping Systems

Bookkeeping: The recording part of the accounting process. Bookkeeping records income, charges, and disbursements. There are three types of manual bookkeeping systems: single-entry, double-entry, and pegboard.

Single-entry system: The oldest bookkeeping system, requiring only one entry for each transaction. This straightforwardness makes it the easiest system to learn and use. Because it is not self-balancing, however, it is the hardest system in which to spot errors. It includes several basic records, such as:

- Daily log to record charges and payments. See Figure 9-1.
- Patient ledger cards
- Payroll records
- Cash payment journal
- Petty cash records

Double-entry system: Based on the accounting equation *assets = liabilities + owner equity*. The materials required for a double-entry bookkeeping system are inexpensive, but the system requires more skill and knowledge of accounting procedures than the single-entry system. It is also more time-consuming to use. After each financial transaction, the medical office using a double-entry system must debit one account and credit another account. For example, when the practice charges for a medical service, the patient's account is debited and the appropriate account for the practice is credited.

Pegboard system: This system consists of daysheets, ledger cards, patient charge slips, and receipt forms or superbills. It is the mostly commonly used manual medical accounts receivable system and the most expensive to maintain. A pegboard system usually includes a lightweight board with pegs on the left or right edges and is sometimes called a "one-write"

Dr. _____		Date _____		
Hour	*Patient*	*Service Provided*	*Charge*	*Paid*
	1			
	2			
	3			
	4			
	5			
	6			
	7			
	8			
	9			
	10			
	11			
	12			
	13			
	14			
	15			
	16			
		Totals		

Figure 9-1. *A daily log is used to record charges and payments.*

system. See Figure 9-2. A pegboard system has several main advantages:

- The system is efficient and time-saving.
- The daysheet provides complete and up-to-date information about accounts receivable status at a glance.
- The system is easy to learn.

Posting to Records

General journal: A record of the physician's practice. It includes records of services rendered, charges made, and monies received. The general journal is also known by the names daily log, daybook, daysheet, daily journal, and charge journal. This journal is also called the book of original entry because it is where all transactions are first recorded.

Ledger: A record of charges, payments, and adjustments for individual patients or families. Figure 9-3 on p. 214 is an example of a patient ledger card.

Accounts receivable ledger: Includes all the individual patients' financial accounts on which there are balances.

Posting: The process of copying or recording an amount from one record, such as a journal, onto another record, such as a ledger—or from a daysheet onto a ledger card.

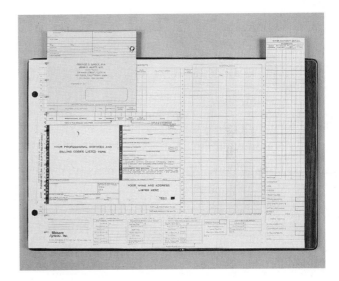

Figure 9-2. *A pegboard system allows information to be written once and transferred simultaneously onto several bookkeeping forms.*

Manual posting: Facilitated by a section at the bottom of each daysheet and a check register page at the end of each month, plus monthly and annual summaries. Accounting records must show every amount paid out, date and check number, and purpose of payment.

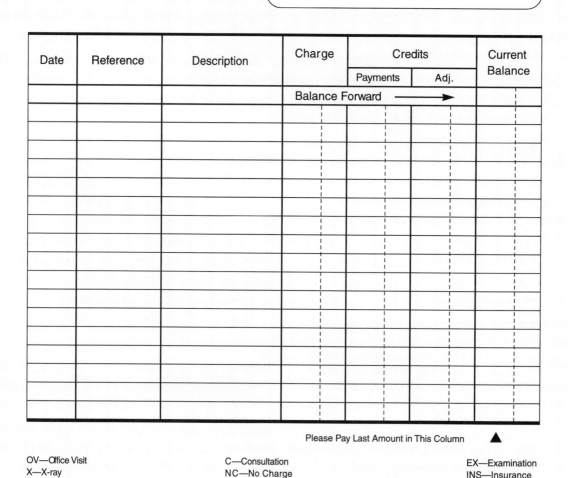

Patient's Name ___Jonathan Jackson___

Home Phone ___(612) 555-9921___ Work Phone ___(612) 555-1000___

Patient's ID No. ___111-21-4114___

Employer ___Ashton School District___

Insurance ___National Insurance Co.___

Policy # ___123-4-56-788___

Person Responsible for Charges (if Different from Patient) _____

JONATHAN JACKSON
123 Fourth Avenue
Ashton, MN 70809-1222

Date	Reference	Description	Charge	Credits		Current Balance
				Payments	Adj.	
		Balance Forward ⟶				

Please Pay Last Amount in This Column ▲

OV—Office Visit C—Consultation EX—Examination
X—X-ray NC—No Charge INS—Insurance
ROA—Received on Account MA—Missed Appointment

Figure 9-3. *Patient ledger cards are used to show how much each patient owes.*

Computer posting: Using a computer to to keep track of and print accounts receivable and accounts payable. Computers are also used to print the check as well as payment information.

Accrual basis accounting: Recording income when it is earned and expenses when they are incurred.

Trial balance: A method of checking the accuracy of accounts. It should be done once a month after all posting has been completed and before preparing the monthly statements. The purpose of a trial balance is to disclose any discrepancies between the journal and the ledger.

Account Balances

Equity: The net worth of the medical office. Equity equals the practice's total assets minus the total liabilities.

Balance: The difference between the debit and credit totals.

Adjustment column: An account column, sometimes included to the left of the balance column, used for entering discounts, debits, credits, refunds, and write-offs.

Balance column: The account column on the far right that is used for recording the difference between the debit and credit columns.

Debit: An amount usually representing things acquired for the intended use or benefit of a business. It is recorded in the column to the left of the credit column. In each journal entry, the dollar amount of the debit must be equal to the dollar amount of the credit. A debit is also called a charge. Debits are incurred when the practice pays for something, such as medical supplies.

Credit: An amount constituting an addition to a revenue, net worth, or liability account. It is recorded in the column to the right of the debit column. Credits constitute payments received by the practice, such as from patients or third-party insurance providers.

Credit balance: Money owed to the patient that results when a patient has paid in advance and there has been an overpayment.

Refunds: Debit adjustments. If a patient wishes to have an overpayment refunded, write a check for the amount due and enter the transaction on the daysheet.

Credit bureau: A company that provides information about the creditworthiness of a person seeking credit. If a patient's credit history is in question, you may request a report from a credit bureau. A sample credit bureau report is shown in Figure 9-4 on p. 216.

Payables: Amounts owed to others.

In balance: Accounts are in balance when the total ending balances of patient ledgers equals the total of accounts receivable.

Receipts: Money received.

Petty cash fund: A fund maintained to pay small, unpredictable cash expenses.

Reconciliation of bank statement: The process of verifying that the bank statement and the checkbook balances are in agreement. As you reconcile the bank statement with your accounts, be aware of outstanding checks, outstanding deposits, and any service fees the bank may have charged.

Superbill: A combination charge slip, statement, and insurance reporting form. A superbill includes the charges for services rendered on a day, an invoice for payment or insurance copayment, and all the information for submitting an insurance claim. It is also called an encounter form. See Figure 9-5 on p. 217.

Banking

Medical business: A medical practice is a business that must produce a profit—that is, its income must exceed its expenses. Bookkeeping and banking are essential and must be 100% accurate.

Absolute accuracy: Necessary when working with bank deposits, reconciliation of statements, and all bookkeeping activities. The medical assistant acts as the agent for the physician.

Banks: Maintain checking and savings accounts for their customers.

Banking functions: Basic bank-related activities carried out by a medical practice include:

- Depositing funds
- Withdrawing funds
- Reconciling statements
- Using auxiliary services

Types of Bank Accounts

Types of bank accounts: Medical practices typically use three types of bank account:

- Regular checking account
- Interest-earning, or interest-bearing, checking account
- Savings account

Regular checking account: Most medical practices have a regular checking account for office expenses. This account does not pay interest but offers availability and flexibility.

Interest: Money paid to a depositor by a bank or other financial institution for the use of the depositor's money.

Electronic banking: Banking with the use of computers. Electronic banking has several advantages over traditional banking: It can improve productivity, cash flow, and accuracy. The computer screen can display all checks and deposits that were logged into the register in the order they were posted. In electronic banking, someone must still be responsible for recording and physically depositing checks.

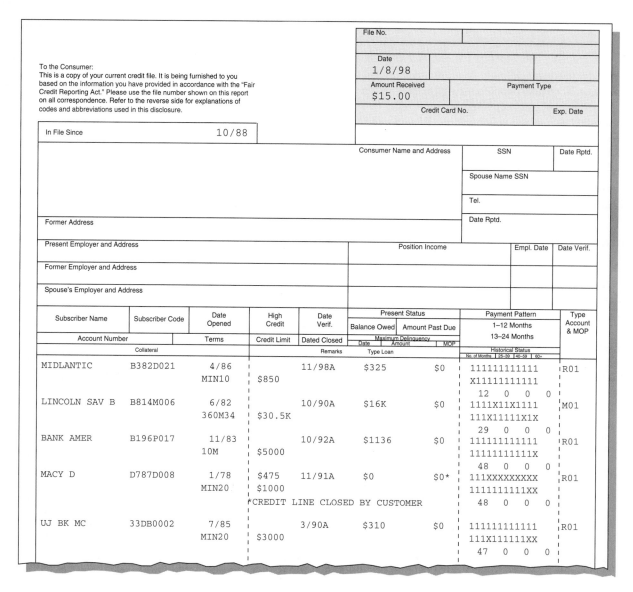

Figure 9-4. *Credit reports are generated by credit bureaus.*

Bank statements: All contain certain basic information, including:

- Closing date
- Caption
- List of checks processed
- List of deposits

Caption: A summary of the account activity that has taken place during the month up to the closing date. It includes the beginning balance, total value of checks processed, total amount of deposits made, service charges, and ending balance.

Checks

Check: A written order to a bank to pay or transfer money. It is payable on demand and is considered a negotiable instrument. The person who writes the check is called the payer or drawer.

Types of checks: Cashier's checks, certified checks, money orders, limited checks, traveler's checks, voucher checks, bank drafts, and warrants.

Cashier's check: Written using the bank's own check form and signed by a bank representative. The funds for payment of the check are debited from the payer's account at the time the check is written. A service charge is usually added. Another term for a cashier's check is treasurer's check.

Certified check: A certified check is written on the payer's own check form and verified by the bank with an official stamp. The bank withdraws the money from the payer's account when it certifies the check. The stamp indicates that the bank certifies the availability of the funds.

Money order: A certificate of guaranteed payment. It is purchased for the cash value printed on the certificate plus a nominal handling fee. Money orders may be purchased from banks, post offices, and some conven-

☐ **PRIVATE** ☐ **BLUECROSS** ☐ **IND.** ☐ **MEDICARE** ☐ **MEDI-CAL** ☐ **HMO** ☐ **PPO**

PATIENT'S LAST NAME		FIRST	ACCOUNT #	BIRTHDATE / /	SEX ☐ MALE ☐ FEMALE	TODAY'S DATE / /
INSURANCE COMPANY		SUBSCRIBER		PLAN #	SUB. #	GROUP

ASSIGNMENT: I hereby assign my insurance benefits to be paid directly to the undersigned physician. I am financially responsible for non-covered services. SIGNED: (Patient, or Parent, if Minor) DATE: / /	RELEASE: I hereby authorize the physician to release to my insurance carrers any information required to process this claim. SIGNED: (Patient, or Parent, if Minor) DATE: / /

✔	DESCRIPTION	M/Care CPT/Mod	DxRe	FEE	✔	DESCRIPTION	M/Care CPT/Mod	DxRe	FEE	✔	DESCRIPTION	M/Care CPT/Mod	DxRe	FEE
	OFFICE CARE					PROCEDURES					INJECTIONS/IMMUNIZATIONS			
	NEW PATIENT					Tread Mill (In Office)	93015				Tetanus	90718		
	Brief	99201				24 Hour Holter	93224				Hypertet	J1670 90782		
	Limited	99202				If Medicare (Set up Fee)	93225				Pneumococcal	90732		
	Intermediate	99203				Physician Interpret	93227				Influenza	90724		
	Extended	99204				EKG w/Interpretation	93000				TB Skin Test (PPD)	86585		
	Comprehensive	99205				EKG (Medicare)	93005				Antigen Injection-Single	95115		
						Sigmoidoscopy	45300				Multiple	95117		
	ESTABLISHED PATIENT					Sigmoidoscopy, Flexible	45330				B12 Injection	J3420 90782		
	Minimal	99211				Sigmoidos. , Flex. w/Bx.	45331				Injection, IM	90782		
	Brief	99212				Spirometry, FEV/FVC	94010				Compazine	J0780 90782		
	Limited	99213				Spirometry, Post-Dilator	94060				Demerol	J2175 90782		
	Intermediate	99214									Vistaril	J3410 90782		
	Extended	99215									Susphrine	J0170 90782		
	Comprehensive	99215				LABORATORY					Decadron	J0890 90782		
						Blood Draw Fee	36415				Estradiol	J1000 90782		
	CONSULTATION-OFFICE					Urinalysis, Chemical	81005				Testosterone	J1080 90782		
	Focused	99241				Throat Culture	87081				Lidocaine	J2000 90782		
	Expanded	99242				Occult Blood	82270				Solumedrol	J2920 90782		
	Detailed	99243				Pap Handling Charge	99000				Solucortef	J1720 90782		
	Comprehensive 1	99244				Pap Life Guard	88150-90				Hydeltra	J1690 90782		
	Comprehensive 2	99245				Gram Stain	87205				Pen Procaine	J2510 90788		
	Dr.					Hanging Drop	87210							
	Case Management	98900				Urine Drug Screen	99000				INJECTIONS - JOINT/BURSA			
											Small Joints	20600		
	Post-op Exam	99024									Intermediate	20605		
						SUPPLIES					Large Joints	20610		
											Trigger Point	20550		
											MISCELLANEOUS			

DIAGNOSIS:	ICD-9										
___ Abdominal Pain	789.0	___ Gout	274.0	___ C.V.A. - Acute	436.	___ Electrolyte Dis.	276.9	___ Herpes Simplex	054.9
___ Abscess (Site)	682.9	___ Asthma	493.90	___ Cere. Vas. Accid. (Old)	438	___ Fatigue	780.7	___ Herpes Zoster	053.9
___ Adverse Drug Rx	995.2	___ Asthmatic Bronchitis	493.90	___ Cerumen	380.4	___ Fibrocys. Br. Dis	610.1	___ Hydrocele	603.9
___ Alcohol Detox	291.8	___ Atrial Fib.	427.31	___ Chestwall Pain	786.59	___ Fracture (Site)	829.0	___ Hyperlipidemia	272.4
___ Alcoholism	303.90	___ Atrial Tachi.	427.0	___ Cholecystitis	575.0	___ Open/Close		___ Hypertension	401.9
___ Allergic Rhinitis	477	___ Bowel Obstruct.	560.9	___ Cholelithiasis	574.00	___ Fungal Infect. (Site)	110.8	___ Hyperthyroidism	242.9
___ Allergy	995.3	___ Breast Mass	611.72	___ COPD	492.8	___ Gastric Ulcer	531.90	___ Hypothyroidism	244.9
___ Alzheimer's Dis.	290.1	___ Bronchitis	490	___ Cirrhosis	571.5	___ Gastritis	535.0	___ Labyrinthitis	386.30
___ Anemia	285.9	___ Bursitis	727.3	___ Cong. Heart Fail.	428.9	___ Gastroenteritis	558.9	___ Lipoma (Site)	214.9
___ Anemia - Pernicious	281.0	___ Cancer, Breast (Site)	174.9	___ Conjunctivitis	372.30	___ G.I. Bleeding	578.9	___ Lymphoma	202.8
___ Angina	413.9	___ Metastatic (Site)	199.1	___ Contusion (Site)	924.9	___ Glomerulonephritis	583.9	___ Mit. Valve Prolapse	424.0
___ Anxiety Synd.	300.00	___ Colon	153.9	___ Costochondritis	733.99	___ Headache	784.0	___ Myocard. Infarction (Area)	410.9
___ Appendicitis	541	___ Cancer, Rectal	154.1	___ Depression	311.	___ Headache, Tension	307.81	___ M.I., Old	412
___ Arterioscl. H.D.	414.0	___ Lung (Site)	162.9	___ Dermatitis	692.9	___ Migraine (Type)	346.9	___ Myositis	729.1
___ Arthritis, Osteo.	715.90	___ Skin (Site)	173.9	___ Diabetes Mellitus	250.00	___ Hemorrhoids	455.6	___ Nausea/Vomiting	787.0
___ Rheumatoid	714.0	___ Card. Arrhythmia (Type)	427.9	___ Diabetic Ketosis	250.1	___ Hernia, Hiatal	553.3	___ Neuralgia	729.2
___ Lupus	710.0	___ Cardiomyopathy	425.4	___ Diverticulitis	562.11	___ Inguinal	550.9	___ Nevus (Site)	216.9
		___ Cellulitis (Site)	682.9	___ Diverticulosis	562.10	___ Hepatitis	573.3	___ Obesity	278.0

DIAGNOSIS: (IF NOT CHECKED ABOVE)

SERVICES PERFORMED AT: ☐ Office ☐ E.R. ☐ ☐	☐ CLAIM CONTAINS NO ORDERED REFERRING SERVICE	REFERRING PHYSICIAN & I.D. NUMBER

RETURN APPOINTMENT INFORMATION: 5 - 10 - 15 - 20 - 30 - 40 - 60 [DAYS] [WKS.] [MOS.] [PRN]	NEXT APPOINTMENT M - T - W - TH - F - S DATE / / TIME:		AM PM	ACCEPT ASSIGNMENT? ☐ YES ☐ NO	DOCTOR'S SIGNATURE

INSTRUCTIONS TO PATIENT FOR FILING INSURANCE CLAIMS:

1. Complete upper portion of this form, sign and date. 2. Attach this form to your own insurance company's form for direct reimbursement. **MEDICARE PATIENTS - DO NOT SEND THIS TO MEDICARE. WE WILL SUBMIT THE CLAIM FOR YOU.**	☐ CASH ☐ CHECK # _____ ☐ VISA ☐ MC ☐ CO-PAY	TOTAL TODAY'S FEE
		OLD BALANCE
		TOTAL DUE
		AMOUNT REC'D. TODAY

INSUR-A-BILL ® BIBBERO SYSTEMS, INC. • PETALUMA, CA • UP. SUPER. © 6/94 (BIBB/STOCK)

Figure 9-5. *A superbill is a form that can also be used as a charge slip and invoice and can be submitted with insurance claims.*

ience stores. International money orders can be acquired in U.S. dollars to be cashed in foreign countries.

Limited check: Issued on a special check form that displays a preprinted maximum dollar amount for which the check can be written. This type of check often is used for payroll or insurance payments.

Traveler's check: A check purchased for a small fee for a specified amount of money. It is designed for people who are traveling where personal checks may not be accepted and for people who don't want to carry large amounts of cash. Traveler's checks are also available in foreign currencies. They can be purchased at a bank.

Voucher check: Contains a detachable voucher form. It is frequently used for payroll checks because additional information about the transaction can be supplied to the payee. The voucher portion is used to itemize the purpose of the check, deductions, or other information.

Bank draft: A check written by a bank against its funds in another bank.

Warrant: A nonnegotiable check. It is a statement issued to indicate that a debt should be paid, for example, by an insurance company.

ABA number: Part of a coding system originated by the American Bankers Association (ABA). It is always located in the upper right corner of a printed check to identify the location of the bank at which the check is to be redeemed.

MICR code: Stands for *magnetic ink character recognition* code, which appears along the bottom of a check and consists of numbers and characters printed in magnetic ink.

Accepting checks: The majority of bills are paid by personal checks drawn on patients' bank accounts. Some checks may be considered risky, such as third-party checks, postdated checks, checks drawn on an out-of-town bank, and checks marked *Paid in full* that do not represent the total due. Cashing such checks should be avoided.

Postdated check: A check that bears a date in the future and cannot be cashed until then.

Predated or **backdated check:** A check made out with a date in the past. Predated checks can be accepted so long as the date shown is no more than 6 months before the date on which it is cashed.

Third-party check: A check written by an unknown party to a payee (e.g., your patient) who wishes to release the check to you for payment of an outstanding balance. Government and payroll checks used in this way are also third-party checks.

Canceled check: A check that has been cashed and thus cannot be issued again.

Deposits

Deposits: Cash or checks placed into a bank account. They can be made to either checking or savings accounts. Checks should be deposited promptly for the following reasons:

- They may be lost, misplaced, or stolen.
- There is the possibility of a stop-payment order.
- They may have a restricted time for cashing.

Endorsement: A check must be endorsed to transfer the funds from one person to another. Endorsement is accomplished by signing or rubber-stamping the back of the check, in ink, at the left end. When you accept a check, immediately endorse it and write the words *For deposit only* on the back. See Figure 9-6.

Types of endorsement: There are four principal kinds of endorsement: blank, restrictive, special, and qualified. Blank and restrictive endorsements are the most commonly used.

Blank endorsement: A signature only. Also known as an open endorsement, it is the simplest and most common type of endorsement on personal checks.

Restrictive endorsement: The words *For deposit only* followed by the account number and signature.

Limited endorsement: The words *Pay to the order of* and the name, followed by a signature. A check with a limited endorsement functions as a third-party check. For example, a patient might give you a check that was originally made out to someone else, who has signed the check over to the patient using a limited endorsement. This original payee would become a third-party payer if the practice were to accept the check from the patient.

Qualified endorsement: Used to disclaim future liability of the endorser, generally consisting of the words *Without recourse* above the signature. It is most commonly used by lawyers who accept checks on behalf of clients.

Deposit slip: After endorsing the check, fill out a deposit slip as shown in Figure 9-7.

Methods of deposit: There are three different ways to deposit funds: in person, by mail, or at commercial night depositories. Making deposits in person is the most direct method, and banks immediately provide a receipt to verify transactions. Avoid sending cash through the mail, but if it is absolutely necessary to do so, use registered mail.

Returned checks: Occasionally, the bank returns a deposited check because of some problems such as a missing signature or missing endorsement. It is also returned if the payer has insufficient funds on deposit to cover the check.

NSF: Abbreviation for *not sufficient funds*, meaning that there is not enough money in the account on which a check has been drawn to cover the amount of the check.

Handling returned checks: If a check is returned, begin by contacting the person who gave you the check. If payment is not made, or if you cannot track down the person, turn the account over to a collection agency.

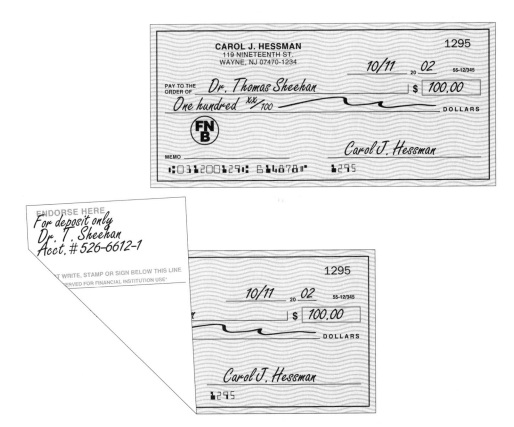

Figure 9-6. *After verifying that a patient's check is correct, immediately endorse it with the words* For deposit only, *the name of the practice, and the bank account number.*

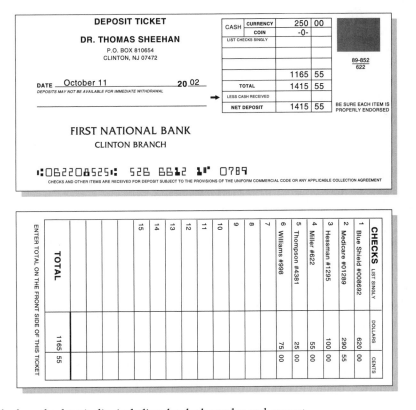

Figure 9-7. *List each check on the deposit slip, including the check number and amount*

Bill Payment

Bills: All bills should be paid by check for documentation and control purposes. For small payments, such as public transportation costs, petty cash may be used.

Office banking policy: Should indicate who is responsible for writing and signing all checks. For good control, one person should write the checks and another person should be authorized to sign them. Sometimes two authorized signatures are required in order to transfer funds from one account to another or to write checks over a certain amount, such as $1,000.

Check writing: Checks are printed on sensitized paper so that erasures are easily noticeable. The bank has the right to refuse payment on any check that has been altered. You must not cross out, erase, or change any part of a check.

Check stub: The part of a check that remains in the checkbook after the check has been written and removed.

Payee: The person to whom the check is payable.

Payer: The person who signs the check to release the funds to the payee.

Lost and stolen checks: Occasionally, an outgoing check may be lost or stolen after it has been issued. You must report this situation to the bank promptly. The bank will place a warning on the account, and signatures on cashed checks will be carefully inspected to detect possible forgeries. A stop-payment order should be issued, and the stop-payment notice should be attached to the check stub. The amount of the check should be added to the current checkbook balance. A new check can be issued to replace the one lost.

Billing and Collections

Medical Billing

Billing duties of a medical assisting: To be an effective account manager, follow these rules:

- Do not be embarrassed to ask for payment for services. The physician or facility has the right to charge for the care and services provided.

- Practice good judgment.

- Give personal attention and consideration to each patient.

- Show a desire to help patients with financial difficulties.

Payment at the time of service: Every practice should encourage time-of-service collection. There will be no further billing and bookkeeping expenses if patients get into the habit of paying their current charges before they leave the office.

Payment plans and extensions of credit: For procedures and services involving large fees, such as surgery and long-term care, inform patients of:

- What the charges will be
- What services these charges cover
- Credit policies of the facility:
  - When payment is due
  - Circumstances in which the practice requires payment at the time of service
  - When or whether assignment of insurance benefits is accepted
  - Whether insurance forms will be completed by the office staff
  - Collection procedures, including circumstances in which accounts will be sent to a collection agency

It is a good idea to have credit policies in writing, for example, included in a new patient brochure.

Balance billing: Billing the patient for the difference between the fee and the amount the insurance company allows. Whether balance billing is acceptable depends on the contract with the insurance company.

Exceptions and rules: Although there will be exceptions, there must be rules, which should be conveyed in writing to the patient at the outset of the relationship. Any patient who needs special consideration can be counseled individually.

Internal billing: In a practice with only a moderate number of accounts, the medical assistant handles the preparation and mailing of statements. A printed statement may be computer-generated, based on a superbill, typewritten, or photocopied from the ledger card.

Statement: Should show the service rendered on each date, the charge for each service, the date on which a claim was submitted to the insurance company, the date of payment, and the balance due from the patient. A regular system of mailing statements should be put into operation. Time limits must also be observed in billing third-party payers. Bills for minors must be addressed to parents or legal guardians.

Cycle billing: A common billing system that bills each patient once a month but spreads the work of billing over the month. In this system, invoices are sent to patients whose names begin with A–D on one day, those whose names begin with E–H on another day, and so on.

Fair Credit Billing Act: A federal law mandating that billing for a balance due or reporting a credit balance of one dollar or more must occur every 30 days.

Collection Policies and Procedures

Standard payment period: Normally, people are expected to pay bills within 30 days.

Open-book account: The most typical account for patients of a medical practice, in which the account is open to charges made occasionally. It uses the last date of payment or charge for each illness as the starting date for determining the time limit on that debt.

Written-contract account: An account in which the physician and patient sign an agreement stating that the patient will pay the bill in more than four installments.

Single-entry account: An account with only one charge, as is created, for example, when an out-of-town vacationer consults a local physician for an illness.

Delinquent accounts: Payment is the most difficult to collect from two groups of patients: those with hardship cases and those who have moved and have not received an invoice.

Hardship cases: Accounts of patients who are poor, uninsured, underinsured, or elderly and on a limited income. Physicians may decide to treat such patients at a deep discount or for free.

Payment collection: Evaluation of the success of collections is based on (1) the collection ratio and (2) the accounts receivable ratio.

Collection ratio: Measures the effectiveness of the billing system. The basic formula for figuring the collection ratio is to divide the total collections by the net charges (gross charges minus any discounts) to reach the percentage figure.

Accounts receivable ratio: Measures how fast outstanding accounts are being paid. The formula for figuring the accounts receivable ratio is to divide the current accounts receivable balance by the average gross monthly charges.

Aging accounts receivable: A procedure for classifying accounts receivable by age from the first date of billing. It should list all patient account balances, when charges were incurred, the most recent payment date, and any notes regarding the account. The age analysis is a tool to show, at a glance, the status of each account.

Reasons for collecting delinquent accounts: The main reasons to try to collect all delinquent accounts are:

- Physicians must be paid for services so that they can pay expenses and continue to treat patients.

- Although a patient cannot be "fired" for nonpayment (in the sense that necessary treatment cannot be withheld because of an inability to pay), failure to collect payment can result in the termination of the established patient-physician relationship.

- Noncollection of medical bills may imply guilt and a malpractice suit may result.

- Abandoning accounts without collection follow-up encourages nonpayment; as a result, the paying patients indirectly subsidize the cost of medical care for those who can pay but do not.

Collection techniques: Include telephone collection calls, collection letters or statements, and personal interviews. Send the first letter or statement when the account is 30 days past due, then follow up at 60 days, at 90 days, and again at 120 days. Table 9-2 on p. 222 lists laws governing credit and collections. If you call the patient, make sure that you do so in private and

during reasonable hours. Always be respectful and professional, and demonstrate your willingness to help the patient meet his or her financial obligation. Get a definite answer from the patient if you can, and follow up later if the payment has not been received. Do not call the patient's place of work, especially if you don't know whether or not the patient can take personal calls at work. When writing collection letters, make sure that the first few letters simply remind the patient about a possible oversight of debt, and make sure that each letter is specific to the individual situation.

Illegal collection techniques: It is illegal to harass a debtor. Harassment includes making threats or calls late at night (after 9 p.m.). It is also illegal to threaten action that cannot be legally taken or that is not intended to be taken.

Statute of limitations: A statute that limits the time in which rights can be enforced by action. After the statute of limitations expires, no legal collection suit may be brought against a debtor. This time limit depends on the state in which the debt was incurred.

Outside collection assistance: When you have done everything possible internally to follow up on an outstanding account and have not received payment, there are still steps you can take:

- Use a collection agency. If the patient has failed to respond to your final letter or has failed to fulfill a second promise on payment, send the account to the collector without delay. After an account has been released to a collection agency, your office makes no further collection attempts.

- Collect through the court system. Most physicians believe that it is unwise to resort to the courts to collect medical bills unless there are extraordinary circumstances.

Collection agencies: Medical practices should be careful to avoid collection agencies that use harsh collection practices. Once an account has been turned over to an agency, do not send bills or discuss the account with the patient. If the agency is unable to collect the money, the physician should decide whether to write off the debt or to take the matter to court.

Accounts Payable

Accounts payable: Amounts the physician owes to others for equipment and services. Examples:

- Office supplies
- Medical supplies and equipment
- Equipment repair and maintenance
- Utilities
- Taxes
- Payroll
- Rent

Law	Requirements	Penalties for Breaking the Law
Equal Credit Opportunity Act (ECOA)	• Creditors may not discriminate against applicants on the basis of sex, marital status, race, national origin, religion, or age. • Creditors may not discriminate because an applicant receives public assistance income or has exercised rights under the Consumer Credit Protection Act.	• If an applicant sues the practice for violating the ECOA, the practice may have to pay damages, penalties, lawyers' fees, and court costs. • If an applicant joins a class action lawsuit against the practice, the practice may have to pay damages of up to $500,000 or 1% of the practice's net worth, whichever is less. (In a class action lawsuit, one or more people sue a company that wronged all of them in the same way.) • If the Federal Trade Commission (FTC) receives many complaints from applicants stating that the practice violated the ECOA, the FTC may investigate and take action against the practice.
Fair Credit Reporting Act (FCRA)	Credit bureaus are required to supply correct and complete information to businesses to use in evaluating a person's application for credit, insurance, or a job.	• If one applicant sues the practice in federal court for violating the FCRA, the practice may have to pay actual damages, punitive damages (punishment for intentionally breaking the law), court costs, and lawyers' fees. • The FTC may investigate and take action against the practice if it receives too many complaints.
Fair Debt Collection Practices Act (FDCPA)	Debt collectors are required to treat debtors fairly. Certain collection tactics are also prohibited, such as harassment, false statements, threats, and unfair practices.	• If it is sued by a debtor, the practice may have to pay damages, court costs, and lawyers' fees. • In a class action lawsuit, the practice might have to pay damages of up to $500,000 or 1% of the practice's net worth, whichever is less. • The FTC may investigate and take action.
Truth in Lending Act (TLA)	Creditors are required to provide applicants with accurate and complete credit costs and terms, in clear and understandable language.	• If it is sued by a debtor, the practice may have to pay damages, court costs, and lawyers' fees. • The FTC may investigate and take action against the practice if it receives too many complaints.

Table 9-2

Accounts payable records: Include purchase orders, packing slips, and invoices.

Payroll

Payroll: The total direct and indirect earning of all employees. Federal, state, and local laws require records to be kept of all salaries and wages paid to employees.

Payroll tasks: Include calculating the amount of wages or salaries paid and amounts deducted from employees' earnings. Other payroll tasks involve writing checks, tracking data for payroll taxes, and filling out payroll tax forms.

Retention of payroll records: The physician is required by law to keep payroll data for 4 years. The records should include the following information:

- Employee's Social Security number
- Number of withholding allowances claimed
- Gross salary
- Deductions for Social Security tax; Medicare tax; federal, state, and other tax withholding; state disability insurance; and state unemployment tax

Employer tax identification number (EIN): Every employer, no matter how small, must have an EIN for reporting federal taxes. It is obtained by completing

Form SS-4, Application for Employer Identification Number.

Employee identification: Employees are identified for tax purposes by their Social Security numbers.

Payroll register: A list of all employees and their earnings, deductions, and other information. See Figure 9-8.

Employee earnings: Either salaries or wages, plus indirect forms of payment, such as paid time off and employee benefit and service programs.

Salary: A fixed amount paid to an employee on a regular basis regardless of the number of hours worked.

Wages: Pay based on a specific rate per hour, day, or week.

Payroll deductions: Amounts regularly withheld from a paycheck, such as those for federal, state, and local taxes, as well as those for such options as a 401(K) plan, life insurance, or savings bonds.

Methods for calculating payroll checks: Include the manual, the pegboard, and the computer system. Regardless of the accounting system used, attention to accuracy in bookkeeping is necessary. In addition, it is necessary to maintain confidentiality in matters related to employees' wages and salaries.

Net earnings: Gross earnings minus total deductions.

Payroll services: Some offices hire an outside payroll service to process all payroll checks and withholding payments, as well as to keep records.

Tax

Types of tax: The federal government mandates payment of the following taxes through withholding:

- Social Security
- Medicare
- Federal income tax

These taxes are based on a percentage of the employee's total gross income.

Withholding: Amounts of salary held out of payroll checks for the purpose of paying government taxes or for employee benefits.

Form W-4: In order to determine the amount of money to be withheld from each paycheck, each new employee must complete a Form W-4, and each employee should update the W-4 regularly. Figure 9-9 on p. 224 shows a Form W-4, which asks for the (1) employee's name and current address, (2) Social Security number, (3) marital status, and (4) number of allowances the employee claims that should be used in calculating withholding.

Social Security (FICA): The Federal Insurance Contribution Act governs the Social Security system. The employee pays half of the contribution, and the employer pays the other half. IRS *Circular E* lists the FICA tax percentages that should be applied, based on the level of taxable earnings, length of the payroll period, marital status, and number of withholding allowances claimed.

Federal Unemployment Tax Act (FUTA): Requires employers to pay a percentage of each employee's income, up to a specified dollar amount, to fund an account used to pay employees who have been laid off for a specified time while they are seeking new employment. Although FUTA is based on employees' gross income, it must not be deducted from employees' wages. Payments into a state unemployment fund can generally be applied as credit against the FUTA tax amount. FUTA deposits are calculated quarterly. See Figure 9-10 on p. 225.

State unemployment tax: All states have unemployment compensation laws. Most states require only the employer to make payments to the unemployment insurance fund. However, a few states require both the employer and employee to make a payment. In some states, the employer does not have to make unemployment compensation payments if there are very few employees (4 or fewer).

Pay Period 6/1–6/14

Emp. No.	Name	Earnings to date	Hrly. Rate	Reg. Hrs.	OT Hrs.	OT Earnings	TOTAL GROSS	Earnings Subject to Unemp.	Earnings Subject to FICA	Social Security (FICA)	Medicare	Federal W/H	State W/H	Health Ins.	Net Pay	Check No.
0010	Scott, B.	9,823.14	14.00	70.00			980.00	980.00	980.00	60.50	14.10	147.92	15.10	25.00	717.38	11747
0020	Wilson, J.	14,290.38	17.00	70.00	6.50	153.00	1343.00	1343.00	1343.00	83.26	19.47	160.45	15.85	67.50	996.47	11748
0030	Diaz, J.	2,750.26	5.50	46.25			254.37	254.37	254.37	15.77	3.68	38.20	3.75		192.97	11749
0040	Ling, W.	2,240.57	6.80	30.00			204.00	204.00	204.00	12.66	2.96	26.02	3.12		159.54	11750
0050	Harris, E.	2,600.98	10.00	23.50			235.00	235.00	235.00	14.57	3.41	33.52	3.36		180.14	11751

Figure 9-8. *A payroll register is designed to summarize information about all employees and their earnings.*

Form W-4 (2000)

Purpose. Complete Form W-4 so your employer can withhold the correct Federal income tax from your pay. Because your tax situation may change, you may want to refigure your withholding each year.

Exemption from withholding. If you are exempt, complete only lines 1, 2, 3, 4, and 7, and sign the form to validate it. Your exemption for 2000 expires February 16, 2001.

Note: *You cannot claim exemption from withholding if (1) your income exceeds $700 and includes more than $250 of unearned income (e.g., interest and dividends) and (2) another person can claim you as a dependent on their tax return.*

Basic instructions. If you are not exempt, complete the **Personal Allowances Worksheet** below. The worksheets on page 2 adjust your withholding allowances based on itemized deductions, adjustments to income, or two-earner/two-job situations. Complete all worksheets that apply. They will help you figure the number of withholding allowances you are entitled to claim. **However, you may claim fewer (or zero) allowances.**

Child tax and higher education credits. For details on adjusting withholding for these and other credits, see **Pub. 919,** How Do I Adjust My Tax Withholding?

Head of household. Generally, you may claim head of household filing status on your tax return only if you are unmarried and pay more than 50% of the costs of keeping up a home for yourself and your dependent(s) or other qualifying individuals. See line **E** below.

Nonwage income. If you have a large amount of nonwage income, such as interest or dividends, you should consider making estimated tax payments using **Form 1040-ES,** Estimated Tax for Individuals. Otherwise, you may owe additional tax.

Two earners/two jobs. If you have a working spouse or more than one job, figure the total number of allowances you are entitled to claim on all jobs using worksheets from only one Form W-4. Your withholding usually will be most accurate when all allowances are claimed on the Form W-4 prepared for the highest paying job and zero allowances are claimed for the others.

Check your withholding. After your Form W-4 takes effect, use Pub. 919 to see how the dollar amount you are having withheld compares to your projected total tax for 2000. Get Pub. 919 especially if you used the **Two-Earner/Two-Job Worksheet** on page 2 and your earnings exceed $150,000 (Single) or $200,000 (Married).

Recent name change? If your name on line 1 differs from that shown on your social security card, call 1-800-772-1213 for a new social security card.

Personal Allowances Worksheet (Keep for your records.)

A Enter "1" for **yourself** if no one else can claim you as a dependent . . . . **A** _____

B Enter "1" if:
- You are single and have only one job; or
- You are married, have only one job, and your spouse does not work; or
- Your wages from a second job or your spouse's wages (or the total of both) are $1,000 or less.

. . **B** _____

C Enter "1" for your **spouse.** But, you may choose to enter -0- if you are married and have either a working spouse or more than one job. (Entering -0- may help you avoid having too little tax withheld.) . . . . **C** _____

D Enter number of **dependents** (other than your spouse or yourself) you will claim on your tax return . . . . **D** _____

E Enter "1" if you will file as **head of household** on your tax return (see conditions under **Head of household** above) . . **E** _____

F Enter "1" if you have at least $1,500 of **child or dependent care expenses** for which you plan to claim a credit . . . **F** _____

G **Child Tax Credit:**
- If your total income will be between $18,000 and $50,000 ($23,000 and $63,000 if married), enter "1" for each eligible child.
- If your total income will be between $50,000 and $80,000 ($63,000 and $115,000 if married), enter "1" if you have two eligible children, enter "2" if you have three or four eligible children, or enter "3" if you have five or more eligible children   **G** _____

H Add lines A through G and enter total here. Note: *This may be different from the number of exemptions you claim on your tax return.* ▶ **H** _____

For accuracy, complete all worksheets that apply.
- If you plan to **itemize or claim adjustments to income** and want to reduce your withholding, see the **Deductions and Adjustments Worksheet** on page 2.
- If you are **single,** have **more than one job** and your combined earnings from all jobs exceed $34,000, OR if you are **married** and have a **working spouse or more than one job** and the combined earnings from all jobs exceed $60,000, see the **Two-Earner/Two-Job Worksheet** on page 2 to avoid having too little tax withheld.
- If **neither** of the above situations applies, **stop here** and enter the number from line H on line 5 of Form W-4 below.

- - - - - - - - - - - - - - - - - - Cut here and give Form W-4 to your employer. Keep the top part for your records. - - - - - - - - - - - - - - - - - -

Form **W-4**
Department of the Treasury
Internal Revenue Service

Employee's Withholding Allowance Certificate

▶ **For Privacy Act and Paperwork Reduction Act Notice, see page 2.**

OMB No. 1545-0010

2000

1 Type or print your first name and middle initial	Last name		2 Your social security number

Home address (number and street or rural route)	3 ☐ Single ☐ Married ☐ Married, but withhold at higher Single rate. **Note:** *If married, but legally separated, or spouse is a nonresident alien, check the Single box.*
City or town, state, and ZIP code	4 If your last name differs from that on your social security card, check here. **You must call 1-800-772-1213 for a new card** . . . ▶ ☐

5	Total number of allowances you are claiming (from line **H** above **OR** from the applicable worksheet on page 2)	**5**
6	Additional amount, if any, you want withheld from each paycheck	**6** $

7 I claim exemption from withholding for 2000, and I certify that I meet **BOTH** of the following conditions for exemption:
- Last year I had a right to a refund of **ALL** Federal income tax withheld because I had **NO** tax liability **AND**
- This year I expect a refund of **ALL** Federal income tax withheld because I expect to have **NO** tax liability.

If you meet both conditions, write "EXEMPT" here . . . . ▶ **7**

Under penalties of perjury, I certify that I am entitled to the number of withholding allowances claimed on this certificate, or I am entitled to claim exempt status.

Employee's signature
(Form is not valid unless you sign it) ▶ _____   Date ▶ _____

8 Employer's name and address (Employer: Complete lines 8 and 10 only if sending to the IRS.)	9 Office code (optional)	10 Employer identification number

Cat. No. 10220Q

Figure 9-9. *Update all Employee's Withholding Allowance Certificates (Forms W-4) at least once a year.*

Form 940

Department of the Treasury
Internal Revenue Service (99)

Employer's Annual Federal Unemployment (FUTA) Tax Return

► **See separate Instructions for Form 940 for information on completing this form.**

OMB No. 1545-0028

1999

T	
FF	
FD	
FP	
I	
T	

Name (as distinguished from trade name)   Calendar year

Trade name, if any

Address and ZIP code   Employer identification number

A Are you required to pay unemployment contributions to only one state? (If "No," skip questions B and C.) ☐ Yes ☐ No

B Did you pay all state unemployment contributions by January 31, 2000? ((1) If you deposited your total FUTA tax when due, check "Yes" if you paid all state unemployment contributions by February 10. (2) If a 0% experience rate is granted, check "Yes." (3) If "No," skip question C.) . . . . ☐ Yes ☐ No

C Were all wages that were taxable for FUTA tax also taxable for your state's unemployment tax? . . . . . ☐ Yes ☐ No

If you answered "No" to any of these questions, you must file Form 940. If you answered "Yes" to all the questions, you may file Form 940-EZ, which is a simplified version of Form 940. (Successor employers see **Special credit for successor employers** on page 3 of the instructions.) You can get Form 940-EZ by calling 1-800-TAX-FORM (1-800-829-3676) or from the IRS's Internet Web Site at **www.irs.gov.**

If you will not have to file returns in the future, check here (see **Who Must File** in separate instructions), **and complete and sign the return** . . . . ► ☐

If this is an Amended Return, check here. . . . . ► ☐

Part I Computation of Taxable Wages

1 Total payments (including payments shown on lines 2 and 3) during the calendar year for services of employees **1**

2 Exempt payments. (Explain all exempt payments, attaching additional sheets if necessary.) ► **2**

3 Payments of more than $7,000 for services. Enter only amounts over the first $7,000 paid to each employee. Do not include any exempt payments from line 2. The $7,000 amount is the Federal wage base. Your state wage base may be different. **Do not use your state wage limitation** . **3**

4 Total exempt payments (add lines 2 and 3) **4**

5 **Total taxable wages** (subtract line 4 from line 1) . . . . ► **5**

Be sure to complete both sides of this form, and sign in the space provided on the back.

For Privacy Act and Paperwork Reduction Act Notice, see separate instructions.   Cat. No. 11234O   Form **940** (1999)

DETACH HERE

Form 940-V

Department of the Treasury
Internal Revenue Service

Form 940 Payment Voucher

Use this voucher only when making a payment with your return.

OMB No. 1545-0028

1999

Complete boxes 1, 2, 3, and 4. Do not send cash, and do not staple your payment to this voucher. Make your check or money order payable to the "United States Treasury". Be sure to enter your employer identification number, "Form 940", and "1999" on your payment.

1 Enter the amount of the payment you are making

► $.

2 Enter the first four letters of your last name (business name if partnership or corporation)

3 Enter your employer identification number

Instructions for Box 2

—Individuals (sole proprietors, trusts, and estates)— Enter the first four letters of your last name.

—Corporations and partnerships—Enter the first four characters of your business name (omit "The" if followed by more than one word).

4 Enter your business name (individual name for sole proprietors)

Enter your address

Enter your city, state, and ZIP code

Figure 9-10. *Taxes submitted with the FUTA tax return (Form 940) provide money to workers who are unemployed.*

a Control number		OMB No. 1545-0008		
b Employer identification number			**1** Wages, tips, other compensation	**2** Federal income tax withheld
c Employer's name, address, and ZIP code			**3** Social security wages	**4** Social security tax withheld
			5 Medicare wages and tips	**6** Medicare tax withheld
			7 Social security tips	**8** Allocated tips
d Employee's social security number			**9** Advance EIC payment	**10** Dependent care benefits
e Employee's name, address, and ZIP code			**11** Nonqualified plans	**12** Benefits included in box 1
			13	**14** Other

15 Statutory employee ☐	Deceased ☐	Pension plan ☐	Legal rep. ☐	Deferred compensation ☐

16 State	Employer's state I.D. no.	**17** State wages, tips, etc.	**18** State income tax	**19** Locality name	**20** Local wages, tips, etc.	**21** Local income tax

Form **W-2** Wage and Tax Statement **2000**

Copy 1 For State, City, or Local Tax Department

Department of the Treasury- Internal Revenue Service

Figure 9-11. *Each employee's Wage and Tax Statement (Form W-2) records the total amount of taxes withheld during the previous year.*

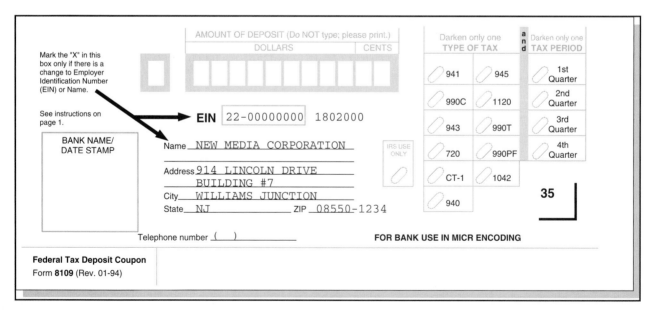

Figure 9-12. *Practices that do not submit taxes electronically must submit federal income and FICA taxes with a Federal Tax Deposit (FTD) Coupon (Form 8109).*

State disability insurance: Some states require a certain amount of money to be withheld from the employee's check to cover a disability insurance plan. This plan covers employees in the event of injury or disability.

Insurance withholding: Money may also be withheld, as requested by the employee, for health insurance, life insurance, and disability insurance that are available from the employer as employee benefits.

Form W-2: Must be completed at the end of each year and given to each employee, with copies to the federal and state governments. The W-2 lists the total gross income; total federal, state, and local taxes withheld; taxable fringe benefits; tips; and the employee's total net income. The amount of wages taxable under Social Security and Medicare must be listed separately on the W-2. See Figure 9-11.

Deposit requirements: Federal tax withholding and FICA payments must be made to a federal deposit account in a Federal Reserve Bank or authorized banking institution at regular intervals, at least monthly. The Internal Revenue Service (IRS) imposes a severe penalty for failure to deposit this money.

Employer's quarterly federal tax return: Form 941 (see Figure 9-12) must be filed quarterly to report federal income and FICA taxes withheld from employees' paychecks. It is due before the last day of the first month after the end of a quarter: April 30, July 31, October 31, and January 31.

Instructions:

Answer the following questions. Check your answers in the *Answer Key* that follows this section.

1. A list of all employees and their earnings, deductions, and other information is called
   A. Employee earnings
   B. Payroll tasks
   C. Accounts payable
   D. Payroll register
   E. Employee financial listing

2. A payer's own check that is guaranteed by the bank is called a
   A. Counter check
   B. Cashier's check
   C. Money order
   D. Guaranteed check
   E. Certified check

3. Recording financial transactions in a bookkeeping or accounting system is called
   A. Ledger
   B. Superbill
   C. Posting
   D. Trial balance
   E. Deducting

4. Paper towels are considered
   A. Incidental items
   B. Durable items
   C. Capital equipment
   D. Clinical supplies
   E. Expendable items

5. Amounts charged with suppliers or creditors that remain unpaid are referred to as
   A. Bookkeeping
   B. Accounts receivable
   C. Account balances
   D. Accounts payable
   E. Assets

6. A collection ratio is
   A. The amount of money collected this year divided by the amount of money collected last year
   B. The total collections divided by net charges
   C. The total collections divided by gross charges
   D. The total amount of money collected divided by any discounts
   E. None of the above

7. The portion of salary held back from payroll checks for the purpose of paying government taxes is known as
   A. W-4 forms
   B. Federal Unemployment Tax Act
   C. Withholding
   D. Annual tax returns
   E. FICA

8. Which of the following may be used by a payer as a third-party check?
   A. Payroll check
   B. Cashier's check
   C. Bank draft
   D. The payer's personal check
   E. Traveler's check

9. A billing statement should include

   A. The patient's name and address
   B. Services rendered on each date
   C. Balance due to the patient
   D. Both B and C
   E. All of the above

10. Which of the following due dates for Employer's Quarterly Federal Tax Returns is <u>not</u> correct?

    A. July 31
    B. January 31
    C. October 31
    D. April 30
    E. June 30

11. Aging accounts receivable

    A. Means that the physician must collect the receivables on time
    B. Is not necessary in a single-physician office
    C. Is a tool to show the status of each account
    D. Involves writing off accounts that are over 1 year past due
    E. Involves writing off accounts that are over 5 years past due

12. A piece of paper describing a purchase and the amount due is known as a(n)

    A. Inventory
    B. Disbursement
    C. Vendor
    D. Packing slip
    E. Invoice

13. Evaluation of collection is based on

    A. The collection ratio
    B. The accounts receivable ratio
    C. The bank statement balance
    D. Both A and B
    E. All of the above

14. Which of the following statements regarding state unemployment tax is correct?

    A. Only employees must make a payment
    B. Only employers must make a payment
    C. A few states require both employees and employers to make a payment
    D. A few states do not make it available
    E. None of the above

15. The accounts receivable ratio shows

    A. The dollar value of the services performed
    B. How fast outstanding accounts are being paid
    C. The number of outstanding accounts
    D. Both B and C
    E. Both A and B

16. What is the trial balance?

    A. A daily summary
    B. A way of checking the accuracy of accounts
    C. An accounting system
    D. Accrual accounting
    E. Bookkeeping

17. Cash amounts that are paid out are called

    A. Disbursements
    B. Statements
    C. Receivables
    D. Payables
    E. None of the above

18. A vendor's invoice should be kept on file for at least how long?

   A. 1 year
   B. 3 years
   C. 5 years
   D. 10 years
   E. As long as the practice exists

19. The reviewing of financial data to verify accuracy and completeness is called

   A. Withholding taxes
   B. Auditing
   C. Annual tax returns
   D. Accounts payable
   E. Taking a trial balance

20. Which of the following does *debit* mean?

   A. Total
   B. Subtract
   C. Charge
   D. Subtotal
   E. Balance

21. When new supplies are received, you should

   A. Throw out the old ones
   B. Place them in the front of the supply area
   C. Place them in the back of the supply area
   D. Inventory all supplies
   E. Both A and D

22. A bank draft is a check drawn by a bank

   A. That is not limited
   B. That can be used as a third-party check
   C. That is less reliable than a cashier's check
   D. On the guaranteed funds of a depositor
   E. On its funds in another bank

23. The credit policies of a medical facility

   A. Should include a specification of when the practice requires payment
   B. Should be in writing
   C. Should vary depending on a patient's circumstances
   D. Both A and B
   E. Both B and C

24. Petty cash may be used

   A. For paying minor incidental expenses such as public transportation fares
   B. For paying an invoice for supplies ordered
   C. For paying the electric bill for the medical facility
   D. Only by the physician
   E. Only in emergencies

25. Which type of check is frequently used for payroll because it itemizes the purposes for the check and deductions?

   A. Bank draft
   B. Voucher check
   C. Limited check
   D. Certified check
   E. Cashier's check

26. An amount that constitutes an addition to revenue is called

   A. Debit
   B. Credit
   C. Payables
   D. Equity
   E. Charge

27. A disadvantage of single-entry bookkeeping is that it

   A. Is the most expensive system to set up
   B. Is hard to learn
   C. Makes errors hard to spot
   D. Is time-consuming
   E. Is very rare in medical practices

28. Which of the following statements is true about a typical purchasing procedure in a medical office?

   A. An authorized person should be in charge of purchasing
   B. Receipts of goods should be recorded
   C. High-quality goods should be ordered at the lowest price
   D. Shipments should be checked against packing slips
   E. All of the above

29. Which of the following is an appropriate collection technique?

   A. Calling patients at work to remind them of their financial obligation and to offer to work with them to help pay their debt
   B. Threatening legal action, even though your office rarely undertakes legal action to collect, because the threat makes patients more likely to pay quickly
   C. Calling patients at home after 10 p.m.
   D. Sending a payment reminder in the form of a statement or letter when the account is 30 days past due
   E. None of the above is an appropriate collection technique

CHAPTER 9 REVIEW

ANSWER KEY

1.	D	16.	B	
2.	E	17.	A	
3.	C	18.	D	
4.	E	19.	B	
5.	D	20.	C	
6.	B	21.	C	
7.	C	22.	E	
8.	A	23.	D	
9.	E	24.	A	
10.	E	25.	B	
11.	C	26.	B	
12.	E	27.	C	
13.	D	28.	E	
14.	C	29.	D	
15.	B			

CHAPTER 10

Medical Insurance

CHAPTER OUTLINE

Medical Insurance Terminology

Types of Insurance

Types of Medical Plans

Government Plans
Private Plans
Managed Care

Coding and Claim Processing

Diagnostic Coding
Procedural Coding
Claim Processing
Legal Considerations

AREAS OF COMPETENCE

AAMA—ROLE DELINEATION STUDY AREAS OF COMPETENCE

Administrative

Administrative Procedures

- Understand and apply third-party guidelines
- Obtain reimbursement through accurate claims submission
- Monitor third-party reimbursement
- Understand and adhere to managed care policies and procedures

General (Transdisciplinary)

Legal Concepts

- Document accurately
- Follow employer's established policies dealing with the health care contract

(Chart continued on next page.)

AMT—RMA CERTIFICATION EXAM TOPICS

Insurance

- Terminology
- Plans
- Claim forms
- Coding
- Financial aspects of medical insurance

Financial Bookkeeping

- Patient billing

Medical Insurance Terminology

Premium: The amount charged for a medical insurance policy. The insurer agrees to provide certain benefits in return for the premium. It is also called coverage cost.

Insurance benefits: Payments for medical services that can be submitted by an insurance company under a predefined policy issued to an individual or group of individuals.

Rider: An addition to an insurance policy, often attached on a separate piece of paper.

UCR: The *u*sual, *c*ustomary, and *r*easonable fee. It is determined by comparing the actual fee charged by a physician, the fee charged by most physicians in a community, and the amount determined to be appropriate for the service.

Usual fee: The fee an individual physician most frequently charges for a service to private patients.

Customary fee: The range of fees charged by most physicians in the community for a particular service.

Reasonable fee: The generally accepted fee a physician charges for an exceptionally difficult or complicated service. A charge is considered reasonable if it is deemed acceptable after peer review even if it does not meet the criteria for a customary fee or prevailing charges.

Prevailing charges: The most frequently charged fees in an area by a specialty group of physicians.

Fee schedule: The price list for the medical practice, which lists the services offered and the corresponding charges for those services.

Payment: Cash, a check, or a money order received for professional services rendered.

Assignment of benefits: An authorization to an insurance company to make payment directly to the physician.

Acceptance of assignment: An agreement by a physician to accept the amount established by Medicare, Medicaid, or a private insurer as full payment for covered services. The patient is not billed for the difference.

Allowed charge: The maximum charge an insurance carrier or government program will cover for specific services. The allowed charges are detailed in an insurance carrier's explanation of benefits (EOB). In managed care, a participating (PAR) provider agrees to accept allowed charges in return for various incentives, such as fast payment. If a participating provider normally charges more for a service than the allowed charge, the physician must write off the difference, and the patient may not be billed for this amount. However, nonparticipating (nonPAR) providers may bill patients for this difference.

Coordination of benefits: Prevents duplicate payment for the same service. For example, if a child is covered by both parents' insurance policies, a primary carrier is designated to pay benefits according to the terms of its policy, and the secondary plan may cover whatever charges are still left. If the primary carrier pays $105 dollars of a $150 charge, the most the secondary carrier will pay is $45.

Medical provider: A licensed professional who performs medical procedures.

Participating (PAR) provider: A physician or other health care provider who participates in an insurance carrier's plan. Participating providers must write off (cannot charge a patient for) disallowed charges and charges not eligible for payment.

Nonparticipating (nonPAR) provider: A physician or other health care provider who has not joined a particular insurance plan. Patients who obtain services from nonPAR providers generally must pay more of the cost than those who obtain services from PAR providers.

Subscriber: The person named as the principal in an insurance contract.

Beneficiary: The person named in an insurance policy to receive the benefits.

Overpayment: Payment by the insurer or by the patient of more than the amount due.

Schedule of benefits: The list of services that are paid for and the amounts that are paid by the insurance carrier. For example, the schedule of benefits may say that the insurance carrier will pay only 80% of all medical fees for surgeries, making the subscriber responsible for payment of coinsurance, the remaining 20% of the medical fees. Such a plan is often referred to as an 80:20 plan.

Explanation of benefits (EOB): A document from an insurance carrier that shows how the amount of the benefit was determined.

Waiting period: The initial period of time when a newly insured individual is not eligible to receive benefits.

Deductible: An amount that a subscriber must pay for covered medical services before insurance benefits are payable. The insurance carrier, not the medical practice, keeps a running account of these payments. Until the deductible has been met, the physician may bill the patient for the amount listed as deductible on the explanation of benefits.

Copayment (copay): The amount of money due from the subscriber to cover a portion of a bill. For most health maintenance organizations (HMOs), this amount is usually a small fixed fee, such as $10, per office visit.

Coinsurance: A percentage of the total cost for which the subscriber is responsible. This item is usually called a copayment in managed care plans. The physician may bill for coinsurance that was not collected at the time of service.

Services not covered: A subscriber is required to pay for services not covered by the insurance policy.

Utilization review: Examination of services by an outside group. A utilization review committee reviews individual cases to make sure that the medical care services are medically necessary.

Peer review organizations: Groups of practicing physicians paid by insurance companies to review medical records with respect to effectiveness and efficiency. The purpose of reviewing is to monitor the validity of diagnoses and the quality of care and to evaluate the appropriateness of hospital admissions and discharges.

Types of Insurance

Basic medical: Covers some or all nonsurgical services provided by a physician, whether in the office, the patient's home, or a hospital. Each time service is received, there is usually a copayment or coinsurance charge as well as a deductible amount payable by the patient. Some insurance plans cover pathology, X-ray, and diagnostic lab fees.

Major medical: A policy designed to offset heavy medical expenses resulting from catastrophic or prolonged illness or injury.

Hospital coverage: Pays for a hospital room, board, and special services in total or in part. Often a maximum number of days in the hospital or a maximum amount payable per day is set by hospitalization policies.

Surgical coverage: Covers suturing, fracture reduction, aspiration, removal of foreign bodies, excisions, and incisions performed in a doctor's office, a hospital, or elsewhere. Part or all of a surgeon's and possibly an assistant surgeon's fees are paid for by surgical coverage.

Disability protection: Covers loss of income that results from illness. It is not to be used for payment of specific medical bills, and it is paid directly to the patient.

Dental care: Employers' benefit packages often include dental coverage, usually based on an incentive and copayment program. Often a company's portion of a copayment increases by the year, until 100% coverage is achieved.

Vision care: Reimburses for all or some costs for frames, lenses, and eye exams.

Liability insurance: Covers people injured in their homes or cars. The many types include homeowner, business, and automobile policies.

Life insurance: A plan that pays benefits to a beneficiary in case of loss of life.

Types of Medical Plans

Indemnity plans: The insurer pays the subscriber a set amount for each service or procedure performed because of illness or injury. These fees are usually paid directly to the insured unless previous arrangements have been made for them to go straight to the provider. This type of plan does not pay for complete services rendered, and there is often a difference between the physician's fee and the amount the insurance company pays out. A fee schedule is given to the purchaser at the beginning of the contract, and benefits are determined on a fee-for-service basis.

Group policies: Cover groups of people under a master contract, which is generally issued to an employer for the benefit of the employees. Such a plan usually provides greater benefits at lower premiums than an individual plan. Every person in a group contract has identical coverage. Physical examinations are not required in order to receive coverage.

Individual policies: Individuals who do not qualify for group policies may apply for individual policies. Premiums will probably be greater and the benefits less than in group policies. Individual policies usually require applicants to pass physical examinations in order to receive coverage.

Service benefit plans: Cover certain medical or surgical services without any additional cost to the insured. There are no scheduled set fees.

Government Plans

Government policies: Government-sponsored insurance coverage for eligible individuals. The federal government provides coverage under Medicare, Medicaid, TRICARE or CHAMPUS, and CHAMPVA.

Medicare Plans

Medicare: Provides health insurance to citizens aged 65 and older and to younger patients who are blind or widowed or who have serious long-term disabilities, such as kidney failure. Medicare Part A covers hospital, nursing facility, home health, hospice, and inpatient care. Those who are eligible for Social Security benefits are automatically enrolled in Medicare Part A. Medicare Part B covers outpatient services, services by physicians, durable medical equipment, and other services and supplies. Medicare Part B coverage is optional. Everyone eligible for Part A can choose to enroll in Part B by paying monthly premiums. Deductibles must be met in Parts A and B before payment benefits begin.

Diagnosis-related groups (DRGs): Groups of procedures or tests related directly to a diagnosis. The fixed fees paid by Medicare Part A are based on DRGs. In other words, Medicare uses DRGs to determine appropriate reimbursement for medical diagnoses and procedures, as do many private insurers. DRGs are assigned in the hospital when a patient is discharged.

Medicare fee schedule (MFS): Providers participating in Medicare must accept the charges listed in this schedule as payment for covered services. The MFS is developed using the Resource-Based Relative Value Scale (RBRVS). The participating physician may bill the patient for coinsurance and deductibles but may not collect excess charges.

Resource-Based Relative Value Scale (RBRVS): A system used by Medicare since 1992 to determine uniform payments for medical services that take geographic differences into account. A relative value unit is determined for each medical service, based on the physician's work, time and skill, and on the provider's expenses such as the costs of running the office and malpractice insurance.

Medicare supplements (Medigap policies): Private insurance contracts that supplement regular Medicare coverage. They are kept uniform in their benefits so as not to be confusing to purchasers. These supplemental plans pay for a beneficiary's deductibles, coinsurance, and in some cases for services not covered by Medicare. If the subscriber has Medigap insurance, Medicare is still the primary payer, which means that claims must be filed with Medicare first. If a patient has both Medicare and Medicaid, charges must be filed with Medicare first, and Medicaid is the secondary payer.

Medicaid Plans

Medicaid: A health benefit program designed for low-income people (people receiving welfare payments or other forms of public assistance) who cannot pay their medical bills. People covered under Medicaid are categorically needy, medically needy, or medically indigent. Eligibility for coverage might vary from month to month based on the recipient's income. Medicaid is a health cost assistance program, not an insurance program, and physicians may choose to accept or not to accept Medicaid patients. By treating Medicaid patients, physicians accept Medicaid reimbursement for covered services and cannot charge patients for any difference. In some states, Medicaid is known by a different name. For example, in California Medicaid is called MediCal. Always ask for a Medicaid card from all patients who state that they are entitled to Medicaid coverage (See Figure 10-1).

Third-party liability: An obligation of a governmental program or insurance plan to pay all or part of a patient's medical costs. Eligibility for Medicaid does not relieve Medicare of its responsibility to cover health care costs. In other words, Medicaid is always a secondary carrier or a payer of last resort.

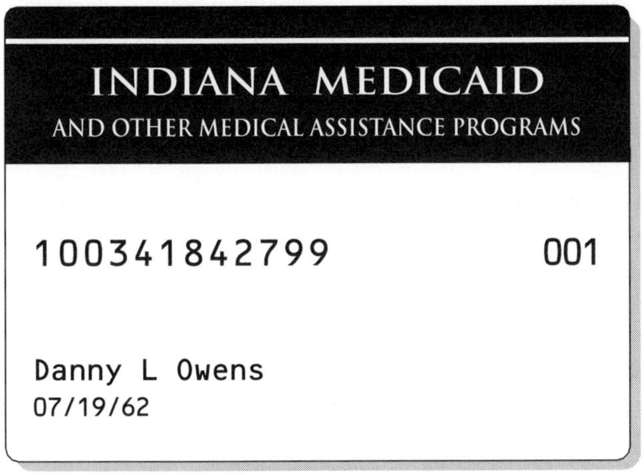

```
INDIANA MEDICAID
AND OTHER MEDICAL ASSISTANCE PROGRAMS

100341842799          001


Danny L Owens
07/19/62
```

Figure 10-1. *A Medicaid card gives the patient's name and identification (or Social Security) number.*

TRICARE (CHAMPUS) and CHAMPVA

CHAMPUS: Stands for *C*ivilian *H*ealth *A*nd *M*edical *P*rogram of the *U*niformed *S*ervices. It was a health care benefit for families of uniformed personnel and retirees from the uniformed services (the Army, Navy, Marines, Air Force, Coast Guard, Public Health Service, and National Oceanic and Atmospheric Administration).

TRICARE: A new program that replaced CHAMPUS and offers managed care benefits at three different levels: TRICARE Standard, TRICARE Extra, and TRICARE Prime. These programs feature various annual deductibles, enrollment fees, and reimbursement percentages.

CHAMPVA: Stands for *C*ivilian *H*ealth *A*nd *M*edical *P*rogram of the *V*eterans *A*dministration. It covers the expenses of the families of veterans with total, permanent, service-connected disabilities. It also covers surviving spouses and dependent children of veterans who died in the line of duty.

DEERS: Stands for Defense Enrollment Eligibility Reporting System, maintained by the Department of Defense. DEERS is a worldwide database of people covered by CHAMPUS.

Payments under CHAMPUS and CHAMPVA: Payments on assigned claims are made directly to the physician. As with Medicaid, the physician who does not participate has the option to accept assignment on a case-by-case basis.

Cost-share: The term CHAMPUS and CHAMPVA use for coinsurance.

Catastrophic cap: The maximum amount a beneficiary might need to pay out as coinsurance within a span of a year. When the cap is reached, CHAMPUS and CHAMPVA pay all allowed charges for the rest of the year.

Avoiding duplication: CHAMPUS and CHAMPVA are primary payers when an insured individual also has Medicaid. If the insured is also covered under Medicare, claims must be filed with Medicare first. CHAMPUS and CHAMPVA also do not pay for illnesses or injuries covered by workers' compensation unless compensation benefits have been exhausted. Claims must be filed within one year from date of service.

Private Plans

Coverage with private insurance companies: Physicians and medical societies control neither the premiums paid nor the benefits received from such policies. Insurance payments may be made to the subscriber and not to the physician.

Blue Cross and Blue Shield (BCBS) Association: A nationwide federation of local nonprofit service organizations that offer prepaid health care services to subscribers. Under a prepaid health coverage plan, the carrier will pay for specified medical expenses if premiums are paid in advance. The Blue Cross part of BCBS covers hospital services, outpatient and home care services, and other institutional care. Blue Shield covers physician services and dental, vision, and other outpatient benefits. Some local BCBS organizations help the government administer Medicare, Medicaid, and TRICARE programs.

Local BCBS organizations: Operate under the laws of the states in which they are located. There are 86 local BCBS plans in the United States, each with its own claim form. Plans make direct payments to member physicians, but payments may be made to the subscriber (patient) if the physician is a nonmember. Many small groups and individuals who may not be able to get coverage elsewhere can join a Blue Cross and Blue Shield Plan. Some plans offer coverage regardless of medical condition during special periods of time. Plans must also get permission from the state to raise their rates.

Customary maximum: The term BCBS plans use to describe the fee based on actual fees charged by most physicians in the community.

Fixed fee schedule: A list used by BCBS plans of maximum fees allowed for specific services.

Blue card: An agreement among BCBS plans through which a local plan may provide benefits for any out-of-town BCBS plan subscriber.

Kaiser Foundation Health Plan: A type of prepaid group practice (HMO). The Kaiser Foundation was a pioneer of nonprofit prepaid group practice beginning in California in 1933. The plan owns the medical facilities and directly employs the physicians and other providers.

Workers' compensation: A contract that insures a person against on-the-job injury or illness. The employer is responsible for the premium payment. See Table 10-1 on managing workers' compensation cases.

If your medical practice accepts workers' compensation cases, you should follow this procedure when contacted by a patient:

- Call the patient's employer to verify that the accident occurred on the employer's premises.

- Obtain the employer's approval to provide treatment.

- Ask the employer for the name of the workers' compensation insurance company.

- Remind the employer to report the accident or injury to the state labor department.

- Contact the insurance company to verify that the employer has a policy in good standing.

- Obtain a claim number from the insurance company.

- Create a patient record.

Table 10-1

Managed Care

Managed care organizations: Organizations that manage, negotiate, and contract for health care with the goal of keeping costs down. Managed care organizations sign up health care providers who agree to charge a fixed fee for services. These fixed fees are set by the managed care organization or by the governmental agency responsible for managed care.

Cost-containment practices: Developed by insurance carriers such as managed care organizations to keep premiums as low as possible. Such practices may include, for example, requiring fewer overnight stays after certain surgeries or requiring preauthorization of a service before the procedure is performed.

Health maintenance organization (HMO): A type of managed care program that provides specific services to enrollees. Enrollees are expected to receive treatment only from participating providers, and they may see specialists only when referred by their primary care physicians, who act as gatekeepers.

Group model HMO: Physicians in this type of an arrangement see both members of the HMO and non-member patients, and they remain self-employed. Physicians receive fixed payments from the HMO for each member patient, rather than reimbursement for the services provided. This fixed fee is paid to the physician monthly regardless of the number of times the patient visits the physician. This type of reimbursement is called capitation. Examples of a group model HMO include independent practice associations (IPAs) and network model HMOs.

Staff model HMO: Under this arrangement, the physicians are employees of the HMO and work full-time seeing member patients. In this type of HMO, a primary care physician is assigned as the gatekeeper for patients.

Preferred provider organization (PPO): A type of managed care plan in which enrollees receive the highest level of benefits when they obtain services from a physician, hospital, or other health provider designated by their program as a preferred provider. Enrollees receive reduced benefits when they obtain care from a provider who is not designated as a preferred provider by their program. PPO patients may see specialists without prior authorization from their primary care physicians. HMOs offering point-of-service options are more like PPOs.

Point-of-service: An option added to some HMO plans that allows patients to choose a physician outside the HMO network and to pay increased deductibles and coinsurance.

Physician-hospital organization (PHO): An approach to coordinating services for patients, in which physicians join hospitals to create an integrated medical care delivery system. This union then makes arrangements for insurance with a commercial carrier or an HMO.

Fee-for-service: A system of retrospective reimbursement in which the physician or other provider bills for each service that is provided. Blue Cross and Blue Shield is a fee-for-service plan.

Capitation: A system of payment used by managed care plans in which physicians and hospitals are paid a fixed, per capita amount for each patient enrolled over a stated period of time, regardless of the type and number of services provided.

Withhold: A portion of the monthly capitation payment to physicians retained by an HMO until the end of the year to create an incentive for efficient care. If the physician exceeds utilization norms, he or she will not receive this portion.

Relative value scale (RVS): A system of assigning values to medical services based on an analysis of the skill and time required to provide them. Both indemnity plans and many managed care plans are moving to this approach for assigning allowed charges. The relative value scale assigns numerical values to medical services, which then have to be multiplied by a dollar conversion factor to calculate fees.

Precertification: A call to the patient's insurance carrier to find out whether the treatment, surgery, tests, or hospitalization is covered under the patient's health insurance policy.

Preauthorization: Permission by the insurance carrier that must be obtained before giving a certain treatment to a patient.

Utilization management: A process, based on established criteria, of reviewing and controlling the medical necessity for services and providers' use of medical care resources. In managed care systems such as HMOs, reviews are done to establish medical necessity.

Referrals: In managed care, the primary care physician needs to refer a patient to a specialist before that patient can make an appointment with the specialist. A referral form must be completed, showing the following information:

- Referring physician
- Specialist to whom the patient is being referred
- Diagnosis
- Treatment (past and present, including medications)
- Chart notes
- Minor surgical procedures

Types of referrals: There are three types of referral:

- Regular referral, which usually takes 3–10 days.
- Urgent referral, which usually takes 24 hours.
- STAT referral, which can be done on the phone immediately.

Authorization: A referral that is approved.

Processing authorizations: Follow these guidelines in processing authorizations:

- Always review the authorization before providing services.
- Deny unauthorized procedures.
- Unauthorized services provided cannot be billed to the patient, and the practice will eventually have to write off the charges.
- Obtain the patient's signature on an agreement to pay for services not covered by insurance.

Formulary: A list of medications that are covered by a health plan.

Member services: A department designed to assist patients with inquiries and/or concerns that may arise.

Provider relations: This department is designed to assist the physician's office with inquiries about capitation, contracts, credentialing, physician appeals, formularies, and so forth.

Coding and Claim Processing

Claims department: A department primarily designed to process all medical claims. The set-up varies among medical groups.

Insurance claim form: The Health Care Financing Administration (HCFA) has designed a form called the HCFA-1500 to handle Medicare and Medicaid claims. It is the most commonly used insurance claim form and is accepted by most private insurers. (Two records are particularly useful for completing the form: the patient information form and the patient's superbill.) Form HCFA-1500 is divided into two main sections. Blanks 1 through 13 are used for patient and insured information, and blanks 14 through 33 are used for physician or supplier information. See Figure 10-2 on p. 240. When you know that the claim form is to be scanned, follow a number of guidelines in preparing it, such as using only capital letters and avoiding the use of symbols or punctuation. After completing the form, the medical assistant acting as the medical insurance specialist should:

- Proofread the form.
- Photocopy the form and place a copy in the patient's medical records.
- Enter the date sent, the patient's name, and the name of insurance carrier in the insurance log (if any).
- Enter the date and the words *Insurance filed* in the patient ledger.
- Transmit the form.

Electronic media claim (EMC): A computerized insurance claim transmitted using a modem or an optical scanner.

File acknowledgment: Immediate feedback that lets the physician's office know that the file has arrived at the insurance carrier's claims department.

Format rejection: Immediate feedback that the file has details missing or incorrect information, such a required field left blank.

National Standard Format (NSF): The most widely accepted format for transmitting HCFA forms electronically.

Advantages of electronic claim submission:

- Immediate transmission and feedback about errors.
- Faster payment and electronic funds transfer.
- Faster explanation of benefits and appeal resolution.
- Easier tracking of claim status.

APPROVED OMB-0938-0008

PLEASE DO NOT STAPLE IN THIS AREA

CARRIER

PICA

HEALTH INSURANCE CLAIM FORM

PICA

1. MEDICARE (Medicare #) MEDICAID (Medicaid #) CHAMPUS (Sponsor's SSN) CHAMPVA (VA File #) GROUP HEALTH PLAN (SSN or ID) FECA BLK LUNG (SSN) OTHER (ID)

1a. INSURED'S I.D. NUMBER (FOR PROGRAM IN ITEM 1)

2. PATIENT'S NAME (Last Name, First Name, Middle Initial)

3. PATIENT'S BIRTH DATE MM DD YY SEX M F

4. INSURED'S NAME (Last Name, First Name, Middle Initial)

5. PATIENT'S ADDRESS (No., Street)

6. PATIENT RELATIONSHIP TO INSURED Self Spouse Child Other

7. INSURED'S ADDRESS (No., Street)

CITY STATE

8. PATIENT STATUS Single Married Other

CITY STATE

ZIP CODE TELEPHONE (Include Area Code) ( )

Employed Full-Time Student Part-Time Student

ZIP CODE TELEPHONE (INCLUDE AREA CODE) ( )

9. OTHER INSURED'S NAME (Last Name, First Name, Middle Initial)

10. IS PATIENT'S CONDITION RELATED TO:

11. INSURED'S POLICY GROUP OR FECA NUMBER

a. OTHER INSURED'S POLICY OR GROUP NUMBER

a. EMPLOYMENT? (CURRENT OR PREVIOUS) YES NO

a. INSURED'S DATE OF BIRTH MM DD YY SEX M F

b. OTHER INSURED'S DATE OF BIRTH MM DD YY SEX M F

b. AUTO ACCIDENT? PLACE (State) YES NO

b. EMPLOYER'S NAME OR SCHOOL NAME

c. EMPLOYER'S NAME OR SCHOOL NAME

c. OTHER ACCIDENT? YES NO

c. INSURANCE PLAN NAME OR PROGRAM NAME

d. INSURANCE PLAN NAME OR PROGRAM NAME

10d. RESERVED FOR LOCAL USE

d. IS THERE ANOTHER HEALTH BENEFIT PLAN? YES NO *If yes*, return to and complete item 9 a-d.

READ BACK OF FORM BEFORE COMPLETING & SIGNING THIS FORM.

12. PATIENT'S OR AUTHORIZED PERSON'S SIGNATURE I authorize the release of any medical or other information necessary to process this claim. I also request payment of government benefits either to myself or to the party who accepts assignment below.

SIGNED ______ DATE ______

13. INSURED'S OR AUTHORIZED PERSON'S SIGNATURE I authorize payment of medical benefits to the undersigned physician or supplier for services described below.

SIGNED ______

PATIENT AND INSURED INFORMATION

14. DATE OF CURRENT: MM DD YY ILLNESS (First symptom) OR INJURY (Accident) OR PREGNANCY(LMP)

15. IF PATIENT HAS HAD SAME OR SIMILAR ILLNESS. GIVE FIRST DATE MM DD YY

16. DATES PATIENT UNABLE TO WORK IN CURRENT OCCUPATION FROM MM DD YY TO MM DD YY

17. NAME OF REFERRING PHYSICIAN OR OTHER SOURCE

17a. I.D. NUMBER OF REFERRING PHYSICIAN

18. HOSPITALIZATION DATES RELATED TO CURRENT SERVICES FROM MM DD YY TO MM DD YY

19. RESERVED FOR LOCAL USE

20. OUTSIDE LAB? YES NO $ CHARGES

21. DIAGNOSIS OR NATURE OF ILLNESS OR INJURY. (RELATE ITEMS 1,2,3 OR 4 TO ITEM 24E BY LINE)

1. ___ . __

2. ___ . __

3. ___ . __

4. ___ . __

22. MEDICAID RESUBMISSION CODE ORIGINAL REF. NO.

23. PRIOR AUTHORIZATION NUMBER

24. A DATE(S) OF SERVICE From MM DD YY To MM DD YY	B Place of Service	C Type of Service	D PROCEDURES, SERVICES, OR SUPPLIES (Explain Unusual Circumstances) CPT/HCPCS MODIFIER	E DIAGNOSIS CODE	F $ CHARGES	G DAYS OR UNITS	H EPSDT Family Plan	I EMG	J COB	K RESERVED FOR LOCAL USE
1										
2										
3										
4										
5										
6										

25. FEDERAL TAX I.D. NUMBER SSN EIN

26. PATIENT'S ACCOUNT NO.

27. ACCEPT ASSIGNMENT? (For govt. claims, see back) YES NO

28. TOTAL CHARGE $

29. AMOUNT PAID $

30. BALANCE DUE $

31. SIGNATURE OF PHYSICIAN OR SUPPLIER INCLUDING DEGREES OR CREDENTIALS (I certify that the statements on the reverse apply to this bill and are made a part thereof.)

SIGNED DATE

32. NAME AND ADDRESS OF FACILITY WHERE SERVICES WERE RENDERED (If other than home or office)

33. PHYSICIAN'S, SUPPLIER'S BILLING NAME, ADDRESS, ZIP CODE & PHONE #

PIN# GRP#

PHYSICIAN OR SUPPLIER INFORMATION

790-0115 (12/90) (OCR) 1 pt.

(APPROVED BY AMA COUNCIL ON MEDICAL SERVICE 8/88)

PLEASE PRINT OR TYPE

FORM HCFA-1500 (12-90) FORM OWCP-1500 FORM RRB-1500

Figure 10-2. *The HCFA-1500 is the universal health insurance claim form accepted by most insurers, even if they have their own forms.*

Coding: It is extremely important to know exactly how to use the code books. Directions accompany each section of each book and should be followed precisely. Because coding is revised annually, the medical assistant responsible for coding should attend at least one CPT and one ICD-9 class each year.

Diagnostic Coding

Diagnostic coding: ICD-9-CM *(International Classification of Diseases, 9th Edition, Clinical Modification)* is a three-volume system for classifying diseases and surgical procedures to facilitate collection of uniform, comparable health information. It is used to list what is wrong with the patient and what initially brought the patient to see the doctor. It is published by the World Health Organization, and an Official Authorized Addendum is published each October.

Diagnostic coding of Medicare claims: ICD-9-CM coding is required on all Medicare claims, whether the physician is Medicare-participating or not.

Coding levels: The ICD-9-CM uses three-digit codes for broad categories of diseases, injuries, and symptoms. Fourth- and fifth-level codes are created by the addition of a decimal point followed by a one- or two-digit subclassification suffix. Such subclassification permits the specification of a diagnosis as exactly as possible (e.g., 380.01 represents a fifth-level diagnostic code). In addition, some codes begin with a *V* indicating visits for reasons other than illness or injury (e.g., annual physical examinations or treatments for already diagnosed conditions, such as chemotherapy for cancer). Codes beginning with an *E* indicate the external cause of an injury.

Primary diagnosis: The main condition for which the patient is being treated.

Secondary condition: Medical conditions that are present at the same time with the primary diagnosis and affect the treatment or recovery from the condition described by the primary diagnosis. It's important to realize that if a person with cancer comes into the office complaining of an ear infection that is not related to the patient's cancer, the primary diagnosis will be the ear infection, not cancer. In some cases, the diagnostic code contains both the primary and secondary conditions. The primary diagnosis must be listed first on the insurance claim form, followed by secondary conditions.

Superbill: A custom-made form used by physicians to note diagnosis and treatment. It is also known as the encounter form or charge ticket. Superbills often list the ICD-9-CM codes for the most frequently used diagnoses. The codes on the superbill should be checked against the annual updates of codes.

Five steps to diagnostic coding:

1. Locate the diagnosis in the patient's medical record.

2. Find the diagnosis and corresponding code in the ICD's Alphabetical Index. Look for the condition first, then for any descriptors that make the condition more specific.

3. Look in the ICD's Tabular List and locate the code from the Alphabetical Index.

4. Read all information and subclassifications to get the code that most closely corresponds to the patient's specific condition. It is best to get fourth- or fifth-level codes. Note requirements and exclusions listed.

5. Record the diagnostic code on the insurance claim form and proofread the numbers.

Procedural Coding

***Physicians' Current Procedural Terminology* (CPT):** A procedural code book using a numerical system updated annually by the American Medical Association. The terminology provides a uniform language that accurately identifies medical, surgical, and diagnostic services and is used for reliable nationwide communication among physicians, patients, and third parties. CPT codes are five-digit numbers, organized into six sections: Evaluation and Management, Anesthesiology, Surgery, Radiology, Pathology and Laboratory, and Medicine. See Figure 10-3 on p. 242. To find the correct procedure codes using the CPT, look for the service in the index. Read section guidelines and notes to determine the accurate codes and appropriate modifiers.

HCPCS: Stands for Health Care Procedural Coding System. Pronounced "hic-pics," it is an alphanumeric coding system used for Medicare claims, mandated by Congress, published by HCFA, and updated annually. Level I codes duplicate CPT codes. Level II HCPCS codes are issued by HCFA in the *Medicare Carriers Manual*. These codes are used for supplies and for new procedures not yet added to CPT.

Modifiers: Two-digit numbers appended to the main five-digit CPT code. The use of a modifier shows that some special circumstance applies to the service the physician performed. More than one modifier can be used on one main code (e.g., 19366-99-20-50, which represents bilateral breast reconstruction using microsurgical technique).

Unlisted procedure: If a procedure is unlisted, there are guidelines at the beginning of each section on what codes to use on the insurance form. In these cases, a special report must be attached to the claim to describe and explain the extent of and the reasons for the service.

Critical care codes: Intended for all critical care services that require the constant attention of the physician. Critical care includes treatment for cardiac arrest, shock, bleeding, respiratory failure, and postoperative complications. Critical care is usually given in an intensive care unit, respiratory care unit, or emergency

Surgery
Integumentary System

Skin, Subcutaneous and Accessory Structures

Incision and Drainage

(For excision, see 11400, et seq)

(10000-10020 have been deleted. To report, see 10060, 10061)

10040* Acne surgery (eg, marsupialization, opening or removal of multiple milia, comedones, cysts, pustules)

10060* Incision and drainage of abscess (eg, carbuncle, suppurative hidradenitis, cutaneous or subcutaneous abscess, cyst, furuncle, or paronychia); simple or single

10061 complicated or multiple

10080* Incision and drainage of pilonidal cyst; simple

10081 complicated

(For excision of pilonidal cyst, see 11770-11772)

(10100, 10101 have been deleted. To report, see 10060, 10061)

10120* Incision and removal of foreign body, subcutaneous tissues; simple

10121 complicated
(To report wound exploration due to penetrating trauma without laparotomy or thoracotomy, see 20100-20103, as appropriate)

(To report debridement associated with open fracture(s) and/or dislocation(s), use 11010-11012, as appropriate)

10140* Incision and drainage of hematoma, seroma or fluid collection

(10141 has been deleted. To report, use 10140)

10160* Puncture aspirations of abscess, hematoma, bulla or cyst

10180 Incision and drainage, complex, postoperative wound infection
(For secondary closure of surgical wound, see 12020, 12021, 13160)

Excision—Debridement

(For dermabrasions, see 15780-15783)

(For nail debridment, see 11720-11721)

(For burn(s), see 16000➡16035◀)

11000* **Debridement** of extensive eczematous or infected skin; up to 10% of body surface

+ 11001 each additional 10% of the body surface
(List separately in addition to code for primary procedure)

(Use 11001 in conjunction with code 11000)

11010 Debridement including removal of foreign material associated with open fracture(s) and/or dislocation(s); skin and subcutaneous tissues

11011 skin, subcutaneous tissue, muscle fascia, and muscle

11012 skin, subcutaneous tissue, muscle fascia, muscle, and bone

11040 Debridement, skin, partial thickness

11041 skin, full thickness

11042 skin, subcutaneous tissue

Figure 10-3. *To be sure of your coding on a claim form, you must check the most recent edition of the* Physicians' Current Procedural Terminology *(CPT) manual. (CPT codes and descriptions are © 1996, American Medical Association. All rights reserved.)*

department. Examples of noncritical procedures include joint reduction, casting, and bladder tapping.

Levels of Evaluation and Management codes: Offer a way to code for different levels of service based on:

- Type of patient history taken
- Type of examination conducted
- Complexity of the medical decision-making
- Counseling given
- Coordination of care
- Nature of the patient's problem
- Amount of time the physician spent with the patient

The lowest code level usually assumes a minor problem, for which the patient gave only a brief history, the examination was limited to the affected body area or organ system, the physician spent only about 10 minutes with the patient, and the diagnostic decision was made without too many additional tests. In addition to the level of service, insurance carriers also want to know whether a patient is a new patient (NP) or an established patient (EP). Emergency patients are neither new nor established. It also matters where the service is performed—in the physician's office, a hospital, a nursing facility, or the patient's home.

Surgery and laboratory procedures: Surgical packages and laboratory panels should be coded as single procedures rather than broken down into component parts.

Consultation codes: Referral services are those performed for a patient whose care has been transferred from one physician to another. Consultation services are those provided by a second physician in response to a request for advice by an attending physician. The CPT lists several codes for consultations at various levels depending on the time and effort that went into the coordination of consultations.

Four steps to using CPT:

1. Find the services listed on the superbill.
2. Look up the procedure code. Remember that the number listed in the index is not a page number but a five-digit code. Resist the temptation of recording the procedure directly from the index. Go the specific code's explanation to find the main numbers and modifiers that most accurately reflect the service performed.
3. Determine appropriate modifiers.
4. Record the procedure code on the insurance claim and proofread it.

Claim Processing

Insurance claim reimbursement criteria: There are four bases for determining payment:

- Usual, customary, and reasonable (UCR) charges

- The Medicare Resource-Based Relative Value Scale (RBRVS)
- Fee schedules
- Diagnosis-related groups (DRGs)

The most common reason for the return of insurance claim forms is missing or mistyped information. To minimize the chance of errors, it is extremely important always to proofread all claims before submitting them.

Steps in claims processing: Following are the general steps in processing a claim:

1. Gather health insurance information from the patient and verify insurance coverage.
2. Complete the HCFA-1500 claim form.
3. Base the claim on the superbill, which lists the name and address of the patient, the name of the insurance carrier, the insurance identification number, a brief description of each service by code number, the fee for the service, the place and date of service, the diagnosis, the physician's name and address, and the physician's signature. You should also have the current editions of the ICD-9-CM and CPT, for diagnostic and procedural coding.
4. If possible, use electronic claims submission. Prepare claims on a computer and submit them via modem to the insurance carrier's computer system. Such claims are also called electronic media claims (EMCs).
5. Track insurance claims. Follow up with the insurance company until the claim is paid in a timely manner.
6. Remember that if a claim form is not sufficiently detailed, complete, and accurate, it will be rejected by the insurance company.

Tracing: If after 30 days the insurance company has not paid the claim or responded to a claim, the choices are to bill again or to call the carrier. Because second billings are sometimes rejected as duplicates, the medical office can send a tracer, a letter to the insurance company containing the basic billing information.

Rebilling: Make a copy of the original claim form submitted and write *SECOND BILLING* in red letters at the top. Reasons to rebill:

- The insurance company is delinquent in responding to a claim.
- A mistake has been made in billing.
- Charges must be detailed to receive maximum reimbursement.
- A claim was overlooked by the physician's office.
- The carrier asked for rebilling because the wrong diagnosis or procedure codes were submitted, some information was incomplete or missing, or the charges did not total properly.

Reasons why claims are denied or payments are delayed:

- The claim is not for a covered contract benefit. Bill the patient.
- The patient's preexisting condition is not covered. Bill the patient.
- The patient's coverage has been canceled. Bill the patient.
- Workers' compensation is involved, and the case is under consideration. Check on the claim's progress every 30 days.
- The insurance company considers the physician's procedure to be experimental. Call the carrier to discuss options. Peer review may be requested.
- No preauthorization was obtained. Review the patient's contract and what the sanctions are. Write a letter of appeal if appropriate.
- The physician provided services before the patient's health insurance contract went into effect. Bill the patient.
- The carrier asks for additional information. Send the carrier the requested information and follow up in 30 days.

Claim appeal: A written request to the insurance carrier to review reimbursement. It is usually filed if the preauthorization was not obtained because unusual circumstances exist, the reimbursement was inadequate for a complicated procedure, the physician disagrees that the patient's condition was preexisting, or the patient has unusual circumstances that affect medical treatment.

Medicare claims processing: Guidelines for processing Medicare claims are:

- Providers are required by law to file the HCFA-1500 for all eligible patients.
- Providers may be participating or nonparticipating.
- Participating providers accept assignment on Medicare claims and receive the allowed fee.
- Nonparticipating providers are not required to accept assignment; therefore, the patient is responsible for the balance after Medicare makes its payment. See Table 10-2.
- The allowable payment to nonparticipating providers is less than the payment to participating providers.
- Medicare forms must be signed by both the patient and the physician.
- Claims for Medicare must be filed by December 31 of the year following that in which the services were rendered.

Medicaid claims processing: Guidelines for processing Medicaid claims are:

- A physician is free to accept or refuse to treat a patient under Medicaid.
- A patient's eligibility should be verified prior to the delivery of medical service.
- Preauthorization may be required for the service.
- Claims should be filed on the HCFA-1500.
- There is always a time limit for filing claims, according to state regulations.

Medi/Medi (Medicare plus Medicaid) claims processing: Guidelines for processing Medi/Medi claims are:

- A physician must always accept assignment.
- A claim form is first processed through Medicare and is then automatically forwarded to Medicaid.
- It is not necessary to prepare two claim forms. The combined claim is sometimes referred to as a crossover claim.

Blue Cross and Blue Shield claims processing: Guidelines for processing Blue card claims are:

- Claims should be submitted as soon as possible after the service is provided.
- Like Medicare, the Blue plans have arrangements with participating and nonparticipating providers. Usually a participating provider is paid directly for covered services and agrees not to bill the patient for any difference.
- Blue plans have provider manuals that describe coverage and coding features of the plan.

TRICARE claims processing: Guidelines for processing a TRICARE claim are:

- Use the HCFA-1500.
- If the physician accepts assignment (i.e., the physician is a participating provider), the medical office files the insurance claim and the patient can be billed for the entire deductible and the coinsurance portion of the allowed charge.
- If the physician does not accept assignment, the patient must submit claim forms to the insurance company and is responsible for all charges.
- The claims must be filed no later than December 31 of the year following that in which services were provided.
- Participating providers are paid within 21 days after submitting a claim, and only participating providers may appeal a claims decision.

CHAMPVA claims processing: CHAMPVA claims follow the same guidelines as TRICARE claims.

Participating Provider		Nonparticipating Provider	
Physician's standard fee:	$120.00	Physician's standard fee:	$120.00
Medicare PAR fee:	$ 60.00	Medicare nonPAR fee:	$ 57.00
Medicare pays 80% of Medicare fee:	$ 48.00	Medicare pays 80% of nonPAR fee:	$ 45.60
Patient or supplemental plan pays:	$ 12.00	Patient or supplemental plan pays:	$ 11.40
Provider writes off:	$ 60.00	Provider writes off:	$ 63.00

Table 10-2   Note: These charges do not represent realistic or accurate medical service fees. They are used here merely as an example.

Workers' compensation claims processing: Follow these guidelines:

- Records of the workers' compensation case should be kept separate from the patient's regular history.
- The insurance carrier is entitled to receive copies of all records pertaining to the industrial injury.
- The injured person's records must be personally signed by the physician.
- The insurance carrier may supply its own billing forms.
- Payment is usually made on the basis of a fee schedule.
- At the termination of the treatment, a final report and bill are sent to the insurance carrier.
- Do not bill the patient.

Legal Considerations

Legal and ethical issues: There are a variety of legal and ethical issues associated with processing claims:

- Stay current on the laws that affect medicine.
- It is the physician's responsibility to identify the procedures that have been performed. Only code for procedures that appear in the medical records. If you think that a certain procedure has been left out by accident, tell the physician to update the medical records before you file a claim.
- An incorrect code used for billing a service can be considered fraud.
- Obtain patient signatures permitting insurance billing.
- Obtain proper authorization from the insurance carrier whenever required.

Fraud: Occurs when someone intentionally misrepresents facts to receive a benefit illegally. A person who cooperates in a fraudulent situation becomes personally liable, or legally responsible. Some fraudulent actions include:

- Altering a patient's chart to increase the amount reimbursed.
- Upgrading or falsifying medical procedures to increase the amount reimbursed.
- Billing primary or secondary insurance carriers while at the same time collecting payment from the patient.
- Under Medicare law, not to attempt to collect a required payment from a Medicare patient.

Because an incorrect code can seem like fraud, it is very important to code accurately and keep good records of the coordination of benefits.

STRATEGIES TO SUCCESS

▶ *Test-Taking Skills*

Circle key words!
  Don't get a question wrong just because you misread what it was asking you. Circle key words in the question such as *best*, *not*, *except*, *always*, *never*, *all*, and any other words that relate to the main point in the question. Doing so will force you to focus on the central point so that you can untangle even more complicated questions.

Instructions:

Answer the following questions. Check your answers in the *Answer Key* that follows this section.

1. The range of fees charged by most physicians in a community is called the
   A. Customary fee
   B. Reasonable fee
   C. Usual fee
   D. Premium
   E. Average fee

2. If a child is covered by both of her parents' insurance and the total medical charges come to $365, $280 of which is covered by the primary insurance, how are the rest of the charges handled?
   A. The parents are billed for $85
   B. A claim is submitted to secondary insurance for $85
   C. A claim is submitted to secondary insurance for $365
   D. The doctor writes off $85, and no one is charged
   E. A claim is submitted to secondary insurance for $280

3. Which of the following is an example of fraud?
   A. Miscoding a diagnosis unintentionally
   B. Leaving a field blank on the HCFA-1500 by mistake
   C. Altering a patient's chart to increase the amount reimbursed
   D. Releasing patient's medical records without the patient's consent to the patient's wife because you feel morally obligated to do so
   E. All of the above

4. A participating provider in a managed health care program must write off
   A. Disallowed charges
   B. Coinsurance
   C. Copayments
   D. Deductibles
   E. Amounts due from the carrier

5. Which of the following Medicare programs covers hospital charges?
   A. Part A
   B. Part B
   C. Part C
   D. Both Parts A and B
   E. None of the above

6. Which of the following code books is published by the World Health Organization?
   A. ICD-9-CM
   B. CPT
   C. HCPCS
   D. RBRVS
   E. None of the above

7. Assume that John Smith got an X-ray through Dr. Jones, a participating provider in Mr. Smith's HMO. The allowed charge for such an X-ray is $75, but Dr. Jones's usual fee is $100. John Smith's copayment due for each office visit is $15. How much can Dr. Jones collect from Mr. Smith?
   A. $25
   B. $10
   C. $15
   D. $0
   E. $75

8. If a person is covered under both Medicare and Medicaid, to which program should the claim be sent first?
   A. Medicaid
   B. Medicare
   C. Both should get it at the same time
   D. Neither; the patient has to be billed
   E. Neither; claims are sent to an independent government agency to decide

9. The amount due from the patient for covered services from a participating provider is the difference between
   A. The allowed charge and the physician's fee
   B. The allowed charge and the patient's deductible and/or coinsurance
   C. The physician's fee and the coinsurance
   D. The physician's fee and the deductible
   E. The physician's fee and the capitation

10. Which of the following types of medical insurance is designed to offset medical expenses resulting from prolonged injury or illness?
    A. Basic medical
    B. Hospital coverage
    C. Disability protection
    D. Liability insurance
    E. Major medical

11. Because coding is revised annually, medical assistants responsible for coding should
    A. Attend at least one CPT class each year
    B. Attend at least one ICD-9 class every two years
    C. Attend at least one ICD-9 and one CPT class every two years
    D. Attend at least one CPT and one ICD-9 class each year
    E. Review codes in their spare time; there is no need to attend classes

12. Which of the following is true about Blue Cross and Blue Shield?
    A. It offers prepaid health services
    B. It helps Medicare to determine covered health services
    C. It follows a fee-for-service reimbursement plan
    D. Both A and C
    E. All of the above

13. Capitation is
    A. Payment at the time of service
    B. Fixed prospective payment for services provided
    C. Fixed payment made for each enrolled patient rather than reimbursement based on the type and number of services provided
    D. Various payments for specific services provided during a specified time period
    E. A reduction in payment if services are not provided to a minimum number of enrolled patients

14. Providers are required by law to file which of the following for all eligible Medicare patients?
    A. HCFA
    B. HCPCS
    C. ICD-9
    D. RBRVS
    E. HCFA-1500

15. If a nonparticipating provider's charge for a service is $65 and the allowed charge is $50, the amount due from the patient is
    A. $10
    B. $65
    C. $50
    D. $15
    E. $115

16. The most common insurance claim form is the
    - A. Superbill
    - B. Charge sheet
    - C. HCFA-1500
    - D. ICD-9
    - E. None of the above

17. If a policy holder of an 80:20 plan had foot surgery that cost $3,600, how much of this bill is the subscriber responsible to pay?
    - A. $450
    - B. $720
    - C. $180
    - D. $2,880
    - E. $3,600

18. An authorization to the insurance company to make payments directly to the physician is called
    - A. HCFA-1500 claim form
    - B. Assignment of benefits
    - C. Tracker
    - D. Coordination of benefits
    - E. Service benefit plan

19. The primary difference between an HMO and a PPO is that
    - A. An HMO locks patients into receiving services from providers with whom it has contracts, whereas a PPO allows patients to choose among providers in return for higher deductibles and copayments
    - B. In an HMO patients may select specialists, whereas in a PPO patients must see specialists to whom they were referred
    - C. HMOs pay for all services completely except preventive check-ups, whereas PPOs do not pay for services completely but do partially cover preventive medicine
    - D. An HMO has fee-for-service contracts with providers, whereas a PPO has a capitation model for reimbursement
    - E. All of the above

20. TRICARE is a health care benefit program for all of the following except
    - A. The Coast Guard
    - B. The National Oceanic and Atmospheric Administration
    - C. The Navy
    - D. Families of uniformed personnel
    - E. Families of veterans with service-related disabilities

21. Fee-for-service reimbursement is
    - A. Retroactive payment made after services are provided
    - B. Fixed prospective payment for services provided during a specified time period
    - C. Payment at the time of service
    - D. Various payments for specific services provided during a specified time period
    - E. Fixed payment made each month for an estimated total of services provided, which is calculated according to the number of member patients

22. A patient's medical fees come to a total of $600 from a participating provider, and the EOB lists the following information.

Charges:	$78
Not Eligible for Payment:	$15
Allowed Charge:	$63
Applied to Deductible:	$ 7
Coinsurance:	$ 5
Amount Due From Carrier:	$51

    What amount is the patient required to pay?
    - A. $7
    - B. $5
    - C. $27
    - D. $12
    - E. Nothing

23. In the point-of-service option,
    A. Plan members can see out-of-network providers for additional fees
    B. Providers are employees of the HMO
    C. The HMO has capitation contracts with provider groups
    D. Contracts exist with an administrative group of physicians that in turn contracts with its provider-members
    E. Physicians receive fixed payments for each nonmember patient rather than reimbursement for the services provided

24. In the group network model,
    A. Providers are employees of the HMO
    B. The HMO has capitation contracts with provider groups
    C. Contracts exist with an administrative group of physicians that in turn contracts with members
    D. Plan members can see out-of-network providers for additional fees
    E. Providers are paid on a fee-for-service basis

25. Which of the following statements is true of the Kaiser Foundation Health Plan?
    A. It insures persons against on-the-job injury
    B. It is a nonprofit organization that offers out-of-town benefits through what is called a Blue card
    C. It is a prepaid group practice in which providers are employees
    D. Patients can receive care from providers of their choice while deductibles and premiums are kept low
    E. None of the above

ANSWER KEY

1.	A		14.	E
2.	B		15.	D
3.	C		16.	C
4.	A		17.	B
5.	A		18.	B
6.	A		19.	A
7.	C		20.	E
8.	B		21.	A
9.	B		22.	D
10.	E		23.	A
11.	D		24.	B
12.	D		25.	C
13.	C			

CLINICAL

MEDICAL ASSISTING KNOWLEDGE

Theory Review

SECTION OUTLINE

Blood-Borne Pathogens and Principles of Asepsis

AREAS OF COMPETENCE

AAMA—ROLE DELINEATION STUDY AREAS OF COMPETENCE

Clinical

Fundamental Principles

- Apply principles of aseptic technique and infection control
- Comply with quality assurance practices

General (Transdisciplinary)

Legal Concepts

- Follow federal, state, and local legal guidelines
- Maintain awareness of federal and state health care legislation and regulations

AREAS OF COMPETENCE (cont.)

- Maintain and dispose of regulated substances in compliance with government guidelines
- Comply with established risk management and safety procedures

AMT—RMA CERTIFICATION EXAM TOPICS

Medical Secretarial-Receptionist

- Office safety

Asepsis

- Terminology
- Universal blood and body fluid precautions
- Medical asepsis
- Surgical asepsis

Sterilization

- Terminology
- Sanitization
- Disinfection
- Sterilization

Instruments

- Care and handling

Laboratory Procedures

- Safety

STRATEGIES TO SUCCESS

▶ Study Skills

Prepare for class!

You can understand a lecture better and retain more information if you take time before class to read the material that is going to be covered. If your instructor tells you which chapters will be discussed on a certain date, you should have plenty of time to review the information beforehand. Even if you don't have time to read a whole chapter, you should scan it for key concepts and headings. This background information will make the lecture material more comprehensible and perhaps even provide an outline for your notes in class.

Blood-Borne Pathogens

Pathogen: Any microorganism that causes a disease.

Blood-borne pathogens: Disease-causing microorganisms that spread from one person to another via blood. The most common blood-borne pathogens are the hepatitis B virus (HBV) and human immunodeficiency virus (HIV), but blood-borne pathogens are not limited to these two pathogens.

Potentially infectious body fluids: Include body fluid visibly contaminated with blood; seminal and vaginal secretions; cerebrospinal, mucous, amniotic, and other body fluids; and tissue cultures.

Contaminated: Exhibiting the presence of blood or other potentially infectious materials.

Biohazard: Anything that poses a risk to the human body or other living organism, such as blood (which can cause the spread of infections), chemical materials, or ionizing radiation.

Biohazard container: A leakproof, puncture-resistant container that is color-coded red or labeled with a biohazard symbol and is used to store and dispose of contaminated supplies and equipment. When a biohazard container is filled to the three-quarter mark, it should be placed in a locked storage area until pickup. All biohazard containers must have a fluorescent orange or orange-red label with the biohazard symbol and the word *BIOHAZARD* in a contrasting color. Every container must have a lid that is replaced after use. These containers are used for disposable gowns, table covers, items contaminated with blood and body fluids, dressings, gloves, needles, and sharp objects.

Sharps: Needles, scalpels, scissors, or other objects that could cause wounds or punctures to individuals handling them.

Needlestick injuries: Accidental skin punctures resulting from contact with hypodermic syringe needles. These injuries can be dangerous, particularly if the needle has been used in a patient with a severe blood-borne infection. Needles should never be recapped or broken. They must be discarded immediately into a biohazard container. If an injury occurs, wash your hands, cover the injury, report and document the injury, and get the injury treated.

Exposure potential: The possibility of bodily contact with a safety hazard, a hazardous chemical, blood, or other potentially infectious material.

Hazardous chemical: A chemical that is explosive, unstable, flammable, carcinogenic, or irritating, or that contains toxic agents.

Occupational exposure: Contact with blood or other potentially infected body fluids that occurs as a result of the normal duties of an employee at work.

Disease Profiles

Hepatitis

Hepatitis: Inflammation and infection of the liver that may be caused by several factors, such as drugs, toxins, and microorganisms. The most common cause of hepatitis is a virus. There are six known hepatitis viruses, designated A, B, C, D, E, and G.

Hepatitis A: Transmitted by fecal-oral contamination and caused by the hepatitis A virus (HAV). Hepatitis A is not generally considered to be an important risk to health care workers. It is also called acute infective hepatitis.

Hepatitis B: Inflammation of the liver caused by the hepatitis B virus (HBV). It is the main blood-borne hazard for health care workers. HBV can be transmitted through contaminated serum and plasma; contaminated needles (involved in needlestick injuries or IV drug use); cuts caused by contaminated sharps; sexual contact with an infected person; and splashes of contaminated material onto the eyes, mouth, nose, or broken skin. HBV is also transmitted from infected mothers to newborns. It is a severe infection that may cause a prolonged illness and become a chronic disease resulting in destruction of liver tissues, cirrhosis, or death. It is also known as serum hepatitis. The virus is capable of surviving for at least a week in a dried state on environmental surfaces.

Acute hepatitis B: Approximately one-third of all patients are asymptomatic. The initial symptoms, if present, last from 2 to 14 days. There is no specific treatment or drug that kills the hepatitis virus. About 90% of patients recover fully after the acute phase.

Chronic hepatitis B: About 10% of patients who do not recover from the acute phase go on to develop chronic hepatitis. These patients face an increased risk of liver damage, cirrhosis of the liver, liver cancer, or liver failure.

Hepatitis B vaccine: Approximately 90% effective in providing immunity for at least 7 years. The vaccine is recommended as a series of three intramuscular doses in infants, children, adolescents, and adults. Employers must offer this vaccine within 10 days of employment if there is a reasonable expectation of exposure to the virus. At the present time, a routine booster dose is not recommended. The hepatitis B vaccine is recommended for the following individuals:

- Health care workers in high-risk occupations, such as physicians, dentists, dental hygienists, medical assistants, nurses, and laboratory personnel
- Staff members of residential institutions
- Sexually active homosexual men
- Intravenous drug users
- Persons with hemophilia
- Hemodialysis patients
- Household members or sexual contacts of hepatitis B carriers

Hepatitis C (non-A, non-B hepatitis): A chronic disease transmitted largely by blood transfusion or intravenous drug use (sharing needles). Diagnosis is made by detecting HCV antibodies.

Hepatitis D: Also called delta hepatitis, a form of viral hepatitis that occurs only in patients infected with hepatitis B; consequently, it can be prevented by hepatitis B vaccination. The hepatitis D virus (HDV) is transmitted through needle-sharing and sex. Diagnosis is made by detecting HDV serum antibodies. It is not common in the United States.

Hepatitis E: A common acute infection of the liver, similar to hepatitis A, seen mainly in Southeast Asia, South America, and Africa. Hepatitis E is frequently seen in the rainy season or after natural disasters because of fecally contaminated water or food. There is no serologic test available for the detection of the hepatitis E virus (HEV). The disease is most dangerous in pregnant women and increases the mortality rate among them.

HIV and AIDS

HIV: The human immunodeficiency virus that causes AIDS. It is passed from one person to another through blood-to-blood and sexual contact. Infected pregnant women can pass the virus to their babies during pregnancy or delivery or by breast-feeding. It is not spread through casual contact. HIV infects and destroys T lymphocytes (T cells) of the immune system.

HIV transmission: HIV has been isolated in blood, semen, saliva, tears, breast milk, cerebrospinal fluid (CSF), amniotic fluid, urine, and vaginal secretions. No cases of AIDS have been reported as a result of exposure to saliva or tears.

AIDS: Acquired immunodeficiency syndrome, caused by HIV. It is a fatal disease that attacks the immune system and is characterized by severe opportunistic infections and rare cancers. Approximately 70% of HIV-infected people develop AIDS within 10 years. An HIV-infected person is diagnosed as having AIDS after development of one of the indicator illnesses or on the basis of certain blood tests.

Risk factors for HIV transmission: The risk factors for HIV transmission are generally the same as the risk factors associated with HBV. People at risk include:

- Those with multiple sexual partners
- Those who have had unprotected anal, vaginal, or oral sex
- Intravenous drug users who share needles
- Sexual partners of an infected person
- Infants born to HIV-positive women

Stages of AIDS: A person who is HIV-positive without any symptoms for months or even years is known as a carrier of HIV. The AIDS virus infection cycle has four stages: acute HIV infection, asymptomatic latency period, AIDS-related complex (ARC), and full-blown AIDS.

Acute HIV infection: Lasts from 3 days to a month. Symptoms are often mistaken for those of other viral infections and include fever, sweats, fatigue, loss of appetite, diarrhea, pharyngitis, myalgia, arthralgia, and adenopathy.

Asymptomatic latency period: A long incubation period, sometimes lasting for years. During this period, the infected individual is asymptomatic. The only evidence of infection during this phase is the body's production of HIV antibodies. These HIV antibodies, however, are unable to destroy the virus. This period is a confounding factor in tests for the presence of HIV infection, because testing may fail to detect HIV for as long as 3 to 6 months after an individual has been infected.

AIDS-related complex (ARC): A syndrome resulting from HIV infection but lacking an opportunistic infection or Kaposi's sarcoma. Patients with ARC often have chronic systemic symptoms including enlarged lymph nodes, fever, diarrhea, weight loss, fatigue, and dementia. Most people with ARC progress to having full-blown AIDS.

Final stage of AIDS: Full-blown AIDS is characterized by the presence of opportunistic infections and unusual cancers. A severe pneumonia caused by *Pneumocystis carinii* is commonly seen in AIDS patients, and Kaposi's sarcoma, a rare type of cancer, frequently occurs.

Opportunistic infections: Occur when normal immunity is altered. If the immune system cannot respond to a microbe that it would normally eliminate, the infection that results is termed opportunistic. These infections cause most of the morbidity and mortality in AIDS because they attack many different organs of the body. See Figure 11-1. These infections also play a major role in the diagnosis of AIDS. The lungs are the most commonly involved organ system in AIDS and are the principal target for *Pneumocystis carinii* and atypical tuberculous bacteria.

Kaposi's sarcoma: A malignancy of the skin and lymph nodes that often occurs in AIDS patients. It is the most common HIV-related cancer and usually appears as painless nodules and reddish purple to dark blue colors on the body.

***Pneumocystis carinii* pneumonia:** A type of pneumonia caused by the parasite *Pneumocystis carinii*, usually seen in patients with HIV infection. Its symptoms include fever, tachypnea, cough, and cyanosis. The diagnosis is not easy to make. The mortality rate in untreated patients is approximately 100%.

Serologic tests: The only readily available method to detect evidence of HIV infection. There are two serologic tests used to detect antibodies to HIV: enzyme-linked immunosorbent assay (ELISA) and western blot technique.

HIV antibody testing: Since 1992, recommendations issued by the Centers for Disease Control and Prevention (CDC) have called for the voluntary testing of people who are at high risk for HIV infection. HIV antibody testing is federally mandated for all military applicants and is also required for those who donate organs, tissue, sperm, or blood.

Inactivation of HIV: It is readily destroyed by heat treatment and exposure to disinfectants. The most common disinfectant is 10% NaClO (sodium hypochlorite, the active ingredient in household bleach).

Other Blood-Borne Pathogens

Syphilis: A sexually transmitted disease caused by the spirochete *Treponema pallidum*. The incubation period is 10 to 90 days. There are three stages. The first stage (primary syphilis) is marked by a single lesion, called a chancre. Syphilis can be treated with penicillin.

Malaria: A severe infectious disease caused by one or more of four species of the protozoan genus *Plasmodium*. The disease is transmitted by mosquitoes.

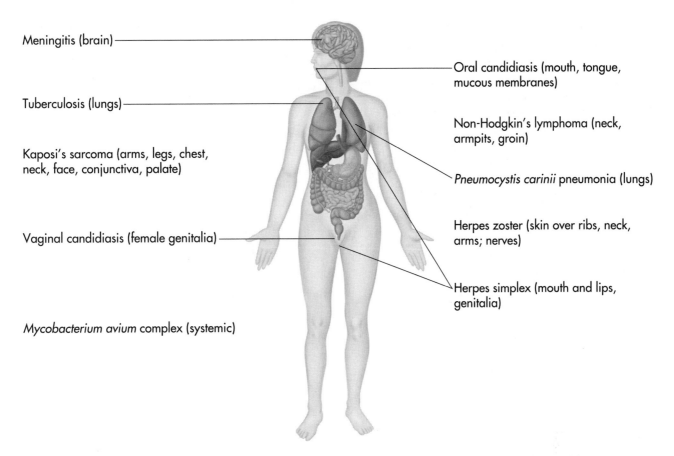

Figure 11-1. *The AIDS patient may contract a variety of opportunistic infections, which affect many different parts of the body.*

Labels (clockwise from top left):
- Meningitis (brain)
- Tuberculosis (lungs)
- Kaposi's sarcoma (arms, legs, chest, neck, face, conjunctiva, palate)
- Vaginal candidiasis (female genitalia)
- *Mycobacterium avium* complex (systemic)
- Oral candidiasis (mouth, tongue, mucous membranes)
- Non-Hodgkin's lymphoma (neck, armpits, groin)
- *Pneumocystis carinii* pneumonia (lungs)
- Herpes zoster (skin over ribs, neck, arms; nerves)
- Herpes simplex (mouth and lips, genitalia)

It can also be spread by blood transfusion from an infected patient or by the use of an infected hypodermic needle.

Brucellosis: Caused by the gram-negative coccobacillus *Brucella*. It is most prevalent in rural areas among farmers, veterinarians, meat packers, and livestock producers. The ingestion of unpasteurized milk from infected stock can also cause brucellosis.

Leptospirosis: An acute infectious disease caused by the spirochete *Leptospira interrogans*, transmitted in the urine of wild or domestic animals, especially dogs and rats. Human infections arise directly from contact with an infected animal's urine or tissue or indirectly from contact with contaminated water or soil.

Toxoplasmosis: Caused by *Toxoplasma gondii* transmitted in cat feces. Pregnant women and AIDS patients should not handle cat litter boxes. During pregnancy, the mother may pass the infection to her fetus through the placenta. Toxoplasmosis can result in spontaneous abortion, retardation, and malformation. It can also cause blindness, deafness, and brain damage.

Cytomegalovirus: One of the most common infections. As many as 80% of adults have been exposed to it. In AIDS patients it may cause severe lung disease. Pregnant women may transmit this infection to the fetus through the placenta, which results in brain damage, mental retardation, blindness, deafness, or death.

Medical and Surgical Asepsis

Medical asepsis: Also referred to as the clean technique, used to maintain cleanliness in order to prevent the spread of microorganisms and to ensure that there are as few microorganisms in the medical environment as possible. This technique is usually used for noninvasive procedures.

Surgical asepsis: Also referred to as the sterile technique, used to create a completely sterile environment without the presence of any microorganisms. This procedure is used for invasive or surgical techniques. When performing the sterile technique, it is important that nothing interrupts this process and that things are done in the correct order. If there is any question that an area might be contaminated, consider it contaminated and sterilize again.

Aseptic Precautions

Office procedures: The following procedures help promote asepsis:

- Separate areas in the waiting room for well and sick patients
- Maintenance of a well lit, well ventilated, draft-free office with a room temperature of approximately 72°(F)

- Prohibition of eating and drinking in the office
- Disposal of trash as often as needed
- Elimination of insects from the office
- Signs asking patients to use tissues, to put waste in the trash cans, to report safety or health hazards, and to tell the receptionist if they are nauseated or need to use the restroom

Cross-contamination: Perform procedures in a way that avoids cross-contamination. For example, do not place the lid of a sterile container face down on a surface, and do not pour tablets or capsules into your hand.

Hand washing: One of the most important methods of medical asepsis. Wash your hands:

- At the beginning of the day
- After breaks
- Before and after using the restroom
- Before and after lunch
- Before and after using gloves
- Before and after handling specimens or waste
- Before and after handling clean or sterile supplies
- Before and after performing any procedure
- After blowing your nose or coughing
- Before leaving for the day

Aseptic hand washing: Removes accumulated dirt and microorganisms that could cause infection. Table 11-1 describes how to perform aseptic hand washing,

and Figures 11-2 and 11-3 show two important steps in washing your hands.

Surgical scrub: Similar to aseptic hand washing, with the following differences:

- A sterile scrub brush is used instead of a nail brush.
- Hands and forearms are washed.
- Hands are held above the elbows so that water cannot run from the arms onto washed areas.
- Sterile towels are used instead of paper towels.
- Sterile gloves are put on immediately after the hands are dried.

Transfer forceps: Used to move sterile items onto a sterile field. See Figure 11-4.

Infection Control

Sanitization: Reducing the number of microorganisms on an object or surface to a fairly safe level by scrubbing it with hot, soapy water. It is used to clean items that touch only healthy, intact skin, such as:

- Blood pressure cuff
- Ophthalmoscope
- Otoscope
- Penlight
- Reflex hammer
- Stethoscope

AT A GLANCE	Aseptic Hand Washing Method
Remove all jewelry, except plain gold wedding bands.	
Turn on faucets using a paper towel, and adjust the temperature to moderately warm.	
Wet your hands and apply liquid soap. Liquid soap in a foot pump dispenser is less likely to accumulate dirt.	
Work the soap into a lather, and make sure that both of your hands are covered in lather. Rub vigorously in circular motions for at least 2 minutes. Keep your hands lower than your forearms so that the dirty water flows into the sink instead of back onto your arms. Interlace your fingers, and clean the palms and between the fingers.	
Use a nailbrush or orange stick to dislodge dirt from the cuticles and nails.	
Rinse your hands well, keeping your hands lower than your forearms and not touching the sink or faucets.	
With the water still running, dry your hands with clean, dry paper towels, and then turn off the faucets using a clean, dry paper towel. Discard the paper towels.	

Table 11-1

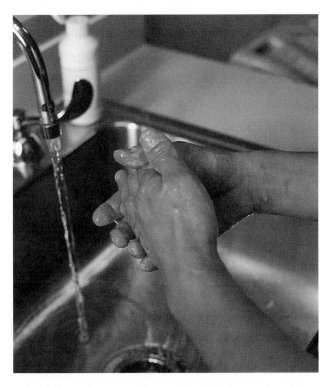

Figure 11-2. *When you wash your hands, be sure to clean all surfaces, including the palms and between the fingers.*

Figure 11-3. *The nails and cuticles require additional attention to ensure that all dirt is removed.*

- Tape measure
- Tuning fork

Ultrasonic cleaning: Used to sanitize delicate instruments and those with moving parts. It involves placing the instruments in a special bath that generates sound waves through a cleaning solution.

Disinfection: The process of destroying infectious agents by chemical or physical means. It is used for instruments that do not penetrate a patient's skin or that come in contact only with a patient's mucous membranes or other surfaces not considered sterile, such as:

- Enamelware
- Endotracheal tubes
- Glassware
- Laryngoscopes
- Nasal specula

Disinfectants: Cleaning products that reduce or eliminate infectious organisms on instruments or equipment. Common disinfectants are chemical germicides, household bleach, boiling water, and steam.

Antiseptics: Cleaning products used on human tissues as anti-infection agents.

Germicides: The use of soap in the process of disinfection is less important than the scrubbing and rinsing steps. Germ-killing additives may increase the effectiveness of soap.

Sterilization: A destruction of all living microorganisms. It is required for all instruments and

Figure 11-4. *Grasp the sterile supplies or instrument, pointing the forceps downward and avoiding contact with the sterile container or field.*

supplies that penetrate a patient's skin or come in contact with any normally sterile areas of the body. It is also required for instruments that will be used in a sterile field. Examples of items that need to be sterilized are:

- Curettes
- Needles
- Syringes
- Vaginal specula

Autoclave: A device that forces the temperature of steam above the boiling point of water in order to sterilize instruments and equipment.

Autoclave procedures: Take the following steps when using the autoclave:

1. Wrap sanitized and disinfected instruments and equipment, and label each pack. See Figure 11-5.
2. Clean and preheat the autoclave.
3. Perform quality control procedures.
4. Load the instruments and equipment, allowing adequate space around the items.
5. Set the autoclave for the correct time.
6. Run the autoclave through the cycle, including the drying time.
7. Remove the instruments and equipment.
8. Store the instruments and equipment for the next use.
9. Clean the autoclave and the surrounding work area.

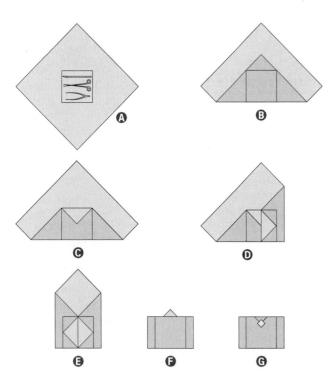

Figure 11-5. *Follow this sequence when you wrap instruments in a paper or fabric pack for sterilization in an autoclave.*

Sterilization indicators: Tags, inserts, tapes, tubes, or strips that confirm that the items in the autoclave have been exposed to the correct volume of steam at the correct temperature for the correct length of time.

Chemical sterilization: Used on instruments that would be damaged by prolonged exposure to the high temperatures in a steam autoclave.

Dry heat sterilization: Used on items that would be damaged by immersion in chemical solution or by exposure to steam.

Gas sterilization: Uses ethylene oxide, a hazardous gas. It may be performed only in hospital and manufacturing environments.

Microwave sterilization: The fastest method, using low-pressure steam with radiation.

OSHA Requirements

OSHA: The U.S. Department of Labor's Occupational Safety and Health Administration, which requires basic safety practices, including infection control, and develops federal regulations that aim to protect health care workers from health hazards on the job, particularly from accidentally acquiring infections.

OSHA Bloodborne Pathogens Standard of 1991: A set of regulations to protect health care workers, patients, and other visitors from health hazards. It:

- Requires employers to identify, in writing, tasks, procedures, and job classifications where occupational exposure to blood occurs.
- Mandates universal precautions, emphasizing engineering and work practice controls.
- Requires employers to provide and employees to use personal protective equipment.
- Requires a written schedule for cleaning, identifying the method of decontamination to be used, and specifies methods of disposing of regulated waste.
- Specifies procedures to be made available to all employees who have had an exposure incident, including a confidential medical evaluation.
- Requires warning labels, including the biohazard symbol, to be affixed to containers of regulated waste and other containers used to store or transport blood or other potentially infectious materials.
- Mandates training within 90 days of the effective date of assignment and annually thereafter.
- Calls for confidential medical records of employees to be kept for the duration of employment plus 30 years.

Failure to comply with OSHA standards: Could result in a maximum penalty of $7000 for the first violation, and up to $70,000 for repeated violations. See Table 11-2.

Type of Violation	Characteristics of Violation	Penalties for Violation
Other than serious violation	Direct relationship to job safety and health but would probably not result in death or serious injury	Fine of up to $7,000 (discretionary)
Serious violation	Substantial probability that death or serious physical harm could result and employer knew or should have known of the hazard	Fine of up to $7,000 (mandatory)
Willful violation	Violation committed intentionally and knowingly	Fine of up to $70,000, with a $5,000 minimum; in the event of the death of an employee, possible additional penalties including 6 months' imprisonment
Repeated violation	Substantially similar violation found upon reinspection (not applicable if initial citation is under contest)	Fine of up to $70,000
Failure to correct	Initial violation was not corrected	Fine of up to $7,000 for each day prior violation the violation continues after the date it was supposed to stop

Table 11-2

Universal Precautions: An approach to infection control, in which all human blood and certain other human body fluids are treated as if they were known to be infectious for HIV, HBV, and other blood-borne pathogens. Universal Precautions apply to blood and blood products; human tissue; semen and vaginal secretions; saliva from dental procedures; cerebrospinal, synovial, pleural, peritoneal, pericardial, and amniotic fluids; and other body fluids if visibly contaminated with blood or of questionable origin in the body. See Figures 11-6 and 11-7 on p. 260.

Standard Precautions: A combination of Universal Precautions and rules to reduce the risk of disease transmission by means of moist body substances. Standard Precautions apply to blood, other body fluids, secretions, excretions (except sweat), nonintact skin, and mucous membranes. Standard Precautions are used in hospitals for the care of all patients. In medical offices, you use Universal Precautions when dealing with patients.

Work practice controls: Controls that reduce the likelihood of exposure by altering the manner in which a task is performed, such as prohibiting the recapping of needles using two hands.

Category I tasks: Tasks that expose a worker to blood, body fluids, or tissues, such as assisting with removal of a cyst, and tasks that have a chance of spills or splashes. These tasks always require special protective measures.

Category II tasks: Tasks that usually do not involve a risk of exposure but that may involve exposure in certain situations. An example is giving mouth-to-mouth resuscitation. These tasks require precautions to be taken.

Category III tasks: Tasks that involve no exposure to blood, body fluids, or tissues and therefore do not require special protection. An example is giving a patient nose drops.

Postprocedure cleanup: OSHA requires the following steps:

- Decontaminate all exposed work surfaces with bleach or a germ-killing solution.
- Replace protective coverings on surfaces and equipment that have been exposed.
- Decontaminate receptacles.
- Pick up broken glass with tongs.
- Discard all potentially infectious waste materials in appropriate biohazardous waste containers.

 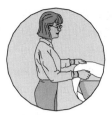   

❶ Decontaminate exposed work areas.　❷ Replace exposed protective coverings.　❸ Decontaminate receptacles.　❹ Pick up broken glass.　❺ Discard infectious waste.

Figure 11-6. *Follow these OSHA guidelines to clean and decontaminate the medical environment after each procedure or treatment.*

Ⓐ　Ⓑ　Ⓒ　Ⓓ　Ⓔ　Ⓕ　Ⓖ　Ⓗ

Figure 11-7. *These OSHA guideline icons represent (A) hand washing, (B) gloves, (C) mask and protective eyewear or face shield, (D) laboratory coat or gown, (E) reusable sharps container, (F) sharps disposal, (G) biohazardous waste container, and (H) disinfection.*

Engineering controls: Controls, such as sharps disposal containers and self-sheathing needles, that isolate or remove the hazard of blood-borne pathogens.

Hand washing facility: A facility providing an adequate supply of running potable water, soap, and single-use towels or hot-air drying machines.

Personal protective equipment: Specialized clothing or equipment worn by an employee for protection against a hazard. It includes gloves, lab coats, protective eyewear, face shields, surgical gowns, and shoe covers. See Figure 11-8.

Hazard warning label: Each hazardous chemical should identified by a hazard warning label that displays the following information:

- A stated requirement that the chemical be kept in its original container
- A color code (blue for health hazards, red for flammability, yellow for reactivity, and white for specific hazards such as radioactivity)
- A numerical rating superimposed on each colored area of the label indicating a level of hazard from 0 (no hazard) to 4 (extreme hazard)

Decontamination: A term used by OSHA to describe the use of physical or chemical means to remove, inactivate, or destroy blood-borne pathogens on a surface or item to the point where they are no longer capable of transmitting infection and the surface or item is rendered safe for handling, use, or disposal.

Regulated waste: Liquid or semi-liquid blood or other potentially infectious materials; contaminated items that would release blood or other potentially infectious materials in a liquid or semi-liquid state if compressed; items that are caked with blood or other potentially infectious materials and are capable of releasing these materials during handling; contaminated sharps; and pathological and microbiological wastes containing blood or other potentially infectious materials.

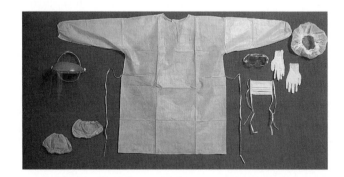

Figure 11-8. *Health care workers may need to use various types of personal protective equipment including gloves, masks and protective eyewear or face shields, gowns, and other protective clothing.*

Storing biohazardous materials: OSHA regulations prohibit medical personnel from doing any of the following activities in a room where potentially infectious materials are present:

- Eating
- Drinking
- Smoking
- Chewing gum
- Applying cosmetics
- Handling contact lenses
- Chewing pencils or pens
- Rubbing eyes

You should have separate refrigerators in separate rooms for food and for biohazardous materials.

Refrigerators: To prevent spoilage or deterioration of testing kits and specimens, the temperature of the laboratory refrigerator should be maintained between 36° and 46°F (2° and 8°C).

CHAPTER 11 REVIEW

Instructions:
Answer the following questions. Check your answers in the *Answer Key* that follows this section.

1. Potentially infectious body fluids include all of the following except
   A. Blood
   B. Vaginal secretions
   C. Sweat
   D. Cerebrospinal fluid
   E. Semen

2. Which color code for hazard warning labels is not correct?
   A. Blue for health hazards
   B. White for radioactivity hazards
   C. Yellow for radioactivity hazards
   D. Red for flammability
   E. All are correct

3. How long is hepatitis B virus capable of surviving in a dried state on environmental surfaces?
   A. One day
   B. One week
   C. Two days
   D. Two weeks
   E. One month

4. Clean technique is another term for
   A. Medical asepsis
   B. Surgical asepsis
   C. Hand washing
   D. Sterilization
   E. Sanitization

5. Instruments that penetrate a patient's skin should be
   A. Sanitized
   B. Disinfected
   C. Sterilized
   D. Treated with antiseptics
   E. Cleaned ultrasonically

6. Instruments that come in contact only with a patient's mucous membranes should be
   A. Sanitized
   B. Disinfected
   C. Sterilized
   D. Treated with antiseptics
   E. None of the above

7. Instruments that touch only healthy, intact skin should be
   A. Sanitized
   B. Disinfected
   C. Sterilized
   D. Treated with antiseptics
   E. Cleaned

8. The vaccine against hepatitis B provides immunity for at least
   A. 3 years
   B. 4 years
   C. 5 years
   D. 6 years
   E. 7 years

9. A syndrome resulting from HIV infection that generally involves chronic systemic symptoms but lacks an opportunistic infection or Kaposi's sarcoma is known as
   A. AIDS-related complex (ARC)
   B. Acute HIV infection
   C. AIDS
   D. Asymptomatic latency period
   E. None of the above

10. Which of the following is the only readily available method to detect evidence of HIV infection?
    A. Patient history
    B. Signs and symptoms
    C. Serologic test
    D. Urinalysis
    E. None of the above

11. Which of the following organ systems is the most commonly involved in AIDS?
    A. Kidneys
    B. Ovaries
    C. Lungs
    D. Liver and spleen
    E. Stomach

12. Kaposi's sarcoma is a malignancy of the
    A. Skin and lungs
    B. Skin and brain
    C. Skin and kidneys
    D. Skin and bones
    E. Skin and lymph nodes

13. Anything that poses a risk to the human body or a living organism is called
    A. A pathogen
    B. An occupational exposure
    C. A biohazard
    D. Blood-borne
    E. A virus

14. Which of the following is a possible means of transmission of HIV?
    A. Saliva
    B. Tears
    C. Intact skin
    D. Blood
    E. Hair

15. OSHA standards require which of the following?
    A. A written schedule for cleaning
    B. Cleaning only when needed
    C. Cleaning only after procedures
    D. Cleaning by cleaning staff only
    E. Both A and D

16. Treating all human blood as if it were infectious is known as

    A. Engineering controls
    B. Work practice controls
    C. Asepsis
    D. Universal Precautions
    E. Isolation methods

17. Hand washing is necessary at which of the following times?

    A. Before using gloves
    B. Before leaving for the day
    C. After performing a procedure
    D. After using gloves
    E. All of the above

18. After you have rinsed your hands using the aseptic hand washing method, what step should you take next?

    A. Using a nailbrush or orange stick, dislodge the dirt from your nails
    B. Turn off the faucets using your hands
    C. Hold your hands above the elbows to prevent water from running onto washed areas
    D. Put on sterile gloves
    E. Dry your hands with clean paper towels and turn off faucets using a clean paper towel

19. Which of the following is <u>not</u> an example of personal protective equipment?

    A. Gloves
    B. A lab coat
    C. A surgical coat
    D. A uniform
    E. A face shield

20. To dispose of a contaminated needle,

    A. Recap it and drop it into the nearest biohazardous waste container
    B. Drop it into the biohazardous waste container for sharps
    C. Wash it, recap it, and drop it into the biohazardous waste container for sharps
    D. Sterilize it and put it into the biohazardous waste container
    E. Drop it in the nearest trash can

21. Surgical scrub involves washing

    A. Hands and forearms
    B. Hands
    C. Forearms
    D. Hands, forearms, and face
    E. All parts of the body before surgery

22. The autoclave
    A. Is used for instruments that would be damaged by prolonged exposure to high temperatures and steam
    B. Involves the use of soap and scrubbing to disinfect instruments
    C. Forces the temperature of steam above the boiling point of water in order to sterilize equipment
    D. Uses ethylene oxide and may be operated only in the hospital or a manufacturing environment
    E. Is used for items that would be damaged by immersion in a chemical solution or by exposure to stem

23. Standard Precautions are
    A. Used in all medically-related fields
    B. Used mainly in hospitals
    C. Used mainly in medical offices
    D. Never used, because they are outdated
    E. The same as Universal Precautions

ANSWER KEY

1.	C		13.	C
2.	C		14.	D
3.	B		15.	A
4.	A		16.	D
5.	C		17.	E
6.	B		18.	E
7.	A		19.	D
8.	E		20.	B
9.	A		21.	A
10.	C		22.	C
11.	C		23.	B
12.	E			

Preparing the Patient

CHAPTER OUTLINE

AREAS OF COMPETENCE

AAMA—ROLE DELINEATION STUDY AREAS OF COMPETENCE

Clinical

Fundamental Principles

- Apply principles of aseptic technique and infection control
- Comply with quality assurance practices

Diagnostic Orders

- Collect and process specimens
- Perform diagnostic tests

Patient Care

- Obtain patient history and vital signs
- Prepare and maintain examination and treatment areas
- Prepare patient for examinations, procedures, and treatments
- Assist with examinations, procedures, and treatments

Communication Skills

- Treat all patients with compassion and empathy
- Adapt communications to individual's ability to understand
- Recognize and respond to verbal and nonverbal communications

Legal Concepts

- Maintain confidentiality
- Practice within the scope of education, training, and personal capabilities
- Prepare and maintain medical records
- Document accurately

Instruction

- Instruct individuals according to their needs
- Explain office policies and procedures
- Locate community resources and disseminate information

AMT—RMA CERTIFICATION EXAM TOPIC AREAS

Patient Education

- Patient instruction
- Patient resource materials

Medical Secretarial-Receptionist

- Oral and written communications
- Charts
- Supplies and equipment management
- Office safety

(Chart continued on next page.)

AREAS OF COMPETENCE (cont.)

Asepsis

- Medical asepsis
- Surgical asepsis

Sterilization

- Sanitization
- Disinfection
- Sterilization

Instruments

- Identification
- Usage
- Care and handling

Vital Signs

- Blood pressure
- Pulse
- Respiration
- Height and weight
- Temperature

Physical Examinations

- Problem-oriented records
- Positions
- Methods of examination
- Specialty examinations
- Visual acuity
- Allergy testing

Minor Surgery

- Surgical supplies
- Surgical procedures

Review frequently!

As soon as possible after your lecture, it's important to spend some quiet time organizing and clarifying your notes. Doing so will help you to retain and understand material much better than waiting until the night before the exam to take out your notes. Also review by rereading your notes throughout the course of your study. Test yourself on the material you should already know. If your class does not give midterm exams, give yourself one to check on your progress. As you learn new information, try to link it to things you've already learned. For example, before reading the section on conducting medical interviews, you should go back and review the section on patient communication.

Medical Interview

Patient interview: The first step in the examination process. It establishes a relationship between the medical assistant and the patient, and it allows the medical assistant to collect information and data pertinent to the patient's well-being.

Chief complaint: A subjective statement made by the patient describing the patient's most significant symptoms or signs of illness.

Patient chart: A legal document that contains medical information about the patient.

Six Cs of charting:

- Client's words—The patient's own phrasing must be recorded exactly.
- Clarity—Use precise medical terminology.
- Completeness—The chart must contain all pertinent information.
- Conciseness—Use abbreviations where you can to save time and space.
- Chronological order—Date all entries.
- Confidentiality—Protect the patient's privacy.

Interviewing successfully:

- Do your research before the interview. Review the patient's medical history.
- Plan the interview. Plan what types of questions you want to ask.
- Approach the patient and request an interview. Make the patient feel part of the process.

- Make the patient feel at ease. Use icebreakers and casual conversation.
- Listen to the patient.
- Conduct the interview in private without interruption.
- Deal with sensitive topics with respect.
- Do not diagnose or give a diagnostic opinion. Never go beyond the scope of your knowledge.
- Formulate a general picture. Summarize key points, and let the patient ask questions.

Methods that can further help you collect patient data include asking open-ended and hypothetical questions; mirroring the patient's explicit responses and verbalizing the implied responses; focusing on the patient; encouraging the patient to take the lead; encouraging the patient to provide additional information; and encouraging the patient to evaluate the situation. Make sure that you do not challenge the patient or probe in a manner that invades the patient's privacy.

Detect nonverbal clues: During the preexamination interview, you may note things that patients have not communicated to you verbally, such as anxiety, depression, signs of physical or psychological abuse, and signs of drug or alcohol abuse. If you suspect abuse, bring it to the physician's attention immediately. Provide such patients with support, advice, and the appropriate hotline number for your area if they want to seek help. Please have community resources such as hotline numbers and informative brochures or literature available for such situations.

Vital Signs

Vital signs: Also known as cardinal signs. They indicate that life is present. They are also indicators of the body's ability to maintain homeostasis. The vital signs include temperature (T), pulse (P), respiration (R), and blood pressure (BP). For normal ranges of vital signs, see Table 12-1.

Taking vital signs: OSHA has specific guidelines that must be followed in measuring vital signs. See Table 12-2.

Temperature

Celsius (°C): A scale for measurement of temperature in which 0°C is the freezing point of water and 100°C is the boiling point of water at sea level. Celsius is also known as centigrade.

Fahrenheit (°F): A scale for measurement of temperature in which the boiling point of water is 212°F. The freezing point of water is 32°F at sea level.

Converting Fahrenheit to Celsius: Subtract 32 from the Fahrenheit temperature, multiply the remainder by 5, and divide by 9. (See Table 12-3 on p. 272.)

Normal Ranges for Vital Signs

	0–1 year	1–6 years	6–11 years	11–16 years	Adult	Elderly
Temperature (°F)						
Oral	96–99.5	98.5–99.5	97.5–99.6	97.6–99.6	97.6–99.6	97.2–99.6
Rectal	99–100	99–100	98.5–99. 6	98.6–100.6	98.6–100.6	96.8–98.5
Pulse (beats per minute)	80–160	75–130	70–115	55–110	60–100	60–100
Respirations (per minute)	26–40	20–30	18–24	16–24	12–20	12–24
Blood Pressure (mm Hg)						
Systolic	74–95	80–100	84–110	94–120	90–139	100–140
Diastolic	50–65	50–70	54–76	62–76	60–90	60–90

Table 12-1

AT A GLANCE **OSHA Guidelines for Taking Measurement of Vital Signs**

Situation	OSHA Guideline
Before and after all patient contact	Clean the examination area according to OSHA standards.
Taking temperature orally or rectally, contact with a patient with lesions, contact with a patient suspected of having an infectious disease	Wear gloves.
	Use biohazard bags to dispose of thermometer sheaths, otoscope tips, alcohol swabs, dressings, and bandages.
In the presence of a patient suspected of having an airborne infectious disease	Wear a mask.
	The patient should be weighed, measured, and examined in a room away from staff and other patients.
	Wear protective clothing.
	Use biohazard bags for disposal of wastes.

Table 12-2

Converting Celsius to Fahrenheit: Multiply the Celsius temperature by 9, divide by 5, and add 32. It's important that you know how to use these conversion formulas. See Table 12-3 on p. 272.

Body temperature: Controlled by the hypothalamus, located in the brain, and maintained through a balance of the heat produced in the body and the heat lost from the body. Most heat is produced in the body by muscle contractions and cell metabolism. Fever and strong emotional states increase heat production in the body. Radiation, conduction, and convection all cause loss of heat from the body. Body temperature is measured with a thermometer.

Normal body temperature range: The range is from 97°F to 99°F (36°C to 37.2°C). The average temperature is 98.6°F (37°C).

Pyrexia: Fever, which is defined as any body temperature above 100.4°F (38°C). Causes of fever include

Converting From Celsius to Fahrenheit	Converting From Fahrenheit to Celsius
$°F = (°C \times 9/5) + 32$	$°C = (°F - 32) \times 5/9$

Table 12-3

infection, heat stroke, neoplasms, drug hypersensitivity, and central nervous system damage. Fevers are classified in five levels. See Table 12-4.

Hyperpyrexia: A temperature reading above 105.8°F (41°C). A body temperature above 106.0°F (41.1°C) is generally fatal.

Hypothermia: Occurs when the temperature falls below 97°F (36°C). In general, a body temperature below 93.2°F (34°C) is fatal.

Febrile: Having a body temperature above the normal range.

Afebrile: Having a body temperature within the normal range.

Types of thermometers: There are four types: mercury, electronic, tympanic, and chemical. Figure 12-1 shows the three styles of mercury thermometers.

Oral temperature: The average normal value is 98.6°F (37°C). Taking temperature orally is the most convenient method. The thermometer should be placed in the mouth for at least 3 minutes.

Aural temperature: Tympanic thermometers are used in the ear. Their benefits are speed and patient comfort. Accurate readings are obtained in approximately two seconds.

Axillary temperature: The thermometer is placed in the middle of the axilla, with the shaft facing forward. The average normal value is 97.6°F. It is the least accurate measurement site for body temperature and takes 10 minutes.

Rectal temperature: Rectal temperature is the most accurate measurement of body temperature. Rectal temperature is 1°F higher than oral. A rectal thermometer is used if a patient is unconscious, has had oral surgery, is very young, has dyspnea, or is uncooperative. The process takes 5 minutes.

Antipyretic: Pertaining to a substance that reduces fever.

Pulse Rate

Pulse: The throbbing of an artery caused by the flow of blood when the heart beats.

Pulse rate: The number of times the heart beats in a minute. The normal pulse rate in adults is 60 to 100 beats per minute. Several factors affect the pulse rate: age, sex, body size, physical exercise, health status, and medications. Infants and children have a faster pulse than adults. The pulse is usually faster in women than in men. Exercise increases the pulse rate. Anxiety, fever, anger, cancer, pregnancy, and hyperthyroidism can increase the pulse rate. Epinephrine increases and digitalis decreases the pulse rate.

Tachycardia: A pulse rate above 100 beats per minute.

Bradycardia: A pulse rate below 60 beats per minute.

Pulse sites: There are many locations on the body to take a pulse, including the temporal, carotid, brachial, radial, and femoral arteries. See Figure 12-2.

Level	Fahrenheit (°F)	Celsius (°C)
Slight	99.6–101.0	37.5–38.3
Moderate	101.0–102.0	38.3–38.8
Severe	102.0–104.0	38.8–40.0
Dangerous	104.0–105.0	40.0–40.5
Fatal	Over 106.0	Over 41.1

Table 12-4

Figure 12-1. *There are three styles of mercury thermometers.* **A.** *An oral thermometer has a long, slender tip.* **B.** *The stubby, or security, thermometer, currently the most popular style of mercury thermometer, has a short, rounded tip and can be used to take either oral or rectal temperatures.* **C.** *Rectal thermometers have a pear-shaped tip.*

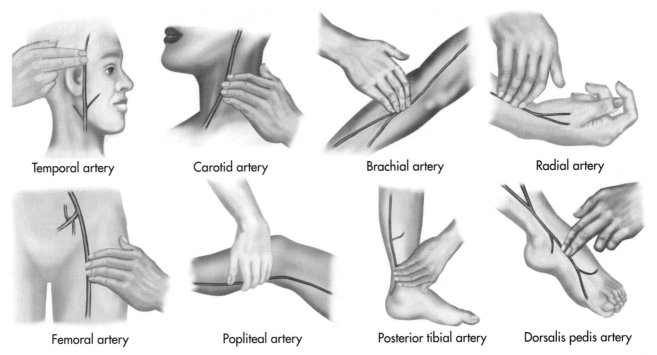

| Temporal artery | Carotid artery | Brachial artery | Radial artery |

| Femoral artery | Popliteal artery | Posterior tibial artery | Dorsalis pedis artery |

Figure 12-2. There are many locations on the body where major arteries are close enough to the surface to allow a pulse to be felt and counted.

Temporal artery: Located at the temple area of the skull. It is seldom used as a pulse site.

Carotid artery: Located between the larynx and the sternocleidomastoid muscle in the neck. This site is used in emergencies and during CPR.

Radial artery: Found in the groove on the thumb side of the inner wrist. It is the most commonly used site for measuring the pulse rate.

Apical pulse: The pulse at the apex of the heart, located in the left fifth intercostal space on the midclavicular line. It must be heard with a stethoscope. This site is used commonly for infants and children. See Figure 12-3.

Pulse deficit: The difference between the apical pulse rate and the radial pulse rate.

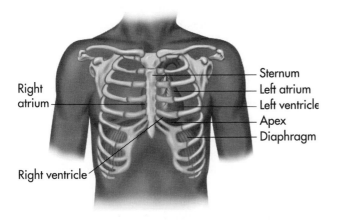

Right atrium —

Right ventricle —

— Sternum
— Left atrium
— Left ventricle
— Apex
— Diaphragm

Figure 12-3. A stethoscope is used over the apex of the heart to listen for the pulse in patients in whom pulse is not otherwise detectable.

Blood stasis: Lack of circulation due to a stoppage of blood flow.

Respiration Rate

Respiration: The exchange of oxygen and carbon dioxide between living organisms or tissues and their surroundings. Also, breathing (inhaling and exhaling, or inspiration and expiration). The control center for breathing is in the medulla oblongata (in the brain). There are two types of respiration: external and internal.

External respiration: The exchange of O_2 and CO_2 in the lungs.

Internal respiration: The exchange of O_2 and CO_2 at the tissue level.

Characteristics of respiration: The best way to check respiration is by watching the movement at the patient's chest, back, abdomen, or shoulders. There are three important characteristics that must be noted: rate, rhythm, and depth.

Respiratory rate: The number of respirations per minute. The normal adult range is 14–20 cycles per minute.

Increased respiratory rates: Occur because of asthma, heart attack, fever, hemorrhage, high altitudes, allergic reactions, nervousness, obstruction of air passages, shock, and pain.

Decreased respiratory rates: May occur as a result of the action of certain drugs (morphine), a decrease of CO_2 in the blood, stroke, and coma. The respiratory rate can also be affected by factors such as age.

Emphysema: An abnormal pulmonary condition with loss of lung elasticity, resulting in difficulty in exhaling.

Cyanosis: Bluish discoloration of the skin and mucous membranes due to oxygen deprivation.

Apnea: Temporary cessation of respiration or periods of no respiration that last more than 15 seconds.

Bradypnea: Slow respiration in an adult, fewer than 10 cycles per minute.

Hyperpnea: Rapid and deep breathing.

Dyspnea: Difficult or painful breathing.

Orthopnea: Difficulty in breathing when lying down.

Tachypnea: Fast breathing, more than 35 respirations per minute.

Depth of respiration: The amount of air being inhaled and exhaled.

Rales: Abnormal breath sounds that occur during the inspirational portion of breathing.

Stertorous: Characterized by a deep snoring sound that occurs with each inspiration.

Rhonchi: Whistling sounds made in the throat, also called gurgles or wheezes. They are heard in patients with various respiratory disorders or conditions such as asthma or chronic obstructive pulmonary disease.

Spirogram: A visual record of respiratory movement made by a spirometer and used in the assessment of pulmonary function and capacity.

Spirometer: An instrument that measures and records the volume of inhaled and exhaled air.

Blood Pressure

Heart sounds: There are two basic heart sounds: The first, produced at systole, is dull, firm, and prolonged (a "lubb" sound); the second, produced at diastole when the heart valves close, is shorter and sharper (a "dupp" sound). A "lubb dupp" is the sound of one heartbeat.

Blood pressure (BP): The pressure of the blood against the walls of the arteries. There are two blood pressure readings: systolic pressure and diastolic pressure. Readings of BP give the systolic measure first, then the diastolic measure, in millimeters (mm) of mercury (Hg). Blood pressure readings should routinely be started at the age of five years.

Normal blood pressure: Depends on age. The average normal blood pressure in healthy persons of different ages is listed in Table 12-5.

Pulse pressure: The difference between the systolic and the diastolic pressure readings.

Korotkoff's sounds: Heard during the taking of blood pressure using a sphygmomanometer and stethoscope. As air is released from the cuff, pressure on the brachial artery is reduced, and the blood is heard pulsing through the artery.

Factors affecting BP: There are five physiological factors that affect blood pressure: blood volume, peripheral resistance of the vessels, condition of the heart muscle, vessel elasticity, and blood viscosity.

Blood volume and blood viscosity: Blood pressure elevates as the blood volume increases. Polycytopenia

AT A GLANCE	Normal Blood Pressure at Different Ages	

Age	Average (mm Hg)
Newborn	50/25
6–9 years	95/65
10–15 years	100/65
Young adult	118/76
Adult	120/80 (Normal range: 90/60 to 140/90)

Table 12-5

increases BP. Hemorrhage causes volume and BP to drop.

Peripheral resistance: The relationship of the lumen of the vessel and amount of blood flowing through it. Fatty cholesterol deposits narrow the lumen, resulting in high BP.

Heart muscle condition: The strength of the heart muscle affects the volume of blood flow.

Elasticity of vessels: The ability of blood vessels to expand and contract. It decreases with age.

Hypertension: High blood pressure, defined as systolic pressure consistently above 140 mm Hg and diastolic pressure above 90 mm Hg. There are several factors that contribute to hypertension, including hyperthyroidism, heart and liver disease, rigidity of blood vessels, smoking, anxiety, stress, and race. There are two types of hypertension: primary (essential) and secondary (nonessential). Hypertension should be found on at least two occasions before the patient is placed on medications, unless the diastolic reading is over 120 mm Hg.

Essential hypertension: The vast majority of patients with hypertension (90%) have essential hypertension. The actual cause of essential high blood pressure is not known. It may be genetic.

Nonessential hypertension: Caused by disorders of other organs in the body, such as the kidney, as well as endocrine disorders.

Malignant hypertension: The most fatal form of hypertension. It is characterized by rapidly and severely elevated blood pressure that commonly damages the intima of small vessels, the brain, the retina, the heart, and the kidneys. It is more common among African Americans and may be caused by genetic predisposition, stress, obesity, smoking, the use of contraceptives, and aging.

Hypotension: An abnormal condition in which the blood pressure is not adequate for full oxygenation of the tissues. Several factors may be the cause of hypotension. They include anemia, dehydration, shock, hemorrhage, cancer, starvation, infection, high fever, and certain medications. The common drugs that affect blood pressure and cause hypotension are analgesics, narcotics, antihypertensives, and diuretics.

Orthostatic hypotension: Abnormally and temporarily low blood pressure. It occurs when a patient rapidly moves from a lying to a standing position and is also called postural hypotension.

Stethoscope: A diagnostic instrument that amplifies sound, used to detect sounds produced by blood pressure as well as heart sounds. This instrument consists of a chest piece consisting of a diaphragm and/or bell, flexible tubing, binaurals, a spring mechanism, and ear pieces. See Figure 12-4.

Sphygmomanometer: An instrument used to measure blood pressure. The components are the manometer, inflatable rubber bladder, cuff, and bulb. There are three types of sphygmomanometer: mercury, aneroid, and electronic. The mercury type is the most accurate and must be recalibrated every 6 to 12 months. The aneroid type must be checked and calibrated every 3 to 6 months.

Manometer: A scale that registers the actual blood pressure reading.

Blood pressure cuffs: A thigh cuff is available when an adult arm is too large for the large arm cuff. When using a thigh cuff, the popliteal artery is palpated for a pulse.

Measuring blood pressure: Wrap the cuff around the upper arm, just above the pulse point of the brachial artery. Inflate the cuff to the maximum inflation level, then release the air, and listen with the stethoscope as you watch the manometer. The point at which the heartbeat is first heard is the systolic pressure; the point at which the sound disappears is the diastolic pressure.

Height and Weight

Mensuration: A general term for the measurement of weight and height. Mensuration for infants also includes measuring the circumference of the head.

First visit: Provides baseline or normal values for the patient's current condition. Weight and height measurements are taken at each office visit. Any sudden changes may be an indication of a medical problem.

Measuring weight (adult): See Figure 12-5.

1. Identify the patient and introduce yourself.

2. Wash your hands and explain the procedure.

3. Check to see whether the scale is in balance by moving all the weights to the left side. The indicator should be level with the middle mark. If you are using a scale equipped to measure both kilograms and pounds, check to see that the scale is set to measure the desired units and that the upper and lower weights show the same units.

4. Place a disposable towel on the scale.

5. Ask the patient to remove shoes.

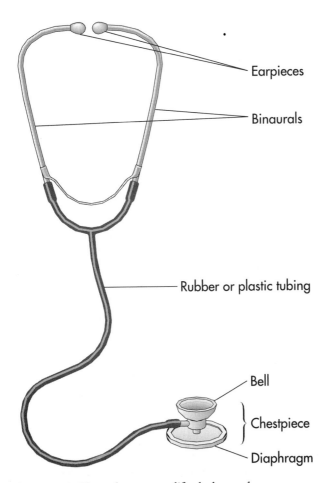

Figure 12-4. *The stethoscope amplifies body sounds.*

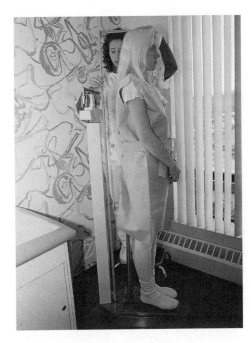

Figure 12-5. *The scale with attached height bar is used for measuring the height and weight of children and adults.*

6. Ask the patient to step on the center of the scale, facing forward.

7. Place the lower weight at the highest number that does not cause the balance indicator to drop to the bottom.

8. Move the upper weight slowly to the right until the balance bar is centered at the middle mark, adjusting as necessary.

9. Add the two weight measurements together.

10. Record the patient's weight to the nearest quarter of a pound or tenth of a kilogram.

Measuring height (adult):

1. Raise the height bar well above the patient's head and swing out the extension.

2. Ask the patient to step on the center of the scale and stand up straight.

3. Gently lower the height bar until the extension rests on the patient's head.

4. Have the patient step off the scale before reading the measurement.

5. If the patient is fewer than 50 inches tall, read the height on the bottom part of the ruler. If the patient is more than 50 inches tall, read the height on the top, movable part of the ruler. Note that the numbers increase in opposite directions on the top and bottom, so make sure that you read the height in the right direction.

6. Record the patient's height.

Physical Examination

Purpose of the physical examination: The determination of the general state of health of the patient. The purpose of the general physical examination is also to diagnose any medical problems and diseases the patient may have. The physician uses a variety of devices and laboratory tests to complete the physical findings. The majority of physicians usually start at the patient's head and end at the feet. Sometimes the physician may order some additional tests or procedures such as blood sample testing, the collection of culture specimens, or X-rays.

Complete physical examination: Includes vital signs, examination of the patient's entire body, laboratory tests (CBC and urinalysis); and diagnostic tests (X-rays).

Duty of a medical assistant: Room and equipment preparation, readiness of the patient, and assisting the physician.

Emotional preparation: Begin by explaining what will happen during the examination. This step is especially important when dealing with children.

Physical preparation: The medical assistant is responsible for obtaining and recording weight and height, facilitating the examination, asking the patient to empty his or her bladder and bowel, asking the patient to disrobe completely, dressing the patient in a full gown, and providing a drape sheet.

Examination methods: Six methods for examining a patient are a part of a complete physical examination. They are inspection, palpation, percussion, auscultation, manipulation, and mensuration.

Inspection: Observing the patient's outer body and certain mental characteristics.

Palpation: Feeling with the fingers or hand to verify data seen during inspection.

Percussion: Tapping with the fingers and listening for sounds, particularly in the abdomen, back, and chest.

Auscultation: Listening to sounds with a stethoscope.

Manipulation: Skillfully using the hands in therapeutic or diagnostic procedures.

Symptoms: Subjective changes in the body felt or observed by the patient, such as headache, blurred vision, or dizziness.

Signs: Objective findings as perceived by another person such as a physician or medical assistant. Examples of signs include fever, blood pressure, and heart murmurs.

Diagnose: To determine the cause and nature of an abnormal condition. It's important to remember that diagnosis is not within the scope or training of a medical assistant. You should never give a diagnosis to a patient. If patients ask you, refer them to the physician.

Clinical diagnosis: Based on the signs and symptoms of a disease.

Differential diagnosis: The process of ruling out certain possibilities, used to determine the correct diagnosis when two or more diagnoses are possible.

Prognosis: The outcome of a disorder, or a predication of the probable course of a disease in an individual and the chances of recovery.

Equipment

Examination tables: Usually adjustable to enable the patient to assume various positions. Tables are usually covered with disposable papers that must be changed after each patient.

Surfaces: Must be disinfected with products approved by the Environmental Protection Agency (EPA), such as 10% NaClO (sodium hypochlorite, the active ingredient in household bleach).

Accessibility: The ease with which people can move in and out of a space. The Americans with Disabilities Act of 1990 (ADA) requires:

- A doorway at least 36 inches wide to allow for the use of wheelchairs

- A clear space in rooms and hallways 60 inches in diameter to allow persons using a wheelchair to make a 180° turn

- Stable, firm, slip-resistant flooring
- Door-opening hardware that can be grasped with one hand and does not require the twisting of the wrist to use
- Door closers adjusted to allow time for a person in a wheelchair to enter and exit
- Grab bars in the lavatory

Instrument: A surgical device or tool to assist the physician in performing a specific function such as measuring, examining, grasping, holding, cutting, or suturing. Some commonly used instruments are shown in Figure 12-6 on p. 278.

Gloves: Should always be worn if the hands will come in contact with a patient's nonintact skin, blood, body fluids, or moist surfaces and if the patient is suspected of having an infectious disease.

Tongue depressors: Used in the examination of the mouth and tongue.

Gooseneck lamp: A movable light used to focus on a body area for increased visibility during physical examination.

Penlight: A small flashlight used to provide additional light during an examination, for example, to check pupil response.

Reflex hammer: A percussion mallet with a rubber head, used to tap tendons, nerves, or muscles to elicit reflex reactions.

Lubricants: Used in examination of the rectum and female genitalia.

Anoscope: An instrument used to open the anus for examination.

Speculum: An instrument that expands and separates the walls of a cavity (such as the ear, nose, and vagina) to make examination possible.

Nasal speculum: Used to enlarge the opening of the nose to permit viewing. This type of speculum may consist of a reusable handle with a disposable speculum tip, or it may be a disposable one-piece unit.

Vaginal speculum: Used to enlarge the vagina to make the vagina and the cervix accessible to visual examination and specimen collection.

Thermometer: Used to measure body temperature.

Otoscope: An instrument used to examine the external ear canal and tympanic membrane.

Ophthalmoscope: A hand-held instrument, equipped with a light, used to view inner eye structures.

Tuning fork: A small, metal instrument consisting of a stem and two prongs that produces a constant pitch when either prong is struck. It is used by physicians as a screening test of air and bone conduction.

Inspecting and maintaining instruments: Prior to examination, check all instruments and sanitize, disinfect, and sterilize as appropriate. Also make sure that all of them are in good working order, and replace or repair instruments as necessary.

Arranging instruments: Arrange instruments so the physician may find them easily.

Disposable supplies used in physical examinations: These supplies are used once and then they are discarded. They include:

- Cervical scraper
- Cotton balls
- Cotton-tipped applicators
- Curettes
- Disposable needles
- Disposable syringes
- Gauze, dressings, and bandages
- Glass slides
- Gloves, both sterile and nonsterile
- Paper tissues
- Specimen containers
- Tongue depressors

Consumable supplies: Supplies that can be emptied or used up in an examination. They include:

- Sprays (chemical spray used to preserve specimens)
- Isopropyl alcohol (used to cleanse the skin)
- Lubricants

Positioning and Draping

Draping: The placing of a sheet of fabric or paper during an examination to protect and cover all or a part of a patient's body, for the comfort and privacy of the patient.

Positioning: For physical examinations, the patient may need to be placed in a variety of positions to facilitate the examination of various parts of the body. The physician indicates which positions are needed for specific examinations, and the medical assistant helps the patient assume the positions. Cover the patient with a drape that will help keep the patient warm and maintain privacy. The patient can remain draped and gowned until the physician begins the examination, at which time only the part of the body being examined should be uncovered.

Positions: Many positions are used for medical examinations, including sitting, supine, dorsal recumbent, lithotomy, Trendelenburg's, Fowler's, prone, Sims', knee-chest, proctologic, jackknife, and standing. See Figure 12-7 on p. 279.

Sitting position: The patient sits at the edge of the examination table without back support. This position is used for examination of the head, neck, chest, heart, back, and arms. In this position, the physician can evaluate the patient's ability to fully expand the lungs and can check the upper body parts for symmetry. The drape is placed across the lap of male patients and the chest and lap of female patients.

Supine position: Also called the recumbent position. The patient lies flat on the back (face up). This posi-

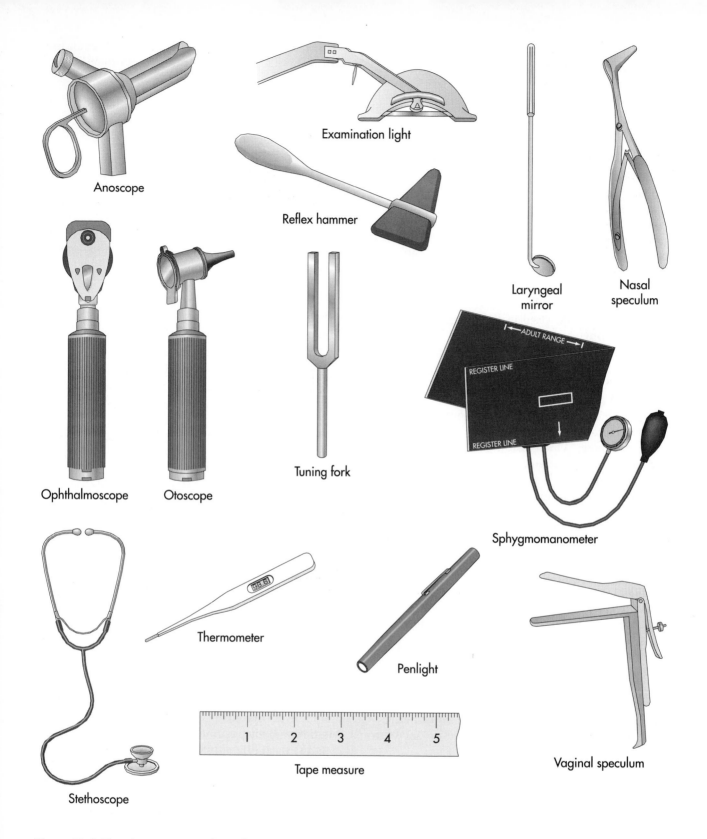

Anoscope

Examination light

Reflex hammer

Laryngeal mirror

Nasal speculum

Ophthalmoscope

Otoscope

Tuning fork

REGISTER LINE

ADULT RANGE

REGISTER LINE

Sphygmomanometer

Stethoscope

Thermometer

Penlight

Tape measure

Vaginal speculum

Figure 12-6. *These instruments may be used in a general physical examination.*

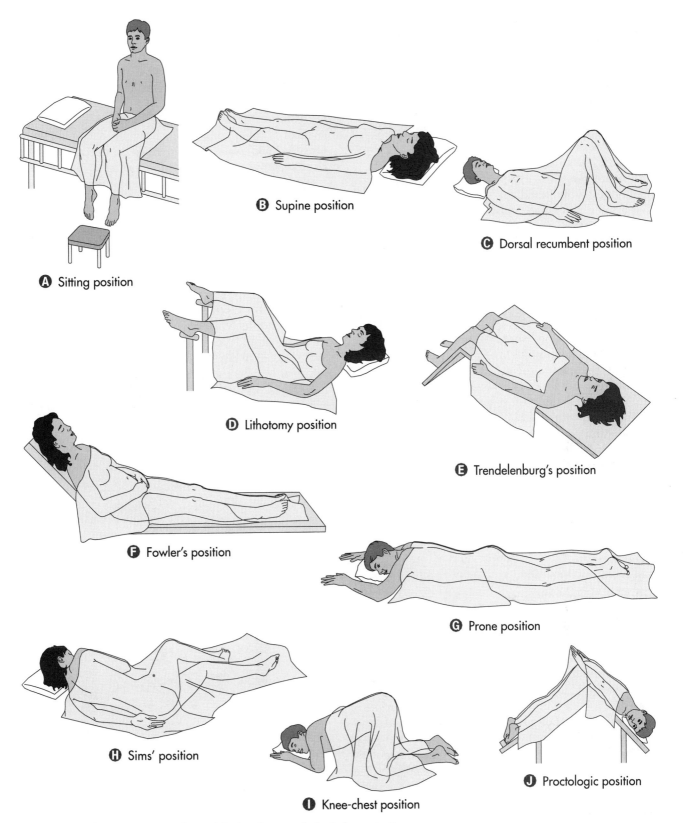

A Sitting position

B Supine position

C Dorsal recumbent position

D Lithotomy position

E Trendelenburg's position

F Fowler's position

G Prone position

H Sims' position

I Knee-chest position

J Proctologic position

Figure 12-7. *These positions may be used during the general physical examination.*

tion is used for examination of the head, neck, chest, heart, abdomen, and arms and legs. The patient is normally draped from the neck or underarms down to the feet.

Dorsal recumbent: The patient lies face up while flexing the knees, with the soles of the feet flat on the table. This position is the same as the supine position except that the patient's knees are drawn up. It is used for examination of the head, neck, chest, heart, and lower extremities (vaginal, rectal, and perineal areas).

Lithotomy position: The patient lies on the back with the knees sharply flexed and the feet placed in stirrups that are set wide apart and away from the table. This position is used for examination of the vaginal and perineal areas. It is an embarrassing and physically uncomfortable position for most women, so you should not ask the patient to stay in this position any longer than necessary.

Trendelenburg's position: The patient lies flat on the back with the head lower than the legs. This position is used for abdominal surgery and for treatment of patients who are in shock.

Fowler's position: The patient lies face up on the examination table with the head elevated. Although the head of the table can be raised to 90°, the most common position is 45°. This position is used for examination and treatment of the head, neck, and chest. This position is best for people with lower-back injury or for those experiencing shortness of breath.

Prone position: The patient lies face down on the table. This position is used for examination of the back and feet. It is not suitable for patients who are obese, are pregnant (in the late stage), are elderly, or have difficulties of the respiratory system.

Sims' position: Also called the lateral position. The patient lies on the left side with the left arm placed behind the body and the left leg slightly flexed. The right arm is flexed toward the head, and the right leg is flexed. This position is used for examination of the rectum.

Knee-chest position: The patient rests on the knees and chest with the thighs slightly separated. Patients who have difficulty in maintaining this position can be placed in a knee-elbow position. The knee-chest position is used for examination of rectal, sigmoid, and vaginal areas.

Proctologic position: The patient lies face down with both the torso and the legs lowered. The hips of the patient are flexed at a 90° angle. Adjustable tables can be raised in the middle with both ends sloping down. This position is used for rectal examination.

Jackknife position: The patient lies face up with both the torso and the legs raised. The hips of the patient are flexed at a 90° angle.

Standing position: Used for examination of the musculoskeletal system, the neurological system, hernias, and the peripheral vascular system.

Eye and Ear Examination

Eye

Optometrist: A specialist who measures the eye's refractive power and prescribes correction of visual defects when needed.

Ophthalmologist: A medical doctor who is an eye specialist.

Ophthalmic assistant: Provides administrative and clinical support for an ophthalmologist; works with patients; assists with surgery; keeps instruments and equipment in proper working order; and may conduct distance acuity, near acuity, and color perception tests.

Visual acuity test: Used to measure the degree of clarity or sharpness of vision. There are many types of tests for visual acuity. The test most commonly used in the medical office and performed by the medical assistant is the Snellen eye test.

Snellen letter chart: A chart used to test the distance vision of adults. The distance between the patient and the chart should be 20 feet. Normal vision is recorded as 20/20. Have the patient read the chart, and record the smallest line read. If the patient misses only one or two letters on a line, record the results with a minus sign. For example, if one letter is missed on the 30-foot line from 20 feet away with the right eye, the result would be recorded as O.D. 20/30 –1. See Figure 12-8.

Color blindness: The congenital or acquired inability to distinguish certain colors. Congenital color blindness is more common. This condition is seen in males more frequently than in females.

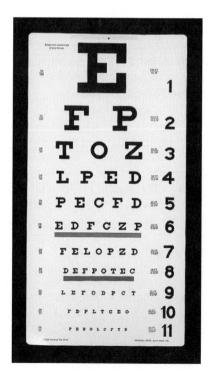

Figure 12-8. *The Snellen letter chart is used to test the ability to see objects that are relatively far away.*

Color vision acuity test: Measures the patient's ability to determine and differentiate between colors. The medical assistant may be responsible for administering the color vision test. There are two common color tests, Ishihara and Richmond pseudoisochromatic, in which the individual must distinguish a figure made up of colored dots from a background made up of dots of another color. A score of 10 or above indicates average color vision. A score of less than 7 may represent a color vision deficiency.

Tonometer: An instrument used in measuring tension or pressure of the intraocular region. It is used for the detection of glaucoma.

Eye irrigation: The flushing of foreign materials from the eye, using a sterile solution formulated for this purpose.

Ear

Audiologist: A specialist who evaluates and corrects hearing problems.

Hearing loss: An inability to perceive the entire range of sound heard by a person with normal hearing. There are two types: conductive and sensorineural.

Conductive hearing loss: Caused by damage to the middle ear.

Sensorineural hearing loss: Caused by damage to the inner ear (the cochlea or the auditory nerve).

Audiometer: An electronic device that measures hearing acuity by producing sounds in specific frequencies and intensities.

Audiology tests: Determine the presence of conduction defects or nerve impairment. They are used to evaluate hearing loss and disturbances in equilibrium.

Weber's test: A method of evaluating auditory acuity. The test is performed by placing the stem of a vibrating tuning fork against the center of a person's forehead, or the midline vertex. The loudness of the sound is equal in both ears if hearing is normal.

Rinne test: Compares bone conduction hearing with air conduction hearing. A vibrating tuning fork is held on the mastoid process of the ear until the patient no longer hears it. Then it is held close to the external auditory meatus.

Ear irrigation: Flushing of the ear canal to remove impacted cerumen, to relieve inflammation, or to remove a foreign body. The solution used should be warmed to room temperature before administration. To perform the irrigation for adults, the ear lobe should be pulled upward and outward. For infants and children, the ear lobe should be pulled down and back.

Ear instillation: Applying eardrops to treat an ear disorder. The medication should be warmed to room temperature before application.

Cardiovascular Examination

Cardiologist: A physician trained in the treatment of heart diseases.

Medical assistant's role: To assist with and perform tests, to keep equipment properly maintained and calibrated, to educate patients about diet and exercise, and to provide emotional support to patients.

General cardiovascular examination: Taking a blood pressure reading, palpating the heart and chest wall and the vessels in the extremities, and recording an electrocardiogram.

Cardiac stress test: Recording an electrocardiogram while a patient is exercising on a treadmill, stationary bicycle, or stair-stepping ergonometer. The test determines the capacity of a patient to respond to an increased demand for energy. Performing this test helps diagnose diseases of the heart.

Electrocardiogram (ECG or EKG): The measurement of electrical activity generated by the heart muscle. It is a safe procedure that is used in the diagnosis of heart diseases. The medical assistant performs the ECG and assists with stress tests.

Echocardiography: The process of obtaining echoes with the use of ultrasound and recording them on paper. It is used to evaluate the inner structures of the heart.

Phonocardiography: A process that graphically records the cardiac cycle sounds as heard through a stethoscope.

Cardiac catheterization: A diagnostic procedure in which a catheter is introduced through an incision into a large vein (in the arm or leg) and sent to the chambers of the heart. The procedure takes about 1 to 3 hours.

Holter monitor cardiography: A portable monitoring system used to record the cardiac activity of a patient over a 24- or 48-hour period. The patient should perform regular daily activities and note those activities that cause stress. The process is also called ambulatory electrocardiography.

Angioplasty: The reconstruction of blood vessels damaged by disease or injury.

Respiratory System Examination

Eupnea: Normal breathing.

Throat culture: A commonly performed diagnostic test for determination of infection.

Sputum culture: Difficult to obtain. The patient must cough deeply and expectorate material from the lungs.

Pulmonary function tests: Done to measure the amount of air a patient can inhale and exhale.

Spirometer: An instrument that measures the air taken into and expelled from the lungs.

Spirometry: The measuring of breathing capacity.

Forced vital capacity (FVC): The greatest volume of air that can be expelled when a person performs rapid, forced expiration.

Total lung capacity (TLC): The total volume when lungs are maximally inflated.

Laryngoscope: An endoscope for examining the larynx.

Bronchoscopy: Visual examination of the tracheo-bronchial tree using the standard rigid, tubular metal bronchoscope. The procedure may also be used for suctioning or biopsy.

Cheyne-Stokes respiration: A breathing pattern marked by a period of apnea lasting 10 to 60 seconds, followed by gradually increasing depth and frequency of respirations.

Gastrointestinal System Examination

Gastroenterologist: A physician who diagnoses and treats disorders of the gastrointestinal tract.

Proctology: The branch of medicine concerned with treating disorders of the colon, rectum, and anus.

Medical assistant's role: To tell patients how to prepare for examinations, to order informational brochures, and to answer patients' questions.

Endoscopy: Visual examination of the interior of cavities and organs of the body with an endoscope. The purpose of this procedure is the diagnosis of disorders. Endoscopy can also be used for biopsy. See Figure 12-9.

Gastroscopy: Examination of the stomach and abdominal cavity using a type of endoscope called a gastroscope.

Sigmoidoscopy: Inspection of the rectum and sigmoid colon with the aid of a sigmoidoscope.

Colonoscopy: Visual examination of the large intestine by means of a colonoscope inserted through the anus.

Anoscope: A speculum used to examine the anus and lower rectum.

Proctoscopy: Examination of the lower rectum and anal canal by means of a protoscope.

Cholecystogram: An X-ray of the gallbladder, made after injection of a radiopaque substance, usually a contrast medium containing iodine.

Barium swallow: Also called an upper GI series, used to diagnose abnormalities in the esophagus, stomach, and small intestine. The patient swallows a liquid containing barium, and X-rays are taken to record the diagnostic images.

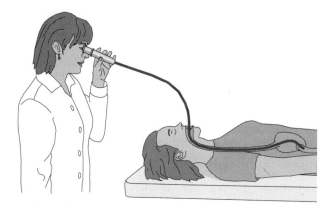

Figure 12-9. *To perform peroral endoscopy, the physician inserts a scope into the patient's mouth.*

Barium enema: Also called a lower GI series, used to detect abnormalities in the large intestine. Barium is given as an enema.

Gastric lavage: Obtaining a sample of stomach contents with an orogastric tube, which suctions the contents up for analysis.

Occult blood test: A chemical test or microscopic examination for blood, especially in the feces, that is not apparent on visual inspection.

Laparotomy: Surgical incision into the peritoneal cavity.

Urinary System Examination

Urologist: A physician who specializes in the study of the urinary system.

Medical assistant's role: It is important to be thorough in taking a patient's history in order to obtain information about changes in frequency or urgency of urination, difficulty or pain with urination, and incontinence.

Urinalysis: Physical, chemical, and microscopic examination of urine to find bacteria, blood, or other substances and to monitor for dysfunctions of the prostate gland and for sexually transmitted diseases. The medical assistant collects the urine specimen for chemical or physical analysis.

Urine culture: The placement of urine samples on special media that promote the growth of microorganisms and thus facilitate bacterial analysis. It requires special training and equipment but may be performed in the office.

Cystoscopy: Visual examination of the bladder using a special instrument called a cystoscope.

Pyelogram: An X-ray image of the bladder made using an opaque dye for visualization. The dye may be injected into the patient's vein, or the physician may insert a small catheter into the urethra through a cystoscope and inject the dye through the catheter.

Urinometer: A device for determining the specific gravity of urine. It is also called a urometer.

Vasectomy: A sterilization procedure for men in which a section of each vas deferens is removed.

Gynecology and Obstetrics

Obstetrician/gynecologist (OB/GYN): A physician who specializes in the female reproductive system.

Role of the medical assistant: The medical assistant collects a urine specimen; interviews the patient about her health and any changes in appetite, weight, and emotional status; and asks about the date of the patient's last menstrual period. If the doctor is male, a female medical assistant should be present during the examination not only to assist but also to provide legal protection.

Pelvic examination: The physician checks the external genitalia, cervix, vaginal wall, internal reproductive organs, and rectum via palpation and inspection with a speculum.

Papanicolaou test (Pap smear): Used to determine the presence of abnormal or precancerous cells in the cervix and vagina. A Pap test is done during the pelvic examination. The patient is instructed not to douche, use vaginal medications, or have intercourse within 48 hours before the examination. The test should not be done during a patient's menstrual period.

Pregnancy test: A test to determine whether the hormone *human chorionic gonadotropin*, which is produced during pregnancy, is present in a woman's blood or urine. False negatives and false positives can occur.

Ultrasonography: The process of imaging deep structures of the body by measuring and recording the reflection of pulsed or continuous high-frequency sound waves. It is a valuable tool to diagnose fetal abnormalities, gallstones, heart defects, and tumors. It is also called sonography.

Mammogram: A low-dose X-ray of a woman's breasts to detect early cancer. A mammogram is first taken between the ages of 35 and 40 years.

Colposcopy: The examination of the vagina and cervix with a colposcope.

Schiller's test: Iodine staining of cervical and vaginal areas to diagnose cancer of the cervix or vagina.

Laparoscopy: Examination of the abdominal cavity with a laparoscope through one or more small incisions in the abdominal wall. The incisions are usually at the umbilicus. A general anesthetic is used. This procedure is also called an abdominoscopy.

Skin Examination

Dermatologist: A physician who diagnoses and treats skin diseases and disorders.

Medical assistant's role: To assist with positioning and draping during a skin examination, to take skin scrapings and wound cultures, to administer sunlamp treatments, to apply topical medications, and to instruct patients about caring for a skin condition or wound at home.

Whole-body skin examination: An examination of the entire surface of the skin, including the scalp and the areas between the toes, to look for lesions, especially suspicious moles or precancerous growths.

Wood's light examination: A type of dermatological examination in which a physician inspects the patient's skin under an ultraviolet lamp in a darkened room.

Tuberculin skin test: Administered intradermally. This test is routinely performed on all individuals who have contact with children, on those working in health care fields, and on patients with a positive X-ray suggestive of infection. The tine test, a common tuberculin skin test, is performed by cleansing the skin on the inside of the forearm and then pressing tuberculin-coated tines into the skin while pulling the skin taut. The skin is observed for results after 48 to 72 hours.

Scratch test: A test for specific allergies. The skin is scratched with a sterile lancet, and a drop of allergen (antigen) is added to the site. Results are recorded in 30 minutes.

Patch test: A test for hypersensitivity allergy. Antigens are applied to the skin and covered with gauze patches and tape. The site is checked in 48 hours, and results are recorded. This type of test is used to discover the cause of contact dermatitis.

Tissue biopsy: There are three types or methods: excision biopsy, punch biopsy, and shave biopsy.

Neurology Tests

Neurologist: A physician who diagnoses and treats diseases and disorders of the central nervous system and associated systems.

Medical assistant's role: To ready equipment for use; to position the patient; to hand tools and other items to the physician; to perform visual acuity tests or audiometry; to assist with electroencephalography; and to instruct and educate patients and their families about procedures, disorders, and treatments.

Neurological examination: A complete examination evaluates cognitive function, cranial nerves, the motor system, reflexes, and the sensory system.

Myelogram: An X-ray taken after the injection of a radiopaque medium into the subarachnoid space to demonstrate any distortions of the spinal cord.

Magnetic resonance imaging (MRI): Medical imaging that uses radio-frequency radiation as its source of energy. It has become an important tool in musculoskeletal and pelvic imaging.

Computed tomography (CT): A radiographic technique that produces a film representing a detailed cross section of tissue structure.

Electroencephalogram (EEG): A graphic chart on which is traced the electrical potential produced by the brain, detected by electrodes placed on the scalp. The resulting brain wave patterns are called alpha, beta, delta, and theta rhythms.

Carotid angiogram: A radiographic image of the carotid artery, into which a contrast medium has been injected.

Alpha-fetoprotein testing: Measurements of AFP in amniotic fluid are used for early diagnosis of fetal neural tube defects, such as spina bifida and anencephaly.

Lumbar puncture: A diagnostic and therapeutic procedure done by a physician, involving the introduction of a hollow needle and stylet into the subarachnoid space of the lumbar part of the spinal canal.

Infants and Children

Pediatrician: A physician who specializes in the health care of children, monitoring their development and diagnosing and treating their illnesses. Subspecialties include surgery and oncology.

Medical assistant's role: To prepare the child for examination; to discuss eating habits, sleep patterns, daily activities, immunization schedules, and toilet training with the caregiver or child; and to help relieve the child's fear by calmly explaining procedures.

Well-baby examination: Regular checkups when the infant is 2 weeks, 1 month, 2 months, 4 months, 6 months, 9 months, 1 year, 15 months, and 18 months old. Starting at age 2, children should have checkups every year.

Scoliosis examination: An assessment of a child of 10 years or older for abnormal curvature of the spine. See Figure 12-10.

Child abuse and neglect: Watch for signs of physical injury, dirty or neglected appearance, hunger, extreme sadness or fear, or inability to communicate. Note suspicions on the chart, and report them to the doctor. Physicians are legally responsible for reporting suspected child abuse or neglect to your community's child protection agency or to the police.

Immunizations: Usually given during routine office visits to protect children against hepatitis B, diphtheria, tetanus, pertussis, poliomyelitis, measles, mumps, rubella, chickenpox, and influenza. The child should not have an illness or fever at the time of immunization.

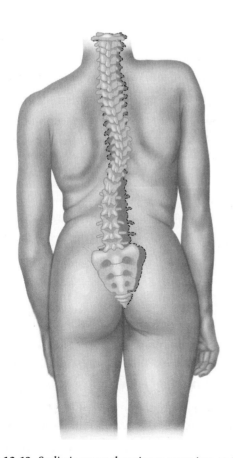

Figure 12-10. *Scoliosis causes the spine to curve into an S shape.*

Minor Surgery

Surgery: The branch of medicine that treats diseases, injuries, and deformities by removal or operative methods. Also, the surgical treatment or procedure itself. Generally, the place for major surgery is in a hospital, but minor surgery commonly is performed in a doctor's or dentist's office. Minor surgery may include removal of a sebaceous cyst, wart, or foreign object. Other minor surgeries include circumcision, vasectomy, skin biopsy, dilation and curettage, or insertion of an IUD.

Medical assistant's role: To complete forms for insurance; to obtain signed informed consent forms from the patient; to explain the procedure to the patient; to answer questions; to make sure that the doctor is informed about medications the patient is taking; to make sure that the patient knows how to follow presurgical instructions for diet and fluid intake; to make sure that the room is clean; to make sure that all supplies are clean, disinfected, or sterilized, as appropriate, and that all supplies are properly arranged; possibly to assist with the surgery; to help dress the wound and perform other postoperative care; to clean the room and prepare it for the next patient.

Outpatient surgery: A surgical procedure that requires less than one day and for which the patient does not need to stay in the facility overnight.

Ambulatory surgery: A surgical procedure for which the patient is able to walk into and out of the surgical facility on the same day.

Invasive procedure: A diagnostic or therapeutic technique that requires entry into a body cavity or interruption of normal body functions. Examples include the Pap test, sigmoidoscopy, colonoscopy, and intravenous pyelography.

Anesthesia: Partial or complete loss of sensation. It is induced to permit the performance of surgery or other painful procedures. Local anesthesia provides loss of sensation in a particular location without loss of consciousness; it is used for diagnostic procedures or minor surgery. Techniques for administering local anesthetics include topical application, infiltration (injection into tissue), and block (injection into or around a nerve). Types of block anesthesia include regional, spinal, epidural, and saddle, which affect a group of nerves. General anesthesia is used for major surgery.

Anesthetic: A drug or agent used to prevent the sensation of pain and, depending on the situation, to achieve adequate muscle relaxation during surgery, to calm fear and anxiety, and to produce amnesia for the event.

Needle biopsy: The removal of a segment of living tissue for microscopic examination by inserting a hollow needle through the skin or the external surface of an organ or tumor.

Cauterization: The destruction of tissue with a cautery.

Cautery: A means of destroying tissue, such as a caustic agent, a hot instrument, an electric current, or a laser beam.

Electrocautery: The cauterization of tissue by means of an electrode that consists of a red-hot piece of metal, such as a wire, in a holder.

Electrosurgery: The use of electrical current in surgical procedures such as electrocoagulation to cauterize blood vessels and electrocision to excise tissue.

Cryosurgery: The destruction of tissue (e.g., abnormal cells) by the use of freezing temperatures.

Laser: The acronym for *l*ight *a*mplification by *s*timulated *e*mission of *r*adiation. Thermal lasers are used to heat tissue at a microscopic level, causing vaporization and coagulation of the target area.

Surgical Asepsis

Disinfection: The destruction or inhibition of pathogenic organisms by physical means or by chemical germicides. Two common disinfectants are zephrin chloride and chlorophenyl. Contaminated instruments are completely immersed in a germicidal solution for from 1 to 10 hours. The chemical disinfection process is referred to as a "cold" process because no heat is used.

Surgical asepsis: Used when sterility of supplies and the immediate environment is required. This technique is necessary during any invasive procedure. It requires sterile hand washing (surgical scrub), sterile gloves, special handling procedures, and sterilization of materials. Most dangerous bacteria are destroyed at a temperature of 50° to 60°C (122° to 140°F). Pasteurization of a fluid, which is the application of heat at about 60°C, destroys pathogenic bacteria. However, temperatures of 120°C are usually required to destroy spore cells. A sterile object that touches anything nonsterile is automatically considered contaminated and must not be used in surgery.

Surgical scrub: The purpose of performing a surgical scrub (hand washing) is to remove dirt and microorganisms from the surface of the skin and the fingernails. Materials needed include a sterile surgical scrub brush, a dispenser with surgical soap, orange sticks, and sterile towels. The physician or surgical assistant must remove all jewelry, turn on warm water, keep the hands higher than the elbows, use surgical soap, scrub the hands with the scrub brush for 2 minutes, rinse the hands, apply more surgical soap, and again scrub the hands for at least 3 minutes. Total hand washing time should be approximately 10 minutes.

Sterilization: The process of destroying all microorganisms and their pathogenic products. Methods of sterilization include the application of steam under pressure, dry heat, bactericidal chemical compounds (in liquid or gas form), and radiation.

Moist heat sterilization: Uses steam under pressure. This method kills all pathogens and spores and it is the best and most accepted type of sterilization.

Autoclave: An appliance used to sterilize medical instruments. It allows steam to flow around each article placed in the chamber. The vapor penetrates cloth or paper used to package the articles being sterilized. Autoclaving is one of the most effective methods for destruction of all types of microorganisms. The amount of time and the temperature necessary for sterilization depend on the articles to be sterilized and whether they are wrapped or left directly exposed to the steam under pressure. Wrapped items autoclaved with steam under pressure require 30 pounds of pressure at 132°C (270°F) for 20 minutes. Unwrapped items require only 10 minutes of autoclaving, which is known as flashing. The autoclave chamber must be cleaned after each load.

Dry heat sterilization: A method of sterilization that uses heated dry air at a temperature of 160° to 180°C (320° to 356°F) for 90 minutes to 3 hours.

Sterilization indicator: Any material that undergoes a change in appearance (usually a color shift) when it is exposed to a predetermined combination of temperature, pressure, and time. Indicators are used to confirm that the sterilization process has been completed. The most common forms of indicator include autoclave tape and sterilization indicator strips.

Autoclave indicator: A change of color or the appearance of dots on an indicator strip, tube, tape, or tag shows that steam has entered the chamber, not that the instruments are sterile. Autoclave indicator tape turns black after autoclaving.

Shelf-life: The amount of time during which an item may be expected to retain its useful characteristics (such as sterility). Packages that have been autoclaved are stored with the date visible, and the oldest package is placed in front so that it is used first. Sterilized instruments are considered to have a shelf-life of approximately one month. Autoclaved packages cannot be re-autoclaved without washing, rinsing, drying, and re-wrapping the items.

Surgical setup tray: Instruments that may be required for a specific minor surgical procedure should be gathered together into a pack, sterilized, and made ready for use as needed. Specialized trays are used for such procedures as incision, vasectomy, suture removal, and laceration repair. See Figure 12-11.

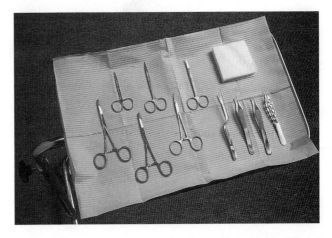

Figure 12-11. *This laceration tray contains scissors, several pairs of forceps, a needle holder, suture material, and sterile gauze.*

Clean gloves: Worn to protect health care personnel from urine, stools, blood, saliva, and drainage from patients' wounds and lesions.

Sterile gloves: Used to prevent contamination of areas that need to be sterile on the patient. See Figures 12-12 to 12-15.

Sterile field: The area immediately around a patient that has been prepared for a surgical procedure. The sterile field includes the scrubbed team members, who are properly attired, and all furniture and fixtures in the area.

Formalin: A dilute solution of formaldehyde used to preserve biological specimens.

Instruments

Surgical scissors: A sharp instrument composed of two opposing cutting blades, held together by a central pin on which the blades pivot, used to dissect and cut tissues. See Figure 12-16.

Operating scissors: Straight or curved, with a combination of blades such as sharp/sharp (s/s), blunt/blunt (b/b), or sharp/blunt (s/b).

Suture scissors: Used to remove sutures. The hook on the tip aids in getting under a suture, and the blunt end prevents puncturing of the tissues.

Bandage scissors: Inserted beneath a dressing or bandage to cut it for removal.

Scalpel: A small, straight surgical knife consisting of a handle and a sharp blade that has a convex edge used to make surgical incisions. There are both reusable and disposable scalpels. Blades are numbered according to size. A number 15 blade is often used in performing minor surgeries.

Retractors: Used to hold tissue aside to improve the exposure of operative areas. See Figure 12-17.

Probes: Long, slender instruments used to explore wounds or body cavities.

Forceps: A surgical instrument with two handles, each attached to a dull blade, used to grasp, compress, pull, handle, or join tissue, equipment, or supplies. See Figure 12-18 on p. 288. Grasping types include thumb forceps and tissue forceps. (The word *forceps*, like *scissors*, is plural.)

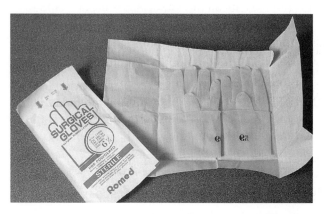

Figure 12-12. *You can put these sterile gloves on without reaching across the sterile surfaces of the gloves or the sterile inner wrap of the pack.*

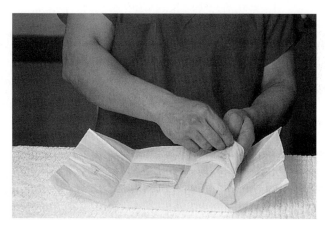

Figure 12-13. *Your palm should face up as you slide your dominant hand into the first glove.*

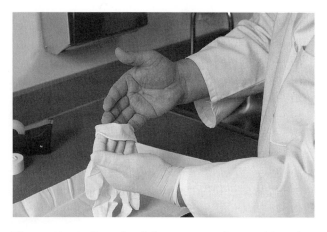

Figure 12-14. *Your gloved fingers secure the remaining glove while you slip it over your nondominant hand.*

Figure 12-15. *Unfold the cuff over your arm while touching only the sterile surface of the glove.*

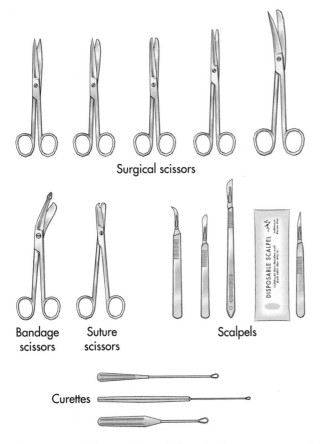

Surgical scissors

Bandage scissors **Suture scissors** **Scalpels**

Curettes

Figure 12-16. *These cutting and dissecting instruments are typically used in minor surgical procedures.*

Thumb forceps: Also called smooth forceps, used to pick up tissue or to grasp tissue between the adjacent surfaces of the blades.

Splinter forceps: Thumb forceps with sharp points that are useful in removing foreign objects.

Tissue forceps: Have teeth to prevent them from slipping. They are used to grasp tissue.

Holding forceps: Have handles that can lock the blades closed.

Dressing forceps: Used in the application and removal of dressings.

Hemostatic forceps or **hemostats:** Used for clamping and grasping blood vessels.

Towel forceps: Used to keep towels in place during a surgical procedure.

Needle holders: Surgical forceps used to hold and pass a suturing needle through tissue. They are also called suture forceps.

Surgical suture needle: A sharp instrument used for puncturing and suturing. The needle carries suture material, also called ligature. Needles vary in their piercing ability (pointed or blunt-tipped), shape (straight or curved), and size, depending on their use. A swaged needle has no eye; instead, the needle and suture material are combined in one length. See Figure 12-19.

Suturing: Using sterile suture material and a needle to close a wound. Ligature (suture material) is of two types: absorbable and nonabsorbable.

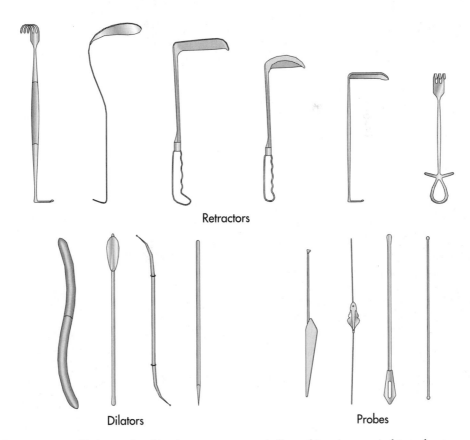

Retractors

Dilators **Probes**

Figure 12-17. *These retracting, dilating, and probing instruments are typically used in minor surgical procedures.*

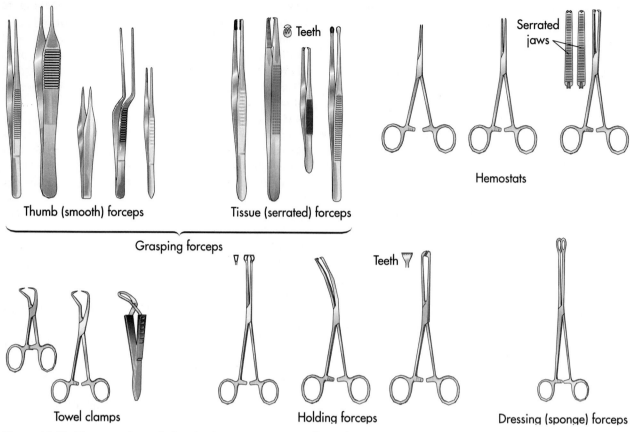

Figure 12-18. *These grasping and clamping instruments are typically used in minor surgical procedures.*

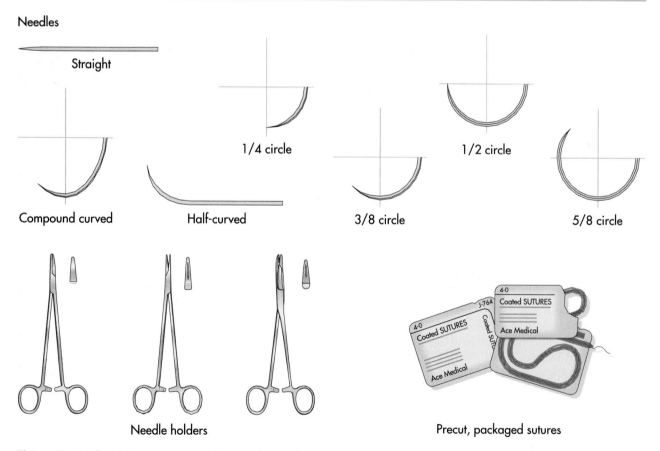

Figure 12-19. *These instruments are typically used in suturing.*

Absorbable sutures: Used for internal suturing. They are digested by tissue enzymes and absorbed by the body tissues. Absorption usually occurs 5 to 20 days after insertion. Surgical catgut made from the intestinal lining of sheep is used for the bladder, intestines, and subcutaneous tissue.

Nonabsorbable sutures: Generally used for outer tissues of the body. These types of suture must be removed after the wound begins healing. They may be made of polyester, steel, silk, or nylon.

Suture size: In the U.S., the size designation of sutures decreases as the thickness (diameter) decreases. Size 7 is the largest generally available. Size 3 is thinner; size 0 is thinner still. Sizes smaller than 0 are indicated by additional 0s: 00 (or 2-0), 000 (or 3-0), and so on. Few sutures are smaller than size 11-0. Sizes 2-0 through 6-0 are the most commonly used.

Staple: A piece of stainless steel wire used to close certain surgical wounds. It is used in major surgery and is the strongest of all suture material.

Suture removal: After surgery, nonabsorbable sutures generally remain in place from 5 to 6 days and then have to be removed. If they are not removed, they can cause infection and skin irritation.

Wounds and Bandaging

Puncture: A wound made by a sharp-pointed object, such as a needle, bullet, carpentry nail, knife, or animal tooth, that pierces the skin layers.

Laceration: A wound in which the tissues are torn apart rather than cut. The edges of the wound are irregular. Dull knife blades and other objects that tear into the skin produce lacerations.

Abrasion: A wound in which the outer layers of the skin are rubbed off, resulting in an oozing of blood from ruptured capillaries. Many falls cause abrasions, such as skinned knees and elbows.

Incision: A clean, smooth cut, as is caused by a sharp knife edge, a razor, or a piece of glass. Also, a cut produced surgically with a sharp instrument that creates an opening into an organ or space in the body. There are two types of incisions: superficial and deep. Generally, a deep incision is accompanied by profuse bleeding with damage to tissues such as muscles, tendons, and nerves.

Contusion: A wound in which the tissues under the skin are injured, as by a blunt object. Blood vessels rupture, allowing blood to seep into the tissue.

Wound healing: The healing process serves to restore the structure and function of the damaged tissue. This process takes place in three phases: lag, proliferation, and maturation.

Lag phase: During the initial phase, bleeding is reduced because of blood vessel constriction.

Proliferation phase: During the second phase, new tissue forms.

Maturation phase: The last phase involves the formation of scar tissue.

Dressing: Sterile material used to cover a surgical or other wound.

Bandage: A strip of woven material used to wrap or cover a part of the body. A bandage causes pressure to control bleeding, protects a wound from contamination, holds a dressing in place, or supports or immobilizes an injured part of the body.

Types of bandage: Three types of bandage are often used in the medical office: roller, elastic, and triangular.

Roller bandages: Long strips of soft material that are coiled to form rolls. They are often used to apply pressure (i.e., as pressure bandages).

Elastic bandages: Made of woven cotton containing elastic fibers. They are typically used on swollen extremities or joints, on the chest to treat empyema, on fractured ribs, and on legs to support varicose veins. They are expensive, but they can be washed and reused.

Triangular bandages: Usually made of muslin and measuring approximately 55 inches across the base and 40 inches along the sides. They are frequently used in first aid.

STRATEGIES TO SUCCESS

▶ Test-Taking Skills

Answer the easy ones first!

Answering all the questions you know first will give you confidence and momentum to get through the rest of the exam. As you go through the exam, make a mark next to any questions that you want to come back to—questions you are uncertain about or difficult questions you don't want to answer right away. Go back to these questions once you've answered all the questions that you thought were easy. Often you will be surprised how your subconscious mind has continued to work on these questions, or perhaps how something later in the test has jogged your memory, and these hard questions don't seem that difficult any more.

Instructions:

Answer the following questions. Check your answers in the *Answer Key* that follows this section.

1. Which of the following is one of the six Cs of charting?

   A. Clerical
   B. Client's words
   C. Consult
   D. Counsel
   E. Court

2. The normal pulse rate (in beats per minute) for adults is

   A. 40–60
   B. 60–100
   C. 80–100
   D. 100–120
   E. 120-140

3. A small surgical clamp for grasping blood vessels is called

   A. Tissue forceps
   B. Thumb forceps
   C. Smooth forceps
   D. Hemostatic forceps
   E. Dressing forceps

4. Which of the following thermometers is considered the most accurate indicator of body temperature?

   A. Oral
   B. Aural or tympanic
   C. Axillary
   D. Rectal
   E. Both A and B

5. Which suture size listed below is the thickest?

   A. 0-0
   B. 5-0
   C. 7-0
   D. 1-0
   E. 15-0

6. The position in which the patient is lying flat on the back is known as

   A. Prone
   B. Sims'
   C. Supine
   D. Fowler's
   E. Lithotomy

7. Needle holders are also called

   A. Staples
   B. Thumb forceps
   C. Suture forceps
   D. Hemostatic forceps
   E. Dressing forceps

8. The artery most commonly used for taking a patient's pulse is

   A. Carotid
   B. Apical
   C. Temporal
   D. Celiac
   E. Radial

9. During the preexamination interview, you notice some cuts on an adult patient's arm that you suspect might be signs of abuse or even of attempted suicide. You try to ask the patient about it, but the patient doesn't want to talk to you. What should you do?

   A. Press the patient and explain how important it is that all your questions be answered
   B. Call the police immediately and report that you have a victim of abuse whom they need to talk to
   C. Tell the examining physician, and prepare a list of community resources that can provide advice and support to the patient even if the patient isn't ready to talk to you
   D. Ignore the problem, because the patient obviously does not want to talk about it, and go on with assisting the physician as if you didn't see anything
   E. Transfer the patient to a mental institution and notify immediate family members

10. Which of the following positions is used for vaginal and perineal area examination?

    A. Lithotomy
    B. Fowler's
    C. Supine
    D. Jackknife
    E. Trendelenburg's

11. You've taken a patient's temperature and recorded it as 96.9°F. Later, the physician asks you to convert this measurement to Celsius. What is the patient's temperature in Celsius?

    A. 21.8
    B. 116.8
    C. 36.1
    D. 37.9
    E. 25.8

12. Which of the following is not considered a vital sign?

    A. Blood pressure
    B. Pulse rate
    C. Body temperature
    D. Respiration rate
    E. Weight

13. Which of the following positions requires the examination table to be raised in the middle with both ends pointing down?

    A. Fowler's
    B. Proctologic
    C. Knee-chest
    D. Sims'
    E. None of the above

14. Surgical procedures that require less than one day to perform, with no overnight stay for the patient, are called

    A. Outpatient surgery
    B. Ambulatory surgery
    C. Surgery without anesthesia
    D. Cryosurgery
    E. Daily surgery

15. A patient has an oral temperature of 100.5°F. The medical term for this condition is

    A. Hyperpyrexia
    B. Pyuria
    C. Pyrexia
    D. Hypothermia
    E. Normal

16. Color blindness is more common in

    A. Children
    B. Adults
    C. Elderly individuals
    D. Females
    E. Males

17. Which of the following respiratory terms means "difficult breathing"?

    A. Bradypnea
    B. Orthopnea
    C. Dyspnea
    D. Apnea
    E. Eupnea

18. Minor cauterization procedures are performed in the medical office with all of the following means except

    A. Lasers
    B. Hemostats
    C. Hot instruments
    D. Electric currents
    E. Caustic agents

19. The best and most accepted method of sterilization is

    A. Dry heat sterilization
    B. Zephrin chloride
    C. Bactericidal solution
    D. Moist heat sterilization
    E. Ultrasound sterilization

20. A tonometer is used to detect

    A. Nerve impairment of the ears
    B. Breathing capacity
    C. Contact dermatitis
    D. Glaucoma
    E. Heart rate

21. When temperature is taken rectally, the thermometer should be left in the rectum for how long?

    A. 3 seconds
    B. 3 minutes
    C. 5 minutes
    D. 10 minutes
    E. 15 minutes

22. The time needed for dry heat sterilization is

    A. 30 to 90 minutes
    B. 90 minutes to 3 hours
    C. 30 minutes to 3 hours
    D. 30 to 60 minutes
    E. 10 to 20 minutes

23. The shelf-life of a sterile package is

    A. 1 week
    B. 3 weeks
    C. 4 weeks
    D. 12 weeks
    E. 1 year

24. The adult normal range of respiration cycles per minute is

    A. 12–16
    B. 14–20
    C. 16–30
    D. 20–30
    E. 20–50

25. All of the following are responsibilities of the medical assistant in the physical preparation of the patient except

    A. Dressing the patient in a full gown
    B. Asking the patient to empty his or her bladder and bowel
    C. Obtaining and prescribing medications that are not expired
    D. Obtaining and recording the patient's weight and height
    E. Obtaining the vital signs

26. Autoclave indicator tape changes color (after autoclaving) to

    A. Red
    B. Blue
    C. Yellow
    D. Green
    E. Black

27. A method of screening auditory acuity by placing the stem of a vibrating tuning fork against the center of the patient's forehead (to evaluate whether hearing is the same in both ears) is known as

    A. Weber's test
    B. Audiology test
    C. Audiometer
    D. Schiller's test
    E. None of the above

28. The absence of respiration for periods lasting more than 15 seconds is called

    A. Bradypnea
    B. Hyperpnea
    C. Shock
    D. Cheyne-Stokes
    E. Apnea

29. The scalpel blade size often used to perform minor surgeries is number

    A. 5
    B. 10
    C. 15
    D. 25
    E. 30

30. Blood pressure readings should routinely be started at age

    A. 5 years
    B. 10 years
    C. 15 years
    D. 20 years
    E. 25 years

31. The general term for a surgical suture is

    A. Staple
    B. Ligature
    C. Needle biopsy
    D. Pointed needle
    E. Gauge

32. A Holter monitor is also called

    A. Phonocardiograph
    B. Echocardiograph
    C. Cardiac stress testing
    D. Cardiogram
    E. Ambulatory electrocardiograph

33. You should wear gloves

    A. All the time
    B. If the patient is suspected of having an infectious disease and if your hands might come in contact with the patient's intact skin
    C. If your hands might come in contact with the patient's nonintact skin or body fluids
    D. Only when directed by the physician
    E. In surgery only

34. Surgical hand washing is performed

    A. By scrubbing for 2 minutes
    B. With a nail brush and germicidal soap
    C. For 10 minutes using a clean hand brush
    D. For 10 minutes using a sterile hand brush
    E. For 20 minutes

35. In which of the following positions, used for the examination of the rectum, does the patient lie on the left side with the left leg slightly flexed?

    A. Sims'
    B. Prone
    C. Lithotomy
    D. Dorsal recumbent
    E. Trendelenburg's

ANSWER KEY

1.	B		19.	D
2.	B		20.	D
3.	D		21.	C
4.	D		22.	B
5.	A		23.	C
6.	C		24.	B
7.	C		25.	C
8.	E		26.	E
9.	C		27.	A
10.	A		28.	E
11.	C		29.	C
12.	E		30.	A
13.	B		31.	B
14.	A		32.	E
15.	C		33.	C
16.	E		34.	D
17.	C		35.	A
18.	B			

Administration of Medication

AREAS OF COMPETENCE

AAMA—ROLE DELINEATION STUDY AREAS OF COMPETENCE

Clinical

Patient Care

- Prepare and administer medications and immunizations
- Maintain medication and immunization records

(Chart continued on next page.)

AMT—RMA CERTIFICATION EXAM TOPICS

Clinical Pharmacology

- Terminology
- Injections
- Prescriptions
- Drugs

STRATEGIES TO SUCCESS

▶ Test-Taking Skills

Form study groups!

Find one or two well-prepared students in your class and arrange to meet for a study or homework session if possible. Working your way through questions and problems with other students will make you feel better about your own difficulties, and it will give you a chance to pose questions to your fellow students and combine your collective knowledge to help you understand material covered in class. You may find that another student can explain something better to you than the instructor could, or you may gain confidence in finding yourself explaining concepts to others that you didn't even realize you knew. During these study sessions, it's important that you know exactly why you are meeting. For example, you may want to work through some difficult practice questions, or you may want to review material covered in a chapter. Don't get bogged down on minor points or stray from the original goal of your meeting.

Drug Classifications

Drug classification: One method of classifying drugs is based on the form in which they are prepared (liquid or solid). See Table 13-1. Please also review this section in Chapter 5, *Pharmacology*.

AT A GLANCE	Classification of Drugs Based on Preparation Form	
Class	**Definition**	**Example**
LIQUID		
Aerosol	A pressurized dosage form in which solid or liquid drug particles are suspended in a gas to be dispensed in a cloud or mist	*Proventil*® inhaler
Elixir	A drug that is dissolved in a solution of alcohol and water	*Tylenol*® elixir
Emulsion	A mixture of oils in water	Cod liver oil
Liniment	A drug combined with oil, soap, alcohol, or water and applied externally	Camphor liniment

Table 13-1

Class	Definition	Example
Lotion	An aqueous preparation that contains suspended ingredients	*Nutraderm®* lotion
Spirit	A drug combined with an alcoholic solution that is volatile	Aromatic spirit of ammonia
Spray	A fine stream of medicated vapor (to treat the nose and throat)	*Dristan®* nasal spray
Syrup	A drug dissolved in a solution of sugar and water	*Robitussin®* cough syrup
Tincture	An extract of a therapeutic material in alcohol	Tincture of benzoin
SOLID		
Capsule	A drug contained in a gelatin capsule that is water soluble	*Benadryl®* capsule
Cream	A drug combined in a base that is generally nongreasy, resulting in a semisolid preparation	*Aristocort®* topical cream
Ointment	A drug combined with an oil base, resulting in a semisolid preparation	*Polysporin®* ointment
Suppository	A drug mixed with a firm base, such as cocoa butter, that is designed to melt at body temperature	*Nupercainal®* suppository
Tablet	Powdered drugs that have been pressed into a disc shape	Aspirin tablet

Table 13-1, continued

Measuring Medication and Dosage Calculations

Systems of measurement: Medical assistants must be familiar with the measurement of drug dosage. Three systems of measure are used in the United States for prescribing and administering medication: the metric system, the apothecaries' system, and the household system. They each have units of weight, volume, and length. Several common containers for measuring doses are shown in Figure 13-1 on p. 298.

Metric system: The most commonly used, most accurate, and easiest to use of all the measuring systems. The metric system is used for most scientific and medical measurements, and all pharmaceutical companies now use the metric system for labeling medications. It employs a uniform decimal scale (based on powers of 10). The basic metric units of measurement are the gram, liter, and meter. Prefixes added to the words *gram*, *liter*, and *meter* indicate smaller or larger units in the system. For example, the centimeter is 1/100th of a meter. For a list of prefixes used in the metric system, see Table 13-2. The unit abbreviations of the metric system are summarized in Table 13-3 on page 299.

Gram: The basic metric unit of weight (for solids).

Liter: The basic metric unit of volume (for liquids).

Meter: The basic metric unit of length.

Cubic centimeter (cc): The amount of space occupied by 1 milliliter: 1 mL = 1 cc.

Apothecaries' system: An older and less accurate measuring system than the metric system. The basic unit of weight in the apothecaries' system is the grain (gr), derived from the weight of a large grain of wheat. The remaining units of increasing weight are the scruple (scr), dram (dr), ounce (oz), and pound (lb). The pound, which equals 12 apothecaries' ounces, is not generally used in the administration of medication. The smallest unit of measurement of liquid volume is the minim (min), meaning "the least." A minim is approximately equivalent to a volume of water weighing one grain. The remaining units of increasing

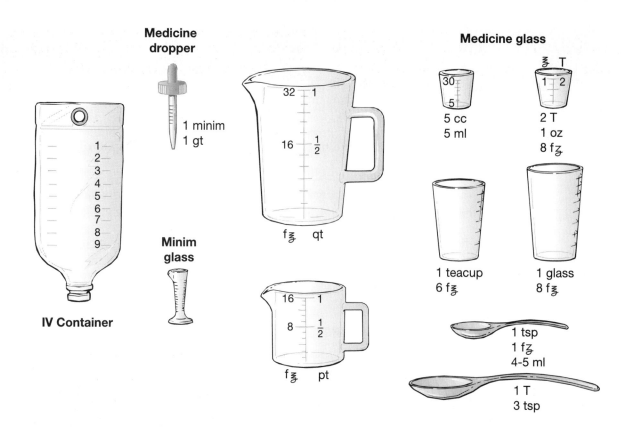

Figure 13-1. *Containers for measuring doses.*

AT A GLANCE		Prefixes in the Metric System	
Prefix	**Meaning**	**Prefix**	**Meaning**
deca-	× 10	kilo-	× 1000
deci-	÷ 10	milli-	÷ 1000
hect- / o	× 100	mega-	× 1,000,000
centi-	÷ 100	micro-	÷ 1,000,000

Table 13-2

volume are the fluidram (fl dr), fluid ounce (fl oz), pint (pt), quart (qt), and gallon (gal). Sixty grains equal one dram, and eight drams equal one ounce. In the apothecaries' system, dosage quantities are written in lowercase Roman numerals. By convention, the Roman numerals are written with a bar over them after the unit of measurement. For example, gr x̄ means 10 grains.

Household system: More complicated and less accurate for administering liquid medication than the other systems. The only household units of measurement used in the administration of medication are based on volume. The basic unit of liquid volume in the house-

hold system is the drop (gt, plural gtt). One drop is approximately equal to 0.6 mL in the metric system and 1 minim in the apothecaries' system. The remaining units, in order of increasing volume, are the teaspoon, tablespoon, ounce, teacup, and glass or cup. See Tables 13-4 and 13-5. (There are also units called the ounce and cup for measuring dry weight; do not confuse them with the units of liquid volume.)

Conversions Between Systems of Measurement

Conversion chart: Lists approximate, not exact, equivalents between systems. Check the chart several times, and place a ruler under the applicable line to be sure that you are reading it correctly. For a list of approximate conversions between the metric and apothecaries' systems, see Table 13-6.

Ratio method: *To convert aspirin gr x̄ to metric measurement (e.g., mg), follow these steps:*

1. Set up the first ratio:

    unknown quantity : known quantity

    x : 10 gr

2. Set up the second ratio to show the standard equivalence between the desired unit of measurement (mg) and the given unit of measurement (gr). There are 60 mg in 1 grain, so the second ratio is:

    60 mg : 1 gr

AT A GLANCE	Metric System Unit Abbreviations
Unit	**Abbreviation**
WEIGHT	
Microgram	μg
Milligram	mg
Gram	g
Kilogram	kg
VOLUME	
Milliliter	ml or mL
Cubic centimeter	cc
Liter	l or L
LENGTH	
Millimeter	mm
Centimeter	cm
Meter	m

Table 13-3

AT A GLANCE	Household System Liquid Equivalents
Measurement	**Equivalent**
1 teaspoon	60 drops
1 tablespoon	3 teaspoons
1 ounce	6 teaspoons = 2 tablespoons
1 teacup	6 ounces
1 glass or cup	8 ounces

Table 13-4

AT A GLANCE	Household System Abbreviations
Measurement	**Abbreviation**
Drop	gt
Teaspoon	tsp, t
Tablespoon	tbs, T
Ounce	oz
Cup	C

Table 13-5

AT A GLANCE	Approximate Conversions Between the Metric and Apothecaries' Systems
Metric System	**Apothecaries' System**
2 g (2000 mg)	30 gr
1 g (1000mg)	15 gr
600 mg (0.6 g)	10 gr
100 mg (0.1 g)	$1\frac{1}{2}$ gr
60 mg (0.06 g)	1 gr
30 mg (0.03 g)	$\frac{1}{2}$ gr
1 mg (0.001 g)	$\frac{1}{60}$ gr
0.1 mg (0.0001 g)	$\frac{1}{600}$ gr
Approximation formulas:	
grains $\times$ 60 = milligrams	
milligrams $\div$ 60 = grains	
grams $\times$ 15 = grains	
grains $\div$ 15 = grams	

Table 13-6

3. Create a proportion using the ratios:

   x mg : 10 gr :: 60 mg : 1 gr ("x milligrams are to 10 grains as 60 milligrams are to 1 grain")

   Note that the x, which stands for our unknown measurement in mg, is in the same place in relationship to the 10 gr as the 60 mg is to the 1gr. Your job now is to solve for x.

4. Multiply the outer and then the inner parts of the proportion and set them equal to each other:

   $x \times 1$ gr = 10 gr $\times$ 60 mg

5. Divide both sides of the equation by 1 gr, and then do the arithmetic.

   $x = 600$ mg

   So 10 grains of aspirin is the same as 600 milligrams of aspirin. 10 gr = 600 mg.

Fraction method: *To convert 300 mg of aspirin to an apothecaries' measure, follow these steps:*

1. Set up a fraction with the known dose as the numerator (on the top) and the unknown amount, representing grains, as the denominator (on the bottom):

   $\dfrac{300 \text{ mg}}{x}$

2. Set up a fraction with the standard equivalent, making sure that the units of measurement are in the same positions as in the first fraction:

   $\dfrac{60 \text{ mg}}{1 \text{ gr}}$

3. Set up a proportion with both fractions; in other words, set the two fractions equal to each other:

   $\dfrac{300 \text{ mg}}{x} = \dfrac{60 \text{ mg}}{1 \text{ gr}}$

4. Cross multiply:

   $x \times 60$ mg = 300 mg $\times$ 1 gr

5. Divide both sides of the equation by 60 mg, and then do the arithmetic.

   $x = 5$ gr

(Notice that the two methods are interchangeable. The ratio method uses : and :: where the fraction method uses / and =, and the initial placement of the unknown quantity differs. But the results are the same.)

Calculating Drug Doses

Calculating drug doses: On occasion, it is necessary to calculate drug doses when the drug is not available in the exact amount the physician has prescribed. Drug doses can be calculated with either the ratio method or the fraction method.

Ratio method: If a physician orders 500 mg of a drug that comes in tablets of 250 mg, follow these steps to find the number of tables you will need for the correct dose:

1. Set up a ratio of the unknown quantity (in this case, representing tablets) to the known quantity:

   x : 500 mg

2. Set up a ratio of the known conversion equivalence:

   1 tab : 250 mg

3. Put the ratios into a proportion:

   x : 500 mg :: 1 tab : 250 mg

4. Multiply the outer and then the inner parts of the proportion:

   $x \times 250$ mg = 500 mg $\times$ 1 tab

5. To solve for x, divide both sides of the equation by 250 mg, and then do the arithmetic.

   $x = 2$ tabs

Fraction method: If a physician orders 30 mg of a drug that comes in capsules containing only 10 mg, follow these steps:

1. Set up a fraction with the dose ordered and the unknown number of capsules:

   $\dfrac{30 \text{ mg}}{x}$

2. Set up a fraction with the known conversion equivalence. Make sure that the units of measurement are in the same position as in the first fraction:

   $\dfrac{10 \text{ mg}}{1 \text{ cap}}$

3. Set the two fractions equal to each other:

   $\dfrac{30 \text{ mg}}{x} = \dfrac{10 \text{ mg}}{1 \text{ cap}}$

4. Cross multiply:

   $x \times 10$ mg = 30 mg $\times$ 1 cap

5. To solve for x, divide both sides of the equation by 10 mg, and then do the arithmetic.

   $x = 3$ caps

Methods of Administering Medications

"Seven rights" of drug administration: Never deviate from these seven principles: right patient, right drug, right dose, right time, right route, right technique, right documentation.

Right patient: Always check the name on the order, then ask the patient to tell you his or her name.

Right drug: Read the drug label before you take the container off the shelf, before you administer the drug, and before you put the container back on the shelf. Make sure to check the expiration date, and never use a drug that has passed this date.

Right dose: Compare the dose on the order with the dose you prepare.

Right time: If a drug must be taken after a meal, make sure that the patient has eaten recently.

Right route: Make sure that the route you are preparing to use matches the route the doctor ordered.

Right technique: Always use the proper administrative technique.

Right documentation: Document the procedure immediately after administering the drug. Include the date, time, drug name, dose, administration route, patient reaction, education of the patient about the drug, and your initials.

Route of administration: Medication may be administered by numerous routes, including oral, sublingual, buccal, inhalation, topical, rectal, urethral, vaginal, parenteral (intramuscular, subcutaneous, intradermal, or intravenous), ophthalmic, and otic.

Oral administration: The drug is given by mouth in either a solid form (tablet, capsule, or powder) or a liquid form (water-based solution, suspension, or alcohol solution). The drug is absorbed into the bloodstream through the lining of the stomach and intestine. This method is easy, safe, and economical, but drug absorption is slow and may be affected by the presence of food. Some medications may also cause nausea or stomach discomfort.

Sublingual administration: The medication must be placed under the tongue until it dissolves. See Figure 13-2. This method is faster than the oral method.

Buccal administration: The medication is placed in the mouth and absorbed in the buccal area. The patient should not chew or swallow the medication. See Figure 13-3.

Inhalation administration: The medication is given in the form of gases, sprays, or aerosol mists (fluid droplets). The respiratory tract absorbs medication more rapidly than any other mucous membrane. One inhalation medication that should be kept in every medical practice is oxygen.

Topical administration: Used in treating skin disorders. The medication is applied directly to affected areas of the skin. Topical medications come in the form of sprays, creams, lotions, ointments, transdermal patches, and compresses.

Transdermal drug delivery (TDD): A method of applying a drug to unbroken skin. The drug is absorbed continuously through the skin and enters the bloodstream. It is used particularly for the administration of nicotine, nitroglycerin, and scopolamine. To promote adhesion to the skin, the patch should be applied to a clean, dry area without hair.

Rectal administration: Useful if the patient is nauseated, vomiting, or unconscious. The best time to administer a rectal drug is after a bowel movement or the elimination of an enema. A suppository must be inserted about 2 inches above the internal anal sphincter.

Urethral administration: A solution is instilled into the bladder using a catheter.

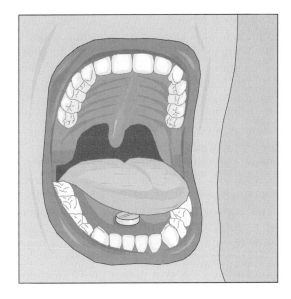

Figure 13-2. *Place a sublingual drug under the tongue.*

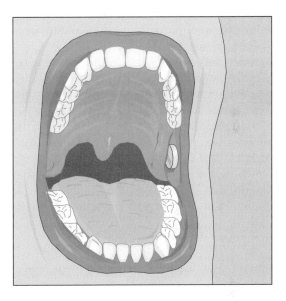

Figure 13-3. *Place a buccal drug between the cheek and gum.*

Vaginal administration: A liter or more of a solution of medication in warm water is introduced as a douche into the vagina under low pressure. Other forms of medication are inserted into the vagina with an applicator.

Parenteral administration: A medication is given in the form of an injection. Drugs are absorbed more rapidly and completely than by most other routes. In some cases, injection is the only way a drug can be given (for example, to an unconscious patient). The disadvantages of the parenteral route are that all equipment must be sterile; that the method is often expensive, painful, and awkward for patients to administer themselves; and that there is a danger of injecting a drug incorrectly into a vein, which could cause serious harm or even death.

Intradermal injection: Given into the dermal layer of the skin. A very short needle of small gauge is used. The angle of insertion is 15 degrees, nearly parallel to the skin. Absorption is slow. Only a small amount of medication may be injected (0.01 to 0.2 cc). The anterior forearm is the most common area for injection. See Figure 13-4. The gauge is usually 25 to 27. When an intradermal injection is correctly administered, a small wheal is raised on the skin. See Figure 13-5. The most common uses of intradermal injections are to administer allergy tests and tuberculin skin tests.

Subcutaneous (SC) injection: Given into the layer of fatty tissue that lies just below the skin. The most common sites for subcutaneous injections are the upper lateral part of the arm, anterior thigh, upper back, and abdomen. See Figure 13-6. The needle length varies from 1/2 to 5/8 inch, and the gauge ranges from 23 to 25. The needle should be inserted at a 45 degree angle to the skin. Drugs given subcutaneously must be isotonic, nonviscous, water-soluble, and nonirritating. The amount of drug injected through the subcutaneous route should not exceed 2 cc. Medications commonly administered through this route include insulin, local anesthetics, epinephrine, and allergy treatments.

Intramuscular (IM) injection: Given deep into a muscle. Muscles can absorb a greater amount of fluid without discomfort to the patient, and intramuscular injections are preferred for substances that can irritate the skin. The most common muscles used for this method of injection are the deltoid, gluteus medius, and vastus lateralis. See Figure 13-7. For injection of the gluteus muscle site, the patient must be in the prone position. For injection of the vastus lateralis site, the patient may be sitting or in the recumbent

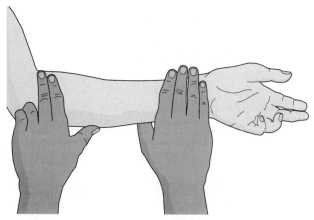

Figure 13-4. *This space is available for intradermal injection sites.*

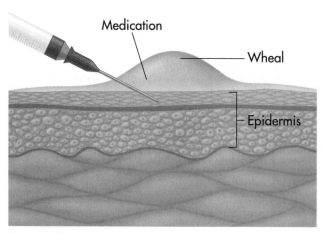

Figure 13-5. *Medication collects under the skin, forming a wheal, during an intradermal injection.*

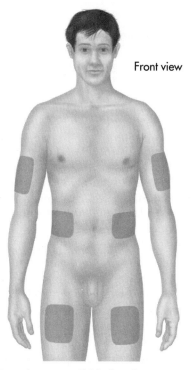

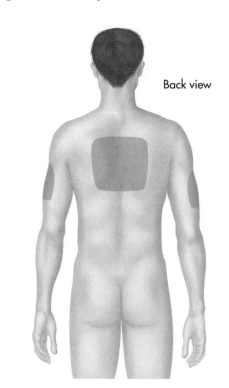

Figure 13-6. *Many sites are available for subcutaneous injections.*

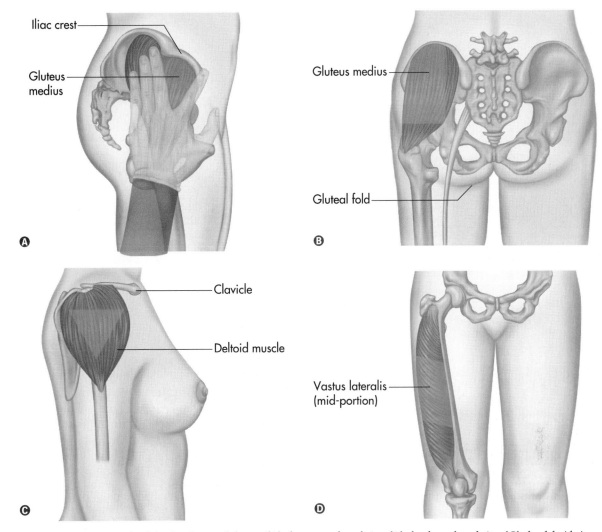

Figure 13-7. *For intramuscular injection in an adult, use (A) the ventrogluteal site, (B) the dorsogluteal site, (C) the deltoid site, or (D) the vastus lateralis site.*

position. The needle should be 1 to 3 inches in length or sometimes longer. The gauge of the needle ranges between 18 and 23. The angle of insertion is 90 degrees. Dosage may vary from 0.5 to 5 mL. For medications that are irritating to subcutaneous tissue and skin tissue or that may cause discoloration of the skin, the Z-track method should be used. See Figure 13-8 on page 304. The vastus lateralis muscle in the thigh is the preferred injection site for children under 3 years of age. Penicillin is often injected intramuscularly.

Intravenous (IV) injection: Given directly into a vein. Intravenous injection is usually used in an emergency situation for an immediate effect. The disadvantage is that painful infection may result. Rotation of the sites is necessary if injections are given repeatedly. Needles are 1 to 1-1/2 inch in length. The gauges are usually between 20 and 21.

IV drip: The insertion into a vein of a tube or a needle through which fluids are slowly added to the bloodstream over a period of time. It is also called infusion. The IV drip should not be confused with intravenous injection.

Ophthalmic administration: Drugs are placed into the patient's eye.

Otic administration: Drugs are placed into the patient's ear.

Needles and Syringes

Needle: Consists of several parts: hub, shaft, lumen, point, and bevel. See Figure 13-9 on page 304.

Needle gauge: The inside diameter of the needle. A larger gauge indicates a smaller diameter. The common range for administering medication is between 18 and 27 gauge.

Needle length: Ranges between 3/8 of an inch and 3 inches.

Syringe: Used for inserting fluids into the body. It is usually made of plastic. A syringe consists of three parts: barrel, flange (rim), and plunger. See Figure 13-10 on page 305.

Hypodermic syringes: Available in 2-, 2.5-, 3-, and 5-cc sizes. They are commonly used to administer intramuscular injections.

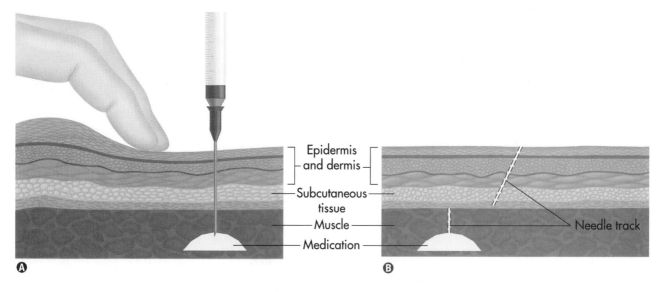

Figure 13-8. *Use the Z-track method for IM injection of irritating solutions. (A) Pull the skin to one side before inserting the needle. (B) After injecting the drug, release the skin to seal off the needle track.*

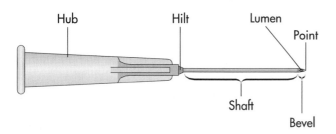

Figure 13-9. *Understanding the parts of a needle will help you use it correctly.*

Insulin syringe: Designed for an insulin injection. It is calibrated in units (U); 100 U = 1 mL. The most commonly used size is the 100 U syringe (with a capacity of 100 units), divided into increments of 2 units. Syringes are also available in 40 U and 80 U sizes.

Tuberculin syringe: Has a capacity of 1 cc. The calibrations are divided into tenths (0.1) and hundredths (0.01) of a cubic centimeter.

Prefilled syringe: Known as a cartridge. It is a sterile, disposable syringe. Needle units are packaged by the manufacturer with a single dose of medication inside, ready to administer.

Ampule: A small, sealed glass container that holds a single dose of medication.

Vial: A closed glass container with a rubber stopper protected by a soft metal cap. There are two types: single- and multiple-dose.

Deltoid muscle: Located at the top of the arm on the upper, outer surface. It is a good site for a small amount of medication. The deltoid is commonly used for injections of tetanus boosters in adults, rabies vaccine after exposure, and vitamin B_{12}. Major blood vessels and nerves in the upper arm are located in the posterior portion of the arm. A 23-gauge, 1-inch needle is most frequently used for the injections in the deltoid muscle. A 25-gauge, 5/8-inch needle is used for a small arm.

Gluteus medius muscle: Most commonly used for deep intramuscular injections, for injections of viscous medications (antibiotics), and for injections of irritating drugs. This site should not be used in infants.

Medication Orders

Medication order: A directive issued by a physician telling a nurse or another health care worker which drug to administer. These orders should be written down so that there is little chance of error. In an emergency situation, when there is no time to give written instructions, the order should be written down and signed by the physician within 24 hours. Orders are written on the physician's order sheet in a patient's chart. No medication should ever be given out without an order.

Prescription pads: Used to write medication orders for outpatients.

Medication order components: The patient's full name, date of the order, name of the drug preceded by the abbreviation *Rx*, dosage, route of administration, time and frequency, physician's signature (without which the medication order is not legal), number of refills and quantity (preceded by the word *repetatur*), and the physician's DEA number on all prescriptions for controlled substances.

Types of Drug Orders

Routine order: Specifies that a drug be administered until a discontinuation order is written or until a specified termination date is reached.

Standing order: Outlines a specific condition for which the drug is to be administered. These orders are

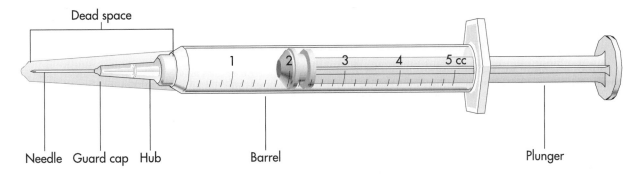

Dead space

Needle Guard cap Hub   Barrel   Plunger

Figure 13-10. *Know the parts of a standard syringe.*

frequently used in critical care units, where the patient's condition changes rapidly, and in long-term care facilities.

PRN order: Specifies that a drug be given only when the patient needs it, such as for pain or before an operation or diagnostic procedure. (PRN stands for *pro re nata*, roughly "for a circumstance that has come to be" or "as the situation requires.")

Stat order: A single order that is administered immediately, written usually for emergencies.

Setting up Medications

Diligence: In setting up medication to be administered, be sure to observe the "seven rights" of drug administration. Get information from the Kardex, medication record, or medicine cart, and concentrate on nothing but the task at hand. Do not engage in a conversation with someone else while you are trying to prepare and administer the medication.

Cleanliness: Clean up by washing your hands, and try not to touch the drugs at all. Never give a pill that has fallen on the floor. Keep unit doses sealed until you are ready to give them.

Tablets: After you have calculated the correct dose, you may find that you need only half or a quarter of a tablet. If you need to divide a tablet, use a pill cutter or a knife to make a quick, clean break. If you have to touch the pill to break it, use a tissue. Never open the tablet package until you administer the medication to the patient. If you need tablets from a bottle, pour them into the medicine cup without touching them. Sometimes tablets must be crushed or capsules opened. Check the reference book to make sure that such a procedure is permissible. Never crush enteric-coated or sustained-action medications.

Liquid medications: Remove the cap and place it upside down to prevent contamination. Hold the bottle so that the label is against the palm of your hand in order to prevent medication from running down the side of the bottle and damaging the label. Place the medication cup on a stable, flat surface at eye level to ensure accuracy. Do not hold the cup at eye level, because you might tip the cup as you pour.

Recording Medication Administration

Kardex file: A card-filing system that serves as a quick reference to the needs of a patient. Each card is folded once and lists up-to-date information about medications, treatments, and care. All information is written in pencil, so it can be erased and updated.

Medicine card: Used to record the patient's name, room and bed number, name of the drug, dose, route, and time at which the drug is to be given. One medicine card is written for each type of drug the patient is to receive; the information is copied over from the Kardex file.

Medication administration record (MAR): A convenient way to document all the drugs administered to a patient every day, especially if there are several drugs given at different times. If the drug is to be given regularly, a complete schedule is written for all administration times. Each time a dose is administered, the health care worker checks off the time at which it was given and initials the entry.

Patient chart or **medical record:** All events related to the treatment of a patient, including the administration of medications, need to be recorded in the patient's chart as a permanent record of care received. When medication is administered, you must record the drug's name, the strength and amount, the route, the times at which it is given, and the initials and signature of the health care worker who administered it.

Vaccinations

Immunization: The process of rendering a person immune to a disease.

Artificial immunity: Produced by the administration of vaccines or other forms of immunization.

Vaccines: Made from dead or harmless infectious agents. They trigger the immune response in the body to manufacture antibodies against the particular disease-causing agent. The childhood immunization schedule is summarized in Figure 13-11. For a recommended schedule of vaccinations for adolescents 11 to 12 years of age, see Table 13-7 on page 307.

Recommended Childhood Immunization Schedule
United States, January - December 1997

Vaccines[1] are listed under the routinely recommended ages. [Bars] indicate range of acceptable ages for vaccination. [Shaded bars] indicate *catch-up vaccination:* at 11-12 years of age, hepatitis B vaccine should be administered to children not previously vaccinated, and Varicella vaccine should be administered to children not previously vaccinated who lack a reliable history of chickenpox.

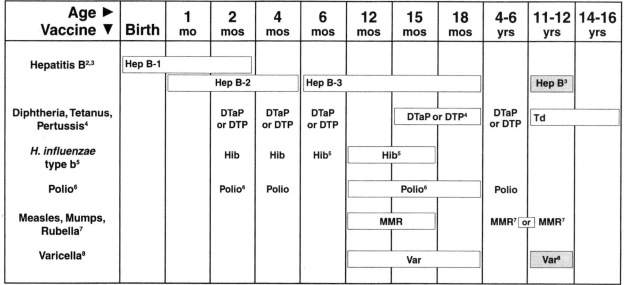

Age ▶ Vaccine ▼	Birth	1 mo	2 mos	4 mos	6 mos	12 mos	15 mos	18 mos	4-6 yrs	11-12 yrs	14-16 yrs
Hepatitis B[2,3]	Hep B-1										
		Hep B-2			Hep B-3					Hep B[3]	
Diphtheria, Tetanus, Pertussis[4]			DTaP or DTP	DTaP or DTP	DTaP or DTP		DTaP or DTP[4]		DTaP or DTP	Td	
H. influenzae type b[5]			Hib	Hib	Hib[5]	Hib[5]					
Polio[6]			Polio[6]	Polio		Polio[6]			Polio		
Measles, Mumps, Rubella[7]						MMR			MMR[7] or	MMR[7]	
Varicella[8]						Var				Var[8]	

Approved by the Advisory Committee on Immunization Practices (ACIP), the American Academy of Pediatrics (AAP), and the American Academy of Family Physicians (AAFP).

IS 5081

(For **necessary footnotes** and important information, see reverse side.)

[1] This schedule indicates the recommended age for routine administration of currently licensed childhood vaccines. Some combination vaccines are available and may be used whenever administration of all components of the vaccine is indicated. Providers should consult the manufacturers' package inserts for detailed recommendations.

[2] **Infants born to HBsAg-negative mothers** should receive 2.5 μg of Merck vaccine (Recombivax HB) or 10 μg of SmithKline Beecham (SB) vaccine (Engerix-B). The 2nd dose should be administered ≥ 1 mo after the 1st dose.
Infants born to HBsAg-positive mothers should receive 0.5 mL hepatitis B immune globulin (HBIG) within 12 hrs of birth, and either 5 μg of Merck vaccine (Recombivax HB) or 10 μg of SB vaccine (Engerix-B) at a separate site. The 2nd dose is recommended at 1-2 mos of age and the 3rd dose at 6 mos of age.
Infants born to mothers whose HBsAg status is unknown should receive either 5 μg of Merck vaccine (Recombivax HB) or 10 μg of SB vaccine (Engerix-B) within 12 hrs of birth. The 2nd dose of vaccine is recommended at 1 mo of age and the 3rd dose at 6 mos of age. Blood should be drawn at the time of delivery to determine the mother's HBsAg status; if it is positive, the infant should receive HBIG as soon as possible (no later than 1 wk of age). The dosage and timing of subsequent vaccine doses should be based upon the mother's HBsAg status.

[3] Children and adolescents who have not been vaccinated against hepatitis B in infancy may begin the series during any clinic visit. Those who have not previously received 3 doses of hepatitis B vaccine should initiate or complete the series during the 11-12 year-old visit. The 2nd dose should be administered at least 1 mo after the 1st dose, and the 3rd dose should be administered at least 4 mos after the 1st dose and at least 2 mos after the 2nd dose.

[4] DTaP (diphtheria and tetanus toxoids and acellular pertussis vaccine) is the preferred vaccine for all doses in the vaccination series, including completion of the series in

children who have received ≥1 dose of whole-cell DTP vaccine. Whole-cell DTP is an acceptable alternative to DTaP. The 4th dose of DTaP) may be administered as early as 12 months of age, provided 6 months have elapsed since the 3rd dose, and if the child is considered unlikely to return at 15-18 mos of age. Td (tetanus and diphtheria toxoids, absorbed, for adult use) is recommended at 11-12 years of age if at least 5 years have elapsed since the last dose of DTP, DTaP, or DT. Subsequent routine Td boosters are recommended every 10 years.

[5] Three *H. influenzae* type b (Hib) conjugate vaccines are licensed for infant use. If PRP-OMP (PedvaxHIB [Merck]) is administered at 2 and 4 mos of age, a dose at 6 mos is not required. After completing the primary series, any Hib conjugate vaccine may be used as a booster.

[6] Two poliovirus vaccines are currently licensed in the US: inactivated poliovirus vaccine (IPV) and oral poliovirus vaccine (OPV). The following schedules are all acceptable by the ACIP, the AAP, and the AAFP, and parents and providers may choose among them:
    1. IPV at 2 and 4 mos; OPV at 12-18 mos and 4-6 yr
    2. IPV at 2, 4, 12-18 mos, and 4-6 yr
    3. OPV at 2, 4, 6-18 mos, and 4-6 yr
The ACIP routinely recommends schedule 1. IPV is the only poliovirus vaccine recommended for immunocompromised persons and their household contacts.

[7] The 2nd dose of MMR is routinely recommended at 4-6 yrs of age or at 11-12 yrs of age, but may be administered during any visit, provided at least 1 month has elapsed since receipt of the 1st dose and that both doses are administered at or after 12 months of age.

[8] Susceptible children may receive Varicella vaccine (Var) at any visit after the first birthday, and those who lack a reliable history of chickenpox should be immunized during the 11-12 year-old visit. Children ≥ 13 years of age should receive 2 doses, at least 1 mos apart.

Immunization Protects Children

Regular checkups at your pediatrician's office or local health clinic are an important way to keep children healthy.

By making sure that your child gets immunized on time, you can provide the best available defense against many dangerous childhood diseases. Immunizations protect children against: hepatitis B, polio, measles, mumps, rubella (German measles), pertussis (whooping cough), diphtheria, tetanus (lockjaw), *Haemophilus influenzae* type b, and chickenpox. All of these immunizations need to be given before children are 2 years old in order for them to be protected during their most vulnerable period. Are your child's immunizations up-to-date?

The chart on the other side of this fact sheet includes immunization recommendations from the American Academy of Pediatrics. Remember to keep track of your child's immunizations—it's the only way you can be sure your child is up-to-date. Also, check with your pediatrician or health clinic at each visit to find out if your child needs any booster shots or if any new vaccines have been recommended since this schedule was prepared.

If you don't have a pediatrician, call your local health department. Public health clinics usually have supplies of vaccine and may give shots free.

American Academy of Pediatrics

The information contained in this publication should not be used as a substitute for the medical care and advice of your pediatrician. There may be variations in treatment that your pediatrician may recommend based on individual facts and circumstances.

Figure 13-11. *This schedule shows recommended ages for various childhood immunizations.*

Recommended Schedule of Vaccinations for Adolescents 11–12 Years of Age

Vaccine	Indications	Dose	Frequency	Route
Hepatitis A	An increased risk of hepatitis A infection or its complications	720 ELISA Units/0.5 mL	A total of two doses at 0* and 6–12 months	IM
		25 U/0.5 mL	A total of two doses at 0 and 6–18 months	IM
Hepatitis B	No previous vaccination for hepatitis B	5 μg/0.5 mL	A total of three doses at 0, 1–2, and 4–6 months	IM
		10 μg/0.5 mL	A total of three doses at 0, 1–2, and 4–6 months	IM
Influenza	An increased risk for complications caused by influenza or contact with persons at increased risk for these complications	0.5 mL	Annually (September–December)	IM
Measles, mumps, and rubella (MMR)	Adolescents not vaccinated previously with two doses of measles vaccine at $\geq$ 12 months of age.	0.5 mL	One dose	SC
Tetanus and diphtheria toxoids (Td)	No vaccination within the previous 5 years	0.5 mL	Every 10 years	IM
Varicella	No previous vaccination and no reliable history of chickenpox	0.5 mL	One dose (two doses at 0 and 4–8 weeks for those $\geq$ 13 years of age)	SC

*0 represents the time of the initial dose, and subsequent numbers represent time units after the initial dose.

Table 13-7

Rabies

Rabies: There are two types of rabies immunizing products. Rabies vaccines induce an active immune response that includes the production of neutralizing antibodies. Rabies immune globulins (RIG) provide rapid, passive immune protection that persists for only a short time (a half-life of approximately 21 days).

Exposure to rabies: Rabies can be transmitted only when the virus is introduced into open cuts or wounds in skin or mucous membranes. Two categories of exposure (bite and nonbite) should be considered.

Bite: Any penetration of the skin by teeth constitutes a bite exposure. Bites to the face and hands carry the highest risk, but the site of the bite should not influence the decision to begin treatment.

Nonbite: Scratches, abrasions, open wounds, or mucous membranes contaminated with saliva or other potentially infectious material (such as brain tissue) from a rabid animal constitute nonbite exposure. If the material containing the virus is dry, the virus can be considered noninfectious.

Rabies vaccine: Studies conducted in the United States by the CDC have shown that a regimen of one dose of HRIG and five doses of HDCV over a 28-day period is safe and induces an excellent antibody response in all recipients. The schedule of the HDCV vaccinations is:

- 1st dose at 0 days
- 2nd dose 3 days after the first
- 3rd dose 7 days after the first
- 4th dose 14 days after the first
- 5th dose 28 days after the first

Intramuscular injection of rabies vaccine should be administered only in the deltoid muscle for post-exposure. Subcutaneous injection should be administered for pre-exposure.

Hepatitis

Hepatitis A vaccine: Should be stored and shipped at temperatures ranging from 35.6°F (2°C) to 46.4°F (8°C) and should not be frozen. The vaccine should be administered intramuscularly into the deltoid muscle. A needle length appropriate for the patient's age and size should be used.

Meningitis

Neisseria meningitidis: Causes both endemic and epidemic disease, principally meningitis and meningococcemia. As a result of the control of *Haemophilus influenzae* type b infections (which can result in meningitis), *Neisseria meningitidis* has become the leading cause of bacterial meningitis in children and young adults in the United States. The incidence of meningococcal disease peaks in late winter to early spring. Attack rates are highest among children 3 to 12 months of age and then steadily decline among older age groups. Persons who have certain medical conditions are at increased risk for developing meningococcal infection. Persons who have other diseases associated with immunosuppression (e.g., HIV or *Streptococcus pneumoniae* infection) may be at higher risk for acquiring meningococcal disease and for disease caused by some other encapsulated bacteria.

Meningococcal vaccine: Routine vaccination with the quadrivalent meningococcal polysaccharide vaccine is not recommended because of its relative ineffectiveness in children less than 2 years of age (among whom risk for endemic disease is highest) and its relatively short duration of protection. However, the polysaccharide meningococcal vaccine is useful for controlling serogroup C meningococcal outbreaks.

Indications for use: In general, the use of polysaccharide meningococcal vaccine should be restricted to persons 2 years of age or older; however, children as

young as 3 months of age may be vaccinated to elicit short-term protection against serogroup A meningococcal disease (two doses administered 3 months apart should be considered for children 3-18 months of age). Routine vaccination with the quadrivalent vaccine is recommended for certain high-risk groups, including persons who have terminal complement component deficiencies.

Administration: Primary vaccination, for both adults and children, is administered subcutaneously as a single 0.5 mL dose. The vaccine can be administered at the same time as other vaccines but at a different anatomical site (i.e., deltoid muscle or buttocks).

Pneumonia

Pneumococcal polysaccharide vaccine: Administer pneumococcal vaccine to children who are at risk and to adolescents who have chronic illnesses associated with increased risk for pneumococcal disease or its complications. Use adolescents' visits to providers to ensure that the vaccine has been administered to persons for whom it is indicated. One dose of 0.5 mL, IM or SC.

Typhoid Fever

Incidence of Typhoid Fever: The incidence of typhoid fever declined steadily in the United States from 1900 to 1960 and has since remained low.

Typhoid vaccine: Three typhoid vaccines are currently available for use in the United States.

Indications for use: Routine typhoid vaccination is not recommended in the United States. However, vaccination is indicated for the following groups:

- Travelers to areas in which there is a recognized risk of exposure to *Salmonella typhi*—The risk is greatest for travelers to developing countries.
- Persons with intimate exposure to (e.g., household contact with) a documented *S. typhi* carrier
- Microbiology laboratory technicians who work frequently with *S. typhi*—No evidence indicates that typhoid vaccine is useful in controlling common-source outbreaks.

Cholera

Incidence: Since 1961, cholera caused by the El Tor biotype has been epidemic throughout much of Asia, the Middle East, and Africa, and in certain parts of Europe.

Transmission: Infection is acquired primarily by consuming contaminated water or food; person-to-person transmission is rare.

Cholera vaccine: Cholera vaccines, whether prepared from Classic or El Tor strains, are of limited usefulness.

Indications for use: The Public Health Service no longer requires cholera vaccination for travelers coming to the United States from cholera-infected areas, and the World Health Organization (WHO) no longer recommends cholera vaccination for travel to or from cholera-infected areas.

Tuberculosis

Tuberculin skin test: Several methods are used. The most common are the Mantoux test and the tine test.
Mantoux test: Administered using an intradermal needle and syringe. It must be read within 48 to 78 hours. The amount of solution that is injected is 0.1 mL. A short needle with a gauge of 26 to 27 is used.
Mantoux tuberculin skin test results: Induration of less than 5 mm is considered a negative reaction. According to the American Lung Association, induration of 5 mm or more is considered a positive reaction for infants, children, adults who have had close contact with active tuberculosis, persons with known or suspected HIV infection, and persons whose immune systems are suppressed. Induration of 10 mm or more is considered a positive reaction in persons who are foreign-born from high-prevalence countries; persons with other medical risk factors; health care workers; migrant workers; and residents of long-term care facilities, nursing homes, and correctional institutions. Induration of 15 mm or more is considered a positive reaction in all other persons.
Tine test: Uses a sterile plastic unit containing four stainless steel tines for puncturing the skin.
Induration: An area of hardened tissue.
BCG vaccine: A live vaccine derived from a strain of *Mycobacterium bovis*. Many different BCG vaccines are available worldwide.
Indications for BCG use: The presence or size of a postvaccination tuberculin skin-test reaction does not predict whether BCG will provide any protection against TB. BCG vaccination should be considered for an infant or child who has a negative tuberculin skin-test result in the following circumstances:

- The child is exposed continually to an untreated or ineffectively treated patient who has infectious pulmonary TB, and the child cannot be separated from the presence of the infectious patient or given long-term primary preventative therapy.

- The child is exposed continually to a patient who has infectious pulmonary TB caused by *Mycobacterium tuberculosis* strains resistant to isoniazid and rifampin, and the child cannot be separated from the presence of the infectious patient.

BCG vaccination is not recommended for children infected with HIV.
Complications: Although BCG vaccination often results in local adverse effects, serious or long-term complications are rare. The most serious complication of BCG vaccination is disseminated BCG infection. Postvaccination BCG-induced tuberculin reactivity ranges from no induration to an induration of 19 mm at the skin-test site.

Yellow Fever

Yellow fever: An enzootic viral disease transmitted among nonhuman primate hosts by various mosquito vectors. At present, yellow fever occurs only in the African and South American jungles.
Yellow fever vaccine: Yellow fever vaccine is a live, attenuated virus preparation. The vaccine should be stored at temperatures between 5°C (41°F) and –30°C (–22°F)—preferably frozen, below 0°C (32°F)—until it is reconstituted by the addition of diluent sterile, physiologic saline supplied by the manufacturer. Unused vaccine should be discarded within 1 hour after reconstitution.
Primary vaccination: For persons of all ages, a single subcutaneous injection of 0.5 mL of reconstituted vaccine is used.
Booster doses: The International Health Regulations require revaccination at intervals of 10 years.

STRATEGIES TO SUCCESS

▶ Test-Taking Skills

Use all of the time allotted!
It may be tempting to hand in your exam after you have answered the last question, but your score can be improved if you use all the time you are given. Look over your exam and make sure that you answered every question, that the choices are clearly marked, and that the answer sheet numbers match the exam question numbers. If you have time, cover up your answers and rework some of the problems. Especially rework problems involving math or questions you originally thought were difficult. If a question still seems too complicated to decipher, try rephrasing and expressing it in your own terms. When a question involves math, make sure that you understand what the question is asking for. What do you need to calculate? Break down the question into its elements, list all the known variables, and name the unknown variable. Check your math to make sure that you didn't make any mistakes.

CHAPTER 13 REVIEW

Instructions:

Answer the following questions. Check your answers in the *Answer Key* that follows this section.

1. The basic unit of liquid volume in the household system is the
   A. Grain
   B. Teaspoon
   C. Drop
   D. Minim
   E. Gram

2. A prefilled syringe is also known as a(n)
   A. Tuberculin syringe
   B. Hypodermic syringe
   C. Insulin syringe
   D. Cartridge
   E. Flange

3. Which of the following is an advantage of intramuscular injections?
   A. IM injections cause less irritation of the skin than SC injections
   B. It's easy to tell that they have been correctly administered, because a wheal forms on the skin
   C. One can give a greater amount of medication in an IM injection
   D. Both A and C
   E. All of the above

4. Which of the following sites for injection should not be used for infants?
   A. Vastus lateralis muscle
   B. Abdominal muscle
   C. Gluteus medius muscle
   D. Anterior thigh
   E. B and D

5. Which of the following injection methods should be chosen for medications that are irritating or may cause discoloration of the skin?
   A. Subcutaneous
   B. Intravenous
   C. Z-track
   D. Intradermal
   E. Intramuscular

6. Medication applied in patch form is called
   A. Buccal
   B. Topical ointment
   C. Tine test
   D. Mantoux test
   E. Transdermal

7. The needle gauges usually used for intravenous injections are
   A. 18–19
   B. 20–21
   C. 23–24
   D. 26–27
   E. 28–32

8. Which of the following is a unit of weight in the metric system?
   A. Gram
   B. Liter
   C. Grain
   D. Minim
   E. Pound

9. A drug combined with an oil base, resulting in a semisolid preparation, is a(n)
   A. Cream
   B. Ointment
   C. Tablet
   D. Suppository
   E. Liniment

10. The doctor has ordered a dose of medicine to be 300 mg, but the medicine is available only in 50 mg tablets. What is the correct dose?
    A. 5 tablets
    B. 6 tablets
    C. 320 mg
    D. 75 mg
    E. None of the above

11. The doctor has ordered 120 mg of a drug that comes only in 30 mg tablets. How many tablets constitute a dose?
    A. 3
    B. 4
    C. 6
    D. 12
    E. 15

12. The metric system employs a uniform scale based on powers of
    A. 1
    B. 10
    C. 50
    D. 100
    E. None of the above

13. Which of the following is the oldest and least accurate type of measurement system for drugs?
    A. Household
    B. Metric
    C. Apothecaries'
    D. English
    E. Both A and B

14. In the household system, one glass is equal to
    A. 2 ounces
    B. 4 ounces
    C. 6 ounces
    D. 8 ounces
    E. 12 ounces

15. How far above the internal anal sphincter must a suppository be inserted?
    A. 1 inch
    B. 2 inches
    C. 3 inches
    D. 4 inches
    E. 5 inches

16. The most commonly used size of insulin syringe is the
    A. 20 unit
    B. 40 unit
    C. 60 unit
    D. 80 unit
    E. 100 unit

17. The angle of insertion for intradermal injections is
    A. 5 degrees
    B. 15 degrees
    C. 45 degrees
    D. 90 degrees
    E. 30 degrees

18. Which of the following needle gauges is used for the Mantoux test?
    A. 16–17
    B. 19–20
    C. 20–22
    D. 23–24
    E. 26–27

19. The physician asks you to convert 30 grains of medication into the metric system. Which of the following represents an accurate conversion?
    A. 2 grams
    B. 2 drams
    C. 1 gram
    D. 3 ounces
    E. 3 grams

20. The last vaccination for rabies must be scheduled no later than how long after the first vaccination?
    A. Two weeks
    B. Four weeks
    C. Eight weeks
    D. Twelve weeks
    E. Sixteen weeks

ANSWER KEY

1.	C		11.	B
2.	D		12.	B
3.	D		13.	C
4.	C		14.	D
5.	C		15.	B
6.	E		16.	E
7.	B		17.	B
8.	A		18.	E
9.	B		19.	A
10.	B		20.	B

CHAPTER 14

Electrocardiography

CHAPTER OUTLINE

Anatomy and Physiology of the Heart

The Electrocardiograph

> Administering an ECG
> Troubleshooting
> Interpreting the ECG

Other Tests

Other Heart Conditions and Procedures

AREAS OF COMPETENCE

AAMA—ROLE DELINEATION STUDY AREAS OF COMPETENCE

Clinical

Patient Care

- Prepare patient for examinations, procedures, and treatments
- Assist with examinations, procedures, and treatments

AMT—RMA CERTIFICATION EXAM TOPICS

Electrocardiography

Standard, 12-lead ECG

- Mounting techniques
- Other ECG procedures

Link to reality!

It might help you to remember concepts and terms better if you relate them to real life. Create a scenario in which you might need the information. What would your responsibilities be as a medical assistant? If the concept is a procedure, are there any situations in which there might be an exception to the established guidelines? Since reality is never as straightforward as textbook cases, can you think of situations in which it might be hard to decide what to do? Discuss these issues with your instructor, your coworkers, and your fellow students. The more you think about these concepts, practice them at work, and talk about them with the people around you, the better prepared you will be for the exam.

Anatomy and Physiology of the Heart

Heart structures: The heart wall consists of three layers: endocardium, myocardium, and epicardium.

Endocardium: The innermost layer of the heart. It lines the inside of the heart muscle and covers the heart valves.

Myocardium: The middle and thickest layer of the heart. It is responsible for contraction of the heart.

Epicardium: Also known as visceral pericardium. It is the outermost layer of the heart.

Heart valves: There are two types of valves: atrioventricular (AV), consisting of bicuspid/mitral and tricuspid, and semilunar, consisting of pulmonic and aortic.

Tricuspid valve: Separates the right atrium and right ventricle.

Mitral valve: Separates the left atrium and the left ventricle.

Aortic valve: Located between the left ventricle and the aorta.

Pulmonic valve: Located between the right ventricle and the pulmonary artery.

Conduction system: Specialized electrical or pacemaker cells in the heart that are arranged in a system of pathways. Cardiac muscle differs from skeletal muscle in that it is able to contract rhythmically and conduct impulses.

Coronary arteries: Supply blood and oxygen to the myocardium. There are two arteries: right and left.

Cardiac cells: There are two types: myocardial cells and pacemaker cells (specialized cells of the electrical conduction system). Cardiac cells have four primary characteristics: excitability (irritability), automaticity, conductivity, and contractility.

Pacemaker cells: Described as slow cells, because their depolarization is dependent on calcium entry into the cells through slow channels. The primary properties of pacemaker cells of the heart are automaticity and conductivity.

Myocardial cells: Described as fast cells, because their depolarization is dependent on sodium entry into the cells through fast channels. The primary property of myocardial cells is contractility.

Excitability: The ability of cardiac muscle cells to respond to an outside stimulus. Excitability may be increased as a result of epinephrine and norepinephrine secretion by the adrenal medulla. All cardiac cells are characterized by excitability.

Automaticity: The ability of cardiac pacemaker cells to spontaneously initiate an electrical impulse without being stimulated from another source.

Contractility: The ability of cardiac cells to shorten, causing cardiac muscle contraction in response to an electrical stimulus. Contractility can be enhanced through the use of certain medications such as dopamine, epinephrine, and digitalis.

Conductivity: The ability of a cardiac cell to receive an electrical stimulus and conduct that impulse to an adjacent cell.

Action potential: Each muscle cell in the heart is stimulated to contract by going through an electrical process called the action potential. The action potential process is composed of five phases. These phases correlate with waveforms of the cardiac cycle recorded on the ECG. The recognition of abnormalities in the size of the waves or the various time intervals can aid in the diagnosis of certain types of heart problems.

Base of the heart: The top of the heart, located at approximately the level of the second intercostal space.

Septum: Separates the left and right halves of the heart (each containing one atrium and one ventricle).

Coronary veins: Carry deoxygenated blood from the myocardium. They empty into the coronary sinus. The coronary sinus empties into the right atrium.

Apex: The point of a cone or conical structure, such as the distal point of the left ventricle of the heart at the level of the fifth intercostal space.

Atrial kick: The surge of blood pushed into the ventricles as a result of atrial contraction.

Sinoatrial node: Specialized nerve tissue located at the junction of the superior vena cava and the right atrium, which is the portion of cardiac electrical tissue that establishes the beat. It is a site of impulse formation, also called the cardiac pacemaker. (Any cardiac conduction system cell can potentially function as a pacemaker.)

The Electrocardiograph

Electrocardiograph: An instrument that measures the waves of electrical impulses that are responsible for the cardiac cycle. There are several types.

12-lead electrocardiograph: The standard machine, which simultaneously records the electrical activity of the heart from 12 different views.

Single-channel electrocardiograph: Records information from one lead, giving one view of the heart's electrical activity.

Electrocardiogram (ECG or EKG): A record of the electrical impulses associated with cardiac contraction and relaxation. The two functions recorded are the amount of voltage generated by the heart and the time required for the voltage to travel through the heart.

Lead: An electrical connector (wire) between a specific combination of electrodes (sensors) attached to the body. Leads are used to record electrical activity. Each lead is given a specific designation and code. There are two types of lead: limb and precordial.

Limb lead: Six leads directly monitor electrodes on the arms and legs. Three are standard leads, and three are augmented leads.

Standard lead: Also called a bipolar lead because it directly monitors two electrodes. Leads I, II, and III are standard limb leads.

Augmented lead: Also called a unipolar lead because it directly monitors only one electrode (and two others less directly). The electrical activity recorded by an augmented lead is very slight. Leads aVR, aVL, and aVF are augmented limb leads.

Precordial lead: Also called a chest lead. The anodes, or positive (+) electrodes, of these six unipolar leads are placed across the chest in a specific pattern, along specific intercostal spaces. Each precordial lead is identified by the corresponding electrode, designated by the letter V with a numeral (V_1, V_2, V_3, V_4, **V5**, and V_6). See Figure 14-1.

Unconventional leads: If P waves cannot be seen on the conventional 12-lead ECG, unconventional leads can be created. The intra-atrial lead is an example of an unconventional lead.

Intra-atrial lead: A specifically designed electrode wire (V lead) advanced intravenously (from the internal jugular, subclavian, or femoral vein) into the right atrial cavity.

Stylus: A pen-like instrument that moves on the ECG paper to record the impulses that are received through electrodes as a result of the electrical activity of the heart.

Telemetry: The transmission of ECG signals via radio waves.

Administering an ECG

Electrocardiograph controls: Certain function controls are common on electrocardiographs: the stan-

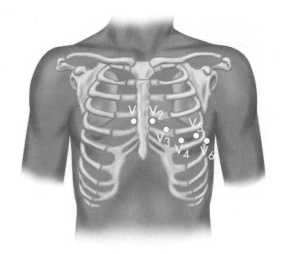

V_1 Fourth intercostal space (between the ribs), to the right of the sternum (breastbone)
V_2 Fourth intercostal space, to the left of the sternum
V_4 Fifth intercostal space, on the left midclavicular line
V_3 Fifth intercostal space, midway between V_2 and V_4
V_6 Fifth intercostal space, on the left midaxillary line
V_5 Fifth intercostal space, midway between V_4 and V_6

Figure 14-1. *Six precordial electrodes are arranged in specific positions on the chest. Note that electrode V_4 must be positioned before V_3 and V_6 before V_5.*

dardization control, speed selector, sensitivity control, lead selector, centering control, stylus temperature control, marker control, and on/off switch. Some may need to be activated or adjusted before use.

Preparing the patient's skin: Wash the skin with alcohol and rub it vigorously. If necessary, shave the areas where the electrodes will be attached.

Electrode: A device that detects electrical charges. A reusable electrode may be cleaned with steel wool, warm water, or alcohol. Electrodes are also known as sensors.

Types of electrodes: There are three main types of electrodes: metal plates, suction bulbs, and disposable electrodes.

Anode: The positive electrode of an ECG lead.

Applying electrodes: Apply electrodes first to the fleshy portions of the limbs; then apply the precordial electrodes. You must position electrodes at ten locations on the body. See Figure 14-2.

Electrolyte: Material applied to the skin to enhance contact between the skin and an electrode.

Attaching electrodes: Use electrolyte gel, lotion, or solution before placing reusable electrodes, and secure the electrodes with rubber straps or bulbs. For disposable electrodes, peel off the backings and press them into place.

Positioning electrodes: Precordial electrodes must be placed at specific locations, whereas the positions of limb electrodes need not be exact. Limb electrodes are most commonly placed on the inside of the fleshy part of the calf muscle and on the outside of the upper arm.

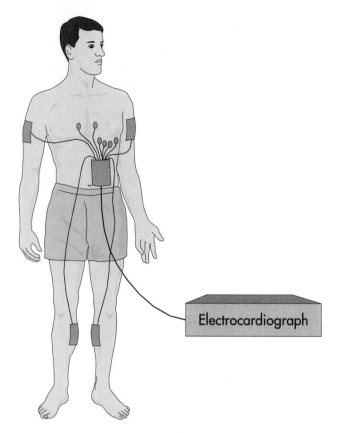

Figure 14-2. *There are ten electrode positions for electro-cardiography.*

Einthoven's triangle: Electrodes placed on the right arm, left arm, and left leg form Einthoven's triangle. Leads I, II, and III record electrical activity between their two respective electrodes. One of these electrodes is always positive, and one is negative. The positive electrode is the recording electrode. The third electrode is a ground, which minimizes electrical activity from other sources. The right leg is never used for ECG tracings; it serves as an electrical ground. See Table 14-1.

Attaching the wires: Connect the limb wires first, then the precordial wires in sequence from V_1 to V_6.

Make sure that the wires follow the patient's body contours and lie flat against the body. Drape the wires to avoid putting tension on the electrodes.

Polarity: A positive or negative electrical state.

Polarization: The electrical state of the heart at rest, in which the electrical charge on the outside of muscle cells is negative in relation to the inside.

Depolarization: A change of polarity. It is the electrical discharge that precedes contraction.

Baseline: An indication, as on an ECG tracing, of no electrical charge or activity. It is also known as an isoelectric line.

Repolarization: The restoration of a cell to its original pattern of charge. It is a return to polarization from the depolarized state (a return to rest).

Cardiac cycle: A complete phase of atrial contraction and ventricular contraction, followed by relaxation. It occurs about 60 to 100 times per minute. The contraction of the heart muscle is called systole. The ECG tracing of one heartbeat produces a pattern of waves designated as P, Q, R, S, T, and sometimes U, which correspond to certain electrical activities. See Figure 14-3.

P wave: A small upward curve that represents the contraction of the atria and is thus a measure of the atrial rate.

QRS complex: The Q, R, and S waves, which correlate with the contraction of the ventricles.

Q wave: A downward deflection.

R wave: A large upward spike.

S wave: A downward deflection.

T wave: An upward curve that represents the recovery (or repolarization) of the ventricles.

U wave: A small upward curve sometimes found after the T wave. The U wave represents the slow recovery (or repolarization) of Purkinje fibers, as seen in patients who have low potassium levels in their blood. It occurs between the T wave and the following P wave. A U wave taller than 2 mm is considered abnormal and may suggest hypokalemia or the effects of digoxin or quinidine on the conduction system.

P-R interval: Includes the P wave and the straight line connecting it to the QRS complex. It represents that

AT A GLANCE	**Standard Limb Leads**	
Lead	**Positive Electrode**	**Negative Electrode**
I	Left arm	Right arm
II	Left leg	Right arm
III	Left leg	Left arm
MCL1	Right side of sternum, 4th intercostal space	Left arm

Table 14-1

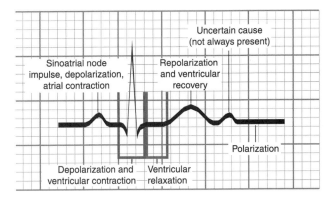

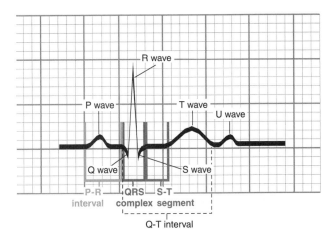

Figure 14-3. *This ECG tracing shows the pattern of one cardiac cycle in a normal heart. These specific electrical impulses (top) represent the cycle of cardiac contraction and relaxation. The waves and lines (bottom) represent specific parts of the pattern.*

time it takes for the electrical impulse to travel from the SA node to the AV node.

Q-T interval: Includes the QRS complex, S-T segment, and T wave. It represents the time it takes for the ventricles to contract and recover, or repolarize.

S-T segment: Connects the end of the QRS complex with the beginning of the T wave. It represents the time between contraction of the ventricles and recovery.

Asystole: Absence of cardiac electrical activity, represented as a straight (isoelectric) line on the ECG.

Cardiac rate: The pulse rate; the number of beats or contractions per minute.

Deflection: Deviation up or down from zero on the isoelectric line.

Refractory period: The period during repolarization when cells cannot respond normally to a second stimulus.

Cardiac output: The amount of blood ejected by the left ventricle into the aorta in one minute.

Amplitude: The height of a waveform on the ECG, showing the degree of voltage variation from zero (the baseline) up or down. It is measured in millimeters and is normally calibrated so that 10 mm represent 1.0 mV.

Troubleshooting

Artifacts: Deflections caused by electrical activity from sources other than the heart. They are irregular and erratic markings caused by poor conduction, outside interference, improper handling of a tracing, a patient's movement (or talking), or dirty sensors. There are several types of artifacts: wandering baseline, flat line, and extraneous marks.

Wandering baseline: A shift in the baseline from the center position for that lead. Its causes include muscle movement and mechanical problems.

Flat line: A flat line on the tracing of one of the leads is typically caused by a loose or disconnected wire. If flat lines occur on more than one lead, two of the wires may have been switched. If flat lines occur on all leads, there are two possible causes: The electrocardiograph unit or the connection to it is faulty, or the patient is in cardiac arrest.

Extraneous marks: Any marks on the paper that are not part of the tracing. The ECG graph paper is sensitive to heat and pressure. It can be easily damaged.

Interpreting the ECG

Heart rate: Can easily be determined by counting the number of QRS complexes in a 6-second strip of the ECG tracing (30 large squares at 25 mm per second) and multiplying by 10.

Heart rhythm: The ECG is the best way to assess heart rhythm and the regularity of the heartbeat. A normal heart rhythm is indicated on the ECG by regularly spaced complexes (repeated intervals, such as between one P wave and the next P wave or between one R wave and the next R wave). The patient's rhythm is usually assessed by viewing the rhythm strip, the ECG tracing from lead II.

Arrhythmia: An irregularity, disturbance, or abnormality in heart rhythm. It is also called a dysrhythmia. Some arrhythmias do not cause problems.

Ectopy: Placement outside the usual location.

Ectopic beat: A beat having an ectopic focus.

Ectopic focus: A site of impulse formation located somewhere other than the sinoatrial (SA) node.

Bigeminy: A type of arrhythmia in which every other beat is ectopic or premature (or both).

Premature beat or **premature contraction:** A contraction that occurs early. Premature contractions are of three types: premature atrial contractions (PACs), premature junctional contractions (PJCs), and premature ventricular contractions (PVCs).

Premature ventricular contraction (PVC): Can occur normally in healthy persons with apparently normal hearts. Causes of abnormal PVCs include hypoxia; an increase in catecholamines; stimulants such as alcohol, tobacco, and caffeine; acid-base imbalance; electrolyte imbalance; digitalis toxicity; and drugs such as epinephrine, dopamine, phenothiazines, or isoproterenol.

PVCs can cause ischemia, myocardial infarction, or congestive heart failure.

Acardia: The absence of the heart.

Acardiac rhythm: The absence of cardiac rhythm. It is also called asystole.

Bradyarrhythmia: An abnormally slow and irregular cardiac rhythm; irregular bradycardia.

Bradycardia: A heart rate slower than 60 beats per minute.

Tachyarrhythmia: An abnormally fast and irregular cardiac rhythm; irregular tachycardia.

Tachycardia: A heart rate faster than 100 beats per minute.

Atrial fibrillation: Incomplete, irregular, and rapid contraction of the atria between 350 and 500 times per minute. The ventricular rate may also be rapid, or it may be relatively normal.

Atrial flutter: Contraction of the atria between 250 and 350 beats per minute. The ventricular rate varies.

Ventricular fibrillation: Cessation of coordinated ventricular contraction. Untreated ventricular fibrillation leads to cardiac arrest.

Ventricular flutter: Contraction of the ventricles between 150 and 300 times per minute. It is a dangerous rhythm and should be reported immediately.

Sinus rhythm: A heart rhythm established by impulses from the sinoatrial (SA) node. Irregularities include sinus bradycardia, sinus tachycardia, sinus arrest, and sinus arrhythmia.

Sinus arrest: The failure of the sinoatrial (SA) node to function. It is also called sinus pause. The complete cardiac complex is absent from the ECG tracing.

Sinus arrhythmia: A usually benign fluctuation of the heart rate occurring within the normal range of 60 to 100 beats per minute, distinguished by a vagally influenced slowing of the cardiac rate during respiratory expiration and an increase in the cardiac rate during inspiration.

Agonal rhythm: The rhythm of a dying heart, usually ventricular, extremely slow and irregular and becoming slower to the point of asystole. A rate of less than 10 beats per minute is common.

Other Tests

Holter monitor: A portable (ambulatory) electrocardiography device that includes a small cassette recorder worn around a patient's waist to record the heart's electrical activity during normal daily activities. This test is given over a 24-hour period. The tape is analyzed by a microcomputer in the physician's office or at a reference laboratory.

Exercise electrocardiography: Assessment of the heart's conduction system during physical exertion such as exercise. It is also known as stress testing. The patient is required to walk on a treadmill, pedal a stationary bicycle, or walk on a stair-stepping ergonometer while ECG readings are taken.

Echocardiography: Tests the structure and function of the heart through the use of reflected sound waves, or echoes. The echoes can indicate structural defects and fluid accumulation, among other conditions.

Heart catheterization: A diagnostic method in which a catheter is inserted into a vein or artery in an arm or leg and passed through blood vessels into the heart, so that blood samples may be taken, the pressure in the heart's chambers measured, and/or the heart's motions viewed.

Angiography: The X-ray examination of a blood vessel, after the injection of a contrast medium, to evaluate the function and structure.

Other Heart Conditions and Procedures

Cardiodynia: Pain in the heart. It is also called cardialgia.

Cardiomalacia: Softening of the heart.

Cardiomegaly: Enlargement of the heart.

Cardioplegia: Paralysis of the heart.

Cardiolith: A stone in or on the heart.

Cardiectasia: Stretching of the heart.

Cardiorrhexis: Rupture of the heart wall.

Dextrocardia: Location of the heart in the right thorax as a result of a congenital defect or displacement by disease.

Cardioptosis: Drooping or falling of the heart at the normal location.

Hypertrophy of the heart: An increase in the size of the heart due to growth of the heart muscle tissue without an increase in the size of the heart chambers.

Heart blocks: Damage to the conduction system of the heart results in abnormal conduction patterns, causing dysrhythmias known as heart blocks. There are four types: first-degree; two variants of second-degree (Wenckebach, or Mobitz I, and Mobitz II); and third-degree, or complete.

Aortic aneurysm: Ballooning of the aorta.

Capture: The successful depolarization of an atrium or ventricle achieved, for example, by an artificial pacemaker.

Cardioversion: The administration of timed electrical shocks for the purpose of correcting certain arrhythmias or restoring normal rhythm, particularly in the ventricular beat.

Cardioplasty: Surgical repair of the heart.

Cardiorrhaphy: The suturing of the heart muscle.

Cardiomyopexy: A surgical procedure in which the blood supply from the nearby pectoral muscles of the chest is diverted directly to the coronary arteries.

STRATEGIES TO SUCCESS

▶ Test-Taking Skills

Come prepared!

Always bring all the supplies you need to the exam. Bring a few number 2 pencils with you and a working eraser. Don't depend on someone else to give these supplies to you. Make sure that you have the CMA or RMA admission card you received after registering for the exam. You also need to bring at least two forms of identification, one of which should have a photo.

Instructions:

Answer the following questions. Check your answers in the *Answer Key* that follows this section.

1. The medical term meaning transmission of ECG signals via radio waves is
   - A. Telepathy
   - B. Telemetry
   - C. Telediagnosis
   - D. Telocentric
   - E. Telecardio

2. On an ECG tracing, an indication of the absence of electrical charge or activity represents
   - A. Sinoatrial node
   - B. QRS complex
   - C. Baseline
   - D. Repolarization
   - E. None of the above

3. A beat arising from a focus outside the heart is known as
   - A. Ectopic beat
   - B. Escape beat
   - C. Uncontrolled beat
   - D. Fusion beat
   - E. Bigeminy

4. Which of the following is the epicardium?
   - A. Heart muscle
   - B. Heart wall
   - C. Inner lining of the myocardium
   - D. Right atrium
   - E. Outermost layer of the heart

5. The sudden rush of blood pushed into the ventricles as a result of atrial contraction is known as
   - A. Apex kick
   - B. Atrial kick
   - C. Acardia
   - D. Repolarization
   - E. Ventricular contraction

6. The U wave represents
   - A. Repolarization
   - B. Depolarization
   - C. Baseline
   - D. Ectopic beat
   - E. Contraction

7. Which of the following is not necessary in administering an ECG?
   - A. Sterilizing the leads
   - B. Activating the standardization control
   - C. Washing the patient's skin
   - D. Selecting the speed
   - E. Both B and D

8. Which type of lead is lead III?
   - A. Bipolar limb lead
   - B. Unipolar (augmented) limb lead
   - C. Precordial lead
   - D. Intercostal lead
   - E. None of the above

9. Which of the following is represented by the Q-T interval?
   - A. Low potassium in the blood
   - B. One ventricular contraction and recovery (repolarization)
   - C. The depolarization of the atria
   - D. The repolarization of the atria
   - E. Unusually frequent articular contraction due to high blood sugar

10. Leads aVR, aVL, and aVF are
    - A. Standard leads
    - B. Limb leads
    - C. Intercostal leads
    - D. Augmented leads
    - E. Both B and D

11. Successful depolarization of the atria or ventricles by an artificial pacemaker is called
    - A. Cardioplasty
    - B. Capture
    - C. Atrial kick
    - D. Apex kick
    - E. None of the above

12. All of the following are causes of artifacts except

    A. A patient's talking
    B. Clean sensors
    C. Outside interference
    D. Poor conduction
    E. Improper handling of a tracing

13. Augmented leads are also called

    A. Standard leads
    B. Bipolar leads
    C. Unipolar leads
    D. Nonstandard leads
    E. None of the above

14. The QRS complex represents

    A. Contraction of the atria
    B. Recovery of the atria
    C. Contraction of the heart
    D. Recovery of the ventricles
    E. Contraction of the ventricles

15. The coronary sinus empties into the

    A. Left atrium
    B. Right atrium
    C. Left ventricle
    D. Right ventricle
    E. Both B and D

16. The medical term meaning a falling or drooping of the heart is

    A. Cardioplegia
    B. Cardiomyopathy
    C. Cardiomyopexy
    D. Cardioptosis
    E. Cardiolith

17. Which of the following is the measurement of the atrial rate on the ECG tracing?

    A. The PR intervals
    B. The P waves
    C. The R waves
    D. The QRS complexes
    E. None of the above

18. Lead II is a(n)

    A. Chest or precordial lead
    B. Bipolar limb lead
    C. Augmented or unipolar limb lead
    D. Intercostal lead
    E. None of the above

19. The heart's conduction system is measured by which of the following?

    A. Heart catheterization
    B. Angiography
    C. Exercise electrocardiography
    D. Echocardiography
    E. Action potential

20. Which of the patient's limbs serves as an electrical ground?

    A. Right leg
    B. Left leg
    C. Right arm
    D. Left arm
    E. Either arm

21. Depolarization of fast cells is dependent on which of the following electrolytes?

    A. Calcium
    B. Potassium
    C. Magnesium
    D. Chloride
    E. Sodium

ANSWER KEY

1.	B		12.	B
2.	C		13.	C
3.	A		14.	E
4.	E		15.	B
5.	B		16.	D
6.	A		17.	B
7.	A		18.	B
8.	A		19.	C
9.	B		20.	A
10.	E		21.	E
11.	B			

CHAPTER 15

Radiography

AREAS OF COMPETENCE

AAMA—ROLE DELINEATION STUDY AREAS OF COMPETENCE

Clinical

Diagnostic Orders

- Perform diagnostic tests

Patient Care

- Prepare patient for examinations, procedures, and treatments
- Assist with examinations, procedures, and treatments

General (Transdisciplinary)

Instruction

- Instruct individuals according to their needs

(Chart continued on next page.)

AMT—RMA CERTIFICATION EXAM TOPICS

Patient Education

- Patient Instruction

Physical examinations

- Positions
- Methods of examination
- Specialty examinations

STRATEGIES TO SUCCESS

▶ *Study Skills*

Attend every class; read every assignment!
This tip might seem self-explanatory, but many people don't realize how truly important it is to make sure that you go to every class, read the assigned chapters, and complete any exercises your instructor gives you. In this way you will not fall behind and will have ample time to review for the certification exam. Reading the chapters before you come to class has two advantages: It will enable you to ask more relevant questions in class, and the background information it gives you will make the lecture more comprehensible. In class, try to sit near the front and maintain eye contact with the instructor. Make lists of what your instructor emphasizes in class, and review these lists often. If your instructor points out that certain material is always on the exams, make a point to remember these items. Your instructor and your class time are valuable resources you can use to find answers to questions about topics that seem confusing and to get a feel for what will be covered on the exams.

Terminology

Radiology: The study of the uses of radioactive substances for visualizing the internal structures of the body in order to diagnose and treat disease. It is divided into three specialties: diagnostic radiology, radiation therapy, and nuclear medicine.

X-ray: An electromagnetic wave with a high energy level and short wavelength that can penetrate solid objects. X-rays can be used in diagnosis and therapy.

Magnetism: The ability of certain materials to attract iron and other metals.

Radioactive: Capable of emitting radiant energy; or giving off radiation as the result of the disintegration of the nucleus of an atom.

Nuclear energy: Energy produced by fission of an atomic nucleus.

Radiopaque: Refers to something that does not permit the passage of X-rays. Bones are relatively radiopaque.

Contrast media: Radiopaque substances used in radiography to permit visualization of internal structures. Contrast media include liquids, powders, and gases. They are administered orally, parenterally, and rectally. A positive contrast medium is more dense than the surrounding tissue. A negative contrast medium is less dense than the surrounding area in the body. Barium sulfate and iodine are positive contrast media. Air is a negative contrast medium.

Adverse effects of contrast media: Oral agents may cause skin rash, vomiting, diarrhea, abdominal pain, or constipation. Intravenous agents can cause urticaria, skin reddening, anaphylaxis, or death. Some individuals have allergies to iodine.

X-ray film: A special material with a sensitive emulsion layer that reacts when it is exposed to radiation and thereby produces an image. Single-emulsion film is used to create images of the extremities and the breasts.

Radiograph: An image recorded on film that has been exposed. An older term for radiograph is roentgenogram, named after the discoverer of X-rays.

Film fog: An unwanted increase in the density of the emulsion either before or after exposure to radiation. Heat, light, chemicals, and extraneous radiation can produce fogging, which appears as darkened areas on the finished radiograph.

Artifacts: Extraneous marks and areas of increased or decreased density on film. Artifacts interfere with the diagnostic value of the radiograph.

Cassette: A light-proof container that holds X-ray film and serves to intensify the image.

Contrast: The visible difference between any two areas of radiographic density.

Roentgen: A unit used to measure X-ray dosage in air.

Rem: A unit used to measure X-ray dosage in human beings. It is an abbreviation of "Roentgen equivalent (in) man."

Rad: A unit used to measure the actual absorbed dose of radiation.

Ionization: The process by which an atom becomes ionized (gains or loses electrons).

Ionizing radiation: Radiation that causes ionization in the tissues that absorb it.

Scan: An image produced on film by a sweeping beam of radiation.

Isotopes: Variants of a single chemical element that have different atomic weights and different charges.

Frequency: The repetition rate of electromagnetic radiation, measured in Hertz.

X-ray machine: Has four basic parts: table, control panel, X-ray tube, and high-voltage generator. The table is usually adjustable. The most important part of the machine is the tube.

Invasive procedure: Some radiologic tests are invasive in that they require a radiologist to insert a catheter, wire, or other testing device into a patient's blood vessel or organ through the skin or body orifice. All invasive procedures require surgical aseptic technique.

Types of Radiography

Diagnostic radiology: The use of X-ray technology for diagnostic purposes. It also includes the use of magnetic resonance imaging (MRI), ultrasound, computed tomography (CT), and nuclear medicine technologies, such as positron emission tomography (PET), among others.

Magnetic resonance imaging (MRI): Uses a combination of nonionizing radiation and a strong magnetic field to produce images of internal structures and soft tissues. It is used for diagnosing cancer and other masses. It is contraindicated in patients with pacemakers or metallic prostheses.

Ultrasound: Directs high-frequency sound waves through the skin and produces an image based on the echoes. Ultrasound has many medical applications, including fetal monitoring, imaging of internal organs, and color imaging of blood vessels.

Tomography: Also called sectional imaging and body-section radiography. It allows the visualization of an organ or the body in cross-section.

Computed tomography (CT scan): A radiographic technique that shows a detailed, 360° cross-section of tissue structure. It is a painless procedure.

Nuclear medicine: A branch of medicine that uses radionuclides in the diagnosis and treatment of disorders.

Positron emission tomography (PET): Involves the injection of isotopes combined with other substances, such as glucose. Positrons are emitted, which are processed by a computer and displayed on a screen. It is useful for diagnosis of brain-related conditions, such as epilepsy and Parkinson's disease.

Angiography: X-ray visualization of blood vessels after the intravascular introduction of contrast media.

Arthrography: Used for joint conditions. It requires a contrast medium. Arthrography is performed by a radiologist and is usually done for knee, shoulder, or hip injuries. It also requires a local anesthetic.

Barium enema: The rectal infusion of barium sulfate (a radiopaque contrast medium), which is retained in the lower intestinal tract during X-ray studies. It is also called a contrast enema.

Barium meal, or **barium swallow:** The ingestion of barium sulfate. It is used for the radiographic examination of the esophagus, stomach, and intestinal tract. Before the test, the patient should have nothing to eat or drink for at least 8 hours.

Cholecystography: Radiologic study of the gallbladder, not as frequently done as in the past. The preceding evening meal must be low-fat, and an oral contrast medium is taken 12 to 15 hours before the procedure. The exam takes about 15 minutes.

Cholangiography: Similar to cholecystography and performed by a radiologist. The contrast medium is injected directly into the common bile duct (during gallbladder surgery).

Fluoroscopy: Radiologic study, performed by a radiologist, that allows both structural and functional visualization of internal body structures directly on a screen. A contrast medium is needed. It is also called radioscopy.

Intravenous pyelography (IVP): Radiologic study of the urinary system in which a series of X-rays is taken after a contrast medium has been injected into a vein. It is also known as excretory urography.

Mammography: Radiologic study of the breast. It is used for the early diagnosis of breast cancer.

Myelography: Radiologic study of the spinal cord. The radiologist performs a lumbar puncture, removes some cerebrospinal fluid, and injects some radiopaque, water-soluble contrast medium. It is no longer used very often; tomography and magnetic resonance imaging have largely replaced it.

Retrograde pyelography: Similar to IVP, except that the radiologist injects the contrast medium through a urethral catheter and takes a series of X-rays.

Sialography: Radiologic study of the salivary gland duct. The patient sucks on a lemon wedge to open the duct. A catheter is inserted into the duct and a contrast medium is introduced. The exam takes about 1 to 2 hours.

Stereoscopy: A rarely used X-ray procedure to study (primarily) the skull.

Thermography: A heat-sensing technique used for the detection of tumors. An infrared camera is used, which records variation in skin temperature. Warm areas appear light, and cool areas appear dark.

Xeroradiography: A diagnostic X-ray technique in which an image is produced electrically rather than chemically. It permits shorter exposure times and lower radiation levels than ordinary X-rays. It is also called xerography. Xeroradiography is used primarily for mammography.

Therapeutic Uses of Radiation

Radiation therapy: The use of radiation to treat diseases such as cancer by preventing cellular reproduction.

Teletherapy: Radiation therapy administered by a machine that is positioned at some distance from the patient. Teletherapy permits deeper penetration and is used primarily for deep tumors. It is done on an outpatient basis.

Brachytherapy: The implanting of radioactive sources into localized tumor tissues that are to be treated for a specific period of time.

Radioiodine: A radioactive isotope of iodine used in nuclear medicine and radiotherapy. It is used especially in the treatment of some thyroid conditions.

Medical Assistant's Role

Extent of participation by the medical assistant: Varies by state. The responsibilities of the medical assistant may involve simply assisting the radiologic technologist or radiologist, or they may involve operating certain X-ray equipment.

Timing of procedures: Procedures that require the patient to fast, such as barium enemas, are best scheduled in the morning, so that the patient sleeps through most of the period during which the digestive tract is empty.

Preprocedure care: Involves providing preparation instructions, such as diet restrictions or requirements; explaining the procedure to the patient; obtaining a medication history and other information from the patient; and instructing the patient to remove clothing, jewelry, and any other metals and to put on a gown.

Preparation for arthrography: Ask patients about possible allergies to contrast media, iodine, or shellfish. No other special preprocedure preparations are necessary.

Preparation for barium enema or intravenous pyelography: Ask the patient about possible allergies to contrast media, iodine, or shellfish. The patient should follow an all-liquid diet starting the morning before the procedure and should take a prescribed amount of electrolyte solution or other laxative on a specified schedule. The patient may have one cup of coffee, tea, or water on

the morning of the barium enema but should have no food or liquids after midnight before the IVP.

Preparation for cholecystography: Ask the patient about possible allergies to contrast media, iodine, or shellfish. The patient should eat a fat-free dinner the evening before the examination and should not smoke or have any foods or liquids after midnight. The oral contrast medium should be taken about 2 hours after dinner; tablets should be taken 5 minutes apart.

Preparation for tomography or CT scan: Ask the patient about possible allergies to contrast media, iodine, or shellfish. The patient must lie still while the scans are taken. For a CT scan, the patient may breathe normally, but it is necessary for the patient to hold his or her breath for a tomogram.

Preparation for MRI: If a contrast medium will be used, ask the patient about possible allergies to contrast media, iodine, or shellfish. Ask whether any internal metallic materials are present, such as a pacemaker, clips, shunts, heart valves, or slivers or chips from working with metal. Patients should avoid caffeine for 4 hours before the examination, and they should not wear eye makeup during the procedure.

Preparation for mammography: Avoiding caffeine for a week or 10 days prior to the procedure will reduce the possibility of swelling and soreness that will heighten discomfort. The patient should not use deodorant, powder, or perfume on the underarm area or breasts before the examination.

Position: Patients need to be positioned in different ways, depending on the specific body part being X-rayed. The most common positions for taking X-rays are anteroposterior, posteroanterior, oblique, and lateral. See Figure 15-1.

Postprocedure care: Have the patient assume a comfortable position while the films are being developed. If the films are satisfactory, have the patient get dressed and give the patient information on how to find out about the test results.

Safety and Storage

Safety

Radiosensitivity: The susceptibility of cells, tissues, or any living substances to the effects of radiation. Also, a biological organism's measure of response to radiation. Immature, nonspecialized cells and cells that are growing rapidly are the most radiosensitive; mature, specialized cells are the most radioresistant.

Exposure: Exposure to radiation is cumulative, meaning that it adds up to a total dosage over the years. The amount of exposure is measured in units called roentgens.

Absorbed dose: The amount of radiation energy absorbed in tissue.

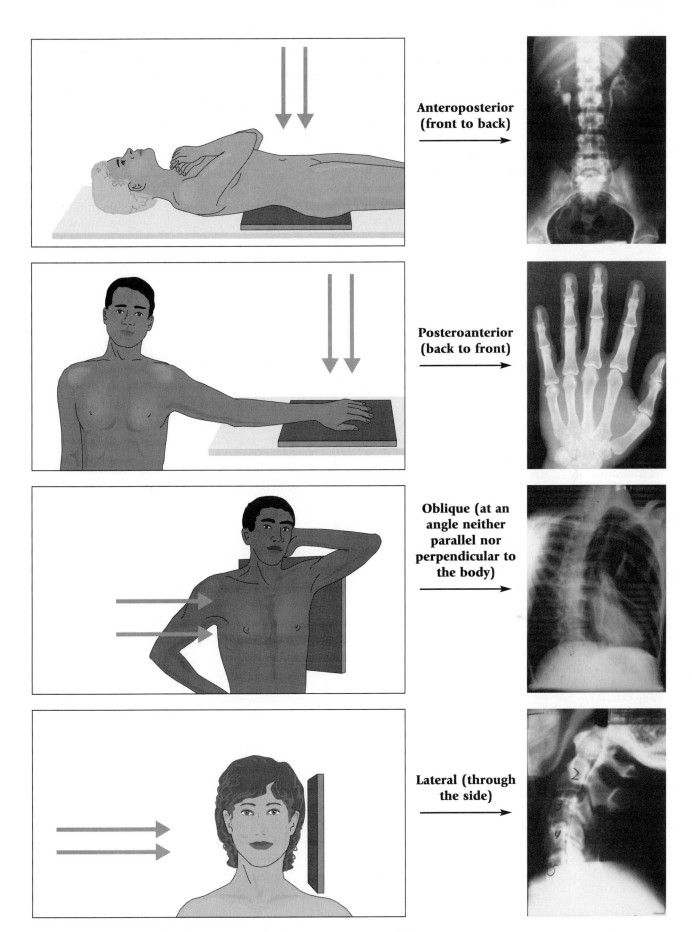

Figure 15-1. *Pathways and resulting projections for the most common types of X-rays.*

Overexposure: Not likely from routine X-rays, especially if precautions are taken. It can produce a variety of symptoms, including nausea, fatigue, and bleeding.

Personnel safety: All medical personnel who work in facilities that perform radiologic tests should wear radiation exposure badges, make sure that equipment is in good working order, and wear a lead shield when equipment is operating.

Radiation exposure badge: A sensitized piece of film, in a holder, that indicates the amount of radiation to which the individual has been exposed. The badge should be checked regularly. It is also called a dosimeter.

Patient safety: The medical assistant must follow all rules governing patient safety from radiation exposure, including providing a lead shield. Among the factors to check are how much exposure the patient has received in the past and whether a female patient is pregnant.

Storage

Radiographic film: Sensitive to X-rays, heat, chemical fumes, light, moisture, and pressure. Fresh film must be kept on hand at all times. It must be properly stored and carefully handled.

Sensitometry: The measurement or study of how radiographic film responds chemically to radiation exposure and to processing conditions.

Film storage: Radiographic film should be stored in a cool, dry place. The best temperature for film storage is between 60 and 70 degrees Fahrenheit. The best relative humidity is between 40% and 60%. Store packages on end; do not stack them on top of each other.

Ownership of radiographs: X-ray radiographs are the property of the radiology department where they are taken. They do not belong to the patient.

Documentation: Document the X-ray information on the patient record card or in the record book.

Labeling: Verify that film is labeled with the referring doctor's name, the date, and the patient's name.

Filing: Place the processed film in a film-filing envelope, and file the envelope in the correct place in the filing cabinet.

Instructions:

Answer the following questions. Check your answers in the *Answer Key* that follows this section.

1. A measurement of the actual absorbed dose of radiation is called
   A. Rem
   B. Rad
   C. Roentgen
   D. Contrast media
   E. Ray

2. An image produced on film by a sweeping beam of radiation is known as
   A. MRI
   B. Cassette
   C. Radioactive
   D. Isotopes
   E. Scan

3. The study of the gallbladder by X-ray with an oral contrast medium is called
   A. Cholecystosonography
   B. Cholecystitis
   C. Cholecystokinin
   D. Cholecystography
   E. Cholangiography

4. Which of the following statements regarding myelography is not correct?
   A. The radiologist performs a lumbar puncture
   B. It is fluoroscopy of the central nervous system
   C. The radiologist removes some cerebrospinal fluid
   D. It is fluoroscopy of the spinal cord
   E. A contrast medium is used

5. Radiation therapy for deeper tumors done on an outpatient basis is known as
   A. Brachytherapy
   B. Cryotherapy
   C. Thermotherapy
   D. Teletherapy
   E. Xeroradiography

6. The best temperature for film storage is between
   A. 40 and 50 degrees Fahrenheit
   B. 50 and 60 degrees Fahrenheit
   C. 60 and 70 degrees Fahrenheit
   D. 70 and 80 degrees Fahrenheit
   E. None of the above

7. Film artifacts are
   A. Areas that interfere with the diagnostic value of the radiograph
   B. Desirable
   C. Films that are beyond their expiration dates
   D. Diagnostic areas of interest
   E. None of the above

8. The frequency of electromagnetic radiation is measured in
   A. Watts
   B. Volts
   C. Rays
   D. Cycles
   E. Hertz

9. Excretory urography is also known as
   A. Sialography
   B. Cystography
   C. Intravenous pyelography
   D. Arthrography
   E. None of the above

10. A type of diagnostic radiology that uses high-frequency sound waves is
    A. Magnetic resonance imaging, or MRI
    B. X-ray
    C. Tomography
    D. Arthrography
    E. Ultrasound

11. Positions that are neither parallel nor perpendicular to the body are called
    A. Supine
    B. Oblique
    C. Prone
    D. Recumbent
    E. Both A and B

12. The front-to-back position in radiology is known as
    - A. Posteroanterior
    - B. Lateral
    - C. Anteroposterior
    - D. Oblique
    - E. Supine

13. The process in which an atom may gain or lose electrons is called
    - A. Ionization
    - B. Radiation
    - C. Fractionation
    - D. Potential difference
    - E. Oxygenation

14. Which of the following statements is not correct in regard to radiosensitivity?
    - A. Mature cells are the least radiosensitive
    - B. Immature tissues are the most radiosensitive
    - C. Cells that are rapidly growing are the most radiosensitive
    - D. Nonspecialized cells are the most radiosensitive
    - E. Specialized cells are the most radiosensitive

15. Before a mammogram, a woman should
    - A. Drink coffee
    - B. Use body lotion
    - C. Avoid wearing deodorant
    - D. Fast after midnight
    - E. Avoid exercise

16. In preparing patients for such tests as barium enemas and CT scans, the medical assistant should
    - A. Tell them that they will have to hold their breath
    - B. Tell them to eat a fat-free dinner the night before
    - C. Ask them whether internal metals are present
    - D. Ask them whether they are allergic to contrast media, iodine, or shellfish
    - E. Ask them whether they are wearing body lotion

17. Safety precautions are necessary because
    - A. Radiation exposure is cumulative
    - B. Radiation exposure is always fatal
    - C. Overexposure is likely from routine X-rays
    - D. Both A and C
    - E. All of the above

18. Xeroradiography is used primarily for
    - A. Cholecystography
    - B. Arthrography
    - C. Mammography
    - D. Intravenous pyelography
    - E. Cardiography

ANSWER KEY

1.	B		10.	E
2.	E		11.	B
3.	D		12.	C
4.	B		13.	A
5.	D		14.	E
6.	C		15.	C
7.	A		16.	D
8.	E		17.	A
9.	C		18.	C

CHAPTER 16

Physical Therapy

CHAPTER OUTLINE

Terminology

Patient Assessment

Treatment

Thermotherapy
Cryotherapy
Other Therapy

Mobility-Assisting Devices

AREAS OF COMPETENCE

AAMA—ROLE DELINEATION STUDY AREAS OF COMPETENCE

Clinical

Patient Care

- Prepare patient for examinations, procedures, and treatments
- Assist with examinations, procedures, and treatments

General (Transdisciplinary)

Instruction

- Instruct individuals according to their needs

AMT—RMA CERTIFICATION EXAM TOPICS

Therapeutic Modalities

- Modalities
- Patient instruction

Terminology

Physical medicine: The branch of medicine that uses physical devices or agents therapeutically for the diagnosis, treatment, management, and prevention of diseases. It is also called physiatry.

Rehabilitation: Restoration of those functions that have been affected by a patient's injuries or disease.

Sports medicine: The branch of medicine that specializes in the prevention and treatment of injuries caused by athletic participation. More than 1 million people are treated for sports injuries each year in the United States. Most sports injuries involve muscle strains, sprains, and tears. Sports medicine uses a number of different modalities that enable the patient to recover quickly and return to high levels of activity with minimal loss of fitness.

Physiatrist: A physician specializing in physical medicine and rehabilitation.

Fitness: Overall good physical condition, including cardiovascular strength, muscular strength, and flexibility.

Range of motion (ROM): The degree to which a joint is able to move, measured in degrees with a protractor-like device called a goniometer.

Flexion: The bending movement allowed by certain joints of the skeleton, such as the elbow, that decreases the angle between the two adjoining bones.

Extension: The straightening movement allowed by certain joints of the skeleton, such as the knee, that increases the angle between the two adjoining bones.

Hyperextension: The position of maximum extension, or the extension of a body part beyond its normal limits.

Reduction: The correction of a fracture, dislocation, or hernia.

Lordosis: Exaggerated anterior curvature of the lumbar spine.

Kyphosis: Abnormally increased convex curvature of the thoracic spine. It is also colloquially called hunchback or humpback.

Scoliosis: Lateral deviation in the normal vertical curve of the spine.

Osteoporosis: A reduction in the mass of bone per unit of volume that interferes with the mechanical support function of bone, causing bone fractures in situations that would not normally damage the skeleton.

Luxation: Complete dislocation of the bone from the joint.

Subluxation: Incomplete dislocation of the bone from the joint.

Tendonitis: Inflammation of tendons. Tendonitis is one of the most common causes of acute pain in the shoulder.

Quadriplegia: Paralysis of all four extremities of the body and the trunk. This disorder is usually caused by spinal cord injury, especially in the area of the fifth to the seventh cervical vertebrae. Automobile accidents and sporting mishaps are common causes.

Paraplegia: Paralysis of the lower portion of the body, usually caused by spinal cord injury or disease. Paraplegia commonly results from automobile and motorcycle accidents, sporting accidents, falls, and gunshot wounds.

Hemiplegia: Paralysis of one side of the body. The three types of hemiplegia are cerebral, facial, and spastic.

Hemiparesis: Muscular weakness of one half of the body.

Cerebral palsy: Nonprogressive paralysis due to defects in or trauma to the brain, especially at birth. Spastic cerebral palsy is characterized by hyperactive reflexes, rapid muscle contraction, muscle weakness, and underdevelopment of the limbs. Mental retardation, seizure disorders, and impaired speech are also common with this condition. Treatment may include the use of braces, adaptive appliances, and range of motion exercises.

Patient Assessment

Gait: A style of walking. A normal gait consists of two phases: stance and swing. See Figure 16-1. Generally, a physician or physical therapist assesses a patient's gait. The patient is asked to walk away, turn around, and walk back. Assessment includes an appraisal of the patient's length of stride, balance, coordination, direction of knees (inward or outward), and direction of feet (inward or outward).

Goniometry: The measurement of joint mobility. Goniometric tests are noninvasive. The movements measured by goniometry are explained in Table 16-1.

Goniometer: A device used to measure the degree of joint movement. See Figure 16-2 on p. 334.

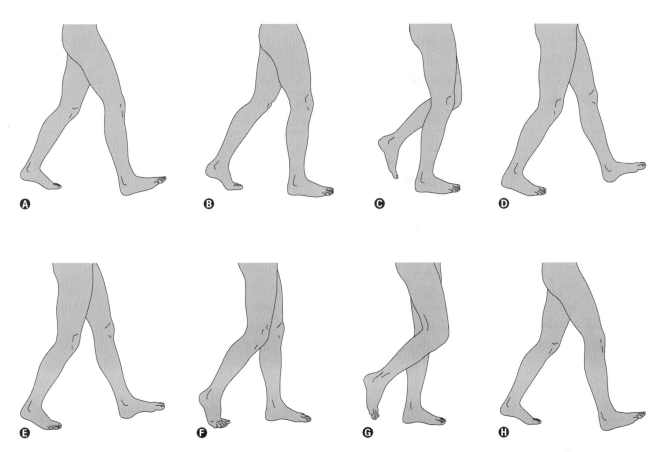

Figure 16-1. *The two phases of gait. Illustrations (A) through (D) show the movements of the stance phase for the right leg; illustrations (E) through (H) show the movements of the swing phase: (A) right heel strike, (B) flat right foot, (C) midstance, (D) push-off with the right foot, (E) right foot poised, (F) left heel strike, (G) midswing, (H) right heel strike.*

AT A GLANCE	Movements Measured by Goniometry	
Term	**Description**	**Example**
Abduction	Movement away from the midline of the body or away from the axis of a limb	Raising an arm straight out to the side
Adduction	Movement toward the midline of the body or toward the axis of a limb	Lowering a raised arm to the side
Circumduction	Circular movement of a body part	Performing arm circles
Dorsiflexion	Upward or backward movement of a body part	Flexing a foot so that the toes point upward
Eversion	Outward movement of a body part	Moving an ankle so that the sole of the foot turns outward
Extension	Movement that spreads two body parts or that opens a joint	Straightening a leg by unbending the knee
Flexion	Movement that brings together two body parts or that closes a joint	Bending a leg at the knee

Table 16-1 (table continued on the next page)

Term	Description	Example
Inversion	Inward movement of a body part	Moving an ankle so that the sole of the foot turns inward
Plantar flexion	Downward movement of a body part	Flexing a foot so that the toes point downward
Pronation	Twisting movement that brings a palm facing downward	Turning a wrist so that the palm faces downward
Rotation	Movement of a body part around its axis	Turning the head from side to side
Supination	Twisting movement that brings a palm facing upward	Turning a wrist so that the palm faces upward

Table 16-1, continued

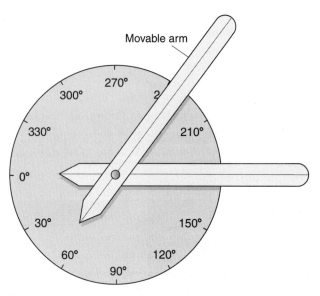

Figure 16-2. *A universal goniometer is a protractor with a movable pointer that measures degrees of joint movement.*

Using a goniometer: The medical assistant may be asked to assist with or perform goniometry. Have the patient move each body part in a specified manner, and position the goniometer to measure degrees of movement.

Muscle testing: Consists of range of motion tests (with a goniometer), strength tests, and task skill tests.

Muscle strength testing: Determines the amount of muscle force. This test is usually done from head to foot, usually in combination with ROM testing. The patient is asked to resist pressure that the physician or medical assistant applies to each muscle or group of muscles. Strength is rated according to a five-point scale, as shown in Table 16-2.

Posture testing: The physician looks at the patient's spinal curve from the sides, back, and front; notes the symmetry of alignment of the shoulders, knees, and hips; assesses alignment and degree of straightness as the patient bends at the waist; and assesses knee position by having the patient stand with both feet together.

Electromyography (EMG): A process of electrically recording muscle action potentials. The patient may receive sedation before this test because the electric current can be painful. Abnormal EMG test results can indicate a congenital or an acquired disease condition of the muscles.

Treatment

Physical therapy: The treatment of disorders with physical agents and methods such as massage, manipulation, therapeutic exercise, cold, heat, hydrotherapy, and electrical stimulation. Physical therapy includes rehabilitative treatment to restore function after an illness or an injury. It is also called physiotherapy.

Physical therapist: An allied health professional who has completed at least a 4-year baccalaureate training program in physical therapy and has received state licensure. He or she deals primarily with movement dysfunction and works with body parts that have been injured by accident, amputation, or disease. As a medical assistant, you may be asked by a physician to assist with some forms of physical therapy including applying cold and heat; teaching basic exercises; preparing patients; and demonstrating how to use canes, walkers, crutches, and wheelchairs.

Thermotherapy

Thermotherapy: The treatment of disease by the application of heat. Thermotherapy is used to relieve pain,

Muscle Response	Rating	Meaning
No response	0	Paralysis
Slight contraction felt	1	Severe weakness
Passive ROM when resistance is removed	2	Moderate weakness
Active ROM against gravity or light resistance	3 or 4	Mild weakness
Active ROM against heavy resistance	5	Normal strength

Table 16-2

to relax spasms of muscles, to relieve localized swelling, to increase tissue metabolism and repair, and to increase drainage from an infected area. A temperature of 116°F (47°C) or above can cause burning. Heat therapy should not be used on pregnant or menstruating women, and it also should not be used longer than ordered by the physician.

Types of heat therapy: The main types are dry heat, moist heat, and diathermy.

Dry heat therapy: Includes the use of heating pads, hot-water bottles, chemical hot packs, heat lamps, and fluidotherapy.

Heating pad: The physician should specify the heating pad temperature and the length of time the pad should be applied. Cover the pad with a pillowcase or towel, make sure that the cord is not frayed, make sure that the patient's skin is dry, plug the cord into an outlet, and turn on the pad. The patient should not lie on top of a heating pad.

Hot-water bottle: Water temperature should not exceed 125°F for adults and 115°F for children and elderly patients. Fill the bottle halfway, and expel the air. Cover the bottle with a cloth or pillowcase before applying.

Chemical hot pack: A disposable, flexible pack of chemicals that becomes hot when kneaded or slapped. After activating the pack, cover it with a cloth and place it on the patient's skin in the area being treated.

Heat lamp: Uses an infrared or ultraviolet bulb. Place the lamp 2 to 4 feet from the area being treated. Treatment usually lasts 20 to 30 minutes.

Infrared therapy: Treatment by exposure to various wavelengths of infrared radiation. Infrared treatment is performed to relieve pain and to stimulate blood circulation.

Ultraviolet therapy: Used in the treatment of rickets and certain skin conditions such as psoriasis. This therapy is also useful in the control of infectious airborne bacteria and viruses. Ultraviolet ray lamp treatments must be carefully controlled because they can cause severe sunburn and even second- or third-degree burns. The time and the distance of the lamp from the patient must be controlled. Treatment is prescribed by the second, for example, 10 or 20 seconds of exposure. The patient should cover his or her eyes with dark goggles.

Fluidotherapy: A relatively new technique in which the patient places the hand or foot in a container of glass beads that are heated and agitated with hot air.

Moist heat therapy: There are several types of moist heat applications, including hot soaks, hot compresses, hot packs, and paraffin baths.

Hot soak: Usually used on arms or legs. A container of plain or medicated water is heated to not more than 110°F, and the patient places the body part in the container. A hot soak should last about 15 minutes.

Hot compress: Soak the gauze or cloth in hot water, wring it out, and apply it to the area being treated. Either place a hot-water bottle on top of it or frequently rewarm the compress in hot water.

Paraffin bath: Utilizes a receptacle of heated wax and mineral oil to reduce pain, muscle spasms, and stiffness in patients with arthritis. A thick coat of wax remains on the area for about 30 minutes and then is peeled off.

Diathermy: The production of heat in body tissues for therapeutic purposes by high-frequency currents that are insufficiently intense to destroy tissues. Diathermy is useful in treating muscular disorders, tendonitis, arthritis, and bursitis. Diathermy cannot be used in patients with metal implants, such as hip replacements, because of the electrical field it creates and the consequent danger of burns. Patients must remove all metal jewelry and buckles before treatment, which usually lasts from 15 to 30 minutes. There are three basic methods of diathermy: ultrasound, microwave, and shortwave.

Ultrasound: Projects high-frequency sound waves that are converted to heat in muscle tissue. The most common type of diathermy, it is administered by rubbing a gel-covered transducer over the skin in circular patterns. It is used to treat sprains, strains, and other acute ailments. Ultrasound treatments should not be used in areas where bones are near the skin's surface.

Microwave: Electromagnetic radiation that is converted into heat in tissues. It should not be used on patients with pacemakers, in combination with wet dressings, or near metal implants.

Shortwave: Provides heat deep in the body by means of radio waves that travel between two condenser plates. It is used to treat chronic arthritis, bursitis, sinusitis, and other conditions.

Cryotherapy

Cryotherapy: Treatment using dry cold or wet cold applications to

- Prevent swelling by limiting fluid accumulation in body tissue
- Control bleeding by constricting blood vessels
- Reduce inflammation by slowing blood and fluid movement
- Provide an anesthetic effect by reducing inflammation
- Reduce pus formation by inhibiting microorganisms
- Lower body temperature

For best results, cryotherapy should be used frequently, for example, about 20 minutes every hour for acute conditions or injuries (during the first 48 hours).

Dry cold applications: Ice bags (or ice collars) and chemical ice packs.

Ice bag or **ice collar:** Place ice chips or small ice cubes in the device, filling it two-thirds full; compress the container to expel air; dry the container; and cover it with a towel to absorb moisture.

Chemical ice pack: A flat plastic bag containing semi-fluid chemicals. Most chemical ice packs remain cold for 30 to 60 minutes; some are disposable, and some are reusable. Check the pack for leaks, and shake or squeeze it to activate the chemicals. Cover the pack with a towel.

Wet cold applications: Cold compresses and ice massage.

Cold compress: Place large ice cubes and a small amount of water in a basin. Place a washcloth or gauze square in the basin to moisten it, wring it out, and apply it to the area being treated.

Ice massage: Wrap an ice cube in a plastic bag, or freeze water in a paper cup, then use the device to massage the area.

Administering cryotherapy: Place the cryotherapy device on the affected body part. Ask the patient how the device feels. Leave the device in place for as long as ordered by the physician. Check the skin for color, feeling, and pain periodically, and have the physician examine an area that becomes excessively pale or blue, numb, or painful. After treatment, check for reduced swelling, redness, and pain.

Other Therapy

Hydrotherapy: The use of water in the treatment of various disorders. Hydrotherapy may include continuous tub baths, wet sheet packs, or shower sprays.

Whirlpool: A tank in which water is agitated by jets of air under pressure, used to relax muscles and to increase circulation.

Contrast bath: Two baths, one filled with hot water and the other with cold water. The patient quickly moves the affected body part from one to the other. It is used to induce relaxation, to stimulate circulation, and to improve mobility.

Underwater exercises: Generally performed in a warm swimming pool by patients with joint injuries, burns, and arthritis.

Exercise therapy: A technique for helping patients prevent deformities, regain body movement, improve muscle strength, stimulate circulation, retain neuromuscular coordination, and resume normal daily activities. Therapeutic exercises are ordered by the physician after complete evaluation of the physical problem.

Medical assistant's role in exercise therapy: To provide information for the patient and family, to provide support and encouragement, to assist with range of motion exercises, and to teach the patient how to perform them at home.

Active mobility exercises: Self-directed exercises a patient performs without assistance to increase muscle strength and function. They may require such equipment as a stationary bicycle or treadmill.

Passive mobility exercises: Used for patients with neuromuscular disabilities or weaknesses. The physical therapist or a machine moves the body part.

Aided mobility exercises: Self-directed exercises performed with the help of such devices as exercise machines or therapy pools.

Active resistance exercises: The patient works against resistance, which is provided by a therapist or by an exercise machine, to increase muscle strength.

Isometric exercises: The patient relaxes and then contracts the muscles while in a fixed position. These exercises are used to maintain muscle strength when a joint is temporarily or permanently immobilized.

Range of motion exercises: Exercises that slowly move each joint through its full range of motion. They may be active (performed by the patient without assistance) or passive (performed with the help of another person or a machine). Typical range of motion exercises are shoulder abduction, back rotation, hip flexion, and toe abduction.

Electrical stimulation: The delivery of controlled amounts of low-voltage electric current to motor and sensory nerves to stimulate muscles. It is used to help retrain a patient to use injured muscles.

Massage: The application of pressure with the hands on the soft tissue of the body through stroking, rubbing, kneading, or tapping, in order to increase circulation, improve muscle tone, and relax the patient. It is one of the oldest known methods for promoting healing. The most common sites for massage are the back, knees, elbows, and heels. Stroking is the most common massage modality used in the medical office.

Immobilization: The restriction of movement of a body part in order to promote healing. Devices such as splints and slings are prescribed by the physician and used by the physical therapist to immobilize damaged tissues and bones.

Manipulation: The application of rapid thrusting motions in order to stabilize, stretch, or reposition a joint.

Traction: The process of pulling or stretching a part of the body. It is applied by a physical therapist to create proper bone alignment, reduce joint stiffening and abnormal muscle shortening, correct deformities, relieve compression of vertebral joints, and reduce or relieve muscle spasms.

Mobility-Assisting Devices

Cane: A sturdy wooden or aluminum shaft or walking stick, used to give support and greater mobility to a person who is ambulatory but needs some assistance.

Standard cane: A cane with a single leg, used by someone who needs only a small amount of support in walking.

Tripod and quad-base canes: Canes with bases having three and four legs, respectively, that provide greater support and stability.

Cane height: When the patient is holding the cane and standing up straight, the cane should be level with the top of the patient's femur, and the elbow should be bent at a 30° angle.

Teaching a patient to use a cane: The medical assistant may be asked to teach a patient how to use a cane. Table 16-3 on p. 338 explains how to use a cane to stand up, walk, and climb stairs.

Crutch: A metal or wooden staff used to aid a person in walking. It is important that the person be taught how to use the crutch(es) safely and how to achieve a stable and acceptable gait.

Types of crutches: The two basic kinds of crutches are axillary crutches (which reach from the ground almost to the armpit) and forearm crutches (which reach from the ground to the forearm and are also called Lofstrand or Canadian crutches).

Measuring a patient for crutches: Crutches must be measured to fit the patient. Crutches that are too long or too short can cause muscle weakness, back strain, or imbalance. To confirm that the fit is correct, make sure that the patient is wearing the type of shoes that will be worn when walking. When the patient is standing erect, with feet slightly apart, and the crutch tips are positioned 2 inches in front of the feet and 4 to 6 inches to the side of each foot, there should be 2 to 3 finger-widths between the axillary supports and the armpits (for axillary crutches), and the handgrips should be positioned to create a 30° flexion at the elbows.

Using crutches: In teaching patients how to use crutches, emphasize the following points:

- Support body weight with the hands.
- Stand erect.
- Look straight ahead.
- Move crutches no more than 6 inches at a time.
- Wear flat, well fitting, nonskid shoes.
- Remove throw rugs and other unsecured articles from traffic areas.
- Check the tips regularly for wear and wetness.
- Check all wing nuts and bolts for tightness.

Crutch gaits: Begin with the standing or tripod position, in which the patient places the crutch tips 4 to 6 inches in front of the feet and 4 to 6 inches away from the side of each foot. Patients should use a slow gait in crowded areas or when feeling tired.

Four-point gait: A slow gait used by persons who can bear weight on both legs. The patient should begin in the tripod position, then move the right crutch forward, move the left foot forward to the level of the left crutch, move the left crutch forward, and move the right foot forward to the level of the right crutch.

Three-point gait: Used by persons who can bear full weight on one leg and no weight on the other. It requires good muscle coordination and arm strength. The patient begins in the tripod position, moves both crutches and the affected leg forward, then balances weight on both crutches and moves the unaffected leg forward.

Two-point gait: A faster gait used by persons who can bear some weight on both feet and have good muscle coordination and balance. The patient begins in the tripod position, the moves the left crutch and right foot forward at the same time, followed by the right crutch and left foot.

Swing-to gait: A modified three-point gait often used by persons with physical disabilities. The patient begins in the tripod position and then moves both crutches forward at the same time. The patient then lifts the body and swings it to the crutches.

Swing-through gait: Also often used by persons with physical disabilities. It is like the swing-to gait, but the patient swings the body past the crutches.

Walker: An extremely light, movable apparatus, about waist high, made of metal tubing (usually aluminum), used to aid a patient in walking. There are two types: standard (with four widely placed legs ending in rubber tips) and rolling (with wheels).

Walker height: The top of the walker should be just below the patient's waist or at the same height as the top of the hip bone, so that when the patient holds the handgrip, the elbow is bent at a 30° angle.

Standing from a chair

1. Instruct the patient to slide his buttocks to the edge of the chair.
2. Tell the patient to place his right foot against the right front leg of the chair and his left foot against the left front leg of the chair.
3. Instruct the patient to lean forward and use the armrests of the chair to push upward. Caution the patient not to lean on the cane.
4. Have the patient position the cane for support on the strong side of the body.

Walking

1. Teach the patient to hold the cane on the strong side of her body with the tip(s) of the cane 4 to 6 inches from the side of her strong foot. Remind the patient to make sure to keep the tip(s) flat on the ground.
2. Have the patient move the cane forward approximately 12 inches and them move her affected foot forward, parallel to the cane.
3. Next have the patient move her strong leg forward past both the cane and her weak leg.
4. Observe as the patient repeats this process.

Going up stairs

1. Instruct the patient always to start with his strong leg when going up stairs.
2. Advise the patient to keep the cane on the strong side of his body and to use the wall or rail for support on the weak side.
3. After the patient steps on the strong leg, instruct him to bring up his weak leg and then the cane.
4. Remind the patient not to rush.

Going down stairs

1. Instruct the patient always to start with her weak leg when going down stairs.
2. Advise the patient to keep the cane on the strong side of her body and to use the wall or rail for support on the weak side.
3. Have the patient use the strong leg and wall or rail to support her body, bending the strong leg as she lowers her weak leg and cane to the next step. She can move the cane and weak leg simultaneously, or she can move the cane first, followed by the weak leg.
4. Instruct the patient to step down with the strong leg.

Table 16-3

Using a walker: Although a physical therapist usually trains patients in the use of walkers, medical assistants may be asked to do it or to reinforce the information. Table 16-4 provides information on how to teach a patient to use a walker.

Wheelchair: A mobile chair equipped with large wheels and brakes. If long-term use of the chair is expected, a physical therapist may prescribe particular features, such as seat size and height, left- or right-hand propulsion, brake type, armrest height, footrest style (e.g., fixed, swing-away, elevating), and special seat pads.

Using a wheelchair: To get into the wheelchair, the patient should lock the chair and fold back the footplates, then back into the chair, supporting himself or herself on the armrests while lowering the body into the chair.

Transferring a patient from a wheelchair to a table: If the patient is weak, heavy, or unstable, ask for help. Make sure that the wheelchair is in the locked position and that the patient is sitting at the front of the wheelchair seat. Face the patient, spread your feet apart, and bend slightly at the knees. Have the patient hold on to your shoulders, and place your arms around the patient under the arms. At the count of "3," lift and pivot the patient to bring the back of his or her knees against the table. Gently lower the patient into a sitting or supine position on the table.

Teaching a Patient How to Walk with a Walker

1. Instruct the patient to step into the walker.
2. Tell the patient to place her hands on the handgrips on the sides of the walker.
3. Make sure that the patient's feet are far enough apart so that she feels balanced.
4. Instruct the patient to pick up the walker and to move it forward about 6 inches.
5. Have the patient move one foot forward and then the other foot.
6. Instruct the patient to pick up the walker again and to move it forward. If the patient is strong enough, explain that she may advance the walker after moving each foot rather than waiting until she has moved both feet.

Table 16-4

STRATEGIES TO SUCCESS

▶ *Test-Taking Skills*

Do a mind dump!
   As soon as the exam starts, you may find it helpful to do a mind dump. Briefly look over the questions and quickly write down all the information that is fresh in your head. Write out any lists that you have memorized. All the concepts and formulas that you always had trouble remembering and those that you were still going over and memorizing as the exam began should be written down as soon as possible so that you don't forget them. Then you can focus on the exam with more confidence. A mind dump doesn't work for everyone, and it should not take valuable time away from your exam.

CHAPTER 16 REVIEW

Instructions:

Answer the following questions. Check your answers in the *Answer Key* that follows this section.

1. The branch of medicine that is also a key component of rehabilitation is
   A. Physical therapy
   B. Physiatry
   C. Sports medicine
   D. Manipulation
   E. None of the above

2. The degree to which a joint is able to move is known as
   A. Goniometer
   B. Goniometry
   C. Range of motion
   D. Range of reach
   E. Universal goniometer

3. Lateral deviation in the normal vertical curve of the spine is called
   A. Kyphosis
   B. Lordosis
   C. Scoliosis
   D. Luxation
   E. None of the above

4. Which of the following is paralysis of the lower portion of the body?
   A. Hemiplegia
   B. Paraplegia
   C. Quadriplegia
   D. Hemiparesis
   E. Parapraxia

5. Which of the following is a type of heat therapy?
   A. Moist heat
   B. Dry heat
   C. Reduced heat
   D. Both A and B
   E. Both B and C

6. In thermotherapy, which of the following temperatures can cause burning?
   A. 105°F
   B. 110°F
   C. 112°F
   D. 114°F
   E. 116°F

7. How long does diathermy usually last?
   A. 5 to 10 minutes
   B. 10 to 15 minutes
   C. 15 to 30 minutes
   D. 60 to 90 minutes
   E. 2 to 3 hours

8. Cryotherapy is used for all of the following purposes <u>except</u>
   A. To lower body temperature
   B. To reduce swelling
   C. To reduce bleeding
   D. To reduce pus formation
   E. To reduce clotting

9. Muscular weakness of one side of the body is called
   A. Hemiparesis
   B. Hemiplegia
   C. Hemimelia
   D. Hemiopia
   E. Hemiphelia

10. Patients instructed on how to use crutches should be told to
    A. Move crutches no more than 6 inches at a time
    B. Look down at the ground to check where they place the crutches
    C. Balance their body weight between their feet and hands
    D. Move crutches approximately a foot at a time
    E. Stand bent over the crutches at a 30° angle for increased support

11. Physical therapists are allied health professionals who have completed at least
    A. Medical school
    B. A four-year baccalaureate training program
    C. A two-year associate degree program
    D. Postgraduate work
    E. A certificate program

12. Movement allowed by joints to decrease the angle between two adjoining bones is called
    A. Range of motion
    B. Extension
    C. Flexion
    D. Gait
    E. Luxation

13. Correction of a fracture, dislocation, or hernia is called
    A. Reduction
    B. Luxation
    C. Subluxation
    D. Relocation
    E. Casting

14. Electromyography (EMG) is the process of electrically recording muscle
    A. Contraction
    B. Relaxation
    C. Action potentials
    D. Energy production
    E. Flexion

15. Diathermy is useful in treating all of the following conditions except
    A. Tendonitis
    B. Myocarditis
    C. Muscular disorders
    D. Arthritis
    E. Bursitis

16. How far from the area being treated should a heat lamp be placed?
    A. 6 to 8 feet
    B. 4 to 6 feet
    C. 2 to 4 feet
    D. 1 to 2 feet
    E. Less than 1 foot

17. Which of the following heat therapies uses radio waves to provide heat deep in the body?
    A. Shortwave diathermy
    B. Microwave diathermy
    C. Ultrasound diathermy
    D. Infrared diathermy
    E. Chemical diathermy

18. A way of assessing the patient's walking behavior is called
    A. Muscle strength testing
    B. Walking test
    C. Goniometry
    D. Electromyography
    E. Gait testing

19. When using a chemical hot pack in heat therapy, you should
    A. Place it on the patient's skin on the area being affected
    B. Plug the pack's heating cord into an outlet and turn the pad on
    C. Knead the pad and then cover it with cloth before placing it on the patient
    D. Fill the pack halfway with water, expel the air, and cover it with a pillowcase before applying
    E. Both B and D

20. How high should the top of a cane be?
    A. Axillary height
    B. Waist level
    C. Any height, because patients can use it well regardless of height
    D. 30 inches from the ground
    E. Level with the top of the femur

ANSWER KEY

1.	B		11.	B
2.	C		12.	C
3.	C		13.	A
4.	B		14.	C
5.	D		15.	B
6.	E		16.	C
7.	C		17.	A
8.	E		18.	E
9.	A		19.	C
10.	A		20.	E

Medical Emergencies and First Aid

AAMA—ROLE DELINEATION STUDY AREAS OF COMPETENCE

Clinical

Fundamental Principles

- Apply principles of aseptic technique and infection control

Patient Care

- Adhere to established triage procedures
- Recognize and respond to emergencies

AMT—RMA CERTIFICATION EXAM TOPICS

Asepsis

- Universal blood and body fluid precautions
- Medical asepsis
- Surgical asepsis

First Aid

- First aid procedures
- Legal responsibilities

STRATEGIES TO SUCCESS

► *Study Skills*

Rephrase!

When a concept seems complicated, look up any words you don't understand in a medical dictionary or a reference book, and try rephrasing the definition in your own words. Be sure that you only make the definition more clear and that you are not actually changing what the definition says. Rephrasing will help you understand the subject matter, and the concept will be easier to recall on an exam.

Emergencies

Medical emergency: A situation in which an individual suddenly becomes ill or has an injury that requires immediate attention and help by a health care professional.

First aid: Immediate care given to a person who has suddenly become injured or ill. First aid can save a life,

reduce pain, prevent further injury, reduce the risk of permanent disability, and increase the chance of early recovery.

Emergency Medical Services (EMS): A network of qualified police, fire, and medical personnel who use community resources and equipment to provide emergency care to victims of injury or sudden illness. Post the EMS telephone number, which is 911 in many communities, at every telephone and on the crash cart or first-aid tray.

Involving the EMS: To involve the EMS in an emergency, it is necessary to

1. Recognize that an emergency exists.
2. Decide to act.
3. Call the local emergency telephone number for help.
4. Provide care until help arrives.

Handling Emergencies

Medical assistant's responsibilities: You may be responsible for providing first aid, but you are never responsible for diagnosing or providing other medical care. Note the presence of serious conditions and take the appropriate action. Perform only procedures that you have been trained to perform. See Table 17-1.

Emergency triage: The classification of injuries according to severity, urgency of treatment, and place for treatment. If you receive an emergency call from a patient or patient's family member, follow the practice's triage protocols. Stay calm; reassure the patient; and act in a confident, organized manner.

Personal protection: When administering first aid and other emergency treatment, assume that all blood and body fluids are infected with blood-borne pathogens, and follow Universal Precautions, including wearing gloves and other personal protective equipment. Minimize your contact with blood by avoiding touching objects unnecessarily that have been contaminated with blood or other body fluids. Minimize the splattering or spraying of blood. Don't touch your face, eyes, nose, or mouth while providing emergency medical care. If you have been exposed to blood or other body fluids, tell the physician so that you can obtain post-exposure treatment.

Documentation: Document all office emergencies in the patient's chart, including information on assessment, treatment, and response.

Good Samaritan law: Permits emergency care on the condition that it is within the scope of competence of the person administering first aid. It holds individuals giving first aid responsible for any injury they cause as a result of negligence or failure to exercise reasonable care. If the victim is conscious or a family member is present, obtain verbal consent. If the victim is unconscious, consent is implied. State laws also apply.

Crash cart: A rolling cart that contains basic drugs, supplies, and equipment for medical emergencies. Most crash carts also contain a first-aid kit with supplies for managing minor injuries and ailments. See Table 17-2.

AT A GLANCE — Performing Emergency Assessment

1. Wash your hands and put on examination gloves if possible.
2. Talk to the patient to determine level of consciousness.
3. If the patient can communicate clearly, ask what happened. If the patient can't talk, ask someone who observed the incident.
4. If you cannot determine the patient's medical history by talking to the patient, check for a medical identification card or a bracelet.
5. Assess the patient's ABCs (airway, breathing, and circulation), and begin rescue breathing or cardiopulmonary resuscitation (CPR) as needed.
6. Assess for injury, observing the body from head to toe. Palpate gently.
7. Observe the skin for pallor (paleness) or cyanosis (a bluish tint). If the patient is dark-skinned, observe for pallor or cyanosis on the inside of the lips and mouth.
8. Check the pulse for regularity and strength.
9. Check the eyes for pupil size. Using a penlight, assess pupil response to light.
10. Document your findings and report them to the doctor or emergency medical technician (EMT).
11. Assist the doctor or EMT as requested.
12. Remove the gloves and wash your hands.

Table 17-1

AT A GLANCE — Stocking the Crash Cart

1. Review the office protocol for a list of items that should be on the crash cart.

2. Check the <u>drugs</u> on the cart against the list. Restock as necessary, and replace any drugs that have passed their expiration date. The following drugs are often included on the cart:
   - Activated charcoal
   - Amobarbital sodium (*Amytal Sodium*®)
   - Apomorphine hydrochloride
   - Atropine
   - Dextrose 50%

Table 17-2 (table continued on the next page)

- Diazepam (*Valium*®)
- Digoxin (*Lanoxin*®)
- Diphenhydramine hydrochloride (*Benadryl*®)
- Epinephrine, injectable
- Furosemide (*Lasix*®)
- Glucagon
- Glucose paste or tablets
- Insulin (regular or a variety)
- Intravenous dextrose in saline and intravenous dextrose in water
- Ipecac syrup
- Isoproterenol hydrochloride (*Isuprel*®), aerosol inhaler and injectable
- Lactated Ringer's solution
- Lidocaine (*Xylocaine*®), injectable
- Metaraminol (*Aramine*®)
- Methylprednisolone tablets
- Nitroglycerin tablets
- Phenobarbital, injectable
- Phenytoin (*Dilantin*®)
- Saline solution, isotonic (0.9%)
- Sodium bicarbonate, injectable
- Sterile water for injection

3. Check the <u>supplies</u> on the cart against the list. Restock used items, and make sure that all packaging of supplies on the cart is still intact. Crash cart supplies typically include:
   - Adhesive tape
   - Constricting band or tourniquet
   - Dressing supplies (alcohol wipes, rolls of gauze, bandage strips, bandage scissors)
   - Intravenous tubing, venipuncture devices, and butterfly needles
   - Padded tongue blades
   - Personal protective equipment
   - Syringes and needles in various sizes

4. Check the <u>equipment</u> on the crash cart against the list, and examine everything to make sure that it is in working order. Restock equipment that is missing or broken. The equipment usually consists of:
   - Airways in assorted sizes
   - *Ambu-bag*™, a trademark for a breathing bag used to assist respiratory ventilation
   - Defibrillator (electrical device that shocks the heart to restore normal breathing)
   - Endotracheal tubes in various sizes
   - Oxygen tank with oxygen mask and cannula

5. Check <u>miscellaneous items</u> on the cart against the list, and restock as needed. These items usually include:
   - Orange juice
   - Sugar packets

Table 17-2, continued

Injuries Caused by Extreme Temperatures

Hypothermia: A medical emergency in which the body temperature is dangerously reduced below the normal range, below 96°F (rectal, child/adult) or 97.5°F (rectal, newborn). Major symptoms include mild shivering, cool skin, and pallor. Minor character-istics include tachycardia, cyanosis, and hypertension. Risk factors include exposure to a cool or cold environment, trauma, malnutrition, consumption of alcohol, specific medications, decreased metabolic rate, aging, and inactivity.

Hyperthermia: Body temperature elevated above the normal range. Skin is warm to the touch and appears flushed. Tachypnea, tachycardia, seizures, or convulsions may be seen. Major factors include exposure to a hot environment, vigorous activity, medications or anesthesia, increased metabolic rate, trauma or illness, and dehydration. Individuals who are in poor health, alcoholic, obese, very young, or elderly are less able to tolerate heat waves and constant high temperatures.

Frostbite: The traumatic effect of extreme cold on skin and subcutaneous tissues, particularly the toes, fingers, ears, and nose. Vasoconstriction of blood vessels causes anoxia, edema, vesiculation, and necrosis. Symptoms include white, waxy, or grayish yellow skin that may feel crusty, with possible softness in the underlying tissue. The body part experiences sensations of cold, tingling, and pain. To treat frostbite, wrap warm clothing or blankets around the affected body part, or place the affected area in warm but not hot water. Do not rub or massage the affected area. Obtain medical assistance.

Heatstroke: A severe and sometimes fatal condition generally caused by prolonged exposure to high temperatures. Symptoms include hot, dry skin; high body temperature; altered mental state; rapid pulse; rapid breathing; dizziness; and weakness. To treat heatstroke, call the EMS system. Move the patient to a cool place and remove the patient's outer clothing. Cool the patient, using any means available. Keep the patient's head and shoulders slightly elevated.

Heat cramps: Painful spasms of the voluntary muscles in the leg, abdomen, or arm, which may be caused by depletion in the body of both water and salt. It occurs in an extremely hot environment.

Heat exhaustion: Characterized by muscle cramps, weakness, nausea, dizziness, and loss of consciousness, caused by depletion of body fluids and electrolytes. It

is the most frequent heat-related injury. Treatment includes removing the patient to a cool place and starting fluid and electrolyte replacement.

Burns

Burn: An injury to the tissues of the body caused by heat, electricity, chemicals, radiation, or gases. The severity of a burn depends on the depth of the burn and the percentage of the body involved. Burns are classified according to the depth of tissue injured. There are three types: first-degree, second-degree, and third-degree (See Figure 17-1).

First-degree burns: Also called superficial burns. They are the most common type of burn. They cause pain and make the surrounding skin turn red. A first-degree burn damages only the epidermis and causes edema. Sunburn is a common example of a superficial burn. To treat first-degree burns, apply cold-water dressings to the burn, or immerse the affected area in cold water. Gently pat the area dry, and apply a dry, sterile dressing. Do not use greasy ointments, butter, or other substances.

Second-degree burns: Also known as partial-thickness burns. These burns extend deeper into the skin than first-degree burns, damaging the epidermis and dermis. The injured area appears blistered, with redness and pain. The blisters should not be broken. They prevent infection of the burned area. They are usually very painful and heal within 3 to 4 weeks. To treat a second-degree burn, immerse the burned area in cold water until the pain subsides, pat the area dry, and apply a

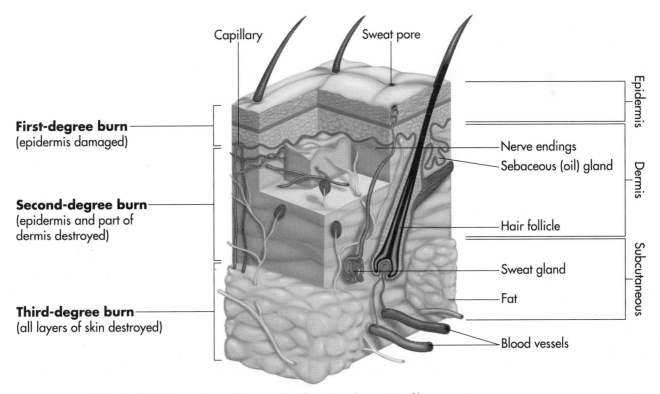

First-degree burn
(epidermis damaged)

Second-degree burn
(epidermis and part of dermis destroyed)

Third-degree burn
(all layers of skin destroyed)

Capillary

Sweat pore

Nerve endings

Sebaceous (oil) gland

Hair follicle

Sweat gland

Fat

Blood vessels

Epidermis

Dermis

Subcutaneous

Figure 17-1. *The depth of skin damage is one factor used to determine the severity of burns.*

dry, sterile dressing. Do not apply antiseptic ointment unless the physician orders it.

Third-degree burns: Also called full-thickness burns. These burns involve all layers of skin and completely damage both the epidermis and the dermis, extending into the underlying connective tissues such as fat, muscle, and even bone. A third-degree burn is an emergency condition. Spontaneous healing is impossible. These burns require the removal of scars and the application of skin grafts. Full-thickness burn victims may not feel any pain because of damage to the nerve endings in the skin. The most severe and major complication is infection. To treat a third-degree burn, call the EMS system. While waiting for the EMS team, do not remove charred or adhered clothing. Cover the burns and adhered clothing with thick, sterile dressings; keep the patient warm; and check to see whether the patient is suffering from smoke inhalation. If so, move the patient into a sitting position.

Estimating the extent of the burn: To calculate the amount of skin surface burned on an adult, use the rule of nines. Each of the following parts of the body is considered to be 9% of the body's surface: the head and neck, each upper limb, the chest, the abdomen, the upper back, the lower back and buttocks, the front of each lower limb, and the back of each lower limb. The remaining 1% is the genital area. See Figure 17-2, which also shows the percentages to use when making calculations in children.

Chemical burns: To treat a chemical burn, flood the area with large amounts of water, and cover it with a dry dressing. Call the EMS system.

Thermal burns: Caused by contact with hot liquids, steam, flames, radiation, excessive heat from fire, or hot objects. Call the EMS system. Use water to cool a burning substance, or use a wet cloth or blanket to put out a flame.

Sunburn: Causes redness, tenderness, pain, swelling, blisters, and peeling skin and can lead to skin damage or cancer. To treat sunburn, soak skin in cool water and apply cold compresses and calamine lotion. Have the patient elevate the legs and arms, drink plenty of water, and take a pain reliever.

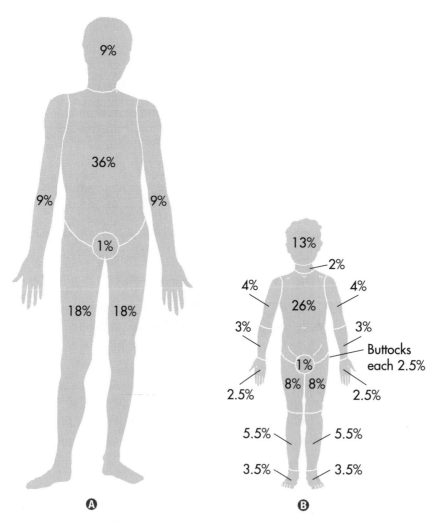

Figure 17-2. *A. Use the rule of nines to calculate the percentage of body surface affected by burns in adults. Except for the genital region, percentage figures combine front and back surfaces. B. In children, use the percentages based on the Lund and Browder chart. These numbers take into account that children's body proportions differ from those of adults.*

Wounds

Wound: A physical injury in which the skin or tissues under the skin are damaged. There are two types of wounds: open and closed.

Open wounds: Include punctures, lacerations, abrasions, and incisions (See Figure 17-3).

Incision: A clean and smooth cut.

Laceration: A cut with jagged edges.

Treating incisions and lacerations: See Table 17-3 for the way to treat minor incisions and lacerations. For deeper wounds that involve muscle, tendons, the face, the genitals, the mouth, or the tongue, control the bleeding with direct pressure to the wound, elevation, and the use of pressure points; contact the physician or EMS system.

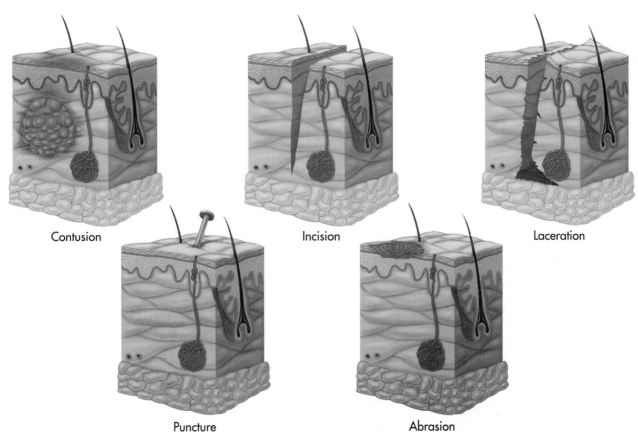

Contusion   Incision   Laceration

Puncture   Abrasion

Figure 17-3. *Different types of wounds produce different degrees of tissue damage.*

AT A GLANCE   **Cleaning Minor Wounds**

1. Wash your hands and put on examination gloves.
2. Dip several gauze squares in a basin of warm, soapy water.
3. Wash the wound from the center outward to avoid bringing contaminants from the surrounding skin into the wound. Use a new gauze square for each cleansing motion.
4. As you wash, remove debris that could cause infection.
5. Rinse the area thoroughly, preferably by placing the wound under warm, running water.
6. Pat the wound dry with sterile gauze squares.
7. Cover the wound with a dry, sterile dressing. Bandage the dressing in place.
8. Properly dispose of contaminated materials.
9. Remove the gloves and wash your hands.
10. Instruct the patient on wound care.
11. Record the procedure in the patient's chart.

Table 17-3

Abrasion: A scraping of the skin. Wash with soap and water, making sure to remove all dirt and debris. Use a bandage on a large abrasion. See Figure 17-4.

Puncture: A small hole created by a piercing object. Allow the wound to bleed freely for a few minutes, then clean it with soap and water and apply a dry, sterile dressing. A tetanus immunization may be required.

Closed wound: An injury that occurs inside the body without tearing the skin. Closed wounds are called contusions or bruises. They are caused by a sudden blow or force from a blunt object. Apply cold compresses to reduce swelling.

Bites and Stings

Animal bites: May range in severity from minor to serious. A wound that tears the skin should be seen by a physician and may need to be reported to the police, animal control office, and local health department. If the animal can be found, it should be checked for rabies.

Treating animal bites: If the bite is a puncture wound, try to make it bleed to flush out bacteria. Wash the area thoroughly with antiseptic soap and water. Apply an

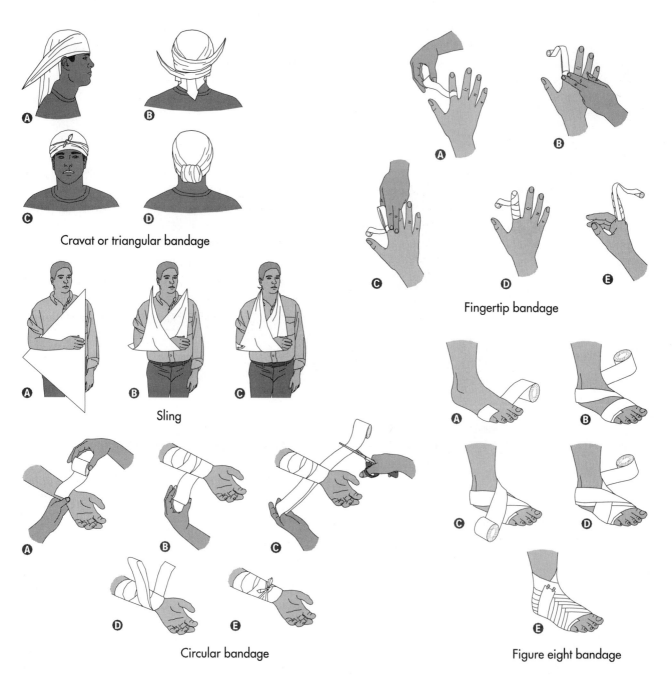

Cravat or triangular bandage

Sling

Fingertip bandage

Circular bandage

Figure eight bandage

Figure 17-4. *Apply a bandage, as needed, to a wound.*

antibiotic ointment and a dry, sterile dressing. The physician will administer a tetanus shot if the patient has not had one for 7 to 10 years.

Rabies: A viral infection normally transmitted through the saliva of rabid animals. Dogs, cats, skunks, squirrels, raccoons, bats, and foxes are more likely to carry rabies than other animals. Prevention involves vaccinating house pets. Immunization of a person who has been exposed to rabies should be started as soon as possible, because treatment is ineffective once clinical symptoms develop. If left untreated, rabies can cause paralysis and death.

Insect sting: An annoyance to most patients, insect stings can be deadly to those who are allergic to the insect venom. The site of an insect sting can become red, swollen, itchy, and painful. To remove the stinger, scrape the skin with a flat, hard, sharp object, being careful not to release more venom. If you cannot remove the stinger, call the physician. Wash the skin with soap and water, apply ice to reduce pain and swelling, and apply a paste of baking soda or a dressing soaked in aloe vera or vinegar to reduce discomfort.

Snakebite: A wound resulting from penetration of the skin by the fangs of a snake. Not all snakebites are poisonous. Symptoms of a poisonous snakebite include puncture marks, pain, swelling, rapid pulse, nausea, vomiting, and possibly unconsciousness and seizures. Bites from snakes known to be nonvenomous are treated as puncture wounds. Bites from poisonous or unidentified snakes require immediate attention. Call a doctor or the EMS system. The bitten area should be immobilized and positioned below heart level, and the patient should not walk. Wash the bite area with soap and water. Do not apply a tourniquet or ice, and do not cut or suction the wound.

Spider bite: A puncture wound produced by the bite of venomous spiders, which in the United States include the black widow and the brown recluse. Symptoms include swelling, pain, nausea, vomiting, rigid abdomen, fever, rash, and difficulty breathing or swallowing. Any patient bitten by a spider should be seen by a doctor. Wash the area thoroughly with soap and water, apply an ice pack, and keep the area below heart level.

Orthopedic Injuries

Strain: Overstretching of muscles or tendons caused by trauma. The muscles of the neck, back, thigh, and calf are the most common sites that can be injured by excessive physical force. Strains do not usually cause the intense symptoms associated with fractures, dislocations, and sprains.

Sprain: An acute partial tear of a tendon, muscle, or ligament, characterized by pain and edema. The joints most commonly sprained are ankles, knees, wrists, and fingers. Treatment requires elevation, mild compression, and immediate application of ice. After 24 to 36 hours, application of mild heat is usually indicated. The patient should also rest the affected area.

Dislocation: The displacement of a bone from its normal articulation with a joint. It is caused by a violent pulling or pushing force that tears the ligaments. Symptoms include deformity of the joint, pain, edema, and loss of function.

Fracture: A break in a bone. Review this section in Chapter 3, *Pathophysiology*.

Treating fractures and dislocations: To reduce pain and continuing damage to soft tissue, immobilize the body area by the application of a splint or cast. In some cases, it is necessary to move the bone back into the proper position.

Splint: An orthopedic device for immobilization or support of any part of the body. It may be rigid (made of metal, plaster, or wood) or flexible (made of leather, rolled newspapers, or magazines). The body part should be splinted in the position in which it was found. The splint should immobilize the area above and below the injury.

Cast: A rigid external dressing, usually made of plaster or fiberglass, that is molded to the contours of the body part. The basic elements of cast care, which should be communicated to the patient, are:

- Tell the physician about any pain, swelling, discoloration, lack of pulsation and warmth, or inability to move exposed parts.
- Keep the extremity elevated for the first day.
- Avoid allowing the affected limb to hang down for any length of time.
- Take care to avoid indenting the cast until it is dry.
- Restrict strenuous activity for the first few days.
- Do not put anything inside the cast.
- Keep the cast dry.

Head and Related Injuries

Head injury: Scalp hematoma, scalp laceration, concussion, contusion, fracture, and intracranial bleeding. Some head injuries can be life-threatening.

Scalp hematoma: A bump on the head caused by a buildup of blood under the skin. The swelling can be reduced by applying ice.

Scalp laceration: A wound that usually bleeds profusely. Direct pressure should be applied to stop the bleeding.

Concussion: A jarring injury to the brain, the most common type of head injury. Symptoms include loss of consciousness, temporary loss of vision, pallor, listlessness, memory loss, and vomiting. Symptoms may disappear rapidly or last up to 24 hours. The patient should refrain from strenuous activity, rest, and then return to regular activity gradually. Unless the physician approves using other pain medications, only acetaminophen should be used. The patient should eat lightly, and a family member should check on the patient every few hours.

Severe head injuries: Contusions, fractures, and intracranial bleeding. Mortality in severe injury approaches 50% and is only slightly reduced by treatment. Symptoms are more profound than in concussions and also include leakage of clear or bloody fluid from the ears or nose, seizures, and respiratory arrest. The patient requires immediate hospitalization to treat such an injury. Maintain the patient's airway and begin rescue breathing or CPR if needed.

Fainting: A brief loss of consciousness, also called syncope, that can result from a variety of causes. The most common direct cause of syncope is decreased cerebral blood flow. Before fainting, a patient may feel weak, dizzy, cold, or nauseated and may perspire or look pale and anxious. Have the patient lower his or her head between the legs and breathe deeply. Lay a patient who has fainted on his or her back with feet slightly elevated; loosen tight clothing, and apply a cold cloth to the face. Notify the physician.

Convulsions: May be caused by injury, trauma, fever, infection, hypocalcemia, hypoglycemia, or idiopathic factors. Convulsions, also called seizures, usually last only a few minutes. To treat convulsions, remove objects in the environment that may cause injury. Lay the patient on the floor on his or her side. Loosen restrictive clothing. Protect the patient from injury, but do not try to hold the patient still. If necessary, begin rescue breathing.

Cerebrovascular accident (CVA): An abnormal condition of the brain characterized by occlusion by an embolus, thrombus, or cerebrovascular hemorrhage. It is also known as stroke. Possible effects of stroke include paralysis, weakness, speech defects, aphasia, and death. Notify the physician and call the EMS system. Turn the patient's head toward the affected side to maintain the airway. Loosen tight clothing. If directed by the physician, monitor vital signs and administer oxygen.

Diabetic Emergencies

Diabetes: A fairly common disorder of carbohydrate metabolism, diabetes can cause hyperglycemia and hypoglycemia, both of which may become medical emergencies.

Hypoglycemia: A lower than normal level of glucose in the blood, usually caused by the administration of too much insulin, excessive secretion of insulin by the pancreas, or dietary deficiency. Symptoms of hypoglycemia include weakness, headache, hunger, ataxia, anxiety, and visual disturbances. Untreated hypo-

glycemia can result in delirium, coma, and death. The treatment is the administration of glucose in orange juice by mouth; if the patient is unconscious, an intravenous glucose solution must be started.

Insulin shock: Very severe hypoglycemia. The symptoms include weakness, tachycardia, cold skin, tremors, convulsions, restlessness, confusion, and fainting. The treatment is the administration of some form of sugar.

Hyperglycemia: A higher than normal level of blood glucose. Symptoms include dry mouth, intense thirst, muscle weakness, and blurred vision.

Diabetic coma: The end result of severe hyperglycemia. Symptoms are rapid breathing; flushed, warm, dry skin; thirst; acetone breath; and disorientation or confusion. If diabetic coma is suspected, a physician should be notified and the patient transported to a hospital.

Cardiovascular Emergencies

Shock

Shock: A life-threatening state associated with failure of the cardiovascular system. It prevents the vital organs from receiving blood and can bring all normal metabolic functions to a halt. Several types of shock are possible, such as hypovolemic, cardiogenic, neurogenic, septic, and anaphylactic.

Hypovolemic shock: Inadequate intravascular volume producing diminished ventricular filling and reduced stroke volume, which results in decreased cardiac output. It occurs after an injury that causes major fluid loss. Patients should be transported to an emergency facility immediately.

Cardiogenic shock: Results from reduction in cardiac output due to factors other than inadequate intravascular volume (e.g., cardiac tamponade, pulmonary embolism, myocardial infarction, myocarditis, drugs, tachycardia, and bradycardia).

Neurogenic shock: May occur following severe cerebral trauma or hemorrhage.

Septic shock: May be partly due to the effects of endotoxin or other chemical mediators on resistance vessels, resulting in vasodilation and decreased vascular resistance.

Anaphylactic shock: Occurs following allergic reactions. It is also called anaphylaxis.

Symptoms of shock: Restlessness; irritability; fear; rapid pulse; pale, cool skin; and increased respiratory rate.

Treating shock: Elevate the patient's feet 8 to 12 inches, unless there is head injury, in which case, keep the patient flat or elevate the head and shoulders. Monitor airways, breathing, and circulation, and control bleeding if necessary. Wrap the patient in a blanket, and call the EMS system.

Bleeding

Bleeding: The release of blood from the vascular system as a result of damage to a blood vessel. It is also called hemorrhaging and can be minor or very severe. A loss of 25 to 40 percent of a patient's total blood volume (approximately 2 to 4 pints of blood for the average adult) can be life-threatening and potentially fatal. There are two types of bleeding: external and internal.

Internal bleeding: Hemorrhaging from an internal organ or tissue, such as intraperitoneal bleeding into the peritoneal cavity, or intestinal bleeding into the bowel.

Hematemesis: The vomiting of bright red blood, indicating rapid upper gastrointestinal bleeding. The most common causes are esophageal varices and peptic ulcer.

Hemoptysis: The coughing up of blood from the respiratory tract.

Controlling internal bleeding: Cover the patient with a blanket, keep the patient quiet and calm, and get medical help immediately.

External bleeding: Bleeding that can be seen outside the body, such as bleeding from wounds, open fractures, and nosebleeds (epistaxis). The type of blood vessel that has been injured determines the classification of external bleeding: arterial, venous, or capillary. The most common type of external bleeding is capillary bleeding. The most serious and least common type of external bleeding is arterial.

Epistaxis (nosebleed): A common type of external bleeding usually caused by trauma, hypertension, exposure to high altitudes, or an upper respiratory infection.

Controlling external bleeding: If time permits, wash your hands and put on personal protective equipment. Apply direct pressure over the wound, using a clean or sterile dressing. Apply an additional dressing on top if blood soaks through. Elevate the body part that is bleeding. If bleeding does not stop, apply pressure over the nearest pressure point between the bleeding and the heart. See Figure 17-5.

Heart Attack

Chest pain: A physical complaint that requires immediate diagnosis and evaluation. Chest pain may be indicative of cardiac disease such as myocardial infarction, angina pectoris, or pericarditis; of respiratory disorders such as pleurisy, pneumonia, or pulmonary embolism; or of nonmyocardial infarction. Another source of chest pain can be cocaine use.

Myocardial infarction (MI): Ischemic myocardial necrosis of a portion of the cardiac muscle caused by obstruction in a coronary artery. It is also known as a heart attack. In more than 90% of patients with acute MI, an acute thrombus, often associated with plaque rupture, occludes the coronary artery. Chest pain is the major symptom of a heart attack. The pain may radiate down the left arm or into the jaw, throat, or both shoul-

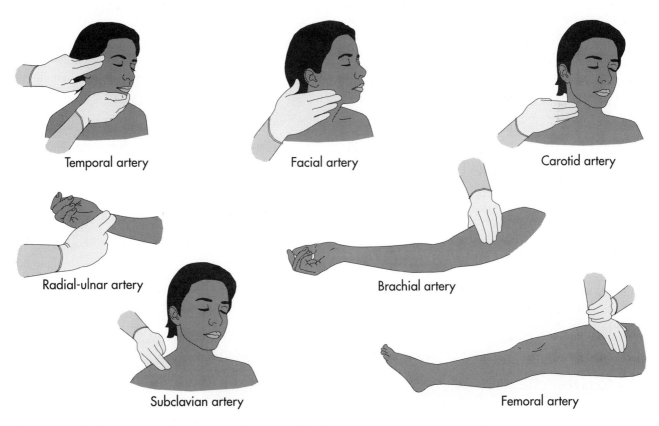

Temporal artery

Facial artery

Carotid artery

Radial-ulnar artery

Brachial artery

Subclavian artery

Femoral artery

Figure 17-5. *Apply pressure on these pressure points to stop bleeding.*

ders, and it may be accompanied by shortness of breath, sweating, nausea, and vomiting. When symptoms start, notify the physician and EMS system immediately, and do not let the patient walk. Loosen tight clothing, and have the patient sit up. The physician may direct you to administer oxygen. If cardiac arrest occurs, start CPR immediately.

Cardiac arrest: The sudden cessation of cardiac output and effective circulation, usually followed by ventricular fibrillation or ventricular asystole. It is also called cardiac standstill. Immediate initiation of cardiopulmonary resuscitation (CPR) is required to prevent heart, lung, kidney, and brain damage.

Cardiopulmonary resuscitation (CPR): In collapsed or unconscious persons, the state of ventilation and circulation must be determined immediately. Speed, efficiency, and proper application of CPR directly affect success. Tissue anoxia for more than 4 to 6 minutes can result in irreversible brain damage or death. After establishing unresponsiveness of the victim, call for help, note the exact time of arrest, and position the victim horizontally on a hard surface. Do a primary survey by assessing the patient's ABCs: airway, breathing, and circulation. CPR involves three basic components: opening the airway, rescue breathing, and chest compressions. See Figures 17-6 through 17-10. Table 17-4 gives a step-by-step procedure for performing CPR. CPR must be continued until the cardiopulmonary system is stabilized, the patient is

pronounced dead, or resuscitation cannot be continued (because of rescuer exhaustion). Resuscitation efforts can be divided into basic life support (BLS), which is carried out with techniques and equipment that are immediately available, and advanced cardiac life support (ACLS), which involves drug therapy, cardiac monitoring, and other specialized techniques and equipment.

Figure 17-8. *Perform mouth-to-mouth rescue breathing.*

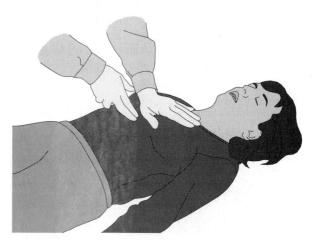

Figure 17-9. *Place your hands at the xiphoid process.*

Figure 17-6. *Use the head tilt-chin lift maneuver to open an airway.*

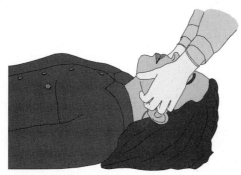

Figure 17-7. *Use the jaw thrust maneuver for a patient with a neck injury.*

Figure 17-10. *Align your shoulders directly over the victim's sternum, with your elbows locked.*

1. Wash your hands and put on examination gloves if possible.
2. If the patient is not on her back, roll her whole body over.
3. Open the patient's airway by lifting her chin gently with one hand while pushing back on her forehead with the other hand. See Figure 17-6.
4. If you suspect a neck injury, use the modified jaw thrust instead. Put your fingers behind the jawbone just below the ear, and push the jaw forward. See Figure 17-7.
5. Place your ears close to the patient's mouth, and keep your eyes on her chest and stomach. Look for chest and abdominal movement. Listen for the sound of air moving. Feel for breath on your cheek. These signs indicate that the patient is breathing.
6. If you do not see, hear, or feel breathing, begin rescue breathing. Turn the hand you are resting on the patient's forehead so that you can also use it to pinch her nose. See Figure 17-8.
7. Place a mouth shield over the patient's mouth, and take a deep breath. Place your mouth on the shield over the patient's mouth, making a seal. You may need to use the patient's nose, nose and mouth together (for a child), or tracheal stoma (for someone with a tracheostomy). Then blow into her mouth (or nose or stoma). Pause and then blow into her mouth (or nose or stoma) again. Watch to see that the patient's chest rises with the breaths.
8. Locate the carotid pulse to check for a heartbeat. If you do not feel a pulse, start artificial circulation. NOTE: The American Heart Association has revised its guidelines and they no longer recommend to check for a pulse before starting chest compressions.
9. Locate the end of the sternum, called the xiphoid process. Run your fingers across the lower margin of the ribs to the notch where they meet. Place your index and middle fingers flat on the chest at this spot. Place the heel of your other hand on the midline of the sternum, next to the index finger. See Figure 17-9.
10. With the heel of your hand in place, place your other hand on top of it and interlace the fingers. Straighten your arms and lock your elbows. Position your shoulders directly over your hands so that you thrust downward. See Figure 17-10.
11. Depress the sternum $1\frac{1}{2}$ to 2 inches for an adult. Release the compression completely, but keep your elbows locked and your hands on the chest.
12. Do four sets of 15 compressions and 2 breaths over a 1-minute period.
13. Assist EMS personnel as requested.
14. Remove the gloves and wash your hands.

Table 17-4

Defibrillator: A device that delivers an electrical shock at a preset voltage to the myocardium through the chest wall. It is used for restoring the normal cardiac rhythm and rate when the heart has stopped beating or is fibrillating. The office defibrillator is portable and is powered by standard 110V current or batteries.

Respiratory Emergencies

Choking: A condition in which the respiratory passage is blocked by an obstruction, usually food in the trachea. If the victim is coughing forcefully, do nothing but observe. If the victim is conscious but cannot speak, breathe, or cough, the Heimlich maneuver should be used. Give upward sub-diaphragmatic abdominal thrusts until the foreign body is expelled. See Figure 17-11. If the victim loses consciousness, lay

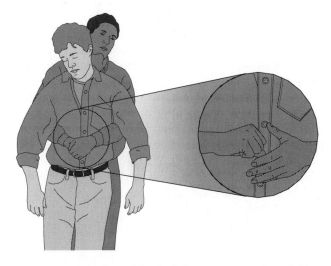

Figure 17-11. *Perform abdominal thrusts on a conscious choking victim.*

the person down slowly on his or her back. Check the mouth for a foreign body, and sweep it out with your fingers if possible. Continue to administer upward abdominal thrusts, with the heel of one hand between the xiphoid process and the navel and the second hand on top of the first, until the foreign body is expelled. If the person is still not breathing independently when the airway is clear, perform CPR. The objectives of emergency treatment are (1) removal of the obstruction and (2) resuscitation if necessary.

Respiratory arrest: Lack of breathing, usually preceded by symptoms of respiratory distress. If a patient shows such symptoms, notify the physician immediately. If the patient develops respiratory arrest, call the physician and the EMS system, and perform CPR.

Asthma: A respiratory disorder characterized by (1) airway constriction that is reversible, either spontaneously or with treatment; (2) airway inflammation; and (3) increased airway sensitivity to a variety of stimuli. If a patient has an asthma attack, notify the physician. If the patient has a respiratory inhaler, help the patient use it.

Hyperventilation: Breathing too rapidly and too deeply, which can cause patients to feel light-headed and as if they cannot get enough air. Move the patient to a quiet area, and have the patient breathe into a paper bag that is held tightly around the nose and mouth. Encourage the patient to take slow, normal breaths.

Poisoning

Poison: A substance that impedes biological functions when taken into the body. The majority of accidental poisonings occur at home to children under the age of 5 years. A poison may enter the body by ingestion, absorption, injection, or inhalation. Clinically, poisons are divided into those that respond to specific antidotes or treatment and those for which there is no specific treatment.

Symptoms of ingested poisons: Abdominal pain; cramping; nausea; vomiting; diarrhea; odor, stains, or burns around the mouth; drowsiness; and unconsciousness.

Treating ingested poisons: Call a poison control center, hospital emergency room, physician, or the EMS system for instructions. Help the patient drink one or two glasses of water or milk as quickly as possible, and turn the patient on his or her left side.

Inducing vomiting: Induce vomiting only if directed to do so by a medical authority. Use ipecac syrup to induce vomiting. When vomiting has stopped, administer 30 to 50 g of activated charcoal to absorb residual poison.

Symptoms of absorbed poisons: Rash, swelling, burning eyes, headache, fever, and abnormal pulse or respiration.

Treating absorbed poisons: Call a poison control center. Have the patient remove all contaminated clothing. Wash infected skin thoroughly with soap and water, drench it with alcohol, and rinse well. Apply wet compresses soaked in calamine lotion and suggest a bath in colloidal oatmeal or the application of a paste of baking soda and water to soothe the itching.

Symptoms of inhaled poisons: Headache, tinnitus, angina, shortness of breath, muscle weakness, nausea, vomiting, confusion, dizziness, blurred or double vision, unconsciousness, and cardiac arrest. Carbon monoxide is the most commonly inhaled poison.

Treating inhaled poisons: Get the patient into fresh air. Call the EMS system or a poison control center. Loosen tight-fitting clothing, and wrap the patient in a blanket to prevent shock.

Digestive Emergencies

Abdominal pain: Although many diseases can produce abdominal pain, acute and severe pain nearly always is a symptom of intra-abdominal abnormality (pathology). It may be the most important indication that an emergency operation or treatment is needed, such as for appendicitis, perforated peptic ulcer, intestinal obstruction, general peritonitis, twisted ovarian cyst, or ectopic pregnancy.

Treating abdominal pain: Call for transport, and have the patient lie on the back with the knees flexed. Keep the patient warm and quiet. Do not apply heat. Monitor the patient's pulse and consciousness, and check for signs of shock.

Vomiting: A common symptom of many disorders that can lead to dehydration and electrolyte imbalances. Notify the physician, and use a basin to collect the vomit. Place a cool compress on the patient's forehead, and offer water and a towel to clean the mouth.

Acute diarrhea: Can cause dehydration and electrolyte imbalances and can lead to shock. The patient should lie on his or her back and elevate the legs. The physician may direct you to assist in administering intravenous fluids.

Melena: Abnormal black, tarry stool that has a distinctive odor and contains digested blood. It usually results from bleeding in the upper gastrointestinal tract. In adults, it is often a sign of peptic ulcer or small bowel disease.

Reproductive System Emergencies

Vaginal bleeding: If a patient experiences gushing vaginal bleeding, call the EMS system, and have her lie down with her feet elevated.

Emergency childbirth: If a physician is not present, the medical assistant should summon help and begin the procedure. Ask the woman how far apart her contractions are, whether her water has broken, and whether she feels straining or pressure as if the baby is coming. Always explain to the woman what you are doing and reassure her. Do a visual examination of the vagina to see whether there is crowning (a bulging caused by the baby's head). If the head is crowning, childbirth is imminent. Place clean cloths under the woman, and use sterile sheets or towels (if available) to cover her legs and stomach. Wash your hands thoroughly, and put on examination gloves if possible. If a physician is available, position yourself at the woman's head and provide emotional support and help if she vomits. If no physician is available, position yourself at the woman's side so that you can see the vaginal opening. Place one hand below the baby's head as it is delivered. Never pull on the baby. If the umbilical cord is wrapped around the baby's neck, gently loosen it and slide it over the head. If the amniotic sac has not broken, use your finger to puncture the membrane and pull the membranes as well as blood and mucus away from the baby's mouth and nose. After the feet are delivered, lay the baby on his or her side, with the head slightly lower than the body. Keep the baby at the same level as the mother until you cut the umbilical cord. The infant must be breathing independently before you clamp and cut the cord. Wait several minutes until the pulsation of the umbilical cord stops, then use clamps or pieces of string to close off the cord in two places: 6 and 12 inches from the baby. Cut the cord between the two clamps with sterilized scissors. Within 10 minutes of birth, expulsion of the placenta will begin. Keep it in a plastic bag for further examination. Keep the mother and baby warm by wrapping them in towels and blankets. Massage the mother's abdomen just below the navel every few minutes to control internal bleeding.

STRATEGIES TO SUCCESS

▶ Test-Taking Skills

Survey the test!

Before you begin answering questions, glance at the exam. Find out how long it is exactly. How many questions are there in each section? Are you missing any pages? Take note of how long you have to complete the exam. Quickly figure out the halfway time and the halfway question number. This information will help you to pace yourself. So on each exam, you actually have less than a minute to answer each question. Make sure that as you are taking the exam, you keep track of your progress. If you fall behind, don't panic. Try to answer questions more quickly, and don't skip questions without answering them. Make educated guesses and move on. Come back to these questions if you finish early.

CHAPTER 17 REVIEW

Instructions:

Answer the following questions. Check your answers in the *Answer Key* that follows this section.

1. What percentage of the body is involved in a burn that covers one arm and the head of an adult?
   A. 1%
   B. 9%
   C. 18%
   D. 36%
   E. 40%

2. The Good Samaritan law explicitly allows medical assistants
   A. To administer first aid within the scope of their competence
   B. To call the EMS system and stay with the victim until EMS personnel arrive
   C. To act freely in an emergency situation to save the victim's life
   D. To diagnose the patient at the scene of an accident or emergency
   E. Only to call the EMS system and wait for authorized personnel but not to touch or communicate with an accident victim

3. In emergency childbirth, at what point should the umbilical cord be tied and cut?
   A. When the infant is fully out
   B. Within 10 minutes of birth
   C. When the infant starts breathing
   D. When the mother and baby get to the hospital
   E. When the baby is ready to nurse

4. To treat frostbite, a medical assistant can
   A. Massage the affected area gently
   B. Rub the affected area with a warmed towel
   C. Keep the patient's head and shoulders slightly elevated
   D. Wash the area with soap and water
   E. Place warm clothing and blankets around the affected area

5. Which of the following are symptoms of heat-stroke?
   A. The body tingles, and the patient feels pain
   B. There is a white, waxy, or grayish yellow build-up on the skin, and the patient has a high body temperature
   C. The skin feels moist and hot, and the patient feels dizzy with a possibly altered mental state
   D. The pulse is rapid, the skin is hot and dry, and the patient feels weak
   E. The patient has a strange metallic taste in his or her mouth and feels hot

6. When treating a second-degree burn, a medical assistant should
   A. Break blisters to relieve the patient's pain
   B. Immerse the burned area in cold water
   C. Remove charred or adhered clothing
   D. Apply medical ointments to the affected area
   E. Apply a wet, sterile dressing

7. When Bill Williams scraped his skin, he most likely got a(n)
   A. Incision
   B. Laceration
   C. Abrasion
   D. Puncture
   E. Bruise

8. Irreversible brain damage can be caused by tissue anoxia lasting
   A. More than 2 minutes
   B. More than 3 minutes
   C. More than 6 minutes
   D. More than 45 minutes
   E. More than 3 hours

9. Which of the following is a correct way to treat a snakebite?

    A. Administer activated charcoal
    B. Walk the patient to a hospital
    C. Suction the wound and apply ice
    D. Immobilize the bitten area and wash it with soap and water
    E. Cut out the affected area

10. If a patient is bleeding from the lower arm and direct pressure and elevation do not stop the bleeding, where should pressure be applied?

    A. Radial-ulnar artery
    B. Brachial artery
    C. Subclavian artery
    D. Carotid artery
    E. Phrenic artery

11. One possible cause of stroke is

    A. Occlusion in the brain by a thrombus
    B. Decreased cerebral blood flow
    C. Ingested poisons
    D. Hypocalcemia
    E. Hyperthermia

12. White, waxy, or grayish yellow skin that also feels crusty and softness in tissue beneath the skin could indicate

    A. Heatstroke
    B. Frostbite
    C. Contusion
    D. Hypothermia
    E. Shock

13. Which of the following is a possible treatment of syncope?

    A. Having the patient lower his or her head between the legs
    B. Laying the patient flat on the patient's back with the feet slightly elevated
    C. Loosening tight clothing and applying a cold cloth to the patient's face
    D. Both B and C
    E. All of the above

14. The Heimlich maneuver is used for which of the following?

    A. Convulsion
    B. Epistaxis
    C. Hematemesis
    D. Shock
    E. Choking

15. Anaphylactic shock occurs following

    A. Hemorrhage
    B. Allergic reaction
    C. Toxemia of pregnancy
    D. Cardiac arrest
    E. None of the above

16. Which of the following should not be done by a patient with a concussion?

    A. Eat
    B. Take aspirin
    C. Take acetaminophen
    D. Rest
    E. Gradually resume normal activities

17. The most severe and major complication for burn victims is

    A. Pain
    B. Anemia
    C. Infection
    D. Malignant fever
    E. Both B and C

18. Which of the following should not be done when a patient complains of abdominal pain?

    A. Have the patient lie on the back
    B. Apply heat to the patient's abdomen
    C. Have the patient flex the knees
    D. Monitor the patient's pulse
    E. Check for signs of shock

19. Closed wounds are called

    A. Bruises or contusions
    B. Lacerations
    C. Abrasions
    D. Scrapes
    E. None of the above

20. When administering CPR, how many compressions should you do?

    A. 15 in 1 minute
    B. 20 in 1 minute
    C. 25 in 2 minutes
    D. 60 in 1 minute
    E. 30 in 2 minutes

21. According to Good Samaritan laws,

    A. Emergency care is required of all medical personnel in all situations
    B. Emergency care is permitted only with the verbal consent of the patient
    C. Emergency care is permitted when it is within the scope of competence of the person
    D. Possible negligence is never a factor in providing emergency care
    E. Both B and D

22. Chest pain might indicate

    A. Cocaine use
    B. Myocardial infarction
    C. Epistaxis
    D. Both B and C
    E. Both A and B

23. When you suspect neck injury, what action should you take to open the patient's airway before administering rescue breathing?

    A. Place your mouth over the patient's nose and blow air into it until the patient's chest rises
    B. Put your fingers behind the jawbone just below the ear and push the jaw forward
    C. Wait for EMS personnel, and do not administer rescue breathing
    D. Hold the patient's neck rigidly while you lift the patient's chin up and push back on the forehead
    E. Open an airway in the patient's neck with a sterile instrument

24. Treat hypoglycemia by

    A. Administering glucose
    B. Giving the patient plain orange juice
    C. Loosening the patient's restrictive clothing and elevating the patient's head
    D. Administering immunization as soon as possible
    E. None of the above

ANSWER KEY

1.	C		13.	E
2.	A		14.	E
3.	C		15.	B
4.	E		16.	B
5.	D		17.	C
6.	B		18.	B
7.	C		19.	A
8.	C		20.	D
9.	D		21.	C
10.	B		22.	E
11.	A		23.	B
12.	B		24.	A

Laboratory Procedures

CHAPTER OUTLINE

Collecting and Testing Blood

Hematology
Serology and Immunology
Collecting Blood
Testing Blood
Conditions Identified by Phlebotomy

Collecting and Testing Urine

Physical and Chemical Composition and Function
Obtaining Specimens
Urinalysis

Medical Microbiology

Collecting Specimens
Examining Specimens
Culture Media

AREAS OF COMPETENCE

AAMA—ROLE DELINEATION STUDY AREAS OF COMPETENCE

Clinical

Fundamental Principles

- Apply principles of aseptic technique and infection control
- Comply with quality assurance practices
- Screen and follow up patient test results

Diagnostic Orders

- Collect and process specimens
- Perform diagnostic tests

(Chart continued on next page.)

AMT—RMA CERTIFICATION EXAM TOPICS

Laboratory Procedures

- Safety
- Quality control
- Laboratory equipment
- Urinalysis
- Blood
- Other specimens
- Specimen handling
- Records
- Microbiology

STRATEGIES TO SUCCESS

► Study Skills

Take study breaks!
Long periods of uninterrupted studying can dull your concentration, make your mind wander, and lead you to daydream. So, after a few hours of studying, treat yourself to a mental break. Giving yourself short, well-defined breaks will help prevent burnout and keep your energy focused. Take a walk outside, read an article in a magazine, or do something that relaxes and refreshes you. Then get back to studying.

Collecting and Testing Blood

Medical assistant's role: Depending on the laws of the state in which you live, you may collect and process blood specimens, conduct blood tests, and complete necessary paperwork.

Hematology

Hematology: The study of blood and blood-forming tissues.

Functions of blood: To distribute oxygen, nutrients, and hormones to body cells; to eliminate waste products from body cells; to attack infecting organisms or pathogens; to maintain the body's acid-base balance; and to regulate body temperature.

Hematopoiesis: The normal formation and development of blood cells in the bone marrow.

Whole blood: Consists of plasma and the formed elements. In adults, total blood volume normally makes up 7% to 8% of body weight, or 70 ml/Kg of body weight in men and about 65 ml/Kg in women. Blood is pumped through the body at a speed of about 30 cm/second, with complete circulation in 20 seconds.

Plasma: The liquid in which the other components of blood are suspended. Plasma accounts for 55% of the body's total blood volume. Water makes up about 90% of plasma. About 9% is protein and 1% is other substances including carbohydrates, fats, gases, mineral salts, protective substances, and waste products. Free of its formed elements and particles, plasma is a clear, yellow fluid. When a tube of blood is centrifuged, the plasma rises to the top.

Formed elements, or **blood cells:** Red cells (erythrocytes), white cells (leukocytes), and platelets (thrombocytes). Blood cells constitute about 45% of the body's total volume of blood. An older term for a formed element is blood corpuscle. See Figure 18-1.

Blood gas: Dissolved gas in the liquid part of the blood. Blood gases include oxygen, carbon dioxide, and nitrogen.

Bone marrow: Found in the cavities of all bones. It may be present in two forms: red and yellow. Yellow marrow is inactive and is composed mostly of fat tissue. Red marrow is active in the production of most types of blood cells. By age 18, red marrow is found only in the vertebrae, ribs, sternum, skull bones, and pelvis.

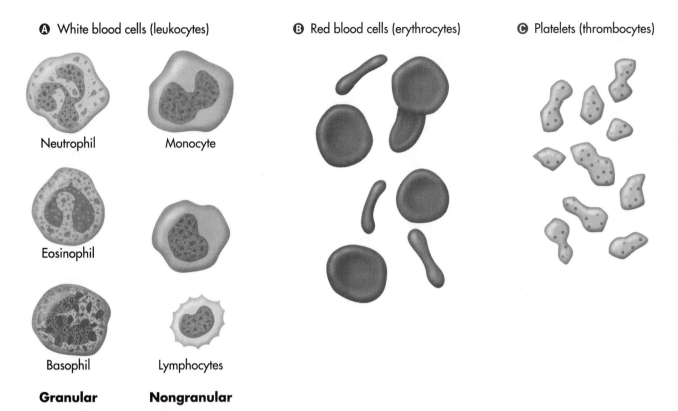

Ⓐ White blood cells (leukocytes)   Ⓑ Red blood cells (erythrocytes)   Ⓒ Platelets (thrombocytes)

Neutrophil   Monocyte

Eosinophil

Basophil   Lymphocytes

Granular   Nongranular

Figure 18-1. *The formed elements of the blood are (A) white blood cells, (B) red blood cells, and (C) platelets.*

Erythrocytes

Erythrocyte: Also known as a red blood cell (RBC). A mature red blood cell is made up of lipids and proteins to which hemoglobin molecules are attached. RBCs play a vital role in internal respiration, the exchange of gases between blood and body cells. They are disk shaped and have concave sides.

Erythropoiesis: The process of erythrocyte production. This process develops in the embryonic yolk sac, liver, and spleen. It is ultimately located in the red bone marrow during late fetal development, childhood, and adult life.

Erythropoietin: A glycoprotein hormone, produced primarily by the kidneys and also secreted by the liver, that stimulates erythropoiesis. It can cross the placental barrier.

Reticulocyte: The last stage of the immature erythrocyte. This cell lacks a nucleus and is found in both the bone marrow and peripheral blood.

Transferrin: A specific transport protein in the blood. It binds iron and transports it back to the bone marrow for hemoglobin synthesis.

Hemoglobin: The iron-containing pigment of red blood cells that carries oxygen from the lungs to the tissues.

Hemagglutination: The coagulation of erythrocytes.

Hemagglutinin: A type of antibody that agglutinates erythrocytes.

Rouleaux formation: A configuration of red blood cells having the appearance of stacked coins.

Leukocytes

Leukocyte: Also known as a white blood cell (WBC). Through phagocytosis, it protects the body against infection. Leukocytes are divided into two groups: granular and nongranular.

Granular leukocytes: Basophils, eosinophils, and neutrophils.

Basophils: Produce histamine, which plays a major role in allergic reactions.

Eosinophils: Capture invading bacteria and antigen-antibody complexes through phagocytosis.

Neutrophils: Attack invaders and release pyrogens, which cause fever.

Nongranular leukocytes: Lymphocytes and monocytes.

Lymphocytes: The smallest leukocytes, which contain the largest nuclei. They include B cells and T cells. B lymphocytes produce antibodies to combat specific pathogens. T lymphocytes regulate the immune response.

Monocytes: Large leukocytes in the bloodstream with oval or horseshoe-shaped nuclei. Their major functions are phagocytosis and synthesis of various biological compounds, including transferrin, complement, interferon, and certain growth factors.

Macrophages: Monocytes that mature outside the circulatory system, distributed in tissues throughout the body. They have a variety of names (often depending on their location in the body), such as histiocytes, Kupffer cells, osteoclasts, and microglial cells.

Phagocytes: Cells that have the capacity for phagocytosis. Macrophages, as well as most of the leukocytes, are phagocytes. Large phagocytes can destroy worn-out red blood cells or bacteria. They are found in the spleen, thymus, and lymphoid tissues.

Phagocytosis: The process by which cells engulf and ingest microorganisms.

Thrombocytes

Platelets: Metabolically active anuclear cell fragments produced in the bone marrow that assist in blood coagulation and clotting. They are also called thrombocytes. Normally, between 130,000 and 400,000 platelets are found in 1 cubic milliliter of blood.

Megakaryocytes: Precursors of platelets. They are the largest cells found in the bone marrow, and they have a nucleus with many lobes. They are normally not present in circulating blood.

Serology and Immunology

Serology: The study of blood serum based on antigen-antibody reactions in vitro.

Serum: The liquid portion of blood that remains after the clotting proteins and cells have been removed. It differs from plasma in that it does not contain fibrinogen, a protein involved in clotting.

Antigen: A substance on cells whose presence in the body stimulates the body's immune response. Antigens produced by the body itself are autoantigens; antigens on other cells are foreign antigens.

Antibody: A protein produced in response to a specific antigen. It defends the body against infection.

Serology abbreviations: Common abbreviations are listed in Table 18-1.

Coagulation: The process of clumping together of blood cells to form a clot. It may occur in vitro, intravascularly, or when a laceration allows the escape of blood from a blood vessel.

Agglutination: An antigen-antibody reaction in which a solid antigen clumps together with a soluble antibody.

Agglutinin: An antibody that interacts with antigens, resulting in agglutination.

Agglutinogen: Any antigenic substance that causes agglutination.

Opsonization: A process by which antibodies or complements render bacteria more susceptible to phagocytosis by leukocytes. It is also called opsonification.

Immunology: The study of the reaction of immune system tissues to antigenic stimulation.

Immune: Protected by antibodies against infective or allergic disease.

Immune response: A defense function of the body that produces antibodies to destroy invading antigens and cancer cells.

Antiserum: A serum of animal or human origin that contains antibodies against a specific disease. It is also called immune serum. Antiserums (or antisera) do not provoke the production of antibodies. There are two types: antitoxin and antimicrobial.

Complement: Protein molecules that are chief humoral mediators of antigen-antibody reactions in the immune system. Complement proteins stimulate phagocytosis and inflammation.

Classification of immunoglobulin: In response to specific antigens, immunoglobulins are formed in the bone marrow, the spleen, and all lymphoid tissue of the body except the thymus. All antibodies are immunoglobulins.

AT A GLANCE	Serology Abbreviations
Ab	Antibody
ABO	Classification system for the four blood groups
ACT	Activated coagulation time
Ag	Antigen
A/GR	Albumin-globulin ratio
Alb	Albumin
Alc	Alcohol
B	Blood (whole blood)

Table 18-1

BCA	Breast cancer antigen
BT	Bleeding time
CA	Cancer antigen
CBC	Complete blood (cell) count
CRP	C-reactive protein
Diff	Differential (blood cell count)
GTT	Glucose tolerance test
Hb, Hgb	Hemoglobin
HCG, hCG	Human chorionic gonadotropin
HCV	Hepatitis C virus
HIV	Human immunodeficiency virus
HSV	Herpes simplex virus
MCV	Mean cell volume
Monospot test	Mononucleosis test
P	Plasma
PLT	Platelet
PRL	Prolactin
PV	Plasma volume
RBC	Red blood cell, red blood cell count
S	Serum
WB	Western blot
WBC	White blood cell, white blood cell count

Table 18-1, continued

Collecting Blood

Collecting blood: The two common ways to collect blood are phlebotomy and capillary puncture. Some, but not all, states permit medical assistants to obtain blood samples. You should know the appropriate laws of your state.

Phlebotomy: The insertion of a needle or tube into a vein to draw blood. It is also called venipuncture or venesection. Phlebotomy is the most common method of collecting blood for hematologic testing. The most common site for venipuncture is the median cubital vein. The cephalic vein of the forearm, the basilic vein of the forearm, and the veins in the back of the hand are also sometimes used. See Figure 18-2 on p. 366.

Capillary puncture: A superficial puncture of the skin with a sharp point that releases a smaller amount of

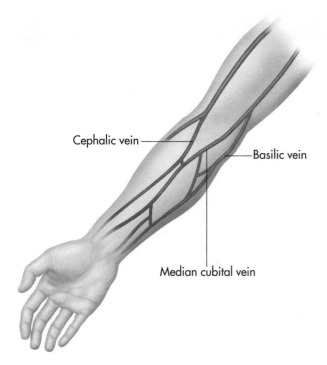

Figure 18-2. *Veins commonly used for venipuncture include the cephalic vein, the basilic vein, and the median cubital vein.*

blood than venipuncture. It is also called a finger stick. Capillary puncture in adults and children is usually performed on the great (middle) finger or the ring finger. Try to use the patient's nondominant hand, and do not reuse a previous puncture site. Capillary puncture in infants is usually performed on one of the outer edges of the underside of the heel. The rear curve of the heel should never be punctured. An alternate site for both children and adults is the lower side of a non-pierced earlobe. A puncture should not be deeper than 2.4 mm (0.1 in).

Quality Control Procedures

Quality control: When taking a blood specimen, follow quality control procedures:

1. Review the request form, verify the procedure, and prepare the equipment, paperwork, and work area.

2. Identify the patient, confirm the patient's identification, and explain the procedure.

3. Confirm that the patient has followed pretest preparation requirements.

4. Collect the specimen properly, using sterile equipment and proper technique.

5. Use the correct specimen collection containers and preservatives.

6. Immediately label the specimens with the patient's name, date and time of collection, test name, and the name of person collecting the specimen.

7. Follow correct procedures for disposing of hazardous waste and decontaminating the work area.

8. Prepare the specimen for transport in the proper container, following OSHA regulations.

Documentation: Maintain the quality control log, reagent control log, equipment maintenance log, reference laboratory log, and daily workload log, as applicable.

Quality control log: Shows the completion of every quality control check conducted on a piece of equipment. The testing equipment must be calibrated regularly in accordance with manufacturer's guidelines. Calibration routines are performed on a set of standards, the values of which are already known.

Control sample: A specimen with a known value that is used every time a patient sample is processed. Using a control sample serves as a check on the accuracy of the test.

Reagent: A chemical or chemically treated substance that reacts in specific ways when exposed under specific conditions.

Reagent control log: Shows the quality testing performed on every batch or lot of reagent products. Control samples or standards are run every time you open a new supply of testing products, such as staining materials, culture media, and reagents.

Equipment maintenance record: Documents any maintenance done on laboratory equipment.

Reference laboratory log: Lists specimens sent to another laboratory for testing.

Daily workload log: Shows all procedures completed during the workday.

Patient record: Record test results in the patient's record, and properly identify any unusual findings. Remember that only a physician is qualified to interpret test results, so these results should not be communicated to the patient until the physician has had an opportunity to review the information.

Blood Collecting Equipment

Equipment needed: Typically includes a syringe, tube, or lancet to draw blood; alcohol and cotton balls or alcohol wipes; sterile gauze; adhesive bandages; and a tourniquet.

Blood lancet: A small, sterile, disposable instrument used for skin or capillary puncture.

Automatic puncturing device: A spring-loaded mechanism equipped with a disposable lancet for capillary puncture.

Micropipette: A calibrated glass tube for measuring small, precise volumes of fluids used in capillary puncture.

Unopette®: A disposable micropipette blood-diluting system used to perform manual blood counts. (It is manufactured by Becton Dickinson Vacutainer® Systems.)

Reagent strip: Used with freshly collected blood droplets in capillary puncture. It is also referred to as a dipstick. Blood is dropped or smeared on the strip. Some of the blood tests performed in this way are those for determining blood glucose levels, sickle cell anemia, infectious mononucleosis, and rheumatoid arthritis.

Smear slide: A prepared microscope slide to which freshly collected blood is applied.

Butterfly needle set: A device used to collect blood samples from individuals with small or fragile veins. It consists of a needle with plastic wings, flexible tubing, an adapter, and a collection device. A 21–25-gauge needle is used. Once inserted, the needle remains completely undisturbed while the collection device is manipulated. Because it is motionless, the needle causes less trauma to the vein and surrounding tissue. See Figure 18-3. With butterfly systems, avoid using large evacuation tubes because they may cause the vein to collapse.

Evacuation tube: The most common evacuation system is the Vacutainer® system (manufactured by Becton Dickinson Vacutainer® Systems). It uses a special needle, a needle holder/adapter, and collection tubes that have been sealed to maintain a slight vacuum (See Figure 18-4). Some tubes are prepared with additives needed to process the blood sample for testing, such as anticoagulants. The tube stoppers are color-coded according to the type of additive used (See Table 18-2). Expired tubes may no longer have a vacuum.

Collection tubes: No matter which method is used to collect blood, the samples must immediately be mixed with the appropriate additives in the correct collection tubes before they are transported to the laboratory for testing. Each laboratory may choose which tubes to use for a particular test.

Anticoagulants: Substances that prevent blood clotting. Three anticoagulants commonly used in the hematology laboratory are heparin, sodium citrate, and ethylenediaminetetraacetic acid (EDTA).

Heparin: A substance produced naturally by basophils and mast cells. Heparin acts in the body as an antithrombin factor to prevent intravascular clotting. As an additive in blood collection, heparin is used in electrolyte studies and tests for arterial blood gasses. Heparin is also used as an anticoagulant in the prevention and treatment of thrombosis and embolism.

Sodium citrate: A white granular powder, used as an anticoagulant in transfusions and coagulation studies.

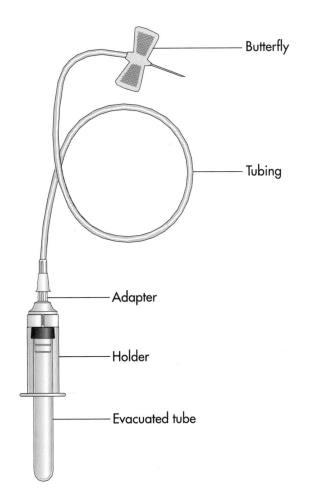

Figure 18-3. *Once inserted, the needle of a butterfly system remains undisturbed during specimen collection.*

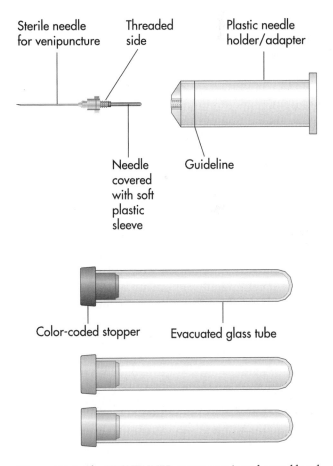

Figure 18-4. *The VACUTAINER system uses interchangeable collection tubes that allow you to draw several blood specimens from the same venipuncture site.*

Color	Additive	Test Types
Red	None	Blood chemistries, AIDS antibody tests, viral studies, serologic tests, blood grouping and typing
Yellow	Sodium polyanetholesulfonate	Plasma cultures
Green	Sodium heparin (anticoagulant)	Electrolyte studies, arterial blood gas tests
Blue	Sodium citrate (anticoagulant)	Coagulation studies
Lavender	EDTA (anticoagulant)	Hematology studies, such as complete blood count, white blood cell differential, and platelet count
Gray	Potassium oxalate or sodium fluoride (anticoagulant)	Blood glucose tests
Red/black (tiger stripes or marbled)	Silicone serum separator	Tests requiring blood serum

Table 18-2

EDTA: Used as an anticoagulant additive in hematology studies. It is also used to treat exposure to toxic chemicals; it chemically "grasps" toxic substances, thereby making them nonactive. Excessive EDTA produces a shrinkage of the erythrocytes.

Antiseptic: A substance that inhibits the growth and reproduction of microorganisms. Some examples of antiseptics are 70% isopropyl alcohol, povidone-iodine (*Betadine*®), and benzalkonium chloride (*Zephiran*®).

***Betadine*®:** An antiseptic recommended for use in arterial blood gas studies and blood culture draws.

***Zephiran*®:** A trade name for benzalkonium chloride, used in blood collection to detect alcohol levels.

Labeling containers: After blood is drawn, all tubes, slides and other containers should be labeled with the patient's name, the date and time of collection, the initials of the person who collected the specimen, and any other required information, such as the patient's identification code.

Tube size: Tubes range in size from 15 mL down. Most tubes used for adults range from 3 to 10 mL, and those for children range from 2 to 4 mL. Microcapillary collection tubes hold less than 1 mL.

Tourniquet: A device used to control hemorrhage or to distend veins for the withdrawal of blood. A tourniquet increases resistance in the venous blood flow. It should not remain on the patient's arm longer than 1 minute. Tourniquets are available in many materials. They are placed on the upper arm of the patient, 3 to 4 inches above the elbow.

Gloves: Made from a variety of materials, such as vinyl, latex, and nitrile. Latex gloves are the most commonly used, but some individuals are highly allergic to latex. Nitrile gloves are more tear-resistant and feel more comfortable on the hand.

Needle disposal: Needles must be properly disposed of into appropriate biohazard containers. They should not be laid down or placed on any surface and should not be recapped.

Procedures

Assembling equipment and supplies: After reviewing the test order, make sure that you have the appropriate equipment to collect the required samples.

Preparing patients: After greeting the patient, ask for the patient's full name to verify that the patient is the one listed on the order. Confirm that the patient has followed any pretest restrictions, such as fasting before the appointment.

Universal Precautions: It is important to follow Universal Precautions during all phlebotomy procedures. Before collecting blood, make sure to wash your hands and put on examination gloves. When you have finished drawing blood, properly dispose of used supplies and disposable instruments, disinfect the area, remove the gloves, and wash your hands.

Steps in venipuncture or phlebotomy: The following steps describe how to perform venipuncture using the evacuation method:

1. Prepare the needle holder/adapter assembly, and push the collection tube into the open end of the needle holder/adapter. Do not puncture the stopper yet. You usually use a 19–23 gauge needle for venipuncture.

2. Ask the patient which arm he or she prefers you to use, and make sure that the arm is positioned slightly downward.

3. Apply tourniquet to the patient's upper arm.

4. Palpate the site, using your index finger to locate the vein.

5. Clean area with a cotton ball moistened with antiseptic or an antiseptic wipe. Let site dry.

6. Remove cap from outer point of the needle.

7. Ask the patient to make a fist.

8. Hold the patient's skin taut above and below the insertion site. Holding the needle at approximately a 15° angle, use a steady and quick motion to insert the needle into the vein to a depth of $\frac{1}{4}$ to $\frac{1}{2}$ inch.

9. Seat the collection tube firmly into place over the needle, puncturing the stopper.

10. Once blood is flowing steadily, ask the patient to release the fist, and untie the tourniquet. Switch tubes as needed, using a smooth and steady motion. Fill each tube until the blood stops running. An evacuation tube containing an additive must be filled completely.

11. As you withdraw the needle in a smooth and steady motion, place a sterile gauze square over the insertion site. Have the patient hold the gauze in place and keep the arm straight and slightly elevated.

12. If the collection tubes contain additives, invert them slowly several times to mix the chemical with the blood.

13. Check the patient's condition and the puncture site for bleeding, and replace the gauze square with a sterile adhesive bandage.

Steps in capillary puncture: The following steps are taken in capillary puncture using the finger stick method:

1. Examine the patient's hand to determine which finger to use for the procedure. If necessary, warm the hands to improve circulation. Keep the hand below heart level.

2. Prepare the finger by gently rubbing it, and clean the area with a cotton ball and antiseptic or an antiseptic wipe.

3. Hold the patient's finger between the thumb and forefinger of one hand.

4. Hold the lancet at a right angle to the pad of the patient's finger (the part that leaves a fingerprint).

5. Puncture the skin with a quick, sharp motion.

6. Allow a drop of blood to form. If it is slow in forming, apply steady pressure, but do not milk the finger.

7. Wipe away the first droplet of blood.

8. Fill the collection devices.

9. When the samples have been collected, wipe the patient's finger with a sterile gauze square.

10. Check the site for bleeding. If necessary, apply a sterile adhesive bandage.

Chain of custody: A means of ensuring that a specimen obtained from a patient is correctly identified, is under the uninterrupted control of authorized personnel, and has not been altered or replaced. It is established for blood samples drawn for drug and alcohol analysis as well as for specimens taken in cases of medicolegal importance such as rape. Because donating a specimen for drug and alcohol testing is potentially self-incriminating, the patient must sign a consent form for the testing.

Handling an exposure incident: Following Universal Precautions should reduce your risk of exposure, but accidents sometimes still happen. If you suffer a needle stick or other injury that results in exposure to blood or blood products from another person, report the incident to the appropriate staff members immediately. Wash the injured area carefully, and apply a sterile bandage. Record the time, date, and nature of the incident and the names of the people involved. You may have to undergo further blood testing and to receive medications depending on the type of incident. OSHA requires every employer to have an established procedure for handling exposure incidents.

Complications of Blood Collection

Syncope: Fainting, usually caused by pain, fright, and the sight of blood. Syncope lasts only 1 to 2 minutes. If fainting occurs, the procedure must be terminated immediately. The patient should be placed lying down, with legs elevated. The event should be completely documented on the laboratory log. Assistance should be called for, and the patient should never be left alone.

Failure to obtain blood: There are several factors that may make blood collection impossible. It is important to remain calm and to determine the cause of the problem. If you cannot collect a good sample on the second try, do not make a third attempt. Ask for assistance.

Scarred and sclerosed veins: Do not draw blood from injured or diseased areas.

Hematoma: A pooling of blood just under the skin. It is caused by blood leaking into the tissues. When it happens, pressure should be applied to the area for 3 minutes, and then ice should be applied.

Hemorrhage: Excessive bleeding.

Petechiae: Tiny red spots appearing on the skin as a result of small hemorrhages within the dermal layer. They may be a complication of keeping a tourniquet in place for longer than 2 minutes.

Testing Blood

Hematology

Hematologic tests: May be performed on venous or capillary whole blood specimens. These tests include blood cell count, morphologic studies, coagulation tests, and the erythrocyte sedimentation rate test. See Table 18-3 for normal ranges of selected blood tests.

Erythrocyte sedimentation rate (ESR, or sed rate) test: Measures the rate at which red blood cells settle out in a tube of unclotted blood, expressed in millimeters per hour. The test determines the degree of inflammation in the body. There are several testing systems available, and it is important to adhere to the manufacturer's instructions in using each test. Results are sensitive to temperature and freshness of the samples, precise position of the sample tube, and vibrations. The normal rate at which red blood cells fall is 1 mm every five minutes. Elevated sedimentation rates are not specific for any disorder but indicate the presence of inflammation. Certain noninflammatory conditions, such as pregnancy, are also characterized by high sedimentation rates.

Bleeding time test: Gives information about the integrity of the patient's platelet function. A prolonged bleeding time indicates such conditions as low platelet count and dysfunction of the platelets. Aspirin impairs the platelets' ability to form aggregates. Antihistamines also interfere with bleeding time.

Blood smears: Used to obtain a differential cell count and to reveal abnormal red blood cell morphology for anemia. To prepare a blood smear slide, apply a drop of blood to the slide, $\frac{3}{4}$ inch from the frosted end, and use a spreader slide at a 30° to 35° angle to spread the blood droplet. See Figures 18-5, 18-6, and 18-7.

AT A GLANCE	Normal Ranges for Selected Blood Tests	
Test	**Blood Component**	**Normal Range**
Red blood cells	Whole blood	Men: 4.3–5.7 × 10⁶ cells/μL Women: 3.8–5.1 × 10⁶ cells/μL
White blood cells	Whole blood	4.5–11.0 × 10³ cells/μL
Platelets	Whole blood	150–400 × 10³ cells/μL
Hematocrit (Hct)	Whole blood	Men: 39%–49% Women: 35%–45%
Hemoglobin (Hb, Hgb)	Whole blood	Men: 13.2–17.3 g/dL Women: 11.7–16.0 g/dL
Bleeding time	Whole blood	2–7 minutes
Cholesterol, total	Serum, plasma	Men: 158–277 mg/dL Women: 162–285 mg/dL
Glucose (fasting blood sugar, FBS)	Serum	74–120 mg/dL
Insulin	Serum	<17 μU/mL
Iron, total	Serum	Men: 65–175 μg/dL Women: 50–170 μg/dL
Uric acid	Serum	Men: 4.4–7.6 mg/dL Women: 2.3–6.6 mg/dL

Table 18-3

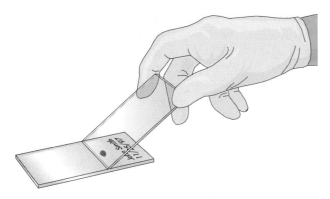

Figure 18-5. *Hold the spreader slide at a 30° to 35° angle. Pull the spreader slide toward the frosted end until it touches the drop of blood.*

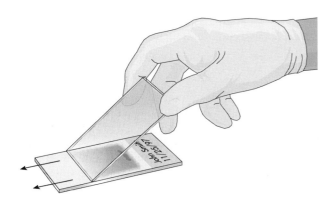

Figure 18-6. *When the drop covers most of the spreader slide edge, push the spreader slide back toward the unfrosted end of the smear slide.*

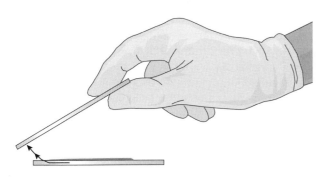

Figure 18-7. *Lift the spreader slide away from the smear slide, maintaining a 30° to 35° angle. The smear should be thicker on the frosted end of the slide.*

Stains: Used to selectively color microscopic objects and tissues for study. Some common stains are listed in Table 18-4 on p. 372.

Morphologic studies: Used in the examination of a blood smear for the purpose of recording the appearance and shape of cells, with special note made of abnormal cell size, shape, or content and abnormal organization of cells.

Coagulation tests: Used to identify bleeding problems, generally scheduled before surgery or to monitor therapeutic drug levels.

Hemoglobin (Hgb or Hb) tests: Measure the concentration of hemoglobin in the blood. Hb testing can be performed on either venous or capillary whole blood specimens. Among the types of hemoglobin are hemoglobin A, hemoglobin F, and hemoglobin S. Hemoglobin level is high at birth but declines during childhood. It then increases at different ages.

Hemoglobin A: Normal adult hemoglobin.

Hemoglobin F (HbF): Fetal hemoglobin, the normal hemoglobin of the fetus and the predominant hemoglobin variety in the fetus and neonate. Most HbF is replaced by hemoglobin A in the first days after birth.

Hemoglobin S: Sickle-shaped hemoglobin, found in sickle cell anemia and also in sickle cell trait. It is found exclusively in persons of African descent. About 8% of African Americans in the United States are affected.

Blood count: The complete blood count (CBC) is the most common laboratory procedure ordered on blood. It includes the red blood count (RBC), white blood count (WBC), differential white blood cell count, and platelet count, as well as a hematocrit determination and a hemoglobin determination.

Hematocrit (Hct): The relative volume of red blood cells in a blood sample after the sample has been spun in a centrifuge (packed cell volume), expressed as a percentage. The erythrocytes collect at the bottom of the tube. Above the packed erythrocytes is a layer of leukocytes and thrombocytes. This layer is called the buffy coat. Above the buffy coat is the plasma, which is free of cell elements.

Serology

Serologic tests: Used to detect the presence of specific substances in blood serum (e.g., disease antibodies, drugs, hormones, and vitamins) and to determine blood types. See Table 18-5.

Amylase test: Amylase is an enzyme of the exocrine pancreas. Its function is to break down starches into dextrin and maltose during the digestive processes. Blood serum is tested for increased amylase levels, which may occur in patients with a perforated ulcer, salivary gland disease, obstruction of the pancreas duct, or cancer of the pancreas. Decreased amylase levels are seen in patients with extensive destruction of the pancreas and hepatic insufficiency.

Western blot: Confirms the presence of the human immunodeficiency virus (HIV).

Stain	Use
Acidic	To stain basic elements of cells
Basic	To stain the nucleic or acidic elements of cells
Contrast	To color one part of a tissue or cell
Differential (e.g., Gram's stain)	To differentiate among various types of bacteria
Giemsa's	To stain tissues that include blood cells, Negri bodies, and chromosomes
Wright's	To stain blood smears

Table 18-4

Substance Identified or Quantified	Blood Component Tested	Indication, Disease, or Disorder
ABO antigens and Rh factor (indicated by clumping reactions that occur when the blood specimen is mixed with serum containing different antibodies)	Whole blood	Possible transfusion or transplant reaction; hemolytic disease of the newborn
Acetone	Serum, plasma	Diabetic conditions or fasting metabolic ketoacidosis
Antistreptolysin O (ASO) antibodies	Serum	Streptococcal infection (which may indicate rheumatic fever, glomerulonephritis, bacterial endocarditis, or scarlet fever)
Bilirubin	Serum	Liver disease, fructose intolerance, or hypothyroidism
Blood urea nitrogen (BUN)	Serum, plasma	Indicates kidney disorders
Cancer antigens and tumor-associated glycoprotein	Serum	Cancer of a specific type depending on the antigen found

Table 18-5

Substance Identified or Quantified	Blood Component Tested	Indication, Disease, or Disorder
Cholesterol	Serum, plasma	Hyperlipoproteinemia, coronary artery disease, or atherosclerosis
Creatine kinase	Serum	Muscular dystrophies, Reye's syndrome, heart disease (particularly myocardial infarction), shock, or some neoplasms
Epstein-Barr virus	Serum	Infectious mononucleosis
Erythrocyte (RBC) count	Whole blood	Anemia
Erythrocyte sedimentation rate (ESR)	Whole blood	Infectious diseases, malignant neoplasms, or sickle cell anemia
Leukocyte (WBC) count	Whole blood	Leukemia, infection, or leukocytosis
Phenylalanine	Plasma	Hyperphenylalaninemia, obesity, or phenylketonuria
Potassium and sodium	Serum	Fluid-electrolyte balance
Prostatic acid phosphatase (PAP)	Serum	Prostate cancer
Rheumatoid factor (RF)	Serum	Rheumatoid arthritis
Treponema pallidum antibodies	Plasma, serum, spinal fluid	Syphilis The most common tests are the VDRL (Venereal Disease Research Laboratories) test and the rapid plasma reagin (RPR) test.

Table 18-5, continued

Blood Bank Tests (Immunohematology)

ABO blood group test: Determines blood groups and type. For a summary of the ABO system and Rh groups, see Table 18-6 on p. 374.

Rh blood groups: Blood that has the Rh (or D) antigen on the surface of its red blood cells is Rh positive (Rh+), and blood that does not have the antigen is Rh negative (Rh–). If an individual with Rh– blood receives a transfusion of Rh+ blood, anti-Rh agglutinin forms, and subsequent transfusions may result in serious reactions.

Crossmatching: A test to establish blood compatibility before transfusion that simulates the transfusion in a test tube by mixing donor cells with recipient serum or plasma. A compatible crossmatch is one in which no reaction occurs between cells and serum at room and body temperature.

Universal donor blood: Uncrossmatched blood, which may be requested from a blood bank by a physician in emergency situations. This uncrossmatched blood is usually group O, Rh– with packed red blood cells.

Clinical Chemistry

Clinical chemistry: The use of computerized instruments to perform one or more tests on a single blood sample. Tests are conducted for such substances as alcohol, potassium, sodium, cholesterol, lead, phenobarbital, and cocaine.

Glucose testing: Can be performed on whole blood, plasma, or serum, but plasma and serum free of hemolysis are preferred. Glucose concentration is stable for up to 8 hours at room temperature and up to 72 hours under

Type	Antigen on Erythrocytes	Serum Antibodies
A	A	Anti-B
B	B	Anti-A
AB	Both antigen A and antigen B	None
O	None	Both anti-A and anti-B
Rh+	D	No anti-D
Rh–	No D	Anti-D

Table 18-6

refrigeration. Blood should be centrifuged and separated from the clot and cells as soon as possible or within 30 minutes, unless a specific additive (such as fluoride) is used. If the blood must be stored for several hours, fluoride-oxalate is the anticoagulant mixture of choice.

Glucose tolerance test: Performed by giving a certain amount of glucose to a patient, then drawing blood samples at specified intervals and measuring the blood glucose level in each sample. Patients with diabetes may have normal fasting blood glucose levels, but they may be unable to produce a sufficient amount of insulin when needed to metabolize normal loads of carbohydrates. In these cases, blood glucose levels rise to abnormally high levels and remain high for a long period of time.

Arterial blood gas: Oxygen and carbon dioxide in arterial blood are measured by various methods to assess the adequacy of ventilation and oxygenation and the acid-base balance. Oxygen saturation of hemoglobin is normally 95% or higher.

Arterial pH: The hydrogen ion concentration of arterial blood. The normal range is 7.35 to 7.45.

Neonatal blood collection: Neonatal screening tests are commonly conducted to detect increased bilirubin, phenylketonuria (PKU), and hypothyroidism. PKU and thyroid tests are required by law in the United States. The common site for collection of blood is the infant's foot. Care must be taken not to damage the heel bone, which could cause osteomyelitis in the newborn.

PKU screening: Tests the infant's ability to metabolize phenylalanine. Increased phenylalanine in the blood can result in brain damage and mental retardation.

Blood Testing Equipment

Microscope: The instrument most often used in the physician's office laboratory (POL). Microscopes are used to examine blood smears, to perform blood cell counts, and to identify body fluid samples. See Figure 18-8. In using a microscope, follow these steps:

1. Clean the lenses and oculars with lens paper.
2. Place the specimen slide on the stage, sliding the edges under the slide clips.
3. Adjust the distance between the oculars so that you see a merged field.
4. Adjust the objectives so that the low-power objective points directly at the specimen slide.
5. Turn on the light, and adjust the amount of light illuminating the specimen.
6. Lower the body tube to move the objective closer to the specimen slide.
7. Use the coarse focus control to slowly adjust the image.
8. Use the fine focus control to adjust the image.
9. Switch to the high-power objective.
10. Apply immersion oil to the specimen slide.
11. Switch to the oil-immersion objective, and examine the specimen. Figure 18-9 shows the pattern to follow for counting leukocytes under the oil-immersion objective.

Oil-immersion objective: The objectives of a microscope contain magnifying lenses that increase the magnification of the oculars by another 10X to 40X. The oil immersion objective is designed to be lowered into a drop of immersion oil placed directly over the prepared specimen under examination. This design eliminates the air space between the microscope slide and the objective, thereby reducing the loss of light and creating images that are sharper and brighter.

Centrifuge: A laboratory machine used to separate particles of different densities within a liquid by spinning them at very high speeds.

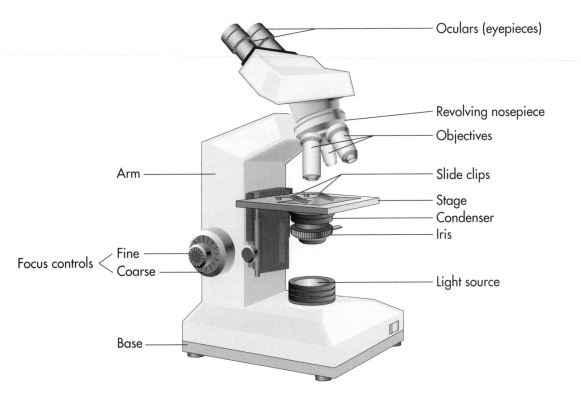

Figure 18-8. *The microscope is the most heavily used piece of equipment in the physician's office laboratory.*

Hemocytometer: A special microscope slide used primarily for counting blood cells that can also be used for counting platelets, sperm, and other cells. The most commonly used hemocytometer is the Neubauer type. The hemocytometer is thicker than the average microscope slide, with a raised platform shaped like a capital H, which forms two separate counting chambers. A coverslip is placed over the chambers to distribute the specimen to a uniform depth. See Figure 18-10. Each chamber is inscribed with a grid measuring 3 mm by 3 mm, subdivided into nine squares measuring 1 mm by 1 mm each. The four corner squares are subdivided into 16 smaller squares measuring 0.25 mm by 0.25 mm. The center square is subdivided into 25 smaller squares, each of which is further subdivided into 16 still smaller squares. See Figure 18-11 on p. 376.

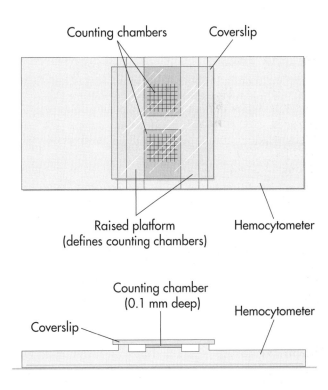

Figure 18-10. *You can count the number of blood cells in a blood specimen by using a hemocytometer.*

Figure 18-9. *Follow this pattern when counting leukocytes visible in the field under the oil-immersion objective of the microscope.*

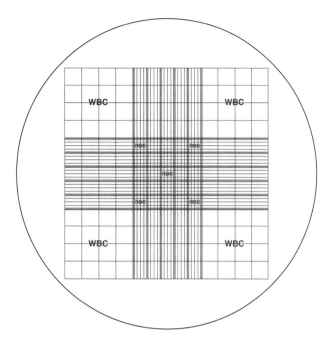

Figure 18-11. *Different areas of the hemocytometer grid are used for counting white blood cells (WBCs) and red blood cells (RBCs). Red blood cells are counted under higher magnification than are white blood cells.*

Conditions Identified by Phlebotomy

Hyperglycemia: A higher than normal blood glucose level. The most common cause of hyperglycemia is diabetes mellitus. Other conditions that can cause hyperglycemia are hyperthyroidism, Cushing's syndrome, acromegaly, obesity, severe liver or kidney damage, alcoholism, and elevated levels of the hormones estrogen, epinephrine, or norepinephrine.

Hypoglycemia: Abnormally low levels of glucose in the blood, below 50 mg/dL. The most common cause of hypoglycemia is insulin overdose in patients with unstable insulin-dependent diabetes mellitus.

Hemophilia: A hereditary disorder of clotting factors, in which blood fails to coagulate at a wound site.

Hyperlipidemia: A higher than normal level of lipids, especially cholesterol, in the blood.

Visual indications: Hyperlipidemia gives plasma or serum a milky, or turbid, appearance. Sometimes the plasma or serum will have a pale, watery appearance as a result of protein disorders or kidney disease. In certain types of cancers, the color of the serum may be green, attributable to heme (part of hemoglobin).

Extramedullary hematopoiesis: In abnormal circumstances, the spleen, liver, and lymph nodes revert back to producing immature blood cells. This reversion can be the result of aplastic anemia, infiltration by malignant cells, leukemia, or hemolytic anemias.

Anemia: A reduction in the number of circulating red blood cells per cubic millimeter. Hemoglobin content is less than that required to provide the oxygen needed by the body.

Abnormal erythrocytes: Vary from the norm in terms of size, shape, and color. Normal mature erythrocytes are biconcave and disc-shaped and lack a nucleus.

Anisocytosis: An abnormal condition characterized by excessive inequality in the size of erythrocytes.

Macrocyte: An abnormally large erythrocyte.

Megalocyte: An erythrocyte that is larger than average.

Microcyte: An abnormally small erythrocyte.

Poikilocytosis: Variation in the shapes of erythrocytes.

Schistocyte or **schizocyte:** An erythrocyte that has been fragmented during circulation.

Ovalocyte: An erythrocyte that is oval in shape. It is also called an elliptocyte.

Spherocyte: An erythrocyte that is spheroid in shape, having a decreased ratio of surface area to volume.

Target cell: An abnormally thin red blood cell with a dark center and a surrounding ring of hemoglobin. Also called leptocytes, target cells occur in anemia and jaundice.

Sickle cell: An erythrocyte that is sickle- or crescent-shaped. Such cells are produced by the polymerization of hemoglobin and occur in hereditary anemias.

Hypochromia: A condition in which cells have decreased hemoglobin.

Polycythemia: An above normal concentration of erythrocytes in the circulating blood. It is also called erythrocytosis.

Polycythemia vera: A blood dyscrasia (disease) characterized by abnormally increased levels of erythrocytes, leukocytes, and thrombocytes. It is also called erythremia.

Neutropenia: A severe decrease in the number of neutrophilic granulocytes in the peripheral blood.

Neutrophilia: A significant increase in the number of neutrophilic granulocytes in the peripheral blood.

Leukocytosis: An increase in the number of leukocytes in the blood, generally caused by infection and usually transient.

Leukemia: A neoplastic, proliferative disease characterized by an overproduction of immature or mature cells of various leukocyte types in the bone marrow or peripheral blood.

Lymphoma: A solid, malignant tumor of the lymph nodes and associated tissue or bone marrow.

Infectious mononucleosis (IM): An acute, infectious disease commonly called mono or the kissing disease, in which there is an abnormally high number of mononuclear leukocytes in the blood. Most cases are caused by the Epstein-Barr virus. The most common serological test is the rapid slide test.

Hemolytic disease of the newborn: A neonatal disease generally caused by Rh incompatibility between mother and child, occurring when an Rh– woman carries an Rh+ fetus. Symptoms are anemia, jaundice, liver and spleen enlargement, and generalized edema. It can be controlled during pregnancy and may require intrauterine transfusion or early induced labor.

Bloodletting: The therapeutic opening of an artery or vein to withdraw blood from a particular area. Also called therapeutic phlebotomy, it is sometimes performed to treat polycythemia or congestive heart failure. One pint is collected and discarded.

Blood lavage: The removal of toxic elements from the blood by the injection of serum into the veins.

Collecting and Testing Urine

Role of the medical assistant: To help collect, process, and test urine specimens. These activities involve dealing with potentially infectious body waste, so following Universal Precautions is generally required.

Physical and Chemical Composition and Function

Urinary system or tract: Consists of two kidneys, two ureters, a bladder, and a urethra. The kidneys remove excess water from the body and waste products from the blood in the form of urine, which then drains through the ureters into the urinary bladder. The bladder stores urine until it leaves the body through the urethra.

Nephron: The basic unit of the kidney. See Figure 18-12. Each kidney contains approximately one million nephrons. Nephrons filter blood to produce urine. One of the main functions of the nephron is to remove waste material from the body. It also allows reabsorption of water and some electrolytes back into the blood.

Urinary meatus: The external opening of the urethra.

Chemical composition of urine: Approximately 95% water and 5% waste materials and other components, which include urea, ammonia, uric acid, creatinine, urobilinogen, and a few white and red blood cells. The presence of a few sperm cells in the urine of males is normal.

Urea: The end product of protein metabolism after ammonia is broken down by the liver.

Urochrome: The yellow pigment that gives urine its color. It is produced by the breakdown of hemoglobin.

Urination: The act of passing urine. It is also called micturition.

Urgency: An immediate need to urinate.

Urinary retention: The inability to empty the bladder.

Urinary frequency: Increased frequency can often be a symptom of a urinary tract infection, but there may also be other causes.

Incontinence: The inability to prevent release of urine. Some causes include an overfilling of the bladder and stress caused by laughing, sneezing, coughing, or lifting.

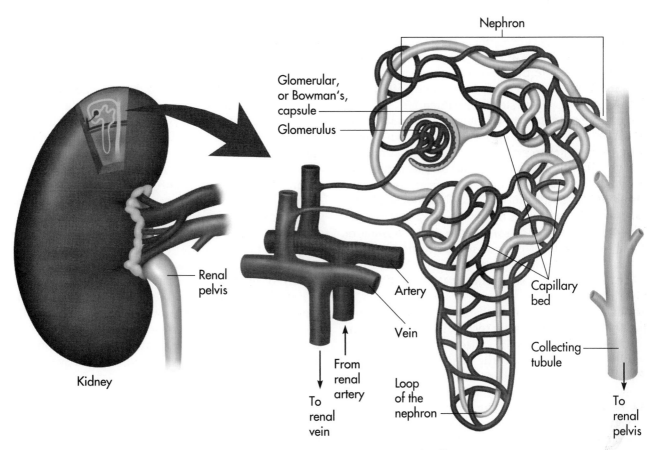

Figure 18-12. *Urine is formed in the nephron, a long tubular structure, during a complex filtering process.*

Enuresis: The involuntary discharge of urine after the age at which bladder control is normally established.

Nocturnal enuresis: Urinary incontinence during the night, also called bedwetting, which can be a symptom of a neurological disorder.

Dysuria: Painful or difficult urination, symptomatic of cystitis, infection, and many other conditions.

Polyuria: Increased output of urine.

Uropathy: Any disease or abnormal condition of any structure of the urinary tract.

Obtaining Specimens

Urine collection: Urine tests require between 30 and 50 mL of the specimen. When it is collected, it must be properly labeled with the patient's name, the date, and the time. Urine tests for females should be avoided during menstruation. Any medication taken by the patient must be recorded on the laboratory requisition and the patient's chart.

Home collection: Instruct patients on how to obtain the specimen. Tell them to urinate into an appropriate container, one that has a wide opening, and not to add anything else to the container. However, if you provide a container that contains preservative, caution them not to throw out the preservative. Instruct them to refrigerate the container and to keep the lid on it.

Random specimen: A single urine specimen taken at any time. A random specimen is the most common type of sample. If collection is done in a doctor's office, provide a urine specimen container, show the patient to the restroom, and ask the patient to void a few ounces of urine into the specimen container and leave it on the sink. Transport the specimen to the laboratory immediately, or refrigerate the specimen.

Clean-catch midstream specimen: A method of urine collection that may be ordered to diagnose urinary tract infections or to evaluate the effectiveness of drug therapy. The purpose of this type of collection is to obtain a urine specimen that is free from contamination. Patients completing this procedure independently need written instructions on how to make sure that the container and the urine specimen remain uncontaminated. When assisting patients, use antiseptic towelettes to clean the perineal area or the penis. Make sure that you rinse away any soap residue that might affect the pH of the specimen.

Timed specimen: Collected over a predetermined time period to obtain more specific information. Such specimens are sometimes collected 2 hours after a meal to test for diabetes. The patient should discard the first specimen and then collect all urine for the specified time, making sure that the urine does not mix with stool or toilet paper. The sample should be kept refrigerated until it is brought to the doctor's office or laboratory.

24-hour specimen: Collected to measure the amount of urine output in a 24-hour period. The urine will be tested for substances that are released sporadically into the urine. It is extremely important to avoid using a bedpan, urinal, or toilet tissue, which could retain the substances for which the test is being done. The first specimen should be discarded. Over the next 24 hours, the patient should urinate directly into the small collection container and then pour the urine into the large container. Between two collections, the small container must be sanitized with soap and warm water. This type of collection is helpful in diagnosing renal disease, dehydration, urinary tract obstructions, and pheochromocytoma.

First-voided morning specimen: Collected after a night's sleep. It contains greater concentrations of substances that collect over time than do specimens taken during the day. A urine specimen container or clean, dry jar is used. It is best for pregnancy testing, microscopic examination, and culturing.

Catheterization: Insertion of a sterile plastic tube into the bladder, ureter, or kidney to withdraw urine. It is used to obtain a sterile urine specimen from a patient, to obtain a specimen from a patient who cannot void naturally, or to measure the amount of residual urine in the bladder after normal voiding, among other reasons. Catheterization is not routinely used because it can introduce infection. In some states, the medical assistant may not perform catheterization.

Drainage catheter: Used to withdraw fluids.

Splinting catheter: Used after plastic repair of a ureter.

Urinalysis

Urinalysis: The examination of urine to obtain information about body health and disease, done as part of a general physical examination or for a specific reason. The testing may be physical, chemical, or microscopic. Table 18-7 lists normal values for tests done on urine.

Physical testing of urine: Provides information about color, volume, odor, and specific gravity.

Color: Normal urine ranges from pale yellow to dark amber, depending on food and fluid intake, medications and vitamin supplements, and waste products present in the urine.

Clarity: Urine can be clear, or it can range from slightly cloudy to very cloudy. Cloudiness is also known as turbidity and sometimes indicates an abnormal condition. Causes of urine color and cloudiness are listed in Table 18-8 on p. 380.

Urine volume: Normal adult urine output is 600–1800 mL per 24-hour period, with an average of 1250 mL per 24 hours.

Oliguria: Decreased output of urine often resulting from dehydration, decreased fluid intake, shock, or renal disease.

Anuria: The complete suppression of urine formation by the kidney. It may be a result of renal or urethral obstruction or renal failure.

Test	Value
Acetone	None
Albumin, qualitative	Negative
Albumin, quantitative	10–140 mg/L (24 hours)
Bacteria (culture)	< 10,000 colonies/mL
Blood, occult	Negative
Calcium, quantitative	100–300 mg/24 hours
Color	Pale yellow to dark amber
Creatine, nonpregnant women/men	< 6% of creatinine
Creatine, pregnant women	≤ 12% of creatinine
Creatinine, men	1.0–1.9 g/24 hours
Creatinine, women	0.8–1.7 g/24 hours
Crystals	Negative
Ketones	Negative
Lead	0.021–0.038 mg/L
Odor	Distinctly aromatic
pH	4.5–8.0
Phenylpyruvic acid	Negative
Protein	Negative
Specific gravity, single specimen	1.005–1.030
Specific gravity, 24-hour specimen	1.015–1.025
Turbidity	Clear
Volume, adult females	600–1600 mL/24 hours
Volume, adult males	800–1800 mL/24 hours
White blood cells	0–8/high-power field

Table 18-7

Color and Turbidity	Pathologic Causes	Other Causes
Colorless or pale straw color (dilute)	Diabetes, anxiety, chronic renal disease	Diuretic therapy, excessive fluid intake (water, beer, coffee)
Cloudy	Infection, inflammation, glomerular nephritis	Vegetarian diet
Milky white	Fats, pus	Amorphous phosphates, spermatozoa
Dark yellow, dark amber (concentrated)	Acute febrile disease, vomiting or diarrhea (fluid loss or dehydration)	Low fluid intake, excessive sweating
Orange-yellow, orange-red, orange-brown	Excessive RBC destruction, bile duct obstruction, diminished liver-cell function, bilirubin	Drugs (such as pyridium and rifampin), dyes

Table 18-8

Urine odor: Can provide clues about the body's condition. Diseases, the presence of bacteria, and certain foods can change the odor.

Urine specific gravity: A measure of the amount or concentration of a substance dissolved in urine. It is calculated by dividing the weight of the sample by the weight of an equal amount of distilled water. The specific gravity of normal urine ranges from 1.005 to 1.030. The specific gravity of urine is lower in cases of chronic kidney disease, diabetes insipidus, overhydration, and systemic lupus.

Measuring specific gravity: Three methods are used to measure specific gravity: urinometer, refractometer, and reagent strip (dipstick).

Urinometer: A sealed glass float with a calibrated scale on the stem that measures specific gravity. At least 15 mL of urine is required. See Figure 18-13.

Refractometer: An optical device that measures the refraction of light as it passes through a liquid. The degree of refraction is proportional to the amount of dissolved material in the liquid. It is faster and easier to use than the urinometer and requires only a drop of urine. It must be calibrated daily. See Figure 18-14.

Reagent strips, or **dipsticks:** Plastic strips to which one or more pads containing chemicals are attached. The pads react to substances in the urine and change color; a chart enables you to interpret the color changes. They are available for many tests: specific gravity, pH, protein, glucose, ketones, leukocytes, erythrocytes, nitrite, bilirubin, urobilinogen, and phenylketones.

Chemical testing of urine specimens: Usually performed with reagent strips or tablets. These tests can measure liver or kidney function, metabolism of carbohydrates, acid-base balance, and urinary pH. They also show the presence of drugs or infections, ketone bodies, blood, hemoglobin, myoglobin, bilirubin, urobilinogen, glucose, protein, nitrite, phenylketones, and leukocytes.

Using reagent strips or tablets: It is important to follow the directions of the manufacturer. Keep strips or tablets in tightly closed containers in a cool, dry area, and do not remove them until immediately before testing. Never use expired strips or tablets. A dipstick or tablet may be used only once.

Urinary pH: A measure of the acidity or alkalinity (hydrogen ion concentration) of urine. The normal pH of urine is 4.5 to 8.0.

Proteinuria: The presence of protein, such as albumin, in the urine. Protein is not normally found in the urine. Its presence may signal renal disease, heart failure, hypertension, or fever, or it may be the result of heavy exercise.

Uremia: A high level of urea in the blood. Excessive amounts of urea and other nitrogenous waste products in the blood are seen in renal failure.

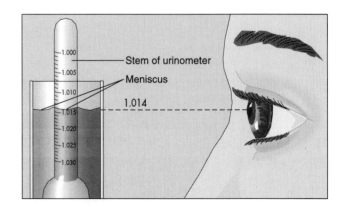

Figure 18-13. *Read the value on the scale where the bottom of the meniscus touches the stem.*

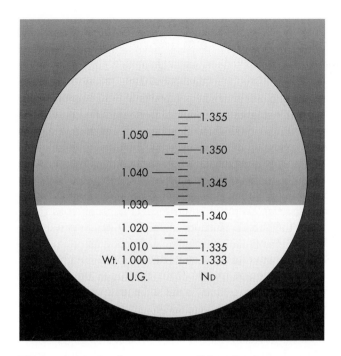

Figure 18-14. *A refractometer uses light refraction to measure specific gravity.*

Uremic: Pertaining to a toxic level of urea in the blood.

Uric acid: The end product of the metabolism of purine, an important constituent of nucleic acids. A high level of uric acid in the urine may be associated with urinary calculi or gout.

Urobilinogen: A colorless compound formed in the intestines after the breakdown of bilirubin by bacteria. Some of this substance is excreted in feces, and some is reabsorbed and excreted again in bile or urine.

Urobilin: A brown pigment formed by the oxidation of urobilinogen. It is normally found in feces and in small amounts in urine.

Bilirubin: An orange-colored pigment in bile. Jaundice is a result of the accumulation in tissues of excess bilirubin in the blood.

Pyuria: The presence of pus in the urine, which may be evidence of renal disease.

Hematuria: The presence of blood in the urine, which may be a result of menstruation, urinary tract infection, or trauma or bleeding in the kidneys.

Hemoglobinuria: The presence of free hemoglobin in the urine, caused by a transfusion or drug reaction, malaria, snakebite, or severe burn.

Myoglobinuria: The presence of myoglobin in the urine caused by injured or damaged muscle tissue.

Glycosuria: The presence of sugar (glucose) in the urine.

Nitrite: Occurs in urine when bacteria break down nitrate. It indicates a urinary tract infection.

Ketosis: An accumulation of large amounts of ketone bodies in the tissues and body fluids as a result of dehydration, starvation, uncontrolled diabetes, or taking too much aspirin. Ketones are sometimes present after general anesthesia has been administered.

Creatinine: A waste product of the metabolism of creatine. Increased quantities are found in the urine in advanced stages of renal disease.

Pregnancy test: Detects an increase in the concentration of human chorionic gonadotropin (HCG) in the plasma or urine. The presence of increased HCG can also indicate ectopic pregnancy; a hydatidiform mole of the uterus; choriocarcinoma; or cancer of the lung, breast, pancreas, stomach, or colon. The first-voided morning urine has the highest concentration of HCG.

Microscopic examination of urine: May show formed elements and can also determine the presence of cells, casts, crystals, bacteria, and other microorganisms. The first step is to use a centrifuge to obtain sediment for analysis. See Figures 18-15 and 18-16.

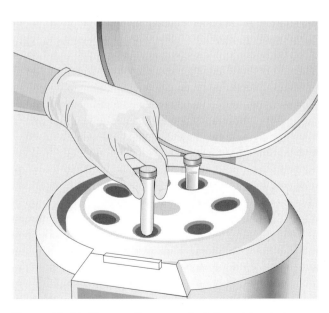

Figure 18-15. *The centrifuge must be balanced by placing test tubes on opposite sides.*

Figure 18-16. *Make sure that you do not lose any sediment when you pour off the urine.*

Crystals: Commonly found in urine specimens. They usually do not indicate a significant disorder. They are found in large numbers in patients with renal stones.

Urinary casts: Cylinder-shaped elements that form when protein accumulates in the kidney tubules and is washed down into the urine.

Mucous threads: Found in normal urine. Increased amounts usually indicate urinary tract inflammation. They are examined under low-power magnification.

Special Considerations

Pregnant patients: Pregnancy normally increases urinary frequency. Pregnant women are also prone to urinary tract infections. At each prenatal visit, they must have their urine checked for abnormal levels of glucose (indicative of diabetes) and abnormal levels of protein (preeclampsia or renal problems).

Elderly patients: Bladder muscles weaken with age, often leading to incomplete bladder emptying and chronic urine retention, which can cause urinary tract infections, nocturia, and incontinence.

Pediatric patients: Ask whether there are any problems with diaper rash (indicative of renal dysfunction), excessive thirst (possible diabetes), crying during urination (urinary tract infection), or bedwetting or enuresis (stress or urinary tract infections).

Medical Microbiology

Diagnosing infections: There are six steps in diagnosing infections: examining the patient, obtaining one or more specimens, examining the specimen, culturing the specimen, determining the culture's antibiotic sensitivity, and treating the patient. The medical assistant should work closely with the other members of the medical team.

Collecting Specimens

Guidelines for collecting specimens: Following these guidelines will make it possible to collect specimens properly:

- Try to avoid causing the patient harm, discomfort, or undue embarrassment.

- If the patient is to collect the specimen, provide clear, detailed instructions and the proper container.

- Collect the material from a site where the organism is most likely to be found and where contamination is least likely to occur.

- Obtain the specimen at a time that allows optimal chance of recovery of the microorganism.

- Use appropriate collection devices, specimen containers, transport systems, and culture media. Follow aseptic techniques.

- Obtain a sufficient quantity of the specimen.

- Obtain the specimen before antimicrobial therapy begins.

- Label the container, and include the proper requisition form.

Throat culture: A frequently performed microbiologic procedure that is often performed when the patient shows signs or symptoms of an upper respiratory, throat, or sinus infection. In most cases, a throat culture is obtained to determine whether the patient has strep throat. Left untreated, strep throat can lead to rheumatic fever. To obtain sterile specimens, such as those used for throat cultures, a sterile swab is used. See Figure 18-17.

Sputum specimen: The patient should cough deeply and expectorate mucus from the lungs into a sterile container. The patient should be instructed to avoid contaminating the specimen with saliva. Follow Universal Precautions when handling sputum specimens, and wear a face shield or mask and goggles.

Wound specimens: The procedure for obtaining specimens from infected wounds is similar to that for a throat culture. Obtain representative material from a deep area and a surface area without contaminating the swab by touching areas outside the site.

Stool culture: Ordered if the physician suspects that the patient has certain diseases such as cancer or colitis or bacterial, protozoal, or parasitic infections. Patients can collect stool specimens on a clean paper plate, in a clean waxed-paper carton, or in a collection container or collection tissue. Collection containers for stool cultures do not have to be sterile. The container must be clean and the stool should not be contaminated with urine.

O and P specimen: A type of stool sample examined for the presence of parasites and their ova (eggs). Both a fresh and a preserved specimen are required.

Preparing specimens for an outside laboratory: If testing is to be done by an outside laboratory, be sure to follow the collection procedures and use the collec-

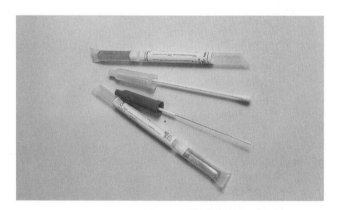

Figure 18-17. *Sterile swabs vary in size and in material.*

tion device required by the laboratory. Maintain the samples in a state as close to their original as possible. Ensure that the container has a tight-fitting lid, and place the container in a secondary container or zipper-type plastic bag.

Transporting the specimen: Specimens can be transported to an outside laboratory during a regularly scheduled daily pickup by the laboratory, during an as-needed pickup, or through the mail.

Mailing specimens: The U.S. Postal Service will accept microbiologic specimens with a total volume of less than 50 mL that are packaged according to strict regulations of the U.S. Public Health Service. See Figure 18-18.

Examining Specimens

Direct examination: Examination of the specimen under a microscope to identify the presence of microorganisms. There are two types of procedure: preparing wet mounts and preparing potassium hydroxide (KOH) mounts.

Wet mount: A type of mount that is easy to prepare and enables quick determination of many microorganisms. It requires mixing a small amount of the specimen with a drop of normal saline (0.9% sodium chloride) on a glass slide. Then a coverslip is placed over the mixture. The physician can examine the slide directly under the microscope.

Potassium hydroxide (KOH) mount: A type of mount used for identification of a fungal infection of the skin, nails, or hair. The procedure involves the following steps:

1. Suspend the specimen in a drop of 10% potassium hydroxide on a glass slide.
2. Apply a coverslip.
3. Let the specimen sit for 30 minutes at room temperature.
4. Examine the slide under the microscope.

Stained specimens: Microorganisms can be seem more clearly when stained with a dye or group of dyes.

Smear: The first step in preparing a stained specimen is to prepare a smear. Apply a small amount of the specimen to a glass slide. Allow the sample to dry, then briefly heat the slide to fix the sample to the slide. Stain the smear.

Gram's stain: The stain most commonly used in examining bacteriologic specimens. It involves a simple procedure, shown in Figure 18-19 on p. 384. If the bacteria have a deep purple color, they are gram-positive. If the bacteria exhibit a pink or red color, they are gram-negative.

Acid-fast: Not readily susceptible to decolorization by acids during the staining procedure. The acid-fast nature of certain microorganisms, such as those of the genus *Mycobacterium*, allows microscopic examination and differentiation.

Culture Media

Culture media: Liquid, semisolid, and solid substances used to foster the growth of bacteria. Semisolid media are most commonly used in medical offices.

Agar: A gelatinlike substance extracted from algae that gives a semisolid culture medium its consistency.

Petri dish or **plate:** A covered glass or plastic dish that holds the culture medium. Handle Petri dishes only on the outside, so as to avoid contaminating them. Store them with the bottom (agar side) up.

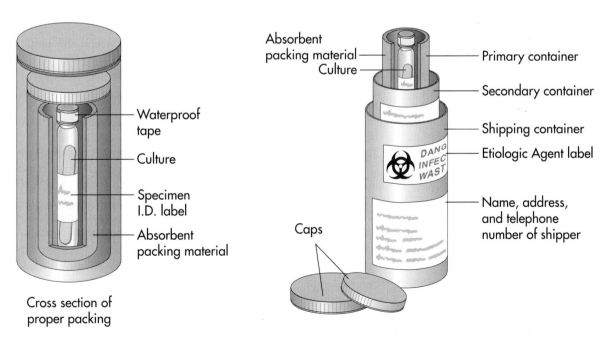

Figure 18-18. *When packaging and labeling a specimen for mail delivery, you must follow the procedures set by the CDC, based on U.S. Public Health Service regulations.*

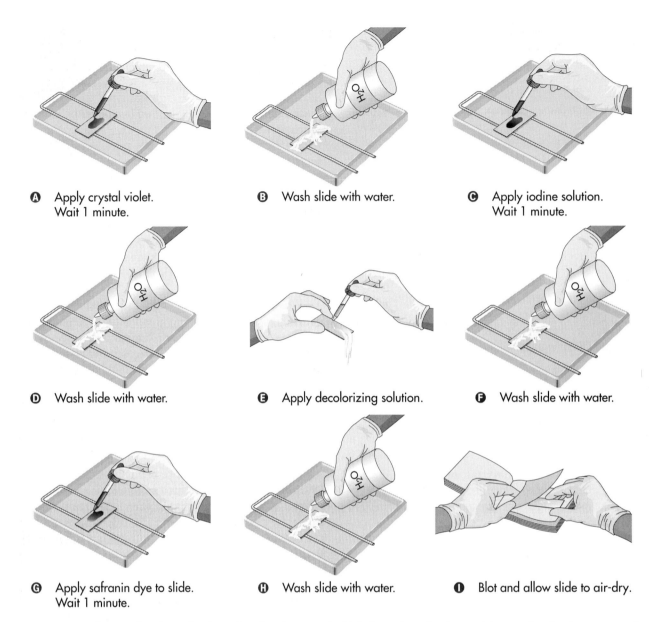

A Apply crystal violet. Wait 1 minute.

B Wash slide with water.

C Apply iodine solution. Wait 1 minute.

D Wash slide with water.

E Apply decolorizing solution.

F Wash slide with water.

G Apply safranin dye to slide. Wait 1 minute.

H Wash slide with water.

I Blot and allow slide to air-dry.

Figure 18-19. *The procedure for performing a Gram's stain on a microbiologic specimen involves applying a series of stains, water washes, and alcohol in a specific order, for precise periods of time.*

Culturette® Collection and Transport System: A sterile, self-contained unit that holds a polyester swab and a small, thin-walled glass vial of transport medium in a plastic sleeve. It is used for obtaining and transporting specimens. (It is manufactured by Becton Dickinson Microbiology Systems.)

Selective culture media: Culture media that allow the growth of only certain kinds of bacteria. They are commonly used for specimens that normally contain bacteria, such as stools or vaginal samples.

Nonselective culture media: Media that support the growth of most organisms. For example, blood agar is a nonselective culture medium used to culture a throat swab specimen.

Special culture units: Commercially prepared units with specific purposes, such as performing rapid urine cultures or culturing vaginal specimens.

Preparing the plate: Before inoculating a culture plate, label it on the bottom (agar side) with the patient's name, doctor's name, source of the sample, date and time of inoculation, and your initials.

Bacitracin: An antibiotic used in cultures to give an early indication of the presence of group A streptococci.

Qualitative analysis: The determination of the type of pathogen by its appearance. Inoculate the plate as shown in Figure 18-20.

Quantitative analysis: The determination of the number of bacteria present in a sample.

Incubation: After inoculating the plate, put it in an incubator set at 35°C to 37°C, with the bottom (agar side) up, for 24 to 48 hours.

Colony: A visible growth on a culture plate, usually resulting from a single type of bacteria.

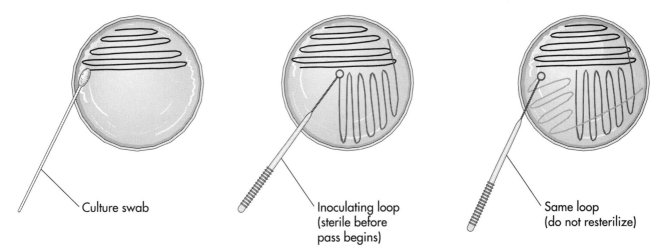

Culture swab

Inoculating loop
(sterile before
pass begins)

Same loop
(do not resterilize)

Figure 18-20. *When inoculating a plate for qualitative analysis, roll and streak the culture swab or inoculating loop of specimen material across one-third of the surface of the culture plate. Begin the next pass with a sterile loop.*

Culture isolation: One isolated, pathogenic-appearing colony is transferred from the primary culture plate. The secondary culture plate is incubated at 37°C to allow a pure culture to grow. A pure culture contains only a single type of organism.

Sensitivity testing: Determines an organism's susceptibility to specific antibiotics in order to enable the doctor to decide which one to use to treat the infection. The test involves the following steps:

1. Suspend a sample of the isolated pathogen in a small amount of liquid medium.

2. Streak the pathogen evenly on the surface of a culture plate.

3. Place small disks of filter paper containing various antimicrobial agents on top of the plate, using sterile forceps or a special dispenser.

4. Incubate the plate at 37°C for one day.

A clear zone around a disk indicates an effective antimicrobial agent, whereas growth next to a disk indicates an ineffective agent.

Quality control: All staining reagents should be checked frequently for effectiveness. All slides must be checked. All devices with temperature controls should be checked every day. All reagents and media must be used before the expiration date and evaluated for sterility. Equipment such as refrigerators, freezers, and incubators should be properly monitored and maintained.

Clinical Laboratory Improvement Amendments of 1988 (CLIA '88): A law enacted by Congress placing all laboratory facilities involved with human health and disease under federal regulations administered by the Health Care Financing Administration (HCFA) and the Centers for Disease Control and Prevention (CDC). As a result, laboratories must meet complex standards, and medical assistants may perform only certain types of tests.

STRATEGIES TO SUCCESS

▶ Test-Taking Skills

Use your anxiety, or overcome it!
Some anxiety is to be expected in any test-taking situation, and often the rush of adrenaline can help keep you energized and focused. However, if you feel that your anxiety is getting in the way of your doing well, learn to control it. Take deep breaths and think positively. Budget your time, but do not let excessive worry over the time limit interfere with your performance. You have studied, and you know your material; now all you need to do is to recall it. You will miss some questions, and some questions will be hard, but if you keep focused, you will pass the certification test.

CHAPTER 18 REVIEW

Instructions:

Answer the following questions. Check your answers in the *Answer Key* that follows this section.

1. Which of the following is an appropriate site for capillary blood collection?

    A. Small toe
    B. Earlobe
    C. Heel
    D. Both B and C
    E. All of the above

2. Which cells play a vital role in internal respiration?

    A. Bone marrow cells
    B. Erythrocytes
    C. Leukocytes
    D. Mast cells
    E. Basophils

3. What is the longest time a tourniquet should remain on a patient's arm?

    A. 1 minute
    B. 2 minutes
    C. 3 minutes
    D. 4 minutes
    E. 5 minutes

4. Dysuria is

    A. Inability to retain urine
    B. Painful or difficult urination
    C. Increased output of urine
    D. Decreased output of urine
    E. Micturition

5. Which of the following devices might be used to collect blood from fragile veins?

    A. A finger stick lancet
    B. A VACUTAINER system
    C. A butterfly needle
    D. An automatic puncturing device
    E. None of the above

6. A blue stopper indicates that a collection tube

    A. Is sterile
    B. Is to be used only for capillary puncture
    C. Contains the additive EDTA
    D. Contains an antiseptic
    E. Contains sodium citrate

7. To test for substances that are sporadically released into urine, a physician might order which type of urine specimen?

    A. 24-hour
    B. Clean catch
    C. Random
    D. First voided
    E. Timed

8. To follow Universal Precautions in phlebotomy, you should

    A. Wash your hands
    B. Wear examination gloves
    C. Recap the needle after blood is drawn, and dispose of it in a biohazard container
    D. Both A and B
    E. All of the above

9. A medical assistant or a phlebotomist should <u>not</u> attempt to obtain blood from any patient more than

   A. One time
   B. Two times
   C. Three times
   D. Four times
   E. Five times

10. The pale color of a urine sample might be an indication of

    A. An insufficient specimen
    B. Diabetes
    C. Excessive fluid intake
    D. Both B and C
    E. All of the above

11. Specific gravity may be measured by all of the following methods <u>except</u>

    A. Dipstick
    B. Urinometer
    C. Microscope
    D. Refractometer
    E. Reagent strip

12. The quality control log

    A. Lists specimens sent to another laboratory for testing
    B. Shows when the testing equipment was last calibrated
    C. Shows all the procedures completed during the workday
    D. Shows the quality testing performed on every batch of reagent product
    E. Documents maintenance done on laboratory equipment

13. Which of the following stains is specific to blood?

    A. Contrast
    B. Gram's
    C. Wright's
    D. Basic
    E. Agar

14. The color code for an evacuation tube that does not contain an additive is

    A. Red
    B. Lavender
    C. Gray
    D. Red and black
    E. Yellow

15. A creatine kinase test is done to help diagnose which of the following conditions?

    A. Muscular dystrophies and heart disease
    B. Infection or leukemia
    C. Cancer
    D. Kidney disorder
    E. Uterine disorder

16. Which of the following describes a centrifuge?

    A. Machine used to count blood cells
    B. Machine used to separate particles
    C. Machine used to heat cultures
    D. Machine used to analyze specimens
    E. Machine used to clean laboratory equipment

17. An erythrocyte sedimentation rate (ESR) test might be used to
    A. Test for specific antibodies in the blood
    B. Determine sickle cell anemia or inflammation and infection
    C. Determine obesity and phenylketonuria
    D. Determine liver disease and hypothyroidism
    E. Determine the type and level of vitamins

18. How should the patient's arm be positioned when drawing blood in phlebotomy?
    A. Above heart level
    B. Bent at the elbow
    C. Hanging down
    D. Slightly upward
    E. Slightly downward

19. Which of the following is used in direct examination of a specimen?
    A. Wet mount
    B. Gram's stain
    C. Agar
    D. Petri dish
    E. Both B and C

20. The venipuncture site most commonly used on adults is the
    A. Basilic vein
    B. Median cubital vein
    C. Cephalic vein
    D. Brachial vein
    E. Iliac vein

21. After preparing a KOH mount,
    A. Examine the slide immediately
    B. Let the specimen sit at room temperature
    C. Refrigerate the specimen immediately
    D. Place the specimen in an incubator
    E. Either A or B

22. Before inoculating a culture plate, you should
    A. Label it on the top
    B. Label it on the bottom, agar side
    C. Label it with the patient's name and your initials only
    D. Both B and C
    E. Both A and C

23. The first step in preparing a culture plate is to
    A. Refrigerate it
    B. Warm it
    C. Add the specimen
    D. Label it
    E. Wash it

24. Albumin found in urine might indicate
    A. Renal disease
    B. Heart failure
    C. Hypertension
    D. Fever
    E. All of the above

25. Urine that is too acidic could indicate
    A. Urinary tract infection
    B. Renal failure
    C. Diabetes
    D. Gout
    E. Incontinence

26. If a drop of blood does not form after capillary puncture, which of the following should be done?

    A. Puncture the skin again
    B. Push repeatedly on the finger as if milking it
    C. Apply a tourniquet
    D. Apply steady pressure
    E. Wait until a drop does form

27. Which of the following causes would give plasma or serum a milky appearance?

    A. Hyperlipidemia
    B. Kidney disease
    C. Cancer
    D. Protein disorder
    E. Vegetarian diet

28. Which of the following is used in preparing a blood smear slide?

    A. Hemoclip
    B. Microhematocrit tube
    C. Lens paper
    D. Automatic puncturing device
    E. Spreader slide

29. Sensitivity testing is used to determine

    A. A pathogen's susceptibility to antibiotics
    B. A patient's susceptibility to antibiotics
    C. A patient's susceptibility to a pathogen
    D. A pathogen's susceptibility to antiseptic agents
    E. None of the above

30. A diaper rash on a pediatric patient may indicate which of the following?

    A. Possible diabetes
    B. Urinary tract infection
    C. Renal dysfunction
    D. Enuresis
    E. Nocturnal enurisis

31. The amylase test is used for disorders related to the

    A. Heart
    B. Brain
    C. Pancreas
    D. Lymphatic system
    E. Endocrine system

32. A physician may order a stool culture if he or she suspects

    A. Cancer
    B. Protozoal infection
    C. Bacterial infection
    D. Colitis
    E. All of the above

ANSWER KEY

1.	D		17.	B
2.	B		18.	E
3.	A		19.	A
4.	B		20.	B
5.	C		21.	B
6.	E		22.	B
7.	A		23.	D
8.	D		24.	E
9.	B		25.	D
10.	D		26.	D
11.	C		27.	A
12.	B		28.	E
13.	C		29.	A
14.	A		30.	C
15.	A		31.	C
16.	B		32.	E

Self-Evaluation

PART

2

| General | Test for Medical Assisting Knowledge |

| Administrative | Test for Medical Assisting Knowledge |

| Clinical | Test for Medical Assisting Knowledge |

SECTION 1
GENERAL

TEST FOR MEDICAL ASSISTING KNOWLEDGE

Self-Evaluation

After you have finished reading Chapters 1 through 7, set aside some time to take this sample exam. There are 250 questions in this section. You can take them all at once or in smaller portions. Try to time yourself and answer about 60 questions in 60 minutes. Read each question carefully and circle the best answer. After you are finished, turn to Part III, p. 459, for answers and rationales.

1. John Smith, a patient at your medical office, has been coming in for cancer treatment. After you send him a bill for the treatment, Mr. Smith's wife calls wondering what kind of treatment her husband has been receiving. What can you tell Mrs. Smith?

   A. Because you think that it's unfair that Mr. Smith has not informed his wife of his condition, you tell her about her husband's disease
   B. You don't tell Mrs. Smith on the phone, but you make sure to leave a message on the couple's answering machine detailing the test results and the reasons for Mr. Smith's visits
   C. You tell Mrs. Smith about her husband's condition, because you are legally required to do so according to public health laws because she is a family member
   D. You tell Mrs. Smith that you are not allowed to release medical information even to family members without the patient's consent and advise her to talk to Mr. Smith.
   E. You tell Mrs. Smith to call the insurance company, who would be able to inform her of all the details.

2. The word "articular" means
   A. The study of joints
   B. Pertaining to speech
   C. Pertaining to a joint
   D. Pain in the joints
   E. Difficulty with speech

3. "Trichoid" means resembling
   A. Nail
   B. Fat
   C. Skin
   D. Mole
   E. Hair

4. The sagittal plane divides the body into
   A. Front and back halves
   B. Left and right halves
   C. Upper and lower halves
   D. Four quarters: upper left, upper right, lower left, lower right
   E. Dorsal and ventral parts

5. The prefix *ambi-* means

   A. Without
   B. Both
   C. Self
   D. Good
   E. Unclear

6. Which of the following is true of DNA?

   A. Contained in the nucleus of a cell, it regulates the cell's activities
   B. It is a rod-shaped organelle that serves as the power plant of the cell
   C. It is a single chain of chemical bases
   D. It is a dense body in the nucleus composed of protein
   E. It contains water, dissolved ions, and nutrients

7. The prefix *ab-* means

   A. Without
   B. Toward
   C. Against
   D. Away from
   E. Underneath

8. The suffix *-ase* means

   A. Enzyme
   B. Noun marker
   C. Lip
   D. Condition
   E. Pain

9. Colpectomy is the excision of the

   A. Colon
   B. Rectum
   C. Vagina
   D. Uterus
   E. Testes

10. Which of the following is a type of cell division?

    A. Diffusion
    B. Osmosis
    C. Endocytosis
    D. Exocytosis
    E. Mitosis

11. Tetracyclines are

    A. Bactericidal antibiotics
    B. Bacteriostatic antibiotics
    C. Antiviral agents
    D. Norepinephrine
    E. Antiepileptic drugs

12. An abnormal decrease in depth and rate of respiration is known as

    A. Dyspnea
    B. Apnea
    C. Auscultation
    D. Hypoxia
    E. Hypopnea

13. An area of necrotic tissue that has been invaded by bacteria is known as

    A. Infarction
    B. Gangrene
    C. Ischemia
    D. Atresia
    E. Inflammation

14. Privileged communication is

    A. The leading physician's conversation with a patient who has a hardship case
    B. The physician's conversation with a judge in a malpractice suit
    C. Communication between the physician and a public health agency
    D. Any conversation among patients in the reception area
    E. Information held confidential within a protected relationship such as between patient and physician or between lawyer and client

15. Which of the following cells release histamine?

    A. Lymphocytes
    B. Monocytes
    C. Basophils
    D. Erythrocytes
    E. Leukocytes

16. The prefix *retro-* means

    A. Behind
    B. Around
    C. Below
    D. Before
    E. After

17. The most common site for cancer incidence in males is

    A. Bladder
    B. Colon
    C. Lung
    D. Prostate
    E. Brain

18. Protection against disease is called

    A. Prognosis
    B. Remission
    C. Pronation
    D. Prophylaxis
    E. Therapy

19. Which of the following types of bacteria is arranged in clusters?

    A. Streptococci
    B. Diplococci
    C. Staphylococci
    D. Protozoa
    E. Spirilla

20. Intentional torts

    A. Include assault, defamation, and invasion of privacy
    B. Are forms of abandonment
    C. Are always considered misdemeanors
    D. Are always forms of negligence
    E. Are a breach of contract

21. The combining form *ren / o* refers to the

    A. Urinary bladder
    B. Rectum
    C. Abdomen
    D. Kidney
    E. Chest

22. Carbohydrate is stored in the liver as

    A. Starch
    B. Sucrose
    C. Disaccharides
    D. Glycogen
    E. Lactose

23. A type of cholesterol that may put patients at risk of heart disease is called

    A. Cholesterolemia
    B. High-density lipoprotein
    C. Low-density lipoprotein
    D. Ketone
    E. Atherosclerosis

24. Saturated fats

    A. Are usually liquid at room temperature and help to lower blood cholesterol levels
    B. Are derived from animal sources and are usually solid at room temperature
    C. Include olive oil and cooking oils made from peanuts
    D. Dissolve in water
    E. Primarily build and repair body tissues

25. "Sexually transmitted disease" is

    A. SD
    B. S
    C. STD
    D. AIDS
    E. Sx

26. Cystalgia is pain in the

    A. Rectum
    B. Vagina
    C. Intestines
    D. Stomach
    E. Bladder

27. Which abbreviation refers to the left ear?

    A. OU
    B. AD
    C. AS
    D. OS
    E. LE

28. A condition characterized by extra fingers or toes is called

    A. Polydipsia
    B. Polyphagia
    C. Polydactyly
    D. Polysomy
    E. Polycoria

29. The shoulder blade is known as the

    A. Sternum
    B. Olecranon process
    C. Pectoral girdle
    D. Scapula
    E. Styloid process

30. A type of trial in which the verdict is decided by the judge is called

    A. Arbitration
    B. Civil
    C. Interrogatory
    D. Disposition
    E. Bench

31. Which of the following is true of the specific immune response?

    A. Controlled by T cells, it is highly changed after exposure to a pathogen
    B. It is responsible for the body's initial inflammation in response to pathogens
    C. It presents antigens to macrophages for destruction via phagocytosis
    D. The response is slower the second time a pathogen invades because of a lack of memory and immune weakness or exhaustion
    E. Both B and C

32. Angioplasty is defined as

32. Angioplasty is defined as

    A. Surgical repair of a blood vessel
    B. Surgical excision of a vein
    C. Surgical excision of an artery
    D. Suturing of a blood vessel
    E. Surgical incision of the heart

33. Vitamin B_9 deficiency may result in which of the following?

    A. Dry skin
    B. Peptic ulcer
    C. Spina bifida
    D. Scurvy
    E. Paralysis

34. Which of these combining forms means the eye?

    A. *opt / o*
    B. *ocul / o*
    C. *phot / o*
    D. *ophthalm / o*
    E. Both B and D

35. What does an antihypertensive drug do?

    A. It regulates the heartbeat
    B. It prevents and controls high blood pressure
    C. It prevents and relieves convulsions
    D. It prevents and decreases perspiration
    E. It controls cholesterol levels in the blood

36. *Res ipsa loquitur* means

    A. "The matter speaks for itself"
    B. "Giving something in return for something else"
    C. "Let the superior answer"
    D. "Within the scope of education and training"
    E. "Negligent in a complicated case"

37. Which of the following nutrients helps prevent edema?

    A. Fats
    B. Carbohydrates
    C. Proteins
    D. Vitamins
    E. Minerals

38. Beriberi may be caused by the lack or deficiency of

    A. Thiamine
    B. Niacin
    C. Riboflavin
    D. Pyridoxine
    E. Vitamin C

39. Biotin is also called

    A. Vitamin K
    B. Vitamin C
    C. Vitamin D
    D. Vitamin H
    E. Vitamin A

40. Which of the following vitamin deficiencies can cause scurvy?

    A. Vitamin B_1
    B. Vitamin B_{12}
    C. Vitamin K
    D. Vitamin B_6
    E. Vitamin C

41. What carries impulses from the spinal cord and the brain to muscles and glands?

    A. Sensory neuron
    B. Afferent neuron
    C. Motor neuron
    D. Neuroglia cell
    E. Dendrite

42. The abbreviation meaning "after meals" is

    A. pc
    B. ps
    C. pm
    D. po
    E. prn

43. Professional negligence is also called

    A. Malpractice
    B. Malfeasance
    C. Malice
    D. Nonfeasance
    E. None of the above

44. The drug of choice for Lyme disease is

    A. Penicillin
    B. Fluconazole
    C. Tetracycline
    D. Metronidazole
    E. Cephalosporin

45. Which part of the brain is responsible for language comprehension?

    A. Parietal lobe
    B. Broca's area
    C. Insular lobe
    D. Occipital lobe
    E. Wernicke's area

46. Cancer of the bone marrow is called

    A. Leukemia
    B. Melanoma
    C. Teratoma
    D. Choriocarcinoma
    E. Adenocarcinoma

47. Any infection or inflammation of the membranes covering the brain or spinal cord is called

    A. Infectious mononucleosis
    B. Meningitis
    C. Parotitis
    D. Diphtheria
    E. Myocarditis

48. Zolpidem is used

    A. As an antihistamine
    B. For the treatment of insomnia and for sedation of elderly individuals
    C. As an antidepressant
    D. As an antiparkinson drug
    E. As a cholinergic

49. The prefix *hypo-* means

    A. Excessive
    B. High
    C. Half
    D. Below
    E. Above

50. What is one of the possible causes of Buerger's disease?

    A. Sickle cell anemia
    B. Polycythemia
    C. A long period of smoking tobacco
    D. A long period of drinking alcohol
    E. Unprotected sex

51. The study of drugs and their actions in the body is called

    A. Pharmacognosy
    B. Pharmacy
    C. Pharmacology
    D. Posology
    E. Pharmacodynamics

52. A drug that has no pharmacologic activity because it contains no active ingredients is known as

    A. Placebo
    B. Teratogen
    C. Synergistic
    D. Melanin
    E. Fluconazole

53. Which of the following drugs is an example of a Schedule V drug?

    A. Diazepam
    B. *Lomotil*®
    C. Amphetamine
    D. Heroin
    E. *Talwin*®

54. Which of the following is not a fat-soluble vitamin?

    A. Vitamin K
    B. Vitamin D
    C. Vitamin B_6
    D. Vitamin E
    E. Vitamin A

55. When is it legal to release medical information about a patient?

    A. When the person asking for it is a close relative or friend
    B. When the patient has verbally consented
    C. When an insurance company calls to request it
    D. When release of the information is ordered by a subpoena
    E. It is never legal to release information about a patient

56. In an emergency situation,

    A. Medically trained personnel can be immune from a liability suit
    B. Consent to allow touching, examination, or treatment by medically authorized personnel is waived
    C. A patient's right to confidentiality can be completely waived even if information released does not directly relate to the emergency
    D. Medically trained personnel are required to help victims according to the Good Samaritan Act
    E. Consent is necessary if the patient is a minor

57. The suffix *-penia* means

    A. Increase
    B. Enlargement
    C. Formation
    D. Abnormal reduction
    E. Pain

58. Something of value that is bargained for in a contract is called

    A. Acceptance
    B. Consideration
    C. Offer
    D. Recipcrocity
    E. Registration

59. Which of the following factors might affect a drug's effect on the patient?

   A. Tolerance
   B. Age
   C. Percentage of body fat
   D. Both A and B
   E. All of the above

60. Which of the following is the role of the umbilical vein in fetal circulation?

   A. It transports oxygen from the placenta to the fetus
   B. It transports blood from the fetus to the placenta to get oxygen and to get rid of carbon dioxide
   C. It carries blood directly to the inferior vena cava
   D. It carries blood directly to the right atrium
   E. None of the above

61. The site of maturation for T lymphocytes is the

   A. Spleen
   B. Thymus
   C. Bone marrow
   D. Liver
   E. Blood

62. A one-sided relationship in which one member benefits and the other is unaffected is called

   A. Symbiosis
   B. Mutualism
   C. Commensalism
   D. Opportunism
   E. Parasitism

63. Costectomy means excision of a

   A. Xiphoid process
   B. Sternum body
   C. Rib
   D. Vertebra
   E. Bladder

64. Which of the following is one of the 5 Cs of communication?

   A. Carrier
   B. Call
   C. Constant
   D. Cohesive
   E. Both C and D

65. How can you communicate to a patient that his or her main idea was understood?

   A. By allowing the patient to reflect
   B. By restating what the patient has said
   C. By being assertive and establishing rapport
   D. By folding your arms across your chest
   E. By shaking your head

66. "Bacteriostatic" means

   A. Inhibiting bacterial growth
   B. Killing bacteria
   C. Without infection
   D. Completely destroying all living organisms
   E. Maintaining a constant amount of bacteria

67. The unauthorized disclosure of client information is called

   A. Invasion of privacy
   B. Battery
   C. Breach of contract
   D. Unethical protocol
   E. None of the above

68. Hydrophobia is also called

   A. Shingles
   B. Rubeola
   C. Rubella
   D. Rabies
   E. Varicella

69. Susan, the new medical assistant, reported to work on her first day and made a mistake in copying some files that her supervisor, John, asked for. When John learned of Susan's mistake, he angrily blurted out that women are always more trouble than they are worth. John was exhibiting

   A. Passive voice
   B. Sexual communication
   C. Unethical discrimination
   D. Gender bias
   E. Negligence

70. Lithiasis refers to

   A. A disease of the liver
   B. The formation or presence of stones
   C. A treatment for kidney failure
   D. An instrument used to examine the bladder
   E. A toxic substance found in the liver

71. Which of the following is part of the patient's bill of rights?

    A. The patient has a right to refuse treatment to the extent permitted by law
    B. The patient has a right to know if treatment is experimental
    C. The patient has a right to expect reasonable continuity of care
    D. Both B and C
    E. All of the above

72. The abbreviation *Tx* means

    A. Prescription
    B. Take
    C. Physical examination
    D. Treatment
    E. Contract

73. A time when signs and symptoms stop is known as

    A. Remission
    B. Prognosis
    C. Prophylaxis
    D. Malaise
    E. Atresia

74. Vitamin D deficiency may cause

    A. Night blindness
    B. Wernicke-Korsakoff syndrome
    C. Hemorrhage
    D. Pernicious anemia
    E. Rickets

75. Formation and excretion of sweat is called

    A. Hydrops
    B. Hydrosis
    C. Hydrolase
    D. Hydropenia
    E. Hydrolysis

76. Quinidine is

    A. An antiarrhythmic drug
    B. Used in the treatment of supraventricular tachycardia
    C. An antiepileptic drug
    D. Both A and B
    E. Both A and C

77. Blaming one's problems on others is a form of

    A. Discrimination
    B. Rationalization
    C. Projection
    D. Repression
    E. None of the above

78. Which of the following drugs is an antihistamine?

    A. Clemastine
    B. Adeparin
    C. Penicillin
    D. Pentobarbital
    E. Lithium

79. Mary Jones is a patient at your medical office. The physician has asked you to explain an upcoming procedure to Mary, but Mary cannot see very well. What should you do?

    A. Use large-print materials and sit close to the patient, speaking clearly
    B. Make sure that there is sufficient lightning in the room
    C. Talk directly and honestly
    D. Both B and C
    E. All of the above

80. The treatment of terminally ill patients generally requires

    A. Geriatrics
    B. Health care proxy
    C. Curative care
    D. Euthanasia
    E. Palliative care

81. Motor neurons are also called

    A. Efferent neurons
    B. Afferent neurons
    C. Receptors
    D. Action potential
    E. Axons

82. The Drug Enforcement Administration (DEA) requires

    A. That physicians register every 2 years
    B. That records be kept when drugs are dispensed
    C. That drugs be disposed of in the presence of a witness
    D. Both B and C
    E. All of the above

83. When dealing with a child, you should
    A. Work directly with the child, without always communicating through the parents
    B. Always communicate directly with the parents
    C. Explain procedures in simple terms and allow the child to examine instruments
    D. Both A and C
    E. All of the above

84. The complete destruction of all microorganisms is called
    A. Sanitization
    B. Sterilization
    C. Antisepsis
    D. Microbial control
    E. All of the above

85. The combining form for the brain is
    A. *cerebr / o*
    B. *encephal / o*
    C. *myel / o*
    D. *poli / o*
    E. *blephar / o*

86. Drugs used to treat narcolepsy and hyperkinesis include
    A. Antidepressants
    B. Antipsychotics
    C. Psychomotor stimulants
    D. Anticoagulants
    E. Diuretics

87. As a good team worker, a medical assistant should
    A. Not gossip
    B. Be ready to compromise
    C. Not adopt or perpetuate negative attitudes
    D. Both A and B
    E. All of the above

88. A 9-year-old girl is picked up at the medical office by her father. Her parents are divorced, and her mother has legal custody. The father would like to see the girl's medical records. Can he see the medical records?
    A. No, not without the mother's written consent
    B. Yes, if the girl gives him permission
    C. Yes, because he is the girl's father
    D. Yes, at the medical assistant's discretion
    E. None of the above

89. The part of the prescription that contains the names and quantities of the ingredients is the
    A. Superscription
    B. Subscription
    C. Inscription
    D. Signature
    E. Drug label

90. What is the term for a drug that is mixed with water to form a milky liquid?
    A. Syrup
    B. Liniment
    C. Emulsion
    D. Lotion
    E. Magma

91. Which of the following defines "privilege"?
    A. Authority granted to a physician by a hospital governing board to provide patient care in the hospital
    B. Authority granted to a hospital to hire physicians
    C. Authority granted to a lawyer by a hospital governing board to protect its physicians in lawsuits
    D. Authority granted to a physician by a patient to perform procedures and treatments
    E. The right granted to physicians by a medical board to make decisions for incompetent patients

92. The alphabetical arrangement of manufacturers is featured in which section of the *Physicians' Desk Reference* (PDR)?
    A. Pink
    B. Blue
    C. Green
    D. White
    E. Yellow

93. Cocaine is a
    A. Schedule I drug
    B. Schedule II drug
    C. Schedule III drug
    D. Schedule IV drug
    E. Schedule V drug

94. What should you do if the physician gets a call from another physician?

   A. Offer to answer any questions he or she might have
   B. Tell him or her to call back after hours
   C. Unless the physician is available to take the call, tell him or her to write a letter to the physician and to mark it *Personal*
   D. Transfer the call to the nurse on duty before transferring it to the physician
   E. Transfer the call to the physician if you can

95. The loss of the sense of smell is known as

   A. Aphonia
   B. Anosmia
   C. Amnesia
   D. Anorexia
   E. Aplastic

96. Legionnaires' disease is a type of

   A. Pneumonia
   B. Anemia
   C. Asthma
   D. Azotemia
   E. Cancer

97. Degeneration of the spinal cord and peripheral nerves may be caused by

   A. Vitamin A deficiency
   B. Excessive intake of vitamin E
   C. Vitamin C deficiency
   D. Excessive intake of vitamin A
   E. Vitamin D deficiency

98. A telephone inquiry about a bill should be handled

   A. By the patient's physician
   B. By the attending physician
   C. By the medical assistant who answers the phone
   D. By the attending nurse
   E. None of the above

99. Which of the following medical terms is misspelled?

   A. Abscess
   B. Homestasis
   C. Aerobic
   D. Neuron
   E. None of the above

100. As a medical assistant, what should your goals be in patient education?

   A. To promote patient health by teaching healthful habits and practices such as proper diet and exercise
   B. To help patients prevent injury
   C. To help patients visualize an upcoming procedure
   D. Both A and B, but C is the physician's responsibility
   E. A, B, and C are all responsibilities of the medical assistant

101. Which of the following structures of the eye contains the photoreceptors (rods and cones)?

   A. Choroid
   B. Sclera
   C. Vitreous humor
   D. Retina
   E. Tunic

102. Which type of drug may be refilled 5 times in 6 months when authorized by the physician?

   A. Schedule I drug
   B. Schedule II drug
   C. Schedule III drug
   D. Schedule IV drug
   E. Schedule V drug

103. Carriers of pathogenic organisms are called

   A. Vectors
   B. Viruses
   C. Diseases
   D. Normal flora
   E. Bacteria

104. Which of the following hormones prepares the uterus for pregnancy?

   A. Estrogens
   B. Human chorionic gonadotropin
   C. Progesterone
   D. Androgen
   E. All of the above

105. The plural of *nucleus* is

   A. *Nuclei*
   B. *Nucleuses*
   C. *Nuclea*
   D. *Nucleae*
   E. *Nucleus*

106. What is the term for a group of people who are authorized by law to act as a single person?

    A. Association
    B. Group practice
    C. Corporation
    D. Partnership
    E. Sole proprietorship

107. Confidentiality may be waived

    A. When a third party such an insurance carrier requests a medical examination and pays the physician's fee
    B. When a patient sues a physician for malpractice
    C. When a waiver has been signed by the patient or legal guardian
    D. When a waiver has been signed by the patient's spouse
    E. Confidentiality may never be waived

108. The Johns Hopkins Medical Center calls to report that a patient whom your office referred there has undergone the needed surgery and is doing well. How should you handle this call?

    A. Transfer it to the physician if he or she is available
    B. Take the call yourself
    C. Take a message for the physician if the physician is out, and make sure that the physician talks to the hospital
    D. Either A or B
    E. None of the above

109. Immobility and consolidation of a joint due to disease, injury, or surgical procedure is called

    A. Scoliosis
    B. Kyphosis
    C. Lordosis
    D. Ankylosis
    E. Crepitation

110. According to Kübler-Ross, dying patients go through all of the following stages except

    A. Isolation
    B. Refusing treatment
    C. Depression
    D. Guilt and bargaining
    E. Anger

111. Who owns medical records?

    A. The patient
    B. The physician
    C. The courts
    D. The legal guardian
    E. Both A and B

112. Chronic dilation and distention of the bronchial walls is called

    A. Bronchiectasis
    B. Bronchitis
    C. Bronchiolitis
    D. Atelectasis
    E. Atelencephalia

113. Which of the following diseases can result from antidiuretic hormone deficiency?

    A. Dwarfism
    B. Diabetes mellitus
    C. Diabetes insipidus
    D. Myxedema
    E. Acromegaly

114. Which of the following is included in the SOAP approach to documentation?

    A. Applicable financial information
    B. Opinion of the medical assistant
    C. Problem
    D. System of conditions
    E. Plan of action

115. Rapid movement of the eyeball is known as

    A. Nystagmus
    B. Hyperopia
    C. Presbyopia
    D. Hordeolum
    E. Hashimoto's disease

116. Which of the following words is misspelled?

    A. Scirrhous
    B. Pneumonia
    C. Puritus
    D. Vaccine
    E. Pleurisy

117. Which of the following suffixes means "surgical repair"?

    A. *-stomy*
    B. *-scopy*
    C. *-plasty*
    D. *-tomy*
    E. *-iasis*

118. A patient's failure to follow the physician's instructions may result in

    A. The transfer of the patient to the care of another physician
    B. A civil case between the physician and the patient
    C. Capitation for managed care
    D. Nonmaleficence against the physician
    E. A premature termination of contract

119. Which of the following abbreviations means "every two hours"?

    A. q2h
    B. q2
    C. qid
    D. qod
    E. qh2

120. What body functions does the hypothalamus control?

    A. Body temperature
    B. Water balance
    C. Sleep
    D. All of the above
    E. None of the above

121. Which endocrine gland secretes cortisol?

    A. Anterior pituitary
    B. Thyroid
    C. Adrenal cortex
    D. Ovaries
    E. None of the above

122. Which law controls the distribution and use of all drugs with abuse potential?

    A. Controlled Substance Act of 1970
    B. Drug Regulation and Reform Act of 1978
    C. Orphan Drug Act of 1983
    D. Toxic Drug Act of 1975
    E. Substance Regulation Act of 1980

123. Which of the following can be seen only with an electron microscope?

    A. Molds
    B. Bacteria
    C. Viruses
    D. Pathogens
    E. Internal organs

124. The combining form *cutane / o* means

    A. Sweat
    B. Skin
    C. Nail
    D. Tissue
    E. White

125. Which of the following blood types is considered the universal donor?

    A. Type A
    B. Type B
    C. Type AB
    D. Type O
    E. None of the above

126. Which of the following suffixes means "pain"?

    A. *-ilgia*
    B. *-itis*
    C. *-olgia*
    D. *-otomy*
    E. *-algia*

127. Which of the following blood types is considered to be the universal recipient?

    A. Type A
    B. Type B
    C. Type O
    D. Type AB
    E. None of the above

128. Which of the following tumors consists of multiple cysts ("a bunch of grapes")?

    A. Hydatidiform mole
    B. Adenocarcinoma of the vagina
    C. Adenocarcinoma of the breast
    D. Fibroadenoma
    E. Myeloid sarcoma

129. Bleeding between menstrual periods is called

    A. Menorrhagia
    B. Amenorrhea
    C. Metrorrhagia
    D. Amnesia
    E. Ovulation

130. The plural of *atrium* is

    A. *Atrius*
    B. *Atrium*
    C. *Atriae*
    D. *Atriums*
    E. *Atria*

131. Dermatitis is

    A. Inflammation of the skin
    B. Chronic itching and swelling of the skin
    C. Chronic pain under the skin
    D. Inflammation of the hair follicles
    E. Inflammation of kidneys

132. Which of the following is true about the scope of education and training for medical assistants?

    A. Medical self assistants are allowed to diagnose patients when the physician is absent and the case needs urgent medical attention
    B. Medical assistants can give out diagnostic opinions when performing emergency triage
    C. In some states, medical assistants are not allowed to draw blood
    D. Medical assistants should not be responsible for keeping controlled substances secure
    E. Medical assistants should not be responsible for treating terminally ill patients, especially patients diagnosed with AIDS

133. Which of the following drug types controls nausea, vomiting, and motion sickness?

    A. Antihidrotic
    B. Anticonvulsant
    C. Vasodilator
    D. Antiemetic
    E. Sedative

134. In a malpractice suit that involves accidentally injuring a patient during a surgical procedure, such as removing a healthy body part,

    A. The physician's lawyers will emphasize the concept of *respondeat superior*
    B. The court has the burden of proving the physician's guilt
    C. The Latin phrase *res ipsa loquitur* does not apply
    D. The patient has the burden of proving the physician's guilt
    E. The physician has the burden of proving innocence

135. Which of the following microbes lives only in the absence of oxygen?

    A. Obligate anaerobe
    B. Facultative anaerobe
    C. Heterotroph
    D. Facultative aerobe
    E. Pathogens

136. As a medical assistant working at the receptionist desk in a medical office, you get a call from an angry individual who insists on talking to Dr. Jonezee, a physician at the office. The angry woman on the phone refuses to be identified and insists that she has a right to be heard by her own physician, and she claims that you are just some person in the front office who obviously doesn't know anything and can't help her. What should you do?

    A. Tell her to calm down or you will hang up, and if she still insists on yelling at you and refuses to identify herself, hang up on her without saying anything else
    B. Transfer the call to Dr. Jonezee if she is available, because the physician might be able to calm an angry patient
    C. Tell the caller politely that she needs to tell you who she is in order for you to be able to help her and that if she can't tell you, she should write a letter to the physician and mark it *Personal*
    D. Trace the call to find out who the caller is, and pull her file and try to help her even if she refuses
    E. Offer the caller the option of leaving a message on the physician's voice mail

137. Drugs with a low abuse potential that have an accepted medical use are classified as

    A. Schedule I drugs
    B. Schedule II drugs
    C. Schedule III drugs
    D. Schedule IV drugs
    E. Schedule V drugs

138. Which of the following drugs prevent or inhibit sleep?

    A. Antianxiety
    B. Antihypnotic
    C. Analgesic
    D. Antipruritic
    E. Antitussive

139. Which part of the ear detects motion and governs balance?

    A. Tympanic membrane
    B. Semicircular canal
    C. Cochlea
    D. Cerumen
    E. Auditory ossicles

140. "Intercostal" means

   A. Between two coasts, in reference to the coverage area of some insurance companies
   B. Pertaining to an area between the ribs
   C. Between two joints
   D. Pertaining to an area between the vertebrae
   E. Pertaining to a disease that affects a large geographic area

141. According to the Medical Assisting Code of Ethics, members of the AAMA should

   A. Render service with full respect for the dignity of humanity
   B. Respect confidential information obtained through employment unless legally authorized or required to divulge such information
   C. Participate in additional service activities aimed toward improving the health and well-being of the community
   D. Both A and B
   E. All of the above

142. Koplik's spots in the mouth are a sign of

   A. Chickenpox
   B. Measles
   C. German measles
   D. Warts
   E. Diphtheria

143. Valproic acid may be used to treat

   A. Petit mal epilepsy
   B. Grand mal epilepsy
   C. Parkinson's disease
   D. Viral infections
   E. Heart disease

144. Thrombolysis is

   A. The surgical reconstruction of blood vessels
   B. The blockage of blood vessels
   C. The destruction of a clot
   D. The surgical removal of a clot
   E. An abnormal condition of blood

145. Which of the following receives oxygenated blood from the pulmonary veins?

   A. Right atrium
   B. Left atrium
   C. Right ventricle
   D. Left ventricle
   E. Both A and C

146. Which of the following is usually the only symptom of cancer of the larynx?

   A. Cephalalgia
   B. Aphasia
   C. Dysphonia
   D. Apnea
   E. Dyslexia

147. Which of the following is true of a living will?

   A. A living will is legal if two witnesses have signed it
   B. A living will is legal if there is a do-not-resuscitate (DNR) order
   C. A living will is legal if the patient is competent at the time of its creation
   D. A living will is legal if the patient is competent to create such a will and two witnesses sign it and attest to its accuracy
   E. Both B and D

148. When should you minimize background noise when communicating with a patient?

   A. It is not usually necessary
   B. When dealing with a fearful patient
   C. When dealing with an angry patient
   D. When dealing with a patient who has a visual impairment
   E. When dealing with a patient who has a hearing impairment

149. Retinol is another name for

   A. Vitamin A
   B. Vitamin B_9
   C. Vitamin E
   D. Vitamin B_6
   E. Vitamin B_{12}

150. Which of the following acts provides immunity from liability for any civil damages to volunteers at the scene of an accident?

   A. Self-Determination Act
   B. Good Samaritan Act
   C. Uniform Anatomical Gift Act
   D. Bill of Rights
   E. Medical Liability Emergency Act

151. Absorption of vitamin B_{12} requires

   A. Pepsin
   B. Gastrin
   C. Intrinsic factor
   D. Secretin
   E. Calcium

152. Questions that require elaboration on the part of the patient are referred to as
    A. Long answer questions
    B. Open-ended questions
    C. Direct questions
    D. Yes/no or is/do questions
    E. None of the above

153. Which of the following diseases can be caused by excessive growth hormone in an adult?
    A. Hypothyroidism
    B. Dwarfism
    C. Diabetes insipidus
    D. Acromegaly
    E. Graves' disease

154. When the eyeball is abnormally short, the condition is called
    A. Presbyopia
    B. Myopia
    C. Hyperopia
    D. Strabismus
    E. Binocular vision

155. Which of the following conditions of the eye may elevate pressure within the eye and cause blindness?
    A. Cataract
    B. Glaucoma
    C. Uveitis
    D. Entropion
    E. Myxedema

156. Which of the following cancers is most easily diagnosed in the early stages?
    A. Ovarian cancer
    B. Vaginal cancer
    C. Endometrial cancer
    D. Cervical cancer
    E. Stomach cancer

157. Which of the following muscles extends the thigh?
    A. Gluteus medius
    B. Quadriceps femoris
    C. Hamstrings
    D. Gluteus maximus
    E. Brachialis

158. The deltoid muscle may
    A. Extend the arm
    B. Raise the arm
    C. Flex the arm
    D. Adduct the arm
    E. Abduct the arm

159. Which of the following is one of the four Ds of negligence?
    A. Diminished
    B. Dereliction
    C. Deceit
    D. Decision
    E. Diathesis

160. Iodine deficiency may cause
    A. Hypertension
    B. Anemia
    C. Impaired growth
    D. Renal hypertrophy
    E. Goiter

161. Where does protein synthesis occur?
    A. In the nucleolus
    B. On ribosomes
    C. On lysosomes
    D. On mitochondria
    E. On the Golgi apparatus

162. A term meaning "within a vein" is
    A. Intervenous
    B. Intravenous
    C. Intravenious
    D. Intervenious
    E. None of the above

163. Which of the following procedures would require the patient's written consent?
    A. Removing a splinter from under a nail
    B. Treating a 14-year-old boy for an emergency
    C. Major surgery
    D. Giving a 25-year-old woman a Pap smear
    E. None of the above

164. A statute of limitations limits
    A. The amount of damages collected in a malpractice suit
    B. The amount a physician can charge for a service
    C. The amount of time or deadline for filing a lawsuit or legal action
    D. The type of work medical assistants can perform within the scope of their training
    E. None of the above

165. Which of the following transplants is also called an allograft?
    A. Heterograft
    B. Homograft
    C. Isograft
    D. Autograft
    E. None of the above

166. The second cervical vertebra is called

    A. Atlas
    B. Coccyx
    C. Basilar
    D. Hyoid
    E. Axis

167. The combining form *pulmon / o* means

    A. Artery
    B. Heart
    C. Breathing
    D. Veins
    E. Lung

168. Which of the following is controlled by the autonomic nervous system?

    A. Brain functions such as thinking
    B. Action of glands
    C. Action of the heart
    D. Both B and C
    E. All of the above

169. A substance that inhibits the growth of bacteria is called

    A. Protozoa
    B. Bactericidal
    C. Bacteriostatic
    D. Aflatoxin
    E. Chemotroph

170. What function does the midbrain control in the human body?

    A. Heart rate
    B. Blood pressure
    C. Auditory and visual reflexes
    D. Both A and B
    E. All of the above

171. What is meant by "ectopic"?

    A. Otocleisis
    B. Misplaced
    C. Dilation
    D. Surplus
    E. Maternal

172. "Dorsal" means

    A. Horizontal
    B. Anterior
    C. Frontal
    D. Posterior
    E. Vertical

173. Giardiasis is

    A. Inflammation of the appendix
    B. Infection of the small intestine, also called traveler's diarrhea
    C. Infectious inflammation of the liver
    D. Food poisoning
    E. Hereditary disease that leads to mental and physical retardation

174. Which of the following is a myelocele?

    A. Herniation of a muscle
    B. Herniation of a nerve
    C. Herniation of an umbilicus
    D. Herniation of the spinal cord
    E. Herniation of the diaphragm

175. Which of the following agents is used in the treatment of inflammatory conditions?

    A. Prednisone
    B. Penicillin
    C. Acetaminophen (*Tylenol*®)
    D. *Axid*®
    E. Zolpidem

176. Which of the following might make you liable for invasion of privacy and breaking patient-physician confidentiality?

    A. Releasing medical records in response to a subpoena
    B. Releasing medical records to an insurance company with the patient's written consent
    C. Refusing to disclose any information to the patient's employer even though you believe that the employer should have this information
    D. Leaving a patient's medical chart as well as the patient sign-in sheet in plain view at the office
    E. Releasing information to the appropriate public health agency about a patient who has been diagnosed with AIDS

177. Touching someone to show sensitivity and empathy is

    A. Discouraged for most medical assistants
    B. Usually acceptable on the shoulder, back, or hand
    C. Acceptable, so long as you are aware of cultural and personal differences and adjust your style accordingly
    D. Both B and C
    E. None of the above

178. The suffix that means "flow" or "discharge" is

    A. -ra
    B. -rrhexis
    C. -rrho
    D. -rrhaphy
    E. -rrhea

179. Joe, a 5-year-old patient at your pediatric practice, has been recently coming in consistently bruised, looking malnourished, and too frightened to talk about what has been happening to him. You suspect child abuse; however, when you question the mother of the boy, she claims that Joe is just very accident-prone and has never been a big eater, but there is really nothing else wrong. What should you do?

    A. Report it as suspected child abuse to the physician, and together report it to the authorities
    B. Do not report it, because the parents of the child might later sue you for slander
    C. Make a note of it in Joe's medical records, but acknowledge that you are powerless until Joe comes to you for help
    D. Call the police immediately
    E. None of the above

180. The energy that is necessary to keep the body functioning at a minimal level is known as

    A. Thermogenesis
    B. Catabolism
    C. Basal reaction
    D. Metabolic reaction
    E. Basal metabolism

181. Which of the following antibiotics can discolor soft contact lenses, the urine, saliva, and sweat, causing each to become reddish-orange in color?

    A. Nystatin
    B. Ampicillin
    C. Metronidazole
    D. Rifampin
    E. Vancomycin

182. German measles is also known as

    A. Shingles
    B. Rubella
    C. Pyoderma
    D. Rubeola
    E. Pertussis

183. Which of the following is the plural of *septum*?

    A. *Sepsis*
    B. *Septae*
    C. *Septa*
    D. *Septic*
    E. *Septums*

184. Which of the following tissues provides insulation for the human body?

    A. Muscle tissue
    B. Nerve tissue
    C. Serous membranes
    D. Adipose tissue
    E. Epithelial tissue

185. Transportation of substances out of a cell by means of vesicles is called

    A. Endocytosis
    B. Phagocytosis
    C. Exocytosis
    D. Pinocytosis
    E. Osmosis

186. When on the telephone in the medical office, you should

    A. Speak clearly, use terms that you can pronounce correctly and that are appropriate to the situation, and not overwhelm patients with technical words they might not understand
    B. Be aware of who is in hearing range of your conversation and use discretion in the type of information you discuss
    C. Hold the telephone receiver about an inch away from your mouth and be courteous
    D. Keep any personal conversations to a minimum
    E. All of the above

187. Type A blood has

    A. Type A and type B antigens
    B. Type A antigens
    C. Type B antigens
    D. Neither type A nor type B antigens
    E. Type A antibodies

188. Most drugs are eliminated by the

    A. Liver
    B. Lungs
    C. Kidneys
    D. Colon
    E. Skin

189. Which of the following is the act of intentionally misleading?

A. Tort
B. Fraud
C. Felony
D. Burglary
E. Misdemeanor

190. Performing a physical examination of the patient without the patient's consent would be considered

A. Rape
B. Assault
C. Abuse
D. Battery
E. Violation

191. While on the phone with a patient discussing an appointment, you get interrupted by a second call, which you think might be an important business associate of the physician. How should you handle this situation?

A. Finish your initial conversation with the patient and let the voice mail get the second call; after you hang up with the patient, check the voice mail and return any messages
B. Excuse yourself to the first caller and answer the second call, then return to the first call as soon as possible; minimize waiting for all callers
C. Tell the patient that there is a second call, that it might be an important call you've been expecting, and that you will call back after taking the call
D. Any of the above
E. None of the above

192. Which of the following components moves substances across the surface of the cell?

A. Cilia
B. Centrioles
C. Flagella
D. Cytoskeleton
E. Leukocytes

193. When answering the phone, which of the following greetings is appropriate?

A. "Hello, this is Dr. Jones-Smith's office. My name is George. How may I help you?"
B. "Hello, this is George. How may I help you?"
C. "Hello."
D. "This is 555-5555. How may I help you?"
E. All of the above

194. The contractual relationship between a patient and a physician binds the physician

A. To cure the patient
B. To advise the patient against needless surgery and to provide reasonable care
C. To diagnose all conditions and prescribe treatment
D. Both B and C
E. All of the above

195. When you are a victim of sexual harassment at your workplace, what actions should you take?

A. Report the harassment to your supervisor
B. Tell the harasser to stop
C. Quit immediately
D. Ignore the situation
E. Both A and B

196. A 4-year-old boy fell on a kitchen floor. After the accident, his mother saw his right leg swell and brought him to the E.R. An X-ray showed that the bone is partially bent and partially broken. What type of fracture is this?

A. Comminuted
B. Impacted
C. Greenstick
D. Oblique
E. Incomplete

197. According to Maslow's hierarchy of needs, which of the following can be considered one of the most basic human needs?

A. Shelter
B. Human contact
C. Safety and security
D. Both A and C
E. All of the above

198. The combining form *gon / o* means

A. Genitals
B. Vagina
C. Sexually transmitted disease
D. Uterus
E. Testis

199. Which of the following would be considered a positive form of body language?

A. Looking down and nodding
B. Facing the patient and nodding
C. Folding your arms
D. Both B and C
E. All of the above

200. A transplant of animal tissue into a human is called a(n)

A. Allograft
B. Isograft
C. Homograft
D. Heterograft
E. None of the above

201. A suffix is

A. The main part of a word
B. The last part of a word
C. A word ending that modifies the root
D. A word part at the beginning that modifies the root
E. The first part of a word

202. The oldest antibiotic drug and still one of the most widely used is

A. Tetracycline
B. Kanamycin
C. Penicillin
D. Streptomycin
E. Cephalosporin

203. Quadriplegia results in the paralysis of

A. The lower extremities
B. The right side of the body
C. The upper extremities and the trunk
D. The left side of the body
E. All four extremities and usually the trunk

204. A license to practice medicine is

A. Required by local law
B. Required by the local medical society
C. Required by law in each state
D. A right of every graduate physician
E. Required by federal law

205. Pentazocine is used as a(n)

A. Opioid analgesic to relieve severe acute or chronic pain
B. Nonopioid analgesic to relive mild to moderate pain
C. Anticoagulant used to prevent venous thrombosis
D. Antiarrhythmic drug to slow the heart rate
E. A barbituate used to promote sleep and treat convulsions

206. The increasing resistance to the usual effects of an established dosage of a drug is called

A. Adverse effect
B. Dependence
C. Antagonism
D. Synergism
E. Tolerance

207. A physician is required to report

A. Births
B. Deaths
C. Food poisoning
D. Both A and B
E. All of the above

208. A contraceptive pill that contains only estrogen may cause which of the following side effects?

A. Weight gain
B. Breast tenderness and nausea
C. Depression
D. Hirsutism
E. All of the above

209. Which of the following statements is true of centrally acting muscle relaxants?

A. Examples include baclofen (*Lioresal*®), carisoprodol (*Soma*®), and tizandine (*Zanaflex*®)
B. They are used for therapy of muscle strain and multiple sclerosis
C. They are used for surgical procedures to relax abdominal muscles, and examples include dantrolene
D. Both A and B
E. All of the above

210. What type of fracture is involved when the bone is broken and one of the broken ends is wedged into the interior of the other?

A. Comminuted
B. Open or compound
C. Impacted
D. Oblique
E. Incomplete

211. A corticosteroid is used to treat

A. Asthma
B. Epilepsy
C. Pain
D. Obesity
E. Hypertension

212. Which of the following is a malignant tumor of the connective tissues?

A. Hyperplasia
B. Carcinoma
C. Sarcoma
D. Cretinism
E. Neoplasm

GENERAL

213. Which of the following terms means "complete hearing loss"?

A. Anacusis
B. Tinnitus
C. Sensorineural hearing loss
D. Conductive hearing loss
E. Vertigo

214. A collapse of the cardiovascular system resulting in a dangerous reduction of blood flow throughout the body is called

A. Acute endocarditis
B. Rheumatic fever
C. Cardiac tamponade
D. Shock
E. Aneurysm

215. Which of the following results from the administration of a vaccine with killed or weakened organisms?

A. Natural active immunity
B. Artificial active immunity
C. Artificial passive immunity
D. Natural passive immunity
E. Both C and D

216. Keratinization

A. Is a process by which epithelial cells lose their moisture, which is replaced by protein
B. Is a process that leads to cretinism
C. Forms a translucent band that is found only in thick-skinned individuals
D. Is found at the bottom layer of the cutaneous membrane, beneath the dermis
E. None of the above

217. Which of the following body cavities is divided into the thoracic and the abdominopelvic cavities?

A. Dorsal
B. Transverse
C. Ventral
D. Frontal
E. Sagittal

218. Hay fever, anaphylaxis, asthma, and eczema are examples of which of the following types of hypersensitivities?

A. Type I
B. Type II
C. Type III
D. Type IV
E. Type V

219. Susan Johnson's insurance company calls to request that her medical records be transferred to her new physician. What should you do?

A. Call the other physician to verify the request
B. Tell the insurance company that you need Ms. Johnson's signed consent to release and transfer her medical records
C. Call Ms. Johnson to verify the transfer
D. Transfer the medical records at the request of the insurance company
E. Instruct the insurance company to arrange the transfer with Ms. Johnson, not you

220. In which part or parts of the body are there no sweat glands?

A. Lips
B. Nipples
C. Ears
D. Palms
E. Both A and B

221. When something is without legal force or effect, it is called

A. Void
B. Implied
C. Breached
D. Offered
E. Tort

222. An increase in the number of cells of a body part that results from an increased rate of cellular division is called

A. Mitosis
B. Malignancy
C. Atrophy
D. Hypertrophy
E. Hyperplasia

223. Hashimoto's disease is an abnormal, chronic condition of the

A. Pancreas
B. Adrenal cortex
C. Thymus gland
D. Thyroid gland
E. Heart

224. The fight-or-flight response is

A. Controlled by the cranial and spinal nerves that connect the central nervous system with the skin and skeletal muscles
B. Communication between neurons of the somatic nervous system and the autonomic nervous system
C. The sympathetic part of the autonomic nervous system that acts as an accelerator for organs needed to meet a stressful situation
D. Both A and C
E. All of the above

225. The abbreviation meaning "right eye" is

A. OS
B. OD
C. AD
D. AU
E. RE

226. The abbreviation meaning "nothing by mouth" is

A. Rx
B. n.o.
C. p.o.
D. m.n.o.
E. n.p.o.

227. What is the main muscle involved in the act of inspiration?

A. Larynx
B. Lung
C. Diaphragm
D. Trachea
E. Stomach

228. The pH of water is

A. 3
B. 5
C. 7
D. 9
E. 11

229. A substance that dissolves in a solution is called a(n)

A. Suspension
B. Electrolyte
C. Compound
D. Solute
E. Isotonic

230. Which of the following statements is true about medical law?

A. Because of the doctrine of *respondeat superior,* the physician becomes responsible for all negligent acts of his or her employees even when he or she is not giving them direct orders
B. A case in which a patient negligently refuses to follow a physician's instructions comes under the umbrella of the *res ipsa loquitur* doctrine
C. The physician is contractually bound to cure a patient
D. A physician dispensing controlled substances must be registered with the Drug Enforcement Agency (DEA)
E. All of the above

231. Which of the following is the study of hereditary improvement through the control of genetic characteristics?

A. Genetic screening
B. Gene therapy
C. Eugenics
D. Artificial insemination
E. None of the above

232. A solution that has a higher concentration (e.g., of salt) than the fluids within a cell is called

A. Hypertonic
B. Hypotonic
C. Isotonic
D. Exotonic
E. Endotonic

233. In which part of the lung does the exchange of gases take place?

A. Ventricles
B. Alveoli
C. Trachea
D. Bronchioles
E. Larynx

234. Where does the chemical breakdown of carbohydrates begin within the digestive system?

A. Esophagus
B. Saliva in the mouth
C. Stomach
D. Small intestine
E. Large intestine

235. Which of the following is a difference between the nervous and endocrine systems?

A. The nervous system controls only conscious activities, whereas the endocrine system controls unconscious activities
B. The nervous system is usually quicker to respond than the endocrine system
C. Although the effects of the endocrine system are slower, they are also more prolonged
D. Both B and C
E. All of the above

236. Cushing's syndrome is

A. An inflammatory autoimmune disease that attacks the thyroid gland
B. A tickborne disease characterized by skin lesions, malaise, fatigue, and facial palsy
C. Hyperactivity of the adrenal cortical gland that develops from an excess of the glucocorticoid hormone
D. Inflammation of the pericardium
E. A reduction in the quantity of either red blood cells or hemoglobin in a measured volume of blood

237. Which of the following is an antiviral agent?

A. Levodopa
B. Amantadine
C. Phenytoin
D. Clindamycin
E. *Nembutal*®

238. Which of the following systems removes waste products, salts, and excess water from the blood and eliminates them from the body?

A. Digestive system
B. Cardiovascular system
C. Endocrine system
D. Respiratory system
E. Urinary system

239. Which of the following is the longest part of the digestive system?

A. Small intestine
B. Large intestine
C. Esophagus
D. Anal canal
E. Rectum

240. The patient has a right to

A. Obtain reasonable responses to requests for service
B. Inquire about the practice's financial records
C. Examine his or her bill and have it explained
D. Both A and C
E. All of the above

241. Professional medical liability insurance is used to

A. Prevent fraud and abuse
B. Comply with federal law
C. Provide for legal expenses in medical liability cases
D. Comply with state law
E. Both B and D

242. Bitter tastes are perceived

A. At the back of the tongue
B. A the very tip of the tongue
C. At the sides of the tongue
D. In the middle of the tongue
E. Everywhere on the tongue

243. Butabarbital and secobarbital are which type of drugs?

A. Schedule I
B. Schedule II
C. Schedule III
D. Schedule IV
E. Schedule V

244. The suffix *-emesis* means

A. Pertaining to
B. Binding
C. Record
D. Condition
E. Vomiting

245. Certification is

A. The same as licensure
B. A voluntary process to meet the standards of a profession
C. Required by federal law
D. Required by state law
E. Both A and D

246. In which of the following instances do you usually have to use a combining vowel?

A. When connecting a prefix to a root that begins with a consonant
B. When connecting two word roots
C. When connecting a word root and a suffix that starts with a consonant
D. Both B and C
E. All of the above

247. Drugs that mimic or stimulate the sympathetic nervous system are called

A. Adrenergic
B. Cholinergic
C. Adrenal steroids
D. Glycosides
E. Vasolidator

248. Which of the following vitamins is necessary for formation of prothrombin in the liver and is essential to blood clotting?

A. Vitamin E
B. Vitamin C
C. Vitamin K
D. Vitamin A
E. Vitamin B_{12}

249. A person or group bringing charges in a lawsuit is called a(n)

A. Arbitrator
B. Defendant
C. Lawyer
D. Plaintiff
E. Both A and C

250. The habit of nail-biting is called

A. Onychomalacia
B. Onychectomy
C. Onychopathy
D. Onychotrophy
E. Onychophagia

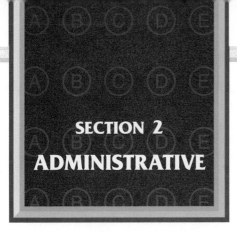

SECTION 2
ADMINISTRATIVE

TEST FOR MEDICAL ASSISTING KNOWLEDGE

Self-Evaluation

After you have finished reading Chapters 8 through 10, set aside some time to take this sample exam. There are 225 questions in this section. You can take them all at once or in smaller portions. Try to time yourself and answer about 60 questions in 60 minutes. Read each question carefully and circle the best answer. After you are finished, turn to p. 477 in Part III for answers and rationales.

1. What should you do with the invoices enclosed with packages?
   A. Check the invoice against the original order
   B. Check the invoice against the packing slip
   C. Pay the invoice unless it has already been paid
   D. Both A and C
   E. All of the above

2. An X-ray with an accompanying letter should be mailed as
   A. Parcel Post
   B. Library Mail
   C. Combination mailing
   D. Standard Mail (B)
   E. Bound Printed Matter

3. Buffer time is
   A. Empty appointment slots that can be filled to maximize office efficiency
   B. Appointment slots held open for emergencies
   C. A pharmaceutical term referring to the waiting period for laboratory test results
   D. Wasted time
   E. Time in a physician's schedule used to make hospital visits

4. In a facility that has several procedure rooms and adequate personnel to staff them, which type of scheduling can be used to build in flexibility?
   A. Wave
   B. Open hours
   C. Grouping
   D. Advance
   E. Computerized

5. Which of the following explanations is a reason to keep medical records?
   A. They are used in malpractice suits
   B. They are used to provide continuity of care
   C. They are used for audits
   D. They are used to evaluate the quality of treatment in a physician's office
   E. All of the above

6. Medical assistants are expected to answer the phone
   A. Only if the answering service doesn't answer it first
   B. By the second or third ring
   C. Rarely, because it is not within their scope of training
   D. To answer diagnostic questions
   E. Only if the call pertains to an administrative matter

7. Which of the following terms is one of the six Cs of charting?
   A. Client's words
   B. Chronicle
   C. Calculation
   D. Computation
   E. Conclusive

8. A referral form should show which of the following information?
   A. Referring physician
   B. Specialist to whom the patient is being referred
   C. Diagnosis
   D. Both A and B
   E. All of the above

9. Bob Johnson goes to his participating HMO provider for a check-up and a flu shot. The allowed charge for a check-up is $80, and the physician's usual fee is $85. The allowed charge for the flu shot is $50, and the physician's usual fee is $40. How much is Mr. Johnson charged for the visit?
   A. Nothing
   B. $5
   C. $15
   D. $40
   E. $130

10. Which accounting system uses the equation *Assets = Liabilities + Owner Equity*?
    A. Pegboard
    B. Single-entry
    C. Double-entry
    D. Daily log
    E. Accounts receivable

11. The balance
    A. Equals debits plus credits
    B. Equals the difference between debits and credits
    C. Is the amount recorded on the left
    D. Is the amount recorded on the right
    E. Both A and C

12. In order to ensure the continuous accuracy of accounts, a medical assistant can
    A. Transfer the amounts in each account from the journals to the ledgers
    B. Keep track of write-offs
    C. Bank electronically
    D. Write only certified checks
    E. Take a trial balance

13. Bills and statements of account should be sent as
    A. Standard Mail (B)
    B. Standard Mail (A)
    C. Express Mail
    D. Priority Mail
    E. First-Class Mail

14. All of the following calls will require the physician's personal attention except
    A. Requests for prescription renewals that have not been preauthorized
    B. Reports from patients concerning unsatisfactory progress or abnormal test results
    C. Calls from insurance companies
    D. Calls from other doctors
    E. Personal calls

15. The fee an individual physician most frequently charges for a service is called the
    A. Usual fee
    B. Customary fee
    C. Reasonable fee
    D. Standard fee
    E. Prevailing charge

16. When you have 300 flyers and circulars to mail out, which mail category should you use?
    A. Standard Mail (A)
    B. Standard Mail (B)
    C. First-Class Mail
    D. Periodicals
    E. Bound Printed Matter

17. Medicare Part B covers
    A. Hospital care
    B. Outpatient services
    C. Hospice care
    D. Nursing facility care
    E. All of the above

18. Michelle Columbus is a patient at your medical facility. She has both Medicare and a type of Medigap insurance. When you file her insurance claim, where should you send the claim?
    A. The claim must be filed with the Medigap insurance carrier first
    B. The claim is not filed at all, because payments from both policies are automatic on a month-to-month basis
    C. The claim must be filed with Medicare first
    D. The charges must be filed with both insurance carriers at once
    E. None of the above

19. Medicaid is
    A. A secondary carrier when the patient has Medicare
    B. Always the primary carrier
    C. A type of Medigap insurance policy
    D. A governmental insurance plan with which all physicians must comply
    E. Both A and C

20. How can you protect your computerized medical office records against both fires and computer viruses?
    A. Do not open attachments from people you don't know
    B. Do not open e-mail messages from people you don't know
    C. Make backup copies of all files nightly
    D. Store backup files off the premises
    E. Both C and D

21. Which of the following types of information is often stored on a medical database?
    A. Provider data
    B. Patient data
    C. Diagnosis codes
    D. Transactions
    E. All of the above

22. What should you do when a bill is 30 days overdue?
    A. Send a letter or a reminder statement to the patient
    B. Call the patient at work to remind him or her of this oversight
    C. Threaten the patient
    D. Ignore the situation, and only call or write once the account is 60 days overdue
    E. Pay a personal visit to the patient to offer help

23. A bank may return a check
    A. If the endorsement is missing
    B. When the check is marked *NSF*
    C. If the endorser is not known or readily identifiable
    D. Both A and B
    E. Rarely, because banks usually do not return checks

24. Physicians are required to keep payroll data for how many years?
    A. 1
    B. 2
    C. 3
    D. 4
    E. 5

25. Employers must submit a report of all taxes owed by a business at least
    A. Every week
    B. Every two weeks
    C. Monthly
    D. Quarterly
    E. Annually

26. HCPCS is the abbreviation for the Health Care Procedural Coding System, mandated by Congress for
    A. Medicare
    B. Medicaid
    C. Blue Cross
    D. CHAMPVA
    E. TRICARE

27. When you have to file an insurance claim for a procedure that is not listed in the *Physicians' Current Procedural Terminology* (CPT), what should you do?

A. File a claim for the procedure that is closest to the unlisted one

B. Look for a code in the ICD-9-CM

C. Read the guidelines for such procedures in each section, and file a special report that describes and explains the extent and reasons for service

D. You cannot file a claim for an unlisted procedure

E. Consult the Health Care Financing Administration (HCFA)

28. Voucher checks are commonly used for

A. Insurance payments

B. Purchasing items that cost less than $100

C. Purchasing items that cost more than $100

D. Cash in foreign countries

E. Payroll

29. FUTA taxes are

A. Deducted from an employee's wages based on gross income

B. Authorized under the Federal Unemployment Tax Act

C. Paid half by employers and half by employees

D. Calculated annually

E. Both A and B

30. Which of the following statements is true of non-participating Medicare providers?

A. The patient pays the provider

B. The patient pays Medicare

C. Medicare pays the provider

D. The provider pays Medicare

E. Either A or C

31. Which of the following statements is true of medical transcription?

A. You should listen all the way through a tape before starting to transcribe

B. You can adjust the transcribing equipment's speed and volume

C. You should write down the time on the digital counter for any problems so that you can find them when you request clarification

D. You should have any needed materials at hand

E. All of the above

32. A method of identifying and separating items to be filed into smaller subunits is called

A. Indexing

B. Creating tickler files

C. Numeric filing

D. Coding

E. Subject filing

33. A matrix is

A. A scheduling system

B. A filing system

C. Blocks of time allotted for activities such as hospital visits, during which the physician is not available for patients

D. Time free to schedule patients

E. A way to organize shifts in the medical office

34. The medical assistant responsible for coding should attend at least

A. One CPT class each year

B. One ICD-9 class each year

C. One ICD-9 and one CPT class each year

D. One CPT and one ICD-9 class every two years

E. One CPT and one ICD-9 class every three years

35. A Form W-2 lists

A. Gross income

B. Taxes withheld

C. FUTA taxes separately

D. Both A and B

E. All of the above

36. What is the maximum size of an item you can mail through the United States Postal Service?

A. Letters should not weigh more than 13 ounces, and parcels should not weigh more than 25 pounds

B. There are size limits only on envelopes, not on Parcel Post

C. There are no size limits on items mailed

D. A combined length and girth of 130 inches and weight of no more than 108 pounds

E. A combined length and girth of 108 inches for mailpieces and weight of no more than 70 pounds

37. Where can you write a service request, such as for a change of address, on an envelope?

    A. Below the return address
    B. Below the postage area
    C. In the upper right corner or in the center of the envelope's flap (the side without any address or postage information)
    D. Both A and B
    E. All of the above

38. Which of the following statements was true of *Special Delivery*?

    A. When something was marked *Special Delivery*, it got delivered as soon as it reached the recipient's post office
    B. It could not be used for items sent to a post office box or to a military address
    C. Special delivery mail got a unique tracking number, and the sender was notified when the mail was received
    D. It alerted postal workers that a package or letter contained unusual contents
    E. Both A and B

39. All of the following benefits are provided under workers' compensation except

    A. Permanent disability income
    B. Life insurance
    C. Rehabilitation benefits
    D. Death benefits
    E. B and D

40. Which of the following is a federation of non-profit organizations offering private insurance plans?

    A. CHAMPVA
    B. Blue Cross and Blue Shield Association
    C. TRICARE
    D. DEERS
    E. Medicare

41. A regular referral from a primary care physician often takes

    A. No time at all, because it is handled over the phone
    B. 24 hours
    C. From 3 to 10 days
    D. About a month
    E. None of the above

42. The HCFA-1500 is

    A. A nonprofit insurance carrier
    B. An agency under Medicare
    C. An agency under Medicaid
    D. A commonly used insurance claim form
    E. A private provider of health care

43. The Blue Cross part of BCBS covers

    A. Physician services
    B. Hospital services
    C. Dental services
    D. Vision services
    E. None of the above

44. A certain patient often comes to your office for cancer treatment. When this patient comes in with a sore throat caused by the flu, what is the primary diagnosis according to the ICD-9-CM?

    A. Cancer
    B. Flu
    C. Sore throat
    D. Both A and B
    E. Both B and C

45. Another name for the encounter form is the

    A. Superbill
    B. Charge ticket
    C. Receipt
    D. Both A and B
    E. Both A and C

46. FICA taxes are paid

    A. Half by the employer and half by the employee
    B. Completely by the employer
    C. Completely by the employee
    D. By the employee if the employer has fewer than 4 workers
    E. Only in special circumstances

47. Transactions are first recorded in the

    A. General journal
    B. Charge journal
    C. Daysheet
    D. Daily log
    E. All of the above

48. The amount charged for a medical insurance policy is the
    A. Customary fee
    B. Usual fee
    C. Copayment
    D. Coinsurance
    E. Premium

49. Preventing duplicate payment for the same service is known as
    A. Cost-share
    B. Insurance fraud prevention
    C. Co-payment
    D. Group policies
    E. Coordination of benefits

50. Where can you go to purchase a money order?
    A. Banks
    B. Convenience stores
    C. Post office
    D. All of the above
    E. None of the above

51. An amount that constitutes revenue would be considered a(n)
    A. Credit
    B. Debit
    C. Accounts payable
    D. Both A and C
    E. Both B and C

52. The endorsement *SPECIAL HANDLING*
    A. Should be used especially on fragile items
    B. Is not required for those parcels sent as First-Class, Express, or Priority Mail
    C. Should printed in capital letters two lines below the postage
    D. Is the same as Special Delivery
    E. Both B and C

53. Certified mail
    A. Offers a guarantee that the item has been mailed and received by the correct party by requiring the mail carrier to obtain a signature on delivery
    B. Is only available for First-Class and Priority Mail
    C. Is the best way to send documents, contracts, mortgages, or bank books that are not valuable intrinsically but would be hard to duplicate if lost
    D. Both A and B
    E. All of the above

54. Blue Shield makes direct payments to
    A. The hospital
    B. Physician members
    C. The patient
    D. Insurance companies
    E. Medicare recipients

55. To maximize communication with children, all of the following guidelines are good practices except
    A. To take their feelings seriously
    B. To work directly with their parents
    C. Explain all procedures, even basic ones, in simple terms
    D. To let them examine instruments
    E. To be truthful

56. Groups of procedures related directly to diagnosis are referred to as
    A. DRGs
    B. MFS
    C. RBRVS
    D. HCFA
    E. HCPCS

57. Amounts of money owed to a medical practice for professional services rendered are
    A. Usual fees
    B. Actual charges
    C. Major medical expenses
    D. Accounts receivable
    E. Accounts payable

58. What is the postal abbreviation for *Circle*?
    A. Cr
    B. C
    C. CIR
    D. Crl
    E. Cre

59. A system of payment used by managed care plans in which physicians and hospitals are paid a fixed, per capita amount for each patient enrolled over a stated period of time, regardless of the type and number of services provided, is called
    A. Premium
    B. Capitation
    C. Medigap
    D. Control plan
    E. Fee management

60. In proofreading, the ∧ mark means
   A. Insert
   B. Delete
   C. Make lowercase
   D. Capitalize
   E. None of the above

61. Medical assistants should
   A. Not have any visible tattoos or wear body-piercing jewelry other than earrings in the ears
   B. Wear perfume and cologne conservatively or not at all
   C. Polish their nails only with natural colors and cut them to an appropriate length
   D. Have clean, neat, and fresh attire
   E. All of the above

62. Under the old mail classification system, manuscript copies and circulars were sent as
   A. First-Class Mail
   B. Second-Class Mail
   C. Third-Class Mail
   D. Fourth-Class Mail
   E. None of the above

63. After opening the mail, a medical assistant should
   A. Date-stamp the letter
   B. Check for enclosures
   C. Annotate mail if necessary by highlighting key information and making notes in the margins
   D. Organize the mail so that the most important letters are on top
   E. All of the above

64. Guidelines that dictate the day-to-day workings of an office are called
   A. Procedures
   B. Planning
   C. Outlines
   D. Policies
   E. Protocols

65. Speaking clearly and articulating carefully is known as
   A. Pronunciation
   B. Enunciation
   C. Volume
   D. Intonation
   E. Salutation

66. When using a postage meter,
   A. Remember to change the date daily
   B. You can save money by printing the exact postage on envelopes
   C. You still have to hand-stamp most envelopes
   D. Both A and B
   E. All of the above

67. When writing a memo, you should
   A. Not use salutations or complimentary closings
   B. Use letterhead
   C. Always use the modified-block letter style
   D. Always indent paragraphs
   E. All of the above

68. In which letter style are all lines flush left except for the dateline, complimentary closing, and signature?
   A. Full-block
   B. Modified-block
   C. Simplified
   D. Center-block
   E. Left-block

69. The term used for the authorization to an insurance company to make payment directly to the physician is
   A. Reasonable fee
   B. Fee schedule
   C. Assignment of benefits
   D. Fee compliance
   E. Accepting fees

70. In postal addresses, *Junction* is abbreviated as
   A. J
   B. JT
   C. JCT
   D. JUNC
   E. JN

71. If you want an envelope to be processed electronically, how should you print the address?
   A. Use single spacing
   B. Use all capital letters
   C. Do not use punctuation
   D. Put the company name first, followed by the *Attention* line
   E. All of the above

72. Which of the following is the correct way to write Mary Jack's title?

   A. Dr. Mary Jack, M.D.
   B. Mary Jack, M.D.
   C. Ms. Dr. Mary Jack
   D. Both B and C
   E. All of the above

73. When dealing with an angry patient, you must learn how to

   A. Return to your work
   B. Stop the patient from talking
   C. Break off communication
   D. Remain calm
   E. Both A and D

74. *Telephone triage* means

   A. Requesting referrals to other doctors
   B. Checking with the insurance company
   C. Determining whether the caller is a new patient
   D. Documenting outgoing calls
   E. Screening and sorting emergency situations

75. Which of the following is a correct form for an inside street address of a business letter?

   A. Fourth Street
   B. 5th Street
   C. One Twelfth Street
   D. 3 Seventh St
   E. Nine Eleventh Dr

76. An independent practice association (IPA) is a type of

   A. Blue Cross and Blue Shield provider
   B. Medicare
   C. Medicaid
   D. HMO
   E. PPO

77. Which of the following is a correct signature block?

   A. Brian Knight, Group Health Physician
   B. Brian Knight
      Group Health Physician
   C. Brian Knight
   D. Group Health Physician
      Brian Knight
   E. Brian
      Group Health Physician

78. Which of the following checks is also available in foreign currency?

   A. Money order
   B. Certified check
   C. Traveler's check
   D. Voucher check
   E. Cashier's check

79. A letter to the insurance company should be signed by

   A. The physician
   B. The medical assistant
   C. Both the physician and the medical assistant working on the claim
   D. The medical insurance specialist or the nurse
   E. The office manager or the lead physician

80. Which of the following envelope sizes is the most commonly used in the medical office?

   A. Number 10
   B. Number 7
   C. Number $6\frac{3}{4}$
   D. Number 5
   E. Both A and C

81. On an envelope, the return address for the sender should always be placed in the

   A. Upper left corner
   B. Middle on the left side
   C. Lower right corner
   D. Lower left corner
   E. Center of the envelope

82. All of the following types of file cabinets are used in the medical office <u>except</u>

   A. Movable
   B. Circular
   C. Open-shelf
   D. Vertical
   E. Both A and C

83. Which device is used to transfer information from one computer to another using telephone lines and servers?

   A. Modem
   B. Scanner
   C. Mouse
   D. Monitor
   E. Windows

84. When performing emergency triage, which of the following conditions would warrant immediate medical help?

   A. Unconsciousness
   B. Pain in the abdomen that will not go away
   C. Persistent headache
   D. Both A and B
   E. All of the above

85. Which of the following is an example of vital supplies?

   A. Rubber bands
   B. Prescription pads
   C. A large, well equipped laboratory
   D. Staples
   E. Laboratory reagents

86. The official record of the proceedings of a meeting is the

   A. Agenda
   B. Minutes
   C. Meeting summary
   D. Itinerary
   E. Meeting report

87. Which of the following determinants can measure the effectiveness of the billing system?

   A. Collection summary
   B. Collection calls
   C. Collection letters
   D. Collection assistance
   E. Collection ratio

88. The abbreviation for "reschedule" is

   A. res
   B. RESC
   C. RS
   D. Rsch
   E. Re

89. The old Second-Class Mail classification was replaced by

   A. Standard Mail (A)
   B. Standard Mail (B)
   C. Periodicals
   D. Bound Printed Matter
   E. Parcel Post

90. Which type of record must be kept permanently?

   A. Financial records
   B. Records of minors
   C. Records needed for civil suits
   D. Immunization records
   E. OSHA records

91. When appointments are made weeks or months in advance, the medical office is using

   A. Advance scheduling
   B. Future scheduling
   C. Wave scheduling
   D. Predictive scheduling
   E. Forward scheduling

92. What is the Medicare fee schedule (MFS) based on?

   A. HCPCS
   B. Diagnosis-related groups
   C. Medicare supplements
   D. The patient's income
   E. Resource-Based Relative Value Scale

93. Carol Jones is a patient with Medicare at your medical office. She has come in for treatment for which the usual fee is $175; however, the MFS allows only $140 for such a service. Carol's copayment is 10% of any treatment. How much do you bill Carol?

   A. $17.50
   B. $14
   C. $49
   D. $3.50
   E. $35

94. Mark Winston's insurance carrier provides an 80:20 plan. When Mark goes to a physician for a service that costs $200, how much will Mark have to pay?

   A. $40
   B. $160
   C. $80
   D. $20
   E. None of the above

95. Which of the following statements about mail is true?

   A. Forwarding is offered free of charge for Priority, First-Class, and Standard Mail (A)
   B. Standard Mail (B) is forwarded out of town without any extra charge
   C. Return service is free for Standard Mail (A)
   D. Certificates of mailing are free
   E. Return service for Standard Mail (B) is charged by weight

96. Which of the following guidelines should you follow when scheduling patients?

   A. Patient preference
   B. Degree of illness
   C. Physician preference
   D. All of the above
   E. None of the above

97. Steps toward having a positive attitude include all of the following except

   A. Smiling
   B. Accepting tips from patients
   C. Using positive statements
   D. Saying something pleasant
   E. Being constructive and refraining from complaining

98. Which of the following mail items may need to be opened by the physician?

   A. Insurance forms
   B. Checks for deposit
   C. Laboratory test results
   D. Letters from attorneys
   E. Bills from suppliers

99. Who keeps a running account of a patient's deductible, and where can you find information on this deductible in order to charge the patient correctly?

   A. The physician keeps a running account of the deductible on the patient superbill
   B. The insurance carrier keeps a running account on the patient superbill
   C. The patient keeps a running account on the explanation of benefits document
   D. The insurance carrier keeps a running account on the explanation of benefits document
   E. None of the above

100. The amount due from the patient for covered services from a nonparticipating provider is

   A. The difference between the physician's fee and the deductible plus copayment
   B. The difference between the allowed charge and the physician's fee plus any coinsurance or copayment
   C. The difference between the deductible and the copayment
   D. The physician's fee plus copayment and a deductible
   E. Nothing

101. You should file business and organizational records based on the

   A. Date of birth
   B. Subject or topic
   C. Patient identification number
   D. Address of the business
   E. Patient name

102. A check written by a bank against its funds in another bank is called a

   A. Voucher check
   B. Money order
   C. Certified check
   D. Third-party check
   E. Bank draft

103. All of the following are procedures to follow if your medical practice accepts workers' compensation cases except

   A. To call the patient's employer to verify that the accident occurred on the employer's premises
   B. To create a report to law enforcement about the accident
   C. To obtain the employer's approval to provide treatment
   D. To create patient records
   E. All of the above are necessary procedures in workers' compensation cases

104. A patient's medical fees come to a total of $90 from a participating provider. What can you bill the patient if the EOB lists the following itemization?

Charges: $90
Not Eligible for Payment: $12
Allowed Charge: $78
Applied to Deductible: $30
Copayment: $10
Amount Due from Carrier: $38

A. $38
B. $10
C. $40
D. $30
E. $42

105. Which of the following is the most secure way to mail something through the United States Postal Service?

A. Certified mail
B. Insured mail
C. Registered mail
D. First-Class Mail
E. Priority Mail

106. Which act funds Social Security?

A. Federal Insurance Contribution Act
B. Federal Unemployment Tax Act
C. Employer Tax Identification Number Act
D. Health Care Financing Administration Act
E. General Accounting Office Act

107. Which special service assures that mail is delivered only to a specific addressee or to someone authorized in writing to receive mail for the addressee?

A. Registered mail
B. Restricted delivery
C. Address service
D. Insured mail
E. COD

108. What action can you take when you realize that you have mailed something you didn't intend to?

A. Nothing; once an item is mailed, it will be delivered
B. Ask the carrier to give you the item back
C. Fill out a written application at the post office to recall the mail, and attach an identically addressed envelope
D. Intercept it before it gets delivered to the addressee
E. Present a receipt of mailing or Certificate of Mailing at the addressee's post office

109. What information should be included in a patient's medical records?

A. Patient registration form
B. Laboratory test results
C. Copies of prescriptions
D. Informed consent forms
E. All of the above

110. When working on medical records, you should

A. Date and initial all entries
B. Not include correspondence about a patient
C. Record the patient's own words, not your interpretation
D. Both A and C
E. Both A and B

111. Which of the following statements is true of medical records?

A. Transferred records from the patient's previous physician are never added to the patient's record
B. Reports from consulting physicians should not be placed in the record until they have been carefully reviewed
C. Only the patient, the attending physician, and the medical assistant are allowed to see the charts without the patient's written consent or a court order
D. Both B and C
E. All of the above

112. Which filing method is useful in keeping patient information highly confidential?

A. Numeric
B. Alphabetic
C. Chronological
D. Color-coding
E. None of the above

113. According to the American Medical Association, how long should you keep patient records after the patient's final visit?

A. 5 years
B. 10 years
C. 3 years
D. 7 years
E. Permanently

114. Which of the following is a type of computer memory?

   A. Read-only
   B. Random-access
   C. Virtual
   D. Cache
   E. All of the above

115. How can you avoid getting carpal tunnel syndrome?

   A. Do not sit in one position too long
   B. Stand up and walk around often
   C. Use a wrist rest
   D. Place your wrist in a neutral position, and take frequent breaks from extended typing
   E. Both C and D

116. TRICARE was formerly known as

   A. CHAMPVA
   B. CHAMPUS
   C. BCBS
   D. RBRVS
   E. Medicaid

117. Which of the following checks can be accepted without risk?

   A. A third-party check
   B. A check drawn on an out-of-town bank
   C. A check postdated 5 days
   D. A check predated 20 days
   E. None of the above

118. Which of the following steps should you take when you receive new supplies?

   A. Inventory all supplies
   B. Send back old supplies to the supplier
   C. Throw out all old supplies
   D. Place them in the front of the supply area
   E. Place them in the back of the supply area

119. What type of software is often used for accounting procedures?

   A. Word processing
   B. Mathematical
   C. Spreadsheet
   D. Graphical
   E. Calculator

120. Which of the following is a slow type of memory that uses the hard disk?

   A. Virtual
   B. ROM
   C. RAM
   D. Cache
   E. None of the above

121. Which of the following publications could serve as a resource in developing an office policies and procedures manual?

   A. Journals
   B. Product literature
   C. Textbooks
   D. Standards publications
   E. All of the above

122. When should you collate patient records?

   A. Once a month
   B. The day before a patient is seen
   C. The day a patient is seen, while the patient is in the waiting room
   D. Once a week
   E. Once a day

123. Which of the following is used for recording the difference between the debit and credit columns?

   A. Balance column
   B. Adjustment column
   C. Trial balance
   D. Credit balance
   E. Journal column

124. In each journal entry in a double-entry accounting system, the dollar amount of a debit must be equal to the dollar amount of a

   A. Receivable
   B. Credit
   C. Balance
   D. Equity
   E. None of the above

125. Which of the following statements is true about coding?

   A. Emergency patients are considered new patients on insurance claim forms
   B. Surgical packages and laboratory panels should be coded as single procedures
   C. Modifiers allow the subparts of a procedure to be generalized into broad categories
   D. Both A and B
   E. All of the above

126. What can you do if an insurance company has not paid a claim yet?
    A. After 2 weeks, you should call the carrier to inquire about the claim
    B. After 30 days, you can bill for the same claim again, send a tracer, or call the carrier
    C. You can bill the insurance carrier again after 2 months
    D. Both B and C are good choices
    E. All of the above are good choices

127. For which of the following reasons might a claim be denied?
    A. No preauthorization has been obtained
    B. The claim is not for a covered benefit
    C. The patient has a preexisting condition that is not covered
    D. Services were provided before the waiting period was up
    E. All of the above

128. An unpredictable small cash expenditure, such as buying a cup of coffee for a visiting physician, can be covered by a(n)
    A. Superbill
    B. Emergency bill
    C. Petty cash fund
    D. Bank draft
    E. Money order

129. If an insurance company has rejected a claim because no preauthorization was obtained, what should your medical office do?
    A. Write a letter of appeal, and review the patient's contract
    B. Bill the patient
    C. Resubmit the claim with proper preauthorization
    D. Call the carrier, and take the company to court if necessary
    E. Write off the claim as a loss

130. Which of the following statements is true about Medicare claims processing?
    A. Providers are encouraged but not required to use the HCFA-1500 form
    B. Medicare forms are signed only by the patient
    C. Nonparticipating providers are required to accept assignment
    D. The allowable payment to nonparticipating providers is less than the allowable payment to participating providers
    E. None of the above

131. When a patient has both Medicare and Medicaid,
    A. You need to prepare two forms and file with Medicare first
    B. Claims are automatically forwarded from Medicare to Medicaid
    C. Claims no longer need to be filed on a HCFA-1500
    D. You need to file with Medicaid and Medicare at the same time, dividing the claim amounts equally
    E. File the claim with Medicaid first and then with Medicare

132. Which of the following statements is true of TRI-CARE claims processing?
    A. The patient may be billed for the entire deductible and the coinsurance portion of the allowed charge
    B. If the office does not accept assignment from TRICARE, the patient has to submit the claim forms
    C. The claim forms are always filed by the office using the HCFA-1500
    D. Both A and C
    E. Both A and B

133. Which of the following practices is allowed in a medical office?
    A. Billing the patient and the insurance carrier at the same time
    B. Billing both the primary and secondary carrier at the same time
    C. Not collecting payment from a Medicare patient
    D. All of the above
    E. None of the above

134. Which of the following mail types will guarantee overnight delivery?
    A. Special Delivery First-Class
    B. Registered First-Class
    C. Certified First-Class
    D. Priority
    E. Express

135. Which of the following statements is true about international mail?

   A. The rates for Canada and Mexico are the same as U.S. standard rates
   B. The rates for all international mail are determined by the USPS
   C. You can use any type of envelope for international mail
   D. Both B and C
   E. Both A and B

136. Rubber bands and staples are

   A. Incidental supplies
   B. Vital supplies
   C. Capital equipment
   D. Clinical supplies
   E. General supplies

137. Open-ended questions

   A. Should never be asked of patients
   B. Should be asked of all patients
   C. Should be asked of adults, but not of children
   D. Should be asked of children, but not of adults
   E. Should be asked of difficult patients only

138. Medicare claims must be filed by which of the following dates for services rendered during the previous year?

   A. February 28
   B. March 31
   C. June 15
   D. September 30
   E. December 31

139. What percentage of a practice's gross income should be devoted to purchasing supplies?

   A. Not more than 3%
   B. Not more than 20%
   C. Not more than 6%
   D. Not more than 15%
   E. Not more than 50%

140. Which of the following items serves as a reminder to the patient?

   A. A legal record
   B. An appointment book
   C. An appointment card
   D. An encounter form
   E. Any of the above

141. Which of the following items should be included in a patient's information packet?

   A. An explanation of the office's payment policy
   B. A summary of the office's lawsuit policy
   C. A list of office hours
   D. Both A and C
   E. All of the above

142. Scheduling two or more patients in the same time slot is called

   A. Wave scheduling
   B. Advance scheduling
   C. Double booking
   D. Modified wave scheduling
   E. Doubled open hours

143. Which of the following statements is true of workers' compensation claims processing?

   A. Records of a workers' compensation case should be kept with the patient's regular medical records
   B. The medical office bills the patient, who then is responsible for submitting claims to the insurance carrier
   C. The injured person's records must be personally signed by the physician
   D. The insurance carrier gets only a claim but no other records
   E. The injured person pays the medical bills and can file claims with the insurance company later

144. When you receive a monthly statement from the practice's bank, you should first

   A. Initial and file the statement with other financial records
   B. Reconcile the bank statement with the practice's own checkbook balances and contact the bank if you notice any discrepancies
   C. Note when the account was opened and compare this date to the date listed in your records
   D. Review the caption for the total value of checks processed, the total amount of deposits made, the account's beginning and ending balance, and that month's closing date
   E. Both B and D

145. A medical practice usually needs which type of bank account?

    A. Checking account

    B. Savings account

    C. Money market (interest-earning) checking account

    D. Both A and B

    E. All of the above

146. Which of the following mail classifications provides First-Class handling for items that weigh more than 13 ounces and no more than 70 pounds?

    A. First-Class Mail

    B. Priority Mail

    C. Standard Mail (A)

    D. Standard Mail (B)

    E. Special combination mail

147. Computer memory is usually measured in

    A. Inches

    B. Cubic centimeters

    C. Processor time

    D. Megahertz

    E. Bytes

148. A nonnegotiable check issued for the payment of debts by an insurance company is called a

    A. Warrant

    B. Voucher check

    C. Bank draft

    D. Limited check

    E. Money order

149. When you receive a check as payment from a patient, you should

    A. Endorse it immediately and write "For deposit only" on its back

    B. Endorse it and deposit it as soon as possible

    C. Use a qualified endorsement by writing *Without recourse* above the signature

    D. Write *For deposit only* on the back and deposit it with your bank

    E. None of the above

150. What should a medical office do when its collection efforts have failed?

    A. Collect through the court system

    B. Collect through a collection agency

    C. Keep sending bills to the patient and also allow a collection agency to follow up with the account

    D. Write off the debt

    E. Either A or B

151. An addition to an insurance policy is called a(n)

    A. Addendum

    B. Rider

    C. Expansion

    D. Premium

    E. Appendix

152. Which of the following acts requires that creditors provide applicants with accurate and complete credit costs and terms, clearly and obviously?

    A. Truth in Lending Act

    B. Fair Credit Reporting Act

    C. Fair Debt Collection Practices Act

    D. Equal Credit Opportunity Act

    E. Reasonable Collection and Credit Act

153. Which of the following accounts is the most typical for patients of a medical practice?

    A. Written-contract account

    B. Single-entry account

    C. Open-book account

    D. Standard payment account

    E. Double-entry account

154. When a mistake has been made in billing, you should

    A. Rebill, noting the changes on the copy of the original form and writing *Second Billing* at the top

    B. Hope that the insurance provider will not notice any mistakes

    C. Wait until the insurance provider asks for corrections

    D. Trace the original claim

    E. Both C and D

155. Educational charts, sound recordings, and films are often sent as
    A. Special Standard Mail
    B. Standard Mail (C)
    C. Library Mail
    D. Standard Mail (A)
    E. Parcel Post

156. Which of the following items is <u>not</u> permitted to be mailed via the USPS?
    A. Pornographic material
    B. Fraudulent material
    C. Hazardous material
    D. All of the above
    E. Only A and B

157. The nonremovable magnetic medium inside a computer where information is stored is called a
    A. Hard drive
    B. Keyboard
    C. Modem
    D. Mouse
    E. CD-ROM

158. The amounts a physician owes to others for equipment and services are called
    A. Payrolls
    B. Accounts payable
    C. Accounts receivable
    D. Delinquent accounts
    E. Payments

159. Which of the following tools is useful in showing the status of each account at a glance?
    A. Single-entry account list
    B. Collection ratio
    C. Accounts receivable ratio
    D. Aging accounts receivable
    E. Open-book account list

160. All of the following are advantages of electronic banking over traditional banking <u>except</u>
    A. Increased productivity
    B. Increased accuracy
    C. Greater control of cash flow
    D. Ease of depositing checks
    E. Computerized check access

161. A physician who participates in an insurance carrier's plan is called a(n)
    A. Coordinator of benefits
    B. Contributor
    C. Acceptor/Coinsurer
    D. Participating provider

162. All of the following are different types of liability insurance <u>except</u>
    A. Business
    B. Automobile
    C. Life
    D. Homeowner's
    E. A and D

163. Which of the following systems is the least structured of all the scheduling systems?
    A. Open hours
    B. Wave scheduling
    C. Advance scheduling
    D. Modified wave scheduling
    E. Double booking

164. Which act requires credit bureaus to supply correct and complete information to businesses to use in evaluating a person's application for credit?
    A. Equal Credit Opportunity Act
    B. Fair Credit Reporting Act
    C. Fair Debt Collection Practices Act
    D. Truth in Lending Act
    E. All of the above

165. Being firm and standing up for oneself while showing respect for others is called
    A. Rapport
    B. Prejudice
    C. Communication
    D. Argumentativeness
    E. Assertiveness

166. Checks should be deposited promptly because
    A. They may be lost, misplaced, or stolen
    B. There is the possibility of a stop-payment order
    C. They may have a restricted time for cashing
    D. Both A and C
    E. All of the above

167. Balance billing refers to
    A. A practice that all participating providers of an HMO engage in
    B. Billing a third-party provider for all delinquent accounts
    C. Billing the patient for the difference between the usual fee and the allowed charge
    D. Auditing the office's billing practices
    E. Comparing the bank statements to the practice's own financial records

168. Which of the following abbreviations refers to a procedural code book using a numerical system updated annually by the American Medical Association?
    A. HCPCS
    B. HCFA
    C. ICD-9-CM
    D. CPT
    E. UCR

169. Which of the following types of file cabinet is the least efficient?
    A. Movable
    B. Open-shelf
    C. Vertical
    D. Office
    E. Upright

170. What will happen when a physician in contract with an HMO plan exceeds the utilization norms set by the HMO?
    A. The physician will not receive a withheld portion of the capitation payment
    B. The physician will lose the contract with the HMO
    C. The physician will have to switch to a fee-for-service payment option
    D. All of the above
    E. None of the above

171. Bank statements contain all of the following information except
    A. List of deposits
    B. Closing date
    C. Fee schedules
    D. Caption
    E. List of checks processed

172. Which of the following is determined by comparing the actual fee charged by physicians in the same specialty?
    A. Fee schedule
    B. Accepting assignment
    C. Usual fee
    D. Usual, customary, and reasonable (UCR) fee
    E. Resource-Based Relative Value Scale

173. The term *point-of-service* refers to
    A. A type of HMO
    B. An option added to some HMO plans that allows patients to choose physicians outside the HMO network
    C. The geographic place where a medical service is performed
    D. The reasons given by a physician for performing a medical service
    E. The preauthorization some HMOs require

174. Which of the following activities provides a method of protecting confidential information on computers?
    A. Creating backup files
    B. Creating passwords unique to each employee and restricting access to certain files depending on the employee's level
    C. Monitoring the computer system through specialized software
    D. All of the above
    E. Both B and C

175. A color-coded filing system breaks the alphabet up into how many different colors?
    A. 2
    B. 3
    C. 5
    D. 7
    E. 9

176. Which type of filing cabinet requires the least amount of room?
    A. Vertical
    B. Movable
    C. Four-drawer
    D. Open-shelf
    E. None of the above

177. When filing identical names, how should you distinguish between two patients?

A. By date of birth
B. By patient identification number
C. You do not need to distinguish between the patients; file them in the same place
D. Either A or B
E. None of the above

178. A single computer that can be accessed by other computers over a network is called a(n)

A. Server
B. Software-driven computer
C. Operating system
D. Modem computer
E. Application computer

179. Which of the following files is used as a reminder?

A. Subject
B. Numeric
C. Inactive
D. Cue
E. Tickler

180. On the outside of an envelope, the postal abbreviation for *Plaza* is

A. Plaz
B. P
C. PL
D. Pla
E. PLZ

181. Seeing which of the following patients would be considered an exception to the practice of regular scheduling?

A. Emergency patients
B. Patients who have a physician referral
C. Elderly patients
D. Both A and B
E. Both A and C

182. When someone calls inquiring about a bill,

A. You should transfer the caller to the nurse on duty
B. You should transfer the caller to the physician
C. Handle the call yourself
D. Transfer the caller to the answering service
E. Transfer the caller to the appropriate insurance provider

183. The worldwide database of people covered by CHAMPUS or TRICARE is called

A. CHAMPVA
B. DEERS
C. BCBS
D. HCPCS
E. EOB

184. How long should copies of all bills and order forms for supplies be kept on file, in case the practice is audited by the IRS?

A. 1 year
B. 3 years
C. 5 years
D. 10 years
E. Indefinitely

185. When a patient has both Medicaid and CHAMPVA,

A. You should file the claim with Medicaid
B. You should file the claim with Medicaid first, then with CHAMPVA
C. You should file the claim with CHAMPVA first, then with Medicaid
D. You should file the claim with both Medicaid and CHAMPVA at the same time
E. The patient is responsible for filing these claims

186. Which of the following programs may offer the highest level of benefits to enrollees when they obtain services from a designated physician, hospital, or other health provider?

A. Health maintenance organization (HMO)
B. Preferred provider organization (PPO)
C. Kaiser Foundation Health Plan (KFHP)
D. Independent practice association (IPA)
E. Indemnity policy

187. Which portion of the HCFA-1500 form contains physician or supplier information?

A. The first part
B. The middle part
C. The last part
D. Both A and B
E. The form does not include physician or supplier information

188. After opening the mail, one of your duties as a medical assistant might be to

A. Enunciate
B. Proofread
C. Edit
D. Rewrite
E. Annotate

189. When performing diagnostic coding, you use the

A. *Physicians' Current Procedural Terminology*
B. Health Care Procedural Coding System
C. *International Classification of Diseases, 9th Revision, Clinical Modification* (ICD–9–CM)
D. National Standard Format
E. Health Care Financing Administration

190. Anesthesiology is a section of which type of coding?

A. CPT
B. ICD
C. DRG
D. RBRVS
E. MFS

191. Each new employee must complete which of the following federal income tax forms at the time of hiring?

A. W-2
B. W-4
C. 941
D. 1099
E. 1094

192. What is the time limit on refiling a denied Medicare charge?

A. 7 days
B. 30 days
C. 3 months
D. 6 months
E. 12 months

193. Whose telephone calls require the immediate attention of the physician?

A. Pharmacists
B. Consulting physicians
C. Hospital staff nurses
D. The physician's family
E. Important patients

194. Which of the following types of correspondence can be signed by the medical assistant?

A. Consultation reports
B. Referral letters
C. Termination letters
D. Letters to other physicians
E. Insurance paperwork

195. Which of the following forms must be filed as the employer's quarterly federal tax return?

A. W-2
B. W-4
C. 941
D. 1099
E. 1094

196. All of the following factors are important in selecting a supplier <u>except</u>

A. Service
B. Location
C. Quality
D. Payment policies
E. Price

197. Which of the following groups present the most common collection problem?

A. Patients with hardship cases
B. Younger adults
C. Partially insured individuals
D. Male patients
E. Foreign patients

198. Which of the following cost-containment practices is commonly employed by HMOs?

A. Allowing fewer overnight stays after certain surgeries
B. Requiring preauthorization of services before a procedure
C. Not allowing patients to see specialists
D. Always reviewing all patient diagnoses and treatment plans
E. Both A and B

199. The body of a business letter begins

A. Two lines below the salutation or subject line
B. On the line immediately below the salutation or subject line
C. Three lines below the salutation or subject line
D. Two lines below the letterhead
E. One line below the inside address

200. Notations on a business letter are placed
    A. Below the letterhead
    B. Two lines below the signature block or identification line
    C. Anywhere at the end of the letter
    D. Below the complimentary closing
    E. At the very bottom of the last page

201. In an accounting system, how should a debit balance on a patient ledger card be entered?
    A. Income
    B. Accounts receivable
    C. Payment
    D. Charge
    E. Debit

202. Which of the following persons is the principal in an insurance contract?
    A. Subscriber
    B. Beneficiary
    C. Insurer
    D. Coordinator
    E. None of the above

203. When a patient consults a physician away from home on vacation, the patient most likely is given
    A. An open account
    B. A single-entry account
    C. A one-time account
    D. A vacation account
    E. A holiday account

204. The numerals appearing in the lower left corner of a check, which are printed in magnetic ink, represent which of the following codes or numbers?
    A. NSF
    B. ABA number
    C. MICR code
    D. dollars
    E. Bank code name

205. All of the following insurance programs are sponsored by the federal government except:
    A. TRICARE
    B. CHAMPVA
    C. Medicaid
    D. Workers' compensation
    E. Medicare

206. The abbreviation NS indicates
    A. New surgery
    B. Nasal cavity
    C. No-show patient
    D. Not submitted
    E. Not sanitized

207. Which of the following ratios measures how fast outstanding accounts are being paid?
    A. Collection ratio
    B. Payment ratio
    C. Accounts receivable ratio
    D. Delinquency ratio
    E. Percentage

208. Before submitting a claim for rebilling, you should
    A. Call the staff of the insurance carrier to alert them to a second billing
    B. Write the words *Second Billing* in red letters at the top of a copy of the original claim form
    C. Review procedures and then write off the debt, because the insurance company will automatically reject a rebilled claim
    D. Make a photocopy of the original claim and send it to the insurance carrier
    E. None of the above

209. In the color-coded filing system, purple includes which part of the alphabet?
    A. E through H
    B. I through N
    C. O through Q
    D. R through Z
    E. A through L

210. Which of the following devices can convert printed matter and images into information that can be interpreted by the computer?
    A. Touch screen
    B. Modem
    C. Keyboard
    D. Hard drive
    E. Scanner

211. On letters and packages, handling instructions such as *Personal* or *Confidential* are printed
    A. Two lines above the address
    B. Three lines below the postage
    C. Three lines below the return address
    D. Across from the address, on the same line
    E. Anywhere on the envelope where there might be room

212. Which of the following is a correct way to write the date on a letter?

    A. December 5, '02
    B. Dec. 5, 2002
    C. 12/5/02
    D. 12/05/2002
    E. December 5, 2002

213. Where does the dateline go on a letter?

    A. Two or three lines below the letterhead, about 15 lines ($2\frac{1}{2}$ inches) down the page
    B. Right below the letterhead, about 12 lines (2 inches) down the page
    C. To the right of the letterhead, at the same level with the last line on the letterhead
    D. One line above the letterhead
    E. None of the above

214. The postal abbreviation for *Expressway* is

    A. EX
    B. EP
    C. EXPY
    D. EW
    E. E

215. You should capitalize

    A. All medical terms
    B. Numbers
    C. Days of the week and names of holidays
    D. Both A and C
    E. None of the above

216. When you need to divide a word in a business letter, which of the following rules can you apply?

    A. You can divide after a prefix
    B. You can divide according to pronunciation
    C. You can divide between two consonants that appear between vowels
    D. All of the above
    E. None of the above

217. The side of the letterhead on which a watermark is readable is

    A. The felt side of the letterhead
    B. The side on which typing and printing should be done
    C. The baronial or executive side of the letterhead
    D. Both B and C
    E. Both A and B

218. A letter in which all the lines are flush left is

    A. In modified-block style
    B. In full-block style
    C. In simplified style
    D. A standard letter
    E. A left-flush letter

219. Which type of check endorsement is "For deposit only"?

    A. Restricted
    B. Limited
    C. Open
    D. Qualified
    E. Certified

220. What type of HMO employs its own physicians?

    A. Group model HMO
    B. Cost containment HMO
    C. Fee-for-service HMO
    D. Staff model HMO
    E. Point-of-service HMO

221. Which of the following guidelines applies to writing business letters in a medical office?

    A. The text in the body of the letter should always be double-spaced
    B. Insert an extra line between paragraphs
    C. On the second page, use letterhead and put the name of the addressee, the page number, the date, and the subject in a header
    D. Both A and C
    E. All of the above

222. The most common insurance claim form is the

    A. CPT form
    B. Charge sheet
    C. Superbill
    D. HCPCS
    E. HCFA-1500

223. Which of the following statements is a reason to collect on delinquent accounts?

    A. A physician needs to be paid for services in order to cover expenses
    B. Noncollection of bills may imply guilt in a malpractice suit
    C. Collecting encourages nonpayment
    D. Both A and B
    E. All of the above

224. Bill Joentis went to a participating provider to receive a single treatment for which the provider usually charges $300. The allowed charge for such a service as prescribed by Bill's insurance carrier is $280, and Bill's copayment is $10 for each visit. How much is the provider allowed to charge Bill?

A. $10
B. $30
C. $20
D. $28
E. $38

225. According to the Labor Standards Act, employee health records should be kept for

A. 1 year
B. 2 years
C. 3 years
D. 5 years
E. 7 years

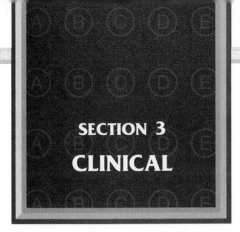

SECTION 3
CLINICAL

TEST FOR MEDICAL ASSISTING KNOWLEDGE

Self-Evaluation

After you have finished reading Chapters 11 through 18, set aside some time to take this sample exam. There are 250 questions in this section. You can take them all at once or in smaller portions. Try to time yourself and answer about 60 questions in 60 minutes. Read each question carefully and circle the best answer. After you are finished, turn to p. 491 in Part III for answers and rationales.

1. If a needlestick injury occurs, you should take all of the following actions <u>except</u>
   A. Washing your hands
   B. Documenting and reporting the injury
   C. Sending the report to the local health department
   D. Covering the injury
   E. Notifying your supervisor

2. Failure to comply with OSHA standards could result in penalties; the maximum penalty for the first violation is
   A. $700
   B. $1,700
   C. $7,000
   D. $10,000
   E. $15,000

3. The most common causes of hepatitis is a(n)
   A. Drugs
   B. Toxins
   C. Bacteria
   D. Viruses
   E. Allergens

4. Which of the following microorganisms is the main blood-borne hazard for health care workers?
   A. Hepatitis B virus
   B. Human immunodeficiency virus
   C. *Treponema pallidum*
   D. Cytomegalovirus
   E. Hepatitis E virus

5. Infected pregnant women can pass all of the following microorganisms to their babies during pregnancy or delivery <u>except</u>
   A. Syphilis
   B. Malaria
   C. The human immunodeficiency virus
   D. AIDS
   E. Hepatitis B virus

6. The average body temperature of adult human beings is
   A. 96.8°F
   B. 97.8°F
   C. 98.6°F
   D. 99°F
   E. 96.6°F

7. Which of the following positions is also called the recumbent position?

   A. Fowler's
   B. Sims'
   C. Lithotomy
   D. Supine
   E. Prone

8. The basic unit of weight in the apothecaries' system is the

   A. Microgram
   B. Milligram
   C. Gram
   D. Grain
   E. Micrograin

9. All of the following vaccines may be injected subcutaneously except

   A. Chickenpox
   B. Hepatitis A
   C. Measles
   D. Mumps
   E. Rubella

10. All of the following are adverse effects of taking contrast media orally except

    A. Skin rash
    B. Diarrhea
    C. Anaphylaxis
    D. Abdominal pain
    E. Sinus headache

11. A measurement of the actual absorbed dose of radiation is called

    A. Rad
    B. Scan
    C. X-ray
    D. Radioactivity
    E. Radioisotope

12. Which of the following crutch gaits can be used by patients who can bear full weight on one leg and no weight on the other?

    A. Swing-to
    B. Four-point
    C. Three-point
    D. Two-point
    E. Both A and D

13. Treatment of frostbite includes all of the following except

    A. Wrapping with warm clothing
    B. Massaging the affected area
    C. Obtaining medical assistance
    D. Both A and C
    E. Both A and B

14. Burns of what severity require removal of scars and skin grafting?

    A. First-degree
    B. Second-degree
    C. Third-degree
    D. Both B and C
    E. Both A and B

15. Mr. Brown, who is 39 years old, received second- and third-degree burns on his chest, abdomen, upper back, and genital area. Which of the following is an estimation of the extent of his burn?

    A. 20%
    B. 28%
    C. 48%
    D. 53%
    E. 68%

16. A cut with jagged edges is called a(n)

    A. Incision
    B. Abrasion
    C. Laceration
    D. Puncture
    E. Contusion

17. The majority of accidental poisonings occur at home to children under the age of

    A. 7 years
    B. 10 years
    C. 5 years
    D. 6 years
    E. 8 years

18. When a patient is using a walker, his or her elbow should be bent at what angle?

    A. 5°
    B. 15°
    C. 30°
    D. 45°
    E. 90°

19. Each of the following is part of the AIDS virus infection cycle except

    A. Acute HIV infection
    B. AIDS-non-related complex
    C. AIDS-related complex (ARC)
    D. Asymptomatic latency period
    E. Full-blown AIDS

20. *Hyperpyrexia* means a body temperature reading above

    A. 98.6°F
    B. 99.6°F
    C. 101.8°F
    D. 105.8°F
    E. 115.8°F

21. Which of the following positions is similar to the jackknife position in that the patient's hips are flexed at a 90° angle?

    A. Trendelenburg's
    B. Proctologic
    C. Knee-chest
    D. Prone
    E. Supine

22. Bronchoscopy may be used for all of the following purposes except

    A. Obtaining a biopsy
    B. Suctioning
    C. Visual examination of the tracheobronchial tree
    D. Visual examination of the alveoli
    E. Removing foreign objects

23. A barium swallow is also called

    A. Barium enema
    B. Lower GI series
    C. Upper GI series
    D. Gastric lavage
    E. Gastric substance

24. A body temperature is generally fatal if it rises to at least

    A. 101.0°F
    B. 103.0°F
    C. 104.0°F
    D. 106.0°F
    E. 116.0°F

25. Destroying abnormal cells by the use of freezing temperatures is called

    A. Electrosurgery
    B. Electrocautery
    C. Laser surgery
    D. Cryosurgery
    E. Heat therapy

26. An example of an emulsion is

    A. Cod liver oil
    B. *Tylenol elixir*®
    C. *Nutraderm lotion*®
    D. Aromatic spirits of ammonia
    E. None of the above

27. In the metric system, 1000 micrograms equal

    A. One milligram
    B. One gram
    C. One kilogram
    D. One grain
    E. One wheat

28. Which of the following ECG curves represents recovery of the ventricles?

    A. P wave
    B. QRS complex
    C. T wave
    D. U wave
    E. QRS

29. The image produced on film by a sweeping beam of radiation is called a(n)

    A. Rad
    B. Scan
    C. Isotope
    D. Frequency
    E. Dose

30. All of the following are open wounds except

    A. Lacerations
    B. Abrasions
    C. Bruises
    D. Incisions
    E. Punctures

31. Epistaxis (nosebleed) can be caused by all of the following except
    A. Trauma
    B. Exposure to high altitudes
    C. Hypotension
    D. An upper respiratory infection
    E. A blood disorder

32. The cardiac cycle is composed of a complete phase of atrial contraction and
    A. Atrial relaxation
    B. Ventricular relaxation
    C. Ventricular contraction
    D. Both B and C
    E. Both A and B

33. The half-life of rabies immune globulins is approximately
    A. 7 days
    B. 21 days
    C. One month
    D. Three months
    E. One year

34. Electrode devices may be cleaned with all of the following solutions or substances except
    A. Warm water
    B. Alcohol
    C. Steel wool
    D. Paper or plastic
    E. B and C

35. One teaspoon of liquid in the household system is equal to how many drops?
    A. 30
    B. 60
    C. 70
    D. 80
    E. 100

36. Attack rates of *Neisseria meningitidis* are highest among which of the following age groups of children?
    A. 1 to 6 months
    B. 3 to 12 months
    C. 1 to 6 years
    D. 1 month to 6 years
    E. 1 year to 6 years

37. All of the following waves on the ECG curve upward except
    A. Q
    B. T
    C. R
    D. P
    E. U

38. All of the following waves are part of one heartbeat on an ECG tracing except
    A. P
    B. V
    C. Q
    D. R
    E. T

39. Which of the following statements is not true regarding the preparation of a patient for MRI?
    A. The patient should avoid caffeine for 4 hours before the examination
    B. The patient should not wear eye makeup
    C. The patient should avoid alcohol for 4 hours before the procedure
    D. The patient should be asked whether any internal metallic materials are present
    E. The patient should not have a pacemaker

40. The basic elements of cast care, which should be communicated to the patient, include all of the following except
    A. Keep the cast wet
    B. Report pain, swelling, or discoloration
    C. Keep the extremity elevated for the first day
    D. Restrict strenuous activity for the first few days
    E. Both C and D

41. Which of the following individuals should not handle cat litter boxes?
    A. Elderly persons
    B. AIDS patients
    C. Blind people
    D. Pregnant women
    E. Both B and D

42. A heart rate more than 150 beats per minute and less than 250 beats per minute is called
    A. Sinus bradycardia
    B. Sinus tachycardia
    C. Atrial bradycardia
    D. Atrial tachycardia
    E. Atrial fibrillation

43. The angle of insertion of a needle for intradermal injections is

   A. 5°
   B. 15°
   C. 30°
   D. 45°
   E. 90°

44. Acardiac rhythm is also called

   A. Ventricular fibrillation
   B. Atrial fibrillation
   C. Asystole
   D. Both A and C
   E. Bradycardia

45. All of the following statements about Weber's test are true except

   A. It is a method of screening auditory acuity
   B. It is performed by placing the stem of a vibrating tuning fork in the center of a patient's forehead
   C. It is performed by placing the stem of a vibrating tuning fork on the mastoid process of the ear until the patient no longer hears it
   D. It evaluates whether the hearing is the same in both ears
   E. Both A and D

46. All of the following are common sites for intramuscular injections except

   A. Serratus anterior
   B. Vastus lateralis
   C. Deltoid
   D. Gluteus medius
   E. Both A and B

47. Which of the following statements is not true of echocardiography?

   A. It evaluates the inner structures of the heart
   B. Echoes are obtained and heard by a stethoscope
   C. Echoes are obtained by ultrasound
   D. Echoes are recorded on paper
   E. Echoes can be used to detect the buildup of fluid

48. Which of the following techniques can show a detailed cross-section of tissue structure?

   A. Magnetic resonance imaging (MRI)
   B. Myelogram
   C. Electroencephalogram (EEG)
   D. Computed tomography (CT)
   E. Mammogram

49. All of the following are topical medications except

   A. Compresses
   B. Patches
   C. Douches
   D. Ointments
   E. Lotions

50. Hypothermia is a reduction in body temperature below the normal range; rectally, the lower limit of this range is

   A. 97.8°F
   B. 97.0°F
   C. 96.0°F
   D. 94.0°F
   E. 91.0°F

51. Total surgical scrub (hand washing) time should be approximately

   A. 2 minutes
   B. 3 minutes
   C. 5 minutes
   D. 10 minutes
   E. 15 minutes

52. Which of the following malignancies is the most common HIV-related cancer?

   A. Osteosarcoma
   B. Kaposi's sarcoma
   C. Melanoma
   D. Leukemia
   E. Bronchogenic carcinoma

53. Destruction of all living microorganisms by specific means is called

   A. Sterilization
   B. Disinfection
   C. Sanitization
   D. Ultrasonic cleaning
   E. Both B and D

54. Which of the following terms is used by OSHA to describe the use of physical or chemical means to remove, inactivate, or destroy blood-borne pathogens?

A. Decontamination
B. Disinfection
C. Sterilization
D. Sanitization
E. Distraction

55. All of the following are common positions for taking X-rays except

A. Posteroanterior
B. Anteroposterior
C. Transverse
D. Lateral
E. Oblique

56. Radiation exposure badges are also called

A. Radiopaques
B. Dosimeters
C. Nuclear energy
D. Scan meters
E. Radiometers

57. Which of the following vaccines is no longer recommended by the World Health Organization?

A. Cholera
B. Yellow fever
C. Meningococcal
D. Pneumonia
E. Chickenpox

58. "Atrial kick" is a term used for the surge of blood that is

A. Pushed into the aorta as a result of ventricle contraction
B. Pushed into the ventricle as a result of atrial contraction
C. Pushed back into the arteries as a result of ventricle contraction
D. Pushed back into the superior and inferior vena cava as a result of atrial contraction
E. Leaving the ventricle

59. Which of the following is also called a bipolar lead?

A. Precordial lead
B. Augmented lead
C. Standard lead
D. Unconventional lead
E. Conventional lead

60. The degree to which a joint is able to move is called

A. Luxation
B. Range of extension
C. Range of flexion
D. Range of motion
E. Range of limitation

61. The style of walking is called

A. Gag reflex
B. Gait
C. Gap phenomenon
D. Gaze
E. Hyperextension

62. The medical assistant may be asked to assist with all of the following forms of physical therapy except

A. Teaching basic exercises
B. Demonstrating how to use a cane, walker, or crutches
C. Demonstrating how to use a wheelchair
D. Correcting a fracture or dislocation in the patient
E. Applying cold or heat

63. The four corner squares of hemacytometers are subdivided into how many squares?

A. 3
B. 4
C. 16
D. 20
E. 25

64. Which of the following instructions for treating snakebite is incorrect?

A. Do not apply a tourniquet
B. Do not cut or suction the wound
C. Do not immobilize the bitten area
D. Do not apply ice on the bitten area
E. Wash the bite area with soap and water

65. All of the following are gram-negative organisms <u>except</u>

    A. Meningococci
    B. Gonococci
    C. Staphylococci
    D. *Escherichia coli*
    E. *Salmonella*

66. All of the following are types of moist heat therapy <u>except</u>

    A. Hot packs
    B. Heat lamps
    C. Paraffin baths
    D. Hot soaks
    E. Hot compresses

67. How many limb leads are used in recording electrocardiograms?

    A. 3
    B. 6
    C. 10
    D. 12
    E. 13

68. In which of the following ranges is the normal specific gravity of urine?

    A. 1.010 and 1.030
    B. 1.015 and 1.035
    C. 1.020 and 1.040
    D. 1.025 and 1.045
    E. 1.025 and 1.050

69. Pneumococcal polysaccharide vaccine is administered to children or adolescents in one dose of 0.5 mL by which of the following routes?

    A. Intramuscular
    B. Intradermal
    C. Subcutaneous
    D. Sublingual
    E. Either A or C

70. All of the following are types of autoclaving <u>except</u>

    A. Boiling
    B. Dry heat
    C. Dry gas
    D. Steam under pressure
    E. Radiation

71. The procedure for obtaining specimens from infected wounds is similar to which of the following?

    A. Pap smear
    B. Urine culture
    C. Sputum culture
    D. Stool culture
    E. Throat culture

72. Which of the following sphygmomanometers used to measure blood pressure is the most accurate?

    A. Electronic
    B. Aneroid
    C. Mercury
    D. Digital
    E. Both A and C

73. In which of the following positions does the patient lie face up with the knees flexed and the feet flat on the table?

    A. Dorsal recumbent
    B. Fowler's
    C. Prone
    D. Sims'
    E. Jackknife

74. All of the following components are important for the stoppage of bleeding <u>except</u>

    A. Blood coagulation factors
    B. Fibrinolysis
    C. Agglutinin
    D. Platelets
    E. Vascular system

75. A body temperature is generally fatal if it is lower than

    A. 96.2°F
    B. 94.2°F
    C. 93.2°F
    D. 91.2°F
    E. 90.2°F

76. Which of the following arteries of the body is seldom used to take the pulse?

    A. Temporal
    B. Carotid
    C. Radial
    D. Femoral
    E. Brachial

77. Which of the following types of gloves are the most commonly used in the medical office?

    A. Nitrile
    B. Vinyl
    C. Sterol
    D. Cotton
    E. Latex

78. Lack of circulation due to a stoppage of blood flow is called

    A. Hypotension
    B. Blood stasis
    C. Myocardial infarction
    D. Stroke
    E. Phlebitis

79. A laboratory test for which of the following requires the use of serum or plasma?

    A. Bleeding time
    B. Hemoglobin
    C. Platelets
    D. Erythrocytes
    E. Cholesterol

80. Most dangerous bacteria are destroyed at a temperature of at least

    A. 112°F to 120°F
    B. 122°F to 140°F
    C. 152°F to 170°F
    D. 182°F to 220°F
    E. 250°F to 280°F

81. Sterilized instruments are considered to have a shelf life for

    A. 7–14 days
    B. 14–21 days
    C. 1 month
    D. 2–3 months
    E. 4–6 months

82. Which of the following forceps have sharp points that are useful in removing foreign objects?

    A. Dressing
    B. Towel
    C. Splinter
    D. Hemostatic
    E. Thumb

83. The presence of an excessive number of platelets in circulating blood is called

    A. Thrombocytopenia
    B. Thrombosis
    C. Thrombocythemia
    D. Thrombophlebitis
    E. None of the above

84. An antistreptolysin O (ASO) test is useful in diagnosis of all of the following conditions except

    A. Bacterial endocarditis
    B. Glomerulonephritis
    C. Rheumatic fever
    D. Scarlet fever
    E. Yellow fever

85. Which of the following sizes of scalpel blade is often used in performing minor surgeries?

    A. Number 10
    B. Number 13
    C. Number 15
    D. Number 18
    E. Number 20

86. All of the following are common sites for subcutaneous injections except

    A. Upper lateral part of the arm
    B. Anterior thigh
    C. Posterior thigh
    D. Upper back
    E. Abdomen

87. Which of the following ECG waves may indicate slow recovery of Purkinje fibers?

    A. P
    B. QRS
    C. T
    D. U
    E. V

88. In which of the following types of anemia may you find hemoglobin S?

    A. Iron-deficiency
    B. Aplastic
    C. Hemolytic
    D. Sickle cell
    E. Megaloblastic

89. Common neonatal tests screen for all of the following except

 A. Hypothyroidism
 B. Phenylketonuria
 C. Increased bilirubin
 D. Increased meconium
 E. Both B and C

90. All of the following are commonly administered subcutaneously except

 A. Epinephrine injections
 B. Tuberculin skin tests
 C. Insulin injections
 D. Allergy injections
 E. Both C and D

91. All of the following may be risks of liver damage from chronic hepatitis B except

 A. Cirrhosis of the liver
 B. Cholecystolithiasis (gallstones)
 C. Liver failure
 D. Liver cancer
 E. Both A and D

92. Urochrome is produced by the breakdown of

 A. Bile
 B. Cholesterol
 C. Vitamin D
 D. Urobilinogen
 E. Hemoglobin

93. Which of the following bandages are used as pressure bandages?

 A. Elastic
 B. Triangular
 C. Roller
 D. Both A and B
 E. None of the above

94. All of the following are phases of wound healing except

 A. Proliferation
 B. Degeneration
 C. Lag
 D. Maturation
 E. Both A and C

95. A physiatrist is a physician who specializes in dealing with

 A. Rehabilitation
 B. Physical medicine
 C. Chemotherapy
 D. Both A and B
 E. Both B and C

96. Abnormal black tarry stools that have a distinctive odor and contain digested blood are called

 A. Melanoma
 B. Melena
 C. Melatonin
 D. Melanin
 E. Megoloblastoma

97. Which of the following bandages frequently is used in first aid?

 A. Roller
 B. Elastic
 C. Triangular
 D. All of the above
 E. None of the above

98. Beginning at what age should children have annual checkups?

 A. One year
 B. Two years
 C. Three years
 D. Five years
 E. Twelve years

99. Alpha-fetoprotein testing from amniotic fluid is used for early diagnosis of which of the following?

 A. Fetal neural tube defects
 B. Fetal alcoholism
 C. Anencephaly
 D. Fetal drug addiction
 E. Both A and C

100. Which of the following types of viral hepatitis is frequently seen in the rainy season, and is a common disease of the liver in Southeast Asia?

 A. Hepatitis D
 B. Hepatitis B
 C. Hepatitis E
 D. Hepatitis C
 E. Hepatitis G

101. Which of the following methods of collecting urine is the most common?

    A. Clean-catch midstream
    B. First-voided morning
    C. 24-hour
    D. Timed
    E. Random

102. Which of the following is the normal respiration rate per minute for newborns?

    A. 14–20
    B. 20–30
    C. 20–40
    D. 20–50
    E. 30–50

103. A dipstick is another name for

    A. Refractometer
    B. Urinometer
    C. Specific gravity
    D. Reagent strip
    E. Both A and B

104. All of the following statements about preparation for mammography are true except

    A. The patient should not use perfume on the underarm area or breasts before the examination
    B. The patient should avoid caffeine for a week
    C. The patient should avoid drinking water 2 hours prior to the procedure
    D. The patient should not use deodorant or powder on the underarm area or breasts before the examination
    E. Both A and D

105. Temporary cessation of respiration is called

    A. Bradypnea
    B. Dyspnea
    C. Apnea
    D. Orthopnea
    E. Tachypnea

106. Annual vaccination may be indicated in some adolescents for which of the following diseases?

    A. Rabies
    B. Chickenpox
    C. Hepatitis A
    D. Influenza
    E. Hepatitis B

107. Which of the following is a slow crutch gait used by patients who can bear weight on both legs?

    A. Swing-to gait
    B. Two-point gait
    C. Three-point gait
    D. Four-point gait
    E. Five-point gait

108. In phlebotomy, at approximately what angle is the needle inserted into the vein?

    A. 10°
    B. 15°
    C. 30°
    D. 45°
    E. 90°

109. Which of the following is the most common type of head injury?

    A. Concussion
    B. Fracture
    C. Intracranial bleeding
    D. Epilepsy
    E. Brain damage

110. Which of the following tests for color blindness may be administered by medical assistants?

    A. Snellen
    B. Weber's
    C. Rinne
    D. Ishihara
    E. Pap smear

111. Which of the following blood types is known as the "universal donor"?

    A. O
    B. AB
    C. B
    D. A
    E. Rh+

112. The smallest leukocytes are

    A. Neutrophils
    B. Eosinophils
    C. Lymphocytes
    D. Basophils
    E. Monocytes

113. Serologic tests are performed on samples collected in evacuation tubes with which stopper color?

    A. Blue
    B. Red
    C. Yellow
    D. Lavender
    E. Black

114. The position used to treat patients in shock is

    A. Jackknife
    B. Sims'
    C. Trendelenburg's
    D. Supine
    E. Standing

115. Which of the following terms means the displacement of bones at a joint?

    A. Sprain
    B. Strain
    C. Dislocation
    D. Fracture
    E. Inflammation

116. Which of the following techniques may prevent the extreme skin irritation and occasional discoloration caused by iron preparations?

    A. The Z-track method
    B. Deep IM injection
    C. IV injection
    D. Intradermal injection
    E. None of the above

117. In which of the following conditions may HCG levels be lower?

    A. First trimester of pregnancy
    B. Ectopic (tubal) pregnancy
    C. Hydatidiform mole
    D. Twin pregnancy
    E. Both A and D

118. Which of the following positions is suitable for the examination of the rectum for both male and female patients?

    A. Sims'
    B. Fowler's
    C. Jackknife
    D. Knee-chest
    E. Standing

119. Organisms that cause disease are called

    A. Fulminate
    B. Pathogens
    C. Acute
    D. Chronic
    E. Inflammation

120. All of the following statements about septic shock are true except

    A. It results in vasodilation
    B. It results in decreased vascular resistance
    C. It is partly due to the effect of exotoxins
    D. It occurs following allergic reactions
    E. Both A and C

121. Which of the following is also called serum hepatitis?

    A. Hepatitis A
    B. Hepatitis B
    C. Hepatitis C
    D. Hepatitis D
    E. Both A and B

122. All of the following factors may cause hypotension except

    A. Cancer
    B. Dehydration
    C. Kidney disease
    D. High fever
    E. Acute hemorrhage

123. What is the minimum temperature usually required to destroy spore cells?

    A. 120°C
    B. 90°C
    C. 60°C
    D. 45°C
    E. 37°C

124. For injection of the vastus lateralis site, the patient may be in which of the following positions?

    A. Recumbent
    B. Knee-chest
    C. Standing
    D. Prone
    E. Trendelenburg's

CLINICAL

125. Which of the following tests requires fasting specimens (that is, specimens taken after the patient has fasted)?

    A. Pregnancy
    B. Creatinine
    C. Hematocrit
    D. Triglyceride level
    E. Hemoglobin

126. A colposcopy is used for which of the following systems?

    A. Reproductive
    B. Respiratory
    C. Digestive
    D. Urinary
    E. Nervous

127. Which of the following instruments is used in measuring pressure of the intraocular region?

    A. Tuning fork
    B. Tonometer
    C. Ophthalmoscope
    D. Snellen chart
    E. Goniometer

128. Which of the following positions is the best for musculoskeletal and neurological examinations?

    A. Knee-chest
    B. Prone
    C. Sims'
    D. Standing
    E. Fowler's

129. Flushing of the ear canal to remove impacted cerumen is called

    A. Ear instillation
    B. Ear irrigation
    C. Tympanectomy
    D. Weber's test
    E. Rinne test

130. What gauge of needle is used for the Mantoux test?

    A. 18 to 19
    B. 20 to 21
    C. 23 to 24
    D. 26 to 27
    E. 28 to 29

131. A score on a color vision acuity test may indicate color vision deficiency only if it is

    A. Less than 7
    B. Less than 10
    C. Greater than 10
    D. Less than 5
    E. Less than 1

132. Which procedure is performed to view an organ in cross-section?

    A. Ultrasonography
    B. Venography
    C. Tomography
    D. Angiography
    E. Pyelography

133. All of the following are invasive procedures except

    A. Intravenous pyelography
    B. Urine pregnancy test
    C. Sigmoidoscopy
    D. Pap test
    E. Venipuncture

134. All of the following positions are used for rectal examination except

    A. Sims'
    B. Trendelenburg's
    C. Knee-chest
    D. Dorsal recumbent
    E. Proctologic

135. One fluid ounce is equal to how many teaspoons?

    A. 3
    B. 6
    C. 8
    D. 12
    E. 16

136. A needle has all of the following parts except

    A. Hub
    B. Shaft
    C. Flange
    D. Bevel
    E. Lumen

137. Which of the following is made from dead or harmless infectious agents?
    A. Immune globulins
    B. Antibodies
    C. Antihistamine
    D. Vaccines
    E. Anticoagulant

138. According to the International Health Regulations, revaccination for yellow fever is required at which of the following intervals?
    A. Every year
    B. Every two years
    C. Every five years
    D. Every ten years
    E. Once per lifetime

139. Which of the following terms means "surgical removal of the gallbladder"?
    A. Colostomy
    B. Cholelithotomy
    C. Cholangiostomy
    D. Cholectomy
    E. Cholecystectomy

140. The action potential of each muscle cell in the heart is composed of how many phases?
    A. 2
    B. 3
    C. 4
    D. 5
    E. 7

141. When a tuberculin test is performed, at which of the following angles is the needle inserted?
    A. 5 degrees
    B. 15 degrees
    C. 30 degrees
    D. 45 degrees
    E. 90 degrees

142. Wrapped items must be autoclaved for 20 minutes and unwrapped items for
    A. 30 minutes
    B. 25 minutes
    C. 20 minutes
    D. 15 minutes
    E. 10 minutes

143. Which of the following procedures requires a general anesthetic?
    A. Pap smear
    B. Colposcopy
    C. Barium enema
    D. Gastric lavage
    E. Laparoscopy

144. A device for determining the specific gravity of urine is called a(n)
    A. Urometer
    B. Tonometer
    C. Manometer
    D. Urinometer
    E. Either A or D

145. Which of the following is the primary property of myocardial cells?
    A. Contractility
    B. Excitability
    C. Automaticity
    D. Conductivity
    E. Both B and C

146. Which of the following is described as a contrast bath?
    A. Two baths, one filled with hot water and the other with cold milk
    B. Two baths, one agitated by jets of air under pressure and the other not
    C. Two baths, one filled with cold water and the other with hot water
    D. Two baths, one dry and the other wet
    E. None of the above

147. The distance between the patient and the Snellen eye chart for visual acuity should be
    A. 3 meters
    B. 5 meters
    C. 10 feet
    D. 20 feet
    E. 25 feet

148. The instrument used to measure blood pressure is called a(n)
  A. Manometer
  B. Tonometer
  C. Sphygmomanometer
  D. Spirometer
  E. Echogram

149. Which of the following temperatures is the most accurate measurement of body temperature?
  A. Rectal
  B. Axillary
  C. Aural
  D. Oral
  E. Tympanic

150. The most appropriate site for performing capillary puncture in infants is
  A. Index finger
  B. Thumb
  C. Earlobe
  D. Heel
  E. Either A or B

151. Treatment using dry-cold or wet-cold applications is called
  A. Diathermy
  B. Cryotherapy
  C. Hydrotherapy
  D. Exercise therapy
  E. Manipulation

152. Which of the following ECG curves represents the time between contraction of the ventricles and recovery?
  A. Q-T interval
  B. P-R interval
  C. S-T segment
  D. QRS complex
  E. U wave

153. A fever in which symptoms disappear completely between paroxysms is called
  A. Remittent
  B. Lysis
  C. Afebrile
  D. Intermittent
  E. Continuous

154. The suture materials carried by surgical suture needles are also called
  A. Ligation
  B. Ligatures
  C. Litigation
  D. Needle holders
  E. Suture forceps

155. Abnormal premature ventricular contractions (PVCs) may occur because of all of the following factors except
  A. Tobacco
  B. Hypoxia
  C. A decrease in catecholamins
  D. Alcohol
  E. Caffeine

156. Which of the following is a treatment in which the patient places the hand or foot in a container of glass beads that are heated and agitated with hot air?
  A. Ultraviolet therapy
  B. Infrared therapy
  C. Hot soak therapy
  D. Fluidotherapy
  E. Cryotherapy

157. Which of the following statements about nonabsorbable sutures is incorrect?
  A. Sizes 2-0 through 6-0 are the most commonly used
  B. They range in thickness from size 16-0 to 0-0
  C. Size 0 is the thickest
  D. They are made of polyester, steel, silk, or nylon
  E. Generally they are used for outer tissues of the body

158. Nicotine and nitroglycerin patches are examples of which of the following methods of drug administration?
  A. Subcutaneous
  B. Intramuscular
  C. Transdermal
  D. Intravenous
  E. Intracapillary

159. Death rates from HIV infection have been declining in the United States mostly as a result of
    A. Immunization
    B. Condom use
    C. Increased research
    D. Antiretroviral therapy
    E. Changes in attitudes about sex among young individuals

160. Which of the following positions is not suitable for patients who are pregnant (late stage), elderly, or obese?
    A. Standing
    B. Trendelenburg's
    C. Sims'
    D. Lithotomy
    E. Prone

161. Wounds in which the outer layers of the skin are rubbed off are called
    A. Lacerations
    B. Abrasions
    C. Incisions
    D. Contusions
    E. Punctures

162. Which of the following medication forms is generally nongreasy?
    A. Cream
    B. Ointment
    C. Suppository
    D. Emulsion
    E. Liniment

163. Which of the following muscles of the body is the preferred injection site for infants?
    A. Gluteus medius
    B. Deltoid
    C. Vastus lateralis
    D. Ventrogluteal
    E. Gluteus maximus

164. Which of the following antibiotics is used in cultures to give an early indication of the presence of group A streptococcus?
    A. Penicillin
    B. Tetracycline
    C. Erythromycin
    D. Amoxicillin
    E. Bacitracin

165. Which of the following conditions may give plasma or serum a milky, or turbid, appearance?
    A. Hyperglycemia
    B. Hyperlipidemia
    C. Hypercalcemia
    D. Hypolipidemia
    E. Hypoglycemia

166. Acetone breath can be smelled in which of the following conditions?
    A. Septic shock
    B. Insulin shock
    C. Diabetic coma
    D. Hyperlipidemia
    E. Hypercalcemia

167. Which of the following conditions may cause plasma outside the body to be pink or red in color?
    A. Hemotomes
    B. Hemoptysis
    C. Hemolysis
    D. Hematoma
    E. Icterus

168. The most common type of diathermy is
    A. Ultrasound
    B. Microwave
    C. Shortwave
    D. Hot compress
    E. Hot soak

169. Muscular weakness in one half of the body is called
    A. Hemiplegia
    B. Paraplegia
    C. Quadriplegia
    D. Hemiparesis
    E. Cerebral palsy

170. What does *cardiomalacia* mean?
    A. Stretching of the heart
    B. Rupture of the heart
    C. Softening of the heart
    D. Hypertrophy of the heart
    E. Drooping of the heart at the normal location

171. BCG vaccination is <u>not</u> recommended for children who are
    A. Infected with HIV
    B. Infected with hepatitis A virus
    C. Anemic
    D. Malnourished
    E. In kindergarten

172. *Cystoscopy* means
    A. Examination of the gallbladder with a special instrument
    B. Examination of the bladder by X-ray
    C. Visualization of the uterus with a special instrument
    D. Inspection of the bladder with a special instrument
    E. Inspection of the gallbladder with contrast medium (iodine)

173. All of the following statements about OSHA regulations are true <u>except</u>
    A. They require employers to identify, in writing, tasks, procedures, and job classifications in which occupational exposure to blood occurs
    B. They require employers to provide and employees to use personal protective equipment
    C. They mandate training within the first week of the effective date of assignment and annually thereafter
    D. They specify procedures to be made available to all employees who have had an exposure incident
    E. They require a written schedule for cleaning and identifying the method of decontamination to be used

174. Which of the following culture media is most appropriate for culturing streptococcus?
    A. Thayer-Martin
    B. MacConkey
    C. Blood agar
    D. Potassium hydroxide
    E. Normal saline

175. The color of serum may be green because of
    A. Hemoglobin
    B. Cholesterol
    C. Albumin
    D. Bilirubin
    E. Ketones

176. The loss of at least what percentage of total blood volume can be life-threatening or fatal?
    A. 5% to 10%
    B. 15% to 20%
    C. 20% to 25%
    D. 25% to 40%
    E. 50% to 70%

177. In sensitivity testing, a clear zone around the disk indicates that
    A. There has been no growth of microorganisms
    B. The antimicrobial agent is ineffective
    C. The antimicrobial agent is effective
    D. The culture medium is outdated
    E. The culture medium has been effective

178. Which of the following is the most common massage modality used in the medical office?
    A. Kneading
    B. Tapping
    C. Rubbing
    D. Stroking
    E. All of the above

179. In preparation for cholecystography, the oral contrast medium should be taken about
    A. 2 hours after dinner
    B. 2 hours before the procedure
    C. 3 hours before the procedure
    D. 3 days before the procedure
    E. 2 hours before dinner

180. Which of the following is <u>not</u> a cause of artifacts?
    A. Poor conduction
    B. Outside interference
    C. Patient's movement
    D. Clean sensors
    E. Patient's talking

181. A prefilled syringe is known as a(n)

    A. Vial
    B. Ampule
    C. Flange
    D. Plunger
    E. Cartridge

182. All of the following procedures are considered minor surgery except

    A. Skin biopsy
    B. Vasectomy
    C. Dilation and curettage
    D. Barium enema
    E. Insertion of an IUD

183. Which of the following can be measured with a urinometer?

    A. Ketone
    B. Albumin
    C. Specific gravity
    D. pH
    E. Glucose

184. Which of the following conditions is referred to informally as hunchback?

    A. Kyphosis
    B. Hyperextension
    C. Lordosis
    D. Scoliosis
    E. Luxation

185. Which of the following is used to destroy blood-borne pathogens in the medical office?

    A. Phenol
    B. Alcohol
    C. Hydrochloric acid
    D. Ammonium hydroxide
    E. Bleach

186. Symptoms of overexposure to X-rays include which of the following?

    A. Bleeding
    B. Fatigue
    C. Nausea
    D. Both B and C
    E. All of the above

187. Which of the following medications may impair the ability of platelets to form aggregates?

    A. *Benadryl*®
    B. *Zantac*®
    C. Aspirin
    D. Acetaminophen
    E. Codeine

188. Leads aVR, aVL, and aVF are

    A. Bipolar leads
    B. Precordial leads
    C. Limb leads
    D. Augmented limb leads
    E. Standard leads

189. The common range of needle gauge for administering medication is between

    A. 13 and 20
    B. 15 and 23
    C. 18 and 27
    D. 20 and 30
    E. Both A and D

190. Which of the following procedures requires surgical asepsis?

    A. Needle biopsy of the breast
    B. Mantoux test
    C. Rinne test
    D. Cryosurgery
    E. Pap smear

191. Which of the following positions is used for abdominal surgery?

    A. Sims'
    B. Fowler's
    C. Lithotomy
    D. Prone
    E. Trendelenburg's

192. All of the following people are considered at risk for HIV transmission except

    A. Injection drug users who share needles
    B. Those with multiple sex partners
    C. Those who need radiation therapy
    D. Infants born to HIV-positive women
    E. Those who have had unprotected anal, vaginal, or oral sex

193. How often should an autoclave be cleaned?

    A. Every month
    B. Every two weeks
    C. Every week
    D. Every day
    E. After each load

194. A prediction of the outcome of a disease is called

    A. Clinical diagnosis
    B. Differential diagnosis
    C. Prognosis
    D. Prevention
    E. Epidemiology

195. Which of the following procedures or techniques involves injecting isotopes combined with glucose?

    A. Computed tomography
    B. Magnetic resonance imaging
    C. Ultrasound
    D. Positron emission tomography
    E. Arthrography

196. Which of the following cells are normally <u>not</u> present in circulating blood?

    A. Erythrocytes
    B. Megakaryocytes
    C. Thrombocytes
    D. Leukocytes
    E. Monocytes

197. Which diagnostic X-ray technique, used primarily for mammography, produces images electrically rather than chemically and permits shorter exposure times and lower radiation levels than ordinary X-rays?

    A. Xeroradiography
    B. Thermography
    C. Xerography
    D. Fluoroscopy
    E. Both A and C

198. Hypodermic syringes are commonly used to administer medication by which of the following routes?

    A. Intravenous
    B. Intramuscular
    C. Intradermal
    D. Subcutaneous
    E. Transdermal

199. Proctology is

    A. The study of disorders of the colon
    B. The study of disorders of the female reproductive system
    C. The study of disorders of the internal body cavities
    D. Concerned with treating disorders of the colon, rectum, and anus
    E. Both A and D

200. Which of the following is used to detect alcohol levels in blood samples?

    A. *Betadine*®
    B. *Zephiran*®
    C. Isopropyl alcohol
    D. Povidone-iodine
    E. Pure iodine

201. Which of the following statements about a Pap smear is false?

    A. The patient should not douche within 48 hours before the test
    B. The patient should not use vaginal medications within 48 hours before the test
    C. The patient should not have intercourse within 8 hours after the test
    D. The test should not be done during a patient's menstrual period
    E. The patient should not have intercourse within 48 hours before the test

202. The first MMR vaccination should be given to a child by which of the following ages?

    A. At birth
    B. 2–4 months
    C. 6–7 months
    D. 12–15 months
    E. 4–6 years

203. Your physician has ordered 120 mg of a drug that comes only in 15 mg tablets. How many tablets constitute a dose?

    A. 4
    B. 6
    C. 8
    D. 10
    E. 12

204. What is meant by a patient's gait?

    A. Style of walking
    B. Vital signs
    C. Muscle tone
    D. Weight
    E. Sharpness and awareness of the patient

205. Which of the following terms means an increased number of white blood cells?

    A. Leukoplakia
    B. Leukopenia
    C. Leukoblast
    D. Leukopoiesis
    E. Leukocytosis

206. Which of the following is the best specimen on which to conduct an occult blood test?

    A. Whole blood
    B. Serum
    C. Plasma
    D. Feces
    E. Sputum

207. Which of the following color codes indicates a blood collection tube containing EDTA?

    A. Purple
    B. Green
    C. Black
    D. Yellow
    E. Red

208. Forearm crutches are also called

    A. Lofstrand crutches
    B. Axillary crutches
    C. Walkers
    D. Canadian crutches
    E. Both A and D

209. All of the following statements about preparing a patient for intravenous pyelography are true except

    A. The patient should be asked about possible allergies to iodine
    B. The patient should take a prescribed amount of electrolyte solution or other laxative
    C. The patient may eat no solid food starting the morning before the procedure
    D. The patient may have one cup of coffee on the morning of the test
    E. The patient should be asked about possible allergies to shellfish

210. On an ECG, which of the following is considered an artifact?

    A. Flat line
    B. Extraneous mark
    C. Wandering baseline
    D. All of the above
    E. None of the above

211. Autoclave indicator tape turns which color after autoclaving?

    A. Red
    B. Yellow
    C. Green
    D. Blue
    E. Black

212. Which of the following types of urine specimen is helpful in diagnosing dehydration and pheochromocytoma?

    A. Random
    B. Clean-catch midstream
    C. Timed
    D. 24-hour
    E. First-voided morning

213. The temperature of an autoclave is commonly set for

    A. 150°F to 180°F
    B. 180°F to 210°F
    C. 210°F to 245°F
    D. 250°F to 270°F
    E. 270°F to 295°F

214. Abnormal, temporary low blood pressure, especially when a patient moves rapidly, is called

    A. Anemic hypotension
    B. Orthostatic hypotension
    C. Very mild hypertension
    D. Very mild hypotension
    E. Hypovolemic shock

215. Which of the following types of shock may occur following allergic reactions?

    A. Cardiogenic
    B. Hypovolemic
    C. Neurogenic
    D. Anaphylactic
    E. Septic

216. Which of the following color codes indicates a tube that does not contain any additive?

A. Lavender
B. Green
C. Red
D. Blue
E. Yellow

217. Which of the following instruments is used to separate particles of different densities within a liquid?

A. Seralyzer
B. Autoclave
C. Ultrasound generator
D. Spectrophotometer
E. Centrifuge

218. Which of the following groups of microorganisms can be seen only with an electron microscope?

A. Fungi
B. Rickettsiae
C. Protozoa
D. Bacteria
E. Viruses

219. What percentage of the U.S. population has Rh negative blood?

A. 35%
B. 25%
C. 20%
D. 15%
E. 10%

220. Treatment for which of the following diseases requires a series of six injections over a four-week period?

A. Rabies
B. Viral meningitis
C. Hepatitis B
D. Influenza
E. AIDS

221. Which of the following items should be used to clean the lenses of a microscope?

A. Soft facial tissue
B. Cotton cloth
C. Paper towel
D. Lens paper
E. Either A or B

222. OSHA regulations require all health care workers who may be at risk to be vaccinated against which of the following diseases?

A. Tuberculosis
B. AIDS
C. Hepatitis A
D. Hepatitis B
E. Hepatitis C

223. The most commonly used site for measuring the pulse rate is the

A. Carotid artery
B. Radial artery
C. Brachial artery
D. Femoral artery
E. Temporal artery

224. A dilute solution of formaldehyde used to preserve biological specimens is

A. Formalin
B. Selective culture medium
C. Fixative
D. Lactated Ringer's solution
E. EDTA

225. Which of the following is a correct estimate of the percentage of body surface represented by the chest, abdomen, right upper limb, and genital areas (according to the rule of nines)?

A. 9%
B. 19%
C. 28%
D. 37%
E. 49%

226. What structure separates each atrium and its respective ventricle?

A. Septum
B. Valve
C. Base of the heart
D. Apex
E. Sinus

227. An X-ray procedure used primarily to study the skull is

A. Stereoscopy
B. Fluoroscopy
C. Myelography
D. Xeroradiography
E. Thermography

228. The Ishihara test is used for which of the following organs of the body?

 A. Gallbladder
 B. Ear
 C. Urinary bladder
 D. Eye
 E. Uterus

229. Which of the following leads is also called unipolar?

 A. Standard
 B. Limb
 C. Precordial
 D. Augmented
 E. Chest

230. The control center for breathing is in the

 A. Chest
 B. Cerebellum
 C. Pons
 D. Hypothalamus
 E. Medulla oblongata

231. Which of the following color codes indicates tubes used for blood cultures?

 A. Red
 B. Yellow
 C. Green
 D. Blue
 E. Black

232. Which of the following colors is used on labels to indicate a health hazard?

 A. Yellow
 B. White
 C. Red
 D. Blue
 E. Black

233. The administration of a drug by placing it under the tongue until it dissolves is called

 A. Transdermal
 B. Sublingual
 C. Buccal
 D. Oral
 E. Topical

234. The coughing up of blood from the respiratory tract is called

 A. Hemolysis
 B. Hemostasis
 C. Hemothorax
 D. Hemopneumothorax
 E. Hemoptysis

235. Which of the following vaccines can be administered at birth?

 A. BCG
 B. Polio
 C. Hepatitis A
 D. Hepatitis B
 E. Measles

236. At present, the incidence of yellow fever is restricted to

 A. North America
 B. South American jungles
 C. South Asia
 D. Africa
 E. Both B and D

237. According to Good Samaritan laws,

 A. Emergency care is permitted when it is within the scope of competence of the person administering first aid
 B. Emergency care is permitted only with the explicit (e.g., verbal) consent of the patient
 C. All medical personnel are required to provide care in all emergency situations
 D. When providing emergency care, medical personnel are protected against possible claims of negligence
 E. The permission of the patient (or the person holding power of attorney) is required in any situation, emergency or otherwise

238. Which of the following colors indicates specific hazards such as radioactivity?

 A. White
 B. Red
 C. Yellow
 D. Blue
 E. Green

239. Administration of a drug by placing it in the mouth between the gums and the cheek is called
    A. Oral
    B. Topical
    C. Sublingual
    D. Transdermal
    E. Buccal

240. Macrophages include all of the following cells except
    A. Kupffer cells
    B. Microglial cells
    C. Histiocytes
    D. Osteoblasts
    E. Osteoclasts

241. The liquid portion of the blood that remains after the clotting proteins and cells have been removed is called
    A. Plasma
    B. Antibody
    C. Serum
    D. Fibrinogen
    E. Anticoagulant

242. In the erythrocyte sedimentation rate (ESR) test, the normal rate at which cells fall is 1 mm every
    A. Minute
    B. Five minutes
    C. Thirty minutes
    D. Hour
    E. Two hours

243. Burns can be caused by temperatures of at least
    A. 106°F
    B. 109°F
    C. 112°F
    D. 114°F
    E. 116°F

244. Long, slender instruments used to explore wounds or body cavities are called
    A. Retractors
    B. Scalpels
    C. Probes
    D. Scissors
    E. Thumb forceps

245. Excessive EDTA causes erythrocytes to
    A. Shrink
    B. Rupture
    C. Swell
    D. Reproduce
    E. Be destroyed

246. A device used to measure the degree of joint movement is called a
    A. Tonometer
    B. Torsiometer
    C. Glucometer
    D. Goniometer
    E. Gonioscope

247. The introduction of a substance into a vein is called
    A. Solution
    B. Infusion
    C. Suspension
    D. Aromatic waters
    E. Liquors

248. What percentage of the U.S. population has Rh+ blood?
    A. 65%
    B. 75%
    C. 80%
    D. 85%
    E. 90%

249. The needle gauge range most commonly used for venipuncture is
    A. 17–19
    B. 19–20
    C. 21–23
    D. 24–25
    E. 17–25

250. After surgery, sutures generally remain in place for how many days?
    A. 2–3
    B. 3–5
    C. 5–6
    D. 8–9
    E. 10–12

Self-Evaluation Answers and Rationales

PART

3

| General | Medical Assisting Knowledge |

| Administrative | Medical Assisting Knowledge |

| Clinical | Medical Assisting Knowledge |

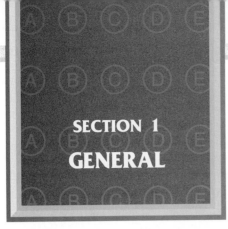

MEDICAL ASSISTING KNOWLEDGE

Self-Evaluation Answers and Rationales

Here you'll find the answers to the test on General Medical Assisting Knowledge in Part II on p. 393. Check your answers and note which questions you missed. Study the rationales for any questions you feel you had difficulty with and if you need more review, go back to the appropriate section in the chapters.

1. **(D)** You should not decide confidentiality on the basis of your personal opinion of the patient. You are not allowed to disclose any information, even to family members, without the patient's signed consent, a subpoena, or an applicable health law. When leaving a message at a patient's home, you should not mention the nature of the call or disclose information that should be considered confidential, such as test results or the nature of doctor visits. State health statues require the reporting of only those diseases that could threaten the health and well-being of the population, such as diphtheria, cholera, plague, smallpox, malaria, AIDS, rubeola, rheumatic fever, tetanus, and sexually transmitted diseases such as gonorrhea, syphilis, and chlamydia.

2. **(C)** *Articulus* and the combining form *arthr / o* both mean "joint." The suffix *-al* means "pertaining to." Another word for *articular* is *arthral*.

3. **(E)** *Trich / o* means "hair."

4. **(B)** The frontal plane divides the body into front and back halves, the sagittal into left and right halves, and the transverse into upper and lower halves. Dorsal and ventral are the two main body cavities.

5. **(B)** *Ambi-* means "both," as in "ambidextrous," "able to use both hands."

6. **(A)** *DNA* stands for deoxyribonucleic acid, and it consists of long, double chains of chemical bases along a sugar backbone. This pattern provides the hereditary information that directs cell activities.

7. **(D)** *Ab-* is a prefix meaning "away from."

8. **(A)** The suffix *-ase* means "enzyme," as in the word "amylase," which refers to a class of digestive enzymes.

9. **(C)** Colpectomy is also called vaginectomy, the surgical excision of the vagina. A surgical incision into the colon is known as a colotomy; surgical excision of the colon is colectomy. A surgical procedure of the rectum is called proctotomy; surgical excision of the rectum is proctectomy. Surgical incision of the uterus is known as hysterotomy; surgical excision of the uterus is hysterectomy. Surgical excision of a testis is orchidectomy or testectomy.

10. **(E)** Mitosis is a type of cell division. All other answers describe a type of movement of substances across the cell.

11. **(B)** Tetracyclines are a group of broad-spectrum bacteriostatic antibiotics that are effective against both gram-negative and gram-positive microorganisms. Tetracyclines inhibit protein synthesis in bacterial cells. Examples: *Aureomycin®*, *Vibramycin®*, and *Achromycin®*. Tetracyclines are commonly used in the treatment of urethritis, cholera, lower respiratory tract infections, meningitis, rickettsiae, and Lyme disease.

12. **(E)** Hypopnea is abnormally slow respiration. Apnea is an absence of spontaneous respiration. Hypoxia is an inadequate supply of oxygen at the cellular level. Auscultation is the act of listening for sounds within the body. Dyspnea is difficult or labored breathing.

13. **(B)** Gangrene is necrosis, or death of tissue, usually as the result of ischemia, bacterial invasion, and subsequent putrefaction. Infarction is a localized area of necrosis in a tissue, caused by an interruption in the blood supply. Ischemia is a decreased supply of oxygenated blood to a body or part. Atresia is the absence of a normal body opening, duct, or canal. Inflammation is the nonspecific defense mechanism, characterized by heat, redness, swelling, and pain.

14. **(E)** Privileged communication is communication of information that is confidential within a protected relationship, such as between a patient and his or her physician and between a client and his or her lawyer.

15. **(C)** Basophils release histamine and thus are active in allergic reactions.

16. **(A)** The prefix *retro-* means "behind," *peri-* means "around," *sub-* means "below," *pre-* means "before," and *post-* means "after."

17. **(D)** According to the American Cancer Society, prostate cancer is the most common site for cancer incidence in males in the United States each year. It is the third leading cause of cancer deaths.

18. **(D)** Prophylaxis is prevention of or protection against disease. Prognosis is a prediction of the probable outcome of a disease. Remission is the partial or complete disappearance of the clinical and subjective characteristics of a chronic or malignant disease. Pronation is the lowering of the medial edge of the foot by turning it outward and, through abduction, movement in the tarsal and metatarsal joints. Therapy refers to treatment of a disease or condition.

19. **(C)** Staphylococci are arranged in clusters. Streptococci are in chains. Diplococci are in pairs. Protozoa, which are single-celled microorganisms, are the lowest form of animal life. Spirilla are spiral-shaped bacteria.

20. **(A)** Intentional torts include civil wrongs committed against a person or property, excluding breach of contract. Intentional torts include assault, battery, defamation of character, and invasion of privacy. Negligence is an unintentional tort.

21. **(D)** *Ren / o* means "kidney," *rect / o* means "rectum," *lapar / o* means "abdomen," *pector / o* means "chest," and both *cyst / o* and *vesic / o* mean "urinary bladder."

22. **(D)** Glycogen is a polysaccharide that is the major carbohydrate stored in animal cells. It is formed from repeating units of glucose and is stored chiefly in the liver.

23. **(C)** Low-density lipoprotein is known as "bad" cholesterol, and in high concentration it may cause atherosclerosis and heart disease. High-density lipoprotein helps transport cholesterol to the liver and is called "good" cholesterol. Cholesterolemia is the presence of excessive amounts of cholesterol in the blood. Atherosclerosis is the most common form of arteriosclerosis, marked by cholesterol, lipid, and calcium deposits in arterial linings. Ketone is a substance that results from the breakdown of fat.

24. **(B)** Saturated fats are usually solid at room temperature and are derived from animal sources. Saturated fats are found in milk, meat, and butter. They tend to raise blood cholesterol levels.

25. **(C)** The abbreviation *STD* stands for "sexually transmitted disease." Although AIDS is a sexually transmitted disease, the abbreviation stands for "acquired immunodeficiency syndrome."

26. **(E)** Cystalgia is pain in the urinary bladder. *Cyst / o* is a combining form that means "bladder," and the suffix *-algia* means "pain."

27. **(C)** *AS (auris sinistra)* is the abbreviation meaning "left ear." *AD (auris dextra)* is the abbreviation meaning "right ear." *OS (oculus sinister)* is the abbreviation meaning "left eye." *OU (oculus uterque)* is the abbreviation meaning "each eye" or "both eyes." LE is not an abbreviation.

28. **(C)** *Dactyl / o* means "finger" or "toe." Polydactyly is the presence of extra fingers or toes. Polydipsia is excessive thirst. Polyphagia is excessive, uncontrolled eating. Polysomy is the presence of a chromosome in at least triplicate form in an otherwise diploid somatic cell. Polychoria is the condition of having more than one pupil in one eye.

29. **(D)** The scapula is one of the pairs of large, flat, triangular bones that form the dorsal part of the pectoral girdle. It is also known as the shoulder blade. The pectoral girdle includes the clavicles (collarbones) and scapulae. The olecranon process is the bony point of the elbow. The sternum forms the anterior portion of the thoracic cavity. The styloid process is a projection on the temporal bone.

30. **(E)** In a bench trial, a judge serves without a jury and rules on the law as well as on the facts.

31. **(A)** The specific immune response is required if the nonspecific immune response cannot cope with invasion or injury. It is directed and controlled by T and B cells. These cells can remember pathogens and respond more quickly in subsequent invasions.

32. **(A)** Angioplasty is the reconstitution of a blood vessel. Venectomy (or phlebectomy) is the excision of a vein. Arterectomy or arteriectomy is the excision of an artery. Angiorrhaphy is the repair by suture of any blood vessel. Cardiotomy is surgical incision of the heart.

33. **(C)** Vitamin B_9 (folic acid) deficiency may result in anemia and spina bifida during fetal development. Scurvy is caused by vitamin C deficiency.

34. **(E)** *Opt / o* refers to vision, and *phot / o* refers to light. *Ocul / o* and *ophthalm / o* both mean "eye."

35. **(B)** Antihypertensive drugs treat high blood pressure or hypertension. Vasodilators, calcium antagonists (e.g. diltiazem and varapamil), sympathetic blocking drugs (e.g., clonidine), and thiazides are a few types of antihypertensive drugs.

36. **(A)** *Res ipsa loquitur* is a Latin phrase that means "the matter speaks for itself." It is also known as the doctrine of common law. This doctrine is usually applied when the physician clearly could have prevented a negligent act, such as leaving foreign bodies (e.g., instruments) inside a patient's body during surgery, damaging healthy tissue during an operation, burning or otherwise unnecessarily injuring the patient while the patient is under anesthesia, or causing an infection by the use of unsterilized instruments.

37. **(C)** Proteins such as albumin help maintain water balance that affects osmotic pressure, which prevents the accumulation of fluids in body tissues, which would cause edema.

38. **(A)** Beriberi is a disease of the peripheral nerves caused by a deficiency of thiamine.

39. **(D)** Biotin is also called vitamin H. It is one of the water-soluble B-complex vitamins that acts as a coenzyme in fatty acid production and in the oxidation of fatty acids and carbohydrates.

40. **(E)** Scurvy is caused by severe ascorbic acid (Vitamin C) deficiency. Vitamin B_1 deficiency causes beriberi. Vitamin B_{12} deficiency may result in pernicious anemia. Vitamin K deficiency may cause hemorrhages. Vitamin B_6 deficiency causes anemia and may cause spina bifida in a fetus.

41. **(C)** Sensory neurons transmit impulses from the sense organs to the reflex center (spinal cord) or the brain. Motor neurons carry impulses to muscle tissue to stimulate contraction. They also carry impulses to glandular tissue to stimulate secretion. They are also called efferent neurons or motoneurons.

42. **(A)** *After meals* is abbreviated as *pc*, from the Latin phrase *post cibum*. The abbreviation *pm (post meridiem)* means "after noon," *po (per os)* means "by mouth," and *prn (pro re nata)* means "as needed." PS is not an abbreviation.

43. **(A)** Professional negligence is the proximate cause of injury or harm to a patient, resulting from a lack of professional knowledge, experience, or skill. It is also known as malpractice.

44. **(C)** Treatment for Lyme disease includes tetracycline or amoxicillin/probenecid for early symptoms. The drug of choice for candidiasis is fluconazole, and for trichomoniasis it is metronidazole. Urinary and respiratory infections are treated with cephalosporin.

45. **(E)** Wernicke's area is responsible for language comprehension. Broca's area is responsible for motor speech and for controlling the mouth, tongue, and larynx. The occipital lobe is responsible for visual recognition. The parietal lobe is responsible for the interpretation of sensory input, such as taste. The insular lobe is responsible for visceral or primitive emotions, drives, and reactions.

46. **(A)** Leukemia is the most common cancer in childhood. It is a cancer of the blood-forming cells in the bone marrow.

47. **(B)** Meningitis is inflammation of the meninges, the membranes covering the brain and spinal cord. Diphtheria affects the mucous membranes of the respiratory tract. Parotitis is mumps, the inflammation of one or both parotid glands. Infectious mononucleosis is an acute infectious disease that changes leukocytes. Myocarditis is an inflammation of the myocardium commonly caused by viruses, bacteria, fungi, or protozoa.

48. **(B)** Zolpidem is a sedative-hypnotic nonbarbiturate used to treat insomnia. Its side effects include nausea, vomiting, diarrhea, and dizziness.

49. **(D)** *Hypo-* means "below" or "under." Hypoglycemia is low blood sugar.

50. **(C)** Buerger's disease is an occlusive vascular condition, usually of a leg or a foot. Men are affected more often than women. Most of the affected men smoke and are between 20 and 40 years of age.

51. **(C)** Pharmacology is the study of the origin, nature, chemistry, effects, and uses of drugs. Pharmacy is the art of compounding, preparing, dispensing, and properly utilizing drugs. Pharmacognosy is the branch of pharmacology dealing with natural drugs. Posology is the study of the amount of a drug that is required to produce therapeutic effects. Pharmacodynamics is the study of the mechanisms of actions of drugs on living organisms.

52. **(A)** A placebo has no pharmacologic activity. A teratogen is any agent that interferes with normal prenatal development, causing the formation of one or more developmental abnormalities in the fetus. Synergism is the joint action of agents in which their combined effect is greater than the sum of their individual effects.

53. **(B)** *Lomotil®* is a trademark for an antidiarrheal drug, classified as a Schedule V drug with low abuse potential and accepted medical use. Diazepam is an example of a Schedule IV drug, amphetamine is listed in Schedule II, and heroin is classified as a Schedule I drug. *Talwin®* is a schedule IV drug.

54. **(C)** Vitamins A, D, E, and K are fat-soluble vitamins. Vitamin of the B complex and vitamin C are water-soluble vitamins.

55. **(D)** When giving out confidential information, you should always get the patient's written consent. Other legally required disclosures include those ordered by subpoena, those dictated by statute to protect public welfare, and those considered necessary to protect the welfare of the patient or a third party.

56. **(B)** Consent to allow touching, examination, or treatment by medically authorized personnel in unnecessary in an emergency situation.

57. **(D)** The suffix *-penia* means "abnormal reduction" (leukopenia), *-osis* means "increase" (leukocytosis), *-megaly* means "enlargement" (cardiomegaly), and *-plasia* means "formation" (dysplasia). The suffix *-algia* means "pain" (neuralgia).

58. **(B)** Contracts have three parts: offer, acceptance, and consideration. The offer sets the stage, and it must be communicated effectively and in good faith. Acceptance involves agreeing to take the offer. The consideration is something of value bargained for as part of the contract.

59. **(E)** Factors that affect individual variation in a drug's effect include age, weight, sex, percentage of body fat, time of day, tolerance, genetic variation, emotional state, placebo effect, presence of a disease, and patient compliance.

60. **(A)** The umbilical vein in fetal circulation transports oxygen from the placenta to the fetus. The umbilical artery transports blood from the fetus to the placenta to get oxygen and to get rid of carbon dioxide.

61. **(B)** The thymus is the primary, central gland of the lymphatic system and is the site of maturation for T cells. The T cells of the cell-mediated specific immune response develop in this gland before migrating to the lymph nodes and spleen.

62. **(C)** Commensalism is a one-sided relationship in which one member benefits and the other is unaffected. Mutualism is a relationship in which both organisms benefit. Symbiosis is the living together of two species. Opportunism is a relationship in which an organism that was previously harmless becomes pathogenic when the host's defenses are weakened. In parasitism, one organism lives at the expense of another organism.

63. **(C)** Costectomy is the surgical removal of a rib.

64. **(D)** The 5 Cs of communication are complete, clear, concise, courteous, and cohesive.

65. **(B)** By restating or repeating what you believe is the main thought or idea expressed in a conversation, you can make sure that you understand what is being communicated. Allowing patients to reflect will not tell them that you understood what they said; it will, however, allow them to think through and answer their own questions. Being assertive involves standing up for yourself while showing respect to others; it has little to do with whether you understood the patient or not. A rapport can develop between you and a patient through good communication skills, but rapport itself won't mean that you specifically understood what the patient has communicated to you. Crossing your arms over your chest or shaking your head is displaying negative body language, which conveys anger, disagreement, or lack of caring.

66. **(A)** *Bacteriostatic* means inhibiting bacterial growth. Bactericidal substances destroy or kill bacteria. *Aseptic* means free of infective material. *Sterile* means free of living microorganisms.

67. **(A)** Invasion of privacy is the intrusion into a person's seclusion or into his or her private affairs. The unauthorized disclosure of medical records or financial or personal information of the patient is considered an invasion of privacy. For example, if you told a patient's employer without the patient's written consent that the patient has AIDS, you would be violating the patient's right to privacy.

68. **(D)** Rabies is also called hydrophobia (fear of water).

69. **(D)** John was exhibiting gender bias. Gender bias is any type of action or language that unjustly favors one gender over another. Discrimination involves acting unfairly based upon bias or prejudice against a certain group or class. For example, if Susan does not get a promotion because John tends to view women unfavorably, then John could be sued for discriminating against her.

70. **(B)** *Lith / o* is a combining form that means "stone," and the suffix *-iasis* means "condition or formation of."

71. **(E)** The patient has the right to all of the choices listed in this question. For all patient rights, review Table 7-3 in Chapter 7, *Medical Law and Ethics*.

72. **(D)** Treatment is abbreviated as *Tx* or *Tr. Rx* is commonly used to mean "prescription"; it is an abbreviation of the Latin verb "recipe," which means "take."

73. **(A)** Remission is the partial or complete disappearance of the clinical and subjective characteristics of a chronic or malignant disease. Prognosis is a prediction of the probable outcome of a disease. Prophylaxis is prevention or protection against disease. Malaise is a vague, uneasy feeling of body weakness, distress, or discomfort, often marking the onset of and persisting throughout a disease. Atresia is the absence or closure of a normal body opening, duct, or canal such as the external ear canal or anus.

74. **(E)** Night blindness is caused by a deficiency in vitamin A. Vitamin B_1 deficiency may lead to Wernicke-Korsakoff syndrome. Hemorrhage can be a symptom of vitamin K deficiency. Pernicious anemia may be caused by vitamin B_{12} deficiency.

75. **(B)** Hidrosis is the production and secretion of sweat. Hydrops is an abnormal accumulation of clear, watery fluid in a body tissue or cavity. Hydrolase is an enzyme. Hydropenia is a lack of water in the body tissues. Hydrolysis is a chemical process of decomposition that involves splitting a bond and adding a hydrogen ion.

76. **(D)** Quinidine (*Cardioquin®*, *Quinidex®*) is an antiarrhythmic drug that depresses the myocardium and the conduction system, thereby slowing the heart rate. It is used to treat supraventricular arrhythmias and supraventricular tachycardia. Phenytoin (*Dilantin®*) is an antiarrhythmic drug that is also used to treat epilepsy.

77. **(C)** Projection is a defense mechanism that involves the attribution of one's own difficulties to external causes. Rationalization is the justification of problems or unacceptable behavior by giving acceptable reasons rather than real ones (i.e., by making up plausible excuses). Repression involves pushing unpleasant thoughts or problems into the unconscious to avoid dealing with them. You should be aware of these defense mechanisms and avoid using them, because they do not lead to effective communication.

78. **(A)** Clemastine (*Tavist®*) counteracts the effects of histamines. Adeparin is an anticoagulant. Penicillin is an antibiotic. Pentobarbital is a sedative. Lithium is an antimanic drug.

79. **(E)** When you talk to patients who have a visual impairment, you should use larger print materials, make sure that there is adequate lightning in the room, and as always talk directly and honestly.

80. **(E)** Geriatrics is the treatment of elder individuals, not necessarily the treatment of individuals with terminal illnesses. Palliative care is care given to make someone, such as a dying person, more comfortable. Patients should never be abandoned. They should have emotional support, pain control, respect for their autonomy, and effective communication.

81. **(A)** A motor neuron is one of various efferent nerve cells that transmit nerve impulses from the brain or from the spinal cord to muscular or glandular tissue.

82. **(D)** The DEA requires physicians to renew their registration every 3 years; to keep records for 2 years about who was given what drug, what dosage, on what date, and for what reason; to keep inventory; and to log the disposal of drugs with a witness present.

83. **(D)** When dealing with children, you should work directly with the children rather than communicating through the parents, take their feelings seriously, explain all the procedures in simple terms, let them examine the instruments, use praise, be truthful, and do not talk down to them.

84. **(B)** Sanitization reduces the number of microorganisms, and antisepsis inhibits the growth and multiplication of microorganisms.

85. **(B)** *Encephal / o* refers to the brain, as in the word *encephalitis*, meaning "inflammation of the brain." *Cerebr / o* refers to the cerebrum, not to the brain as a whole. *Myel / o* means "spinal cord." *Poli / o* means "gray matter." *Blephar / o* means "eyelid."

86. **(C)** Psychomotor stimulants include amphetamines. They are used to treat the first few weeks of depression, narcolepsy, and hyperkinesis. They increase the activity of norepinephrine and dopamine in the brain.

87. **(E)** As part of a medical team, medical assistants should be ready to compromise and admit if they are wrong, treat others with respect, listen to everyone equally, avoid putting others on the defensive, refrain from reinforcing or adopting negative attitudes, work to solve problems, learn from others, and remember the common goal of providing excellent health care to patients.

88. **(A)** The girl's legal guardian, her mother, must give written consent before the girl's medical records are released.

89. **(C)** The inscription lists the names and quantities of the ingredients. The superscription includes the patient's name, address, date, and the symbol *Rx*. The subscription gives directions to the pharmacist. The signature gives instructions to patients. The drug label is not part of the prescription.

90. **(E)** Magmas are made up of heavy particles mixed with water to form a milky liquid. Magmas must be shaken before administration.

91. **(A)** Privilege is the authority granted to a physician by a hospital to provide patient care in the hospital.

92. **(D)** Brand and generic names are located in the pink section. Classification or category names are in the blue section. There are no green or yellow sections. The white section features an alphabetic index by manufacturer.

93. **(B)** Schedule II drugs have high abuse potential but have some accepted medical use. Cocaine is such a drug. Prescriptions for Schedule II drugs cannot be refilled without a new prescription from the physician.

94. **(E)** Calls that require the attention of the physician include emergency calls, calls from other doctors and physicians, calls from patients who want to discuss test results (particularly abnormal results), calls from patients who want to discuss symptoms with the physician, reports from patients concerning unsatisfactory progress, requests for prescription renewals when they have not been previously authorized by the physician, and personal calls. In general, all emergencies should be routed to the physician immediately. Calls from other physicians should also be routed to the doctor immediately if possible.

95. **(B)** Anosmia is the loss or impairment of the sense of smell. Aphonia is a condition characterized by loss of the ability to produce normal speech sounds. Amnesia is a loss of memory caused by brain damage or by severe emotional trauma. Anorexia is a lack or loss of appetite. Something lacking new development or pertaining to the failure of a tissue to produce normal cell division is referred to as aplastic.

96. **(A)** Legionnaires' disease is an acute pneumonia caused by a bacterial infection.

97. **(A)** Vitamin A deficiency causes retarded growth, susceptibility to infection, dry skin, night blindness, xerophthalmia, abnormal gastrointestinal function, dry mucous membranes, and degeneration of the spinal cord and peripheral nerves.

98. **(C)** An inquiry about a bill is an administrative call that can be handled by the medical assistant who answers the phone. Other calls that the medical assistant can handle include appointment scheduling, rescheduling, and canceling; insurance questions; X-ray and laboratory reports; routine reports from hospitals regarding a patient's progress; satisfactory progress reports from patients; requests for referrals to other doctors; questions concerning office policies, fees, and hours; complaints about administrative matters; and prescription refills when they have been previously authorized by the physician.

99. **(B)** *Homestasis* should be spelled *homeostasis*.

100. **(E)** As a medical assistant, you might be required to give patients instructions prior to surgery, a test, or a procedure. It may be easier for patients to visualize the conditions or procedures if you use an anatomical model or a video tape. Other instructional materials include brochures, booklets, fact sheets, educational newsletters, and community directories. Another one of your goals as a medical assistant should be to promote good health behaviors and to teach patients how to prevent common injuries. Encourage patients to eat well, exercise regularly, get adequate rest, limit alcohol consumption, stop smoking, and balance work and leisure to avoid stress.

101. **(D)** The retina is the innermost layer of the eye, composed of delicate nervous tissue that receives images of external objects and transmits visual impulses through the optic nerve to the brain.

102. **(D)** Schedule IV drugs have low abuse potential and an accepted medical use. They may be refilled 5 times in 6 months when authorized by a physician. Examples of Schedule IV drugs include chloral hydrate, diazepam, and alprazolam.

103. **(A)** Vectors are carriers of pathogenic organisms. For example, mosquitoes can be vectors for malaria and encephalitis.

104. **(C)** Progesterone is a natural progestational hormone. It prepares the uterus for pregnancy.

105. **(A)** When a word ends in *-us*, you can usually (not always) form the plural by dropping the *-us* and adding *-i*.

106. **(C)** A corporation is a body formed by a group of people who are authorized by law to act as a single person.

107. **(C)** Confidentiality should not be waived in a malpractice suit, nor by an insurance carrier, nor by the patient's spouse. Confidentiality should be waived only when the patient or his or her legal guardian gives written consent, the medical records are subpoenaed, or there is a statute requiring a waiver to protect the public.

108. **(B)** Routine reports from hospitals regarding a patient's progress can be handled by the medical assistant. Only calls regarding a patient's unsatisfactory progress need to be handled by a physician.

109. **(D)** Ankylosis is the fixation of a joint, often in an abnormal position, resulting from the destruction of articular cartilage and subchondral bone. It is common in rheumatoid arthritis.

110. **(B)** Elisabeth Kübler-Ross defines five stages or responses of dying patients: denial and isolation, anger, bargaining and guilt, depression, and acceptance.

111. **(B)** Physicians are considered the owners of the medical records they have written.

112. **(A)** Bronchiectasis is an abnormal condition of the bronchial tree characterized by irreversible dilation and destruction of the bronchial walls.

113. **(C)** Diabetes insipidus is a metabolic disorder caused by injury of the neurohypophyseal system. It is caused by deficient production or secretion of the antidiuretic hormone (ADH) or the inability of the kidney tubules to respond to ADH.

114. **(E)** SOAP provides a series of steps for dealing with a medical case: the patient's symptoms (subjective data), the diagnosis (objective data), assessment, and plan of action.

115. **(A)** Nystagmus is the involuntary, rhythmic movement of the eyes, in which the oscillations may be horizontal, vertical, rotary, or mixed.

116. **(C)** *Puritus* should be spelled *pruritus*, which means "severe itching."

117. **(C)** The suffix *-stomy* means "the (surgical) creation of a new opening," *-tomy* means "cutting" or "incision," and *-scopy* means "the process of viewing (something) with a scope." The suffix *-iasis* refers to a condition or the formation of something, such as the formation of stones, lithiasis.

118. **(E)** A contract may be prematurely terminated as a result of failing to pay for services, missing appointments, failing to follow the physician's instructions, or obtaining the services of another physician.

119. **(A)** The abbreviation *q2h* is short for *quaque secunda hora*, meaning "every second hour." The abbreviation *qid* (for *quater in die*) means "four times a day." The abbreviation *qod* stands for "every other day."

120. **(D)** The hypothalamus assists in controlling body temperature, water balance, sleep, appetite, emotions of fear and pleasure, and involuntary functions.

121. **(C)** The adrenal cortex secretes aldosterone, cortisol, and androgens. Cortisol increases blood glucose levels and contributes to stress adaptation.

122. **(A)** The Controlled Substance Act of 1970 controls the distribution and use of all drugs of abuse potential as designated by the Drug Enforcement Administration (DEA). It divides narcotics, stimulants, and some sedatives into five classes, called schedules.

123. **(C)** Viruses are infectious agents that are even simpler in nature than prokaryotes. They are composed of a small amount of DNA or RNA wrapped in a protein covering, and they are usually not considered cellular. Only an electron microscope is powerful enough to magnify them sufficiently to be seen.

124. **(B)** *Cutane / o* means "skin," *hidr / o* means "sweat," *onych / o* means "nail," *hist / o* means "tissue," and *albin / o* means "white."

125. **(D)** Type O Rh− blood is the universal donor because it has neither A nor B antigens and has both A and B antibodies.

126. **(E)** The suffixes *-algia* and *-algy* mean "pain" or "painful condition."

127. **(D)** Type AB Rh+ blood is the universal recipient because it has both A and B antigens on red blood cells but neither A nor B antibodies in plasma.

128. **(A)** A hydatidiform mole is an intrauterine tumor mass of grapelike enlarged cysts.

129. **(C)** Metrorrhagia is uterine bleeding other than that caused by menstruation. It may be caused by uterine lesions and may be a sign of a urogenital malignancy, especially cervical cancer. Menorrhagia is abnormally heavy or long menstrual periods. Amenorrhea is the absence of menstruation.

130. **(E)** When a word ends in *-um*, you can usually form the plural by dropping the *-um* and adding *-a*.

131. **(A)** *Dermat / o* means "skin," and the suffix *-itis* means "inflammation." The term dermatitis refers to the inflammation of skin.

132. **(C)** Often, laws dictate what medical assistants may or may not do. For example, in some states it is illegal for medical assistants to draw blood. It is illegal in all states for a medical assistant to diagnose a condition, prescribe treatment, and engage in deception about certification, title, and level of education.

133. **(D)** Antiemetics control nausea, vomiting, and motion sickness. Antihidrotics prevent or decrease perspiration. Anticonvulsants prevent or relieve convulsions. Vasodilators relax and dilate blood vessels. Sedatives have a soothing, relaxing effect.

134. **(E)** In cases involving negligence, the doctrine of *res ipsa loquitur* applies, and the physician has the burden of proving innocence and nonnegligence. This doctrine implies that injury would not have occurred unless someone had been clearly negligent.

135. **(A)** An obligate anaerobe lives only in the absence of oxygen. The majority of microbes are aerobes, meaning that they live and grow in the presence of oxygen.

136. **(C)** In order for you to properly transfer a call, the person calling needs to identify himself or herself and to give you a brief description of the nature of the call. If the person refuses to be identified, you should not put the call through to the physician; instead, ask the person to write a letter to the physician and to mark it *Personal*. Even if the patient is angry, you should remain calm and professional and offer to help solve the caller's problem. Genuinely listen to complaints, and help the patient express his or her anger in a constructive manner.

137. **(D)** Drugs with low abuse potential that have an accepted medical use are classified as Schedule IV drugs.

138. **(B)** Antianxiety drugs depress the central nervous system, analgesics relieve pain, antipruritics relieve itching, and antitussives relieve coughing.

139. **(B)** The semicircular canal is one of three curved passages in the inner ear that detect motion and govern balance. The tympanic membrane transmits sound vibrations. The cochlea is the receptor for hearing. Cerumen is ear wax. The auditory ossicles are three tiny bones in the middle ear: the malleus (hammer), the incus (anvil), and the stapes (stirrup). These bones transmit and amplify vibrations.

140. **(B)** The prefix *inter-* means "between," and *cost / o* means "rib."

141. **(E)** The AAMA publishes a code of ethics for all of its certified medical assistants. According to the AAMA, all its members should be dedicated to the conscientious pursuit of their profession in order to deserve the high regard of the entire medical profession. The AMT holds its certified medical assistants to similarly high standards. Whether you are seeking RMA or CMA certification, you should familiarize yourself with the AAMA Code of Ethics.

142. **(B)** Koplik's spots are small red spots with bluish-white centers on the buccal mucosa, characteristic of measles.

143. **(A)** Valproic acid (*Depakenel*®) is used to treat petit mal epilepsy. Its side effects include nausea, vomiting, tremors, and liver toxicity in young patients.

144. **(C)** *Thromb / o* means "clot," and the suffix *-lysis* means "destruction." Thrombolysis is the destruction or dissolving of a clot.

145. **(B)** The atria are the upper chambers of the heart. The right atrium receives deoxygenated blood through the superior and inferior venae cavae, and the left atrium receives oxygenated blood from the lungs through the pulmonary veins. Blood then passes through the atria to the ventricles. As the ventricles contract, they pump blood through the arteries. The right ventricle pumps blood into the pulmonary artery to the lungs, and the left ventricle pumps blood into the aorta to the rest of the body.

146. **(C)** Dysphonia is any abnormality in the speaking voice. In cancer of the larynx, dysphonia is usually the only symptom.

147. **(D)** In a living will, the individual expresses his or her wishes regarding medical treatment. It may detail circumstances under which treatment should be discontinued, which treatments to suspend, and which to maintain. A living will is legal if the patient is competent to create such a will and two witnesses sign it and attest to its accuracy.

148. **(E)** Minimizing background noise, positioning yourself close to and facing the patient, using body language to supplement your voice, speaking slowly, and using written materials all help you communicate more effectively with an individual who has a hearing impairment.

149. **(A)** Retinol is another name for vitamin A. Carotene is a precursor that is converted to vitamin A in the liver.

150. **(B)** The Good Samaritan Act provides immunity from liability to a volunteer at the scene of an accident for any civil damages in rendering emergency care, so long as the volunteer acts within his or her scope of education and training.

151. **(C)** Intrinsic factor is a substance secreted by the gastric mucosa that is essential for the intestinal absorption of Vitamin B_{12} (cyanocobalamin).

152. **(B)** Open-ended questions usually ask "how" and "why." They allow the patient to describe in detail the symptoms and any related thoughts and feelings he or she may have. Such questions are usually used in a patient interview to obtain more complete information by allowing patients to elaborate on responses they may have previously given to simple yes/no or is/do questions.

153. **(D)** Acromegaly is a chronic metabolic condition characterized by a gradual, marked enlargement and elongation of the bones of the face, jaw, and extremities. This condition mostly affects middle-aged and older persons and is caused by the overproduction of growth hormone.

154. **(C)** Hyperopia is farsightedness, or an inability of the eye to focus on nearby objects. It results from an error of refraction, brought on by the abnormal shortness of the eyeball, which causes rays of light entering the eye to be brought into focus behind the retina.

155. **(B)** Glaucoma is an abnormal condition of elevated pressure within an eye caused by obstruction in the outflow of aqueous humor. The most serious complication of glaucoma is blindness.

156. **(D)** Cervical cancer is a neoplasm of the uterine cervix that can be detected in the early, curable stage by the Papanicolaou test (Pap test or Pap smear).

157. **(D)** The gluteus maximus is a large muscle, originating in the iliac and the sacrum, that acts to extend the thigh. The gluteus medius abducts and rotates the thigh. The quadriceps femoris extends the leg. The hamstrings flex the leg. The brachialis flexes the forearm.

158. **(E)** The deltoid muscle is a large, thick, triangular muscle that covers the shoulder joint. It is the prime mover of the arm for abduction.

159. **(B)** The four *D*s of negligence are *duty, dereliction, direct cause,* and *damage.*

160. **(E)** Iodine deficiency may cause goiter or cretinism. Goiter is more common among women.

161. **(B)** A ribosome is a cytoplasmic organelle composed of ribonucleic acid (RNA) and protein that functions in the synthesis of protein.

162. **(B)** *Intravenous* means "pertaining to the inside of a vein," as of a thrombus or an injection, infusion, or catheter.

163. **(C)** Only major surgery, an invasive procedure, the prescription of experimental drugs, admittance to a hospital, and procedures with high risk would require written expressed consent. Routine procedures such as Pap smears, minor surgical procedures such as removing splinters or broken glass, and emergency situations even when they involve a minor do not require written consent.

164. **(C)** A statute of limitations prescribes a fixed amount of time in which a lawsuit can be filed for an alleged wrongdoing.

165. **(B)** A homograft is also called an allograft. It is the nonpermanent transplant of tissue between individuals of the same species (e.g., from one person to another).

166. **(E)** The axis is the second cervical vertebra, about which the atlas rotates, allowing the head to be turned, extended, and flexed.

167. **(E)** *Pulmon / o* means "lung." The word *pulmonary* means "relating to the lungs."

168. **(D)** The autonomic nervous system controls unconscious activities such as reflexes. It regulates the action of glands, the heart muscle, and the smooth muscles of hollow organs and vessels.

169. **(C)** A bactericidal substance destroys or kills bacteria. A bacteriostatic substance inhibits the growth of bacteria.

170. **(C)** The midbrain, located in the brainstem, controls visual and auditory reflexes such as turning to listen to a loud noise. The medulla oblongata, also located in the brainstem, contains the cardiac center (which controls heart rate), vasomotor center (which controls blood pressure), and respiratory center (which controls the rate, rhythm, and depth of breathing).

171. **(B)** *Ectopic* means "away from the normal location" (i.e., situated in an unusual place). For example, in an ectopic pregnancy, the fertilized egg is implanted somewhere other than in the uterus.

172. **(D)** *Dorsal* means "pertaining to the back" or "posterior."

173. **(B)** Giardiasis is a protozoan infection of the small intestine caused by *Giardia lamblia*, usually acquired from contaminated and untreated water.

174. **(D)** Myelocele is a saclike protrusion of the spinal cord through a congenital defect in the vertebral column.

175. **(A)** Prednisone is prescribed in the treatment of severe inflammation and immunosuppression.

176. **(D)** In order to guard the privacy of patients, you should not leave medical charts, insurance reports, or patient sign-in sheets where patients or office visitors can see them. Imagine a friend or an employer of your patient walking in and finding out that the patient has had multiple appointments for cancer treatment or multiple appointments with an OB/GYN.

177. **(D)** Touching someone on the shoulder, back, or hand can show sensitivity and empathy, but not everyone will be accepting. Be aware of cultural and personal differences, and adjust your style to the preferences of others.

178. **(E)** The suffix *-rrhea* means "flow" or "discharge."

179. **(A)** Child abuse commonly affects children less than 3 years of age, but it can happen at any age. You should not expect children to come to you for help, because they may be unaware that what is happening to them is wrong and that it can and should be stopped, they may not realize that you would be able to help, and they may also be frightened of their abusers. The Child Abuse Prevention and Treatment Act of 1974 mandates the reporting of cases of child abuse. Child abuse should be reported by teachers, physicians, and other licensed health care practitioners. A report should immediately be made to the proper authorities, and a written report is usually required within a specific time frame, such as 72 hours. Depending on state law, failure to report suspected cases of child abuse may be considered a misdemeanor. Those who report child abuse are granted absolute immunity from criminal and civil liability resulting from the reported incident. So even if you turn out to be wrong about Joe's symptoms, the parents will not be able to sue the practice because you had just cause in reporting a suspected case.

180. **(E)** Basal metabolism is the amount of energy needed for the body when it is at digestive, physical, and emotional rest.

181. **(D)** Rifampin is an antibacterial drug prescribed in the treatment of tuberculosis, in meningococcal prophylaxis, and as an antileprotic. Among the more serious adverse reactions to rifampin is liver toxicity. Discoloration of urine, saliva, and sweat and softening of contact lenses commonly occur.

182. **(B)** German measles is also known as rubella. It is a contagious viral disease.

183. **(C)** When a word such as *septum* ends in *-um*, you can usually form the plural by dropping the *-um* and adding *-a*. A septum is a wall dividing two cavities.

184. **(D)** Adipose tissue is a collection of fat cells or loose connective tissue with many cells that contain fat vacuoles. It provides insulation for the human body.

185. **(C)** Exocytosis is the formation of vesicles to transfer substances from inside the cell to the outside of the cell.

186. **(E)** To handle incoming calls, follow these guidelines: answer the telephone by the second or third ring, hold the mouthpiece about an inch away from your mouth and leave one hand free to write with, greet the caller with the name of the office and then with your name, identify the caller, be courteous, pay attention to the caller, use appropriate terminology and enunciate and pronounce correctly, avoid unnecessarily long conversations, and keep personal calls to a minimum.

187. **(B)** Type A blood has type A antigens and type B antibodies. The type A antigens sit on red blood cells, and the antibodies are found in the serum. Type A blood has type B antibodies, type B blood has type A antibodies, type AB has no antibodies, and type O has both types of antibodies. A handy rule to remember is that each blood group has the same type antigen as its name and the opposite antibody.

188. **(C)** There are four basic stages a drug must pass through: absorption, distribution, metabolism, and excretion. Absorption is the process by which a drug is brought into circulation. Distribution is the process by which the circulatory system transports drugs to the affected areas. Metabolism is the process by which drugs are broken down into useful byproducts by enzymes in the liver. The liver is the main body part involved in metabolism. The kidney is responsible for filtering out the drugs from the blood. Drugs are also excreted by the lungs, the sweat glands, and the intestines.

189. **(B)** Fraud is the act of intentionally misleading or deceiving another person by any means so as to cause him or her legal injury. Fraud usually leads to the loss of something valuable or the surrender of a legal right.

190. **(D)** Assault is the threat of bodily harm to another. Battery is an action that causes bodily harm to another. Battery is often broadly defined as the illegal touching of another person. In health care, battery may be charged for unauthorized touching of a patient, including such actions as suturing a wound, administering an injection, performing surgery, or performing a physical examination without consent.

191. **(B)** If you get interrupted by a second call, excuse yourself to the first caller and answer the second call. Determine the identity of the second caller and the nature of the call. Return to the first call as soon as possible and minimize waiting for all callers. In fact, if you have callers on hold, return to them occasionally to reassure them that you have not forgotten about them and to update them on what's going on. For example, if someone is waiting to talk to the physician but the physician is still busy, offer the caller an opportunity to leave a message or have the physician return the call as soon as possible.

192. **(A)** Cilia are membrane-enclosed bundles of microtubules that extend outward from cell membranes. They are short and numerous. Cilia move substances across the surface of the cell.

193. **(A)** Greet callers with the name of the office and then with your name. Do not answer the phone by simply giving the telephone number of your office or by saying "hello."

194. **(B)** The physician must advise patients against needless surgery, and the physician must advise patients of any risks associated with major surgery or a difficult procedure, but the physician is not bound to fully cure a patient or to restore a patient to a previous condition. The physician should not be negligent, but no physician is infallible. The physician is obligated only to treat the patient to the scope of the physician's training and education and to provide reasonable care according to his or her capabilities. For example, an ophthalmologist, trained in the disorders of the eye, might not recognize a disorder of the ear.

195. **(E)** Sexual harassment is persistent, unwanted sexual advances, attention, or communication, and it is prohibited in the workplace. Sexual harassment can be physical or verbal, expressed in gestures, in images, or in written and spoken words. It can occur at any level of the hierarchy within a workplace. It can result in personal distress for the recipient and legal trouble for the medical facility. When faced with sexual harassment, you may find that the easiest way to stop this behavior is to tell the harasser that the behavior has made you uncomfortable and that you wish it to stop. If this approach does not work, you should go to your supervisor or even seek help outside of your employment, either in support groups or with legal counsel.

196. **(C)** In a greenstick fracture, the bone is partially broken and partially bent. This type of fracture commonly occurs in children.

197. **(A)** According to Abraham Maslow's systematized theory of human behavior, all human needs can be organized into five successive categories or levels. The first level includes basic needs, such as for food, water, shelter, and clothing. The second level includes needs for safety and security. The third level includes needs for human companionship and a sense of belonging to a group. The fourth level includes needs for respect and self-esteem. The fifth level includes the need to achieve one's highest level of potential, a concept referred to as self-actualization.

198. **(A)** *Gon / o* means "genitals" or "semen." Gonorrhea is a contagious inflammation of the genital mucous membrane.

199. **(B)** Your body language complements your verbal messages, and it's important that your body language reflect what you are trying to say. Maintain eye contact with the patient when talking to him or her. Eye contact shows interest, attention, and sensitivity. Looking away might imply disinterest, boredom, or anger. Similarly, crossing or folding your arms creates a closed position that implies anger, distrust, and lack of caring. On the other hand, turning and leaning your body toward a person usually shows interest and focuses your attention.

200. **(D)** A heterograft is the transplant of animal tissue into a human. It is also called a xenograft.

201. **(C)** A suffix is word ending that modifies the meaning of the root. Not all words have a suffix. An example of a suffix can be found in the word *ganglionectomy*. *Ganglion* is the root, and *-ectomy* is the suffix.

202. **(C)** Penicillins were the first true antibiotics, and they are the most widely used class of antibiotics. They interfere with the synthesis of bacterial cell walls. As a drug class, penicillins also cause the highest incidence of drug allergy.

203. **(E)** Quadriplegia is the paralysis of the lower and upper extremities (the legs and arms) and the trunk, which results from spinal cord injury in the region of the fifth to seventh cervical vertebrae.

204. **(C)** A license to practice medicine is required by law in each state.

205. **(A)** Pentazocine (*Talwin®*) is an opioid analgesic used to relieve severe acute and chronic pain, pain associated with myocardial infarction, post-trauma, cancer, and chronic inflammatory conditions. Other opioid analgesics include codeine, meperidine, morphine, and propoxyphene. Codeine is also an antitussive drug.

206. **(E)** Tolerance is the increasing resistance to the usual effects of an established dosage of a drug as a result of continued use. Dependence is a state of reliance on a drug, either psychological or physiological, that may result in withdrawal symptoms if drug use is discontinued.

207. **(E)** Physicians are required to submit statutory reports on a regular basis to various governmental agencies. Certain reports are required from all practicing physicians, including reports of births, deaths, and cases of food poisoning and communicable diseases (AIDS, hepatitis, neonatal herpes, Lyme disease, rabies, and sexually transmitted diseases). Physicians also need to report known or suspected abuse of any individual (e.g., child, elderly adult, or battered woman), drug abuse, and evidence of criminal acts (e.g., injuries resulting from violence, such as gunshot or stab wounds).

208. **(B)** The side effects of estrogen include nausea, vomiting, breast tenderness, skin pigmentation, hypertension, and breakthrough bleeding. The side effects of progesterone include weight gain, depression, and hirsutism.

209. **(D)** Centrally acting skeletal muscle relaxants inhibit skeletal muscle contraction by blocking conduction within the spinal cord.

210. **(C)** A comminuted fracture describes a bone that has broken into pieces. In an open or compound fracture, the broken bone creates an external wound that leads to the site of fracture; fragments of the bone commonly pierce through the skin. An oblique fracture is a slanted fracture of the shaft of the bone on its long axis. An incomplete fracture does not continue along the whole bone.

211. **(A)** Corticosteroid is the drug of choice for chronic asthma. Other drugs used to treat asthma include metaproterenol (*Alupent®*), and theophylline.

212. **(C)** Sarcoma is a malignant neoplasm or tumor of connective tissues such as bone or muscle. This type of cancer might affect the bones, bladder, kidneys, liver, lungs, and spleen.

213. **(A)** Anacusis is the term used to describe complete hearing loss. Tinnitus is ringing or buzzing in the ear. Sensorineural hearing loss is the term used to describe hearing loss caused by damage to the inner ear or to the nerve from the ear to the brain. Conductive hearing loss is caused by an interruption in the transmission of sound waves to the inner ear. Vertigo is dizziness.

214. **(D)** Shock is the collapse of the cardiovascular system resulting in a dangerous reduction of blood flow throughout body tissues. Shock can be caused by sepsis, hemorrhage, heart failure, respiratory distress, or anaphylaxis.

215. **(B)** Active immunity is a long-term immunity in which the body produces its own antibodies. Active immunity can be natural or artificial. Natural active immunity results from the exposure to disease-causing organisms. Artificial active immunity results from the administration of a vaccine with killed or weakened organisms. Passive immunity results from the introduction into the body of antibodies that were produced outside the body. Natural passive immunity results when antibodies from the mother cross the placenta to the fetus. Artificial passive immunity results from immunization with antibodies to a disease-causing organism.

216. **(A)** Keratinization is the process by which epithelial cells lose their moisture and are replaced by keratin (protein). The stratum lucidum is the translucent band that is found only in thick-skinned individuals. The subcutaneous layer is the bottom layer of the cutaneous membrane, beneath the dermis, or true skin. The dermis contains hairs, nails, glands, fibers, sense receptors, and blood vessels. Cretinism is a congenital condition characterized by severe hypothyroidism and often associated with other endocrine abnormalities. Typical signs of cretinism include dwarfism, mental deficiency, puffy facial features, dry skin, and a large tongue.

217. **(C)** There are two main body cavities: dorsal and ventral. The dorsal cavity is divided into two separate cavities: the cranial cavity, which contains the brain, and the spinal cavity, which contains the spinal cord. The ventral cavity comprises the thoracic and the abdominopelvic cavities.

218. **(A)** Hypersensitivity is an abnormal condition characterized by an exaggerated response of the immune system to an antigen. High fever, anaphylaxis, asthma, and eczema are examples of type I hypersensitivities.

219. **(B)** You need to have such a request in writing from the patient authorizing the transfer.

220. **(E)** Sweat glands, also called sudoriferous glands, are widely distributed over the body, except for the lips, nipples, and parts of the external genitalia. Sweat glands are abundant on the palms of the hands and on the soles of the feet.

221. **(A)** Void is the correct description for something that is without legal force or effect. An implied contract is an unwritten or unspoken agreement, the terms of which result from the actions of the parties involved.

222. **(E)** Hyperplasia is an increase in the number of cells of a body part that results from an increased rate of cellular division.

223. **(D)** Hashimoto's disease is an autoimmune thyroid disorder. It is characterized by the production of antibodies in response to thyroid antigens.

224. **(C)** The fight-or-flight response is controlled by the sympathetic part of the autonomic nervous system, which acts as an accelerator for organs, especially the adrenal gland, whose functions are needed to meet a stressful situation. Heart rate, respiratory rate, blood pressure, and blood flow increase in response to an emergency situation. In addition, the pupils dilate, sweat glands are stimulated, the liver increases the release of glucose, and there is a reduction in the secretion of enzymes in the digestive system.

225. **(B)** *OD* (*oculus dexter*) is the abbreviation meaning "right eye."

226. **(E)** The abbreviation for "nothing by mouth" is *NPO* or *n.p.o.*, which stands for the Latin phrase *non per os*, "not by mouth." *PO* or *p.o.* stands for *per os*, "by mouth."

227. **(C)** Inspiration is the process of bringing air into the lungs. The major muscle of inspiration or inhalation is the diaphragm, the contraction of which creates negative pressure in the chest, allowing air to fill the lung along a pressure gradient.

228. **(C)** The pH of water is 7. Water is neutral.

229. **(D)** A solute is a substance dissolved in a solution.

230. **(D)** Even with the doctrine of *respondeat superior*, as a medical assistant you can be sued for your own negligent actions unless you were directly ordered to perform a certain task. The *respondeat superior* doctrine makes physicians responsible for the employee's actions; however, supervising someone is not the same as giving an order. You should not act negligently, and you should not go beyond the scope of your education and training. The doctrine of *res ipsa loquitur* applies to cases in which the physician clearly demonstrated negligence, such as by leaving surgical instruments in patients or by injuring a healthy body part during surgery. A physician is not contractually bound to cure every patient and every disease, because to do so would be an impossible task. The physician is contractually bound to perform to the best of his or her capabilities and to provide reasonable care to patients.

231. **(C)** Eugenics is the study of improving a population by selective breeding. This process is considered unethical in humans.

232. **(A)** *Hyper-* means "high," and *-tonic* means "pertaining to tension or contraction." *Hypertonic* applies to solutions that are of higher osmotic pressure than the fluid in cells as well as to muscles that are tense.

233. **(B)** The alveoli are clusters of air sacs at the end of the bronchioles in the lungs. The exchange of gases occurs in the alveoli.

234. **(B)** Food is chewed in the mouth and mixed with saliva to form a moist, soft lump called the bolus. The saliva moistens food and begins the chemical breakdown of carbohydrates.

235. **(D)** The endocrine system coordinates many body functions. Its response to change is slower and more prolonged than that of the nervous system. It would be incorrect to say that the nervous system controls only conscious activities. For example, the autonomic nervous system controls unconscious activities such as reflexes.

236. **(C)** Cushing's syndrome is the hyperactivity of the adrenal cortical gland. The patient experiences fatigue, weakness, fat deposits in the scapular area, a protruding abdomen, hypertension, edema, and hyperlipidemia.

237. **(B)** Amantadine is an antiviral and antiparkinsonian agent. It is prescribed in the prophylaxis and early treatment of the influenza virus and in treatment of parkinsonian symptoms.

238. **(E)** The urinary system removes waste products, salts, and excess water from the blood and eliminates them from the body. The organs of the urinary system include the kidneys, ureters, urinary bladder, and the urethra.

239. **(A)** The small intestine is the longest part of the digestive tract, where the chemical digestion of fats and the final breakdown of carbohydrates and proteins take place. Most of the nutrients in food are absorbed in the small intestine.

240. **(D)** The patient does not have the right to inquire into the practice's financial matters.

241. **(C)** Liability insurance provides legal expenses in the event of a medical liability case, but it is not required by federal or state law.

242. **(A)** There are four basic taste sensations: salty, sweet, sour, and bitter. The very tip of the tongue contains sweet and salty receptors, the sides of the tongue contain sour receptors, and the back of the tongue contains bitter receptors.

243. **(C)** Butabarbital and secobarbital are Schedule III drugs, which have a moderate abuse potential and an accepted medical use. They may be refilled 5 times in 6 months when authorized by the physician.

244. **(E)** Hyperemesis is excessive vomiting.

245. **(B)** Certification (such as, for example, RMA and CMA certification) is a voluntary process to meet the safety and ethical standards of a profession. Licensure is the granting of permission by a competent authority to an individual or organization to engage in a practice or activity that would otherwise be illegal. Licensure is the strongest form of regulation. It gives legal permission, granted by state statutes, to perform specific acts. Licensure is a mandatory credential process established by law, and all physicians are required to be licensed to practice medicine.

246. **(D)** Most prefixes can be connected to other word parts without a combining vowel. When two word roots are connected, a combining vowel is usually used even if vowels are present at the junction. Connecting a word root and a suffix that starts with a consonant usually requires a combining vowel. When a word root and a suffix are connected, a combining vowel is usually not used if the suffix begins with a vowel.

247. **(A)** Adrenergic drugs mimic or stimulate the sympathetic nervous system. They include epinephrine, dopamine, dolutamine, and ephedrine.

248. **(C)** Vitamin K represents a group of fat-soluble vitamins, known as quinones, that are essential for the synthesis of prothrombin in the liver.

249. **(D)** A plaintiff is a person who files a lawsuit, thereby initiating a legal action.

250. **(E)** Nail-biting is the habit of excessively biting and chewing one's fingernails and periungual skin, sometimes leading to cutaneous injury.

MEDICAL ASSISTING KNOWLEDGE

Self-Evaluation Answers and Rationales

Here you'll find the answers to the test on General Medical Assisting Knowledge on p. 415 in Part II. Check your answers and note which questions you missed. Study the rationales for any questions you feel you had difficulty with and if you need more review, go back to the appropriate section in the chapters.

1. **(E)** Check the invoice against the original order and the packing slip, mark it to confirm the order was received, and pay it. The check number, date, and payment amount should then be recorded on the invoice. Invoices should be placed in a special folder until paid.

2. **(C)** Combination mail consists of a letter combined with anything else, such as an X-ray. The letter should be attached to the outside of the package or placed in the package marked *"Letter Enclosed"* just below the space for postage. Separate postage is paid for the parcel and the letter.

3. **(B)** Buffer time refers to appointment slots held open in case of emergencies. Every medical practice should have at least one or two slots open for buffer time each day.

4. **(A)** Wave scheduling can provide flexibility to accommodate unforeseen situations, such as a patient who requires more time or a patient who arrives late. For wave scheduling to work, the medical facility should have multiple procedure rooms and adequate personnel.

5. **(E)** Good medical records help a physician provide continuity in a patient's medical care. They also supply statistical information. Correlation in a new outlook on some phases of medicine can lead to revised techniques and treatments. Medical records can also be used in lawsuits and malpractice cases either to support a patient's claim or to support the physician's defense against such a claim. They can also help to evaluate the quality of treatment a doctor's office provides. Medical records also provide documentation for insurance billing and the basis for defending audits by managed care and government (Medicare and Medicaid) regulatory agencies.

6. **(B)** Medical assistants should answer the phone promptly by the second or third ring. Hold the phone's mouthpiece about an inch away from your mouth and leave at least one hand free to write with. Greet callers first with the name of the office and then with your name. Do not answer the phone by simply repeating the number of your office or by saying "hello." Although the type of calls you usually handle as a medical assistant will be administrative, you will still be expected to answer the phone and transfer the patient to the physician when it is necessary. You should never give a diagnostic opinion to a patient either on the phone or in person.

7. **(A)** In order to maintain accurate patient records, you should keep these six concepts in mind: client's words, clarity, completeness, conciseness, chronological order, and confidentiality.

8. **(E)** In managed health care systems, the primary care physician needs to refer a patient to a specialist before the patient can make an appointment with a specialist. A referral form must be completed, showing the following information: referring physician, specialist being referred to, diagnosis, treatment (past and present including medications), chart notes, and minor surgical procedures.

9. **(A)** In managed care, a participating provider (PAR) agrees to accept allowed charges in return for various incentives, such as fast payment. If a participating provider charges more for a service than what the allowed charge is, the physician must write off the difference. The patient, like Mr. Johnson, may not be billed for this amount.

10. **(C)** The double-entry system is based on the accounting equation: *Assets = Liability + Owner Equity*. This system requires more extensive knowledge of accounting procedures than the simpler single-entry or pegboard systems.

11. **(B)** The balance equals the difference between the debit and credit totals. The balance column is usually on the far right side of a ledger. A debit is recorded on the left side of an account and is also called a charge. A credit is recorded on the right side of an account and is also referred to as revenue or net worth.

12. **(E)** Taking a trial balance is a method of checking the accuracy of accounts. It should be done once a month after all posting has been completed and before preparing the monthly statements. The purpose of a trial balance is to disclose any discrepancies between the journal and the ledger.

13. **(E)** Items that weigh 13 oz or less may be sent as First-Class Mail. First Class Mail that weighs over 13 oz becomes Priority Mail. Anything the post office accepts for mailing can be mailed as First-Class Mail; however, some things *must* be mailed as First-Class Mail (or Priority Mail). Handwritten or typewritten material, bills, statements of account or invoices, and credit cards should be mailed First Class.

14. **(C)** Generally, calls from insurance companies will not require the physician's personal attention.

15. **(A)** The usual fee is what an individual physician most frequently charges for a service to private patients. The customary fee is a range of fees charged by most physicians in the community for a particular service. For example, the range of fees for a check-up could vary from $40 to $50 in a community. The prevailing charges are fees most frequently charged in an area. For example, for a check-up, fees could range from $40 to $50; however, upon closer investigation an insurance company could learn that 10 physicians in the community charge $45, three charge $40, one charges $42, and four charge $50. In this case, the prevailing fee would be $45.

16. **(A)** Standard Mail (A) is designed for printed matter, flyers, circulars, advertising, newsletters, bulletins, catalogs, and small parcels. All Standard Mail (A) must be mailed in bulk. There must be at least 200 pieces of mail or 50 pounds of mail to get this low rate. The periodicals classification is designed for newspapers, magazines, and other periodical publications whose primary purpose is transmitting information to an established list of subscribers or requesters. Periodicals must be published at regular intervals least four times a year from a known office of publication and be formed of printed sheets. There are specific standards for, among other things, circulation, record keeping, and advertising limits. There is a nonrefundable application fee to become authorized for Periodicals mailing privileges.

17. **(B)** Medicare Part B covers outpatient services, services by physicians, durable medical equipment, and other services and supplies. This coverage is optional. Medicare Part A covers hospital, nursing, facility, home health, hospice, and inpatient care.

18. **(C)** Medigap policies are private insurance contracts that supplement regular Medicare coverage. They often pay for the beneficiary's deductibles, coinsurance, and in some cases for services not covered by Medicare. If the subscriber has Medigap insurance, Medicare is still the primary payer, which means claims must be filed with Medicare first.

19. **(A)** Medicaid is a health cost assistance program for needy individuals. Coverage may vary from month to month based on the recipient's income. Physicians are not obligated to treat Medicaid patients, but if they do accept Medicaid patients, they also accept Medicaid reimbursement for covered services and they cannot bill the patients for any differences in cost. Medicaid is always a secondary carrier to Medicare.

20. **(E)** In order to protect essential computerized information, it is important to make regular back ups of files onto disks, CD-ROMs, or zip drives. It's also important to store these back-up files off premises. While not opening an email attachment from someone you don't know or an attachment you did not expect to receive provides good protection against certain computer viruses, it will definitely not protect your computer from a fire. Opening an email is usually harmless, since viruses are usually programs sent as an attachment to emails. Another good way to protect your computers from viruses is by purchasing an up-to-date virus detection and protection program.

21. **(E)** Provider data, patient data, insurance carriers, diagnosis codes, procedure codes, and transactions are usually stored on large medical databases. A database is a collection of related data organized within a specific structure. For example, the procedures code database would contain data needed to create charges such as the *Physician's Current Procedural Terminology* (CPT), as well as place of service (POS). The source of these codes is often the patient superbill.

22. **(A)** You should send out the first collection letter or statement when an account is 30 days overdue, and follow up at 60, 90, and 120 days. You should not call the patient at work nor pay the patient a personal visit. Write a letter that reminds the patient of a possible oversight of debt and call the patient only at home during reasonable hours.

23. **(D)** Occasionally, the bank returns deposited checks because of a problem such as a missing signature, or endorsement, or if the payer has insufficient funds to cover the check's amount. *NSF* is an abbreviation for *not sufficient funds*.

24. **(D)** The physician is required by law to keep payroll data for 4 years. The records should include the employee's Social Security number, the number of withholding allowances claimed, gross salary, and deductions for Social Security tax, Medicare tax, federal, state, and other tax, state disability insurance, and state unemployment tax.

25. **(D)** An employer must file and submit a quarterly federal tax return.

26. **(A)** HCPCS, pronounced "hic-pics", is mandated by Congress for Medicare claims and updated annually. It is a five-digit alphanumerical coding system that can accommodate the addition of modifiers.

27. **(C)** If a procedure is unlisted, there are guidelines at the beginning of each section on what codes to use on the insurance form. In these cases, a special report must be attached to the claim to described and explain the extent and reasons for service. ICD-9-CM refers to the *International Classification of Diseases, 9th revision, Clinical Modification*, which is used to list what is wrong with the patient and what initially brought the patient to see the doctor.

28. **(E)** A voucher check is frequently used for payroll checks since it allows additional information such as deductions to be supplied to the payee.

29. **(B)** FUTA is the Federal Unemployment Tax Act that requires employers to pay a percentage of each employee's gross income. This amount should not be deducted from the employee's wages.

30. **(A)** When a patient goes to a non-participating provider of Medicare, the patient pays the practice, and then the patient receives reimbursement from Medicare.

31. **(E)** To ensure accurate transcription, you should have needed materials at hand, adjust the transcribing equipment's speed, tone, and volume. Listen all the way through before starting to transcribe, write down the time on the digital counter for any problems so that you can find them quickly when requesting clarification, and listen carefully.

32. **(A)** Indexing refers to a method of deciding where to file a letter or paper. Indexing is an organized method of identifying and separating items to be filed into small subunits. Each unit is identified according to unit number. The key individual's unit, unit 1, is the individual's last name. Unit 2 is the individual's first name. Unit 3 is the middle initial. Unit 4 is a title or special name such as Mrs. or Dr.

33. **(C)** The matrix contains times already allotted for other events, which is therefore not available to schedule patients. The first step in preparing an appointment book is to block off these times.

34. **(C)** The medical assistant responsible for coding should attend at least one CPT and one ICD-9 class each year.

35. **(D)** The W-2 form lists the total gross income, total federal, state, and local taxes that were withheld, and taxable fringe benefits such as tips. The amount of wages that were taxable under Social Security and Medicare are listed separately.

36. **(E)** The maximum size for mail pieces is 108 inches in combined length and girth. The maximum mailable weight of any mail piece is 70 pounds. Items mailed as Parcel Post can have a maximum combined length and girth of 130 inches.

37. **(D)** You must write any endorsements legibly and in the proper area. The endorsement and return address must read in the same direction as the delivery address. It should be printed in no smaller than 8-point type, and it must stand out clearly against its background. There must be a $\frac{1}{4}$-inch clear space around the endorsement. The endorsement must be placed in one of these four positions: directly below the return address, directly above the delivery address area, directly to the left of the postage area and below any rate marking, and directly below the postage area and below any rate marking.

38. **(E)** *Special Delivery* allowed mail to be delivered as soon as it reached the recipient's post office. Special delivery stamps could be purchased at the post office. Special delivery was used for regular First-Class, Second-Class, and insured mail. Special delivery could not be used for mail addressed to a post office box or military installation. Please note that this is an outdated service that might still appear on the certification exams.

39. **(A)** Workers' compensation coverage includes temporary disability income, death benefits, rehabilitation benefits, and life insurance. It does not provide permanent disability income.

40. **(B)** The Blue Cross and Blue Shield (BCBS) Association is a nationwide federation of local nonprofit service organizations that offer prepaid health-care services to subscribers.

41. **(C)** A regular referral usually takes 3 to 10 days, an urgent referral takes 24 hours, and STAT referrals are done over the phone and take place immediately.

42. **(D)** The Health Care Financing Administration (HCFA) designed a form called the HCFA-1500 to handle Medicare and Medicaid claims. It is the most commonly accepted insurance form by private insurance providers as well.

43. **(B)** The Blue Cross part of the BCBS covers hospital services, home care services, and other institutional care. Blue Shield covers physician services, dental, vision, and other outpatient benefits.

44. **(B)** The primary diagnosis refers to the main condition for which a patient is treated. When a cancer patient comes in with the flu, the primary diagnosis will be the flu, not cancer.

45. **(D)** The encounter form is also known as a superbill or the charge ticket. The superbill is a custom-made form used by physicians to note diagnosis and treatment. Superbills often list the ICD-9 codes for the most frequently used diagnoses. The codes on the superbill should be checked against the annual update of codes. A superbill also includes the charges for services rendered, an invoice for payment or co-payment, and the information for submitting an insurance claim.

46. **(A)** FICA stands for the Federal Insurance Contribution Act, which funds Social Security. The employee pays half and the employer pays the other half of these taxes. Taxes are applied based on the level of taxable earnings, the length of the payroll period, marital status, and the number of withholding allowances claimed.

47. **(E)** The general journal is known also as the daily log, daybook, daysheet, daily journal, and charge journal. This journal is where all transactions are first recorded.

48. **(E)** The amount charged for a medical insurance policy, in which the insurer agrees to provide certain benefits, is called the premium.

49. **(E)** Coordination of benefits can prevent duplicate payment for the same service.

50. **(D)** Money orders may be purchased from banks, post offices, and some convenience stores.

51. **(A)** A credit is the amount recorded on the right-hand side of an account, constituting an addition to revenue.

52. **(E)** A "*Special Handling*" endorsement is required for parcels whose unusual contents require additional care in transit and handling. Special handling is not required for those parcels sent by First-Class, Express, or Priority Mail. Special handling is available for Standard Mail only, including insured and COD mail. Special handling service is not necessary for sending ordinary parcels even when they contain fragile items. Breakable items will receive adequate protection if they are packed with sufficient cushioning and clearly marked "*FRAGILE.*" If special handling is required, the words "SPECIAL HANDLING," (similar to other mailing notations such as "CERTIFIED," "HAND CANCEL," or "REGISTERED") should be printed in capital letters two lines below the postage.

53. **(D)** Certified mail offers a guarantee that the item has been mailed and received by the correct party by requiring the mail carrier to obtain a signature on delivery. It provides proof of mailing and delivery of mail. The sender receives a mailing receipt at the time of mailing, and a record of delivery is kept at the recipient's post office. A return receipt to provide the sender with proof of delivery can also be purchased for an additional fee. Certified mail is available only for First-Class and Priority Mail. This is the best way to send documents, contracts, mortgages, or bank books that are not valuable intrinsically but would be hard to duplicate if lost. Certified mail is the cheapest way to receive proof of mailing.

54. **(B)** Blue Cross makes direct payment to physician members.

55. **(B)** To maximize communication with children, we must work directly with them, rather than communicating through parents.

56. **(A)** Diagnostic-related groups or DRGs are groups of procedures or tests related directly to diagnosis. The fixed fees paid by Medicare Part A are based on DRGs.

57. **(D)** Accounts receivable are the amounts owed to a business for services or goods supplied.

58. **(C)** The postal abbreviation for Circle is CIR.

59. **(B)** Capitation is a reimbursement type often used in group-model HMOs. A fixed fee is paid to the physician monthly regardless of the number of times the patient visits the physician.

60. **(A)** ∧ is a proofreader's mark meaning *insert*. This mark is usually followed by some text to be inserted or # indicating that a space should be inserted.

61. **(E)** In the medical assisting profession, appearance is very important. Every medical facility will have its own dress code, but these general rules will apply in most places.

62. **(C)** Under the old classification system, third-class mail included books and catalogues of 24 or fewer bound pages, manuscript copies, identification cards, circulars, and other printed materials, as well as all other matter weighing less than 16 ounces that was not sent first or second class.

63. **(E)** In general, mail processing involves sorting, opening, recording, annotating, and distributing. Some physicians prefer to open letters from attorneys or accountants. Mail such as routine office expense bills, insurance forms, and checks for deposit may not need to be opened by the physician. In general, when you transmit letters to the physician, place the most important letters on the top and the least important ones on the bottom. Usually something marked *special delivery* is considered important mail. After opening the mail, medical assistants usually need to date stamp the letters, check for enclosures, and in some cases annotate the letter. You should not open mail marked *personal* or *confidential* unless you have the addressee's explicit permission.

64. **(D)** Guidelines that dictate the day-to-day workings of an office are policies.

65. **(B)** The term *enunciation* means to speak clearly and to articulate carefully.

66. **(D)** Most medical offices use a postage meter that automatically stamps large mailings. The postage can be printed directly onto an envelope with a meter. The advantages of using a postage meter include saving trips to the post office and saving money by providing exact postage without having to provide every denomination of stamps at hand.

67. **(A)** Memos are usually intended for interoffice correspondence. The purpose is to expedite the communication of a message in a manner that provides a record without becoming cumbersome. They are used to inform personnel about meetings and general changes that affect everyone. You should not use salutations and complimentary closes in memos. The standard format for a memorandum contains a to, from, date, and subject line before the body of the memo. The body of the memo starts two blank lines after the subject line and has no paragraph indentations.

68. **(B)** When using a modified-block letter style, all lines begin at the left margin, with the exception of the date line, complimentary closure, and keyed signature, which usually begin at the center position.

69. **(C)** Assignment of benefits is the authorization to the insurance company to make payments directly to the physician.

70. **(C)** *Junction* should be abbreviated as *JCT*.

71. **(E)** The address must be typed on the envelope using single spacing and all capital letters with no punctuation. Put the addressee's name on the first line, the department on the second line, and the company name on the third line. If the letter is being sent to someone's attention at the company, put the company name first and "*ATTENTION*: [*NAME*]" on the second line. The last line in the address must include the city, the two-digit state code, and the zip code.

72. **(B)** For a doctor, the title should read as either *Dr. Mary Jack* or *Mary Jack, M.D.* The form *Dr. Mary Jack, M.D.*, is incorrect. It is also preferable to use a professional degree such as *M.D.* instead of an academic title such as *Dr.* The degree designations should be abbreviated.

73. **(D)** As a medical assistant, you must learn how to remain calm when you deal with an angry patient.

74. **(E)** *Triage* refers to the screening and sorting of emergency situations.

75. **(C)** On the inside address of a business letter, spell out numerical names of streets but use numerals for the street address except for single numbers one through nine, which should be spelled out. Also spell out the words *Street*, *Drive*, *Boulevard*, *Place*, and so on.

76. **(D)** An Independent Practice Association (IPA) is a type of HMO in which a program administrator contracts with a number of physicians who agree to provide treatment to subscribers in their own office for a fixed capitation payment per month.

77. **(B)** The signature block contains the sender's name on the first line and title on the second line. The block should be aligned with the closing and be typed four lines below it to allow for the signature.

78. **(C)** Travelers' checks are designed for people who are traveling where personal checks may not be accepted, and for people who don't want to carry large amounts of cash. Travelers' checks are also available in foreign currencies.

79. **(A)** Things of a routine business nature such as ordering supplies are often signed by the medical assistant; however, medical reports, letters to insurance companies, consultation or referral letters, and letters clinical in nature should be signed by the physician.

80. **(E)** The most common types of envelopes used in the medical office are the Number $6\frac{3}{4}$ and Number 10.

81. **(A)** A return address for the sender should always be placed in the upper lefthand corner.

82. **(B)** There are three types of file cabinets used in the medical office: vertical, lateral, and movable file cabinets.

83. **(A)** Modems may be used to transfer information from one computer to another using telephone lines and servers.

84. **(D)** Unconsciousness, trouble breathing, severe bleeding, pressure or pain in the abdomen that will not go away, poisoning, and snake bites are among the things that would require immediate medical help.

85. **(B)** Vital supplies are absolutely essential to ensure the smooth running of the practice. An example of these supplies is prescription pads.

86. **(B)** Minutes are the official record of the proceedings of a meeting. An agenda is the order of business for a meeting. When keeping minutes, you should note the date, location, time, and purpose of the meeting, the presiding officer, names of people in attendance, the agenda, motions made, and summaries of discussions.

87. **(E)** The collection ratio measures the effectiveness of the billing system.

88. **(C)** *Reschedule* is abbreviated as *RS*.

89. **(C)** Formerly, the periodicals class of mail was called Second-Class mail. This classification is designed for newspapers, magazines, and other periodical publications whose primary purpose is transmitting information to an established list of subscribers or requesters. Periodicals must be published at regular intervals least four times a year from a known office of publication and be formed of printed sheets. There are specific standards for, among other things, circulation, record keeping, and advertising limits. There is a nonrefundable application fee to become authorized for Periodicals mailing privileges.

90. **(D)** According to the National Childhood Vaccine Injury Act of 1986, all immunization records must be kept permanently.

91. **(A)** Advanced scheduling refers to when appointments are made weeks or months in advance.

92. **(E)** The Resource-Based Relative Value Scale (RBRVS) is a system used by Medicare since 1992 to determine uniform payments for medical services that take geographic differences into account. A relative value unit is determined for each medical service, based on the physician's work, which requires time and skill, and the provider's expenses, such as running the office and having malpractice insurance. The MFS is developed using the RBRVS. The participating physician may bill the patient for coinsurance and deductibles but may not collect excess charges.

93. **(B)** Carol Jones can be billed only for 10% of the set fee, which is $140. Therefore, her bill would be for $14. The physician, by accepting Medicare patients, accepts the Medicare fee schedule, and the medical office may not bill the patient for any difference between usual fees and the Medicare assigned fee.

94. **(A)** An 80:20 plan means that the insurance carrier will pay for 80% of all medical fees, making the subscriber, Mark, responsible for coinsurance, 20% of all medical fees. 20% of 200 equals $40. An easy way to calculate this without a calculator is to first determine 10% by moving the decimal point one space to the left (10% of $200 is $20). Then multiply the 10% figure by 2.

95. **(A)** Forwarding is offered free of charge to Priority, First-Class, and Standard Mail (A). Standard Mail (B) is forwarded locally at no charge, but if it is going out of town, extra postage will be due. First-Class and Priority mail is returned at no charge; Standard Mail (A) is returned for a charge based on weight; and Standard Mail (B) return is charged at the appropriate single-piece rate. Return service is free for First-Class and Priority Mail, but Standard Mail (A) is charged First-Class or Priority Mail rates for the return. Certificates of mailing are not free. They can be purchased at the time of mailing.

96. **(D)** Once the matrix has been established, you can schedule patient appointments based on patient need and preference, physician preferences and habits, degree of illness and/or contagion, and available facilities.

97. **(B)** Steps toward having a positive attitude include using positive statements instead of negative statements, smiling instead of frowning, and saying something pleasant instead of complaining.

98. **(D)** Some physicians prefer to open letters from attorneys or accountants. Mail such as routine office expense bills, insurance forms, and checks for deposit may not need to be opened by the physician. Personal letter or letters marked *confidential* also should not be opened unless you have the expressed permission of the addressee. It's always good to check with the physician to find out what mail falls under your responsibility and what mail he or she prefers to open.

99. **(D)** The explanation of benefits (EOB) is a document that the medical practice receives from the insurance carrier, and it shows how the amount of the benefit was determined. The insurance carrier keeps a running account of the deductible, and this deductible will be listed on the explanation of benefits. Until the deductible has been met, the physician may bill the patient for the amount listed as the deductible on the explanation of benefits.

100. **(B)** When a patient goes to a nonparticipating provider, the patient is responsible for any difference between the allowed charge and the physician's usual fee as well as any deductible, co-payment, or coinsurance. If the patient had gone to a participating provider, the physician would not be able to bill the patient for any difference between the physician's usual fee and the allowed charge. Any difference would have to become a write-off for the physician.

101. **(B)** Filing business and organizational records is based on subject and topic.

102. **(E)** Bank drafts are checks written by a bank against its funds in another bank.

103. **(B)** If your medical practice accepts workers' compensation cases, the procedures to follow when contacted by a patient include calling the patient's employer to verify that the accident occurred on the employer's premises, obtaining the employer's approval to provide treatment, and creating a patient record.

104. **(C)** The patient cannot be charged the difference between the allowed charge and the physician's usual fees. So the $12 difference will be a write-off for the practice. However, the patient is responsible for the deductible and the co-payment. The allowed charge is $78 and the carrier will pay $38 of that. The difference is $40, which is the total of the co-payment and the deductible.

105. **(C)** Registered mail is the most secure service offered by the post office. Registered mail provides insurance coverage for valuable items and is controlled from the point of mailing to the point of delivery. This service should be reserved for mailing items of tangible value, such as gifts or items that cannot be replaced in case of loss or damage. Both First-Class Mail and Priority Mail can be registered.

106. **(A)** Federal Insurance Contribution Act (FICA) funds Social Security.

107. **(B)** Restricted delivery means that the mail is delivered only to a specific addressee or someone authorized in writing to receive mail for the addressee. Restricted delivery is available only for registered mail, certified mail, COD mail, and mail insured for more than $50.

108. **(C)** You can recall mail by filling out a written application at the post office and by giving it to the post office along with an envelope that is addressed identically to the one you want to recall. A mail carrier is not permitted to simply give mail back to you.

109. **(E)** For adequate legal protection, a patient's medical record should include the following items: patient registration form, patient medical history, physical examination results, results of laboratory tests, copies of prescription notes on refill authorizations, diagnosis and treatment plan, patient progress reports, follow-up visits, and telephone calls, informed consent forms, discharge summary, and correspondence with and about the patient.

110. **(D)** Make sure you date and initial all entries that go in to the patient's medical records. Always record all signs, symptoms, and other information the patient wishes to share with you in the patient's own words, not your interpretation of them. You should include correspondence about the patient in the medical records. You should not include any flippant or prejudicial comments.

111. **(E)** The following items should not be included in a patient's medical records:

- Reports from consulting physicians should not be placed in the record until carefully reviewed.
- Financial information.
- Transferred records from the patient's previous physician are never added to the patient's record.
- Prejudicial, personal, or flippant comments are never entered into the record.

In order to observe confidentiality, only the patient, the physician, and the medical assistant directly involved with the patient should have access to the patient's medical records.

112. **(A)** The numeric filing system involves the filing of records, correspondence, or cards by number. Such a system is often used when patient information is highly confidential. Numeric filing is used by practically every large clinic or hospital where there are more than 5,000 patients.

113. **(B)** According to the American Medical Association and the American Hospital Association, patient records should be kept for 10 years after the patient's final visit.

114. **(E)** Computer memory is used as operating and storage space for data. Memory is measured in bytes. Random access memory (RAM), read only memory (ROM), virtual memory, and cache memory are all types of memory. Cache memory is the smallest and fastest on any computer.

115. **(E)** If you use the keyboard improperly for extended periods of time, you could get carpal tunnel syndrome, in which tendons around your wrist swell and may require medication or surgery. Proper posture and hand position, using a wrist rest, and taking breaks from repeated typing can help you avoid injury. While typing on the keyboard, your wrist should be in a neutral position to avoid injury. While standing and walking is a good idea, doing so does not directly avoid carpal tunnel syndrome.

116. **(B)** TRICARE was formerly known as CHAMPUS, a health-care benefit for families of uniformed personal and retirees from the uniformed services.

117. **(D)** Accepting a predated check is not a risk unless the check is predated more than 6 months.

118. **(E)** When new supplies are received, you should place them in the back of the supply area.

119. **(C)** A spreadsheet is a computer program that simulates a business or scientific worksheet and performs the necessary calculations when data is changed. It is used most often in accounting procedures.

120. **(A)** Virtual memory is the slowest type of memory that uses the hard disk to store programs and data when all the RAM has been used.

121. **(E)** Developing a manual begins with planning the format and outline, which should be approved by the office manager and physicians. Sources for developing and updating material include journals, product literature, textbooks, and standards publications, among others.

122. **(B)** Collating records involves collecting all records, test results, and information pertaining to the patient who is scheduled to be seen by the physician. This is usually done the day before the patient is seen.

123. **(A)** Balance column is used for recording the difference between the debit and credit columns.

124. **(B)** In a journal entry, the dollar amount of debit must be equal to the dollar amount of the credit. For example, an amount owed by a patient to the medical facility is a debit for the patient and a credit to the facility.

125. **(B)** Surgical packages and laboratory panels should be coded as single procedures rather than broken down into component parts. Insurance carriers usually want to know if the patient was a new patient (NP) or established patient (EP). Emergency patients are neither new nor established. Modifiers allow coders to most accurately reflect the specific service performed.

126. **(B)** If after 30 days the insurance company has not paid a claim or responded to a claim, the choices are to bill again or call the carrier. Since sometimes second billings are rejected as duplicates, the medical office can send a tracer, a letter to the insurance company containing the basic billing information.

127. **(E)** Claims might be denied because a claim is not for a covered benefit, the patient has a preexisting condition that is not covered, the patient's coverage has been cancelled, the physician's procedure was experimental, no preauthorization was obtained, and the physician provided services before the patient's health insurance contract went into effect.

128. **(C)** The petty cash fund is maintained to pay small, unpredictable cash expenditures.

129. **(A)** Your best course of action would be to write a claim appeal, a written request to the insurance carrier to review the reimbursement. Perhaps the patient's condition was an emergency and there was no time to obtain preauthorization. It is best to review the patient's contract with the insurance carrier. You would bill the patient when a claim was rejected for the reasons that the patient's coverage was cancelled or if the physician provided services before the patient's health insurance went into effect. If the claim is rejected because the insurance company considers the physician's procedure experimental, you office might request a peer review or call the carrier to discuss options.

130. **(D)** Claims for Medicare must be filed by December 31 of the year following that in which the services were rendered. Medicare forms must be signed by both the patient and the physician. Nonparticipating providers are not required to accept assignment of benefits, and the allowable payment to nonparticipating providers is less than the payments to participating providers. Providers are required by law to file the HCFA-1500 for all eligible patients.

131. **(B)** When a patient has both Medicare and Medicaid, the claim form is first processed through Medicare, the primary provider, and then the claim is automatically forwarded to Medicaid, the secondary provider. This is sometimes referred to as a crossover claim.

132. **(E)** When processing TRICARE claims and the provider accepts assignment, the patient will be billed for the deductible and any coinsurance. If the provider does not accept assignment, the patient is responsible to file claims with TRICARE.

133. **(E)** All of the actions listed are considered fraud and your medical office should never engage in any fraudulent actions. It is also considered fraud to use an incorrect code for a procedure, to alter a patient's charts to increase the amount reimbursed, and to not obtain the patient's signature permitting insurance billing.

134. **(E)** Express mail is available seven days a week and it guarantees overnight delivery of an item. Federal Express and the United Parcel Service (UPS) also offer next-day delivery.

135. **(B)** The majority of letters to distant foreign countries, such as those located in Central or South America, Europe, Australia, and Africa as well as Mexico and Canada are sent by airmail at international rates determined by the U.S. Postal Service. Window envelopes cannot be used for international mail. Parcel Post is handled according to an agreement with foreign countries that place restrictions on materials that enter their borders.

136. **(A)** Incidental supplies can be clinical, administrative, or general in nature. They do not threaten the efficiency of the office if the supplies run low. Incidental supplies include rubber bands and staples.

137. **(B)** Open-ended questions should be asked of all patients. They allow the patient to elaborate on feelings and symptoms and they help you understand the patient better. Children should be treated with the same respect and attention as adults.

138. **(E)** Claims for Medicare must be filed by December 31 of the year following that in which the services were rendered.

139. **(C)** The average medical practice spends 4 to 6% of its annual gross income on supplies. If costs exceed 6%, reevaluate the office's spending practices and impose some cost-saving measures.

140. **(C)** An appointment card often serves as a reminder to the patient about an appointment scheduled with the medical office.

141. **(D)** Patient information packets include payment policy, office hours, and physician's qualifications.

142. **(C)** Double booking means two or more patients are scheduled into the same time slot.

143. **(C)** The records of the workers' compensation case should be kept separate from the patient's regular history. The insurance carrier is entitled to receive copies of all records pertaining to the industrial injury. The injured person's records must be personally signed by the physician. The insurance carrier may provide its own billing forms. The patient is not billed.

144. **(E)** The bank statement's caption provides a summary of account activity that has taken place during the month up to the closing date. It includes the beginning balance, total value of checks processed, total amount of deposits made, service charges, and an ending balance. You should reconcile this statement with the practice's own records.

145. **(E)** Medical practices typically use three types of bank accounts: checking accounts, interest-earning checking accounts, and a savings account.

146. **(B)** Priority mail provides First-Class handling for items that weigh more than 13 ounces and less than 70 pounds.

147. **(E)** Memory is usually measured in bytes.

148. **(A)** A warrant is a nonnegotiable check, issued to indicate that a debt should be paid, for example, by an insurance company.

149. **(A)** When you accept a check, immediately endorse it and write the words *"For deposit only"* on the back.

150. **(E)** Before writing off the amount, you can try to collect through the court system or through a collection agency. After an account has been released to a collection agency, your medical office should make no further attempts to collect the debt.

151. **(B)** A rider constitutes an addition to an insurance policy, often attached on a separate piece of paper. The premium is the amount charged for a medical insurance policy.

152. **(A)** The Truth in Lending Act (TLA) requires creditors to provide applicants with accurate and complete credit costs and terms, clearly and obviously.

153. **(C)** Open-book accounts are the most typical accounts for patients of a medical practice.

154. **(A)** You should never ignore mistakes made in billing. You should rebill the claim. Waiting for the insurance provider to notice the mistake might take too long and they might not notice the mistake. It is best to correct any mistakes as soon as you catch them.

155. **(A)** Special Standard Mail is generally used for books (at least 8 pages long), film (16mm or narrower), printed music, printed test materials, sound recordings, play scripts, educational charts, loose-leaf pages, binders consisting of medical information, and computer-readable material.

156. **(E)** United States Postal Service prohibits the mailing of fraudulent or pornographic materials. The responsibility for mailing any materials whether they are prohibited, illegal, or hazardous rests with the mailer. Hazardous materials are designated by the U.S. Department of Transportation (DOT) as being capable of posing unreasonable risk to health, safety, and property during transportation. Certain drugs and medicines can be classified as hazardous material. Before mailing anything that might be considered hazardous check with the post office for appropriate labeling procedures. It is not necessarily prohibited to mail hazardous materials.

157. **(A)** The magnetic medium inside the computer where information is permanently stored for later retrieval is known as the hard drive.

158. **(B)** Accounts payable refers to the accounts a physician owes to others for equipment and services.

159. **(D)** Aging accounts receivable is a procedure that classifies accounts by age from the first date of billing. It should list all patient account balances, when charges were incurred, the most recent payment date, and any notes regarding the account. The age analysis is a good tool to show the status of each account at a glance.

160. **(D)** Productivity, accuracy, and cash flow are advantages of electronic banking over traditional banking. A medical assistant is still responsible for recording and depositing checks.

161. **(D)** A participating provider is a physician or other health care provider who participates in an insurance carrier's plan.

162. **(C)** Liability insurance covers people injured in their homes, work, or cars. Life insurance is a plan that pays benefits to a beneficiary in case of loss of life.

163. **(A)** Some providers do not schedule appointments; they prefer to conduct their practices with open office hours. This system is the least structured.

164. **(B)** The Fair Credit Reporting Act (FCRA) requires credit bureaus to supply correct and complete information to businesses to use in evaluating a person's application for credit, insurance, or a job. If an applicant sues the practice in federal court for violating the FCRA, the practice may have to pay damages, punitive damages, court costs, and lawyers' fees.

165. **(D)** Assertiveness means someone being firm and standing up for oneself while showing respect for others.

166. **(E)** All of the reasons listed are good reasons to cash checks promptly.

167. **(C)** Balance billing refers to billing the patient for the difference between the usual and the allowed charges. Whether balance billing is acceptable depends on the physician's contract with the insurance company. Most participating providers of an HMO are not allowed to do any balance billing.

168. **(D)** *Physicians' Current Procedural Terminology* (CPT) is a procedural code book using a numerical system updated annually by the American Medical Association.

169. **(C)** Vertical file cabinets are the least efficient type of cabinet because half of the filing time goes into opening and closing drawers.

170. **(A)** The "withhold" is the portion of the monthly capitation payment to physicians retained by an HMO until the end of the year to create an incentive for efficient care. If the physician exceeds the utilization norms, he or she will not receive this portion.

171. **(C)** Bank statements contain basic information including: closing date, caption, list of checks processed, and list of deposits. Fee schedules are the price lists for the medical practice. The bank's fees are usually not listed on their statements.

172. **(D)** The usual, customary, and reasonable fee is determined by comparing the actual fee charge by physicians in the same geographic area and specialty.

173. **(B)** With increased deductibles and coinsurance, the point-of-service option was added to some HMO plans to allow patients to choose physicians outside of the regular HMO network.

174. **(E)** Passwords and monitoring systems can provide security for confidential files stored on a computer. Creating back-up files might protect against computer viruses, but they will not secure your documents.

175. **(C)** Color-coded filing systems break the alphabet up into five different colors.

176. **(B)** Movable file units allow easy access to large record systems and require less space than either the vertical or lateral (open-shelf) files.

177. **(D)** When filing identical names, use date of birth, patient identification number, or some other form of identification in order to distinguish between two patients.

178. **(A)** A server is a single computer that can be accessed by other computers over a network.

179. **(E)** Tickler files are chronological files used as reminders that something needs to be done on a certain date.

180. **(E)** The postal abbreviation for Plaza is PLZ.

181. **(D)** Exceptions to regularly scheduled patients include emergency patients, acutely ill patients, and physician referrals.

182. **(C)** An inquiry about a bill is an administrative type call a medical assistant should handle.

183. **(B)** DEERS stands for the Department of Defense's Defense Enrollment Eligibility Reporting system.

184. **(D)** Copies of all bills and order forms for supplies should be kept on file for 10 years in case the practice is audited by the Internal Revenue Service (IRS).

185. **(C)** CHAMPVA or TRICARE are primary providers. Medicaid is always a secondary provider. Therefore, claims must be filed with CHAMPVA first, and only then with Medicaid.

186. **(B)** Preferred provider organizations (PPO) can offer the highest level of benefits to enrollees when they obtain services from a physician, hospital, or other health provider.

187. **(C)** The HCFA-1500 is divided into two main sections. Blanks 1 through 13 are used for patient and insured information. Blanks 14 through 33 are used for the physician or supplier information.

188. **(E)** *Annotate* means you must highlight key points of the letter and write comments in the margins.

189. **(C)** The *International Classification of Diseases, 9th Revision, Clinical Modification* (ICD-9-CM) is a three-volume system for classifying diseases and surgical procedures.

190. **(A)** CPT codes are five digit numbers, organized into six sections: Evaluation and Management, Anesthesiology, Surgery, Radiology, Pathology and Laboratory, and Medicine. To find the correct procedure codes using the CPT, look for the service in the index.

191. **(B)** A W-4 form must be completed at the time of hiring.

192. **(D)** A denied Medicare can be reconsidered only within 6 months after denial.

193. **(B)** Consulting physicians should always be transferred to the physician.

194. **(E)** The medical assistant may sign claim forms to insurance carriers and other vendors.

195. **(C)** Form 941 must be filed to report employers' quarterly federal tax returns.

196. **(B)** The type of services, quality, and payment policies are important factors to select a supplier, not the location.

197. **(A)** Hardship cases are patients who are poor, uninsured, underinsured, or elderly, and on a limited income. They are one of the most common collection problems in health care fields. Physicians sometimes decide to treat patients with hardship cases for a reduced fee or for free.

198. **(E)** Common HMO cost-containment practices include requiring fewer overnight stays after certain surgeries and requiring preauthorization before a procedure.

199. **(A)** The body of a letter begins two lines below the salutation or subject line. It is single spaced with double spaces between paragraphs. Leave an extra line above and below a list and indent each item on the list five spaces from the margin.

200. **(B)** Notations include such information as the number and type of enclosures and the names of other people who receive copies of the letter. The notation is typed two lines below the signature or identification line.

201. **(B)** The accounts receivable balance represents the debit balance.

202. **(A)** The subscriber is the principal. A beneficiary is the person who receives the benefits. The terms "insurer" and "coordinator" are not used.

203. **(B)** A single-entry account is an account with only one charge, as, for example, when a vacationer consults a physician for illness.

204. **(C)** The magnetic ink character recognition code (MICR code), appears on the bottom of a check and consists of numbers and characters printed in magnetic ink.

205. **(D)** Government-sponsored insurance coverage for eligible individuals includes Medicare, Medicaid, TRICARE, and CHAMPVA.

206. **(C)** The abbreviation of NS indicates "no-show patient."

207. **(C)** An accounts receivable measures how fast outstanding accounts are being paid. The formula for figuring out the accounts receivable ratio is to divide the current accounts receivable balance by the average gross monthly charges.

208. **(B)** When rebilling is necessary, make a copy of the original claim form submitted and write *"SECOND BILLING"* in red letters at the top. Reasons to rebill include correcting a mistake in billing, a need to detail charges to receive maximum reimbursement, to respond to a carrier's request and supply missing information, or to correct any wrong diagnosis or procedure codes.

209. **(D)** Color coding filing breaks the alphabet up into five different colors: red, yellow, green, blue, and purple. The last color, purple, covers the letters from R through Z.

210. **(E)** A scanner is a device that can convert printed matter and images to information that can be interpreted by the computer.

211. **(C)** Handling instructions should be placed three lines below the return address.

212. **(E)** You should always completely write out the date.

213. **(A)** The date is usually keyed on line 15, or two or three lines below the letterhead.

214. **(C)** *Expressway* is abbreviated as *EXPY*.

215. **(C)** You should capitalize all proper names, all titles, positions, names of organizations, racial, religious, and political designations, proper nouns such as trade names, specific addresses and geographic locations, titles, headings of books, magazines, and newspapers, and the days of the week, months, and holidays.

216. **(D)** You can divide according to pronunciation, compound words between the two words, hyphenated compound words at the hyphen, after a prefix, before a suffix, between two consonants that appear between vowels, being *-ing* unless the last consonant id doubled, in which case divide before the second consonant. Do not divide such suffixes as *-sion*, *-tial*, and *-gion*. Also do not divide a word so that only one letter is left on a line.

217. **(E)** The felt side of letterhead is the side from which the watermark is readable and the side on which printing and typing should be done.

218. **(B)** A full-block letter is typed with all the lines flush left. It is quick and easy to write. It is often used in medical practices.

219. **(A)** A restrictive endorsement includes the words *"for deposit only"* making it impossible for anyone other than the bank to cash the check.

220. **(D)** Under a staff model HMO, the physicians are employees of the HMO and work full-time seeing member patients. In this type of HMO, a primary care physician is assigned as the gatekeeper for patients.

221. **(B)** The body of the letter should be single-spaced. Between paragraphs, use double spacing. For multi-page letters, use letterhead only for the first page and blank quality bond paper for the second page. The second page should contains the name of the addressee, page number, date, and subject in the header.

222. **(E)** The most common insurance claim form is the HCFA-1500.

223. **(D)** The physician must be paid for services so as to be able to pay expenses and continue to treat patients. Not collecting medical bills may imply guilt in a malpractice suit. Abandoning accounts encourages non-payers and other paying patients subsidize the cost of medical care for those who can pay but do not.

224. **(A)** A participating provider is not allowed to charge the patient for any differences between the actual charges and allowed charge. The patient is responsible for the co-payment, coinsurance, and deductible.

225. **(C)** The Labor Standards Act requires that you should keep employee health records on file for 3 years.

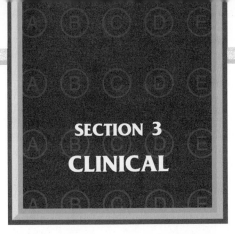

MEDICAL ASSISTING KNOWLEDGE

Self-Evaluation Answers and Rationales

Here you'll find the answers to the test on General Medical Assisting Knowledge in Part II on p. 437. Check your answers and note which questions you missed. Study the rationales for any questions you feel you had difficulty with and if you need more review, go back to the appropriate section in the chapters.

1. **(C)** If an injury occurs, you must take the following actions: wash your hands, cover the injury, report and document the injury, and get the injury treated. It is not necessary to send the report to the local health department.

2. **(C)** Failure to comply with OSHA standards could result in a maximum penalty of $7,000 for the first violation.

3. **(D)** The most common cause of hepatitis is a virus.

4. **(A)** Hepatitis B virus is the main blood-borne hazard for health care workers.

5. **(B)** Infected pregnant women can pass the spirochete of syphilis, HIV, and HBV to their babies during pregnancy or delivery.

6. **(C)** The average body temperature is 98.6°F (37°C).

7. **(D)** The supine position is also called the recumbent position.

8. **(D)** The basic unit of weight in the apothecaries' system is the grain.

9. **(B)** Chickenpox and measles, mumps, and rubella (MMR) vaccines can be administered subcutaneously.

10. **(C)** Oral agents may cause skin rash, vomiting, diarrhea, abdominal pain, or constipation. Intravenous agents can cause urticaria, skin reddening, anaphylaxis, or death.

11. **(A)** A rad is a measurement of the actual absorbed dose of radiation.

12. **(C)** A three-point gait is used by patients who can bear full weight on one leg and no weight on the other.

13. **(B)** Treatment of frostbite includes wrapping warm clothing or blankets around the affected body part and obtaining medical assistance. Do not rub or massage the affected area.

14. **(C)** Third-degree burns require removal of scars and skin grafting.

15. **(B)** To calculate the amount of skin surface burned on an adult, you should use the rule of nines. Mr. Brown's chest, abdomen, and upper back each accounts for approximately 9% of the skin surface; 9% ×3 = 27%. His genital area counts as 1%. The total comes to 28%.

16. **(C)** Lacerations are cuts with jagged edges.

17. **(C)** The majority of accidental poisonings occur at home to children under the age of 5 years.

18. **(C)** The patient's elbow should be bent at a 30° angle.

19. **(B)** The AIDS virus infection cycle has four stages: acute HIV infection, asymptomatic latency period, AIDS-related complex (ARC), and full-blown AIDS.

20. **(D)** A body temperature reading above 105.8°F (41°C) is called hyperpyrexia.

21. **(B)** In both the proctologic and the jackknife position, the hips of the patient are flexed at a 90° angle. In the proctologic position, the patient lies face down with both the torso and the legs lowered. In the jackknife position, the patient lies face up with both the torso and the legs raised.

22. **(D)** Bronchoscopy may be used for visual examination of the tracheobronchial tree and for removal of objects and tissue from it (e.g., by suctioning or biopsy).

23. **(C)** A barium swallow is also called an upper GI series.

24. **(D)** A body temperature above 106.0°F (41.1°C) is generally fatal.

25. **(D)** Cryosurgery can destroy abnormal cells by freezing.

26. **(A)** An example of an emulsion is cod liver oil, which is a mixture of oils in water.

27. **(A)** In the metric system, 1000 micrograms equal one milligram.

28. **(C)** The T wave represents the recovery of the ventricles.

29. **(B)** A scan is an image produced on film by a sweeping beam of radiation.

30. **(C)** Open wounds include punctures, lacerations, abrasions, and incisions. Contusions or bruises are examples of closed wounds.

31. **(C)** Epistaxis (nosebleed) is usually caused by a trauma, hypertension (not hypotension), exposure to high altitudes, or an upper respiratory infection.

32. **(C)** The cardiac cycle is composed of a complete phase of atrial contraction and ventricular contraction.

33. **(B)** The half-life of rabies immune globulins is approximately 21 days.

34. **(D)** Electrode devices may be cleaned with alcohol, warm water, or steel wool.

35. **(B)** One teaspoon of liquid in the household system is equal to 60 drops.

36. **(B)** The incidence of meningococcal disease peaks in the late winter to early spring. Attack rates are highest among children 3–12 months of age and then steadily decline among older age groups.

37. **(A)** On the ECG, the P, R, T, and U waves curve upward. The Q and S waves curve downward.

38. **(B)** One heartbeat produces a pattern of waves designated P, Q, R, S, T, and sometimes U.

39. **(C)** The preparation for an MRI includes asking the patient about possible allergies to contrast media, iodine, or shellfish. You should also ask whether any internal metallic materials are present, and the patient should avoid caffeine for 4 hours before the examination.

40. **(A)** The basic elements of cast care that should be explained to the patient are: keep the cast dry (not wet); report pain, swelling, or discoloration; keep the extremity elevated for the first day; and restrict strenuous activity for the first few days.

41. **(E)** Pregnant women and AIDS patients should not handle cat litter boxes to avoid toxoplasmosis.

42. **(D)** If the rate of the heart is more than 150 beats per minute, and less than 250 beats per minute, this is called atrial tachycardia.

43. **(B)** The angle of insertion of a needle for intradermal injections is 15 degrees.

44. **(D)** Acardiac rhythm is also called asystole or ventricular fibrillation.

45. **(C)** Weber's test is a method of screening auditory acuity. The test is performed by placing the stem of a vibrating tuning fork in the center of a person's forehead. The loudness of the sound is equal in both ears if hearing is normal. Weber's test evaluates whether hearing is the same in both ears. The Rinne test is performed by placing the stem of a vibrating tuning fork on the mastoid process of the ear until the patient no longer hears it.

46. **(A)** The most common sites for intramuscular injection are the vastus lateralis, deltoid, and gluteus medius.

47. **(B)** Echocardiography is recorded on paper. It is obtained by ultrasound (not by stethoscope). It is used to evaluate the inner structures of the heart and can indicate such conditions as fluid accumulation.

48. **(D)** Computed tomography (CT) is a radiographic technique that produces a film representing a detailed cross-section of tissue structure.

49. **(C)** Topical administration is used in treating skin disorders. Topical medications come in sprays, creams, lotions, ointments, patches, and compresses. A douche is a solution administered by the vaginal route.

50. **(C)** Hypothermia is a medical emergency. The body temperature is dangerously below the normal range, less than 96°F (taken rectally in adults) or 97.5°F (taken rectally in newborns).

51. **(D)** Total hand washing time should be approximately 10 minutes.

52. **(B)** Kaposi's sarcoma is a malignancy of the skin and lymph nodes that often occurs in AIDS patients. It is the most common HIV-related cancer.

53. **(A)** Destruction of all living microorganisms by specific means is called sterilization.

54. **(A)** *Decontamination* is a term used by OSHA to describe the use of physical or chemical means to remove, inactivate, or destroy blood-borne pathogens on a surface or item to the point where they are no longer capable of transmitting infection.

55. **(C)** The most common positions for taking X-rays are anteroposterior, posteroanterior, oblique, and lateral.

56. **(B)** Radiation exposure badges are also called dosimeters.

57. **(A)** The cholera vaccine is no longer recommended by the World Health Organization for travelers in cholera-infected areas.

58. **(B)** Atrial kick occurs when blood is pushed into the ventricles as a result of atrial contraction.

59. **(C)** Standard leads are also called bipolar leads because they monitor two electrodes. Leads I, II, and III are standard or bipolar leads.

60. **(D)** Range of motion is the degree to which a joint is able to move.

61. **(B)** Gait is the style of walking.

62. **(D)** The medical assistant may be asked to assist with several forms of physical therapy: applying cold or heat; teaching basic exercise; preparing patients for massage therapy; and demonstrating how to use a wheelchair, cane, or walker.

63. **(C)** The four corner squares of hemacytometers are subdivided into 16 squares.

64. **(C)** For treatment of poisonous snakebites, immediate attention is required. Call a doctor or the EMS system. The bitten area should be immobilized and positioned below heart level. Do not apply a tourniquet or ice, and do not cut or suction the wound.

65. **(C)** Staphylococci are gram-positive organisms.

66. **(B)** There are several types of moist heat applications, including hot soaks, hot compresses, hot packs, and paraffin baths.

67. **(B)** Electrocardiography requires six limb leads, three of which are standard (bipolar) and three of which are augmented.

68. **(A)** The normal range of the specific gravity of urine is between 1.010 and 1.030.

69. **(E)** Pneumococcal polysaccharide vaccine may be administered, IM or SC, to children who are at risk for and to adolescents who have chronic illnesses with increased risk for pneumococcal disease.

70. **(A)** Types of autoclaving include steam under pressure, dry heat, dry gas, and radiation.

71. **(E)** The procedure for obtaining specimens from infected wounds is similar to that of a throat culture.

72. **(C)** There are three types of sphygmomanometers: mercury, aneroid, and electronic. The mercury type is the most accurate.

73. **(A)** In the dorsal recumbent position, the patient lies face up with the knees flexed and the feet flat on the table.

74. **(C)** The stoppage of bleeding depends on the following components: the vascular system, platelets, blood coagulation factors, and fibrinolysis. Agglutinin is an antibody.

75. **(C)** In general, body temperature below 93.2°F (34°C) is fatal.

76. **(A)** The temporal artery is located in the temple area of the skull. It is seldom used to detect a pulse.

77. **(E)** Latex gloves are the most commonly used in the medical office.

78. **(B)** Blood stasis is lack of circulation due to a stoppage of blood flow.

79. **(E)** Tests to measure cholesterol in the blood are done with serum or plasma.

80. **(B)** The most dangerous of bacteria are destroyed at a temperature of 50°C to 60°C (122°F to 140°F).

81. **(C)** Instruments are considered sterile for 21–30 days.

82. **(C)** Splinter forceps have sharp points that are useful in removing foreign objects.

83. **(C)** Thrombocythemia is the presence of an excessive number of platelets in circulating blood.

84. **(E)** An antistreptolysin O (ASO) test is helpful in diagnosing rheumatic fever, glomerulonephritis, bacterial endocarditis, and scarlet fever.

85. **(C)** A number 15 blade is often used in performing minor surgeries.

86. **(C)** The most common sites for subcutaneous injections are the upper lateral part of the arms, the anterior thigh, the upper back, and the abdomen.

87. **(D)** The presence of a U wave that appears after the T wave may be due to slow recovery of the Purkinje fibers.

88. **(D)** Hemoglobin S is found in sickle cell anemia and also in sickle cell trait.

89. **(D)** Common neonatal tests screen for increased bilirubin, phenylketonuria, and hypothyroidism.

90. **(B)** Insulin, epinephrine, and allergy injections are commonly administered subcutaneously. Tuberculin skin tests are administered intradermally.

91. **(B)** Patients with chronic hepatitis face an increased risk of liver damage, such as cirrhosis of the liver, cancer of the liver, or liver failure.

92. **(E)** Urochrome is the yellow pigment that gives urine its color. It is produced by the breakdown of hemoglobin.

93. **(C)** Roller bandages are used as pressure bandages.

94. **(B)** The wound healing process takes place in three phases: lag, proliferation, and maturation.

95. **(D)** A physiatrist is a physician specializing in physical medicine and rehabilitation.

96. **(B)** Melena is an abnormal black tarry stool that contains digested blood.

97. **(C)** Triangular bandages are frequently used in first aid.

98. **(B)** Children two years of age and older should have annual checkups.

99. **(E)** Alpha-fetoprotein testing from amniotic fluid is used for early diagnosis of fetal neural tube defects and anencephaly.

100. **(C)** Hepatitis E is a common disease of the liver in Southeast Asia. It is a self-limited type of hepatitis. HEV is frequently seen in the rainy season or after natural disasters because of fecally contaminated water or food.

101. **(E)** The random specimen is the most common method of urine collection.

102. **(E)** The normal respiration rate in newborns is between 30 and 50 per minute.

103. **(D)** Reagent strips are known informally as dipsticks.

104. **(C)** In preparation for mammography, patients should avoid caffeine for a week and also avoid the use of powder, deodorant, or perfume on the underarm area or breast before the examination.

105. **(C)** Apnea is a temporary cessation of respiration or periods of no respiration that last more than 15 seconds.

106. **(D)** Adolescents who are at increased risk for complications caused by influenza or who have contact with persons at increased risk for these complications can receive an annual influenza vaccine (in the period from September through December).

107. **(D)** A four-point crutch gait is a slow gait used by patients who can bear weight on both legs.

108. **(B)** In phlebotomy, the needle is inserted into the vein at approximately a 15° angle.

109. **(A)** Concussion is a jarring injury to the brain. It is the most common type of head injury.

110. **(D)** The medical assistant may be responsible for administering the Ishihara color vision acuity test.

111. **(A)** Blood type O (in particular, type O, Rh–) is called the "universal donor."

112. **(C)** Lymphocytes are the smallest leukocytes and contain the largest nucleus.

113. **(B)** Serologic tests are performed on samples that do not contain additives, the color code for which is red.

114. **(C)** Trendelenburg's position is the "shock position."

115. **(C)** Dislocation is the displacement of bones at a joint.

116. **(A)** The use of the Z-track method prevents the deposited iron from seeping back into the skin layers.

117. **(B)** HCG levels will be lower in an ectopic pregnancy.

118. **(D)** The rectum is examined in the knee-chest (genupectoral) position for both males and females.

119. **(B)** Pathogens are organisms that cause disease.

120. **(D)** Septic shock may be partly due to the effects of exotoxins or other chemical mediators on resistance vessels, resulting in vasodilation and decreased vascular resistance. Anaphylactic shock occurs following allergic reactions.

121. **(B)** Hepatitis B is also called serum hepatitis.

122. **(C)** Several factors may be the cause of hypotension. They include anemia, dehydration, shock, hemorrhage, cancer, starvation, infection, high fever, and certain medications. Kidney disorders may cause hypertension.

123. **(A)** Temperatures of 120°C or greater are usually required to destroy spore cells.

124. **(A)** For injection of the vastus lateralis site, the patient may be in the recumbent position.

125. **(D)** Triglycerides are simple fat compounds consisting of three molecules of fatty acid. Measuring triglyceride levels in the blood requires fasting specimens.

126. **(A)** Colposcopy is the examination of the vagina and cervix with an optical magnifying instrument. It is commonly performed after a Pap smear to obtain biopsy specimens of the cervix.

127. **(B)** Tonometers are instruments for measuring tension or pressure of the intraocular region. They are used for the detection of glaucoma.

128. **(D)** The standing position is used for musculoskeletal, neurological, and peripheral vascular system examinations.

129. **(B)** Ear irrigation is the flushing of the ear canal to remove impacted cerumen, to relieve inflammation, or to remove a foreign body.

130. **(D)** The Mantoux tuberculin test requires the use of a short needle with a gauge of 26 to 27.

131. **(A)** A score of 10 or above indicates average color vision. A score of less than 7 may indicate color vision deficiency.

132. **(C)** Tomography is the procedure performed to view a cross-section of an organ.

133. **(B)** Invasive procedures are techniques that require entry into a body cavity or interruption of body functions. Examples include the Pap test, colonoscopy, sigmoidoscopy, and intravenous pyelography. The urine pregnancy test is not an invasive procedure.

134. **(B)** For rectal examinations, Sims' position, the knee-chest position, the dorsal recumbent position, and the proctologic position are used.

135. **(B)** One fluid ounce is equal to 6 teaspoons.

136. **(C)** The hub, shaft, lumen, point, and bevel are parts of a needle. The flange (rim) is a part of the syringe.

137. **(D)** Vaccines are made from dead or harmless infectious agents. They trigger the immune response in the body to manufacture antibodies against the particular disease-causing agent.

138. **(D)** The International Health Regulations require a booster dose for yellow fever every 10 years.

139. **(E)** Cholecystectomy means surgical removal of the gallbladder.

140. **(D)** Each muscle cell in the heart is stimulated to contract by going through an electrical process called the action potential. The action potential is composed of five phases.

141. **(B)** The angle of insertion for performing tuberculin tests is 15°, almost parallel to the skin surface.

142. **(E)** Wrapped items autoclaved with steam require 30 pounds of pressure at 132°C (270°F) for 20 minutes. Unwrapped items require only 10 minutes of autoclaving, which is known as flashing.

143. **(E)** Laparoscopy is the examination of the abdominal cavity with a laparoscope through one or more small incisions in the abdominal wall. A general anesthetic is used.

144. **(E)** A device for determining the specific gravity of urine is called a urinometer or urometer.

145. **(A)** The primary property of myocardial cells is contractility.

146. **(C)** A contrast bath is actually two baths, one filled with hot water and the other with cold water. The patient quickly moves the affected body part from one to the other.

147. **(D)** In the distance vision acuity test, which is usually given with the Snellen chart, the distance between the patient and the chart should be 20 feet.

148. **(C)** Sphygmomanometers are the instruments used to measure blood pressure. A manometer is an instrument used to measure the pressure of a liquid or a gas.

149. **(A)** Rectal temperature is the most accurate measurement of body temperature. Axillary temperature is the least accurate measurement.

150. **(D)** The most appropriate site to perform capillary puncture in infants is the heel.

151. **(B)** Cryotherapy is treatment using dry cold or wet cold applications to prevent swelling, to control bleeding, and to reduce inflammation.

152. **(C)** The S-T segment, which connects the end of the QRS complex with the beginning of the T wave, represents the time between contraction of the ventricles and recovery.

153. **(D)** In an intermittent fever, symptoms disappear completely between paroxysms.

154. **(B)** Suture material is also called ligature.

155. **(C)** Premature ventricular contractions are usually normal and can occur in healthy persons with apparently normal hearts. Causes of abnormal PVCs include hypoxia; an increase in catecholamines; and substances such as alcohol, tobacco, and caffeine.

156. **(D)** Fluidotherapy is a relatively new technique in which the patient places the hand or foot in a container of glass beads that are heated and agitated with hot air.

157. **(B)** Nonabsorbable sutures range in thickness from size 11-0 to size 7-0.

158. **(C)** Nicotine and nitroglycerin patches deliver medication by the transdermal route. The drug is absorbed continuously through the skin and enters the bloodstream directly.

159. **(D)** Death rates from HIV infections have been declining in the United States mostly as a result of antiretroviral therapy.

160. **(E)** In the prone position, the patient lies face down. This position is used for examination of the back and feet. It is not appropriate for patients who are obese, pregnant (late stage), or elderly or who have difficulties of the respiratory system.

161. **(B)** Abrasions are wounds in which the outer layers of the skin are rubbed off, resulting in an oozing of blood from ruptured capillaries.

162. **(A)** A cream is a drug combined in a base that is generally nongreasy, resulting in a semisolid preparation.

163. **(C)** The vastus lateralis muscle in the thigh is the preferred injection site for infants and children under 3 years of age.

164. **(E)** Bacitracin is used in cultures to give an early indication of the presence of group A streptococci.

165. **(B)** Hyperlipidemia may give plasma or serum a milky, or turbid, appearance.

166. **(C)** The end result of severe hyperglycemia is the development of diabetic coma. Symptoms are rapid breathing, dry skin, acetone breath, and confusion.

167. **(C)** Hemolysis is the breakdown of red blood cells and the accompanying release of hemoglobin that occurs normally at the end of the life span the cells. In the laboratory, hemolysis sometimes causes plasma to become pink or red in color.

168. **(A)** Ultrasound is the most common type of diathermy. It projects high-frequency sound waves that are converted to heat in muscle tissue.

169. **(D)** Hemiparesis is muscular weakness in one half of the body.

170. **(C)** Cardiomalacia is the softening of the heart.

171. **(A)** BCG vaccination is not recommended for children infected with HIV.

172. **(D)** Cystoscopy is the examination of the bladder by visualization and inspection with a special instrument called a cystoscope.

173. **(C)** OSHA regulations mandate training within 90 days of the effective date of assignment and annually thereafter.

174. **(C)** The appropriate medium for throat cultures (to detect streptococcus) is blood agar.

175. **(A)** Heme (part of hemoglobin) can be responsible for changing the color of serum to green.

176. **(D)** A loss of 25 to 40 percent of a patient's total blood volume can be life-threatening or fatal.

177. **(C)** In sensitivity testing, a clear zone around the disk indicates that the antimicrobial agent is effective.

178. **(D)** Stroking is the most common massage modality used in the medical office.

179. **(A)** In preparation for cholecystography, the oral contrast medium should be taken about 2 hours after dinner.

180. **(D)** Clean sensors usually are not a cause of artifacts.

181. **(E)** Prefilled syringes are known as cartridges.

182. **(D)** Minor surgery is commonly performed in physicians' or dentists' offices. Procedures involving cutting or scraping (such as circumcision or the removal of a sebaceous cyst, wart, or foreign object) are considered minor surgery, as is the insertion of an intrauterine device (IUD). Barium enemas are rectal infusions of barium sulfate, which is retained in the lower intestinal tract during X-ray studies.

183. **(C)** Specific gravity can be measured with urinometers, reagent strips (dipsticks), and refractometers.

184. **(A)** Kyphosis is abnormally increased convex curvature of the thoracic spine. It is also colloquially called hunchback or humpback.

185. **(E)** Blood-borne pathogens in the office can be destroyed by sodium hypochlorite, the active ingredient in household bleach.

186. **(E)** Overexposure is not likely from routine X-rays, especially if precautions are taken. Overexposure can produce a variety of symptoms, including nausea, fatigue, and bleeding.

187. **(C)** Aspirin impairs the ability of platelets to form aggregates.

188. **(D)** Leads aVR, aVL, and aVF are augmented limb leads.

189. **(C)** Needles used for administering medication commonly range in gauge from 18 to 27.

190. **(A)** Needle biopsy of the breast requires surgical asepsis.

191. **(E)** In Trendelenburg's position, the patient lies on the back with the head lower than the legs. This position is used for abdominal surgery and for patients who are in shock.

192. **(C)** The need for radiation therapy is not a risk factor for HIV transmission.

193. **(E)** Autoclaves should be cleaned after each load.

194. **(C)** A prognosis is the likely outcome of a disorder, that is, a prediction of the probable course of a disease in an individual and the chances of recovery.

195. **(D)** Positron emission tomography (PET) involves injecting isotopes combined with other substances, such as glucose. The positrons that are emitted are processed by a computer and displayed on a screen. This technique is useful for diagnosis of brain-related conditions, such as epilepsy and Parkinson's disease.

196. **(B)** Megakaryocytes are precursors of blood platelets, the largest cells found in the bone marrow. They are normally not present in circulating blood.

197. **(E)** Xeroradiography, also called xerography, produces images electrically, permits shorter exposure times, and requires less radiation than standard X-rays.

198. **(B)** Hypodermic syringes are available in 2-, 2.5-, 3-, and 5-cc sizes. They are commonly used to administer intramuscular injections.

199. **(D)** Proctology is a branch of medicine concerned with treating disorders of the colon, rectum, and anus.

200. **(B)** *Zephiran*® (benzalkonium chloride) is used to detect alcohol levels in blood.

201. **(C)** The Papanicolaou test (Pap smear) is used to determine the presence of abnormal or precancerous cells in the cervix and vagina. The patient is instructed not to have intercourse within 48 hours before the test.

202. **(D)** According to recommended childhood immunization schedules, the first measles, mumps, and rubella (MMR) vaccination should be given at between 12 and 15 months, and the second should be given at 4–6 years of age.

203. **(C)** A drug dose of 120 mg administered in 15 mg tablets would require that 8 tablets be taken.

204. **(A)** The patient's gait means the style of walking.

205. **(E)** Leukocytosis is an abnormal increase in the number of circulating white blood cells.

206. **(D)** An occult blood test is a chemical test or microscopic examination for the presence of blood, especially in the feces.

207. **(A)** A blood collection tube containing EDTA is colored purple.

208. **(E)** Forearm crutches are also called Lofstrand or Canadian crutches.

209. **(D)** In preparation for intravenous pyelography, the patient should have no food or liquids after the preceding midnight. Patients who are to be given a barium enema may have one cup of coffee, tea, or water on the morning of the procedure.

210. **(D)** Artifacts include a wandering baseline, a flat line, and extraneous marks.

211. **(E)** Autoclave indicator tape turns black after autoclaving.

212. **(D)** Measuring the amount of urine output in a 24-hour period is helpful in diagnosing renal disease, dehydration, urinary tract obstructions, and pheochromocytoma.

213. **(D)** The autoclave temperature is most commonly set between 250°F and 270°F.

214. **(B)** Orthostatic hypotension is abnormal, temporary low blood pressure. It occurs when a patient moves rapidly from a lying to a standing position. It is also called postural hypotension.

215. **(D)** Anaphylactic shock, or anaphylaxis, may occur following allergic reactions.

216. **(C)** Tubes coded red contain no additive. They are used for blood chemistries, AIDS antibody tests, viral studies, serologic tests, and blood typing.

217. **(E)** A centrifuge is a laboratory machine used to separate particles of different densities within a liquid by spinning them at very high speeds.

218. **(E)** Viruses can be seen only with an electron microscope. They are the smallest microorganisms.

219. **(D)** Rh negative blood is found in 15% of the population in the United States.

220. **(A)** Studies have shown that a regimen of one dose of HRIG and five doses of HDCV over a 28-day period is safe and effective against rabies.

221. **(D)** Lens paper may be used to clean microscope lenses.

222. **(D)** OSHA regulations require hepatitis B vaccination for all health care employees who are at risk.

223. **(B)** The radial artery is the most commonly used site for measuring the pulse rate.

224. **(A)** Formalin is a diluted solution of formaldehyde used to preserve biological specimens.

225. **(C)** According to the rule of nines, the chest counts as 9% of the body surface, the abdomen 9%, the right upper limb 9%, and the genital area 1%, which total 28%.

226. **(B)** The tricuspid valve separates the right atrium and the right ventricle, and the mitral valve separates the left atrium and the left ventricle. The septum separates the left and right halves of the heart (each containing one atrium and one ventricle).

227. **(A)** Stereoscopy is a rarely used X-ray procedure primarily for studying the skull.

228. **(D)** The Ishihara test is used to measure color vision acuity.

229. **(D)** Augmented leads are also called unipolar leads.

230. **(E)** The control the center for breathing is in the medulla oblongata.

231. **(B)** For blood cultures, tubes coded yellow are used.

232. **(D)** Warning labels for health hazards are color-coded blue.

233. **(B)** Sublingual administration is the placement of a medication under the tongue until it dissolves.

234. **(E)** Hemoptysis is the coughing up of blood from the respiratory tract.

235. **(D)** A baby born to a woman who carries the hepatitis B virus must receive the first vaccination at birth.

236. **(E)** At present, yellow fever occurs only in the African and South American jungles.

237. **(A)** Good Samaritan laws permit emergency care on the condition that it is within the scope of competence of the person administering first aid.

238. **(A)** OSHA regulations require that hazard warning labels display a color code. White indicates specific hazards such as radioactivity.

239. **(E)** Buccal administration is the placement of a drug in the mouth between the cheek and gum.

240. **(D)** Macrophages are monocytes (large leukocytes, or white blood cells) that mature outside the circulatory system, distributed in tissues throughout the body. They have a variety of names, such as histiocytes, Kupffer cells, osteoclasts, and microglial cells.

241. **(C)** Serum is the liquid portion of blood that remains after the clotting proteins and cells have been removed. Plasma differs from serum in that it contains fibrinogen, a protein involved in clotting.

242. **(B)** The normal rate (in ESR tests) at which red blood cells fall, often referred to as the sed rate, is 1 mm every five minutes.

243. **(E)** Temperatures of 116°F or above can cause burns.

244. **(C)** Probes are long, slender instruments used to explore wounds or body cavities.

245. **(A)** Excessive EDTA may shrink erythrocytes.

246. **(D)** Goniometers are devices used to measure the degree of joint movement.

247. **(B)** Infusion is the introduction of a substance (such as electrolytes, nutrients, fluids, or drugs) directly into a vein.

248. **(B)** About 85% of the U.S. population has Rh+ blood.

249. **(B)** The most common gauge range of needles used for venipuncture is 19–20.

250. **(C)** After surgery, sutures generally remain in place for 5 to 6 days.

CLINICAL

Index

Note: Generic names are in roman type; product names are in italic type.

Adduction, 18
Adductor magnus muscle, 50
aden / o, 23
Adenocarcinoma, 46, 80
    of vagina, 81
adenoid / o, 28
Adenoma, 46
adenosine triphosphate (ATP), 45
ADH (antidiuretic hormone), 32, 57
ADH (vasopressin), 32, 57, 66
adip / o, 14
Adipose tissue, 45
Adjustment column, 215
ad lib (as desired), 11
Administer, 112
Administration of drugs, 114–115,
    300–305
    "seven rights" of, 300–301
Administrative-issue telephone calls,
    185
Administrative supplies, 211
Adolescents, immunization schedule
    for, 307
Adrenal cortex, 58
Adrenal glands, 56, 66
Adrenal medulla, 54, 58
adrenal / o, 23
Adrenal steroids, 125
Adrenergic blockers, 124
Adrenergic drugs, 122, 124
Adrenocorticotropic hormone
    (ACTH), 25, 57
Adults, meningitis types in, 81
Advance directives, 160
Advance scheduling, 193
Adverse effects
    of contrast media, 324
    of drugs, 111
Aerobe, 101
Aerosol, 112, 296
af-, 3
AF (atrial fibrillation), 27, 318
Afebrile, 272
Aflatoxin, 100
After (p), 12
After noon (PM, p.m.), 12
ag-, 3
Ag (antigen), 77, 364
Agar, 383
Agenda, for meetings, 188
Agglutination, 60, 364
Agglutinin, 60, 364
Agglutinogen, 60
-agon, 25
Agonal rhythm, 318
A/GR (albumin-globulin ratio), 364
Agranulocyte, 60

Agranulocytosis, 86
Aided mobility exercises, 336
AIDS (acquired immunodeficiency
    syndrome), 34, 89, 254, 255.
    See also HIV (human immun-
    odeficiency virus)
AIDS patients, communicating with,
    173
AIDS-related complex (ARC), 254
al-, 3
-al, 6
Alanine, 138
alb-, 3
Alb (albumin), 59, 364
    normal urinalysis value for, 379
Albinism, 78
albin / o, 14
Albumin (Alb), 59, 364
    normal urinalysis value for, 379
Albumin-globulin ratio (A/GR), 364
albumin / o, 31
Alcohol (Alc), 364
Aldosterone, 58, 66
-algesia, 19
-algia, 19
Alimentary canal, 64
Allergic reaction, 109, 111
    to foods, 144
Allergic rhinitis, 86
Allowed charge, 234–235
Alpha-adrenergic blocking agents,
    124
Alpha-adrenergic drugs, 122, 124
Alphabetical filing, 195
Alpha-fetoprotein testing, 283
Alphanumeric filing, 195
ALS (amyotrophic lateral sclerosis),
    20, 83
Alveoli, 63
alveol / o, 28
Alzheimer's disease (AD), 20, 83
am, AM (morning), 11
Amantadine (Symmetrel), 117, 122
ambi-, 3
Ambulatory surgery, 284
Amendments to the Older Ameri-
    cans Act, 156
Amenorrhea, 90
American Hospital Association, 196
American Medical Association, 196
Amino acids
    essential type of, 138
    nonessential type of, 138
Aminoglycoside, 116
Amiodarone (Cordarone), 128
amni / o, 32
Amniocentesis, 160

Amniotomy, 160
Amount (amt), 11
Amphotericin B (Fungizone), 118
Amplitude, 317
Ampule, 112, 304
amt (amount), 11
Amylase test, 371
Amyotrophic lateral sclerosis (ALS),
    20, 83
an-, 3
ana-, 3
Anabolism, 65
Anacusis, 84
Anaerobe, 101
Anal canal, 65
Analgesics, 110, 122–124
Anaphylactic shock, 352
Anaphylaxis, 111
Anatomical model, 189
andr / o, 23
Androgen(s), 58, 111, 129, 130
Anemia, 85, 376
Anencephaly, 160
Anesthesia, 284
Anesthetic(s), 122, 284
Aneurysm, 85
Angina pectoris, 85
angi / o, 26
Angiography, 318, 325
Angioplasty, 281
Angiotensin-converting enzyme
    (ACE) inhibitors, 126
Angiotensin II, 66
Angry patients, 172
Animal bites, treatment of, 350–351
Anion, 44
Anisocytosis, 60, 376
ankyl / o, 16
Annotating mail, 178
an / o, 29
Anode, 315
Anorexia nervosa, 144
Anoscope, 277, 278, 282
Anosmia, 86
Answering service, 185
Answering system, 185
Antacids, 111, 128
Antagonism, 111
ante-, 3
Ante partum, 68
Anterior pituitary, 57
Anteroposterior X-ray, 327
Anthracosis, 86
Anthrax, 82
Antiallergic drugs, 128
Antianginal drugs, 125
Antianxiety drugs, 110

Antiarrhythmic drugs, 111, 126, 127–128
Antibiotics, 110, 115–118
Antibody (Ab), 77, 364
Anticoagulant (EDTA), 368
Anticoagulant agents, 111, 126, 367, 368
Anticonvulsant drugs, 110
Antidepressants, 110, 121
Antidiuretic hormone (ADH), 32, 57
Antidote(s), 113, 114
Antiemetic drugs, 111
Antiepileptic drugs, 110, 121–122
Antifungal agents, 110, 117, 118
Antigen (Ag), 77, 364
Antihidrotic drugs, 110
Antihistamines, 111, 128
Antihypercholesterolemic drugs, 111
Antihypertensive drugs, 111, 125–126, 127
Antihypnotic drugs, 110
Anti-inflammatory drugs, 118
  adrenal steroid type of, 125
Antimicrobials, 115
Antiparkinsonian drugs, 110, 122
Antipruritics, 110, 118
Antipsychotic drugs, 110, 120
Antipyretics, 272
Antisecretory drugs, 110, 128
Antisepsis, 103
Antiseptic(s), 103, 118, 257, 368
Antiserum, 364
Antistreptolysin O (ASO) antibodies, in blood tests, 372
Antitubercular agents, 117
Antitussive drugs, 111
Antivenereal drugs, 111
Antiviral agents, 117
Anuria, 378
Anus, 64, 67, 68
Aorta, 61, 62
  coarctation of, 79
Aortic aneurysm, 318
Aortic arch, 61
Aortic branch, 62
Aortic semilunar valve, 61
Aortic stenosis (AS), 27
Aortic valve, 314
aort / o, 26
ap-, 3
Apex of heart, 314
-apharesis, 27
Apical pulse, 273
Aplastic, 76
Aplastic anemia, 86
Apnea, 274

Apocrine secretion mode, 46
Apothecaries' system, 10, 297–298, 299
  conversion factors for, 10
Appeal, of legal decision, 152
Appendicitis, 87
Appendicular skeleton, 49
append / o, 29
Application software, 200–201
Applying electrodes, 315, 316
Appointment grouping, 193
Appointment scheduling, 189–193
  book for, 189, 191
  cards for, 192
Appointment types, 190
Approved referral (authorization), 239
aq (water), 11
aque / o, 20
Aqueous humor, 55
ar-, 3
-ar, 6
Arbitration, 152
ARC (AIDS-related complex), 254
-arche, 34
ARDS (acute respiratory distress syndrome), 29
ARF (acute renal failure), 32
Arginine, 138
Arranging instruments, 277
Arrhythmia, 317
Arterial blood, 58
Arterial blood gas, 374
Arterial pH, 374
arteri / o, 26
Arteriosclerosis, 85
arter / o, 26
Artery, 48, 62
Arthritis, 82
arthr / o, 16
Arthrography, 325
  preparation for, 326
Articulation, 48
Artifacts
  in ECGs, 317
  in radiography, 324
Artificial active immunity, 77
Artificial immunity, 305
Artificial insemination, 159
Artificial passive immunity, 77
ARU telephone systems, 187–188
as-, 3
AS (aortic stenosis), 27
AS (left ear), 23
Asbestosis, 86
Ascending aorta, 61
ASD (atrial septal defect), 27

As desired (ad lib), 11
-ase, 30
Asepsis, 103
  medical requirements for, 255–258
  OSHA requirements for, 258–261
  surgical requirements for, 255–258, 285–286
Aseptic hand washing, 256, 257
As needed (p.r.n., PRN), 12
ASO (antistreptolysin O) antibodies, in blood tests, 372
Asparagine, 138
Aspartic acid, 138
Aspirin (*Bayer, Bufferin, Anacin*), 123
Assault, 151
Assertiveness, 171
Assets, in bookkeeping, 212
Assignment of benefits, 234
Assumption of risk, 152
ast (astigmatism), 22, 84
-asthenia, 17
Asthma, 86, 356
  medications for, 128, 129
Astigmatism (ast), 22, 84
Astringents, 118
Astrocyte, 52
Asymptomatic latency period, 254
Asystole, 317
at-, 3
Atelectasis, 86
Atherosclerosis, 85
Atlas, 49
Atom, 44
Atomic number, 44
Atomic weight, 44
ATP (adenosine triphosphate), 45
Atresia, 76
Atrial fibrillation (AF), 27, 318
Atrial flutter, 318
Atrial kick, 314
Atrial septal defect (ASD), 27
atri / o, 26
Atrium, 61
Atrophy, 82
Atropine, 122
Atropine sulfate (*Isopto Atropine*), 125
Attaching electrodes, 315
Attaching wires, 316
Attitude, in communicating, 171
AU (each ear), 23
Audiologist, 281
Audiology tests, 281
Audiometer, 281
Auditing accounts, 212

Glucagon, 58
Glucose blood test (fasting blood sugar, FBS), 138, 373–374
　normal range of, 370
Glucose tolerance test (GTT), 25, 365, 374
Glutamic acid, 138
Glutamine, 138
Gluteus maximus muscle, 50, 51
Gluteus medius muscle, 50, 51, 304
Glycine, 138
glyc / o, 24
Glycoprotein, tumor associated type of, 372
Glycosuria, 381
gm (gram), 11, 297, 299
GnRH, 57
Goblet cell, 45
Goiter, 84
Golgi apparatus, 43, 44
Gonad, 66
Gonadal hormones, 129–130
gonad / o, 24
Goniometer, 332, 334
Goniometry, 332, 333–334
gon / o, 33
Gonorrhea, 88
Good Samaritan Act, 155, 345
Gooseneck lamp, 277
Gopher internet tool, 201
Gout, 82
gr (grain), 297, 299
Graafian follicle, 68
Gracilis muscle, 50
Grain (gr), 297, 299
-gram, 6
Gram (g, gm), 11, 297, 299
Gram-negative bacteria, 98–99
Gram-positive bacteria, 98
Gram's stain, 98, 372, 383
　limitations of, 98
　procedure for, 384
Grand mal seizure, 121
Granular leukocytes, 60, 363
Granulocyte, 60
Graphical user interface (GUI), 200
Graphics software, 201
-graphy, 6
Grasping forceps, 288
Graves' disease, 85
-gravida, 34
Greenstick fracture, 83
Greeting patients, 174
Grief, 161
Griseofulvin (Grifulvin), 118
Group insurance policies, 236
Group model HMO, 238

Group practice, 158
Growth hormone (GH), 25, 57
gt (drop), 299
GTT (glucose tolerance test), 25, 365, 374
Guard cap, of syringe, 305
GUI (graphical user interface), 200
Gustatory sense, 54
GYN (gynecology), 34
gynec / o, 33
Gynecologic examination, 282–283
Gynecology (GYN), 34

H

h (hour), 12
H. influenzae vaccine, 306
Haemophilus ducreyi, 98
Haemophilus influenzae, 81, 98
Hair follicle, 48
Hair shaft, 48
Half-life in body, for drug, 111
Haloperidol (Haldol), 120
Hamstring muscle, 51
Handling instructions, on mail, 184
Hand washing, 256
　aseptic procedures for, 103
　facility for, 260
Hard drive, 198–199
Hardship cases, 221
Hardware, of computers, 197–199
Hashimoto's disease, 85
Hazardous materials. See also Bio-hazard(s)
　chemical types of, 253
　mailing of, 176
　penalties for improper disposal of, 259
　warning label for, 260
Hb (hemoglobin), 60, 363, 365
　normal test range of, 370
　tests of, 371
HbF (hemoglobin F), 371
HCG (human chorionic gonadotropin), 34, 365
HCPCS, 241
Hct (hematocrit), 60, 371
　normal test range of, 370
HCV (hepatitis C virus), 365
HD (hemodialysis), 32
HDL (high-density lipoprotein), 138
Head injuries, 351–352
　severe types of, 352
Healing, of wounds, 289
Health care proxy, 161, 162
Health maintenance organization (HMO), 238

Hearing
　loss of, 281
　sense of, 55–56
Hearing impairment, and patient communications, 172
Heart, 54, 61–62, 314
　catheterization of, 318
　muscle condition of, 274
　rhythm of, 317
　sounds made by, 62, 274
　structures in, 314
　valves of, 61, 314
Heart attack, 353–355
Heart blocks, 318
Heart rate, 317
Heat cramps, 347
Heat exhaustion, 347
Heating pad, 335
Heat lamp, 335
Heat stroke, 347
Heat therapy, 335
hect-, 11, 298
hecto-, 298
Height, of patient, 275–276
Heimlich maneuver, 355–356
hema /, 26
Hemagglutination, 363
Hemagglutinin, 363
Hematemesis, 86, 353
hemat / o, 26
Hematocrit (Hct), 60, 371
　normal test range of, 370
Hematologic tests, 370
Hematology, 362–364
Hematoma
　in blood testing, 370
　of scalp, 351
Hematopoiesis, 362
　extramedullary type of, 376
Hematuria, 381
hemi-, 4, 19
Hemiparesis, 332
Hemiplegia, 83, 332
hem / o, 26
Hemochromatosis, 142
Hemocytoblast, 58, 59
Hemocytometer, 375, 376
Hemodialysis (HD), 32
Hemoglobin (Hb, Hgb), 60, 363, 365
　normal test range of, 370
　tests of, 371
Hemoglobin A, 371
Hemoglobin F (HbF), 371
Hemoglobin S, 371
Hemoglobinuria, 381
Hemolytic disease of the newborn, 376

Hemophilia, 376
    classic type of, 78
Hemoptysis, 86, 353
Hemorrhage, in blood testing, 370
Hemostasis, 60
Hemostatic forceps, 287, 288
Hemostats, 287, 288
Hemothorax, 87
Heparin, 367
Hepatitis, 88, 253
Hepatitis A, 253
    vaccine for, 307, 308
Hepatitis B, 253
    vaccine for, 253, 306, 307
Hepatitis C (non-A, non-B hepatitis), 253
Hepatitis C virus (HCV), 365
Hepatitis D, 253
Hepatitis E, 253
hepat / o, 30
Hepatocyte, 65
Hereditary diseases and conditions, 78
Hernia, 88
Herniated disk, 82
Herpes simplex, 89, 255
    virus (HSV) causing, 34, 365
Herpes zoster, 89, 255
Heterograft, 160
Heterotrophs, 101
Hgb (hemoglobin), 60, 363, 365
    normal test range of, 370
    tests of, 371
Hiatal hernia, 88
hidr / o, 14
High-calcium diet, 144
High-density lipoprotein (HDL), 138
High-fat diet, 144
High-fiber diet, 144
High-iron diet, 144
High-phosphorus diet, 144
Hilt, of needle, 304
Hirschprung's disease, 79
Histamine, 128
Histidine, 138
hist / o, 14
Histology, 45
Histoplasmosis, 86
HIV (human immunodeficiency virus), 34, 89, 173, 254, 365. *See also* AIDS
    antibody test for, 254
    drugs for, 118
    transmission of, 254
HIV/AIDS patients, communicating with, 173

HMO (health maintenance organization), 238
Holding forceps, 287, 288
Holocrine secretion mode, 46
Holter monitor cardiography, 281, 318
Home collection of urine, 378
home / o, 24
Homograft, 160
Hordeolum, 84
Hormone replacement therapy, 129
Hormones, 56, 57, 65
    of digestive system, 65
    effects on kidneys of, 66
hormon / o, 24
Hospitalization insurance, 235
Host, 101
Hot compress, 335
Hot soak, 335
Hot-water bottle, 335
Hour (h, hr), 12
24-hour specimen, 378
Household system, 298, 299
hr (hour), 12
h.s. (take medication at bedtime), 12
HSV (herpes simplex virus), 34, 365
Hub
    of needle, 304
    of syringe, 305
Human body
    microbes and, 101–102
    normal flora of, 101, 102
Human chorionic gonadotropin (HCG, hCG), 34, 365
Human immunodeficiency virus (HIV). *See* HIV
Humerus, 48
Humoral immune response, 77
Hydatidiform moles, 90
Hydralazine (*Apresoline*), 126
Hydrocephalus, 79
Hydrochlorothiazide (*Diucardin, Esidrix, HydroDIURIL*), 126, 129
Hydronephrosis, 88
Hydrotherapy, 336
Hyoid bone, 48
hyper-, 4
Hyperextension, 332
Hyperglycemia, 84, 352, 376
Hyperinsulinism, 85
Hyperlipidemia, 376
Hyperopia, 84
Hyperplasia, 79
Hyperpnea, 274
Hyperpyrexia, 272

Hypersensitivity, 77, 78
Hypertension, 274
Hyperthermia, 346–347
Hyperthyroidism, 84
Hypertonic solution, 44
Hypertrophy, 76
    of heart, 318
Hyperventilation, 356
Hypervitaminosis, 140
Hypnotic drugs, 119
hypo-, 4
Hypochromia, 376
Hypodermic syringes, 303
Hypoglycemia, 84, 352, 376
Hypolipidemic drugs, 126
Hypotension, 274–275
Hypothalamus, 53, 56, 57
Hypothermia, 272, 346
Hypothyroidism, 84
Hypotonic solution, 44
Hypovolemic shock, 352
hyster / o, 33

I

-iasis, 6, 30
-iatric, 6
-iatry, 6
Ibuprofen (*Advil, Motrin, Nuprin*), 123
-ic, 6
-ical, 6
Ice bag, 336
Ice collar, 336
Ice massage, 336
Icons, OSHA recommendations for, 260
ICSH (interstitial cell-stimulating hormone), 57
ID (intradermal administration route), 12, 115, 301–302
IDDM (insulin-dependent diabetes mellitus), 25
Identification line, in business letter, 179
Idiopathic, 76
Idoxuridine (*Herplex*), 118
il-, 4
Ileum, 64
Iliac arteries, 62
Ilium, 48
Illegal collection techniques, 221
im-, 4
IM (intramuscular injection route), 12, 115, 302–303, 304
Immediately (stat), 13
Immobilization, 337

PKU screening, 374
Placebo, 111
Placenta previa, 90
Plague, 86
Plaintiff, 151
-plasia, 7
Plasma (P), 59, 362, 365
Plasma hormonal concentration, 69
Plasma volume (PV), 365
plasm / o, 26
Plasmodium species, 100
-plasty, 7
Plate, 383, 384
Platelets (PLT), 362, 363, 364, 365
    normal test range for, 370
Playroom, for reception area,
    174–175
-plegia, 19
Pleurisy, 87
PLT (platelets), 362, 363, 364, 365
    normal test range for, 370
Plunger, of syringe, 305
Plural forms, 8, 183
p.m. (after noon), 12
PMS (premenstrual syndrome), 35
-pnea, 29
pneuma /, 28
pneumat / o, 28
pneum / o, 28
Pneumococcal polysaccharide vac-
    cine, 308
Pneumoconiosis, 86
Pneumocystis carinii, 100, 255
    pneumonia caused by, 89, 254
Pneumonia, 81, 86, 89, 254, 308
Pneumonic plague, 86
pneumon / o, 28
Pneumonoconiosis, 86
Pneumothorax, 87
p.o., PO (take medication by
    mouth), 12
Poikilocytosis, 60, 376
Point, of needle, 304
Pointer, on computer, 200
Point-of-service, 238
Poisons, 113, 114, 356
Polarity, 316
Polarization, 316
Policy and procedures manual,
    201–203
poli / o, 19
Poliomyelitis, 83
Polio vaccine, 306
Politeness, 173
poly-, 5
Polycystic renal disease, 88
Polycythemia, 86, 376

Polycythemia vera, 376
Polydactyly, 78
Polypharmacy, 111–112
Polyunsaturated fats, 138
Polyuria, 378
POMR (problem oriented medical
    records), 158, 195
Pons, 53
POR (problem oriented medical
    records), 158, 195
Position(s), for radiography, 326,
    327
Positioning electrodes, 315
Positioning patient for exam, 277,
    279, 280
Positron emission tomography
    (PET), 325
Posology, 111
Possessive forms, 8
    in writing, 183
post-, 5
Postage meter, 178
Postal money orders, 178
Postcards, 176
Postdated check, 218
Posterior pituitary, 57
Posteroanterior X-ray, 327
Posting entries, in bookkeeping, 213
Postprocedure care, 326
Postprocedure cleanup, 259
Posture
    as communication, 170
    testing of, 334
Potassium (K), 25, 141, 142
    blood tests for, 373
Potassium hydroxide (KOH) mount,
    383
Potassium oxalate, 368
Potassium-sparing diuretics, 129
Potency, of drugs, 111
Potentially infectious body fluids,
    252
Pound (lb), 297
Powder, 112
Power of attorney, durable type of,
    160–161, 162
PPO (preferred provider organiza-
    tion), 238
PR (rectal administration route), 12,
    115, 301
-prandial, 30
-praxia, 19
pre-, 5
Preauthorization, 239
Precertification, 239
Precordial lead, 315
Precut sutures, 288

Predated check, 218
Preeclampsia, 90
Preferred provider organization
    (PPO), 238
Prefilled syringe, 304
Prefixes
    of common medical terms, 3–5
    definition of, 2
    for endocrine system terms, 24
    in metric system, 298
    for nervous system terms, 19
Pregnancy
    ethics and, 159–160
    nutrition during, 142
    termination of, 159–160
    tests for, 283, 381
    urinalysis and, 382
Prejudice, in communicating, 172
Premature beat, 317
Premature contraction, 317
Premature ventricular contraction
    (PVC), 27, 317–318
Premenstrual syndrome (PMS), 35
Premium, 234
Preoperative patient education,
    189
Preparing the plate, 384
Preprocedure care, 326
Prepuce, 67
presby / o, 21
Presbyopia, 84
Prescription (Rx), 13, 112
    abbreviations in, 10–13
    pads for writing of, 304
Presentation software, 201
Pressure points, 353
Pressure receptor, 48
Prevailing charges, 234
Preventive drugs, 110
Primary diagnosis, 241
Primary vaccination, 309
primi-, 5
Printer, 199
P-R interval, 316–317
Priority mail, 175
Privacy
    invasion of, 151
    of patients, 152–153
Private delivery services, 178
Private law, 151
Privilege, of physician, 153
Privileged communication, 153
PRL (prolactin), 25, 57, 365
p.r.n., PRN (as needed), 12
PRN medication order, 305
Probes, 286, 287
Problem calls, 187

Reasonable fee, 234
Rebilling insurance claims, 243
Recalling mail, 178
Receipts, 215
Receiving supplies, 211
Reception area, 174–175
Receptionist position, 173–175
Reciprocity, 157
Reconciliation of bank statements, 215
Record keeping
    of accounts payable, 222
    for drug dispensing, 113
    of equipment maintenance, 366
    of medication administration, 305
    of payroll, 222
    of radiographs, 328
    by receptionist, 174
Rectal administration route (R, PR), 12, 115, 301
Rectal temperature, 272
rect / o, 30
Rectum, 64
Rectus abdominis muscle, 50
Rectus femoris muscle, 50
Red blood cells, 60, 362, 363, 365
    count of (RBC), 365
    normal range count of, 370
Reduction, 332
Reference laboratory log, 366
Referrals, 239
Reflecting, 171
Reflex hammer, 277, 278
Refractometer, 380, 381
Refractory period, 317
Refunds, 215
Regional enteritis (Crohn's disease), 87
Registered mail, 177
Registered trademark (®), 13
Registration
    for drug dispensing, 113
    legal type of, 157
    of new patients, 174
    patient form for, 193, 194
Regressive corpus luteum, 69
Regulated waste, 260
Rehabilitation, 332
Relative value scale (RVS), 239
Rem, 325
REM (rapid eye movement), 22
Reminder cards, 211–212
Remission, 14
Renal calculus, 88
Renal carcinoma, 80
Renal corpuscle, 66

Renal failure, 88
Renal tubule, 66
ren / i, / o, 31
Repeated violation, 259
Replacement drugs, 110
Repolarization, 316
Reproductive system, 66–68
    abbreviations of terms for, 34–35
    combining forms of root terms for, 32–33
    diseases and disorders of, 88–90
    drug types for, 111
    medical emergencies of, 356–357
    pharmacology for, 129–130
    suffixes of terms for, 34
Rescheduling, of appointments, 192
Reservations, for travel, 188
Reservoir host, 102
Res ipsa loquitur, 156
Resistance, 102
Resistance exercises, 336
Res judicata, 156
Resource-Based Relative Value Scale (RBRVS), 236
Respiration, 273
    of microbes, 101
Respiration rate, 273–274
Respiratory arrest, 356
Respiratory center, 63
Respiratory system, 63–64
    abbreviations of terms for, 29
    combining forms of root terms for, 28
    diseases and disorders of, 86–87
    drug types for, 111
    examination of, 281–282
    pharmacology for, 128
    suffixes of terms for, 29
Respondeat superior, 156
Restating, 171
Restricted-copper diet, 144
Restricted delivery, 177
Restricted-fat diet, 144
Restricted-potassium diet, 144
Restricted-sodium diet, 144
Restrictive endorsement, 218
Retention period, of medical records, 196
Reticulocyte, 60, 363
Retina, 55
    detachment of, 84
retin / o, 21
Retinol (vitamin A), 139, 140
    deficiency symptoms of, 141
Retractors, 286, 287

retro-, 5
Retrograde pyelography, 325
Return address, on letters, 184
Returned checks, 218
Return receipt, 177
Return Service Requested, 177
Reye's syndrome, 90
RF (rheumatoid factor), blood tests for, 373
rhabd / o / my / o, 17
Rh+ blood, 60
Rh- blood, 60
Rh blood groups, 373, 374
Rheumatic fever, 85
Rheumatic heart disease, 85
Rheumatoid arthritis, 82
Rheumatoid factor (RF), blood tests for, 373
Rh factor antibodies, in blood tests, 372
Rhinitis, 86
rhin / o, 28
Rhonchi, 274
Rib, 48
Riboflavin (vitamin B_2), 139
    deficiency symptoms of, 141
Ribonucleic acid (RNA), 44
Ribosomes, 43, 44
Ribs, 49
Rickettsia, 99
Rickettsia rickettsii, 99
Rider, 234
Rifampin (*Rifadin*), 117
Right (®), 13
Right atrium, 61
Right documentation, 301
Right dose, 300
Right drug, 300
Right ear (AD), 23
Right eye (OD), 22
Right hemisphere, 52
Right kidney, 66
Right lung, 63
Right lymphatic duct, 63
Right patient, 300
Right pulmonary artery, 61
Right pulmonary veins, 61
Right route, 301
Right technique, 301
Right time, 301
Right-to-know laws, 158
Right ventricle, 61
Rinne test, 281
Risk factors, for HIV transmission, 254
RNA (ribonucleic acid), 44
Rod, 55, 97

thyroid / o, 24
Thyroid-stimulating hormone
    (TSH), 57
Thyrotoxicosis, 85
Thyroxine (T_4), 57
TI (therapeutic index), 112
TIA (transient ischemic shock), 20
Tibia, 48
Tibialis anterior muscle, 50
Tibial nerve, 52
Tickler file, 196
t.i.d., TID (three times a day), 13
Timed specimen, 378
Times (x), 13
Timing, of radiographic procedures,
    326
Tincture, 112, 297
Tinea, 82
Tinea capitis, 82
Tinea corporis, 82
Tinea cruris, 82
Tinea pedis, 82
Tine test, 309
Tinnitus, 84
Tissue(s), 45–46
Tissue biopsy, 283
Tissue donation, ethics and, 160
Tissue forceps, 287, 288
Title VII of the Civil Rights Act of
    1964, 158
TLA (Truth in Lending Act), 222
TLC (total lung capacity), 281
-tocia, 34
Tolerance, of drugs, 111
Tomography, 325
    preparation for, 326
-tomy, 8
Tongue depressors, 277
Tonometer, 281
tonsill / o, 28
Tooth, 64
Topical administration route, 301
Topical route (T), 13, 114
Tort(s), 151, 152
Tortfeasor, 152
Total lung capacity (TLC), 281
Touch, as communication, 170
Touch screen, 199
Tourniquet, 368
Towel clamps, 288
Toxic effect, of drugs, 111
Toxicities, of antiepileptic drugs, 122
Toxicology, 109
Toxoplasmosis, 86, 255
Trace minerals, in diets, 142
Trachea, 63
Tracing insurance claims, 243

Tracing mail, 178
Traction, 337
Trade name, of drug, 112
Transcription, of medical records,
    195
Transdermal administration route,
    113, 114–115
Transdermal drug delivery (TDD),
    301
Transfer forceps, 256, 257
Transferrin, 363
Transferring medical records, 158
Transferring patient, from wheel-
    chair to table, 338
Transferring telephone calls, 185
Transient ischemic shock (TIA), 20
Transitional epithelial tissue, 45
Transmission of cholera, 308
Transplant, 160
Transplantation, ethics and, 160
Transverse fissure, 53
Transverse plane, 46
Trapezius muscle, 50, 51
Travel arrangements, 188
Traveler's check, 218
Treatment
    with physical therapy, 334–337
    of shock, 352
    of wounds, 349–350
Trendelenburg's position, 279, 280
Treponema pallidum, 99
Treponema pallidum antibodies,
    blood tests for, 373
Trespass, 152
TRH, 57
tri-, 5, 24
Triage
    of emergency calls, 186–187
    of medical emergencies, 345
Trial balance, 215
Triangular bandages, 289, 350
Triazolam (*Halcion*), 119
TRICARE, 237
    claims processing for, 244
Triceps brachii muscle, 50
Triceps muscle, 51
Trichinosis, 144
trich / o, 15
Trichomonas vaginalis, 100
Tricuspid valve, 61, 314
Tricyclic antidepressant drugs, 121
Triethanolamine polypeptide oleate-
    condensate (*Cerumenex*), 125
Triflupromazine (*Vesprin*), 120
Trigeminal neuralgia, 84
Triglyceride, 138
Trigone, 66

Triiodothyronine (T_3), 57
Tripod base cane, 337
-tripsy, 32
Troche, 112
-trophy, 17
-tropia, 21
Troubleshooting electrocardiograms,
    317
True ribs, 49
Truth in Lending Act (TLA), 222
Trypanosoma gambiense, 100
Tryptophan, 138
TSH (thyroid-stimulating hormone),
    57
tsp (teaspoon), 299
Tube feeding, 143
Tuberculin skin test, 283, 309
Tuberculin syringe, 304
Tuberculosis (TB), 29, 87, 89, 255,
    309
Tube size, 368
Tubular reabsorption, 66
Tubular secretion, 66
Tumor associated glycoprotein, in
    blood tests, 372
Tunica albuginea, 67
Tuning fork, 277, 278
Turbidity, normal urinalysis value
    for, 379
Turner's syndrome, 78
T wave, 316
12-lead electrocardiograph, 315
Twice a day (b.i.d., BID), 11
Two-point gait, 337
Two-way communications, 171
Tympanic cavity, 56
Tympanic membrane, 55, 56
Tympanitis, 84
tympan / o, 22
Type AB blood, 60
Type A blood, 60
Type B blood, 60
Type B lymphocytes, 60
Type O blood, 60
Type T lymphocytes, 60
Typhoid fever, 308
    vaccine for, 308
Typing injuries, avoiding, 199
Tyrosine, 138

U

UA (urinalysis), 32, 282, 378–382
    standard values from, 379
UCR fee, 234
Ulcerative colitis, 87
Ulcer treatments, 128

Ulna, 48
Ulnar nerve, 52
ultra-, 5
Ultrasonic cleaning, 257
Ultrasonography, 283
Ultrasound, 325
    for physical therapy, 335
Ultraviolet therapy, 335
Umbilical arteries, 62
Umbilical cord, 62
Umbilical hernia, 88
Umbilical vein, 62
Unconventional leads, for electro-
    cardiograph, 315
Underwater exercises, 336
Unemployment taxes, 223, 225
Unguent (ung.), 113
uni-, 5
Unicellular glands, 45
Uniform Anatomical Gift Act, 160
Uniform Donor Card, 160
Unintentional torts, 152
*United States Pharmacopeia Dispens-
    ing Information* (USPDI), 113
United States Postal Service (USPS),
    175–178
    abbreviations for, 182, 184
    current mail classifications of,
        175–176
    old mail classifications of, 175,
        176
    requirements of, 176
    special services of, 176–178
    ZIP codes and, 182
Universal antidotes, 113
Universal blood donor, 60, 373
Universal blood recipient, 60
Universal Precautions, 259, 260,
    368
Unlisted procedures, 241
Unopette®, 366–367
Unsaturated fats, 138
Upper extremity bones, 49
Upper respiratory infection (URI),
    29
Urea, 377
Uremia, 88, 380
Uremic, 381
Ureter, 66, 67, 68
Urethra, 66, 67
Urethral administration route, 115,
    301
Urethral orifice, 67
Urethritis, 88
Urgency, 377
URI (upper respiratory infection), 29
-uria, 25, 32

Uric acid, 381
    normal test range of, 370
Urinalysis (UA), 32, 282, 378–382
    standard values from, 379
Urinary bladder, 54, 66, 67, 68
    cancer of, 80
Urinary casts, 382
Urinary frequency, 377
Urinary meatus, 377
Urinary pH, 380
Urinary retention, 377
Urinary system, 65–66, 377
    abbreviations of terms for, 32
    combining forms of root terms
        for, 31
    diseases and disorders of, 88
    drug types for, 111
    examination of, 282
    pharmacology for, 129
    suffixes of terms for, 32
Urinary tract infection (UTI), 32, 88
Urination, 377
Urine
    chemical composition of, 377
    collection of, 378
    culturing of, 282
    microscopic examination of, 381
    odor of, 380
    specific gravity of, 380
    testing of, 377–382
    volume testing of, 378
urin / o, 31
Urinometer, 282, 380
ur / o, 31
Urobilinogen, 381
Urochrome, 377
Urologist, 282
Uropathy, 378
USPDI (*United States Pharmacopeia
    Dispensing Information*), 113
USPS (United States Postal Service),
    175–178
    abbreviations for, 182, 184
    current mail classifications of,
        175–176
    old mail classifications of, 175,
        176
    requirements of, 176
    special services of, 176–178
    ZIP codes and, 182
Usual fee, 234
Uterine activity, 69
Uterine tube, 68
Uterus, 68
UTI (urinary tract infection), 32,
    88
Utilities software, 201

Utilization management, 239
Utilization review, 235
Uveitis, 84
uve / o, 21
Uvula, 64
U wave, 316

V

VA (visual acuity), 22
    test of, 280
Vaccination(s), 305–309
Vaccine(s), 305–309
Vacutainer system, 367
vag. (vaginal administration route),
    12, 115, 301
Vagina, 68
Vaginal administration route (p.v.,
    PV, vag.), 12, 115, 301
Vaginal bleeding, 356
Vaginal candidiasis, 89, 255
Vaginal speculum, 277, 278
Vaginitis, 89
vagin / o, 33
Vagus nerve, 52
Valine, 138
Valproic acid (*Depakene*), 122
Valve, of heart, 61
valv / o, 26
valvul / o, 26
Vancomycin (*Vancocin*), 116
Varicella (chickenpox), 81
Varicella vaccine, 306, 307
Varicose vein, 85
Vas deferens, 67
Vasectomy, 67, 282
vas / o, 26, 33
Vasoconstrictors, 118
Vasodilator drugs, 111, 125, 126
Vasopressin (ADH), 32, 57, 66
Vastus lateralis muscle, 50
Vastus lateralis site, 303
Vastus medialis muscle, 50
Vector(s), 102
Veins, 48, 62
    used for blood collection, 365,
        366
Vena cava, 61
Vendors, 211
Venipuncture, 365–366
    steps in, 369
ven / o, 26
Venous blood, 58
Ventral cavity, 46
Ventricle, 53, 61
Ventricular fibrillation, 318
Ventricular flutter, 318

Credits and Acknowledgments

Foundations in Microbiology, 3rd Edition, K. P. Talaro
97

Glencoe Administering Medications, 4/e, Becklin & Sunnarborg
47, 48 *top left,* 298 *top,* 301 *both,* 302 *all,* 303, 304 *both,* 305, 306

Glencoe Medical Assisting, Ramutkowki
47 *bottom,* 48 *both,* 50, 52, 56 *bottom,* 61, 63, 64, 66, 67, 68, 89, 102, 137, 143, 157, 170, 171, 174, 179, 180, 181, 182, 185, 189, 191, 192, 193, 194, 197, 198, 199, 200, 202, 213 214, 216, 217, 219, 237, 240, 255, 257 *all,* 258, 260 *all,* 272, 273 *both,* 275, 278, 279, 280, 282, 284, 285, 286, 287 *both,* 288 *all,* 315, 316, 317, 327, 333, 334, 347, 348, 349, 350, 352, 354 *all,* 355, 363, 366, 367 *both,* 371 *all,* 375 *all,* 376, 377, 380, 381 *all,* 382, 383, 384, 385

Glencoe Law and Ethics for Medical Careers, Judson and Hicks
153, 160, 161, 162

Hole's Essential Human Anatomy & Physiology, Shier & Butler
43, 47 *top,* 53, 55, 56 *top,* 59, 69

Forms

W4 Form   224, 1st page

FUTA Form   225

W2 Form   226 *top*

FTD coupon   226 *bottom*